AUTONOMOUS STATE

The Struggle for a Canadian Car Industry from OPEC to Free Trade

Autonomous State provides the first detailed examination of the Canadian auto industry, the country's most important economic sector, in the post-war period. In this engrossing book, Dimitry Anastakis chronicles the industry's evolution from the 1973 OPEC embargo to the 1989 Canada-U.S. Free Trade Agreement and looks at its effects on public policy, diplomacy, business enterprise, workers, consumers, and firms.

Using an immense variety of archival sources, and interviews with some of the key actors in the events, Anastakis examines a fascinating array of topics in recent auto industry and Canadian business and economic history: the impact of new safety, emissions, and fuel economy regulations on the Canadian sector and consumers, the first Chrysler bailout of 1980, the curious life and death of the 1965 Canada-U.S. auto pact, the 'invasion' of Japanese imports and transplant operations, and the end of aggressive auto policy making with the coming of free trade.

More than just an examination of the auto industry, *Autonomous State* provides a rethinking of Canada's tumultuous post-OPEC political and economic evolution, helping to explain the current tribulations of the global auto sector and Canada's place within it.

DIMITRY ANASTAKIS is an associate professor in the Department of History at Trent University.

Autonomous State

The Struggle for a Canadian Car Industry from OPEC to Free Trade

DIMITRY ANASTAKIS

UNIVERSITY OF TORONTO PRESS
Toronto Buffalo London

© University of Toronto Press 2013
Toronto Buffalo London
www.utppublishing.com
Printed in Canada

ISBN 978-1-4426-4504-2 (cloth)
ISBN 978-1-4426-1297-6 (paper)

Printed on acid-free paper

Library and Archives Canada Cataloguing in Publication

Anastakis, Dimitry, 1970–
Autonomous state : the struggle for a Canadian car industry from OPEC
to free trade / Dimitry Anastakis.

Includes bibliographical references and index.
ISBN 978-1-4426-4504-2 (bound). – ISBN 978-1-4426-1297-6 (pbk.)

1. Automobile industry and trade – Canada – History – 20th century.   2. Automobile
industry and trade – Government policy – Canada – History – 20th century.
3. International business enterprises – Canada.   4. Canada – Economic policy –
20th century.   I. Title.

HD9710.C22A53 2013   338.4'7629222097109045   C2012-907085-8

University of Toronto Press acknowledges the financial assistance to its publishing
program of the Canada Council for the Arts and the Ontario Arts Council.

Canada Council   Conseil des Arts
for the Arts   du Canada

ONTARIO ARTS COUNCIL
CONSEIL DES ARTS DE L'ONTARIO
50 YEARS OF ONTARIO GOVERNMENT SUPPORT OF THE ARTS
50 ANS DE SOUTIEN DU GOUVERNEMENT DE L'ONTARIO AUX ARTS

University of Toronto Press acknowledges the financial support of the Government
of Canada through the Canada Book Fund for its publishing activities.

This book has been published with the help of a grant from the Canadian
Federation for the Humanities and Social Sciences, through the Awards to Scholarly
Publications Program, using funds provided by the Social Sciences and Humanities
Research Council of Canada.

Contents

Acknowledgments

In the ten years I worked on this book, I was privileged to have had a number of experiences that helped to shape my view of the global auto industry and Canada's place within it. Along the way I have incurred innumerable debts, only a few of which I can recognize here. Even before I began the project, I underwent an apprenticeship unusual for an historian by taking a position in Ontario's Ministry of Economic Development and Trade, where my work was essentially a practicum for the auto industry-government relations that form the core of my study. The people in the ministry's Automotive Office taught me more than they can imagine about the auto sector, and I wish to thank Babi Bannerjee, Laurie-Ann Hossein, Michael Dube, Fernando Traficante, David Bond, and Bob Seguin.

After leaving the Ontario government, I was fortunate enough to hold a series of post-doctoral fellowships which furthered my education in the auto sector and allowed me to grow as a scholar. As the Canadian Studies Fulbright Chair at Michigan State University, I travelled across the state to visit archives, present papers, tour auto plants, and spend time on the bridges and in the tunnels between Ontario and Michigan, giving me countless hours to think about the interconnectivity of our integrated industry and our two countries. A special thanks to Mike Unsworth, Phil Handrick, Joe Darden, and John Noble.

In Ottawa I held the AUTO21 Postdoctoral Fellowship in Government Policy and the Auto Industry at Carleton University under the supervision of Professor Maureen Molot. Professor Molot is an outstanding mentor and perhaps the most knowledgeable and distinguished scholar of the Canadian auto sector, and I appreciate all she has done for me. I also wish to acknowledge and thank everyone at the

AUTO21 research network in Windsor for their support, especially Dr Peter Frise. At the University of Toronto's Munk Centre, I was fortunate to hold a Social Sciences and Humanities Research Postdoctoral Fellowship. Thanks to Matt Farish for making my time at Munk so enjoyable and productive.

Over the course of the last decade I worked at a number of research institutions across North America, and I would like to thank the staff at these entities for their help. At Library and Archives of Canada, I wish to thank Paulette Dozois, Margaret Dixon, Nathalie Villeneuve, Katherine Legrandeur, Alix MacEwan, Michael MacDonald, Mihaela Ciocarlan, and others who helped me gain access to a wide range of documents, including through the Access to Information and Privacy (ATIP) process. At the Department of Foreign Affairs and International Trade, Greg Donaghy was extremely helpful in facilitating access. In the Privy Council Office, Michel Lortie helped me through my two-year wait for documents under an ATIP request. At the Canadian Auto Workers library and archives, Kathy Bennett provided a very helpful hand. Archivists at the Gerald Ford, Jimmy Carter, and Ronald Reagan presidential libraries, as well as at the National Archives and Records Administration in Washington, D.C., the Bentley Historical Library at the University of Michigan, the National Automotive History Collection at the Detroit Public Library, the Benson Ford Research Center in Dearborn, Michigan, the Walter P. Reuther Library of Urban and Labor Affairs at Wayne State University, the Archives of Ontario, the New Brunswick Archives, and Nova Scotia Archives and Records Management all deserve thanks.

I would also like to acknowledge the help and generosity of a number of individuals. Sam Gindin allowed me to access his private papers and helped me to understand some of the dynamics of auto workers, their organizations, and the auto sector more widely. Greig Mordue also allowed me access to his own research and has been extremely helpful and generous with his time and advice. Over the years Dennis DesRosiers, a forceful voice for the Canadian auto industry and education in Ontario, has been incredibly supportive, not only by sitting for interviews but also by giving me access to his company's materials and his private papers (which he has generously permitted me to use in this book).

At Trent University I have had the good privilege to have a number of supportive colleagues. Special thanks go to Joan Sangster, Keith Walden, Chris Dummitt, Janet Miron, Finis Dunaway, Olga Andriewsky,

Bryan Palmer, and Jim Struthers. My fourth- year seminar, 'The Car in History,' merits a special mention: I learned much from the students and their presentations and papers, which helped to shape my own views and this book. At Trent I had a number of excellent research assistants who deserve thanks: Jeremy Milloy, Stephanie Attley, Meaghan Beaton, and Blair Cullen are all top-flight researchers, teachers, and scholars in their own right. Thank you to Tracy Armstrong for creating the map which graces this book.

In the course of finishing this project, I presented related research at the Business History Conference annual meetings in Toronto, Cleveland, and Sacramento, at the Canadian Historical Association Meetings in Vancouver and Winnipeg, and at the AUTO21 Scientific Conferences in Vancouver and Hamilton. Parts of this book were previously published in the *Urban History Review* (an earlier version of chapter 4), in the *Canadian Historical Review* (a small section of chapter 2), and in the edited collection *Framing Canadian Federalism: Essays in Honour of John T. Saywell* (a small part of chapter 1).

I would like to thank all those who agreed to be interviewed for this project. Thanks also go to Steve Penfold, Tom McCarthy, Peter Norton, Steve High, Penny Bryden, Greg Keenan, Joe Martin, John Holmes, Viv Nelles, Richard White, the late Garth Wilson, and others who provided advice, conversation, and criticism over the years. At the University of Toronto Press, Len Husband has been a great editor and an even better friend. Thanks to him and everyone at the Press for their efforts in seeing this project to completion, and to the two external reviewers, one of whom alerted me to the Tom Paxton song, 'I'm Changing My Name to Chrysler.' Chris Armstrong read the whole manuscript and offered valuable comments. A special thought goes to John Saywell, who read the whole manuscript shortly before he passed away. Without him I would not be the academic or the person I am today.

I wish to acknowledge the research support provided by the AUTO21 Network of Centres of Excellence, the Social Sciences and Humanities Research Council of Canada, and Trent University (including through a Trent Research Fellowship and the Frost Centre for Canadian Studies). Other support came in the form of a Clark Travel-to-Collections Grant from the Benson Ford Research Center, a Gerald R. Ford Foundation Research Grant, and a Mark C. Stevens Researcher Travel Fellowship from the University of Michigan.

Abbreviations Used in Text

AIF	Annual Improvement Factor
AMC	American Motors Corporation
APA	Automobile Protection Association
APAA	Automotive Parts and Accessories Association (U.S.)
APMA	Automotive Parts Manufacturers Association (Canada)
APTA	Automotive Products Trade Agreement (auto pact)
BED	Board of Economic Development (Canada)
BILD	Board of Industrial Leadership and Development (Ontario)
CAFC	Company Average Fuel Consumption (Canada)
CAFE	Corporate Average Fuel Economy (U.S.)
CAJAD	Canadian Association of Japanese Automotive Dealers
CAMI	Canadian Automotive Manufacturing Inc. (GM-Suzuki, Ontario)
CAPTIN	Canadian Auto Parts Toyota Inc.
CAW	Canadian Auto Workers
CDC	Canada Development Corporation
CLC	Canadian Labour Congress
CKD	Complete Knock-Down
CMI	Canadian Motor Industries (Toyota-Nova Scotia)
COLA	Cost-of-Living Allowance
CVA	Canadian Value Added
CVCC	Compound Vortex Controlled Combustion
DOJ	Department of Justice
DNR	Department of National Revenue (Canada)
DOT	Department of Transport (U.S.)
DREE	Department of Regional Economic Expansion (Canada)

DRIE	Department of Regional Industrial Expansion (Canada)
DRO	Duty Remission Order
DVI	Designated Vehicle Importer
EA	External Affairs
EMR	Department of Energy, Mines and Resources (Canada)
EPA	Environmental Protection Agency (U.S.)
EPCA	Energy Policy Conservation Act (U.S.)
ESOP	Employee Stock Ownership Plan
EU	European Union
FIRA	Foreign Investment Review Agency
FDI	Foreign Direct Investment
FTA	Free Trade Agreement
GATT	General Agreement on Tariffs and Trade
GM	General Motors
GMC	General Motors Canada
IEB	International Executive Board (UAW)
ITC	International Trade Commission (U.S.)
IT&C	Department of Industry, Trade and Commerce (Canada)
JAMA	Japanese Automotive Manufacturers Association (Canada)
JIT	Just-in-Time
MFN	Most Favoured Nation
MIT	Ministry of Industry and Tourism (Ontario)
MITI	Ministry of International Trade and Industry (Japan)
MNE	Multinational Enterprise
MOE	Ministry of the Environment (Canada, also Environment Canada)
MOSST	Ministry of State for Science and Technology
MOT	Ministry of Transport (Canada, also Transport Canada)
MVMA	Motor Vehicle Manufacturers Association (both Canada and U.S.)
MVSA	Motor Vehicle Safety Act (Canada)
MVTO	Motor Vehicle Tariff Order (Canada)
NAFTA	North American Free Trade Agreement
NEP	National Energy Program
NHTSA	National Highway and Traffic Safety Agency (U.S.)
NAAO	North American Automotive Operations (Ford Motor Company)
NTMVSA	National Traffic and Motor Vehicle Safety Act (U.S.)
NUMMI	New United Motor Manufacturing Inc. (U.S.-Japan)

OEC	Office of Energy Conservation (Canada)
OECD	Organisation for Economic Co-operation and Development
OEM	Original Equipment Manufacturer
OPEC	Organization of Oil Exporting Countries
R&D	Research and Development
SAGIT	Sectoral Advisory Group on International Trade
SCV	Specialized Commericial Vehicle
SOMA	Société de Montagne Automobile (Quebec)
SUB	Supplemental Employment Benefit
SUV	Sports Utility Vehicle
TNO	Trade Negotiations Office (Canada)
TPS	Toyota Production System
UAW	United Auto Workers
USTR	United States Trade Representative
VER	Voluntary Export Restraint (Canada)
VRA	Voluntary Restraint Agreement (U.S.)
VW	Volkswagen Corporation
WTO	World Trade Organization

List of Tables

List of Illustrations

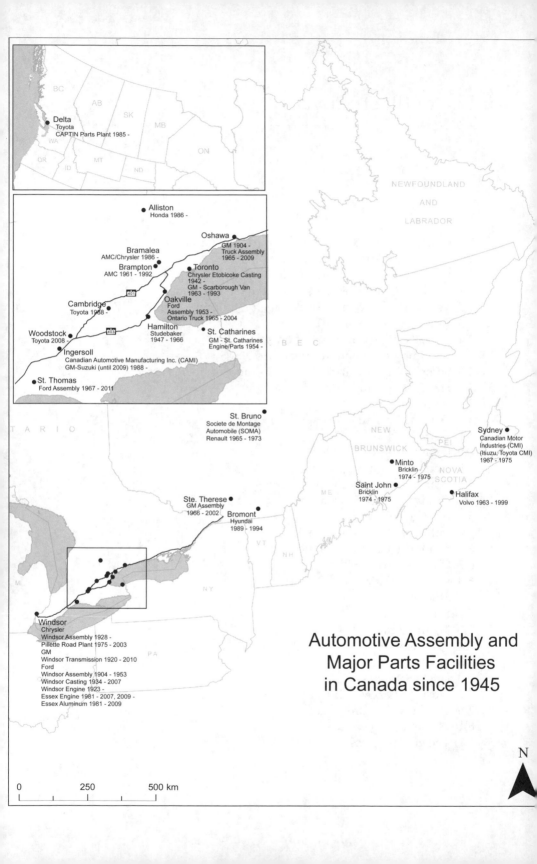

Delta
Toyota
CAPTIN Parts Plant 1985 -

BC
AB
SK
MB
ON
WA
OR
ID
MT
ND

Alliston
Honda 1986 -

Oshawa
GM 1904 -
Truck Assembly
1965 - 2009

Bramalea
AMC/Chrysler 1986 -
Brampton
AMC 1961 - 1992

Toronto
Chrysler Etobicoke Casting
1942 -
GM - Scarborough Van
1963 - 1993

Cambridge
Toyota 1988 -

Oakville
Ford
Assembly 1953 -
Ontario Truck 1965 - 2004

Woodstock
Toyota 2008 -

Hamilton
Studebaker
1947 - 1966

St. Catharines
GM - St. Catharines
Engine/Parts 1954 -

Ingersoll
Canadian Automotive Manufacturing Inc. (CAMI)
GM-Suzuki (until 2009) 1988 -

St. Thomas
Ford Assembly 1967 - 2011

QUEBEC

ONTARIO

St. Bruno
Societe de Montage
Automobile (SOMA)
Renault 1965 - 1973

NEW
BRUNSWICK

PEI

Sydney
Canadian Motor
Industries (CMI)
(Isuzu, Toyota CMI)
1967 - 1975

Minto
Bricklin
1974 - 1975

NOVA
SCOTIA

Saint John
Bricklin
1974 - 1975

Halifax
Volvo 1963 - 1999

Ste. Therese
GM Assembly
1966 - 2002

Bromont
Hyundai
1989 - 1994

ME

VT

NH

NY

MI

Windsor
Chrysler
Windsor Assembly 1928 -
Pillette Road Plant 1975 - 2003
GM
Windsor Transmission 1920 - 2010
Ford
Windsor Assembly 1904 - 1953
Windsor Casting 1934 - 2007
Windsor Engine 1923 -
Essex Engine 1981 - 2007, 2009 -
Essex Aluminum 1981 - 2009

PA

Automotive Assembly and Major Parts Facilities in Canada since 1945

N

0   250   500 km

AUTONOMOUS STATE

The Struggle for a Canadian Car Industry from
OPEC to Free Trade

Introduction: The Ripples of 1973

Sadly, wars happen all the time. Since the Second World War ended in 1945, there has been not a single year without a war raging somewhere in the world. Most of the time, ordinary North Americans, secure in a continental redoubt protected by oceans of distance, barely notice these conflicts, which usually occur in some far-off, little-known country or region. For their part, Canadians are even less affected by wars than Americans, who have been caught up in global events in a way that Canadians have rarely been in the post-war period. Even the long and costly engagements in Iraq or Afghanistan seemed a world away, barely noticeable in most North Americans' everyday lives.

This was probably much the same in 1973. As they watched television reports of yet another far-off war, North Americans could never have predicted that the ripples of this particular war would be more akin to tidal waves in their long-term impact. After all, from a distance it looked as though the Yom Kippur War was just another episode in the seemingly never-ending conflict that had raged between Israel and its Arab neighbours since 1948.

But this war was far different in its consequence and immediacy. Though it lasted less than a month and resolved little, the war had political and economic effects that reached across oceans, continents, and decades. After all was said and done, North Americans understood one thing profoundly about this war: it sparked an oil embargo. In response to the U.S. support of Israel, the Arab-dominated Organization of Petroleum Exporting Countries (OPEC) raised oil prices and cut off exports to the United States from October 1973 until March 1974. The embargo affected North Americans' lives almost instantly, and in unexpected and long-lasting ways.[1]

This was because by the early 1970s, and for most of the previous half-century, oil was nothing less than the lifeblood of the North American economy, tied as it was so intimately to that talisman of modernity: the car. Since the introduction of Henry Ford's Model-T, the automobile had become the single most important economic, environmental, and political force in North American society. Cars had completely reshaped the North American landscape, its economic foundations, the relationships between ordinary people, between citizens, consumption, and the state, and even people's very conceptions of time and place. The 1973 oil embargo was a tremendous shock to a society that had developed around the automobile, since North Americans were, by far, the greatest users of cars on the planet and the continent was the cradle of mass 'automobility.'[2]

Even then, the impact of the embargo was diffuse and uneven, but ubiquitous. Since nearly every adult in North America drove, nearly every North American adult suddenly realized how faraway events could have unexpected and life-altering consequences. The embargo threatened the hegemony of cars, one that underpinned the functioning of a whole society, wedded as it was to seemingly limitless and cheap transportation. Americans felt this more than Canadians, but the impact of significantly and suddenly higher gas prices, pushing inflation skyward, seemed both a symptom and a cause of the broader 1970s economic malaise that was keenly felt north of the border too.

If North Americans were the planet's greatest user of cars, they also built more cars than anywhere else. This is where the most profound impact of the embargo happened, at the intersection between consumers and the auto industry. The giants of car production in North America, Detroit's Big Three of General Motors (GM), Ford, and Chrysler, were less prepared to deal with the embargo than the car-buying public yet faced an even greater challenge than ordinary consumers – the public could simply choose to buy inexpensive cars now readily available from far-off locales. After the embargo, Detroit had to spend billions of dollars to design and build new fuel-efficient vehicles, and it could only hope that the cars it ended up with were actually the ones buyers wanted. In the roller-coaster automotive marketplace of the 1970s, more often than not Detroit guessed wrong, or moved too slowly to the smaller and less gas-hungry vehicles.

Unfortunately for Detroit, 1973's oil spike coincided with another, homegrown, regulatory tidal wave, one that had already been reshaping car safety and emissions since the mid-1960s. Combined with Washington's efforts to lessen America's dependency on foreign oil, these regulations forever changed the North American industry's competitive marketplace. Consumers' desire for vehicles different from those that the Big Three were offering and the emergence of foreign firms (especially Japanese firms) to meet those desires completely reoriented the North American sector. It meant nothing less than a wholesale change in how the Big Three conducted their operations, designed their vehicles, and produced their cars, a change that these giant firms struggled with for decades. The 1973 embargo partially explains Chrysler's near demise in 1980, and the bankruptcy and bailout of Chrysler again in 2009, along with General Motors. For the latter firm, once considered the paragon of American capitalism and technological might, this was an unthinkable event even a few years prior to its restructuring.

The ripples of 1973 deeply affected Canadians too. When it came to the auto industry, far more than any other aspect of North American life, Canadians were connected intimately to the American automotive behemoth and felt every twitch and grunt. After all, not only did they share a continent with Americans, they shared a continental industry. The 1965 Canada-United States Automotive Products Trade Agreement (APTA) or auto pact had completely integrated the two nations' sectors, knocking down the tariff walls that had once protected Canada's industry from its gigantic southern counterpart. In the years between 1965 and 1973, the Canadian industry had, by and large, flourished in this new, integrated, continental dynamic. Yet the embargo, the regulatory changes, and the consequences of these developments not only threatened to corrode whatever gains integration had brought the Canadian sector – they threatened the very survival of the industry itself.

This is a book about public policy and business enterprise, and about states, firms, workers, and consumers in the evolution of the Canadian auto industry from the 1973 OPEC embargo to the 1989 Canada-U.S. Free Trade Agreement (FTA). It makes the case that an activist Canadian state utilized creative and aggressive policies to carve out and grow a 'fair share' of the North American car industry for Canada in this period. Locked as it was in an economic embrace of automotive continentalism, a ballet of diplomacy, daring, and discourse, the Canadian state was largely successful in this endeavour. In most instances, Canadian politicians and policy makers exhibited significant leeway in shaping the direction and nature of their involvement in the continentalized auto industry. When it came to issues as diverse as Canadian auto-emission standards, attracting investment, or external trade matters, Canadians were little constrained by the North American framework of their sector. While the Canadian industry may have been fully integrated into that of the United States, this integration nonetheless still allowed considerable independent action, albeit within a managed capitalist trade regime.

Given integration's inevitable pull, and the lack of any significant Canadian ownership in the sector, how could this be? For decades, Canadians have been told that foreign ownership and continental economic integration would render their state impotent. Yet, in the case of the auto sector, foreign ownership and continental economic integration were the very reasons that Canadians were able to expect and extract their fair share of the industry. Though that industry was tightly linked within a cross-border, integrated sector, the political and economic distance between Windsor and Detroit was far greater than a simple trip across the Ambassador Bridge.

This was because borders still mattered within the borderless industry. While the industry was integrated, the political and economic circumstances each country faced remained different, and shaped each state's response to the dynamics of the continentalized sector.[3] Moreover, in Canada, governments, consumers, and unions saw the bulk of the industry, dominated as it was by U.S.-owned branch-plant operations, in a different light, given that these were 'foreign' enterprises operating in their country. Policy makers, workers, and stakeholders could and did deal with the American-dominated industry differently than they did with domestic firms. Foreign ownership of the industry made it an 'other,' and thus sometimes as much as a helpful target as it was a necessary ally, even if the sector employed as many as one in six Canadians, a mantra repeated almost as often as 'fair share.'

Foreign ownership gave Canadian policy makers a licence to be the *demandeur* in a manner that differed from how Washington attempted to impose its own will on Detroit. The threat of these foreign firms decamping, or more likely being targeted by nationalist dirigisme, was a possibility in Canada (but not in the United States), even though the two countries' industries were integrated. To better understand this dynamic, think, for a moment, as Americans did about foreign firms – mainly the Japanese – in the 1980s. Deeply unhappy at the impact of hundreds of thousands of Japanese imports coming into the United States annually, Americans made demands upon Japanese firms such as quotas and content threats, and expected them be good corporate citizens, since they were, after all, foreign firms.[4] Canadians, of course, also thought this way about the Japanese, but they had for a long time seen American firms operating in Canada in the same light.

Even then, in the case of Canada's continentalized industry, the foreign was domestic, and vice versa. Though these foreign firms operated in Canada, after 1965 they were no longer branch plants in the traditional sense, given the integration of the industry. And after 1973, this reality played a pivotal role in the titanic battle within North America over the billions of dollars of new automotive investment spurred by the tectonic safety, emissions, and fuel-economy regulatory shifts. This battle was fought on three fronts. First, there was an intense competition between states – both national and subnational – to induce firms to invest within their jurisdictions. This dynamic played itself out most notably in a 1978 continental bidding war over a Ford engine plant, and resulted in a stillborn effort by governments to control investment incentives. Second, there was a struggle between states over Chrysler's crisis. Unlike the 'carrot' of investment incentives, the Chrysler case illustrated how the 'stick' of aid, in the form of loan guarantees, could be used by governments to leverage as much as possible out of the troubled company as it spent billions to revamp its production and launch new products in an effort to save itself. Finally, there was a battle over the investment plans of offshore producers. The 1973 embargo's key consequence was that the Japanese would come to North America to build their cars or face barriers to their exports indefinitely. Again, the Canadian state utilized innovative and sometimes provocative methods to demand and ensure that some of these new facilities – 'transplants' – were located north of the border, much to American policy makers' chagrin.

At the end of this nearly two-decade-long battle, the Canadian state willingly surrendered most of the creative policies it had utilized in the auto field, in exchange for what it saw as an even greater opportunity: comprehensive free trade with the United States. The auto industry (and the auto pact itself) played a pivotal role in this decision, and in the debate that surrounded the emergence of the free-trade option. Canadian policy makers chose to embark on a new form of continentalism with free trade, one that departed from and ultimately rendered inoperative the unique and contentious continentalism created by the auto pact. By then, however, Canadians had largely succeeded in building a vibrant and multinational auto sector in Canada which survived the auto pact's 2001 demise and even the bankruptcies of GM and Chrysler in 2009.

The autonomous approach was not confined to Ottawa or Queen's Park, the primary sites for state action. Workers and union leaders also demanded a fair share, and utilized their own techniques to achieve it. Initially, they did so within the constraints of their international union and their internationally bargained collective agreements, but eventually they struck out on their own to create national instruments of collective action. Strikes, battles over concessions, and sharp public debates all figured in their attempts to ensure that Canadian auto workers had a say in the development of the continental industry, and in ensuring their economic interest within it.

Ordinary Canadians' agency within the continental sector was apparent too. Citizens protested against car pollution, marched with auto workers, or complained about car prices on call-in shows on television. They voiced their demands for automotive protectionism or free trade to newspapers, labour leaders, and cabinet ministers. Most profoundly and obviously, they shaped the market with their purchasing choices: they exerted pressure upon the automakers to provide technologically advanced and aesthetically pleasing vehicles, a challenge in any market but even more so in one bedevilled by regulations and external events like the careening price of oil or the influx of import vehicles. In turn, automakers struggled to anticipate consumers' desires, no small gamble when a single car model could cost hundreds of millions or even billions of dollars to develop. Over time, as consumer choices proliferated, citizens' ability to shape the market, and thus the stability of the North American automotive trade under the auto pact, became even more pronounced.[5]

Autonomous State utilizes the auto industry as a vehicle to make a series of other arguments, not just about the state's role in economic policy, though that is the principle focus, but about wider themes as well. While this book is about the auto sector, it is also about economic integration and harmonization, federalism, foreign investment, deindustrialization, worker nationalism, and Canada-U.S. relations. All of these factors shaped and were shaped by the dynamics of the continental auto industry and the agency exhibited by states and other actors within the sector. The resulting impacts of these interactions tell us much about the evolution of the broader North American political economy in this period. Thus, this book attempts, in some ways, to use these ideas to understand Canadian economic and political development in the post-OPEC world.

Other academic works have examined the political economy of the auto industry, and in particular the role of the state. Two studies are particularly important for understanding the issue of state intervention in the auto sector and the relationship between multinational enterprise and host nation in the Canadian context. In *Corporate Power, American Democracy and the Automobile Industry*, the political scientist Stan Luger examines the power relationships between American multinational auto companies and their home country. Luger takes a Marxist approach to argue that, bowing before the industry's power and its allies on Capitol Hill, Washington largely acceded to Detroit's demands in the period between the 1960s and 1980s. His work emphasizes the limits of state power vis-à-vis an entrenched and dominant auto industry in Washington. Luger argues that corporate power 'has a pervasive influence over public policy,' and, using the regulation of safety, emissions, and fuel economy as his examples, he attempts to show that the hegemonic power of the auto industry was rarely curtailed by the state.[6]

A second important book examines the role of multinational automotive corporations in developing states. Helen Shapiro's *Engines of Growth: The State and Transnational Auto Companies in Brazil* makes the case that neither neo-classical market-oriented nor state-centric, institutional approaches can explain the success of Brazilian state intervention in the auto sector in the 1960s and 1970s. The first, market-oriented approach views free trade and a willingness to accept a domestic laissez-faire environment as the best and only way to ensure a viable auto industry. For neo-classicists, state intervention, which is largely predicated on import substitution, can lead only to economic inefficiency and distortions in the marketplace. The statist approach, on the other hand, argues that a government's active role in supporting and seeking outcomes for an industry, including disciplining private industry, is key to the improvement of an auto sector. The Shapiro model for the Brazilian intervention shows that unrestrained market forces and direct state intervention were not the only choices state planners faced in developing policies towards the auto industry.[7]

Autonomous State both builds upon and departs from these interpretations. The Canadian case represents a third way, both in the relations Canada had with multinational firms and in the manner in which the Canadian state shaped the form of its intervention within the auto sector. I depart from Luger's view by arguing that the distance afforded Canadian policy makers from Detroit, one cleaved by an international border and complicated by the interplay of Ottawa's (and Ontario's) position as a third party between Washington and Detroit, gave them an unexpected amount of leeway in their dealings with the Big Three. Instead of weakening its position vis-à-vis multinational firms, because the country acted as nothing more than a host state for foreign entities, the Canadian state's once-removed status increased its bargaining power.

This was, in large part, because of the book's second main departure: whereas many other countries in the post-war period used state-centric approaches to achieve greater *national* control over their industries, Canadian policy makers tied their industry's fate to that of another nation on a *continental* basis. In Brazil (and Mexico, another country where import-substitution and state-centric policies were enacted[8]), auto policies focused upon nationalization, or the threat of nationalization, in the name of greater domestic control. In the Canadian case, the state did *not* utilize traditional import substitution; instead, it employed an ingenious form of managed trade through the auto pact that included mildly protectionist production safeguards but dispensed with tariffs – though, importantly, not the threat of tariff re-imposition. State actors sought to improve Canadian production though increased foreign direct investment, but within the context of a continentally integrated industry, one that reflected the economic and political realities that Canadian policy makers faced in the 1960s and beyond. For Canadian state planners working on the auto industry, their version of economic nationalism ultimately took the form of continentalism, an approach that lies between the opposing models of host country-multinational interaction outlined by Shapiro.

Understanding and exploring Canadian state action in this national/ continental automotive dynamic requires a blend of theoretical and methodological approaches. Though I focus on the Canadian state, this is not a purely institutionalist approach, nor am I arguing that the state was impervious to the influences of non-state actors, particularly the auto firms. The Big Three (and later, foreign firms operating in Canada) did have a privileged position from the perspective of policy makers, but the auto companies did not dictate terms. In fact, in many instances, such as in the case of auto emissions, the Chrysler bailout, the operation of the auto pact, or the inducements granted the Japanese to come to Canada, Ottawa's decisions often directly conflicted with the wishes of the Big Three, the most powerful corporate actors on the continent.

In other matters, the Big Three did hold inordinate sway, as in the case of investment incentives. But in that instance Canadian policy makers faced difficult choices, ones that were shaped as much by domestic imperatives as by Canada's relations with multinational firms operating within a continental industry. Overall, I take the view that politicians and policy makers were sensitive to the motives and desires of ordinary Canadians, of firms, and of workers, and that their actions were affected by both structures and events within the political economy. In that sense, *Autonomous State* is fundamentally pluralist, though it sees the preponderance of power as lying with the state, especially the federal government at Ottawa, at least until the mid-1980s.

At the same time, the nature of this study means that it is a form of trans-border history. Though the auto pact erased tariff walls for producers of cars, in other ways it strengthened the border and made it more meaningful. This is not surprising. As one trans-border scholar has noted, trans-border studies reflect realities that are 'often analytically paradoxical: on the one hand, borderlands history mutes the power of the border as an analytic container; on the other hand, it actually focuses greater attention on the border, moving it from assumed margin to analytic centre.'[9] The North American auto sector operated as a borderless entity on some levels but also simultaneously made the border a vital factor in the kaleidoscope of relations between states, firms, workers, and consumers.

Though this study is, in part, a trans-border story, assessing Canada's place in the continental industry necessarily requires an examination of two countries, and comparable developments within them during the period under study. One approach helpful in such an examination is *histoire croisée*, which can be translated as 'entangled history.' This is, as one Canadian scholar has argued, not 'simply the systematic comparison of two societies ... but rather, the study of the processes of mutual influencing, in reciprocal or asymmetric perceptions, in entangled processes of constituting one another.'[10] In the realm of the Canadian-American automotive political economy, *histoire croisée* most clearly manifests itself in questions surrounding state power and diplomacy, that is, in the relationship between states and multinational enterprises, and between actors in Ottawa and Washington. Untangling these themes is the broader aim of this book.

In doing so, *Autonomous State* addresses three other main themes within the relevant literature. First, the book aims to add to the emerging debate and historiography surrounding Canadian post-war deindustrialization. Stephen High's path-breaking study on the subject, *Industrial Sunset: The Making of North America's Rust Belt, 1969–84*, posits that Ontario's Golden Horseshoe did not suffer the same fate as America's ravaged Midwestern industrial heartland because nationalistic auto workers demanded state action to avoid plant closures and thus protect the Canadian sense of community.[11] *Autonomous State* adds to this debate, and departs from High's view, by arguing that state policy played a more significant role in largely sparing the Canadian industrial and automotive heartland from the fate experienced by its American counterpart. Fair-share policies under the 1965 auto pact regime dictated a minimum level of industrial activity by the Big Three auto producers, which helped to mitigate the worst effects of deindustrialization, and aggressive actions in gaining investment and rescuing Chrysler were far more important in maintaining or growing employment than demands for plant-closing legislation or sit-ins. Moreover, while worker nationalism may have been an element of the discourse employed by auto workers and their unions in the battles of the period, worker self-interest aimed at getting a fair share of the industry's bounty was a much greater motivator than simple flag-waving, as we shall see.

Second, *Autonomous State* aims to add to our understanding of post-1973 Canada-U.S. relations. Here, I utilize the notion of complex interdependence, as postulated by Robert Keohane and Joseph S. Nye in their classic *Power and Interdependence: World Politics in Transition*, to show how states of asymmetrical military or economic power interact and negotiate outcomes beneficial to their own interests. This approach roots itself in established historiographical literature on the Canada-U.S. relationship, which sees that relationship as being based upon both persistent conflict and cooperation.[12] *Autonomous State* will further illustrate the interdependence of the bilateral dyad by examining recent episodes in Canada-U.S. relations.

In so doing, the book builds upon the arguments of works such as Bruce Muirhead's *Dancing around the Elephant: Creating a Prosperous Canada in an Age of American Dominance, 1957–1973*, which illustrated the willingness of Canadian state planners to push the limits of the bilateral relationship for national gain.[13] It also provides a detailed and empirically based example of the persistent tendency of Canadian and American diplomats, for most of the period under examination, to *avoid* linking policy areas together in their cross-border negotiations. This supports the assertions of scholars such as the political scientist Brian Bow in his book *The Politics of Linkage Power, Interdependence, and Ideas in Canada-US Relations*. But at the same time it departs from Bow by offering a case where Canadian automotive policy making was ultimately explicitly linked to another policy, that is, tying the fate of certain auto measures to the negotiation of the 1989 FTA. The price for joining a free-trade agreement was nothing less than the end of creative Canadian automotive policy making, a decision Canadian politicians and policy makers willingly accepted.[14]

Third, and related to the last point, the book aims to contribute to the growing literature and debate surrounding the emergence of post-war free trade and its attendant phenomenon of globalization. Building upon Canadian and international works that examine the emergence of free trade, such as Michael Hart's *A Trading Nation: Canadian Trade Policy from Colonialism to Globalization* and Thomas Zeiler's *Free Trade Free World: The Advent of the GATT*, *Autonomous State* provides the first detailed analysis of the operation of perhaps the most crucial sectoral trade agreement in history, the 1965 auto pact, and its role in the emergence of comprehensive free trade in North America in the 1980s.[15] In this respect, the book joins other efforts that help to contextualize the role of the auto sector in the emergence of free trade.[16] Political debate around the operation of the continental auto industry was pivotal in the emergence of free trade in Canada, and this book is the first attempt to understand exactly how Canadian policy makers and politicians utilized the auto trade to advance the cause of free trade; it also shows how detractors used the Canadian experience under the auto pact to fight free trade.

Finally, I need to address how *Autonomous State* relates to my first book, *Auto Pact: Creating a Borderless North American Auto Industry, 1960–71*. It is, in some ways, a sequel to that effort, though it differs significantly as well. *Auto Pact* was more of a snapshot study of a managed trade agreement's creation, implementation, and impact. *Autonomous State* is about the evolution of an industry under the aegis of that managed trade agreement (paramount among other factors), and the primacy of the state in shaping that evolution. Chronologically, this book overlaps with *Auto Pact* by stretching back into the 1960s, but it mainly takes up the story of the industry where *Auto Pact* left off in the early 1970s and extends it to the free-trade period of the 1980s. It is far more ambitious in its time frame and its scope; it is also dealing with a far more complex industry, one made so by the auto pact's impact upon the sector.

The structure of *Autonomous State* is also very different from *Auto Pact*. This book is basically chronological but takes a much more thematic approach in its organization, with each chapter delving deeply into interconnected themes yet weaving all these elements together to develop an overall, holistic argument. Chapter 1 establishes the foundations of the book by laying out three revolutionary impacts that the auto pact had upon the Canadian sector within its North American context: the integration of the Canadian industry into that of the United States; the consequence of that integration in the form of a growing Canadian parts industry from the 1960s to the 1980s; and the dramatically reshaped relationship between the federal and Ontario governments as both states came to grips with the new continental dynamic faced by the Canadian sector.

Chapter 2 charts the acute disruption caused by the late 1960s safety and pollution movements and capped by the rupture of global oil geopolitics in 1973. The impact upon the continental industry was one of profound dislocation, as the Big Three struggled to respond to the new technological demands of government and the new market realities of the 1970s. Their response was, in part, to launch a massive retooling of and reinvestment in their factories. Chapter 3 traces Canadian efforts to achieve a 'fair share' of the automotive investment pie. This campaign acted as a proxy for more general Canadian views towards the national allotment of the continental industry's bounty, and the analysis of it here challenges traditional interpretations of Canadian attitudes about American foreign investment.

Chapter 4 explores the near demise of Chrysler in 1980, the rhetoric generated by the giant company's brush with death, and the policy implications of that episode. This debate foreshadowed by three decades essentially similar arguments surrounding the near collapse of Chrysler and GM in 2009: by then, Canadian politicians and policy makers were much more comfortable with interventionist actions, already familiar as they were with managing the industry under the auto pact, but the incident reflected uneasiness in the United States over whether Chrysler should even be saved. The contrast between the two approaches is also reflected in the relative success of Canada's efforts in the 1980s to utilize the bailout to further its own ends and achieve an even greater share of North American automotive production.

Chapter 5 focuses on the auto pact itself and its broader meaning within the Canada-U.S. discourse. The agreement's operation, and its many facets, became a site of contention between Washington and Ottawa, and both a symptom and cause of cross-border disputes and disagreements. Yet, through all these difficulties, the auto pact persisted: for policy makers and businesses on both sides of the border, it still served a purpose, for the time being.

Chapter 6 illustrates the willingness of non-state, non-firm actors – namely, the Canadian auto workers – to seek their own fair share of the continental automotive production. By detailing the role of national-ism in the United Auto Workers (UAW), the difficult period marked by conflict, concession, and strikes, and the ultimate decision of Canadian auto workers to leave the American-dominated international in Detroit, it provides a different perspective from that of Ottawa or Washington or even Detroit on how Canada's auto industry functioned within its North American context. In doing so, the chapter helps to explain the tumultuous birth of Canada's most powerful private-sector union, the Canadian Auto Workers (CAW).

Chapter 7 explores the emergence of non-Big Three auto firms in the Canadian sector, both as importers and as manufacturers. Here, I ex-amine the disruptive impact of Japanese imports and production upon the North American industry, and its implications for Canada. Cana-dian policy makers scrambled to contain the disruption, and to take advantage of it by employing a host of innovative, and ultimately – in the American view – unreasonable approaches. In chapter 8, I recount how these policies eventually were challenged and dismantled as the price of a free-trade agreement between Canada and the United States. That new regime would have far-reaching implications for the Cana-dian industry, and for the main policy drivers that had been so pivotal in building a successful sector, especially the auto pact.

The auto industry is the largest, most complex, most competitive, and most challenging industrial sector in North America. There is an *im-mense* amount of information on the automobile and its industry, and the flow is unstoppable: a century of dailies, weeklies, magazines, and reams of raw data from governments and consumer groups, not to mention auto enthusiasts, amateur auto historians, and professional firms whose *raison d'etre* is to analyze the industry. There are whole government departments working on the automotive sector, and the size and scope of the companies involved add a dimension that is not found in most industries. There is also the fact that, although the auto industry is a topic of *historical* interest, its key entities – the auto and parts-making firms – are ongoing business concerns, some more than a century old, that are not keen to share their corporate knowledge. Nor, sometimes, are governments, given the political and economic sensitivity of the automotive sector. In short, there is an automotive data fog, one complicated by inaccessibility to some of its most important sources of information.

It is quite impossible to examine every issue even within the focused period and themes that I have chosen. By necessity I have left a number of issues, elements, and actors out of this book. There is, for instance, little discussion of the retail side of the industry, or the aftermarket, not to mention design, financing, advertising, and marketing (except where necessary in some instances). Nor does the book dwell on automobiles themselves, or deal in any way with specialty manufacturers of heavy trucks, city buses, motor homes, or motorcycles. Snowmobiles, which became very popular and an issue in Canada-U.S. trade in the late 1960s and early 1970s, also do not receive attention.

Some actors are dealt with only from particular angles. For instance, consumers' views are taken into account when these have an impact on the politics, policy, and profitability of the sector. But this is not a consumer-driven view of the industry. The auto workers' union is covered extensively, but less so are the workers themselves – time and space make this unavoidable. The auto industry employed hundreds of thousands of workers; I have done my best to examine their representative institutions and leaders as a way of understanding the motives, concerns, and experiences of many of these men and women. I have also done my best to glean as much information as possible from available sources to analyze the motivations and strategies of firms such as GM, Ford, Chrysler, Volkswagen (VW), Toyota, and Honda, but the paucity of accessible corporate records renders this task difficult.

Even a few significant manufacturers play only a minor role in the book. As the focus is on the Big Three, who controlled over 90 per cent of the industry until the 1980s, companies like the American Motors Corporation (AMC) and International Harvester, though bona fide manufacturers under the auto pact, are not examined in detail. Nor is Hyundai, which was very successful as an importer into Canada in the 1980s and subsequently opened a manufacturing facility in Quebec in 1989. Similarly, some important themes are examined, but only in relation to their place within the book's framework: I explore just a single slice of the complex Canada-U.S. diplomatic relationship, and I study the free-trade debate and agreement only as they pertain to auto issues, and even then only narrowly.

Ultimately, this book does not describe some sort of golden age of statism or interventionist utopia, but it does illuminate a period of active and creative policy making in a highly competitive continental and global economic sector. Indeed, it is undoubtedly true that the Canadian state(s) played a central and positive role in creating and sustaining industrial policies in the auto sector that lasted for two decades, policies that brought great prosperity to Canada, and especially to Ontario. And, although the auto industry was centred in Ontario, the sector's success emanated outwards, and this prosperity was shared by all Canadians through tax revenues, equalization, and employment opportunities. These industrial policies also helped to maintain a cluster of innovation that provided further opportunity in the form of the emerging Canadian-owned parts industry, which generated its own entrepreneurial, research-and-development (R&D), and spin-off opportunities. By the early 2000s, Ontario produced more vehicles than any other jurisdiction in North America including Michigan, and the auto industry today remains its single most important economic driver and the largest value-added Canadian export sector.

The range and sheer audacity of some these policies are difficult to believe in retrospect. In the twenty-first century, when state intervention only seems to come in the form of last-gasp bailouts for firms deemed too big to fail or in direct cash incentives to corporations, it is essential to understand that civil servants once created dynamic public policies by sheer dint of will. Only then can we begin to imagine a world where these types of thoughtful and aggressive approaches can flourish again. After all, productivity and innovation will inevitably lead to fewer jobs, especially in an industry as competitive, technologically advanced, and mature as the automotive sector. But the world still needs to build things, and people will continue to drive cars in the future no matter how they are powered. They might as well be built in Canada, and public policy needs to play a paramount role in ensuring that a vibrant auto sector continues to benefit Canadians, as it unquestionably has for more than a century.

1 Industrial Revolutions: A New Automotive Landscape Emerges

There was no question that change had come. Sometimes slowly and imperceptibly, sometimes quickly and dramatically, Ottawa, Queen's Park, Windsor, Oakville, Oshawa, Sainte-Thérèse and a hundred big and tiny auto towns in between had been transformed in some way. A new regime had emerged in 1965 which sparked revolutions in the automobile industry and the interplay between firms, governments, and the tens of thousands of people who made their livelihoods building cars. The auto pact forever changed the landscape of the sector, though the consequences of this change were not always immediately discernible. In its broadest strokes, however, it was clear that in an industry governed since its inception by John A. Macdonald's tariff wall, a brave new world of opportunity now beckoned. The auto pact had destroyed that wall once and for all, ushering in three fundamental changes that remade Canada's automotive dynamic within the continent's economy.

The first of these revolutions was the integration of the industry. The transformation represented by the emergence of a borderless auto sector was profound, the first significant example of continental economic integration in North America. Where once production, investment, and sales and regulatory considerations of two separate countries had been constrained by borders and tariffs, after 1965 there existed a free-flowing and unencumbered whole. Canada's branch-plant industry was unshackled from its national market and cast into the maw of the great American commercial enterprise. Its assembly plants, now producing for all of North America, boomed in this continental environment. By the early 1970s, production and employment had increased dramatically, and the goals of the auto pact's creators – jobs, investment, and eradicating a persistent automotive trade balance – seemingly had come to fruition.

Yes, opportunity beckoned, yet challenges remained. The industry's integration had a second great revolutionary impact, this one upon the nascent Canadian parts sector. If Canadian assembly lines hummed to a continental tune, they did so with an American accent, since their production and operations were dictated by Detroit and Dearborn. But the auto pact's protectionist provisions gave Canadian parts makers and suppliers a chance to take advantage of new opportunities and new economies of scale. Though they now had to compete and survive in a much harsher environment, Canadian parts makers had the benefit of knowing that the American automakers were required to maintain a Canadian Value Added (CVA) in their production. Accepted by the Big Three and AMC as a price for being allowed to integrate continentally, the CVA requirements held out the possibility that the Canadian parts industry – the only indigenous, Canadian-owned segment of the sector – might survive and even flourish in this new automotive world.

Finally, the industrial integration and transformation of the sector had a galvanizing and long-lasting impact upon the body politic of federalism in Canada. Prior to the Second World War, the auto industry's chief contribution to Canadian political discourse was as a source of conflict over the tariff. After the war, this conflict receded, replaced by a moderately laissez-faire approach as widespread economic prosperity softened regional divisions and allowed the epicentre of the Canadian industry, Ontario (and its government), to enjoy the benefits of a booming sector. By the 1960s, however, the dynamic had shifted dramatically: the economic power of the industry in Ontario and its emergence within a competitive and integrated North American sector following the 1965 auto pact awakened the provincial state to its importance. Whereas only a few years earlier his predecessors were content to largely leave the industry to its federally controlled watertight compartment, the 'auto premier,' William Davis, whose own riding included an assembly plant, became an aggressive and active participant in auto matters. As we shall see, Davis's expanding automotive interest after 1971 paralleled the concordant activism of the federal state, itself awakened by impending technological and economic threats to the industry in the early 1960s. It also competed with the automotive aspirations of Quebec.

Thus, between the end of the Second World War in 1945 and the far-off 1973 Yom Kippur War, a startlingly new Canadian automotive landscape had emerged in North America. From a small and protected industry, one dominated by American multinationals and largely bereft of any potential for growth, there emerged a sector fully engaged with its continental fate. As the Canadian Big Three assemblers shifted gears to catch up to this new reality, indigenous parts makers and activist governments gamely followed suit. A new industrial revolution in Canada emanating from Ontario had begun, and it would be profound.

Ancien Régime Overthrown: The Canadian Auto Industry Transformed, 1945–73

The late 1940s and 1950s are often seen as something of a golden age for the North American auto sector. The Second World War boosted vehicle production to an all-time high, though consumer products were restricted owing to the necessities of wartime output. In the post-war period, pent-up demand led to an automotive surge as veterans returned and Canadian consumers purchased cars in astounding numbers. In 1950 there were less than two million cars registered in Canada; in 1960 that figure had more than doubled to over four million cars. By the late 1950s, Canadians were the second most enthusiastic users of cars on the planet per capita, after Americans.[1]

With massive highway building, suburban expansion, and increasing prosperity driving Canadians to purchase cars in such unprecedented numbers, the passionate automotive tariff battles that had characterized the pre-war period faded into the past, and there remained little regional conflict over the industry. Whereas once western Progressives had railed against auto-industry protectionism, and forced the Liberal government of William Lyon Mackenzie King to rework the tariff schedules to ease the cost of Canadian cars, the booming post-war economy lessened the sting of higher prices. The Canadian sector roared as it had not since the 1920s, and though it was regionally concentrated in Ontario, its success represented the overall spread of prosperity in the country. Between 1946 and 1954, production of vehicles increased from 92,000 to 375,000. Employment in the sector grew from 22,000 to 29,000.[2]

This post-war automotive-production boom was fuelled by more than Canadian consumer demand. As much of the globe recovered from the war in the ten years between 1946 and 1955, the Canadian Big Three of GM, Ford, and Chrysler exported nearly 175,000 autos to Europe and parts of the British Commonwealth. Soon, the value of the country's automotive output made it the most significant industrial element of the Canadian economy. Labour problems, which had wracked the industry since the 1930s, became much less prominent as auto workers gained the benefits of the well-functioning industry. The Treaty of Detroit in

1950, signalling this labour peace, reflected a period of relative consensus within the sector and the growth of Canada's middle class.[3] In exchange for job security, better wages, pensions, and an increasing share of the booming American economic pie, workers became less militant, policed themselves, and established a highly bureaucratic union.

With such flourishing sales, both for domestic consumption and for export, the Canadian industry continued to operate relatively smoothly, notwithstanding its creaking and ancient structure. The pre-war tariff regime that governed the industry, a remnant of the 1879 National Policy, had resulted in a thoroughly branch-plant Canadian industry. It did have the effect of facilitating some indigenous Canadian parts production, though the parts made in Canada were usually significantly more expensive than their U.S. equivalents. At the same time, the duty-free status granted to any parts of a 'class or kind' not made in Canada allowed the major manufacturers to import substantial amounts of expensive parts from their U.S. parent firms. These major parts included main body stampings, not built in Canada because the smaller Canadian market made such production prohibitively expensive. This nineteenth-century tariff structure did not slow down the Canadian subsidiary producers, who by the mid-1950s were producing nearly a half-million vehicles per year, double the pre-war high in the 1920s. The industry saw the expansion or building of dozens of new assembly and parts facilities, including a new Ford assembly operation in 1952 in the Toronto suburb of Oakville, and the adjacent construction of Ford Canada's sparkling new headquarters in 1954.[4]

Yet the Canadian auto industry's post-war success could not forever mask serious structural challenges that began to emerge towards the end of the 1950s. These difficulties stemmed not from regional conflicts over the tariff, as had characterized the pre-war period, but from the operation of the industry itself. The first real sign of trouble was the decline of export markets for Canadian producers. By 1960, the export market had almost entirely dried up, as Europe's automakers (particularly those in Great Britain) re-emerged from the rubble of war. In 1952 Canadian firms had exported nearly 80,000 vehicles; by 1959, this figure had declined to less than 19,000. At the same time, the number of foreign cars coming into Canada skyrocketed. This was true not only of U.S. auto imports (Canadian branch plants could import duty-free some makes that were not built in Canada, like luxury Cadillacs or Lincolns) but also of imports from Great Britain, which had since 1936 entered Canada duty-free. In 1952 Canadians bought 38,000 foreign-built cars; in 1959 they bought 165,000. This led to a growing and massive deficit in the auto trade.[5]

There were also problems on the production side. Canadian plants could not produce the latest complex technologies, such as automatic transmissions, that were becoming increasingly popular with the driving public. Nor did they have the economies of scale to build these new technologies effectively, even if they mastered the production methods. Moreover, by the late 1950s, Canadian consumers expected the same range of models offered their American cousins. As the American Big Three fully embraced GM boss Alfred Sloan's mantra of selling a car 'for every purse and purpose,' the range of brands, styles, and options proliferated. The Canadian factories simply could not maintain this wide range of model production, though they did their best, sometimes even offering Canadian derivatives of U.S. models. But these problems further exacerbated the auto deficit, as Canadian subsidiaries of the Big Three imported whole model lines and costly engines and transmissions from their American parents.[6]

When the inevitable cyclical downturn in the post-war economy occurred, as it did after 1958, the Canadian auto sector was particularly hard hit. The tariff structure and production model the industry operated upon was no match for the complexity of the modern automotive industry and the new challenges it faced. As prime minister between 1957 and 1963, John Diefenbaker realized that something had to be done and was sensitive to the fact that the auto industry, because of the tariff, was a federal matter. Diefenbaker was forcefully reminded of the urgency of the situation by the lobbying of a vocal Canadian United Auto Workers union and the incessant attacks of Liberal Member of Parliament Paul Martin, Sr, who represented auto-dependent Windsor in the House of Commons. Most serious among Martin's charges was that the Canadian auto trade deficit with the United States had increased ominously in the early 1960s and threatened to cripple Canada's current account balance.[7] (See Table 1.2.)

In 1960 Diefenbaker appointed University of Toronto economist Vincent Bladen to head a one-man royal commission on the automotive industry. Bladen's 1961 report resulted in a number of small steps to alleviate the structural problems in the industry. The most important of these was the creation of a duty-remission program to spur growth in the sector by providing a tariff payback on expensive transmissions imported into Canada by GM, Ford, or Chrysler, if these companies boosted their exports of other parts. This duty-remission program, created by Simon Reisman and a small cadre of civil servants committed to helping the industry and lessening the trade imbalance with the United States, was an early example of Canadian willingness to intervene creatively and forcefully in the sector.[8]

The Liberals, too, were keen to improve the auto industry, and took an even more interventionist approach after Lester Pearson's 1963 electoral victory. Their initiatives began a process that resulted in nothing less than an entirely new regime for the Canadian auto industry, and the creation of a vibrant automotive bureaucracy to oversee that regime. Under the aegis of activist ministers such as Walter Gordon and Charles Drury, these measures included the creation of a Department of Industry and an expansion of the Diefenbaker duty-remission plan to include all parts.[9] This scheme induced manufacturers to increase exports from Canada by granting in exchange a remission of duties on imports.[10]

Eventually, these measures resulted in the 1965 Canada-U.S. Automotive Products Trade Agreement. The auto pact was a unique and unprecedented approach to international trade between two countries. Negotiated under the threat of a trade war because of the adverse American reaction to the duty-remission programs (which shifted some Big Three purchasing to Canada from the United States), it created a new model of trade. The agreement contained an element of protection for the Canadian industry sought by the Pearson government (local content requirements and production targets), and at the same time eliminated duties on the cross-border auto trade, sought by U.S. negotiators and the U.S. Big Three. The auto pact heralded a new integrated industry, and between 1965 and 1973 the North American auto sector was transformed.[11]

The auto pact allowed the Big Three to consolidate their operations on a continental basis. Prior to 1965, each country had operated distinct if interdependent auto industries, with separate Big Three operations in both countries manufacturing and selling within each jurisdiction. In order to gain the benefits of a new, open North American market (for production, not consumption – Canadians were still not allowed to buy a car in the United States and bring it back over the border without paying duties), the auto pact required the Big Three and other producers to meet certain requirements. On the Canadian side, the manufacturers had to achieve specific CVA in their production and to build as many cars and trucks as they sold in Canada.[12] The companies also signed Letters of Undertaking with the government, each promising to invest an additional amount in the Canadian sector by 1968 and to maintain a 60 per cent CVA in their production in Canada of any sales increase in the Canadian market. These safeguard requirements were closely watched by the Canadian government, and the penalties for not meeting them could be millions of dollars in tariffs.[13] On the U.S. side, the agreement required a minimum 50 per cent North American content for cars and parts from Canada to be eligible for duty-free entry to ensure that foreign companies did not simply use Canada as a backdoor to import duty-free autos into Canada and then reship them to the United States. The auto pact was a managed trade agreement that solved Canada's massive auto trade deficit and provided for a form of conditional free trade.

Significantly, the agreement was asymmetrical, not only in its requirements for duty-free trade for firms operating on either side of the border, but also in its operation under the General Agreement on Trade and Tariffs (GATT). When Canada and the United States had approached the GATT to gain acceptance for their preferential trade area, the United States received a waiver from the contracting parties. Canada, on the other hand, made the auto pact regime accessible to third-party countries. That is to say, Canadian-based firms other than the Big Three and AMC could, in theory, achieve auto pact status if they fulfilled all the requirements of the agreement.[14] In 1965, when the treaty was implemented and accepted by the GATT, it seemed a remote possibility that any other foreign firms would establish plants in Canada. As we shall see, however, by the 1980s the likelihood of firms other than GM, Ford, and Chrysler being granted this preferential status factored into the auto pact's ultimate demise at the World Trade Organization (WTO) in 2001.[15]

The impact of the auto pact on the sector was profound. The Big Three and many other firms took full advantage of the new opportunities afforded by the agreement by retooling their Canadian operations to produce for the whole of North America. The Canadian subsidiaries, which heretofore had struggled to build a host of models for domestic consumption and imported the remainder, now became far more efficient and maximized their production by building for an entire continent. For instance, after the auto pact, GM produced fewer Pontiacs, Buicks, and Oldsmobiles in Canada but increased its production of Chevrolets; GM Canada made half the previous variety of vehicles in the post-pact period. The story was similar at Ford, which reduced the number of car and truck models produced in Canada from 71 and 227 to 49 and 64 respectively. Another dramatic example was the impact on

Table 1.1
Synopsis of the 1965 Canada-U.S. auto pact

Intergovernmental Agreement
- duty-free treatment on parts and completed automobiles, retroactive to 16 January 1965
- at request of either government, consultations on agreement at any time
- review of agreement in no later than 1 January 1968
- agreement to be of unlimited duration; either country can terminate on twelve months' notice

Annex A (Canadian requirements for duty-free trade):
restricts imports to Canada to bona fide manufacturers who fulfil the following commitments:
- have produced vehicles in pervious twelve-month period
- maintain a ratio of cars produced to cars sold, or at least 75:100 of cars produced to cars sold ('the ratio')
- maintain a base dollar amount of production equal to that of 1 August 1963 to 31 July 1964 ('the base CVA')

Annex B (U.S. requirements for duty-free trade):
- restricts imports to the United States to articles with more than 60% North American content until 1 January 1968, and 50% North American content thereafter

Letters of Undertaking (required by Canadian government of auto manufacturers)
- for increases in production, each manufacturer must increase Canadian Value Added of base year 1963–4 by 60% for automobiles and 50% for commercial vehicles ('the 60% sales increase CVA')
- additionally, the Big Three collectively agreed to boost their total CVA by $260 million in new investments by 1968

AMC's operations. In 1969 AMC's plant in Brampton, Ontario, started producing the Hornet for the eastern half of the continent while AMC's Kenosha, Wisconsin, plant built for the western half.[16]

The results of rationalization and integration were impressive. By the mid-1970s, automotive production in Canada had grown spectacularly. In 1965 Canada produced 853,000 vehicles. By 1976, production had doubled to 1.6 million vehicles, nearly 80 per cent of which were exported south of the border.[17] In 1967 Canadian officials estimated that, because of the content and investment requirements in the agreement, 87 new plants had been built, 164 plants expanded, and a total of over $500 million invested in the industry.[18] Exports, imports, and employment all increased significantly from the pre-auto pact era.

Table 1.2
Canada-U.S. vehicle production summary, 1960–78, in units

Year	U.S. Total	Canadian Total	Canadian % of U.S.
1960	7,894,220	395,855	05.01
1961	6,643,822	390,459	05.87
1962	8,189,402	508,667	06.21
1963	9,100,585	632,172	06.94
1964	9,245,678	669,549	07.24
1965	11,114,213	853,931	07.68
1966	10,363,254	896,119	08.64
1967	8,992,269	939,635	10.44
1968	10,793,744	1,178,186	10.91
1969	10,182,562	1,350,481	13.26
1970	8,262,657	1,189,461	14.39
1971	10,649,666	1,373,108	12.89
1972	11,297,509	1,471,392	13.02
1973	12,662,919	1,589,499	12.55
1974	9,983,934	1,563,850	15.66
1975	8,965,413	1,442,076	16.08
1976	11,485,536	1,646,824	14.33
1977	12,699,086	1,764,987	13.89
1978	12,895,286	1,818,378	14.10

Source: DesRosiers, *Automotive Yearbook 2000*, 112.

Within a decade of the auto pact's implementation, Canada's auto assembly sector was fully and completely integrated into that of the United States. Protected by the ratio and content requirements found in the agreement and the industry-government Letters of Undertaking, while at the same time able to take duty-free advantage of the giant American market, the continentalized Canadian auto industry flourished. Of course, the agreement's benefits were not always evenly distributed, and flowed in different directions at different times. As we shall see, the auto pact may have been a boon to Canadian employment and production, but it left many Americans unhappy with an agreement which they saw as unfairly benefitting Canada. Eventually, Canadians would also become unhappy about the auto pact, and fearful too about what the agreement portended for the future of their industry. But, for now, the auto pact had seemingly, improbably, accorded the Canadian auto industry the fruits of both protectionism and free trade.

The New Industrial Revolutionaries: Building a Viable Canadian Parts Industry, 1965–85

Out of the great, sprawling mass that constituted the North American auto sector, the segment that most keenly felt the integrationist revolution transforming the industry was the Canadian parts sector. After all, the U.S. side of the industry was barely affected by integration. Big Three plants south of the border were not really rationalized as were their Canadian counterparts, though in some instances they shifted production slightly. In Canada, the impact upon Big Three production was obviously more profound, but even then these facilities mostly grew, specialized, and became far more productive.[19] The Big Three Canadian facilities and their workers reaped the benefits of the new regime, yet, unlike a significant segment of the parts industry, they did not face a completely different competitive environment.

The original equipment manufacturer (OEM) Canadian parts industry was made up of three main segments, the first two of which were foreign-owned. First, there were the captive plants of the Big Three in Canada. These included gigantic parts makers such as GM's St Catharines facility, which had once been McKinnon Industries, or Chrysler's Etobicoke parts plant. They largely made stampings and other parts, and eventually complex engines and transmissions, for their parent firms both in Canada and in the United States. Along with these facilities were the Canadian subsidiaries of American independent parts makers. In the 1960s this group constituted the largest segment of the industry that was not Big Three-owned and included the majors of Budd, Rockwell International, Lear, Eaton, Kelsey-Hayes, Dana, Borg-Warner, Bendix, and TRW. These firms also quickly took advantage of the auto pact regime. They had long-standing relationships with the U.S. Big Three and, as subsidiaries of American firms, could easily adapt to the technological, production, and purchasing demands of the new continental regime.[20]

Finally, there were the Canadian parts makers. More than any other segment in the North American industry, these firms were profoundly affected by the changes wrought by the auto pact. A few hundred in number, they were mostly small operations clustered in southern Ontario that made parts generally only for the Canadian Big Three. They included parts makers, tool-and-die operations, and moulders.[21] Before the auto pact they enjoyed a measure of protection since the Canadian tariff for completed autos and parts was 17.5 per cent. The pre-auto pact tariff structure also encouraged assemblers to purchase from Canadian parts makers: duty-free imports of vehicles and parts by an assembly company would be allowed if the company achieved Commonwealth (really, Canadian) content through local purchasing, based on a sliding scale of output.[22] Thus, if an auto company in Canada produced more than 20,000 vehicles a year, it was able to import duty-free only if it achieved 60 per cent Commonwealth content in its vehicles. If a company produced between 10,000 and 20,000 cars, it required 50 per cent Commonwealth content; and below 10,000 vehicles, 40 per cent. Purchases from Canadian firms, often of basic components or by providing unfinished materials, helped to fulfil this content requirement. For instance, Canadian Lamp sold headlights to GM Canada, adding to GM's Commonwealth content (which it also met through labour costs and parts production from its own captive Canadian plants).[23] In turn, by hitting its Commonwealth target, GM could now import parts and cars duty-free.

Despite this protection, the Canadian parts industry was in dire straits by the early 1960s. Since all of the Canadian Big Three and AMC could easily meet their Commonwealth content requirements (even tiny AMC did so while producing 30,000 vehicles in 1963), they could import any other parts they needed duty-free. This not only drove up the Canadian auto trade deficit but, just as important, effectively left Canadian parts makers out in the cold when it came to selling more expensive or higher value-added parts to the Canadian Big Three (selling to the United States directly was virtually unheard of for a Canadian maker). The Canadian parts makers were in a trap. They could keep selling rudimentary parts to the Canadian Big Three so that the latter kept fulfilling their content requirements. But doing so meant that they would never be able to compete for the more lucrative and more complex parts purchases that the Big Three largely filled from their own plants, from the U.S. parts companies in Canada, or from duty-free U.S. imports.

This problem threatened the existence of the Canadian parts sector. In 1960, when Vincent Bladen had asked the industry for submissions for his royal commission, the assemblers were largely in favour of some form of continental integration with the American sector; Canadian parts makers were decidedly not. Their lobby group, the Automotive Parts Manufacturer's Association (APMA), created in 1952, was terrified that opening the door to unrestricted free trade would completely wipe out their membership – both indigenous parts makers and U.S.

He's a road hog, officer!

1.1 The tiny Canadian parts industry feared direct competition with the giant U.S. components sector. *Globe and Mail*, 7 August 1964. Permission granted for reproduction by the *Globe and Mail*.

subsidiaries, which would have no reason to operate in Canada under automotive free trade. Instead, APMA head D.S. Wood took the liberty of submitting a plan to Bladen that gave Big Three manufacturers duty-free credit for imports if they exported more, including exporting more Canadian parts than they purchased. Wood's plan was the seed from which the Canadian government's duty-remission plans eventually grew.[24]

Unsurprisingly, when the auto pact was being negotiated as a consequence of the American fallout from those duty-remission plans, the parts makers were steadfast in their position that any new deal – integrationist or not – had to include continued measures of protection for their segment of the industry. The 'institutional barriers' that Canadian makers faced in selling their parts to Detroit was a key reason Reisman and the Canadians held out for the CVA protectionist safeguards in the auto pact. While the APMA was pleased with the measure of protection afforded by the new agreement, they were also deeply trepidatious: the auto pact also meant that they would now be exposed to a level of competition unlike anything they had ever experienced. As one industry leader stated in 1965, 'the little guy with only one or two engineers and no capital with which to expand just isn't going to be able to compete in the bigger market.'[25]

Canadian parts makers were right to be fearful. In the first decade after the auto pact's implementation, the sector experienced a severe shake-up, as Canadian parts makers failed, were consolidated, or faced devastating competition. Though there was potential for growth in Canadian parts manufacture and sales, a consequence of the CVA and investment requirements under the auto pact, the agreement also meant drastic changes in how the parts sector operated. Its rationalizing aspects shifted all major purchasing decisions of the major manufacturers to the United States, save for GM Canada, which still maintained a significant purchasing capacity in Oshawa owing to its immense size. This resulted in a general reduction in suppliers, which was further compounded by the Big Three move into even greater production at their captive plants in Canada, helping them to meet the CVA requirements 'in house.'[26]

For the remaining independent parts suppliers, because of the new economies of scale, the industry now tended towards fewer, larger firms, operating at a level of size and specialization which most Canadian companies had not yet reached. The industry was also affected by vehicle development changes: it became difficult for newer suppliers to get purchase orders as car companies moved to a six-year vehicle cycle from a three-year cycle by the end of the 1960s. As such, there were now fewer opportunities to source for new models, since some manufacturers preferred to stay with already established relationships. This, in turn, reduced the number of contracts and opportunities for Canadian firms.[27]

By the end of the first post-auto pact boom in the early 1970s, there were concerns about the viability of the Canadian-owned parts sector. Certainly, assembly had increased dramatically, as had Big Three expansion of their own captive parts operations. American parts makers in Canada had also expanded and done well under the new regime. But, after the Big Three had fulfilled their $260 million Letters of Undertaking purchasing and investment commitments by 1968, they no longer needed to source from Canadian firms. Between 1965 and 1969, at least sixty Canadian parts companies failed, simply unable to meet the new competitive regime that required better products, access to capital, and the latest machining and technology. This was a significant chunk of the total Canadian supplier industry (including American firms), which was estimated at nearly 500 companies.[28]

Many companies managed to survive the initial shake-up, but some faced further difficulties when Big Three purchasing switched back to their American sources after 1968. Pilkington Glass in Toronto, which had spent $65 million expanding since 1967 to meet post-auto pact business, complained directly to external affairs (EA) and industry, trade, and commerce (IT&C) ministers Mitchell Sharp and Jean-Luc Pepin that, notwithstanding their 'absolute competitiveness,' 'external influences seem[ed] determined now to transfer the sourcing of massive quantities of glass from Canada back to the United States.' Ford had decided to shift purchasing of its glass away from Pilkington and to Libby Owens in the United States. Duplate Canada also worried when GM decided to shift its glass purchases for Vega production at its assembly plant in Saint-Thérèse, Quebec, to Duplate's parent firm, PPG, in the United States.[29] More threatening were reports that Mexico's newly instituted and much higher content requirements might shift even more purchasing south of the U.S. border as the Big Three fulfilled that country's own harsh local content directives.[30]

In response to these complaints, the Canadian consulate in Detroit investigated whether purchasing decisions were biased against Canadian firms. It found that, in most instances, Canadian suppliers lost out or were dropped because of 'poor service, poor quality, non-competitive prices or simply a lack of aggressiveness.' There was no overt economic nationalism at play here, but Canadian suppliers did have difficulties for more competitively determined reasons.[31]

Clearly, not everyone in the parts industry was happy with how things had developed. There may have been growth in the number of firms and employees, but this was at a cost. Some Canadian parts producers felt that, in retrospect, the auto pact had been a bad deal for the sector. Canada Wire and Cable President J.H. Stevens complained in 1973 that 'we have given up the breadth of operations that we previously had. We have become specialized in a very narrow range of operations.' Perhaps most important, Stevens lamented that 'we have lost one of our main sources of dynamic growth – the entrepreneurial business and development environment of the Canadian-owned automotive parts industry.'[32]

In fact, Stevens was wrong. The auto pact may have led to a shake-up among Canadian parts makers in its initial period, but it also gave opportunities to a whole new generation of auto-parts entrepreneurs. Many of these new parts entrepreneurs were European immigrants, products of the great wave of post-war migration that reshaped Canada. Many of them also had backgrounds as machinists or in tool-and-die making, the skill of making machinery. The 'blueprint' boys, as one journalist has called them, all had backgrounds in skilled trades and a thirst for work.[33]

In the late 1950s and early 1960s, quite a few of these entrepreneurs had started small businesses in the Canadian parts industry or in allied industries, mostly in small towns in southern Ontario. Their skills and entrepreneurial bent, coupled with the province's concentration in auto assembly, its petrochemical, plastics, and steel-making sectors, and its low-cost electricity supply and educated workforce, made the region ideal to supply auto parts. But it was not until after the 1965 auto pact's implementation that these burgeoning entrepreneurs were able to take full advantage of the Canadian content requirements and larger contracts sparked by the agreement to specialize and grow their businesses.

The examples are legion, and legendary. Frank Stronach and Magna remain the most spectacular instance of success in the post-war Canadian auto parts sector, a quintessential rags-to-riches story. Stronach emigrated from Austria in 1954. After working a number of menial jobs, he opened his own tool-and-die shop in Toronto in 1957. His first contract with GM Canada, to make a metal bracket for a sun visor, was worth $30,000. From that point forward, Stronach, obsessively focused on quality machining, and his associate Burton Pabst slowly started to build an auto-parts company. When the auto pact began in 1965, Stronach was well placed to take advantage of the Canadian content requirements and the new competitive environment created by continental integration. The auto pact, according to Stronach biographer Wayne Lilley, 'changed Frank Stronach's life ... the Pact made it possible for him to build a profitable small business into an empire.'[34]

Much of Magna's initial success was in consolidating a diverse and broad range of Canadian parts makers under its corporate umbrella. In 1968 Magna took control of Multimatic Investments, which at the time had five subsidiaries making parts.[35] In the decade after 1968, Magna consolidated a number of firms in the part sector, expanding its product lines and capacity. For instance, in 1969 the company bought an Orillia tool-and-die maker and a small stamping outfit, then a steel fabricator in 1970. In 1972 it bought a muffler maker, and the next year the company became Magna International.[36]

In the 1970s, as the auto pact requirements continued to provide opportunities to Canadian parts firms, business boomed for Magna. When Magna landed a contract for a now continentalized Canadian Big Three manufacturer (and the company maintained relationships with all of the Big Three), the scale of its sales far outstripped what Magna had been doing in the pre-auto pact period. By the end of the decade, a lower Canadian dollar also helped as the company sought out and gained orders directly from the Big Three in the United States. Just as important was Magna's management approach. Utilizing an innovative business philosophy, Magna's plants were organized in a uniquely decentralized structure which gave each individual plant significant autonomy and kept plant sizes small. It also kept unions out. Instead, workers were part of a profit-sharing plan, which included lump-sum payments out of annual profits as well as shares in the company. Magna also maintained recreational and daycare facilities for its workers.[37]

The company devoted a significant amount of funds to research and development, always seeking to achieve high-technology value-added capabilities. This focus led to Magna's ability to build significant components and modules of vehicles when the Big Three began to outsource major parts development. Eventually, Stronach enshrined these principles in a corporate philosophy which became a cornerstone of the 'Magna Way.' By 1977, Magna was exporting nearly 60 per cent of its auto-parts production to the United States, and within a few years it had annual revenues of over $1 billion. According to Lilley, 'under the Auto Pact's free trade, Magna was proving itself to be player, a serious competitor in the major-league US market.' In 1986 the firm had over 100 factories and 10,000 employees, and each car built in North America contained $73 worth of Magna parts.[38]

Similar is the tale of Frank Hassenfratz. Another post-war immigrant, Hassenfratz came to Canada in 1957 as a refugee following the Hungarian uprising. A former army engineer, Hassenfratz started his company Linamar (named after his daughters Linda, Nancy, and his wife, Margaret) in a Guelph basement in 1966 with one lathe bought with borrowed money. His first contract was making fuel pumps for Ford Motor. By the 1970s, Linamar had established itself as a leading manufacturer of close-tolerance metal parts and components such as steering columns, axles, or oil pumps in the auto, defence, and aerospace fields.

Like Magna, Linamar had a unique organizational structure, with each of its subsidiaries (eleven by the early 1980s, employing nearly 2,000 workers) autonomously run, usually by managers who had worked their way up from the shop floor. And like Magna, too, the company was non-unionized. Linamar's healthy growth reflected the new opportunities that an integrated auto sector represented following the auto pact. In the 1980s over 80 per cent of the company's exports were to the United States, and Linamar's largest single contract was with GM in Detroit. Six out of seven of its biggest contracts were North American sole-sourced contracts for auto manufacturers.[39]

Klaus Woerner of Automated Tooling Systems (ATS) was another immigrant machinist. He came to Canada in 1960 from his native Germany and, after taking advanced engineering courses in Montreal, eventually landed a job at Ford, where he gained an interest in automation. The company he started in Kitchener in 1978 building fully integrated automation systems for automotive companies grew to thousands of employees by the 1990s.[40] Like Magna and Linamar, ATS gained the benefit of the continent-wide duty-free market created by the auto pact by getting contracts from Detroit directly.

Suppliers in newer aspects of the parts-making sector also did well under the auto pact regime. Firms such as the ABC Group, created in 1974, specialized in plastic automotive components, particularly injection moulding. By the 1980s, ABC was a major supplier to the Big Three in both Canada and the United States. So was the Woodbridge Group of Mississaugua, Ontario, founded in 1978. Originally the Urethane Foam Division of Monsanto, the company was bought by engineer T. Robert Beamish, Monsanto Canada's president, when the parent company decided to close its subsidiary. Specializing in foam for seating, Woodbridge's largest customers were Ford and GM in the United States and other major American seat suppliers such as the Lear Corporation.[41]

Older Canadian companies did well under the integrated auto pact regime, too. The A.G. Simpson company, founded by Art Simpson, started making bumpers in Scarborough, Ontario, in 1947. Taking advantage of the boom in production at GM's Oshawa facilities after the auto pact, in 1969 the company opened a new facility in Scarborough, and in 1974 it secured a large-scale bumper contract from GM, after which it became one of the largest bumper suppliers in North America. The company's development also reflected the consolidation that occurred in this period within the Canadian sector: in the 1980s it took over a number of smaller Canadian firms, including Comco of Port Perry and Houdaille of Oshawa. The latter had been the site of a brutal labour dispute in 1980.[42]

Wescast, another older company, originally started as Western Foundry in Brantford, Ontario, in 1902, building stoves and furnaces for firms such as the T. Eaton Company. In the 1960s the company shifted to auto parts, which eventually became its core business. In 1980 Wescast received a contract to build exhaust manifolds for the Pontiac Firebird and Chevrolet Camaro, assembled at GM plants in Van Nuys, California, and Norwood, Ohio. By the 1990s, the company had become one of the largest suppliers of exhaust manifolds in the world.[43]

These representative success stories were reflected in overall increases in Canadian parts production. After the culling of less competitive firms, hundreds of Canadian companies increased their production and exports dramatically in the fifteen years following the auto pact's implementation. Simon Reisman estimated in his 1978 royal commission report that, out of this growth, parts exports from Canada to the United States had increased from 13 per cent of total production of $690 million (about $90 million) in 1964 to 69 per cent of total production of $4.4 billion in 1977 – an astounding $3 billion.[44] Much of these exports were intra-company sales within the Big Three between their Canadian captive parts firms and their U.S. operations. Another large percentage was constituted by sales of American parts makers with Canadian subsidiaries selling into the United States.[45] But Canadian parts makers also experienced growth in this period, as the aforementioned company stories can attest. (See Table 1.3.)

The expansion of the sector was also borne out by the increase in the number of firms and in the growth in employment. Before the auto pact, the Canadian parts industry consisted of less than 150 firms. By 1970, even with the shake-up in the sector, the figure had grown to 182 companies. In 1975 the number of establishments was 231, and in 1980 it was 342. By the mid-1980s, there were nearly 500 parts companies operating in Canada.[46] Correspondingly, the number of workers in the parts sector nearly doubled in the fifteen years between 1964 and 1978, and in the mid-1970s surpassed the number of workers at assembly plants in the country. (See Table 1.4; for total auto employment, see Table 6.1.)

Notwithstanding the initial and ongoing challenges faced by the industry, there was no doubt that Canadian parts makers were reaping

Table 1.3
Canadian automotive industry, trade with U.S., 1960–78 (C$ millions)

Year	Vehicle Export	Parts Export	Total Export	Vehicle Import	Parts Import	Total Import	Vehicle Bal.	Parts Bal.	Total Bal.
1960	0	4	4	90	317	407	−90	−313	−403
1961	0	9	9	71	327	398	−71	−318	−389
1962	3	13	16	78	441	519	−75	−428	−504
1963	4	36	40	49	555	604	−46	−518	−564
1964	26	79	105	67	655	723	−41	−576	−617
1965	90	147	237	170	852	1022	−80	−705	−785
1966	493	361	854	409	1103	1511	84	−741	−657
1967	1105	494	1600	807	1310	2117	298	−816	−518
1968	1686	758	2444	1093	1818	2910	593	−1060	−466
1969	2367	950	3317	1154	2344	3498	1213	−1394	−181
1970	2127	1142	3269	934	2131	3065	1193	−989	204
1971	2536	1504	4040	1321	2521	3842	1215	−1017	198
1972	2752	1801	4553	1551	2957	4508	1201	−1156	45
1973	3060	2240	5300	2082	3620	5702	978	−1380	−402
1974	3408	2027	5435	2517	4110	6627	891	−2083	−1192
1975	3790	2113	5903	3125	4599	7724	665	−2485	−1821
1976	4774	3105	7879	3287	5588	8875	1487	−2483	−996
1977	5996	3865	9861	3952	7001	10953	2044	−3136	−1092
1978	7048	4945	11993	4360	8222	12582	2688	−3277	−589

Source: DesRosiers Automotive Yearbook 2000, 190.

the benefits of the integrated sector by the end of the 1970s. The success of the Canadian parts industry was such that it was reported in a 1973 industry journal that U.S. Treasury Secretary George Schultz had ordered American customs officials to apply import regulations with 'increased severity' in an effort to slow down Canadian-made parts coming across the border, and had also allegedly pressured U.S. assemblers to curtail their purchases of Canadian parts.[47] That year, the Canadian parts industry topped $2 billion in sales for the first time. Three-quarters of this production was shipped to the United States.[48] By 1986, auto analyst Dennis DesRosiers estimated that the Canadian-owned segment of the industry was selling $2.5 billion in parts, nearly one-fifth of the total Canadian sector.[49]

As we shall see, the Canadian parts sector remained vigilant in protecting its interest going forward after 1965, especially as the industry continued to face challenges in the 1970s. In 1972 the APMA's D.S.

Table 1.4
Automotive parts manufacturing employment in Canada,
1964–78 (thousands)

Year	Auto Parts & Accessories (SIC 325)	Auto Fabric & Accessories (SIC 188)	Total
1964	30.5	1.3	31.8
1965	35.3	1.9	37.2
1966	37.6	2.7	40.3
1967	37.7	2.6	40.3
1968	37.3	3.1	40.4
1969	40.4	4.1	44.5
1970	36.4	3.7	40.2
1971	41.3	4.3	44.6
1972	41.4	5.2	46.6
1973	48.8	5.8	54.6
1974	45.9	5.7	51.6
1975	41.2	4.8	46.0
1976	46.2	5.6	51.8
1977	48.6	6.5	55.1
1978	52.1	6.9	59.0

Source: Department of Regional Industrial Expansion,
Report on the Canadian Automotive Industry (Ottawa,
1983), 83.

Wood was succeeded by Patrick Lavelle. Lavelle was an energetic and engaged advocate of the parts makers and was given a mandate by the APMA to take on the government. In the 1970s and early 1980s, he continuously pushed for greater Canadian involvement in the industry, especially arguing for increased CVA. As a manufacturing lobby group that could claim significant Canadian ownership in a period of rising economic nationalism, the APMA often had the government's ear on automotive matters (though it represented the independents, too – the APMA's presidency would alternate each year between and an American and a Canadian). It helped, too, that the independent parts industry employed tens of thousands of workers. Such was Lavelle's influence that in 1978 he convinced Industry Minister Jean Chrétien to hold meetings with the largest American independent parts producers in Detroit, ostensibly for the purpose of convincing them to source more from Canada.[50]

These efforts paid dividends for the Canadian parts industry. Within two decades of the auto pact's creation, a handful of Canadian companies such as Magna, Linamar, Wescast, and A.G. Simpson had become Tier I OEM suppliers, selling directly to the assemblers. In many instances these firms were world leaders in areas of production processes such as systems integration and modularization, or production techniques such as hydro-forming or high-precision tooling. Dozens of other Canadian companies followed in their wake as Tier II or III outfits, providing more basic parts and components for the Tier I OEM makers or for aftermarket industries. Many of these firms flourished with the benefit of continental contracts. In Reisman's view, by 1978 'independent parts companies in Canadian hands have been reduced in number, although the survivors are much improved in strength and quality.'[51]

Eventually, the 1960s shock to the Canadian parts sector that the auto pact represented meant that, when the Japanese arrived to establish transplants in North America, Canadian firms were ready to take on the challenge in order to diversify their business.[52] This market would not have been possible without the stimulation provided by the auto pact requirements for Canadian content, or the new continentally competitive environment faced by the new industrial entrepreneurs whom the sector had created and who had helped to create a vibrant and vital new aspect of the Canadian economy.

Quiet Revolutions: State Auto-Policy Capacity and Automotive Federalism, 1960–80

Paralleling the industry's revolution under the auto pact was a transformation in how governments in Canada interacted with the sector. Federally, this transformation had its roots in the emergence of a muscular new attitude towards industrial policy that emerged in Ottawa in the early 1960s with the Diefenbaker government and that gained momentum after the Liberal victory of 1963. The activist approach by both Conservatives and Liberals towards auto policy was accompanied by a new bureaucratic apparatus to implement and oversee the operation of the auto pact. This emerging 'automotive bureaucracy' centred upon the Department of Industry, created by Pearson's government in 1963. To some degree, the department had been spun off from the interdepartmental 'Industry Committee' which itself had emerged from an effort to examine the Bladen Commission's report in 1962. By 1963, many of the people who would direct government policy on the auto industry were working in other departments (mostly Finance and Trade and Commerce) and would take up temporary or permanent positions in industry. Simon Riesman, for instance, was assistant deputy minister in finance until 1964, when he took over the auto negotiations and the position of deputy minister of industry. Initially led by Riesman, this dynamic cadre of civil servants worked to ensure a robust automotive sector from the 1960s onward.[53]

Notwithstanding its vibrant approach to auto issues, the federal government's automotive strategy in the early 1960s also reflected an utter lack of communication between the two levels of government on the industry. All the automotive measures enacted by both the Diefenbaker and Pearson governments, including the auto pact itself, were initiated with virtually no communication between Ottawa and Ontario, home to the bulk of the industry. Worse yet, even as the new regime created by the auto pact was put in place, initially both governments remained tied to a 'watertight compartments' view of the sector – that neither government could, or should, address auto-sector issues outside its jurisdiction.

While Ottawa had at least realized that it needed a policy capability to deal with the new realities of the post-war auto sector, Ontario had not yet awakened to this quickly changing dynamic. When the auto industry ran smoothly, as it had for more than a decade after 1945, Queen's Park paid little attention to the sector. Ontario, after all, did what it had to do within its own jurisdiction to keep the economy humming along. In the auto field, this meant building highways, managing suburban growth, keeping taxes low, and making sure that government largely left private enterprise alone.[54] As Ontario Minister of Economics and Development Robert Macaulay told the provincial legislature in 1963, just as the federal government was ramping up its auto-policy interventionism, 'it is this government's conviction that industry will function best in an atmosphere of limited government control and direction' and that there was no need for 'direct interference' in the economy.[55]

But when things turned sour, governments, particularly the government of Progressive Conservative Ontario Premier Leslie Frost, did not respond well. This became apparent in March 1958, in one of the most telling post-war conflicts between the province and the sector. When a sudden spike in job losses in Windsor reflected the industry's downturn, Frost lashed out at the sector's apparent short-sighted management, focusing on Chrysler Canada's employment practices. Frost felt that Chrysler had simply hired too many people, especially too many

1.2 Premier Leslie Frost seemed ignorant of the challenges of the modern auto industry. *Toronto Star*, 2 April 1960. Copyright Lewis Parker. Used by permission.

people from outside the province (who would now need relief of some sort), and that the company should have seen the downturn coming. His objection was 'not the fact that the auto manufacturers are not now able to employ all the people who had been engaged in motor vehicle production, but the fact that these people were hired a few years ago in what the auto industry should have recognized were excessive numbers.' In response, Chrysler President Ron Todgham challenged the notion that the company's moves were short-sighted, and the assertion by Frost that the company 'collected people from all over the country in Windsor.'[56]

The incident betrayed the premier's profound misunderstanding of the realities of the post-war industry. Canadian consumers demanded the full range of auto styles and models offered in the United States, a demand that Canadian manufacturers attempted to meet but could never really do so adequately. Yet Frost attacked the industry, where, 'in a wild race to expand sales, many methods of sales enticement were used – scores of types and colours of cars, bigger and wider bodies and more horse power.' Unlike the car-buying public, Frost himself felt that 'these frills are not needed by the average car driver.' As a result, 'it should have been obvious to the auto industry that the pace of 1955 and 1956 could not be maintained forever and that when sales slackened, large numbers of workers in the motor vehicle and supplier industries would have been out of work. And this is exactly what has been happening.'[57] Frost's position reflected an unwillingness to engage the auto sector in thinking about ways to alleviate the structural problems of the industry, which were quickly becoming apparent. Canada's small-scale branch plants simply could not keep up with the demand of consumers or with the full model lines offered by their parent companies.

This disconnection between the Ontario government and the new realities of the automotive industry became plain in 1960, Frost's last year as premier. With employment falling and the sector's problems mounting, various stakeholders within the industry pleaded for provincial government assistance (as they did in Ottawa, as well). The APMA's D.S. Wood began a campaign to bring the auto issue more forcefully to the attention of the Ontario premier. Wood felt that the premier and 'members of the Ontario legislature would wish to be informed of this problem which is facing many of their constituents.'[58] Wood's admonitions were soon followed by those of auto-advertising executive William Gent. Gent, a Conservative supporter, was forthright in his plea to the premier for help for the industry: 'It is obvious to me as I am sure it will be to you, that ... the in-roads made in the Canadian market of foreign made automobiles, trucks, and the necessary parts for their continued operation, have seriously affected not only employment in Canada, but basically employment in the Province of Ontario.'

Frost was unmoved. Though Wood and Gent even outlined measures that the premier might take to alleviate the problems of the industry, 'with the hope that our own Ontario government might not only agree with the brief ... but that you might lend the weight of the Provincial government to some means of a fair and more equitable tariff arrangement for Canadian industry and the Canadian worker,' the premier's response was coldly jurisdictional. Frost responded that 'most of the recommendations relate to the tariff structure, which, as you are aware, comes under the jurisdiction of the Federal Government.' With that, he dismissed the matter.[59]

When John Robarts succeeded Frost as premier in 1961, the result was largely the same. Though one enthusiastic member of the provincial legislature declared that the new premier's team had 'vim, vigour, vitality and above all new initiative' to 'make Ontario's economy grow,'[60] this attitude did not apply to auto production. The auto industry may have driven the province's economy and was in the midst of a major transformation, but Robarts was equally disinterested in violating jurisdictional boundaries when it came to helping the sector.

This became abundantly clear when the Studebaker car company was in its final death throes in 1966. Studebaker, founded in 1897 and based in South Bend, Indiana, was one of the last surviving independent car companies. But by the 1960s the post-war auto industry required large capital expenditures, massive economies of scale, and costly product development. Without a large percentage of the market, independents such as Studebaker had trouble remaining profitable. Merging with Packard in 1954 had not helped, as poor quality, work stoppages, and cutthroat competition from the Big Three ravaged the company. By 1962, Studebaker accounted for only 1.33 per cent of the American market, and it had not made a profit in years.[61]

In 1963 Studebaker ceased production in the United States and moved its remaining car-manufacturing operations to its Hamilton, Ontario, plant.[62] The plan was to give Studebaker some benefit in taking advantage of the 1962–4 Canadian remission plans, and the company's chief executive proudly proclaimed the emergence of a truly Canadian auto company. In reality the company's move north was a ploy to ensure that Studebaker avoided lawsuits from its over-extended network of dealers in the event of the end of production. It could do so because its Canadian subsidiary would continue though production had ceased at the U.S. parent plant.[63]

Even with the remission plans and the auto pact, Studebaker could not survive. By 1966, the company was on its last legs. In a final plea, Studebaker president Robert Growcock wrote to Robarts, begging the Ontario premier to help the company by investing directly in the plant in order to save hundreds of jobs. Robarts was indifferent to Studebaker's plight, and the issue was not even discussed in cabinet. He gave Growcock the traditional federal-provincial jurisdictional brush-off: 'If anything in this connection is done, I should think the government at Ottawa should be the jurisdiction which is concerned.'[64]

Within a few years, however, Ontario's approach would utterly change. As one of the key auto-producing jurisdictions in North America, after 1965 Ontario was vulnerable to the vagaries of a continentalized auto industry under the auto pact regime. Nor could the province ignore the size of the sector and its economic impact upon the well-being of so many Ontarians. By the early 1970s, people both inside and outside

Queen's Park were coming to realize that the sector accounted for the largest portion of provincial GDP and that, as many politicians liked to intone, one in six provincial jobs was linked to the health of the industry. Though the Ontario government's response to the new automotive reality in North America was slower in coming than that of Ottawa's, soon the province took a much more vocal and active role in the sector.

This activism was reflected by new Ontario Premier William Davis. Elected in 1971, Davis was a Tory premier different from those before him. A lawyer by trade, Davis was a committed activist on social and economic policy, and, unlike his more laissez-faire predecessors, he was quite willing to wield the power of the state to shape outcomes to benefit the province. As education minister in Robarts's government, Davis had overseen a reorganization of the public-school system and a massive expansion of the provincial college and university sector. His changes had helped to prepare the province for the shift to a growing service economy, while providing a capable workforce for its sprawling manufacturing sector, one that was anchored by the booming auto industry.[65]

Indeed, when it came to the auto industry, Davis was keenly aware of the sector's impact upon his constituents. Representing Brampton, home to AMC's Canadian plant, in the provincial legislature, the new premier was extremely sensitive to any developments that might threaten the industry or the auto pact, and was quite willing to ensure that Ontario's voice was quickly and loudly heard on these matters. He played, in the view of the APMA's Patrick Lavelle, a 'vital role, one which no premier has since played.' In his first year in office in 1971, when reports began to circulate that the federal government was considering changes to the auto agreement at the behest of the U.S. administration of President Richard Nixon, Davis asked Prime Minister Pierre Trudeau 'not to yield to any pressures in this direction.' He also suggested that, 'in view of the singular importance of these matters to the people of Ontario, representatives of my government would welcome an opportunity to participate in discussions.' This was the first time that an Ontario premier had asked to have a direct say in auto-industry matters.[66]

Ontario's 1972 Throne Speech further emphasized the new attitude at Queen's Park. The province was keen to 'make constructive proposals to the federal government, in order to improve intergovernmental cooperation in … areas of concern … relating to competition and foreign trade, including the vital consideration of the auto pact between

1.3 Ontario's auto premier: Bill Davis at the Ford St Thomas plant, 1981, with Ford CEO Phil Caldwell and Bob White of the UAW, celebrating the introduction of EXP and Mercury production, 17 February 1981. Courtesy of Elgin County Archives.

Canada and the United States.' These promises were soon kept. In 1973, when the auto pact was up for renegotiation, one idea being floated to placate the Americans, who were pushing for removal of the safeguards, was a deletion of the 15 per cent tax on vehicles imported from the United States by individual Canadians. Davis pressed the case forcefully that Ontario was 'not very receptive to this approach. Complete free trade in new and or used cars should not be implemented.' He also stressed that it was imperative that the federal government take Ontario's views into account on this matter of vital importance to the province.[67]

Davis's new-found interest was accompanied by the growth of an Ontario automotive apparatus similar to that which had emerged in Ottawa in the 1960s. By the early 1970s, it was clear to senior Ontario civil servants such as James Fleck that the province needed to build a capacity to deal with auto-industry issues. Fleck ran Ontario's 1971–2

Committee on Government Productivity, formed to sort out governmental processes after Davis became premier. With the support of Secretary to Cabinet Edward Stewart, Fleck sought to increase Ontario's capacity to deal with automotive issues. Stewart, for his part, the real 'sparkplug' on the auto issue, had been deputy minister of education during Davis's time in that portfolio. He was from Windsor and his father worked for an auto company.[68]

The government began to add to its auto-analysis capacity, and eventually a new Queen's Park automotive apparatus, centred first in Treasury and then in the Ministry of Industry and Tourism (MIT), began to take shape. This emerging automotive node at Queen's Park drew personnel and expertise from across the government, as had happened during the earlier federal evolution. In the 1970s the government hired, for the first time, dedicated sector analysts, such as Dennis DesRosiers and Gordon Monroe, both of whom worked in Treasury, then in MIT. DesRosiers left government to work at the APMA before the decade was out and eventually started his own auto-consulting business. People like Michael Dube and Felix Pilorusso were also later added. The former remained in government as an adviser in automotive matters for nearly three decades, while the latter eventually left to form a consulting company, often contracted to examine auto issues. In time, MIT would become the main analytical branch providing support for the auto sector, a function performed today under the auspices of the Ministry of Economic Development and Trade.[69]

By mid-decade, then, Queen's Park was ready and raring to play its part. According to one former senior Ontario civil servant, 'Ottawa's intervention sparked the provinces – the provinces wanted to make sure that they were part of' the discussion around automotive programs. This became apparent in 1975. As the auto deficit increased and parts makers continued to call for support, MIT Minister and Ottawa MPP Claude Bennett declared that Ontario would play 'a significant role' in a Canada-U.S. review of the auto pact promised by both federal governments. Bennett's ministry also began to consult frequently with the APMA and individual parts makers, maintaining 'an up-to-date, two-way relationship, which is of value to both parties.' The following year, Bennett met with GM executives 'to discuss their future development plans' in Ontario, a practice that became regular between Davis and the Big Three.[70]

Ontario's activism went beyond simple consultation. The 1976 provincial budget tabled by Treasurer Darcy McKeough included a 'four part action plan to revive the long-term health of the industry.' In 1978 the province published a study indicating its new-found aggressiveness in automotive matters. *Canada's Share of the North American Auto Industry – An Ontario Perspective* was a paean to state intervention, and it also presented the stark demand that Ontario deserved its 'fair share' of the North American sector.[71] In the early 1980s Ontario created a Board of Industrial Leadership and Development (BILD), designed in part to provide $100 million in support to auto part firms in the province. Emerging firms such as Magna and Linamar benefitted significantly from BILD, as they did from an earlier Economic Development Fund, reflecting Ontario's ability to manage these types of programs effectively.[72] By 1981, when Ontario Treasurer Frank Miller became concerned that Ottawa was developing automotive policy without the province's input, he told his cabinet colleague Industry Minister Larry Grossman that 'between our two ministries, we have the knowledge and the expertise to formulate fairly quickly a position to carry to Ottawa.'[73] It was a far cry from the non-interventionist days of Frost and Robarts.

In this capacity development, Ontario had mimicked the earlier evolution in Ottawa, where automotive personnel in the new Department of Industry were drawn from the finance department. In both governments, Finance and Treasury had each hitherto retained the main analytical and policy capacities for economic measures. Now, each government's industry ministry was given more responsibility over automotive policy. Thus, the 1978 appointment of Lynton Wilson as deputy minister of industry came at a key moment and echoed Reisman's appointment as deputy minister of industry in Ottawa at the start of the auto pact era. Wilson, himself a former federal civil servant, took the helm of Ontario's own nascent automotive mandarinate just as it was about enter a dynamic new phase, one that changed the federalism of Canada's automotive industry profoundly.

The new phase reflected a cooperative though sometimes uneasy approach by the federal and Ontario governments towards the auto sector after 1978. While there was no formal arrangement between the two governments to work together on auto issues, an emerging 'automotive cooperative federalism' can be seen by examining two important episodes: the battle to accrue new Big Three automotive investment, particularly around a Ford engine plant in Windsor in 1978, and the 1979 Chrysler bailout. These are the subjects of chapters 3 and 4, respectively. For now, both stories are noteworthy for illustrating the growing capability of the Ontario government on automotive issues, and the policy necessity of working with the federal government to address issues in the sector.

In 1978 Ontario and Ottawa came together to provide a financial incentive that helped to convince Ford to build an engine plant in Ontario instead of Ohio. Although the final amount each government was to provide was decided only after contentious Ontario-Ottawa negotiations, the Ford deal was pivotal in engaging the provincial and federal governments to cooperate to achieve auto investments. For the first time, auto experts from each government worked together to consummate an incentive-package offer that was designed to build the Canadian sector. According to Wilson, the Ontario deputy minister of industry key to making the deal, the Ford investment put Ontario 'on the map' when it came to the continental auto sector.[74]

The second important episode reflective of the new cooperation between the two levels of government, the somewhat more famous bailout of the Chrysler Corporation in 1979–80, differed in that the two levels of government worked together to provide an aid program, as opposed to the Ford incentive package of a few years before. Nonetheless, this required both governments' automotive apparatuses to work together to develop a small but essential part of Chrysler's overall recovery plan. In the fall of 1979 and the spring of 1980, the two governments met on a number of occasions to determine their respective positions on Chrysler. Eventually, after tough negotiations between Queen's Park and Ottawa, the federal government provided $200 million in loan guarantees, while Ontario agreed to co-fund a research facility with Chrysler.[75]

During this period, Ontario and Davis in particular kept a close eye on automotive developments. Davis argued, as he told Trudeau in 1980, that 'a more coordinated policy approach by our two governments is essential if we want the industry to provide more jobs and continued growth in future years.' Trudeau replied that he appreciated 'the spirit of cooperation and support which you have offered in this regard,' and looked forward to the 'continuation of the close cooperation of our two governments in the development of policies affecting this vital segment of the Canadian industry.'[76]

Of course, automotive cooperative federalism was not always successful. The Ontario-Ottawa axis that led to financial incentives and aid to Ford and Chrysler provoked a backlash from Canada's other car-producing province, Quebec. From the 1960s to the 1980s, Quebec had worked assiduously to build its own auto-making capacity, luring foreign carmakers such as Renault and Hyundai, or making its own incentive offers to companies such as GM, often with federal assistance. But the relative success of Ontario in achieving its aims, compared to Quebec's difficulties, sparked intergovernmental conflict during a period of already intense political uncertainty within the federation.

For instance, at the same time that Ontario was successfully courting Ford to build its new engine plant in Windsor, Quebec was offering an even greater incentive to GM to build a new aluminum casting plant in the province, as we shall see in chapter 3. When the negotiations failed, and GM instead decided to spend most of its investment dollars in Ontario, Quebec representatives were incensed. Federal politicians realized that Ontario's success with Ford and GM threatened to break open an already festering sore between Ottawa and Quebec, one that could have dire consequences for the country as the province's separatist Parti Québécois government geared up for its independence referendum.

Ottawa was right to be worried about Quebec's reaction. In 1979 the Quebec government complained vociferously to the new Progressive Conservative government about federal policies towards the industry that favoured Ontario, especially the auto pact. Rodrique Tremblay, René Levésque's minister of industry and commerce, told his federal counterpart, Robert de Cotret, that the auto pact, 'negotiated without consulting the other provinces, had brought the development of an automobile industry in Quebec to a dead stop.' Tremblay cited an Economic Council of Canada study which, he argued, showed that the auto pact had been more beneficial to Ontario's economy 'than all the combined effects of grants and subsidies awarded by the Department of Regional Economic Expansion to the least developed parts of the country.' Further, Tremblay demanded that any assistance to Chrysler be coupled with the condition 'that their future productive investments be located in Quebec in order to make a start on restoring regional equality in that industry.'[77] Automotive cooperation between Ontario and Ottawa could further fray an already stretched federation.

The Ontario-federal auto axis had its own limits, too. When the government of Brian Mulroney embarked upon its campaign to achieve a free-trade accord with the United States in the mid-1980s, it did so without the consent of Ontario. Provincial politicians of all stripes at Queen's Park were deeply concerned that any new trade agreement with the United States would have a detrimental impact upon the auto pact, which had become an article of faith for many politicians, auto workers, and the public. The battle over the auto pact's place within the free-trade negotiations became perhaps the greatest point of conflict between Ottawa and Ontario during the 1980s. As we shall see, Ottawa's decision to achieve a free-trade deal – at the cost of the auto pact and its other automotive programs – ultimately meant the end of nearly three decades of creative and aggressive policy making in the auto field.

Conclusion: Revolutions of a Different Kind

Nineteenth-century policy and politics shaped the Canadian auto industry well into the 1960s. An archaic tariff structure governed the industry, creating small-scale branch-plant assembly operations and resulting in a rudimentary and stilted parts sector, indigenous or otherwise. Politically, an outdated and compartmentalized federalism kept Ottawa aloof, and Ontario from all but ignoring its largest and most important economic driver, one that faced increasingly complex challenges as the nature of the industry quickly evolved.

Continentalism broke this pattern. The auto pact allowed both the assemblers and the parts makers to take advantage of economies of scale unimaginable in the Canadian sector prior to 1965 by granting duty-free access to the largest and most lucrative automotive market in the world. Continentalism liberated the Canadian Big Three, and they blossomed under the new regime, by specializing and increasing production dramatically. The parts industry also grew. Although the journey of Canadian-owned parts makers that were not yet part of the North American automotive firmament was fraught with difficulties, eventually the new continental regime gave them opportunities that allowed them to flourish too.

Continentalism also broke the pattern of federal-provincial automotive relations. Before the auto pact, the federalist discourse surrounding the auto industry in Canada focused on intrastate regional battles between consumers and producers of automobiles, especially in the inter-war period. In the prosperous 1950s, there was little discussion between Ontario and the federal government over the development of the industry. This dynamic continued into the 1960s, even as the Canadian sector faced technological and fiscal challenges that threatened its existence. Though Ottawa took an activist lead tackling the problems of the industry, Ontario was slow to follow.

But the auto pact changed all this. After the end of tariffs, auto issues engaged provincial governments (chiefly Ontario's) to work with the federal government in ensuring a healthy auto industry within a continentally competitive dynamic.[78] This new automotive cooperative federalism fit within the context of broader Ontario-federal cooperation on a number of fronts, including energy and the constitution, and also reflected the generally warm personal relations between Premier Davis and Prime Minister Trudeau. The early continentalization of the auto industry remains unique, as does the sector's pre-eminent place within North America's economy. The emergence of close cooperation between the federal and Ontario governments emphasized the evolution of federalism in this period, one that saw a strong though sometimes contentious Ottawa-Queen's Park accord on the question of the auto sector.

The relationship between Davis and Trudeau set the tone, as federal-provincial cooperation was mostly friendly and ignored partisan divides. Davis's Tories at Queen's Park had little trouble working with Trudeau's Liberals – or Joe Clark's Progressive Conservatives – on Parliament Hill when it came to the auto sector. There were some disagreements over the details, but more often than not the two governments were in accord when it came to the overall direction of the auto sector in Ontario and Canada until the mid-1980s. For instance, during the Chrysler crisis, MIT Minister Larry Grossman remarked that even with a change of government, 'the federal government has been responsive – both the old government and the new government – to ensure not only that new investment goes into Windsor as a result of the discussions with Chrysler but that there isn't necessarily a long or large layoff period from the current situation to 1983 or 1984.'[79] His colleague, Treasurer Frank Miller, kept up a candid and friendly correspondence with federal Liberal Finance Minister Allan MacEachen.[80]

The auto sector also pointed to another emerging development in Canadian federalism in the period: the broader willingness of provinces to engage in economic matters that were clearly federal in nature.[81] While there was much cooperation between Ottawa and Queen's Park, Ontario's engagement in the traditionally federal area of automotive production caused its own problems. As Davis and the province became more aggressive in demanding a say in auto matters, it complicated Ottawa's normal diplomatic functioning. In 1973 Ottawa agreed to allow Davis to see information transmitted by the Canadian embassy in Washington on selected areas of Ontario's interest, including the auto pact. But External Affairs officials quickly realized that some reports, such as the very sensitive discussions with the United States on the agreement's renegotiation, 'were concerned primarily with proposals for resolving *our* problem' with the United States, and were 'not appropriate to hand over to Ontario.'

Instead, External Affairs officials in Ottawa suggested, future missives that might be seen by Ontario should be written in a way that excluded sensitive information. In Washington, Ambassador Marcel Cadieux thought the request 'hardly credible.' If cables left out pertinent information, such as informal talks between the two governments, Ontario was sure to find out eventually, and if that happened the province (and other provinces) might conclude that it 'must have its own man in Washington.' Cadieux questioned the 'appropriateness' of the embassy 'tailoring its reports to suit a variety of audiences.' Only Ottawa could decide what provincial governments should or should not receive.[82] These disagreements reflected the growing overlap and potential conflict that federal-provincial cooperation on issues such as the automotive file represented.

Even after all these developments, the transformation of the Canadian automotive landscape that began in the early 1960s was not complete by the mid-1970s. The wrenching revolutions that had integrated the North American industry, restructured the Canadian parts industry, and reordered the Canadian and Ontario automotive state apparatuses paled in comparison to the coming changes. The new integrated industry soon faced tidal waves of regulatory, technological, and geopolitical challenges that tested the resiliency of the sector both on a continental and a Canadian basis, left Canadian policy makers desperate to gain their 'fair share' of auto investment and production, and threatened the very existence of giant individual firms such as Chrysler. The industrial revolutions of the 1960s were only a prelude. Greater upheavals awaited Canadians in their newly continentalized auto industry, upheavals that would challenge ordinary Canadians, auto workers and their bosses, and politicians and policy makers alike.

2 The New Big Three: Canadian Safety, Emissions, and Fuel Economy in a Continental Industry

Canadians have always loved their cars, so much so that *Maclean's* could once describe Canada as 'a nation driven.' Even in 1977, in the midst of one of the most tumultuous automotive decades – a decade wracked by high gas prices, terrible designs, overweening regulation, and poor-quality vehicles – Canadians remained enamoured of the automobile and all it represented. To be sure, there were problems with the industry, there was pollution, and gas *was* an issue that seemed to generate all kinds of terrible, apocalyptic headlines. But, the magazine argued, virtually all Canadians could agree that cars were wonderful. Even if you hated Pierre Trudeau, the image of him in his 1960 Mercedes 300SL resonated on a level that crossed regional lines or political partisanship: 'This nation, like its Prime Minister, is in love with cars.'[1]

In this, Canadians were no different from Americans. The stunning growth in the automobile's use after 1945 had come to personify a transcontinental dream of post-war consumerism. Auto factories in the United States and Canada assembled an astonishing 150 million new vehicles between 1948 and 1968, many of which were still on the road by the early 1970s.[2] The cars built during the industry's golden age were big, powerful, and focused on styling ahead of safety, fuel economy, or environmental impact. The American Big Three and their Canadian plants competed to build the lowest, longest cars with the biggest engines, the greatest horsepower, and the wickedest tail-fins – it was reported that some 1960 models actually broke Ontario laws regarding the width of passenger cars. By the mid-1960s, the automobile was North America's most important industry, and the car a potent symbol of a very rich society.[3]

2.1 Trudeau gets his car serviced in Ottawa, n.d. Courtesy of Motor Medics Ltd, Ottawa.[4]

But the mass embrace of the automobile had a downside. Lurking just below the love affair was something more serious and more trans-formative than most Canadians realized. Yes, Canadians loved their cars, but the details of the industry – *how* cars were built, cars' impact upon people and place, and the relationships that decided where cars were made – were in the midst of dramatic change. By the early 1960s, North Americans had entered into what auto historian James Flink has called the 'third stage of automobile consciousness,' one that moved beyond simple adoption of the car and its widespread, uncritical ac-ceptance to a critique of its impact.[5] John Keats's 1958 best-seller *In-solent Chariots* attacked the Big Three for their uninspired, conformist designs. Other critics, such as urban thinker Jane Jacobs and consumer-rights advocate Ralph Nader, focused a spotlight on the damage that cars did to cities or the unsafe vehicles pushed by Detroit. The backlash was fuelled by a 1960s counter-culture, anti-establishment ethos which questioned the authority of automobile executives and was personified by Nader's battles with the world's largest and most profitable corporation, General Motors.[6]

Notwithstanding *Maclean's* ode to Canada's love affair with cars, in the post-war period Canadians, like their American neighbours, also began questioning what historian Arthur Lower called the 'Great God Car.'[7] From the battle over the Spadina Expressway to grass-roots campaigns against 'drive-thru' culture, Canadians took part in the North American backlash against the automobile and its impact, a backlash that seemed to gain momentum with every new headline about safety problems, air pollution, smog, and the dependency upon cars so profoundly illustrated by OPEC's embargo.[8]

These concerns resulted in an enormous three-crested regulatory tidal wave in North America which profoundly destabilized the industry and its players. It began with safety in the late 1960s, shifted to emissions in the early 1970s, and then focused almost entirely upon fuel economy after the mid-1970s. Appearing seemingly so suddenly, and extending so deeply into the workings of a hitherto unregulated Detroit, the legislation emanating from Washington was a startling departure from the previous relations between the auto industry and government. Canadians, affected by every ripple through the giant U.S. auto sector because of the integrationist auto pact, faced the possibility that their own ability to regulate would be overwhelmed entirely. After all, by the mid-1970s the North American automobile had become the most regulated, most scrutinized, and, in some instances, most hated (and loved) consumer product in history. When it came to the regulation of the car, ordinary Canadians and their policy makers sometimes conquered the wave, and sometimes struggled against its powerful undertow.

Following in Lockstep: Harmonization of Safety Standards with the United States

Since the first car accident, automobile safety has been a contentious issue, particularly so in the 1920s when an epidemic of auto fatalities became a focus of public attention.[9] As a result, during the interwar period auto companies, led by GM, successfully framed the issue of safety so that the onus of fault was upon the driver. Driver error, as opposed to mechanical problems, overpowered vehicles, or a lack of safety features or regulations, became the standard explanation for accidents. After the Second World War, the Big Three's focus remained upon styling over safety, and post-war notions of family and responsible masculinity continued to uphold the idea that accidents and motor-vehicle deaths were primarily caused by driver mistakes. Detroit argued that it could do little about this except to help educate the public to be better drivers and enforce tough laws against those who drove irresponsibly. This was true in Canada as well. As historian Christopher Dummitt has shown, in the 1950s Vancouver's safety establishment pushed the notion of masculine-oriented driver education as a way to alleviate accidents. A safe driver was a good man, and accidents had almost nothing to do with cars themselves.[10]

By the 1960s, the notion of driver error as the chief cause of automobile accidents was beginning to crash into the horrifying reality of the carnage on the roads. In the 1950s more than 27,000 Canadians lost their lives in motor-vehicle-related accidents. After 1960, 4,500 Canadians a year were being killed on the country's roads and highways, a figure that peaked in 1973 at 6,700. Canadians were slowly realizing that neither driver error nor the simple presence of so many more drivers and cars could solely explain these figures: poorly designed cars were just as culpable as bad drivers, alcohol, and ill-designed roads. An influential 1964 National Film Board Documentary, *Every Second Car*, made the case that every other car on the road would cause an injury-producing accident during its lifetime, and that drivers were less to blame than assumed – 'safety engineering' could reduce fatalities. The film reflected a changing Canadian attitude towards auto safety, one that shifted blame away from drivers to their cars.[11]

Echoing a similar outcry in the United States, where the raw numbers of traffic fatalities were even more appalling – 53,000 auto deaths in 1966 alone – many Canadians demanded that automobiles be redesigned with safety, and not styling, as the main concern. Famous coroner Dr Morton Shulman (who inspired the mid-1960s hit CBC show *Wojeck*) argued that 84 per cent of fatalities were caused by poor auto design, and emphasized the need for production of 'crash worthy vehicles.' This was seconded by the *Toronto Star*, which opined that 'the automobile is potentially a lethal weapon … auto manufacturers understand only one language when it comes to safety devices – compulsion' and called for legislation to regulate car safety. In magazines such as *Chatelaine* or *Canadian Consumer*, Canadians demanded improvements to automobile safety, from equipment improvements like child-safety seats to legislation to mandate behaviour, such as seat-belt laws.[12]

2.2 *Very* early safety belts and seats for children, Alberta, 1972. Courtesy of Glenbow Museum Archives.

The demand for safer cars took root in Ottawa as well. A 1965 report, 'Traffic Accident Death and Injuries in Canada,' endorsed by an inter-party group of MPs, pushed for federal regulation of automobiles, re-search on a prototype 'safety car' to be built by the federal government, and the creation of a national accident-prevention research centre. Cit-ing figures that showed that over half of auto fatalities resulted from passengers being thrown from their cars during accidents, as well as from faulty steering assemblies and instrument panels, the MPs argued that 'automobile injury and death could be very significantly reduced if safety features *already tested and known* were incorporated into the design of the automobile.'[13]

The North American safety revolt ultimately found its champion in consumer- rights activist Ralph Nader. Nader, a Harvard-trained law-yer from Connecticut, began a crusade against poor car safety in the late 1950s. Working in Congress as an assistant to Abraham Ribicoff's (D-Conn.) Senate Subcommittee on Car Safety, in 1965 Nader published *Unsafe at Any Speed*, his muckraking expose of GM's poorly designed Corvair and the safety problems in the auto industry. The book generated headlines and prompted an ill-advised smear campaign by the company against Nader. Nader's battles against GM and the auto industry and his high-profile testimony before Congress resulted in the unanimous congressional passage of the 1966 National Traffic and Motor Vehicle Safety Act (NTMVSA), which created the National Highway and Traffic Safety Agency (NHTSA).[14]

The U.S. regulatory changes (and the immense attention generated by Nader's activities) had a direct impact in Canada. Nader himself was invited to testify before the House of Commons Justice Committee on safety issues, while MPs such as New Democrat Reid Scott and Progressive Conservative Richard Southam both sponsored private members' bills legislating safety standards. Echoing Nader's arguments, Reid's bill would 'counteract the brain-washing of auto makers who have persuaded the public to accept beautiful cars rather than safe cars.'[15] Nader even spawned his own Canadian consumer-advocate clone. In 1968 Phil Edmonston, a former U.S. soldier who had immigrated to Montreal in the mid-1960s, founded the Automobile Protection Association (APA), dedicated to holding manufacturers to account for their shoddy products. The APA was successful in forcing Ford to compensate owners for prematurely rusting cars; Edmonston also published a series of *Lemon-Aid* car guides starting in the 1970s.[16]

The safety crusade found a willing convert in car enthusiast and Prime Minister Pierre Trudeau. Trudeau felt it was important that 'government give a clear public indication in its interest and concern in matters relating to automobile safety, particularly in light of the great public concern' that had emerged with Nader. Following the U.S. regulations enshrined in the NTMVSA seemed the most logical course of action for Canadian politicians and policy makers, since the 1965 auto pact had merged the two countries' automotive sectors into one continental industry. Although the agreement governed aspects of production and trade, it was silent on standards, and said nothing about safety, fuel economy, or emissions. Nonetheless, since Canadian and American plants were both producing for all of North America, it was thought that they would necessarily follow the new U.S. standards given that over 80 per cent of the cars would be sold in the United States; cars sold in Canada would meet these legislative requirements as a consequence of the integrated industry.[17]

Of course, in a federation such as Canada's, there was the question of which level of government should administer any safety regulations. In 1967 the federal cabinet decided that the Ministry of Transport (MOT) would be responsible for motor-vehicle safety, including all safety and emissions regulations. This eventually resulted in the creation of the Motor Vehicle Traffic Safety Branch within MOT, in 1969, headed by engineer Gordon D. Campbell. Cabinet also decided that 'in order to achieve uniformity of motor vehicle safety standards, having particular regard to the Auto Trade Agreement between the two countries, negotiations ... be undertaken with the Motor Vehicle Traffic Safety Bureau of the U.S.A. Department of Transportation,' given the integration of the two countries' industries. In an era of 'cooperative federalism,' subsequent federal-provincial meetings in the late 1960s resulted in an understanding between Ottawa and the provinces that the federal government would indeed legislate safety and other standards for new vehicles, though with some provincial input.[18]

Another consideration was the role of the auto companies in the safety issue. The Canadian industry was almost entirely dominated by the U.S. Big Three, who were already grudgingly dealing with the U.S. safety regulations. MOT officials realized that any new Canadian safety standards would be impossible to legislate without significant cooperation from the carmakers. At the same time, cabinet decided that it could not include 'consultation' in the actual legislation, since that conferred legal obligations upon the government. After drawing up 'proposed' legislation in late 1969, MOT Minister Don Jamieson invited all the assemblers and parts makers in Canada to consult with federal officials on new standards.[19]

The Canadian auto industry descended upon Ottawa in June 1970 to find out what the government had in store for the sector. Over two days of presentations in the recently opened National Archives Building, Minister Jamieson and his deputies laid out the basics of the proposed legislation. Twenty-nine regulations, governing everything from brakes to lighting to tires, were to be put in place and a 'National Safety Mark' affixed to new vehicles. MOT officials also reiterated to company representatives that the Canadian regulations would closely follow U.S. standards, owing to the continentalization of the industry. In 1967, in the wake of Nader and the new U.S. regulations, the companies had already indicated to Ottawa that Canadian-built cars (and obviously those imported from the United States) would meet the NTMVSA standards.[20]

With legislation pending, the Big Three all indicated that, as long as the Canadian standards and practices followed along U.S. lines, they would have no objections. Aside from a few minor variations and questions of interpretation, GM, Ford, and Chrysler were satisfied that the new rules 'achieve[d] the objective' of 'the development of uniform North American standards and regulations.' The head of the Motor Vehicle Manufacturers Association (MVMA), James Dykes, also told MOT that the industry 'was pleased' with the draft legislation. While the automakers faced no difficulties in meeting the new technical requirements, significant lead time was necessary from the publication of the regulations to their enforcement date, so as to deal with the complex paperwork required.[21] On 1 January 1971 the Motor Vehicle Safety Act (MVSA) was proclaimed by the federal government, setting out standards for the design and construction of motor vehicles as well as emission-reduction controls and enforcement.

The new safety standards were not so easily attainable for all automakers in Canada, however. The Société de Montage Automobile (SOMA), a Quebec government-financed plant building Renaults in Saint-Bruno, Quebec, was owned by an offshore producer that could not initially meet the requirements. In early 1972 SOMA officials complained to the government that the new rules meant that they could not export to the United States since their vehicles did not meet the American safety standards, particularly around seat-belt warning systems, which were slightly different from Canada's regulations. Instead, they threatened to close the plant for four months and then resume production at only two-thirds output. The Japanese, who had been importing vehicles into Canada since the 1960s and had started some local production (Toyota had a rudimentary assembly plant in Sydney, Nova Scotia, putting together partially assembled kits), had difficulties meeting some safety standards for Canadian-made 1972 model-year Corollas.[22] As with SOMA, they also needed an extension to meet more stringent bumper standards.[23] Some imports were victims of the new safety rules, too. GM stopped importing British-made Vauxhalls to Canada, since it was not worthwhile to retool the cars to meet the new standards given the vehicle's small sales.[24]

Still, as some automakers struggled to meet the standards, the older way of thinking on auto safety persisted. In a 1971 speech at the University of Western Ontario, AMC Canada president L.G. Rice warned of the costs of meeting safety concerns and wondered whether the public would pay for these measures. He cited the example of his company's efforts to push safety features in the 1950s and 1960s, with little success: 'We tried for years to persuade people to take seat belts as an option. All we asked was that they pay for them. They wouldn't, by and large.'[25]

Even within the government there was scepticism about safety legislation. In 1975 D.W.C. McEwan of IT&C's Motor Vehicle Division agreed with new measures to achieve road-safety goals by 1979, but he warned his superiors that 'driver safety' was where the government's principal efforts should be focused. Vehicle-safety standards could be expensive and 'should be reviewed carefully before being implemented.' After all, in McEwan's view, 'the stronger and heavier a piece of equipment is made, the more it is abused and therefore the more a car is crashable, the less care will the driver take ... legislation for safety features and mandatory recalls can count for very little. It all depends on the driver.'[26]

Notwithstanding McEwans's and Rice's complaints, after 1971 the Canadian regulators largely adopted the U.S. standards, and the industry complied. Whenever there was a change in the NTMVSA, MOT quickly followed suit. A good example is the case of seat belts. Seat belts had been standard equipment on cars in Canada after 1971; the NTMVSA had made the equipment mandatory since 1967. However, the presence of seat belts did not stem the public outcry for mandatory seat-belt *usage* laws, an outcry that reached a height in the early 1970s on both sides of the border.[27] This prompted the United States to legislate the seat-belt ignition interlock for 1973, making a car inoperable unless seatbelts had been fastened. The Canadians quickly followed suit, and changed their laws to meet the U.S. standards. But when a backlash against the interlock forced the U.S. Congress to back down, the Canadians did so as well. There would be no interlock system forcing drivers to buckle up before they started up, on either side of the Canada-U.S. border.[28]

By the 1970s, the safety revolution had redefined the problem of motor-vehicle accidents and responsible driving. The driver was no longer seen as the sole culprit when it came to accidents, as cars themselves became targets of regulation and the focus of safety campaigns. For instance, in its 1975 'Car Check Campaign,' the Canadian Safety Council reasoned that 'one legal and moral obligation all car owners bear is the obligation to make sure their vehicles are maintained in a mechanically safe condition. This won't eliminate all accidents but it will reduce them ... Have your own car checked.'[29] Of course, targeting the car still rankled many. When, in the early 1980s, the administration of U.S. President Ronald Reagan began to roll back some safety regulations, more than a few Canadians were quite happy and demanded that Canada do likewise (which it largely did). One citizen wrote to

2.3 The Canadian Safety Council played its role in making Canadians safe. 1975. W.L. Higgitt (president, Consumer Safety Council of Canada) to Herb Gray, 1 April 1975, LAC, RG 20, file 4956-2-2.

IT&C Minister Herb Gray in 1981: 'I am strongly in favour of this long overdue review of these mostly idiotic, useless, and costly regulations, the bulk of which were instituted by clamouring claques of consumer advocates with little or no knowledge of or respect for sound engineering practices.'[30] By and large, however, most Canadians were content simply to follow along with the U.S. rules, as were the policy makers and the automakers too.

When it came the regulation of cars for safety, in virtually every in-stance the Canadian standards followed those of the United States, and a harmonized North American safety regime was achieved. There were a few minor exceptions, but MOT followed the U.S. agency's de-cisions quite closely and also worked in tandem with American regu-lators to ensure continental compliance of safety standards.[31] In some instances, Canadians were given advance warning of U.S. safety-reg-ulation revisions; at times, Canadian regulators, such as Motor Vehi-cle Traffic Safety Director D.G. Campbell, visited with his American counterparts at NHTSA to consult on auto regulations.[32] When it came to safety regulations, the two countries were in virtual lockstep. This contrasted dramatically with the second great regulatory wave that challenged North America's automakers in the 1970s, the case of auto-motive emissions.

Going for the Bronze: Canada's Unique Emissions Standards in North America

The problem of automotive emissions, and the recognition of this problem, is not a recent phenomenon. As historian Tom McCarthy has shown, from the earliest days of the automobile, auto enthusiasts, observers, and critics all complained about exhaust. Even in the early 1900s, many people wondered whether the 'smoky exhaust' spewing from loud and smelly automobiles was any better than the mountains of excrement created by horses. By the 1920s, some of the problems associated with early engines and gas had been solved, lessening the focus of the car's emissions. The Great Depression, the Second World War, and the booming post-war auto industry pushed cars' environ-mental problems to the periphery.[33]

Yet the problem re-emerged after the war, particularly in California. Los Angeles, owing to its geography and climate, and the fact that it had the highest concentration of automobiles in the world, first encoun-tered smog – smoky fog – in the 1940s. Angelenos and Californians demanded that Detroit provide technological fixes to cut smog-form-ing fumes, and pushed for municipal and state legislation to regulate emissions. Detroit successfully delayed implementing new technolo-gies (which it possessed) until the mid-1960s. Collusive actions to this end led to the Big Three being charged in a civil suit by the anti-trust division of the U.S. Department of Justice, a case that was settled out of court.[34]

In the 1950s scientists determined that there were three main airborne pollutants caused by gasoline use. The first is carbon monoxide, or CO, an odorless, colourless gas that affects the oxygen-carrying ability of blood. The second is hydrocarbons, or HCs, produced by the incomplete burning of gas.[35] HCs constitute a family of substances that react with oxides to form ground-level ozone, which can cause eye irritation, respiratory inflammation, and permanent lung damage. Finally, cars emit nitrogen oxides, or NO_X. In air, these oxidants also form ozone gas, which can thicken the small arteries in the lung, negatively affecting blood flow. The most visible impact of these emissions is the creation of photochemical smog. Smog occurs when ultraviolet rays hit the HCs and NO_X emitted in auto exhaust, changing the chemical composition of these elements to form a heavy, murky black cloud.[36]

By the early 1970s, the issue of smog from cars had become a problem in Canada, particularly in urban areas. Toronto had over 800,000 cars by 1970, a massive increase from the 146,000 registered cars in 1946. The environmental group Pollution Probe, started by University of Toronto students in 1969, took part in a study that showed increased CO blood levels from driving for just an hour on Toronto's streets.[37] By 1972, smog had become so bad that the Association of Professional Engineers of Ontario organized an international conference to examine the problem. The statistics presented were staggering. Cars in Toronto yearly spewed 98 per cent of the city's 437,000 tons of CO, 69 per cent of its 94,000 tons of HCs, and 19 per cent of its 120,000 tons of NO_X. These figures prompted *Globe and Mail* editor Richard J. Doyle to write: 'We have the choice of driving reasonably and with due respect for the city's environment as a whole, or letting [cars] drive us to the cost of ever-wider roadways, more expressways, more unproductive parking space, more unhealthy air.'[38] For its part, the *Toronto Star* launched a special investigation into car pollution and demanded that government 'pull together now' to clean auto exhaust by 1975.[39]

Automobile pollution was a problem across the country. In 1968 the air in Montreal was so bad that the city set up thirty-five air-quality monitoring stations. The municipal health department reported that 1970 levels of CO were high enough to 'cause eye, ear and brain damage in some persons.'[40] In Calgary, anti-pollution protestors took to the streets in 1970, demanding that something be done about the choking smog that seemed to be getting progressively worse. Across Alberta, the urban municipalities association called for compulsory installation of anti-pollution devices for any cars bought in the province. In places

2.4 A 1970 Calgary anti-pollution parade. Courtesy of Glenbow Museum Archives.

like Ottawa, Hamilton, or Vancouver, pollution and the environment gripped the public agenda.[41]

These were not just local concerns, either. In 1969 a Federal-Provincial Committee on Air Pollution was created by the Department of National Health and Welfare to examine the problem and make recommendations.[42] A 1970 poll showed that 70 per cent of Canadians wanted action on air and water pollution, compared to 59 per cent who wanted action on unemployment. The Canadian Labour Congress (CLC) warned that 'pollution has reached such proportions that life in its many forms is seriously menaced.'[43] Federal politicians were starting to pay attention, too. At its 1970 policy convention, the Liberal Party passed Environmental Pollution Resolution 6, which demanded that the government immediately declare a 'War on Pollution.' This war included 'the cessation of untreated stack and automobile exhaust emissions.'[44]

But there were also auto-pollution sceptics. 'No one knows where air pollution comes from and no one can say authoritatively what contribution automotive exhaust have [sic] made to the overall mess,' wrote gadfly Richard Clee of Toronto to the *Globe and Mail*. 'Nor,' Clee continued, 'has there been a single shred of evidence that the quantities of exhaust components present in the atmosphere have harmed any one or any living thing.' Clee advocated killing any notion of regulation 'till we determine that there is a problem, that we are attacking the right problem, that there is a solution available and that we can afford that solution when it's applied. That beats spending a billion bucks a year chasing shadows only to find a decade later it's unproductive when the money could have brought real results instead.' For the president of GM Canada, John Baker, pollution-control devices were 'money not well spent. It's what we call regulatory overkill.'[45]

As with safety, the front lines in the war on pollution were not in Canada but in the United States. The most profound environmental regulatory change in North America's history occurred with the 1970 Clean Air Act. Enforced by a new Environmental Protection Agency (EPA) with the power to regulate emissions, the Clean Air Act meant that 'automakers had to spend whatever it took to invent whatever technology was required in order to meet the standards and safeguard the public health.'[46] The act required a 90 per cent reduction in the emissions of CO and HCs by 1 January 1975, and a 90 per cent reduction of NO_X by 1 January 1976. Practically, this meant a reduction of emissions, per car, to 3.4 grams per mile for CO, .41 grams per mile for HCs, and 3.0 grams per mile for NO_X. (See Table 2.1.) The new regulations set off a storm of controversy in the United States as the automakers claimed that the stricter standards were impossible to meet. Despite this opposition, by 1970 the Big Three had already utilized engine adjustments and some basic emission-control devices to reduce CO and HC emissions by about 60 per cent. But it was true that the remaining emissions were far more difficult to reduce or eliminate.[47]

In the wake of the Clean Air Act, American approaches to emissions were broadly followed by the Canadian government. The establishment of the EPA was echoed in Canada by the creation of a stand-alone Ministry of the Environment (MOE) in June 1971. Heading the new department was Vancouver politician Jack Davis, previously the minister of fisheries. Davis became the world's first environment minister. A new 1971 Canadian Clean Air Act gave Davis the power to 'formulate comprehensive plans and designs for the control and abatement of air pollution.' But it was Transport Minister Don Jamieson who had already announced in 1970 that Canada would follow all twenty-nine standards that the United States had instituted, including those for emissions. While the environment ministry might see the problem of air pollution from cars as one of its greatest policy issues, and 'was designated to carry out the required compliance testing and provide technical advisory services in support of the regulations,' the ultimate decision on emissions standards lay with MOT under the authority of the MVSA.[48] After all, as with safety issues, the integration of cross-border production assumed harmonization of emissions-control technology, or so it was thought.

This view that Canada would simply follow the U.S. legislation when it came to emissions was held by many in government, and by the public as well. In the spring of 1970, Jan Chrystman of MOE's Air Pollution Control Directorate told reporters that 'based on the information we have obtained and observing the decisions made by the EPA, we see no reason why the standards can't be reached. Since automobile production is worldwide, there could be problems if different countries steered away from unified emission standards. So the Canadian standards are similar in approach to the American ones.'[49] That summer, as the regulation battle unfolded in Washington between the automakers and the federal government, the *Globe and Mail* editorialized that Canada was simply following the American lead when it came to the issue: 'In terms of actual control [over emissions regulation], then, the establishment of Canadian standards amounts to little more than a faint cry of "me too!"'[50]

Forced to move on the emissions issue by the enactment of the U.S. Clean Air Act, in 1971 MOT called upon effected ministries to submit their views on what to do, and whether Canada should follow suit with stringent emissions controls. The greatest opposition to following the United States came from the Department of Energy, Mines and Resources (EMR). Voicing the concerns of the oil industry, EMR deputy minister Jack Austin felt that using U.S. emission standards was misguided, given the differences in climate and geography between the two countries.[51] Worse, from EMR's viewpoint, U.S. regulators 'had not worked in close cooperation with the automobile manufacturers and petroleum companies to achieve stepwise improvement in the environment without causing severe economic upset.' EMR instead asked whether Canada should develop its own standards. This position reflected a deep discomfort with the notion of following U.S. emission controls, and illustrated EMR's close relations with the petroleum industry. 'Canada should await developments in the US,' EMR stated, and act only after they have been successfully implemented in that country.'[52]

Swayed by EMR's view, cabinet decided that MOT and MOE (and not the government itself) would announce 'proposed regulations' that matched the U.S. emission standards. But there was to be no official proclamation, giving Canadians a way out if the United States did not end up with the announced EPA standards, a strong possibility in light of the industry-government battle in Washington.[53] In the meantime, the government gave 'interested persons' until 1 July 1972 to make representations on the issue. This opened the door for automakers, oil companies, and a host of others to have their voices heard in the setting of standards. In December 1971, almost one year after the U.S. legislation, the government finally announced its 'proposed regulations' regarding automotive emissions.[54] Jamieson and Davis stated that Canada's proposed regulations would match the U.S. 1975 reduction targets for CO, HCs, and NO_X – a reduction to 10 per cent of current emissions levels.[55]

As representations flowed into Ottawa, most of the auto sector and oil industry argued that going to a different Canadian standard was not only feasible but might be desirable, considering the two countries' differing circumstances. In contrast to his company's views on the safety-standards issue, Chrysler Canada's J.E. Elliot argued that the auto pact was just one consideration and did not preclude different emission standards. Instead, if 'Canadian needs remain as far removed from 1975–76 US regulations as is presently indicated, we believe that there may be ample economic justification to support unique Canadian regulations.'[56] If there were different controls, according to Elliot's boss, Chrysler President Ron Todgham, Canada 'would not face any major production problems in fitting one system for cars destined for the United States and another system for cars to be sold in Canada.'[57]

The idea of a less stringent Canadian emissions standard began to be pushed in earnest following a February 1973 meeting of Big Three and major Canadian oil- company presidents, new Transport Minister Jean Marchand (who replaced Jamieson following the 1972 election), MOE's Davis, IT&C's Alastair Gillespie, and EMR's Donald Macdonald. The auto and oil men reiterated arguments they had made in public against tougher emission standards: the technology was not feasible or cost-effective; no serious air pollution had been demonstrated; and new standards meant fuel-consumption increases and an impact on energy reserves. Importantly, however, GM indicated that it could live with Canada joining the U.S. standards – though this was largely because of advances in its own emission-controlling catalytic converter technology, which it deemed could give it an advantage in the marketplace.[58]

"... you'll notice what a fine sculptured look the new smog-eliminator gives the overall rapier-sweep sleek elegance of total design ..."

2.5 Automakers' claim that a practical technological fix for emissions was impossible had some traction with the public. By Sid Barron, *Toronto Star*, 18 February 1970. Reprinted with permission – Torstar Syndication Services.

Catalytic converters, the industry's emerging solution to the problem, were ceramic containers coated with metal catalysts such as platinum that were attached to a car's exhaust system to intercept HCs and CO and reduce them to carbon dioxide.

Although arguments by the auto and oil representatives' against tighter emission standards were largely refuted by government officials, the idea of unique Canadian standards was appealing to Ottawa. Less stringent Canadian standards had the benefit of giving the automakers more time to develop the technologies to meet the higher, original standards. There was some evidence that this was a good possibility: GM told MOT officials in early 1973 that its catalytic converters were close to meeting the emission standards, and that fuel consumption might even be even improved with the new technology. MOT officials argued that 'the rate of improvement in air quality would not be significantly affected' by this delay.[59]

Moreover, the less stringent Canadian standards offered the government some protection if the United States decided to grant automakers a delay in the 1975/6 standards, which the Big Three had been arguing for in Washington. This strategy proved prudent. In April 1973 the U.S. EPA announced that it was granting a one-year delay for the emission standards and providing new, interim standards for HC and CO levels that were about half of the original requirements (see Figure 1). California, owing to its particular challenges and legislative precedent (it had created its own regulations prior to the U.S. regulations, and therefore could impose its own emission standards), was exempt from the ruling and required the original 1975/6 standards.[60]

In June 1973 MOT decided to push for Canadian standards that were weaker than both Washington's and California's. 'While I could decide to retain the present 1973–74 Canadian automobile exhaust emission standards,' MOT's Marchand told the affected ministers, 'I believe there is merit in considering the second option which would result in further decreases in emissions but would not require the use of catalysts.' There was no chance of Canada following the U.S. standards – not even the less stringent interim U.S. standards. Catalytic converters had not been proven conclusively, Marchand maintained, and in any event this costly device 'was not really justified by Canadian air quality needs.' The devices would, in his view, place an unfair 'financial burden on the petroleum industry and the consumer.' Since MOT had essentially made the decision, Marchand expected his cabinet colleagues to go along (without meeting again to discuss the matter), and asked them to respond as soon as possible to finalize the weaker Canadian targets given 'the extreme urgency to make an announcement.'[61]

Environment Canada disagreed vehemently with Marchand's approach. Its own studies on auto-emission trends found that 'without more stringent emission regulations the total amount of pollutants emitted by automobiles will begin to increase by the end of this decade.'[62] MOE saw only two options: 'Either we stay in lock-step with the US for 1975 or we lag behind them for two or three years by retaining unchanged the present 1973 standards.' Since the Big Three had indicated that they could meet the interim U.S. standards (and GM, the Canadian market leader, had indicated a preference to do so), 'Environment Canada wants the US 1975 standards in Canada in 1975.' Air-quality concerns demanded it, the technology was available to do it, and there was even the opportunity to improve fuel economy with the U.S. standards. Besides, Davis told Marchand, given that GM and the other companies would likely just send cars meeting the U.S. standard north of the border, Canada would get the that standard 'whether we require it or not.'[63]

The battle over the emission standards came to a head in July 1973. Environment's objections forced Marchand to come to a final decision on the issue. Of the six departments involved, only Environment called for the stricter U.S. standards. IT&C, Science and Technology, and EMR all called for either maintaining the 1973 standards or going to a Canadian interim standard, which IT&C and MOT advocated. Health Canada was for either the Canadian standards or the stricter U.S. standards.[64] IT&C's support for the MOT position, and the position of EMR and Science and Technology's call for less stringent standards, reflected the government's ultimate decision. Economic consequences won over environmental concerns when it came to emission standards.

Davis and Environment Canada lost the argument. Instead of hitting the interim U.S. targets of 1.5 grams per mile for HCs, and 15.0 grams per mile for CO (NO_x had remained 3.1, owing to EPA's decision to grant a delay on that standard), the Canadian requirements were 2.0 for HCs and 25.0 for CO. This represented 'a reduction in emissions of about 72% from uncontrolled values,' versus 82 per cent for the United States.[65] Although Ottawa stated that it was taking action because 'the quality of life of the Canadian public was paramount' and the 'levels of these noxious gases are presently of some concern in Canadian urban areas,' it was clear that the Canadians had made the decision with less regard to the environment than claimed.[66] The federal government's decision meant that a new, three-standard North American emissions regime had been established. North American automakers now essentially had to sell to three different automotive markets for the purposes of emissions standards – a U.S. market with about 80 per cent of total sales, one in California with about 10 per cent of the market, and one in Canada with less than 10 per cent of the market.

The Canadian announcement to enforce the least stringent emission standards in North America was met with little reaction. In the House of Commons there were only a few questions lobbed at Davis over the issue, which did not gain traction on the opposition benches.[67] News reports stressed the savings on new cars, given the lack of catalytic converters required to meet U.S. standards.[68] For its part, the Ontario government publicly declared that it would not even bother to enforce the new standards on its highways.[69] The quiet Canadian reaction to the federal decision was even more surprising given that Environment Canada officials had publicly admitted in the spring of 1973 that their studies had shown that average emissions in Canada were higher than those in the United States owing to Canada's generally colder temperatures.[70] Further, with no catalytic converters required on Canadian cars, there was no incentive for Canadian drivers to move more quickly to less damaging unleaded gasoline (in fact, the oil companies ensured that Canadian gas stations would have unleaded gas in small quantities, intended for American tourists driving in Canada). The results were predictable: GM decided in August 1974 to back away from its plan to equip all its Canadian cars with catalytic converters, and instead would offer Canadian customers an emissions package that met the less stringent Canadian standard.[71]

No sooner had the battle over the 1975 standards ended than discussions began between the key players within the government on the issue. In December 1974 Marchand informed affected ministers that a decision on 1976's standards needed to be made. He told his colleagues he intended to tell the automakers that the 1976 standards would remain the same as those for 1975. Marchand advanced several arguments for maintaining the Canadian standards: the automakers needed to make decisions on their emission-control systems as soon as possible; there was 'no longer a need to maintain uniformity with the US Emission regulations'; no improvements in emission control had been proved which required new legislation; and the U.S. Congress might soon change its emission standards again.[72]

Once more, Environment Canada opposed Marchand's position. Although Davis had grudgingly concurred with the decision to maintain the 1975 standards for 1976, he felt that we 'could be doing more.' The government of Canada, Davis implored, 'now had an opportunity to correct' the situation. Davis's plan was to extend the 1975 emission standards for another year, to 1977, giving the automakers time to develop the new technologies required. Then, for 1978 Canada should 'set standards equal to those set by the US EPA for California in 1975.' After three years of the old standards, reasoned Davis, 'there should be reliable, low cost systems available to meet such standards.' The government should also 'keep the original proposed stringent 1975 standards for HC and CO before the manufacturers' as a long-term goal. Davis further stressed that, in light of the fluidity of the situation in the United States, 'if the recommended best practicable technology program is accepted ... the Canadian position could be viewed as lending support to EPA without making Canadian authorities look awkward in trying to follow a changing US position.'[73]

Marchand was sympathetic to the view of a longer-term emission plan, and felt that Davis's proposed plan appeared 'reasonable,' but preached delay. 'I believe,' Marchand told Davis, 'that we must fully and carefully assess [Davis's proposed standards] before reaching a final decision.' Marchand instead made it clear that the economic concerns sparked by the emerging energy crisis following the 1973 OPEC embargo should take precedence over environmental considerations. He informed Davis that 'in Canada there is great concern about the impact of more stringent motor vehicle exhaust emission standard on petroleum demands.' In the meantime, Marchand told the automakers that the 1976 standards would remain the same as 1975.[74]

Davis's plan for Canada to move to California standards had been rejected. Environmental concerns had made little headway against the consumer and industry issues that had dominated the emissions debates, and, with the emergence of the energy crisis, the automobile-pollution problem was shunted aside as fuel economy became the key factor shaping emissions standards. In the July 1974 election, which returned Trudeau's Liberals to a majority, Davis was defeated. By the time Marchand informed new Environment Minister Jeanne Sauvé in November 1974 that he would be keeping the Canadian standards for 1977, the idea of going to the California standard was long past.[75] With the decisions for 1975–7 made, and the focus having shifted to the fuel-economy question, automotive emission standards received little attention for the next two years.

Ironically, unbeknownst to the Canadians, inside the White House advisers in Gerald Ford's administration had, in considering the 1977–81 model years, debated using the much less stringent 1975–6 Canadian standards as a possible option for the U.S. sector. The administration had realized the difficulties of meeting the original standards set out in the Clean Air Act amendments of 1970, especially if the fuel-economy needs of Ford's own 1975 Energy Independence Act were to be achieved to any effective degree (the latter act, though it did not pass, called for a 40 per cent increase in fuel economy). Advocates of moving to the Canadian standard included the chairman of the Council of Economic Advisors, Alan Greenspan, and James T. Lynn, Ford's director of the Office of Management and Budget. Lynn advised the president that going to a Canadian standard meant that companies could dispense with catalytic converters but could still achieve some significant improvements in air quality and fuel economy. But, tellingly, the arguments against the Canadian standard were significant: the administration would face severe criticism in Congress for reversing course on air standards, and the move might not make a positive difference in addressing pollution levels.[76] Ultimately, the United States decided to maintain its standards, and actually made the NO_X figure more stringent.

In February 1976 the decision for 1978–1980 Canadian standards was announced by new Transport Minister Otto Lang and new Environment Minister Jean Marchand. Marchand, so instrumental in ensuring the weaker Canadian standard established in 1973, did not take up Davis's call for stronger regulations. The Canadian emission standards for 1978–80 remained unchanged, though the government did make new regulations regarding the tuning of engines at idle to cut CO, and required manufacturers to label what level of emissions constituted an 'engine in good tune.' Just as before, the decision to retain the weaker standards was not driven by environmental concerns. The ministers noted that, given the developments surrounding oil consumption and costs, 'energy conservation … was a primary concern in their deliberations' over the standards.[77]

By 1978, Canadian standards for emissions had been weaker than those in the United States for nearly five years. Environment Canada's assessment of air-pollution standards across the country showed that, while CO levels had decreased significantly, levels of nitrogen dioxide (N_2O) and ozone (O_3), both resulting from NO_X and HC emissions, had increased dramatically. Its studies found that both of these smog-inducing pollutants had been increasing in urban areas since 1973, 25 per cent in the case of O_3 and 10 per cent for N_2O. Auto emissions accounted for approximately 38 per cent of N_2O and 48 per cent of O_3. At the same time, nitrogen-oxide levels were 'just acceptable and increasing.'[78]

Neither these pollution figures nor a 1977 U.S. strengthening of the NO_X standard could change the Canadian position on emissions. When it came to decide the 1981–5 regulations, MOT remained committed to the weaker Canadian standard, in place since 1975. Department of-

Table 2.1
North American emissions standards, 1975–80

		Emissions, in grams per mile		
		Hydrocarbons (HCs)	Carbon Monoxides (CO)	Nitrogen Oxides (NO$_X$)
Canada	1975–87	2.0	25	3.1
US	1975–6	1.5	15	3.1
	1977–9	1.5	15	2.0
	1980	0.41	7.0	2.0
	1981 on	0.41	3.4	1.0
California	1975–6	0.9	9.0	2.0
	1977–9	0.41	9.0	1.5
	1980 on	0.41	9.0	1.0

Source: Environmental Protection Agency, 'Revised Motor Vehicle Exhaust Emission Standards for Carbon Monoxide (CO) for 1981 and 1982 Model Year Light Duty Vehicles,' *United States Federal Register*, 13 September 1979, 53408; Canada, Motor Vehicle Safety Act (Ottawa, various years).

ficials told Lang that 'the benefits to human health to be gained through further tightening of automobile exhaust emission standards are not known.' But the cost of going to 1977–9 California emissions, which Environment Canada was pushing, was easily identified: $1.7 billion in capital and lifetime costs for the new vehicle standards from 1981 to 1985, and an increase of 820 million gallons of gasoline. After disagreement and delay between the two departments, an isolated Environment Canada (whose position was supported only by Health and Welfare Canada) agreed to maintain the Canadian standards, considering 'the weight of evidence assembled' by MOT. The decision was announced in July 1978, with little fanfare.[79]

The gap between Canadian and U.S. standards would actually grow after 1981. That year, U.S. cars finally met the originally legislated 1975 standards for the first time. The difference meant that, after 1981, Canadian NO$_X$, HC, and CO emission standards allowed three times, five times, and seven times, respectively, greater emissions than those of the United States. Officially, the Canadian standards would not match the U.S. standards until 1988, nearly two decades after EPA's original announcement and almost a quarter-century after the implementation of the auto pact.[80]

Fighting the 'Thirsty Monster': A Voluntary Regime for Fuel Economy

Fuel-economy standards were the third and greatest wave of regulation to reshape the automobile, and had the greatest impact on the industry itself. By the early 1970s, the post-war emphasis on larger vehicles and greater horsepower meant that the Big Three's lumbering cars had an average of only fourteen miles per gallon (mpg).[81] These gas guzzlers were no match for the increased gasoline prices created in the marketplace beginning with the OPEC embargo in 1973 and again after the 1979 Iranian Revolution. Nor could they withstand the regulatory demands of Washington to increase fuel economy through the passage of the 1975 Energy Policy and Conservation Act by the U.S. Congress. These events changed forever the international and North American dynamics of the oil industry, and by implication the auto industry itself, which now bore the brunt of conservation efforts. From a period of cheap and plentiful oil that powered the auto sector and the economy after the Second World War, in short order the United States faced a peak on its domestic production and an international predicament which quadrupled the world price of oil.[82]

The public's reaction to the 1973 embargo has been well documented. The sudden increase in gas prices shocked consumers and helped to boost the spiralling inflation that bedevilled North American economies in the 1970s. Gas shortages caused by the shifting geopolitics of oil created line-ups, irate customers, rationing, and even riots in some places.[83] Many American consumers responded to the new reality by taking a more conservationist approach, and driving less.[84] More likely they decided to purchase smaller, more fuel-efficient autos, often imports from Japan. As a result, sales of big U.S. cars plummeted quickly as snake-like queues formed at gas stations across America. In 1965 the Japanese were barely visible in the North American market, peddling a mere 25,000 vehicles. Yet, by 1973, Americans had snapped up 620,000 Japanese cars. A year later, the number had reached nearly 800,000 – in less than a decade, U.S. imports from Japan had increased an astonishing thirtyfold.[85] As we shall see in chapter 7, the oil embargo opened the door to a massive change in the North American auto market.

In Canada, the gasoline situation was different. Oil prices were lower than those in the United States, owing to the federal government's decision to maintain a 'two-price' system, one for domestic consumption, one for export markets. This meant that gas costs at the pump were lower, but the areas of Canada not sourced from domestic sources (east of the Ottawa River), and therefore dependent on oil imports, were effectively subsidized by the federal government. Ostensibly designed to help Canadian manufacturers, the two-price system chafed many in western Canada who wanted to go to the world price as quickly as possible, especially after the embargo. The Liberal government instead preached gradualism in oil-price increases, though gas prices did begin to rise significantly after 1973. This situation was exacerbated by the fact that in 1975 Canada became a net importer of oil, buying about 100,000 more barrels a year from foreign sources than it sold abroad. Even with cuts to U.S. exports (which became a major source of tension between the two countries), and a plan to meet demand east of the Ottawa River from domestic sources through the construction of a Sarnia-to-Montreal pipeline, Canadian officials predicted that domestic output would not be enough to meet demand by 1982. Canadians could quickly find themselves in the same situation as their American cousins.[86]

As a result, Canadians also experienced some of the consumer shift that the embargo created south of the border. In the context of rising gas prices, the backlash against big cars took to new rhetorical heights. 'With the price of oil going up as mileage goes down,' the *Globe and Mail* harrumphed, 'tomorrow's large-car owner will require, in addition to his tanker trailer, generous trunk space for suitcases stuffed with dollar bills, and a modern street map showing where the gasoline oases are located.' The lampoon continued: 'The owner of such a thirsty monster could, as always, stroll around it, buffing up this part and that with his coat sleeve on a Saturday morning as it sits in the driveway of his home. Best place for it, really – next to a showroom window.'[87]

Yet most Canadians were not as obsessed with the issue as the *Globe*'s diatribe might indicate. Polls in March 1974 showed that the vast majority of Canadians were unconcerned either with the energy crisis or with the potential rise in gas prices.[88] And by the spring of 1974, it seemed that the worst effects of the embargo had passed. One reporter, commenting that the issue had seemingly petered out, wrote: 'Anybody remember the energy crisis? If Canadians do, it's because they came through it with less hardship than most other Western nations.' The *Toronto Star* reported that 'the Big Car is alive and well in Canada.' Import car sales had even slowed, from a high of 21 per cent of the Canadian market in 1971 to just over 15 per cent in 1975.[89] In the United States, the market reaction was similar, and big cars again became the hottest

'It's better this way.'

2.6 Some Canadians had a difficult time with increased gas prices. *Globe and Mail*, 14 June 1975. Permission granted for reproduction by the *Globe and Mail*.

sellers, at least until the Iranian Revolution in 1979, when oil prices spiked anew.[90]

The reaction of Canadian auto companies to the crisis was also somewhat sanguine. Ford Canada's Roy Bennett did not think that gas-price increases would have much of an impact: 'Although there can be a short term psychological reaction, gasoline price is not a factor and we don't perceive it to be a purchase decision.'[91] As early as 1974, Ford dealers were noticing a continuing demand for big cars in Canada, where sales had not been affected to the extent they were in the United States because of fuel shortages. But Bennett was also blunt about what was coming for consumers. Because of the oil situation, the writing was on the wall: 'The escalation in costs that has been occurring is frightening.' Bennett's subordinate, Ford Canada Vice-President William Hawkins, was just as clear: 'The name of the game, more than ever in the industry's history, is miles per gallon, and we're in that game with everything we've got.'[92] Chrysler Chairman John Riccardo expressed the same sentiment, noting that 'the industry is going to be totally different from what it used to be.' 'Consumers,' Riccardo argued, 'are now looking for fuel efficiency and competitive prices, and they are more concerned with reliability, serviceability, and quality than in the past.'[93] The new attitude was reflected in the advertising war over fuel economy, indicating that the companies were convinced about consumers' increasing concerns about efficiency.[94] By 1977, fuel efficiency had taken a hold of the public. One GM dealer in Montreal admitted: 'Even the Cadillac buyers want to know what kind of mileage they can expect.'[95]

The Canadian political reaction to the crisis created by the 1973 OPEC embargo was far more definitive, and had both immediate and longer-term consequences. The first casualty was cleaner air. After 1975, energy conservation was added to the list of reasons against emissions control and provided a justification that ensured that more stringent emission standards were a non-starter, a situation that echoed developments in the United States (which also slowed emission compliance).[96] Within the Canadian government, EMR's Donald Macdonald agreed with MOT's Jean Marchand that there was no need for 'a more restrictive level' when it came to emissions. Macdonald worried about the increased fuel consumption that the emission standards required, which he estimated at between 20 and 40 per cent. Although he still 'supported the need for environmental protections through improved quality of exhaust emissions,' the embargo and the increasing cost of oil meant that 'conflicts have developed between environmental objectives and energy conservation objectives.' The energy minister felt that 'we must work towards reasonable compromises as expediently as possible,' and called for discussions between EMR and MOT to consider the problem. Herb Gray, of Consumer and Corporate Relations, and IT&C's Alastair Gillespie both echoed Macdonald's position – the 'energy crisis' meant that stricter emission controls would take a backseat to energy and fuel-consumption concerns.[97]

When it came to cutting the energy expended by cars, the longer-term Canadian response was very much framed by the new American legislation on fuel economy. The Energy Policy and Conservation Act (EPCA), passed by Congress and signed into law by President Gerald Ford on 22 December 1975, had an impact upon the North American industry as profound as the 1970 Clean Air Act. The EPCA mandated an increase in fleet averages of 18 mpg for 1978, 19 mpg for 1979, 20 mpg for 1980, and 27.5 mpg for 1985.[98] These standards, called the Corporate Average Fuel Economy (CAFE), allowed the companies to keep selling the larger, more profitable vehicles as long as they sold enough fuel-efficient cars to maintain their average. But if companies were over the average even by one mpg, they faced a fine of $50 for every car produced. Given that the car companies produced millions of cars each year, these fines could be substantial.[99]

The CAFE rules presented something of a dilemma for Canadian policy makers. On the one hand, as with safety concerns, it made sense simply to follow the U.S. regulations. It was clear, too, that smaller cars were economically efficient when it came to fuel consumption, especially considering the increase in world oil prices that had resulted in such economic turmoil. Just as important, cars produced in North America would likely meet the U.S. fuel-economy requirements, no matter what Canadians felt – or legislated – on the issue. On the other hand, the fuel-economy rules were also akin to the emissions regulations: many Canadians did not see the need to follow the U.S. regulations, particularly given that Canada did not have the level of dependency on imported oil that the United States did.

But in the wake of the energy convulsions created by the OPEC embargo, the Iranian Revolution, and the continuing increases in oil prices, the federal government realized that steps had to be taken on the issue of automobile-fuel consumption. Canadian cars consumed one-quarter of the country's oil, and government officials predicted that by the early 1980s the country would face a shortfall. In 1975, in meetings between the motor vehicle companies, the MVMA, Transport Canada, and IT&C, the question of fuel-consumption standards was addressed. While 'little reference was made by the manufacturers to the need to follow their parent companies,' Canadian firms' representatives did prefer a 'fleet average' approach (like the United States) as opposed to a minimum fuel-economy standard for their cars. This would give them some leeway in trying to improve fuel economy while still meeting the market demands of consumers.

The carmakers were most concerned that Canada might impose more stringent energy-efficiency standards than the United States, or model-specific figures, which would force them to eliminate entirely certain cars from the Canadian market. Ultimately, however, the Canadian manufacturers appeared 'ready to meet any standard' the government set as long as they received sufficient advance notification. But the companies also 'prefer[ed] to co-operate in developing the standard.' This position held out the possibility of some sort of cooperative or even voluntary program.[100]

Following the government's consultations with the automakers, new EMR Minister Alastair Gillespie pushed to have higher fuel-efficiency standards. Deeply committed to ensuring that Canada became energy self-sufficient, he proposed a minimum average of 27 mpg (imp.), which would have been significantly higher than the 24 mpg (imp.) that the

CAFE regulations called for, as well as an excise tax on heavier cars. In the debate within cabinet, ministers worried about the possible adverse impact upon employment, and upon the industry itself, if Gillespie's proposals were enacted. In the end, cabinet authorized Gillespie to seek fuel-economy goals similar to those in the United States, and the idea of the excise tax was dropped, given the sharp opposition by the Canadian auto sector. The possibility of having stricter fuel-economy standards than those in the United States raised a threat to the Canadian industry. The key worry was that, since over 80 per cent of all cars built in Canada were exported to the United States, more stringent rules on fuel economy could be, in Gillespie's words, 'a disincentive to produce cars in Canada.'[101]

Gillespie's announcement on fuel-economy standards in February 1976 eventually resulted in the Joint Government-Industry Voluntary Fuel Consumption Program. Administered by MOT, the program established that Canadian fuel-economy standards would match those of the United States. All twenty-one Canadian auto manufacturers or importers publicly pledged to comply with the goals of the voluntary program. The program consisted of three main elements: the determination of ratings for all cars sold in Canada, and the publication of those ratings in annual reports (a 'Fuel Economy Guide'); the labelling of all new cars with fuel-consumption ratings; and, most important, the achievement of 'Company Average Fuel Consumption' (CAFC, essentially an equivalent to the U.S. CAFE standards) goals for each year to 1985, which were essentially the same as those of their U.S. parent companies.[102]

At the same time, cabinet also authorized EMR to look at possible contingency legislation if the government eventually decided to require standards instead of continuing with a voluntary regime. This included a request to the Department of Justice (DOJ) to assess the constitutionality of mandatory legislation, an issue that arose from the nature of such standards. In most cases of consumer-product regulation (such as household appliances), each individual product met safety and energy-consumption standards before it could be sold to the public. In this instance, however, the legislation would not regulate individual cars but a company's entire fleet of cars – the 'fleet average.'[103]

This fleet-wide approach created a constitutional quandary. The federal government could legislate standards for cars built and then sold across provincial borders, or across the Canada-U.S. border, an authority that stemmed from section 91(2) of the British North America Act, the 'trade and commerce' clause. The difficulty arose when it came to regulating vehicles built and sold within a single province, such as Ontario (where the vast majority of all Canadian cars were built, and the largest number sold). This was not interprovincial trade, nor was it international trade, where the federal jurisdiction clearly lay. To regulate in-province trade in vehicles meant invading provincial jurisdiction. But leaving those vehicles out of any regulatory scheme, or allowing provinces to set their own standards, made a mockery of any 'national' efforts. Fuel-economy regulation could easily founder on the rocky shoals of Canadian federalism.[104]

One DOJ lawyer made the case that the energy crisis was serious enough to invoke the 'emergency doctrine' that triggered the federal government's 'Peace, Order and Good Government' (POGG) power. This was the federal power's residual grant of authority which had since Confederation been effectively neutered by the courts, and could be used only in the most extreme circumstances, such as war. But the idea was quickly dispatched as unrealistic: the energy crisis was a problem, but the legislation was designed to be permanent (in contrast to temporary, as the POGG's power had come to be seen in that it dealt with 'temporary' crises). The problem could be solved only by having the companies voluntarily report their intra-provincial trade strictly 'for the purposes of administration and statistics,' or by proposing to provinces that they enact complementary legislation.[105]

As DOJ lawyers wrestled with the constitutional problem of enacting a mandatory program, the results from the voluntary program had slowly begun to trickle in, and they were decidedly mixed. The 'Fuel Economy Guide' was a hit among consumers, with 1.5 million copies distributed. At the same time, GM Canada, the country's largest company, announced that its 1977 cars surpassed the fuel-economy standard, hitting 22.3 mpg (imp.) (versus the 'voluntary' requirement of 21.6 mpg), saving twelve million gallons of gas, while Gulf Oil Canada was optimistic that the new program would significantly reduce domestic demand for gasoline in the coming years. Government studies also concluded that 'there is no reason to believe at this time that the industry is not attaining in Canada the fleet average fuel consumption values now required in the US.'[106]

But there were still concerns with the program. When it came to labelling, national surveys showed that only 36 per cent of dealerships had fuel-consumption labels on their cars, and only 21 per cent on cars in actual showrooms. Dealers complained that the ratings posted on the cars were 'completely unrealistic,' and some admitted removing the stickers to avoid complaints from customers. Since the ratings were achieved by test cars (often prototypes) in optimal conditions, with flat and perfect tracks, excellent weather, and controlled speeds, drivers were often getting far less mileage than posted. [107] The Canadian ratings were derived using the automakers' own estimates, with MOT only testing a few vehicles bought from dealers to confirm the figures. Among all of these issues, an even larger problem loomed: EMR officials worried that Canada's success in lowering consumption – estimated at 20 per cent below 1975 standards by 1985 – might lead the United States to dump larger cars into the Canadian market at cheaper prices if mandatory fleet requirements were not established. This would totally skew the averages and negate any progress the Canadians had made on fuel economy.[108]

These problems required a more active approach by government, and EMR's Gillespie was 'anxious to move forward' on the issue. The cabinet decision of December 1975 required some form of contingency legislation, and Gillespie and his officials were keen to oblige. Mandatory legislation would preclude U.S. dumping and ensure that the problems in the program were dealt with. In November 1977 EMR proposed five options to cabinet; two of them continued some form voluntary program, and the other three created mandatory legislation with varying levels of regulatory rigour, particularly on the testing and enforcement side. All of these proposals were based upon matching the U.S. standards.[109]

EMR's enthusiasm for mandatory standards ran headlong into MOT's own preference. It quickly became clear that Gillespie and Transport's Lang had 'a basic difference of opinion' over the issue. Lang was determined to maintain the voluntary program, with contingency legislation to be enacted 'only if needed.'[110] For its part, EMR continued to push for hard standards and embarked on a public-relations campaign for better fuel economy. EMR's Office of Energy Conservation (OEC) even advertised fuel- economy standards in national newspapers showing which brands and models were hitting the minimum average standard. This was an unusual step, since governments rarely pointed out whether certain brands or companies were doing better than others in the marketplace. Moreover, the results themselves were not encouraging: nearly half of all models were below the 24 mpg (imp.) threshold that the government was aiming for by 1980. OEC even set up a booth at the Canadian National Exhibition that allowed visitors to get a computer readout showing their particular car's gasoline consumption and cost for a year in comparison to more fuel-efficient models.[111]

In the end, the government decided to follow Lang and Transport's position. At a January 1978 meeting, cabinet confirmed the continued existence of an expanded voluntary program that would meet the U.S. standards for 1980 and 1985. However, in a nod to Gillespie and EMR, the government also reconfirmed the process to immediately create 'contingency legislation' if Canadians decided to have differing standards from those of the United States.[112] Such a scenario was not welcomed by the manufacturers, who continued to insist that the best approach was a voluntary one that followed the U.S. lead.[113]

Notwithstanding the decision to continue the voluntary program, jurisdictional infighting between Transport, EMR, and Finance plagued the issue. EMR's goal was fuel conservation, while Transport was committed to maintaining its prerogative in regulating cars (one that it had also pushed to maintain with Environment Canada on the issue of emissions). If EMR succeeded in creating contingency legislation, this would remove a very significant aspect of automotive regulation from the MVSA, and thus from MOT's purview. The interdepartmental tug-of-war over fuel consumption pushed back completion of the contingency legislation. These delays were further exacerbated by ongoing questions about the constitutionality of the program and by concerns about the impact of potential new emission standards for the 1980 model year.[114]

Nonetheless, the fuel-economy contingency legislation continued to be worked upon, even after the defeat of the Liberals in the 1979 election and the advent of the new Joe Clark minority Progressive Conservative government. The Conservative interregnum did little to change the discourse surrounding fuel economy, or the government's slow-moving position.[115] However, when the Liberals returned to power in 1980, they promised in their April Throne Speech to legislate mandatory fuel-efficiency standards for automobiles. This was also a part of the broader energy initiative pursued by the Trudeau Liberals through the National Energy Program (NEP).

In the meantime, new Transport Minister Jean-Luc Pepin, along with new EMR Minister Marc Lalonde, announced fuel-consumption objectives for the voluntary program in the summer of 1980. The targets for 1981 and 1982 remained in line with those in the United States. The voluntary program seemed to be working: Pepin noted that all of the car companies met their fleet average objectives for 1980, and that there had been a 36 per cent improvement in the national fleet average since

1973. That year, Canadian cars consumed an average of 16.5 L/100 km., improved to 10.5 L/100 km. in 1980.[116]

The Liberal announcement to legislate mandatory standards generated a flurry of lobbying activity. The MVMA's James Dykes implored Pepin and Lalonde to reconsider going to a mandated fuel-economy standard. Dykes 'hoped and believed' that the two men understood 'the effectiveness of this voluntary program' and so would support its continuation. He also hoped for 'support for the program on the part of your Cabinet colleagues, obviating any need to mandate [fuel-economy] requirements through legislation and regulation.'[117]

Pepin found much to like in Dykes's reasoning. He told Lalonde that he was 'impressed' by the MVMA arguments that legislation was not required, since 'the voluntary government/industry motor vehicle fuel economy program is working and ... the fuel efficiency of automobiles has been improving at a rate exceeding the objectives announced by our Government.'[118] Transport officials also felt that enactment of the mandatory legislation was unnecessary, given 'the success of the voluntary program, the economic problems of the auto industry, and the possible criticism of unnecessary government regulation.' [119] At the same time, similar to emissions, Canadian officials worried (after 1981) that a new Reagan administration would allow CAFE regulations to lapse, leaving the Canadians in a very difficult situation if they had mandated different fuel-economy standards from those in the United States. In the end, Transport 'would have difficulty recommending the Bill over the present successful voluntary program.'[120]

Of course, Canada could go to different standards, ones that might be higher than those in the United States if Reagan let CAFE rules lapse, and that might even significantly cut total consumption. This was, politically, very difficult terrain: What government wanted to tell Canadian consumers that they could not purchase particular models, or even whole classes of cars? Given the difficulties of the auto industry in the late 1970s and early 1980s, no government – and certainly not a Canadian government desperate for automotive investment and employment – wished to be seen as causing the sector further hardship. As we shall see, the Big Three's huge financial losses between 1979 and 1982 and Chrysler's near bankruptcy hovered menacingly above an already volatile situation.

With the idea of mandatory legislation still facing headwinds in the form of MOT's lukewarm support of the fuel-economy aspects of the bill, vigorous lobbying by the MVMA and the auto companies to maintain the voluntary program, and the ongoing challenges facing the industry, the Liberal government decided to incorporate the fuel-economy measures into a larger Energy Security Bill, but not to proclaim them unless necessary. The continuing voluntary regime also remained closely tied to the U.S. rules, and followed American hesitation on efficiency standards thereafter.[121]

Did it make a difference? Was the voluntary program effective? Government officials felt so, though they admitted that the voluntary program confirmed the need to 'monitor representative fuel consumption values of selected models and to provide for thorough investigation of valid public complaints.'[122] The volunteer program had resulted in new vehicle fuel-consumption averages that were 43 per cent less in 1981 than in 1973. The Canadian mpg average for cars had increased from 16.8 mpg in 1973 to 24.8 in 1979. In the United States, the increases were similarly dramatic, even in the first few years after the embargo. The EPA reported that fuel economy for the 1975 model year cars in the United States was 13.8 per cent better than for 1974. The following year, the increase was another 13.8 per cent.[123] Even though Canadians largely remained wedded to their big cars, the voluntary fuel-consumption program had made a difference.[124] By the early 1980s, the broader effects of the energy crisis had profoundly transformed the operation of the North American auto sector.

Conclusion: Harmonization if Necessary, Not Necessarily Harmonization

The regulatory changes in the auto sector after 1966 – safety, emissions, and fuel economy – fundamentally remade the North American auto industry. These regulations reshaped automobiles, both in their internal workings and in their external appearances, and placed new constraints on ordinary consumers in their choice of cars and in the prices they paid. Personal safety, the environment, and global oil geopolitics all had a hand in transforming not only the cars themselves but the very idea of the car as an intellectual and psychological construct. By the 1970s, the automobile had become more than a mode of transport, an expression of freedom, or a harbinger of status – it had become a problem in North American society, one that created an ongoing dialogue between consumers, governments, and industry. Yet the regulatory changes also reflected two deeper currents underlying the political economy of Canada's auto industry.

First, and most obviously, there was the question of harmonization and state autonomy in the area of regulation. Long before free trade in the 1980s, the North American automobile industry was the first significant Canadian economic sector to be integrated into that of the much larger U.S. industry. When it came to legislating standards for the automobile (the most regulated consumer product in history), one might assume that harmonization across the border would inevitably occur, thereby lessening any Canadian policy choice in the regulation of cars. One might further assume that, since the Canadian auto sector was almost entirely U.S.-owned, the Big Three would necessarily follow (or fight) Washington-imposed legislative directives, giving Ottawa even less leeway in regulating cars. Unsurprisingly, this was largely true when it came to safety and fuel economy, areas where Canadians mostly copied American regulations (though, in the latter instance, Canadians maintained a voluntary as opposed to mandatory fuel-economy regime).

Yet the case of emissions control tells an entirely different story, one that challenges any narrative of inevitable harmonization or constrained state autonomy. Not only did Canadians not harmonize with U.S. standards, they actually maintained a *less stringent* standard. As Nancy Olewiler has argued, this is an instance in which there was no 'race to the bottom' to meet weaker U.S. standards.[125] Auto emissions show us that trade agreements do not necessarily interfere with a country's domestic environmental regulation. In this case, the U.S. government (or at least EPA) and the world's largest corporation, GM, would have preferred Canada join the U.S. standard. Canadians and their policy makers chose not to do so, and faced little consequence for their decision.

Why was there no greater push in the 1970s, either from state or societal actors, to *strengthen* Canadian emission standards so as to align them with those of the United States? Perhaps most Canadians did not realize that Canada had weaker standards, and assumed, as many have done since, that Canadians simply followed the United States.[126] One MP, Flora MacDonald, declared in the House of Commons in December 1974 that 'the government failed us, too, in its blind acceptance of US emission standards for automobiles … [it] has decided, in the name of the environment, to apply standards designed to Los Angeles and New York to automobiles in Moose Jaw and Fredericton.'[127] If MacDonald, a future External Affairs minister, had such an erroneous understanding of the regulatory situation, was it reasonable to expect that ordinary Canadians would have a better sense of the situation?

Or perhaps Canadians did not think that the difference was great enough to matter, or that since Canadian policy makers had done *something* about auto emissions, this was good enough for them. After the first great burst of environmental policy making in the early 1970s, the federal government largely retreated on the pollution issue. As Kathryn Harrison writes: 'After 1970 the salience of the pollution issue subsided almost as quickly as it had emerged. It is not entirely surprising that legislative activity declined in the early 1970s, since the recently enacted statutes offered a wide array of new tools to combat pollution.'[128] Moreover, the technical complexity of the issue, the seemingly miniscule amounts of pollution in terms of grams per mile, and the more immediate and obvious problems of fuel economy and the increasing cost of gasoline in the 1970s shifted Canadians' focus from the auto-pollution problem as the decade wore on. At the same time, the lack of concentrated, focused, interest-group pressure, such as that in Los Angeles which pushed automobile emissions to the national stage, mitigated against any sustained interest in the issue – at least until the acid-rain debate of the 1980s.[129]

The emissions case further illustrates the considerable autonomy that Canadian policy makers enjoyed when it came to the regulation of the sector. These policy makers chose to follow American safety standards closely because doing so suited what they judged to be the needs of their constituents and stakeholders. This was also the case with fuel economy, where choices were again made within the constraints of a situation largely not of their making. But in this case, the exception can prove the rule: the autonomy exhibited by the Canadian state on emissions reflected a willingness to bend the rules within the integrated North American sector in an effort to achieve what was 'best' for Canadian consumers and the Canadian industry.

The second significant issue that underlay the regulatory revolution spoke also to a growing fear about the changes required in the production of North America's cars. The fuel-economy standards necessitated entirely new engine and car architectures. This was a much different design and engineering challenge from that involved in issues of safety (which were largely improvements or add-ons) or emissions (again, engine improvements and add-ons such as catalytic converters). Fuel-economy requirements meant a completely new type of vehicle, one that was much smaller and lighter than the behemoths that had come to characterize the Big Three line-ups prevalent in North America from the 1950s onward.

The need for smaller engines and smaller cars to meet Washington's CAFE demands was the greatest demand placed upon the industry since the end of consumer production during the Second World War, and by the late 1970s the shift in car sizes was dramatic. GM led the way in announcing that, for its 1977 model year, the company would cut a foot off its biggest cars and lighten the vehicles by 800 pounds. The full-size 1979 Fords were going to be eleven inches shorter and 600 pounds lighter than their 1978 predecessors. Chrysler cars were between eleven and thirteen inches shorter, and 800 pounds lighter.[130] While ordinary Canadians understood and even championed the need for safety, emissions, and fuel-economy regulations (even if their politicians did not fully embrace such changes), their policy makers recognized early on that the new regime threatened the vitality of their industry – would these cars be built in Canada?

This realization generated a profound fear. The dramatic changes forced by the fuel-economy legislation meant that auto plants would have to be largely rebuilt and modernized to reflect the new designs. Entirely new or retooled facilities and production processes were required, but there was no guarantee that any of these plants would be built in Canada, or that Canadian plants would be retooled to meet the new production. Even with the auto pact, the Big Three were still American companies, and Detroit and Dearborn still made decisions based on American needs first. By the mid-1970s, Canadian policy makers and politicians became increasingly worried that the Canadian industry would be bypassed entirely for these investments. They would again need to exhibit a willingness to bend the rules of their integrated industry, this time not to conform or confound regulations emanating from Washington, but to ensure that jobs and investment continued to flow northward.

3 Fair Share: The Battle over 'Domestic' Automotive Investment in North America

In Canadian history, the late 1960s to the early 1980s are often characterized as a period of intensifying economic nationalism. The emergence of Walter Gordon as the standard bearer for this impulse in the mid-1960s spawned a whole generation of Canadians committed to recapturing Canada from foreign – really, American – economic interests. Their main targets were U.S. multinational enterprises (MNEs), and their main concern was controlling foreign investment, seen as a scourge of political dependence leaching Canada since the 1950s. From Mel Watkins's 1968 *Foreign Ownership and the Structure of Canadian Industry* to Brian Mulroney's 1984 declaration to a New York business audience that Canada was 'open for business,' Canada was seen as being, in Henry Kissinger's view, 'quite tough on foreign investment.'[1]

Kissinger was not entirely correct in this assessment. That Canada had become wholly hostile towards foreign investment is something of a shibboleth. In reality, when it came to the largest and most powerful American MNEs, Canadian policy makers desperately wanted them to invest more in the country. Not only did they fight to convince multinationals to invest in Canada, they did so in a manner that opened a Pandora's box of capital movement, one that still exists to this day. Ironically, instead of containing foreign investment, provocative Canadian actions in the 1970s unleashed a torrent of capital flows, sparked by the financial incentives that governments offered to multinationals.

These efforts were understandable at the time, given legitimate Canadian fears about a lack of investment. The onslaught of automobile regulations coming out of Washington meant that the factories that had pumped out those millions of cars had to be retooled and recapitalized, but it was no sure thing that the Canadian facilities would be the ones chosen. Indeed, by mid-decade, it seemed clear that Canada would get little of this new investment. Just as important, rigorous demands for some of the massive spending planned by the Big Three in the coming years coincided with a growing wariness about the auto pact: the agreement may have been successful in boosting employment and productivity and rationalizing much of the industry, but an emerging and persistent trade deficit by the mid-1970s made it a very qualified success in the eyes of many Canadians.[2] From the Ontario government to Canadian parts-making firms, the pact was seen as not providing the fair share of investment that the Canadian industry deserved.[3]

Inside the federal government, the auto mandarins were coming to that very conclusion. The investment boom that marked the auto pact's first phase between 1965 and 1968 had run its course. With Canadian plants humming along at near capacity, and annual auto pact targets largely being met, there was little incentive for the Big Three to make any further investments in Canada. Such a scenario petrified senior ministers in the Trudeau government, who were told that something had to be done to boost the industry: Canada had to receive its fair share of investment in order for the sector to survive and prosper.[4]

But what, exactly, did 'fair share' mean? There were significantly differing views about this. Patrick Lavelle and the APMA naturally wanted to see a larger share of production and investment in the parts sector. The Canadian UAW was more interested in jobs as the key benchmark, though it understood that investment was intimately connected with jobs – and future jobs. Others, such as Ontario Premier Bill Davis, felt that the growing and persistent trade deficit between the two countries was an indicator that the auto pact and each country's relative share of the North American industry were seriously unbalanced.

Underpinning all of these concerns was the question of new automotive investment tied to the shift to smaller cars. If Canada missed out on the great boom of capital expenditures required by the wrenching regulatory and technological changes being forced upon the industry, there would be little Canadian sector left to worry about in a few years, auto pact or not. Though Canadian policy makers themselves thought that the U.S. companies invested in Canada only by using the earnings of their Canadian subsidiaries, they nonetheless recognized the need to push for additional investment.[5] This meant that the Canadians had no choice but to prompt the major manufacturers by playing the incentives game of offering multinationals direct cash subsidies and bidding against U.S. states. By the late 1970s, the proverbial genie that Canadians had done much to coax was out of the bottle.

Rhetoric and Reality: Economic Nationalism, Investment, and the North American Auto Industry, 1968–78

Economic nationalism emerged as a potent force in Canada in the 1960s and 1970s, led by an unlikely champion, Walter Gordon. Gordon had first gained national attention as chair of the influential 1955 Royal Commission on Canada's Economic Prospects, created to provide direction as Canada charted its economic future in a quickly changing post-war world.[6] Alarmed by the high level of foreign (again, really, American) investment and control in a number of Canadian industrial sectors in the 1950s, the commission called for a much more protectionist approach to wrestle the economy back from external domination. Surprisingly, Gordon was a Liberal at a time when the Liberal Party remained committed to the ideal of free trade and steadfastly allied with the United States. As such, he was seen as something of an interloper in the party of Laurier, King, and Lester Pearson. The Liberals, had, after all, created the continentalizing auto pact.[7]

Eventually, Gordon helped to get Pearson elected in 1963. The new prime minister, himself sympathetic to both free trade and the United States, could not ignore Gordon's contribution to the party, though he may not have been comfortable with his economic ideas. When he became minister of finance in Pearson's first minority government, Gordon was able to put some of his ideas into action. He created a new Department of Industry, advocated punishing taxes on foreign takeovers, and proclaimed the goal of making American-based publicly traded companies in Canada 25 per cent Canadian-owned.[8] With Gordon at Canada's economic helm, there would be no lament for the nation, no silent surrender.

But the mercurial Gordon was difficult to satisfy. Many of his measures were reversed after Gordon's disastrous 1963 budget, which was met by a plunge on the Toronto Stock Exchange. He eventually left, returned, and left Pearson's cabinet again over the issue of foreign control, forever securing himself a place in the pantheon of 1960s economic nationalists. Out of politics after 1966, Gordon turned to propagating his ideas through prolific writing and numerous television appearances. During the decade his nationalistic tomes included titles such as *Troubled Canada: The Need for New Domestic Policies*, dedicated to exposing the influence of American capital in Canada and unsubtly calling for a return to more muscular 'national' economic policies.[9]

Gordon's rhetoric galvanized a wide range of Canadians. In the universities, Watkins, Kari Levitt, Stephen Clarkson, and a host of other academics developed a critique that accused Canada of being economically dependent upon the United States, a perilous situation requiring remedies just such as those demanded by Gordon. With ringing denunciations of American influence, reports such as Watkins's influential study and books such as Levitt's 1971 *Silent Surrender* struck an alarmist tone and generated widespread support, though not all Canadians were convinced.[10] These contributions coincided with a burst of American academic interest in the power of MNEs, as scholars such as Raymond Vernon and Mira Wilkins gained an international following by analyzing and cataloguing the spread and power of American multinational corporations. Their findings fed the growing Canadian fear of foreign investment.[11]

On the ground, Canadians embraced Gordon's nationalism as a predictable result of the patriotism that accompanied Expo '67 and as a reaction to the difficulties America faced in Vietnam and at home. Many Canadians felt the country was finally going its own way and getting out from under the American thumb.[12] The economy was a logical place to start. In 1970 the Committee for an Independent Canada, which included luminaries such as author Peter C. Newman and publisher Jack McClelland among its 10,000 members, generated considerable attention for its stance on American domination. The federal New Democratic Party (NDP) became a bastion of economically nationalist ideas and, for a short time, a home for the ultra-nationalist Waffle movement. In the auto industry, nationalistic auto workers called for the strengthening of Canadian content regulations and demanded that the government force American-owned Canadian companies to build an 'all-Canadian car' or, failing that, create a crown corporation to nationalize the industry.[13]

Other remedies beckoned, both in the popular imagination and, less successfully, in the policy realm. One such remedy was hardening the border to foreign investment and American firms. But the governing Liberals were torn between, on the one hand, their long-standing commitment to lowering trade barriers and their embrace of the United States as a positive influence in Canadian economic affairs, and, on the other, the increasing popularity of Gordon's brand of economic nationalism. This played itself out in the very public *tête-à-tête* between Gordon and the more continentally inclined Liberal heavyweight Mitchell Sharp, when the two men passionately debated the issue during a Liberal convention in 1966.[14]

By the early 1970s, and especially after minority-government Liberals came to depend upon the NDP following the federal election of 1972, it looked as though Gordon had won the debate. Though Pierre Trudeau may not have considered himself a devotee of economic nationalism, his government began advocating a series of measures designed to put Canada on a less continental path. The 1971 Canada Development Corporation, the 1972 'Third Option' in Canadian foreign policy, the 1974 Foreign Investment Review Agency (FIRA), and the 1975 creation of Petro-Canada, combined with Canadian intransigence in economic relations with the United States (on oil and monetary policy, for instance), resulted in a much sharper image of diplomatic and economic independence. Herb Gray himself had authored a 1972 report, *Foreign Direct Investment in Canada*, resulting in the FIRA legislation. Liberals, in part responding to the harsh economic measures adopted by the U.S. administration of Richard Nixon, had taken the path of economic nationalism, or so it seemed.[15]

In Washington the reaction to the Canadian measures was one of caution. In 1974 Henry Kissinger warned President Gerald Ford that 'it would appear clear that the Trudeau Government has decided that Canada's best course lies in gaining greater distance from the United States.' It meant that Canada 'can be expected to give close and continuing attention to all aspects of the bilateral relationship – including issues which may in the past been dealt with solely at the private sector level – seeking in each instance to maximize Canadian advantage.' A year later, Kissinger made his comment that 'Canada is being quite tough on foreign investment' after Ottawa rejected requests by four foreign firms to buy into existing Canadian-owned companies. The move reflected 'Canada's declared intention to gain "economic independence" from foreign control, particularly from the United States.'[16]

Notwithstanding this perceived headlong rush into economic nationalism, in the auto sector the reality for Canadians was far different. When it came to automotive investment, Canadian policy makers did not worry about too much money coming into the country; they were petrified that foreign investment would dry up entirely, something that was already happening by the early 1970s. The three-year $261-million investment boom required by the Letters of Undertaking had run its course by 1968, and from the perspective of the automakers there was little need for new Canadian investment in the foreseeable future. But auto investment was one of the largest sources of foreign capital coming into Canada, and without a steady flow of new money, car manufacturing would eventually grind to a halt.[17]

Numerous assessments bore out this harsh reality for Canadians. The

U.S. congressionally mandated report on the auto pact, the *President's Annual Report*, in 1972 indicated that Big Three new investments in the United States were $1.260 billion, compared to a paltry $59 million in Canada. The figures represented an increase of 5 per cent and a decline of 11 per cent for each country from the previous year, respectively.[18] Canadian government statistics on auto investment were equally grim: between 1965 and 1977, the Big Three and AMC had directed only 6.5 per cent of their investment dollars north of the border, with only $1.3 billion invested in Canada against $20 billion in the United States.[19] A later Canadian report indicated that, when one subtracted reinvestment by the Canadian Big Three, there had been, 'on net, a capital inflow from US sources of only $54.5 million' between 1965 and 1977.[20]

For its part, the Canadian UAW estimated that, between 1965 and 1970, the Big Three and AMC had invested about 7.5 per cent of their North American total in Canada, more than the approximate share of Canada's consumption in that period, which stood at about 6.5–7.0 per cent. But the period between 1971 and 1974 had seen a decline to just over 5 per cent. Canadians, according to Sam Gindin, the union's economist, 'have not been getting our "fair share."' By 1976, the union had come to the conclusion that 'we cannot achieve a fair share of production without a fair share of *investment*.' The UAW put the equation in the starkest terms possible, reflecting broader Canadian views on the question of investment and on the auto trade itself: 'For the concept of "free trade," we substitute the concept of *fair trade*,' which included fairness in investment.[21]

Whatever new investment was trickling in after 1970 was largely a consequence of auto pact requirements. Ford, for instance, had started building the new Pinto at its St Thomas, Ontario, plant in 1970 to maintain car production in a booming Canadian market and avoid paying duties. The facility, called Talbotville, originally opened in 1967 at a cost of $65 million. It, along with two other plants in the United States, was to build the Pinto subcompact,which was designed as a competitor to Japanese and European imports. The cost of retooling St Thomas was estimated at $3.5 million.[22] More significant was the new Chrysler truck plant in Windsor, built in the mid-1970s so that the company could maintain its ratio under the auto pact and continue to import trucks into Canada.[23]

But new money was scarce. However one sliced it (and critics mostly ignored Canada's vehicle trade surplus and the fact that the companies were, after all, *foreign* firms), the statistics indicated a proportionate un-

Table 3.1
General Motors expenditures in plant and equipment, 1965–74

	$ millions Expenditure in U.S.	$ millions Expenditure in Canada	$ millions Expenditure Total	% U.S.	% Canada
1965	990.0	83.4	1,073.4	92.2	7.8
1966	882.2	73.8	956.0	92.3	7.7
1967	732.1	52.0	784.1	93.4	6.6
1968	712.9	27.6	740.5	96.3	3.7
1969	933.7	26.1	959.8	97.3	2.7
1970	941.4	79.3	1,020.7	92.3	7.8
1971	812.5	48.0	855.5	95.0	5.0
1972	749.2	32.4	781.6	95.9	4.1
1973	941.8	45.6	987.4	95.4	4.6
1974	1,185.0	60.1	1,245.1	95.2	4.8
TOTAL $	8,880.8	528.3	9,409.1		
Average %				94.4	5.6

Source: ITC, 'General Motors Corporation Statement on the Automotive Products Trade Act of 1965,' 11 December 1975, LAC, RG 19, vol. 5959, file 8705-08-16, pt. 9, 9.

derinvestment in Canada. According to one report, between 1965 and 1975 the Big Three and AMC invested only 4.2 per cent of their capital in Canada, which accounted for 5.2 per cent of global sales. Another way of looking at it was by individual carmaker: GM's vehicle production in Canada was 8.3 per cent of its North American total, yet its Canadian operations had only 4.2 per cent of the company's employees and gained only 3.9 per cent of its investment. The similar figures for Ford were 13.1 per cent production, 3.5 per cent employees, and 6.6 per cent investment; and for Chrysler, 10 per cent production, 6.5 per cent employees, and 6.0 per cent investment.[24]

GM's own detailed figures illustrated the Canadian dilemma. After the initial burst of investment mandated by the Letters of Undertaking, GM's Canadian investment had slowed down considerably. Though the post-1965 investment was more than the 3.3 per cent average of total Canada-U.S. investment in the period between 1955 and 1964, Canadian policy makers had reason to worry.

Moreover, Big Three investment was largely funded out of retained earnings by their Canadian subsidiaries, a practice that further rankled Canadian policy makers.[25] This was particularly galling given that the Canadian subsidiaries of those firms contributed $230 million a year into their parent firms' coffers – money that was often directed at new investments or research and development activities in the United States.[26] Equally worrying, the lack of investment in the early and mid-1970s did not bode well for production by the end of the decade, or even into the 1980s: the long lead times required by the industry to meet the technological regulations surrounding emissions, safety, and, most important, fuel economy meant that the massive investments needed were already being announced and allocated for the next generation of vehicles.

The capital investments to meet these technology requirements over the next ten years promised to be massive. In 1976 Ford Motor President Lee Iacocca told reporters that the company's capital investment would exceed $2 billion a year for 1977–80 'for North American capacity and North American product programs relating to fuel economy improvement.' At Ford Canada's annual meeting two years later, President Roy Bennett revealed that the parent firm expected to spend between US$15 and US$20 billion by 1985 to retool its plants and produce new vehicles.[27] At its May 1978 shareholder meeting, Chrysler voted to spend US$7.5 billion over the next five years to redesign vehicles and update plants. The decision caused grumbling among many Chrysler shareholders because the company had lost US$120 million in the first quarter, the largest quarterly loss in the firm's history.[28]

These Big Three expansion plans were being closely followed by the Canadian parts industry. If the manufacturers lived up to their word when it came to investment in North America, the APMA realized that there was quite a bit of opportunity for the Canadian parts sector owing to the integration of the industry. As early as 1970, the APMA had proclaimed a goal of increasing parts exports to the United States and the rest of the world by $250 million annually. Since the advent of the auto pact, the APMA estimated that $650 million had been spent on new capital investment, and another $200 million on plant expansions by the industry, but billions more in new investment would be needed to meet this ambitious ten-year, $2.5-billion plan.[29]

Canadian politicians and policy makers were also keenly aware of the astounding investment numbers, and what they meant for the future of the sector. As early as 1972, Ontario NDP leader Stephen Lewis decried the lack of investment in the province, telling the provincial legislature that 'no new investment decisions have been announced. Obviously, we'll lose our competitive edge as the investment in Canada dries up.'[30] Ontario Premier Bill Davis recognized that 'there was an understanding abroad that the industry over the next few years was going to invest something like $50 billion in new capital plants.' He was clear that 'we want our share of that and we're working to see what can be done to get it,' though he warned that not all of this investment was necessarily for new plants.[31]

This pressure seemed to have some impact. At the February 1978 first ministers' meeting, the prime minister and the premiers pledged to take action on the investment issue. The final communiqué of the conference stated that both levels of government would 'provide incentives and take measures to ensure [that] the proportional share of the increasing investment in the new plant for the automotive industry takes place in Canada.'[32] Though it wasn't clear what exactly this meant, the federal government had agreed, in principle, to lend its weight to ensuring new auto investment for Canada.

But this wasn't enough for Oshawa NDP MP Ed Broadbent, the main opposition automotive critic in Ottawa. First elected in 1968, Broadbent was the son of a former GM clerk – nearly his whole family worked at GM – and had a PhD in economics. At GM Local 222's 1978 annual summer picnic in Oshawa, Broadbent warned that of the $60 billion of investment planned by 1985, Canada was 'entitled to 10% of that action in the form of expansion of the Canadian auto industry – but we're not getting it … we're getting less than 5% – less than $3 billion – of that investment here. We should be getting at least $6 billion for new jobs in this country.'[33] Broadbent hammered the investment issue as often and as loudly as he could.

The press also kept up a steady drumbeat of support for the fair-share notion. The *Toronto Star* opined that IT&C Minister Jack Horner 'should stress that if moral suasion doesn't work, he'll consider tougher steps to accomplish a better deal for Canada,' and that unless something was done 'the auto pact will continue to fall short of its promise of a fair and equitable sharing of the auto industry's whole range of activities on both sides of the border.'[34] In the *Globe and Mail* one commenter wrote, 'The big question is: Will the American automotive industry spread this huge capital investment fairly in Canada? … if Ottawa does not push hard the big North American car race will be lost in favor of the United States.'[35] Columnist Ronald Anderson concurred, though he noted that 'a worrisome development in the automotive industry is the competition for new plant investment that is gathering momentum in North America' and pitting states, regions, and countries against one another. He saw this development as a short-term benefit to Canada that would eventually simply lead to more incentives. In this he was prescient.[36]

A flurry of government studies, prompted by worries over the state of the industry and the question of investment, further fuelled the issue of fair share. One of the first was an April 1978 Ontario government report, *Canada's Share of the North American Auto Industry: An Ontario Perspective*, that gained wide publicity for its provocative stance on auto issues, including the auto pact and investment.[37] The Ontario government felt that, while 'Canada has shared the benefits of the auto pact,' it was 'clear that additional production facilities will be required in Canada if an equitable share of these benefits are to be realized.' The report even formalized 'the fair share concept' and argued that Canada was certainly not getting its just portion of investment dollars. The Ontario study was used repeatedly by advocates of stronger measures such as Broadbent to push governments to force the companies to invest in Canada.[38]

The September 1978 federal *Automotive Consultative Task Force* report also voiced serious concern over the future of the Canadian industry. Created in early 1978 to address problems in the industry, the task force reported that the North American sector had entered 'a period of massive technological change to meet government-mandated fuel economy, safety and emission standards.' Factors such as cuts to social programs, instability over Quebec, high inflation, high taxation levels, tougher workplace rules, and FIRA led potential investors to view Canada as a 'high-risk investment,' according to the task force.

The report emphasized the need for 'special treatment' for the auto industry when it came to investment, and noted that foreign investors, including the automakers themselves, saw the Canadian investment climate as 'uncomfortable.' The situation could be improved if Canada utilized either carrots, by playing the incentives game, or sticks, by forcing foreign makers who sold locally to build locally. Unsurprisingly, the Canadian UAW and the parts representatives on the task force disassociated themselves from the report and issued dissenting opinions. The APMA felt that the report gave a plan by Lavelle for an automotive-investment corporation short shrift, while the UAW did not see incentives as a long-term answer to the sector's woes.[39]

Then, finally, came the Royal Commission Inquiry into the Automotive Industry report, *The Canadian Automotive Industry: Performance and Proposals for Progress*, penned by auto pact negotiator Simon Reisman. Also appointed in 1978, and having broader terms of inquiry than the

Automotive Task Force, Reisman essentially overtook the task force in purpose and scope. Initiated under the Inquiries Act as a one-man commission by Trudeau's government, Reisman's efforts echoed the pivotal 1960 commission of Vincent Bladen that had helped to set Canada on the path to the auto pact in 1965. Initially, Reisman's appointment was met with incredulity, especially the three-month time frame allotted for the inquiry. Given the pressing and serious circumstances facing the industry, Ed Broadbent felt that Reisman's 'appointment is just a sham. No one in the industry will take is seriously. It's just trying to buy time for three months.' The UAW saw it as a 'cop out.'[40]

Nonetheless, given his role in creating the original auto pact regime, Reisman's November report was widely anticipated and circulated. Somewhat surprisingly, Reisman argued that Canada had, in fact, no real claim to require as much production as it consumed (or at least a neutral trade balance), as pundits and ordinary people imagined. His recommendations included focusing efforts to develop more effectively the Canadian parts industry, since he did not see significant new assembly operation in Canada's foreseeable future. Reisman also emphasized that reopening the auto pact was a dicey proposition that could lead to unexpected and adverse consequences, a view that was confirmed by officials in Washington.[41]

Instead, investment became a key benchmark for Reisman. In his view, it was clear that 'Canada must cultivate an economic environment which clearly welcomes foreign capital participation that is in the national interest.' Reisman recognized that 'perception and reality may differ greatly in this area, but certainly foreign investors consider that Canada no longer offers the industrial hospitality evident in the mid-1960s.' But he was opposed to investment incentives, which only benefited shareholders and led to 'irrational decision making.'[42]

Reisman's main recommendation, however, was that the government establish a 'designated vehicle importer' (DVI) category for foreign makers allowing them to export from Canada as long as they met auto pact conditions in terms of Canadian Value Added. He also recommended that the government desist with the reborn export-oriented duty-remission orders (DROs) it had granted Volkswagen and others, since these orders could cause intergovernmental irritation or run afoul of U.S. trade laws.[43] Here Reisman was perceptive, for export-remission measures would, in time, prove fateful for the auto pact.

Reisman's recommendations were not universally welcomed. In *Maclean's*, Michael Valpy called it a 'depressing study,' while Mel Wat-

3.1 Simon Reisman: chief architect of the auto pact, royal commissioner, and free-trade negotiator. Image courtesy of Dr J. Reisman, in author's personal collection.

kins felt that attacking the report 'has the quality of flogging a dead horse.' According to the *Globe and Mail*, asking Reisman to investigate the auto industry was 'like asking him to write his own report card.' His 'turgid' assessment may have had some sound proposals but was full of 'expensive ideas.' Moreover, it seemed that the report was being purposely 'buried' under an avalanche of other government announcements: 'Perhaps the Government hoped Mr. Reisman's effort would be overlooked.' The *Toronto Star* was unimpressed, as well. While there were 'some glimmers' of good news, the paper used the opportunity to assert its long-standing fair-share view: 'If the auto industry is to really grow in Canada as the world moves towards safer, energy-efficient cars, then there has to be a direct action to get the Big Three to do their fair share here as well.'[44]

The parts makers, ostensibly the beneficiaries of Reisman's recommendations, were no more enamoured of the report. Lavelle told Trudeau that 'in general we are opposed to the thrust of the Reisman report and find it impossible to support its recommendations,' especially the recommendation to avoid investment incentives. 'Why Canada should refrain from these activities in the face of them being retained by others is not clear,' Lavelle wondered, given that 'almost every country in the world – seeking to find new opportunities for unemployed workers – has engaged this kind of activity.'[45]

Both the federal and Ontario governments were lukewarm towards the report, each picking and choosing among its recommendations but neither fully embracing Reisman's proposals on investment or otherwise.[46] The UAW, for its part, argued that none of the report's recommendations 'came to grips with the problem of solving the fair share for Canada' advocated by the union.[47] The only group enthusiastic about Reisman's report was foreign automakers, who embraced his idea of the DVI.[48] In time, as we shall see, the federal government created a form of production-based duty-remission orders loosely based on Reisman's plan. These remissions would prove pivotal during the free-trade negotiations.

In the midst of this ongoing debate over investment, the Canadian auto trade deficit with the United States continued to worsen significantly from an already alarming $1-billion shortfall in 1977. The gloomy figures prompted NDP MP Derek Blackburn to declare that 'Canada is not getting its fair share of the automotive trade.' Blackburn felt that 'the Auto Pact has become a joke. Canada has had a deficit ten out of the 13 years since the Auto Pact was signed, a deficit that has totaled more than $7.5 billion.'[49]

The question of the future of the sector was tied not only to the growing clamour over the investment shortfall but also to the perceived shortcomings of the auto pact itself. Convinced that something had to be done, the federal government launched an initiative to induce the Big Three to invest in Canada. Its efforts proved only partially successful, but they nevertheless became a wellspring of discontent, on both sides of the Canada-U.S. border.

Fair Shares: The Fight to Get Auto Investment, 1978–80

The growing fear about a lack of automotive investment, both in the public imagination and within government circles, soon prompted action. In June 1978 IT&C Minister Jack Horner announced to the House of Commons that the government was in negotiations with the Big Three and hoped to announce soon at least one new major investment. What Horner did not state was that some candidates for investment were more likely than others. Of the Big Three, Chrysler had announced a $7.5-billion expansion plan essential for its survival yet had not made any overtures for support to the government. Canadian projects included a $72-million expansion of the Windsor van plant, $42 million for its casting plant, and a $173-million engine-plant conversion, but the company's financial woes had put all of these investments in doubt.[50]

Much more promising were GM's and Ford's potential investments in Canada. GM already had a huge presence in Ontario, where its Oshawa Autoplex was one of the largest assembly sites in North America. As part of its retooling, the company was interested in shifting to aluminum engine blocks, which were lighter and thus could help meet fuel-economy regulations. Quebec, being a major aluminum producer, made sense as a potential site for an aluminum engine-castings plant. The notion of such a plant was also looked upon favourably by the federal government, given its emphasis on regional development in the period. The Department of Regional Economic Expansion (DREE) had been established by the Trudeau government in 1969 to facilitate this kind of economic policy.[51]

The idea of a GM aluminum plant dovetailed nicely with the need to 'distribute' more evenly some of the industry's production in Canada. A successfully sourced GM plant in Quebec could also serve as a way to counter the pressing threat represented by René Lévesque and the separatist Parti Québécois following their electoral victory in 1976. As one federal official noted, 'establishment of a GM plant, as a result of major DREE involvement, would be bound to add status to the federal role in Quebec's economic development.'[52]

In December 1977, following discussions with GM representatives, DREE Minister Marcel Lessard proposed a $58.2-million grant to assist the company in building a $486-million aluminum block plant at Valleyfield, Quebec. Though the company had looked at seven sites in the United States, pressure from both the federal and Quebec governments to consider the province had paid off. The locational cost disadvantages of the Quebec site were estimated by the company at $85 million, offset by the DREE grant and another $20 million in incentives offered by the province. When the grant was publicly announced in June 1978, Lessard stated that the potential GM aluminum foundry in Quebec represented an investment of $600 million and approximately 3,300 jobs, and that the proposal qualified for assistance under DREE.[53]

When word leaked that Ontario was willing to provide money to lure two more GM plants, the news prompted a low-grade backlash against the incentives and a call for some sort of agreement to divvy up the investment dollars. A *Globe and Mail* editorial summed up the reaction of many to the idea of investment incentives: 'It is ludicrous to pay millions of dollars to giant automotive companies that already make profits out of the taxpayers who provide the bidding money.' But the paper also realized that 'unfortunately, at the moment it seems the only way of attracting new investments. Until the US and Canada ... [agree that] parts and assembly plants are divided between the two countries in relation to their amount of automotive goods each purchases, the provinces will continue to be forced into attempting these horrendously costly settlements.'[54] For all this hand wringing, the aluminum foundry did not materialize. In the midst of the government's negotiations with GM, the company asked for a ninety-day extension on the deadline for acceptance of the $58-million package to build the plant. This was granted, but the company eventually passed on the entire Quebec proposal.[55]

In July 1979, nearly two months after the official DREE offer had lapsed, GM officials approached Premier Davis about the possibility of putting the aluminum foundry in Sarnia, Ontario. The company envisioned a $650-million plant with 1,500–2,500 jobs, pumping out aluminum components. The site had the advantages of being close to the U.S. border and having ready access to a natural-gas supply. According to GM representatives, the potential plant also had the advantage of not being in Quebec; the company told federal officials that they were unhappy with previous labour difficulties at its Sainte-Thérèse assembly plant. GM was also concerned with the political uncertainty the province's separatist government represented, though it continued talking with Quebec City over potential investment. Still, there were serious competitors for both Canadian sites: a Rome, Georgia, plant was said to have a $40–50 million advantage over Canada, while GM was also looking at a Mexican site which offered a $100-million advantage.[56]

GM's revitalized interest posed a problem. While the federal government could reoffer the original $58-million DREE grant for the Quebec site (which the company did not really prefer), it could not make a similar offer for Sarnia since southern Ontario did not fall within DREE's geographic purview. Moreover, the U.S. government might have been willing to stomach DREE grants, which, in its view, were an unsavory if legitimate use of government intervention. But a federal grant to a wealthy province such as Ontario would be too much. Federal officials agreed – Ontario would have to go it alone if it was to bid for the aluminum plant.

Nonetheless, when word reached U.S. officials that the DREE offer for GM had found a second life, the Americans quietly enquired as to the nature and amount of the offer to the company. The Canadian embassy in Washington politely declined to give them this information, saying it would be prejudicial to the GM's interests, and that DREE grants were acceptable tools of public policy. If it was discovered that the Americans had pushed the question of DREE grants, this would be seen as a 'sensitive issue' for the Canadian public.[57] Moreover, the Canadians worried that, if GM discovered that there had been government-to-government talks about the grant, the company 'could get very nervous about the DREE offer.' Because of this, the Canadians made sure to get in touch with GM officials to tell the company that the government 'stood firm' on its original Quebec offer.[58] By the time the final DREE/Quebec offer had been made, the combined incentive was an astounding $110 million, to be shared 75/25 by the federal and Quebec governments.[59]

Finally, in October 1979, the company announced that it had postponed indefinitely its consideration of the aluminum castings plant. Though it did not disband its site committee, and stated that the project was still an 'outside possibility,' the investment for a new facility was essentially dead.[60] Instead, GM decided to invest up to $2 billion in Canada, primarily in Ontario at already existing facilities ($1 billion to upgrade its Windsor and St Catharines parts plants, another $1 billion for its other facilities). The company told Canadian officials that the Quebec aluminum foundry file should be closed by the federal and Quebec governments. New Prime Minister Joe Clark admitted publicly that he was 'surprised' by GM's decision.[61]

The company's decision to pour nearly $1 billion into the Windsor plant to produce more fuel-efficient front-wheel-drive transmissions for all of its intermediate- sized vehicles for the 1982 model year illustrated how such an investment could trigger even more employment and production and directly affect the independent parts industry in Canada. GM told government officials that it wanted to source about 40 per cent of the die-casting machines for the transmissions from Canadian sources, resulting in over $230 million in potential sales over a decade. The problem was that GM would 'be forced, because of production deadlines associated with the transmission itself, to source the business in the US at captive facilities.' The decision prompted IT&C officials to quickly create a $13-million ad hoc lending program for two Canadian firms to expand to meet these demands and secure the business, with nearly 200 jobs created.[62] Still, some MPs complained that the GM decision was 'only a drop in the bucket' of what Canada was entitled to, considering the reported $38-billion spending plan the company had embarked upon.[63] In the end, GM did not receive major federal or provincial funding for a major new investment in this period, though not for lack of trying on the part of Ottawa, Queen's Park, or Quebec City.

The Ford Motor Company, on the other hand, was the recipient of a massive investment incentive, one that had long-term political and economic consequences. In early 1978 Ford of Canada President Roy Bennett told a Toronto Board of Trade audience that 'if Canada can attract its fair share of the enormous investment to be made, the auto trade deficit could be reduced, auto employment could be increased and further confidence in the general economy could be generated.' Of the estimated $58 billion in investment required to meet the new regulatory demands, Ford was to spend at least $10 billion, and it would be logical for Canada to get some of that investment, according to Bennett.[64] At Ford Canada's annual meeting, he reiterated the possibilities of investment in Canada but warned that 'we in Canada must make ourselves competitive with many of the US states which are seeking to attract new industry by offering a wide range of incentives.'[65]

Not long after Bennett's speech, Ford announced that it planned to build a plant somewhere in North America to produce fuel-efficient engines to meet the new emissions and fuel-economy regulations imposed by Washington. The facility represented an investment of approximately $535 million and potentially 2,600 jobs. The company publicly stated that the plant could go to either Windsor, Ontario, as a new facility or as an addition to an existing plant in Lima, Ohio, which had already offered Ford incentives in competition with other U.S. states.[66] Even though a reported Ford internal assessment indicated that the Ontario site would be initially more expensive than Ohio, the overall cost of the plant was cheaper in Ontario.[67]

But if Ontario was to have a chance at the new facility, it would have to match or better the $30 million in incentives offered by Ohio. Ottawa was keen to oblige. In February 1978, Bennett approached IT&C Minister Jack Horner with the information that the plant might be had if the right incentive was provided. Horner, in turn, brought the idea of a $30-million incentive to win the plant, split 75–25 with Ontario, to the federal cabinet, arguing that if Canada matched the Ohio incentive, he believed 'the company's recommendation would be to favour southern Ontario.' This was the same split agreed to with Quebec for the GM offer. Reaction was positive, though Finance Minister Jean Chrétien thought an outright grant 'politically unacceptable.' Instead of direct funding, Chrétien felt that duty remissions or tax breaks could be offered.[68]

The Ontario government had to be on side too. Initially, Queen's Park was reluctant to participate in investment incentives. In a publicly released letter, Davis told Trudeau that 'we expect a fair deal, not an auction-block deal in which the highest bidder wins.'[69] Ontario Minister of Industry and Tourism John Rhodes balked at the federal government's insistence on a revised 50/50 split for the $75 million that Ford was now looking for.[70] As the federal and Ontario governments tussled over the province's participation and what at a package might look like, Horner was given the go-ahead by cabinet to continue discussions with Ford.[71] In Toronto, Davis and his cabinet determined that, based on the employment figures being considered for a $500-million plant and the taxes generated, a grant of $28 million would return the province's investment within three years.[72]

Meeting at the Calgary Stampede that year, Davis, Trudeau, and Bennett agreed that the two governments should make a proposal to the parent company, with Ford Canada's support.[73] 'It was,' Davis later recalled, 'done very informally,' amidst a crowd of people at Calgary's Petroleum Club: 'There was no written agreement. Mr. Trudeau could trust me, and I could trust him – I use this as an example [of federal-provincial cooperation] when discussing the role of government, not only in the auto sector – it was an important moment.'[74] The three men also all agreed that this pitch needed to be backed by significant incentives if Windsor was to beat out Ohio.

But the price was going up: by mid-June it was clear that Ford was expecting at least $75 million between the two governments to make the Windsor site competitive with Ohio. The escalating price sparked conflict within the federal cabinet, as DREE Minister Lessard felt that reaction in Quebec to the Ford offer would be 'very negative,' given that Ontario already had the lion's share of auto investment. The offer would also 'cut the ground out from under' the ongoing Quebec-GM negotiations. Horner replied that Ontario had a comparative advantage, and if 'the principle of comparative advantage were to be departed from, Western Canada, which now had no automotive industry, could make a strong case for location of plants there.' In the end, cabinet accepted the new figure, though it agreed that the 75/25 federal-provincial split finally decided upon (instead of 50/50, which Ontario refused to accept) was not a precedent-setting formula.[75]

The escalating price provoked strong reactions towards the company from federal politicians. Inside cabinet, Public Works Minister Judd Buchanan felt that 'it should be made clear to Ford that they had valuable assets in Canada and a good market in this country,' and that 'they should therefore place in Canada a fair share of their total investment.'[76] Trudeau felt likewise: Ford officials 'would be obtuse indeed if they did not understand the point that had been made regarding investment in Canada.' Nonetheless, a special '*Ad Hoc* Cabinet Committee of Ministers on the Ford-V6 Program' was created to shepherd the deal through to completion.[77]

Eventually, working together, the two governments' automotive bureaucracies hammered out a proposal with Ford to provide $68 million in incentives for the plant – $40 million from Ottawa and $28 million from Queen's Park – which the company accepted. In return, Ford promised to achieve a minimum production of 1.5 million engines from the 1983 to 1987 period. If it did not achieve this target, the government of Canada's contribution would be 'reduced proportionately to the extent that such production is not achieved.' Out of the company's total investment of approximately $535 million for what eventually became the Essex Engine plant, the two governments provided about 13 per cent of the money, or about $26,000 for each of the 2,600 jobs generated.[78]

Ed Broadbent and the NDP, which had hounded the government for years on the auto file, were unimpressed by the news that the federal government had become involved in a bidding war for the new plant. Broadbent saw Ottawa's incentive efforts as a failure of the government to force Ford and the automakers to live up to their investment obli-

3.2 Auto pact and investment watchdog: Oshawa's NDP MP Ed Broadbent speaks to reporters in 1972. Canadian Press.

gations under the auto pact. Given that Ford had made, according to Broadbent, double the profits in Canada between 1971 and 1975 that it had made elsewhere in the world, this was just an 'attempt to cover up this failure by offering taxpayers' money as subsidies to entice them to do what they ought to have done without subsidy.' Canada was becoming involved, said Broadbent, in a 'blackmail game.'[79] Ontario NDP leader Michael Cassidy echoed Broadbent's harsh language. He felt that 'if Ontario is willing to be suckered into the incentive bidding game, the losers will be the taxpayers of this province.'[80]

Unsurprisingly, the UAW in Canada felt substantially the same way as Broadbent. As early as 1976, the union had come to the conclusion that while Canada 'cannot achieve a fair share of production without a fair share of *investment*,' it opposed 'the corporations' freedom to shift production and plant from one place to another (even within Canada) without having to answer to the social costs imposed on the workers and communities involved.'[81] In 1978 Bob White, the new director of the UAW, made the argument directly to Davis that 'we should not give large amounts of taxpayers' money to wealthy corporations to make what really amounts to Canada's share of investment if the auto agreement is to operate fairly,' a position he reiterated in *Solidarity Canada*, the UAW's newspaper. Like Broadbent, White saw the incentives as a 'failure of government to fight for what is Canada's *by right*.'[82] Although Davis listened to the UAW director, it was clear to White that the Ontario government was 'going to play the game anyway.'[83]

South of the border, White's American brethren had also pushed the case that investment incentives were bad for everyone except the auto companies. The spectacle of Ontario and Michigan bidding over the Ford plant, and potentially putting UAW members on either side of the Canada-U.S. border at odds, was unsettling. UAW International President Douglas Fraser complained to U.S. Special Trade Representative (USTR) Robert Strauss that the Ford plant had gone to the highest bidder, and that the United States must do everything in its power to stop these 'beggar-thy-neighbor' practices. Fraser suggested 'an international treaty to control the use of such subsidies by all levels of government.'[84]

The initial reaction of the U.S. government to the Ford incentive was far more severe. When he learned of the Canadian offer to Ford, U.S. Secretary of the Treasury Michael Blumenthal personally telephoned Henry Ford II in an effort to prevent the plant from being awarded to Ontario.[85] Blumenthal then phoned Chrétien to register his unhappiness with Ford's decision, which he called 'unacceptable.' Blumenthal also wanted 'urgent consultations' on the Ford decision, and on the question of incentives in general. But Chrétien held firm, and made it clear that there would be no withdrawal of the Ford offer. For now, the best the Americans could get was a promise of early consultations, particularly around the Ford and GM incentive offers.[86] For their part, the Canadians intended to use the meetings to hammer home their own unhappiness with existing state and municipal subsidies.[87]

The public was informed of the Ford deal when it was announced at Queen's Park on the evening of 3 August. Bennett unexpectedly called Davis to tell him of the company's decision to locate the $535-million plant in Ontario, contingent upon the federal and Ontario grants. The announcement came just as two senior American officials, the State Department's Julius Katz and Treasury's Fred C. Bergsten, flew north to lodge their protests with the federal government over the Ford incentive.[88] On 14 August, barely two weeks after it was announced that the plant was going to Ontario, Bennett confirmed that Windsor would be the site of the new facility. The largest single expenditure in Ford Canada's seventy-five-year history, the 1.3-million-square-foot Essex Engine plant was now slated to begin producing over 600,000 engines for the 1981 model year, 80 per cent of which were to be exported to the United States. Bennett confirmed that the facility would employ 2,600 workers.[89]

The abrupt Ford decision to announce the Windsor investment caught Ottawa by surprise, and seemed to leave Washington unprepared too. The sudden announcement meant that 'both governments find themselves in an acutely embarrassing position,' since it was unlikely that the two American diplomats heading to Ottawa to discuss the situation 'will have learned of the Ford decision before' they arrived in Ottawa.[90] External Affairs officials speculated on Ford's motives for making the decision so unexpectedly: Ford must have 'decided suddenly to accept it for its own reasons,' a consequence of 'its corporate displeasure with the Administration's attempt to defer or block the decision.'[91]

This indeed was the case. According to one account, inside Ford's Dearborn headquarters there had been serious conflict over the decision. While Henry Ford II and some senior management were in favour of choosing Windsor, Ford's North American Automotive Operations (NAAO) wanted to see the investment go to Ohio. When Blumental phoned Ford personally to register his unhappiness over the rumoured decision to locate in Ontario, the call apparently provoked the auto magnate to immediately decide for the Canadian site.[92] The ultimate decision was made in Dearborn, by Henry Ford II himself, overruling executives in the company's NAAO and in defiance of Washington. In part, Ford II's decision was tied to his concern over the company meeting its auto pact commitments in Canada. According to one Ford insider, Bennett had convinced Ford II that 'if the plant were built in Lima, our Canadian value-added or Canadian investment might fall below the agreed-on floor, potentially wrecking relations with the government of Canada.'[93] Premier Davis, however, recalled differently: the company's decision, as far as he knew from Bennett's discussions with Dearborn, 'was a political and economic decision. There was some auto pact talk, but it was not a basic aspect of the decision.'[94] In any event, as Ford officials worked on the announcement, which was not scheduled for a few more weeks, Ford II, 'irritated by the swirling machinations, told Ford of Canada to get on with the announcement or else.'[95]

Despite the tremendously adverse U.S. government reaction, Ford wasn't done looking for further government incentives. Less than a month after the Ford engine plant announcement, IT&C Minster Lessard visited Detroit to speak with company executives. Lessard was told that Ford was going to build a new engine-testing facility, and that while the obvious location choice was Detroit, Windsor might be considered if an incentive of $13 million was offered. The test facility made sense in Canada, given that the Essex plant would be producing nearly one-third of Ford's V-6 engines for all of North America by 1983.

The facility also had the advantage of being a research centre, something that the Canadians had been demanding for some time. But the offer would have to be made soon, within two weeks. With the bad publicity surrounding the Ford announcement, the haste required to make the decision, brewing unhappiness from both GM and Quebec over the Ford deal, and the simple fact that there was no competing American incentive offer on the table to provide political cover, the new Ford entreaty was simply too much. Lessard, in particular, felt that unless some sort of 'companion project' could be offered to Quebec, he was against offering any funding. Intergovernmental Affairs Minister Marc Lalonde concurred. In late August, cabinet decided to politely decline Ford's new 'offer.'[96]

The Ford engine decision only emboldened the most vigorous advocates of 'fair share.' On the editorial pages of the *Toronto Star*, the newspaper did not pause to celebrate the announcement. Instead, the *Star* called for greater investment by the Big Three or, failing that, an audacious step: if Canada did not receive its fair share of investment and production, it should consider taking an ownership stake in either Ford or Chrysler to force the U.S. parent to ensure that the Canadian subsidiary received its 'fair' allotment: 'Detroit and Washington have to be persuaded that Canada means business.'[97] Once thought outlandish, the notion of direct government ownership of one of the Big Three would soon reappear with the near death of Chrysler (and would eventually be realized in 2009). For now, however, the federal government prepared to face the diplomatic consequences of its investment incentives.

A Mug's Game: The Battle over Investment Incentives

The Canadian decision to offer incentives to induce automotive investment in Canada was not an easy one. But Canadian policy makers felt they had little choice, given the changing circumstances of North American automotive investment. In the pre-auto pact period, tariff barriers constrained production locales; Canadian factories built only for Canadian consumption. After 1965, with the integrationist auto pact regime in place, plants in any jurisdiction in North America could produce for the whole continent. For the first time, states and provinces directly competed with one another when it came to new investment. This dynamic meant that capital in the auto industry flowed 'beyond borders,' as one leading scholar of the new dynamic has termed it.[98] In the case of the Ford incentive, while Ontario was somewhat protected by the production safeguards contained in the auto pact, there was no guarantee of new automotive investment, and the plant could have easily gone to Ohio.

In fact, the Ford incentive battle was not the first such incident pitting subnational jurisdictions in North America against one another for investment. In the mid-1970s, several U.S. states had embarked on an incentive bidding war of their own to lure Volkswagen following the company's 1976 announcement of plans to build an assembly facility somewhere in the United States. The German firm was hoping to take advantage of the growing small car market and capitalize on the company's 1960s Beetle success. A host of cities and states bid for the VW plant and some, such as Baltimore and Atlanta, even took out newspaper ads to woo the German automaker with promises of tax breaks, handouts, and other incentives.[99]

Eventually, VW chose Pennsylvania, lured by nearly $70 million in incentives. The state government bought an unused factory in Westmoreland from Chrysler for $40 million, and leased it back to VW for the next thirty years, the first twenty at a miniscule rental of 1.25 per cent per year. The state also agreed to finance the building of a spur railway line to the factory to the tune of $10 million, while Pennsylvania's pension funds gave VW loans totalling $6 million at favourable rates.[100] The plant, eventually employing 2,500, started producing VW Rabbits in April 1978. As the first ever foreign transplant in the United States, the VW plant reflected the lengths American states such as Pennsylvania were willing to go to secure auto investment.[101]

For Canada, the VW plant in Pennsylvania represented something far more ominous. U.S. states boasted a host of potential tools to convince automakers – domestic or foreign – to build in their jurisdiction. There were state tax incentives, including investment tax credits, federal income-tax exemptions on interest on state and local bonds, job tax credits, and accelerated tax depreciation. The U.S. federal government also had the Domestic International Sales Corporation (DISC) (which encouraged U.S. companies to export), Foreign Trade Zones (which provided assistance to foreign companies to set up in the United States, as had happened in the VW Pennsylvania case), and industrial-development assistance programs offered by agencies such as the Economic Development Administration, the Small Business Administration, and the Export-Import Bank. All of these agencies provided a host of grants, loans, and infrastructure support to industry. At the state and local levels, there were direct grants, bond issues (which often exempted tax on the interest), and concessionary loans or loan guarantees. State and local authorities also could provide land, site assistance, and infrastructure support, along with job training.[102]

Initially, elected officials such as Windsor MP Herb Gray, who became IT&C minister in 1980, questioned the legality of the U.S. incentive packages, wondering whether their existence appeared 'contrary to what both parties specifically agreed to in the Canada-US Automotive Agreement.'[103] His position might have been influenced by the relative paucity of Canadian measures that could compete with the U.S. incentives. The options were few: there were DREE grants, federal and provincial direct subsidies, and support for infrastructure from provincial and municipal governments. With such a potentially meagre arsenal, it might not be so wise to get into a bidding war with the far wealthier and more numerous American states.

Just as daunting was the adverse American reaction to Canadian incentives. Ohio Senator John Glenn, the famous American astronaut, was incensed at the Ford engine-plant decision, especially Ottawa's involvement. He was 'deeply troubled' at how the Canadians had induced the plant away from Ohio, and rattled the saber of countervailing duties under section 303 of the 1930 Tariff Act. In letters to President Jimmy Carter, on the Senate floor, and in the media, Glenn loudly denounced the Ford decision.[104]

The august Ohio senator was not the only one upset with the company's choice. Pennsylvania Representative Robert W. Edgar prepared a report, 'The Canada-Ford Deal: A Case Study in Government Business Incentives,' that was highly critical of the practice.[105] In his 1978 speech to the Windsor Rotary Club, 'The Auto Pact: Who Gets the Benefits?' U.S. Ambassador Thomas O. Enders questioned the usefulness of the auto agreement, given the Ford decision. The Ford announcement also caught GM officials by surprise. They told the Canadians that the Ford decision had 'hurt them' politically, though the company confirmed to a DREE official that the Quebec site was still a 'serious contender.'[106] Even a few Ford employees felt uncomfortable about the decision, or at least how it had been executed.[107]

The Carter administration was extremely unhappy at the decision, too. In front of the House Banking Subcommittee on International Trade, Treasury Secretary for International Affairs Fred Bergsten threw down the gauntlet on the Canadian government's Ford incentives: 'We simply cannot sit by while these interventionist practices are escalated to the federal level.'[108] Secretary Blumenthal had already registered his distaste at the Canadian government's 'intervention,' while Katz and Bergsten had made their feelings known at a rollicking press conference in Ottawa mere hours after the Ford decision. In the wake of the Windsor announcement, the White House was determined to ensure that this open bidding did not happen again. Consultations with the Canadians had to happen, and if nothing was resolved, the threat of countervailing duties was a distinct possibility.[109]

The August 1978 arrival of Bergsten and Katz in Ottawa on the eve of the Ford announcement illustrated just how high the stakes were in the incentive game. The two men had been sent to Ottawa to register American displeasure at the Ford incentive, and were caught unawares when the decision was announced just as they arrived. The *Toronto Star* took a strident tone towards the appearance of the American officials. The two men 'should be told that Canada is determined to get its fair share of new auto industry investment ... Ottawa should tell Carter's emissaries that it's not going to see the US take away Canadian jobs.

If the big US auto companies want Canadians to buy their cars, they'd better make sure Canadians get a fair share of the new investment.'[110] The spat over incentives threatened to turn into a full-fledged cross-border trade war, reminiscent of the 1963–4 battles fought over Canada's original duty-remission orders.

Publicly, Canadian officials downplayed the significance of the Bergsten/Katz meeting, stating that the discussions were of a routine nature. But the U.S. side called the matter an 'urgent consultation.'[111] In Washington, one Commerce Department official claimed that an incentive package such as that given to Ford 'just normally isn't done' and noted that the U.S. Countervailing Duties Act left the Canadians exposed, particularly on a new VW remission program they had instituted to increase VW exports from Canada to the new American plant (discussed in chapter 8). External Affairs officials attempted to understate the incident in advance of the American arrival, but also hoped that it might spark more permanent measures that could provide Canada with future auto investment.

The investment incentives were, according to one External Affairs official, an ad hoc measure which did 'not assure us a fair share of the North American auto industry's investment over the next five years.' Either a renegotiation of the auto pact or a new free-trade agreement – an 'organized free trade agreement,' which would ensure investment and production in Canada – was the best option.[112] This was the view of editorialists as well, who saw the conflict over incentives as a chance for Canadians to assert their prerogatives and push for a renewed look at the industry. According to the *Globe*, the government had been 'much too timid, much too cautious, much too willing to ask Canadians to suffer in silence while the principles and promises on which the auto pact was based [were] increasingly bent out of shape to Canada's loss and to America's advantage.'[113]

It was in this heated atmosphere that Bergsten and Katz arrived in Ottawa. Ostensibly, the consultations had originally been about the operation of the auto pact and the industry in general. But the Ford deal had changed the terms and tenor of the meetings. Both in private talks and publicly, the Americans were clear and cutting: the Ford investment, the reported DREE-GM deal, and rumours about possible aid to leverage a Chrysler investment had 'suggested a pattern' which they found unacceptable. Unless they received reassurance that the Ford agreement was 'a one-shot deal' and that nothing else 'was in the pipeline,' they could not rule out countervailing action. Moreover, they stressed that the White House was under intense political pressure, and that there were calls for the administration to enter the incentives race. After the meeting Bergsten told reporters that incentives were a 'mug's game' which ultimately benefited neither side.[114]

The Canadians held fast in the face of this attack. The dynamics of investment had changed with the regulatory shift, they claimed, and Canada was not to be denied its share of the $40 to $60 billion in automotive investment that was expected in the next five years. With a persistent trade deficit, and the fact that state and municipal governments in the United States were already offering incentives, Canada could not idly stand by. This situation was a 'serious public and political concern.' While the Canadians made clear that the Ford deal was an ad hoc response to a unique opportunity, the problem of automotive investment was an 'ongoing preoccupation' for the federal government, one that it could not ignore. Having established their positions, the two sides agreed that two groups should be struck, one to study incentive programs offered in each country, another to study the 'perceptions' around the auto trade. They also decided that senior officials should consult again when the groups had reported back their findings, and that if any new investments occurred that generated governmental incentives, either of the two sides could call for meetings.[115]

In the wake of the initial Canada-U.S. meeting, the Ontario government remained equally steadfast on incentives. Ontario Treasurer Darcy McKeough was not swayed by the American bluster. Since so many U.S. states were willing to make similar grants, Bergsten's threats were really 'the pot calling the kettle black.' While it was in neither country's interest to continue the incentives game, and Ontario would prefer not to play it, the province had no choice. Instead, McKeough called for cooler heads to prevail: 'We should sit down and say, "look, we are both grown up boys. Let's not play this game.'"[116]

By the time senior officials again reconvened to tackle the incentives problem in December, the working groups had not really resolved any of the underlying issues. In the interim, the Reisman report had been released, adding to the discussions. Both sides had cooled off. In the view of one participant, Bergsten's 'fire (and ire) had considerably diminished' since August. Nonetheless, there were still some sharp edges to the discussion. Katz, for instance, began his comments by attempting to elicit from the Canadian delegation which of them agreed with the APMA or the Ontario government position that Canada had not received its fair share under the agreement. This prompted the Canadian response that the question of fair share was always just below the surface.[117]

When the conversation moved towards incentives questions, the Americans pushed to establish a 'notification' mechanism, which the Canadians saw as unfair. Since the U.S. side claimed it was impossible to provide notification for the dozens of state and municipal government incentive programs, it would amount to a one-sided notification system whereby Canada, with closer federal-provincial working relationships, would do all the notifying. Moreover, such a system might be seen as requiring input by U.S. authorities, particularly around DREE grants. Ultimately, it was unfair to Canada, since federal monies almost always figured in such cases. The Canadians cited the VW Pennsylvania example: the state had not even informed Washington about its incentive package. On the question of notification, the Canadians politely disagreed but emphasized their willingness to consult if another incentive case emerged. For now, the two sides agreed to hold further meetings in the new year.[118]

The Canadian attitude towards the incentive question hardened in the wake of the initial round of talks. In their capacity as leaders of the federal cabinet's Board of Economic Development (BED) ministers, IT&C and finance ministers Jack Horner and Jean Chrétien sponsored a 'Policy for the Canadian Automotive Industry' which stated that the Canadian government 'would not stand idly by while substantial investments are being lost to Canada as a result of incentives available in the US.' 'Special government assistance' was necessary when a particular case did not fall with existing federal programs (as had happened with the Ford package), or when it was beyond the fiscal capacity of a province and thus the potential investment would be lost to Canada. At the same time, however, the BED also agreed that the government 'should pursue on an urgent basis discussions with the United States with a view to negotiating an agreement to control the use of such subsidies.' If both sides could agree to control incentives, the Canadians would go along, but for now they took a hard line in support of incentives.[119]

The hardened federal approach was announced in Windsor at the city's Chamber of Commerce by Horner in March 1979. In developing a new automotive policy, Horner and the government had picked a few of the Reisman recommendations they liked and added a few more. There would be no reopening of the auto pact, and they would consider Reisman's DVI proposal. Yet the government was to continue controversial duty-remission programs – which Reisman had pioneered but which he had recommended dropping in his report. There were also a few other, minor measures, such as a decision to produce annual reports on the industry.[120]

When it came to the issue of incentives, Horner was definitive. The government's policy was clear. Canada did not want to get into the incentives game, was willing to parley with the Americans to find some way to end the practice, and would initiate discussions with Americans to do so. But if U.S. states continued to offer incentives, Canada had no choice but to offer its own incentives packages to ensure that the country was not denied its share of automotive investment: 'The government will not stand by while substantial investment is being lost to Canada because of incentives available in other countries. To offset such incentives, special federal aid will be considered in cases where existing federal programs do not apply and when the assistance needed is beyond the financial capacity of a province.'

Along with Horner's announcement, Prime Minister Trudeau personally reiterated to President Carter that Canada was willing to talk about the incentives issue. But the federal government was not going to back down on the Ford incentive, nor would it 'stand idly by if substantial investments were to be lost to Canada as a result of investments available in the US.'[121] In his own private talks, Premier Davis met with Bergsten in Washington in March 1979. Treasury officials suggested that something needed to be done to stop the incentives, and that it might be beneficial for Ontario to meet with the federal government to push them to end the practice. Davis, while supportive of any notion to end incentives (he also called them a 'mug's game'), emphasized that it would be necessary to get state governments on side as well. He left it to the Americans to organize a meeting with governors William Milliken of Michigan and Jim Rhodes of Ohio to discuss the matter, with little result.[122]

In the wake of the unsuccessful talks to end subsidies, American attitudes hardened, too. Publicly, Bergsten laid out his opposition to the Canadian federal incentives and called for further urgent consultations. At a speech to the Fordham Corporate Law Institute in November of 1978, he declared that 'the international investment policy of the US is based on the premise that the investment process works most efficiently in the absence of government intervention.'[123] Privately, the United States proposed its own working paper outlining its views on incentives. It set down two basic principles: government should not pursue policies 'which draw investments (in industrial capacity) into

3.3 Fair-share fighter: Trudeau speaks with Ford workers in St Thomas, Ont., 20 June 1970. Courtesy of Elgin County Archives.

their territories which would, in the absence of such policies, be made in another country'; nor should government pursue policies 'which distort the economic efficient allocation of global resources.' These two principles were seen by the Canadians as so general and vague as to be unworkable. The Americans eventually withdrew the Treasury-drafted 'principles' in the face of Canadian discomfort with their ambiguity and the fact that, if adopted, these principles would in fact place existing U.S. programs in jeopardy.[124]

The next Canada-U.S. working group meeting on auto incentives, held in May 1979, reflected the two sides' jockeying over the issue. The Americans continued to insist that notification was essential to any control of incentives, while the Canadians pushed for the United States to 'get a handle' on state and municipal subsidies. The Canadians raised the withdrawn U.S. position paper, and reiterated that they could not accede to any agreement which tied Canada's hands. The Canadian policy statement had made it clear that Ottawa did not want to get into a competitive bidding war, 'but of necessity it will meet competition when necessary to maintain a reasonable level of investment in Canada.'[125]

Instead, the Canadians proposed that the two sides consider utilizing instruments such as the 1976 Organisation for Economic Co-operation and Development (OECD) Declaration on Decisions on International Investment and Multinational Enterprises and the GATT's Article XVI codes on subsidies to see if they could be used as constraints on investment incentives.[126] If a further agreement was developed between the two countries specifically on the auto trade (since it was so concentrated, and since it was governed by the auto pact), and which required some type of notification by state governments, Canada would be willing to consider such measures. Initially, the United States countered that the OECD protocol was too weak and that the GATT rules really applied only to subsidies which influenced trade flows, not investment. Even if it could be proven that the incentive influenced trade flows, it would be too late for any recompense. For instance, in the case of the Ford incentive, it would take years before the new plant actually affected trade flows, long after the incentive had been given.[127]

The Americans also felt that the GATT code could not be used to control state and municipal incentives. However, they did think that there might be some potential in the Canadian proposal. As long as the Canadians agreed that new investment incentives automatically had the impact of influencing trade flows and could result in 'serious prejudice' to the sector, the two sides could agree to appropriate countermeasures if the GATT codes did eventually become the instrument by which to control subsidies. These admissions, which amounted to a 'notification, consultation and conciliation' approach, had to be set out in a side agreement between the two countries.[128]

The Canadians retreated to Ottawa to consider the U.S. responses. Using the GATT subsidies code to control incentives in North America meant an explicit acknowledgment that some programs, particularly any 'special ad hoc' incentives programs like the Ford deal, would be illegal and subject to some form of countermeasure, including, perhaps, countervailing duties. This could curtail Canadian action on the investment front significantly and take the federal government entirely out of the equation, a considerable disadvantage for potential Canadian incentives packages. If, however, as Reisman was predicting in his report, the Canadian climate for investment was competitive with the United States owing to lower labour costs and exchange-rate differences, the end of incentives south of the border would work to Canada's advantage. Nonetheless, a clear bottom line remained for the Canadians before they could agree to any incentives regime: 'Canada could not agree to such a system unless the US authorities undertake to notify incentives at the state and municipal levels as well as the federal levels.'[129]

In July 1979 the two sides met again, this time in Ottawa. The tone of this meeting was much more sedate. Privately, the U.S. side told Canadian officials that the departure of Secretary Blumenthal and his replacement by William Miller meant 'uncertainty' in the 'continuity of interest' in the issue. With this uncertainty, 'it was not clear as to how far the present exercise could be advanced.' Nonetheless, the two sides got to work in a 'frank and cordial' atmosphere. The Americans admitted that, when it came to the notification of state and municipal incentives, they could only promise their 'best endeavours,' and that it was simply not possible to 'deliver a commitment that would be binding on states.' The Canadians expressed disappointment that this was the case. They could not be seen as agreeing to a binding mechanism of notification under the GATT Subsidies/Countervailing Codes that prejudiced the federal government's ability to respond to incentives from the United States, if Washington could not control the states. In the Canadian view, 'our ten provinces are not in a position to sustain a bidding war with fifty states ... Canada could not undertake to deliver the provinces if the USA could not deliver the states.'[130]

The Americans accepted that the Canadians could not consent to an 'unbalanced agreement,' in which 'Canada's notification obligations related to both federal and sub-federal levels, while USA's were confined to the federal level, with only best endeavors in respect to states.' Moreover, the U.S. side was hampered by continued interagency wrangling: the Americans had not produced a unanimous position paper, with Treasury continuing to argue for a broad, principles-based approach (as spelled out in the withdrawn April paper) and State and Commerce being in general agreement with the Canadian GATT proposal. The Americans admitted that Canadian thinking was 'well in advance' of that of the United States, reflecting another case of Canadian preparedness on auto-related issues. They agreed that the Canadian-written 'Draft Joint Working Group Report on Containment of Investment Incentives' should go to their respective principals in Washington and Ottawa. But the talks and, it seemed, any serious effort to actually contain incentives in North America went nowhere, foundering upon the American inability to reign in the state and municipal programs, U.S. interagency wrangling, and the uncertainty caused by the arrival of a new treasury secretary.[131]

Despite U.S. fluidity on the file, events outside the negotiations were quickly overtaking the joint efforts to control incentives. The Canadian federal election of May 1979 returned a minority Progressive Conservative government under Joe Clark. The new government needed time to get up to speed on the complex automotive file, and the political uncertainty of a minority government hampered action. By the fall of 1979, most automotive issues had come to a standstill, including the incentives question.[132] In October, officials on the Interdepartmental Committee on Automotive Policy were complaining that 'there exists a certain confusion as to the status and priority of many of the issues' and it was necessary to 'at the very least review the situation and give clear directions as to the work to be undertaking in the next few months.'[133]

More important, events involving Chrysler put all other considerations regarding automotive policy in a new light. With the financial crisis at Chrysler and the company's near bankruptcy, the regulatory and competitive challenges faced by the Big Three in the 1970s came to a crashing climax. Instead of fighting over whether or not governments should entice companies with investment incentives, Canada and the United States were faced with the prospect of having to prop up financially one of the North America's largest firms or see it fail, dragging down with it tens of thousands of jobs and wreaking economic havoc on both sides of the border.

Conclusion: The Prisoner's Dilemma in North American Automotive Investment

For much of the 1960s, Canadians complained about U.S. investment in their country and its impact, with many arguing that ensuring less American control and less American investment was an important step in maintaining Canada's sovereignty. Yet at the very moment when Canadians were making plans to launch nationalization ventures in sectors such as oil and gas and aerospace, they were also fighting tooth and nail to ensure U.S. auto investment. In the battle over automotive investment that emerged after 1973, the Canadian state utilized cash incentives to attract precious auto dollars north of the border, an approach that ran contrary to other Canadian attitudes towards foreign direct investment (FDI). This fight to achieve what Canadians saw as a fair share of automotive investment, and the use of incentives in particular, had three profound and long-lasting implications.

The first of these concerned the very nature of capital flows in North America and the relationship between multinational enterprises and states. The Ford incentive is an excellent example of how capital mobility is a key advantage of mobile, flexible MNEs over territorially immobile states. When it came to automotive investment in the 1970s and beyond, this advantage weakened the state's ability (on both sides of the border) to regulate MNEs. As a leading scholar of capital mobility, Kenneth Thomas, has written, 'as long as different jurisdictions are competing to land new economic activities, or keep existing ones, companies have the potential to improve their outcomes in these bargaining games by using auctions among governments.' Capital mobility has real economic consequences, 'reducing returns to labour and increasing returns to capital.' This results in a situation wherein 'trends in relative bargaining power work *in favour* of multinationals, not in favour of host states.'[134] This explains the American federal government's sharp reaction to the Ford incentive, the UAW's unhappiness, and the Ontario government's reluctance to get into the incentives game.

But what explains the Canadian government's enthusiasm for incentives, given that initiating such a dynamic would ultimately weaken its bargaining position with American automotive capital? In his *Competing for Capital: Europe and North America in a Global Era*, Thomas calls the situation that prevailed in North American automotive investment in the 1970s a 'prisoner's dilemma.' Governments were trapped, like prisoners trying to escape, by their fears of other prisoners' actions.

They could, and should, give up incentives, because the practice weakened their position vis-à-vis capital, but they could not do so unless every other government did. As such, in order to protect themselves, governments offered incentives, making all governments competing for investment weaker in comparison to capital. The dilemma was further exacerbated by the fact that, while cooperation was necessary to escape the problem, both governments feared that they they would weaken themselves by agreeing to a solution. They therefore refused to agree.[135]

Canadians (and Americans) followed this pattern when it came to the automotive sector. They offered incentives that weakened their bargaining position in the face of capital. This was a consequence, in the Canadian view, of a need to ensure, no matter the cost, additional investment (and jobs) for Canada given the new plant requirements necessitated by technological and regulatory imperatives. Canada and the United States also failed to come to any agreement on a mechanism to control incentives, as had been done with some success in the European Union (EU). The EU's European Commission acted as a third party to control incentives by requiring notification of such measures, and the EU made a long-standing effort to curtail or at least lessen these practices.[136] In contrast, Canadian and American diplomats failed to come to a solution that controlled the use of incentives. By the late 1980s, investment incentives became the operating norm in North America, and thereafter no auto plant – either foreign or domestic – has opened on the continent without some sort of 'locational tournament' occurring.[137] After the Ford incentive, the Pandora's box of investment incentives could never be closed: incentives remained one of the few options available to Canadian policy makers. This chapter helps to explain, in part, why this dynamic emerged, and how it helped to shape the relations between states and firms in the North American auto industry.

The incentive battles of the 1970s had other long-term consequences beyond weakening all states vis-à-vis capital. The incentives fight provides an example of how American capital and American firms were effectively decoupled from U.S. government interests. In the post-war period, U.S.-based MNEs and the U.S. government often came into conflict over policies that were designed to restrict capital flows.[138] As yet another example of this dynamic, the Ford incentive fight illustrates how this divergence of interests emerged in the unregulated North American automotive investment market created under the auto pact. Though the reasons surrounding Henry Ford II's decision to put the plant in Windsor are not entirely clear, there is no question that the act was in direct opposition to the wishes of Washington. Canadian policy makers were able to exploit this divergence of interests for short-term gain, allowing them to defy Washington's wishes, too. Yet the longer-term consequences of this decoupling, and of the Canadian willingness to exploit this decoupling, were, as we shall see in chapter 8, eventually self-defeating for Canadian policy makers in the auto field.

Ultimately, the issue of investment incentives and the competition between firms and states over the direction of production and economic outcomes goes to the heart of the post-war global economic order. The Canada-U.S. battle presaged and reflected broader worldwide trends in a period before the formal regionalization and globalization represented by the Canada-U.S. Free Trade Agreement, the North American Free Trade Agreement (NAFTA), and the trade rules put in place by the World Trade Organization. It also underlined the challenges of economic integration and the overcoming of borders by capital. The inability of North American states to regulate auto-capital flows in the 1970s acted as a precursor to the kind of unregulated globalized capital mobility that became so pronounced in the post-war period. The 1970s battle over auto investment in North America was both a cause and symptom of the quickening mobility of capital, particularly automotive capital, which became a mainstay of global economic development in the post-1973 period.

The incentives battle suggests a second important theme. The failure of North American governments to regulate investment incentives was a consequence of federalism, the very structure that allowed them to flourish. A situation report in October of 1979 spelled out the reasons for failure clearly: 'The US government is not in a position to control or even monitor effectively the incentive programs of US state and local levels of government.'[139] Incentives, and the fight over automotive investment more generally, was a problem in Canada as well, but largely for different reasons.

Ontario's preponderant position in the auto sector gave it a privileged position with the federal government in this area of public policy. This had benefits in streamlining automotive policy and providing a coherent and often unified approach between the federal government and Ontario when it came to investment and, later, support for auto firms. But it could also spark interprovincial conflict, especially between Ontario and the other significant auto-producing province, Quebec. This provincial rivalry could be seen in the Ford and GM incentives. Ontario found it unfair that large sections of its province were not eligible for DREE grants, while most of the rest of the country was. This was particularly true in the case of the Ford incentive plan, which did not receive DREE funding – whereas the federal incentive for GM's proposed Quebec plant was a DREE grant. As Ontario Minister of Industry and Tourism Minister Larry Grossman complained in 1978, 'we simply find it hard to see how Montreal can be described as a DREE area.'[140] For their part, Quebec politicians constantly bemoaned what they saw as the unfairness of Ontario's domination in the Canadian industry. They could rightly claim that the Ford deal had played a role in scuttling their GM pitch, and Quebec also had a legitimate gripe, as we shall see, around the efforts to get a VW parts plant into the country in 1979–81, a plant that eventually went to Barrie, Ontario. The battle over auto investment strained federalism during an already difficult period for the federation.

Finally, the battle over Canada's fair share of investment had a third longer-term impact, one that exacerbated an ongoing dilemma for Canadian policy makers. In the mid-1970s the federal state made a great push for investment – one focused almost entirely on production. Ottawa did not make any significant effort to gain research and development facilities. Yet R&D was, ironically, the root cause of the demand for auto investment, given the dramatic evolution of automobile technology, processes, and final products towards lighter, less polluting, safer, and more efficient cars.

A lack of R&D spending in Canada had been identified as a key problem by Canadian policy makers since the 1960s. With over 90 per cent of the Canadian auto industry U.S.-owned, the MNEs operating in Canada felt little need to allocate precious R&D dollars or projects north of the border.[141] In the 1970s, this problem persisted, in both the assembly and parts sectors. In 1977, for instance, IT&C officials estimated that R&D spending in the U.S. sector was $3.4 billion, compared to a paltry $8 million in Canada. Worse from the Canadian perspective, the multinational nature of the industry meant that Canadian subsidiaries paid massive amounts to their U.S. parents for R&D services rendered, totalling approximately $375 million in 1977.[142] Even the largest Canadian parts firms did minimal R&D in the period. Magna's Burton V. Pabst stated that the company performed 'little, if any, R&D in the strict sense.' At that point, Magna 'specialized in working with materials in unique ways through manufacturing process developments. They hire[d] skilled and entrepreneurial tool makers to turn product designs

Table 3.2
Automotive industry research and development expenditures in Canada, 1973–6
(in millions)

	1973	1974	1975	1976
Motor Vehicle Manufacturers	3.3	2.5	2.8	2.1
Parts & Accessories Makers	4.3	4.8	4.5	5.2
Truck and Trailer Makers	0.4	1.1	1.2	1.2
TOTAL	8.0	8.4	8.5	8.5

Source: Robert Latimer to Herb Gray, 'Options Paper,' 10 November 1980, Table 11, LAC, RG 19, vol. 5738, file 3881-01, pt. 3 fp.

into realities.'[143] Total auto R&D expenditures were miniscule, given the industry's size.

In the logic of fair share, some Canadian politicians and policy makers reasoned that the country deserved a much larger slice of the R&D pie. In his 1978 discussions with the automakers, Bill Davis made the case for 'a certain amount of research and development being done here in Ontario.' The premier's 'own view of the auto pact was that it was mutually beneficial. The only objection I had to the auto pact is a matter of principle – we were hewers of wood and drawers of water, but all of the R&D and intellectual property was south of the border. We did not have enough water or wood to make up the difference.' But the automakers had 'counter arguments,' saying that it was difficult to divide up research projects geographically, or that the Canadian research scale was insufficient for Detroit's needs. Davis's response was to argue that specialized-materials research could be done in Canada.[144]

As part of the federal government's revamped 1979 automotive policy, R&D became a focus of Canadian efforts to secure more of a fair share. An interdepartmental committee was created under the chairmanship of the National Research Council to oversee auto R&D efforts, propose possible programs with the OEMs and part makers, and provide funding for any new programs that might develop. At the same time, IT&C initiated discussions with the Big Three to 'encourage them to assign product lines and associated R&D in Canada.' Finally, the Ministry of State for Science and Technology (MOSST) conducted its own study of the regulatory, fleet, and technology needs in North America after 1985, when the current guidelines had run their course. This study was to determine which areas of R&D 'would hold promise' in terms of 'production, employment and trade if pursued in Canada,' and make recommendations to achieve progress in these areas.[145]

The results of these efforts were somewhat uneven. Ontario and the federal government did develop some programs to provide parts makers with funding for research, but this was a drop in the bucket. The vast bulk of North American automotive R&D was being done by the Big Three. GM and Ford were both approached about sourcing some of their R&D needs in Canada. GM's response was rather lukewarm, while Ford was much more receptive and even made a comprehensive submission to its parent company on the possibilities for R&D in Canada. Even this promising start, however, was snuffed out as R&D in Canada became something of an afterthought in the wake of the overall crisis in the industry after 1979.[146]

Indeed, though the Canadian government had some success in gaining automotive investment in Canada in the period, none of it was specifically targeted to R&D. Whether or not this was even possible is a matter of debate. But the fact remains that the government's efforts were focused entirely on production investment – the kinds of jobs that Canada largely already had and had been condemned as 'mere' assembly-line work, with little value added.[147] Few real efforts were made to gain auto R&D, a consequence, perhaps, of what federal politicians and policy makers saw as feasible.

The issue of research and development, the question of automotive investment, and the battle over incentives were all dramatically short-circuited by the end of 1979. The regulatory measures, dramatic changes in the market, and the mistakes of the industry's management conspired to create a new paradigm in the automotive world, one that threatened to deindustrialize the great auto-producing regions of both the American Midwest and the Canadian Golden Horseshoe. Instead of engaging in bidding wars over new automotive investment, states, provinces, and federal governments now plunged into a debate over whether or not to bail out a sector that faced bankruptcy and utter collapse. The new paradigm centred on Chrysler, and the implications for the North American auto industry were tremendous.

4 Nadir: Saving Chrysler and Debating State Intervention in the Auto Sector

For every golden age, there must come a reckoning. By the 1970s, the successes and excesses of the post-war North American automotive industry – with its utter, swaggering confidence – had over time given way to doubt. The doubts of car buyers and consumer activists, fuelled by an untrustworthy Detroit and its unreliable cars, slowly eroded their loyalty to the Big Three. When, after 1973, other seemingly more reliable and sensible automotive options appeared, American consumers, even more than Canadians, embraced these efficient and more cheaply built foreign products.

The American-owned car industry faced a crisis. Clouded by hubris, America's automakers did not remedy their shortcomings, did little to effectively meet the offshore threat, and struggled with the regulatory challenges hoisted upon them by Washington. Within the decade, Detroit's golden aura was replaced by the rust of deindustrialization: as the North American sector restructured and retooled to address the regulatory and market challenges of the decade, the Big Three shuttered plants and cut thousands of jobs. By 1980, the American Midwest had been ravaged by this process, and Canada had started to feel its effects, too. The Canadian struggle for a fair share of any new automotive investment was very much a pre-emptive effort meant to avoid such a fate north of the border.

Deindustrialization became the new scourge of ordinary people and policy makers alike, in both the United States and Canada. Plant closures and the layoffs tore at the fabric of society and portended a harrowing future of economic dislocation. As inflation surged, interest rates spiked, and unemployment persisted, politicians scrambled to contain the creeping rust of industrial decline. In this atmosphere, there was no worse insult than that hurled by Windsor NDP MPP David Cooke, who called Ontario Minister of Industry Larry Grossman the 'Minister of Deindustrialization.'[1]

The epitome of the North American automotive crisis and deindustrialization was Chrysler. The near demise of this giant corporation represented the greatest and most famous example of automotive decline in the post-war period. At the same time, Chrysler's government-supported bailout sparked an intense debate over the merits of state intervention, though with different foci and ultimately different outcomes on the two sides of the border. The Canadian willingness to intervene in Chrysler's case was preconditioned by more than a decade of aggressive state action in the auto field; Americans were far more reluctant to prop up the company, and gained relatively less from the firm's eventual turnaround. Indeed, by the mid-1980s, Chrysler's Canadian operation was disproportionately more successful than its American counterpart and could be said to have led a reindustrialization of the Canadian sector.

In illustrating how the Chrysler bailout represents a way by which state policy makers worked to avoid the emergence of a rust belt in Canada and ultimately strengthened the Canadian auto sector, this chapter touches only briefly upon the larger bailout story, especially on the U.S. side. It does not dwell on the moves made by Chrysler President Lee Iacocca, who in some narratives is given sole credit for 'saving' Chrysler.[2] Nor does it focus on the important role of auto workers and unions in these events. Clearly, the United Auto Workers – both the international union and the Canadian arm of that union – was important in the Chrysler crisis. But the actions of Canadian UAW were not the main factor in preventing the creation of a Canadian rust belt. The focus here is rather on the actions of Canadian state policy makers (both civil servants and politicians) in the Chrysler bailout, and how they played a role in preventing the deindustrialization of Canada's manufacturing heartland.

Chrysler in Crisis, 1974–9

The roots of Chrysler's crisis were multifold. By the end of Detroit's golden age, the American industry was far too dependent on gigantic, gas-guzzling land ships for profit and had not paid enough attention to fuel efficiency or safety. The first deluge had come with the electric charges of consumer-rights activist Ralph Nader in 1966. The industry had clumsily attempted to deflect Nader's allegations that Detroit's cars were 'unsafe at any speed,' resulting in the first real regulatory imposition upon the companies. The Big Three, stung by Washington's new-found willingness to bring America's glamour industry to heel, responded slowly and unsurely. It was the first tangible sign that trouble was brewing for Detroit.[3]

The thunderclap came with the 1973 oil embargo, and then again, in 1979 with the Iranian Revolution. OPEC's decision to cut the flow of cheap gasoline severely checked America's post-war economic hegemony, a trend accelerated by the end of oil supplies from Iran. No sector of American society bore the brunt of the careening energy roller coaster in the 1970s as heavily as the auto industry. Only a few years earlier, Detroit's cars had epitomized the expansive ideals of the sprawling American imagination: the curvy, gleaming chariots that the Big Three pumped out in the millions in the 1950s and 1960s in the United States and Canada quickly became automotive whales stranded in a world where surging oil prices put a premium on small, fuel-efficient cars. These were the very same types of cars that the Japanese had been building since the 1950s, vehicles that Detroit executives had derided as cheap and undesirable. Now these cars flooded into the North American market as consumers struggled to make ends meet in a world seemingly turned upside down. Where big had once been best, now small was beautiful.[4]

The American Big Three learned this lesson painfully, and Chrysler least of all. Although the offshore imports still represented only a slice of the passenger cars sold in the United States, America's once unquestioned loyalty to Detroit's products was cracking. Given Chrysler's ever tentative position in the marketplace, cracks quickly became fissures that mortally threatened the company. As early as 1974, U.S. Federal Bank officials started to worry about Chrysler's economic position and its deepening vulnerabilities in the marketplace.[5] Chrysler's share of car and truck sales – never more than a fraction of their Big Three competitors – dropped from 13.3 per cent to 10.7 per cent, and 14.8 per cent to 12.8 per cent, respectively, between 1976 and 1978.[6] In an industry where even a sliver of market share represented millions in sales, this was a devastating decline. Canada's Chrysler operations, tied now to the U.S. market, also experienced this downturn.

As the smallest of the Big Three, Chrysler officials complained bitterly that government regulations (especially the CAFE demands) fell disproportionately upon them, and that meeting such requirements could prove fatal to a company already barely managing to stay above water. The company lobbied the White House to relax future standards on Chrysler because of the 'special burden' that the regulations placed upon it.[7] During a 1979 press conference, Chairman John Riccardo stated bluntly that 'it's now generally accepted by everyone who has studied the situation that government regulations have hit Chrysler a lot harder than they've hit the bigger manufacturers.' 'Auto regulations,' Riccardo complained, were 'having a double whammy effect on Chrysler's per unit costs – and by virtue of our size, we're the company that's *least* able to afford the skyrocketing costs of regulations to begin with.'[8] To bolster its case, the company released a flood of reports which claimed to show that it was being unfairly punished in comparison to GM and Ford. Riccardo even provided reporters with a handy graphic meant to illustrate the company's plight.

The energy crisis, regulatory demands, and a cyclical downturn in the market were instrumental in pushing Chrysler to the edge. Yet the company also faced a number of problems that were clearly of its own making. During a 1979 Toronto trip, new Chrysler President Lee Iacocca himself admitted that the company had been plagued by weak management in the past: 'We've had problems not only in making decisions, but also in implementing them quickly.'[9] First, management decisions had damaged Chrysler's reputation for quality, well-engineered vehicles. For instance, the company's Volare and Aspen compacts, launched in 1976, were a disaster – poor products with poor launches that resulted in eight recalls within months. Critics pointed to Riccardo's decision to cull the engineering, styling, and marketing departments in the mid-1970s in an effort to trim costs as a direct contributor to the company's woes and the poor product launches. As one Chrysler executive remarked following the cuts, the 'only engineers around were working on government regulations.'[10] This hurt the company's engineering capacity during the 1977–8 period.

Even the introduction of more popular subcompact cars such as the Horizon and Omni did not stop the decline in sales: although the cars were a hit, Chrysler had decided to forgo building small four-cylinder engines in 1976, and opted to instead buy 300,000 from Volkswagen to source their small car, far too few to meet the demand for fuel-efficient vehicles.[11] More ominously, in 1979 *Consumer Reports* rated the Horizon/Omni as 'not acceptable' for safety reasons. Though the National Highway Traffic Safety Administration eventually gave the cars a clean bill of heath, it was not before sales of the vehicles took a huge hit.

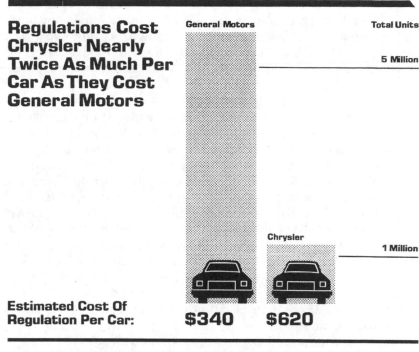

Regulations Cost Chrysler Nearly Twice As Much Per Car As They Cost General Motors

General Motors

Total Units

5 Million

Chrysler

1 Million

Estimated Cost Of Regulation Per Car: $340 $620

Cost figures based on estimates from, "The Impact of Government Regulations on Competition in the U.S. Automobile Industry", H. C. Wainwright & Co., March 23, 1979.

Production figures taken from MVMA Motor Vehicle Facts & Figures, 1979.

4.1 Chrysler's attempts to blame regulation addressed only part of the company's problems. 'The Impact of Government Regulations on Competition in the US Automobile Industry,' 4 May 1979, WRL, D. Fraser Papers, box 51, file 51-9.

The company's production and distribution methods were also problematic. Unlike GM and Ford, which based its production largely on dealer orders, Chrysler built much of its inventory on 'spec,' that is, speculation as to what would sell in the marketplace. This did not bode well in an economy in a sudden downswing, especially one being pummelled by rising gas prices after the 1979 Iranian Revolution. By the summer of 1979, Canadian union leaders complained that Chrysler's decisions left an astounding $750 million worth of cars sitting unsold on dealer's lots. It was no wonder, according to UAW Canada Director

Bob White, that the Windsor car plant, which produced the Chrysler Cordoba (a 4,000-pound, eight-cylinder giant made famous by actor Ricardo Montalban's memorable ads for the car), was in trouble. The cars were well built, but who wanted one in this atmosphere? The company had a 296-day supply of the vehicle, when 60 days was the industry norm.[12]

Then there was the question of Chrysler's dependence on 'gas guzzlers.' More so than any of the Big Three, Chrysler had the reputation for being hooked on the production of big cars with voracious oil appetites. Critics derided the company's decision to continue with big cars even as the reality of the oil embargo hit home for all the carmakers.[13] Although it did introduce small cars such as the Horizon/Omni, the perception of a Chrysler addicted to big vehicles was so widespread that it prompted the company to take out full-page ads in magazines and newspapers across the United States debunking the 'myth' of Chrysler's 'gas guzzlers.'[14] Chrysler Canada President Robert Lander also called the company's dependence on large vehicles a media-generated 'myth,'[15] but there was no denying that Highland Park, the U.S. headquarters, had made poor product decisions in the 1970s.

Chrysler was also burdened by the overseas legacy of Riccardo's predecessor, Lynn Townsend. As Chrysler chief from 1961 to 1975, Townsend had expanded the company's international operations in an effort to emulate the foreign successes of Ford and GM. This strategy included establishing wholly owned Chrysler operations in a host of countries and gaining control or buying into existing firms such as France's Simca (1963), the United Kingdom's Rootes Motors (1964), and the Japanese firm of Mitsubishi (1971). Never fully integrated into the Chrysler operations, by the mid-1970s these companies were a drain on the company's finances: Rootes alone lost over US$100 million in 1974–5.[16]

In a foreshadowing of the parent company's crisis, in 1976 Riccardo threatened to liquidate Rootes and its 55,000 jobs if the British government did not agree to a bailout package of over US$300 million. Reluctantly, the British agreed, but not before they exacted over US$100 million in future investments from the company.[17] By 1978, with massive debts and bleak prospects for further help from its overseas companies, the company announced that it had sold its entire European operations to Peugeot for US$230 million and 15 per cent of Peugeot's stock. Although Chrysler held onto its Mexican and Japanese interests, the company had effectively retreated to its North American stronghold.[18]

In July 1979 Riccardo finally went public with the depth of Chrysler's difficulties. At a dramatic Detroit press conference, he admitted that the company was bleeding red ink. Losses in the second quarter of 1979 reached an unheard of US$207 million. Chrysler owed nearly US$4 billion, to every major bank in America, a total that represented nearly 10 per cent of the entirety of U.S. corporate debt. Eighty thousand unsold vehicles worth over US$700 million sat on dealer lots – an indication of Chrysler's deep malaise in the marketplace. With mounting losses, huge debt, poor products, and government regulatory burdens, the company faced ruin. Even the Canadian subsidiary, which boasted a larger market share in Canada and better financial fundamentals (it did not face the crushing debt burden), had lost $30 million in the first half of 1979. Riccardo called for immediate federal assistance to the tune of a US$1-billion tax holiday, a two-year postponement in federal exhaust-emission standards (worth US$600 million to the company), and concessions from the UAW. Otherwise, he warned, the company would fail.[19]

The bankruptcy of Chrysler would be devastating for the economy. The U.S. Department of Transportation estimated that, if the company went under, 400,000 workers would lose their jobs; unemployment in Detroit would increase from 8.7 per cent to between 16 per cent and 19 per cent. The U.S. economy as a whole would lose US$30 billion of commercial production, or 1.5 per cent of America's entire gross national product (GDP). Welfare costs would increase by US$1.5 billion a year, while US$500 million in Chrysler tax revenues would disappear. At a time when America's trade balance was already in sharp deficit, a Chrysler failure would add a further US$1.5 billion to the country's international trade shortfall.[20] The dreary statistics made headlines across North America, focusing a grim death watch on the company.[21]

A Chrysler failure would be just as devastating north of the border. In Canada, the company was the seventh-largest corporation in the country and employed nearly 14,000 workers (12,000 in Windsor) at five plants in Ontario: Windsor Assembly (Cordoba and Miranda cars); Windsor Pillette Road Truck (vans); a small Windsor spring plant; an Etobicoke aluminum plant; and an Ajax trim facility.[22] Thousands more were employed across the country indirectly through dealerships, parts firms, and secondary manufacturing. In 1979 Chrysler Canada boasted a market share of nearly 22 per cent and revenues of nearly $3 billion. Federal studies showed that, in a worst-case scenario, the failure of Chrysler Canada would result in direct and indirect job losses of 35,000, an increase in the trade deficit of $623 million, and decline in the GDP of $1.5 billion, or 0.5 per cent. Less pessimistic scenarios were not much more favourable, and federal officials agreed that Chrysler's failure might hurt Canada even more than that the United States, since the loss in the Canadian market would be filled by U.S.-based Ford and GM production.[23]

As summer turned to fall, the news from Chrysler was bleak. Third-quarter losses were reported at a staggering US$460 million, bringing the company's loss to date to US$721.6 million. When the final tally was reached, Chrysler's 1979 loss was the largest recorded in U.S. corporate history – US$1.2 billion. By the end of 1979, the company was teetering on the brink of bankruptcy. Lee Iacocca, the company's charismatic new president and chairman, echoed his predecessor and warned that without some sort of federal aid, Chrysler would most certainly fail. Chrysler's impending demise was potentially the largest default in U.S. corporate history, and for many the company's crisis represented the end of American post-war economic hegemony and the deindustrialization of North America.

The Discourse of Demise: Debating Chrysler's Fate in Canada and the United States

While the near death of Chrysler generated a small boom in journalistic prose aimed at explaining the company's attempts to survive, more scholarly appraisals of the bailout remain few and far between. Most interpretations focus on the heroic efforts of Lee Iaccoca to gallantly rescue the company from the jaws of death, and Chrysler's 'miracle' turnaround by the mid-1980s. Less emphasis is placed upon the discourse that emerged over the fate of the company as it teetered on the brink of bankruptcy.[24] Yet the debate over whether or not to save Chrysler, and which form that salvation should take, is just as central to the story as are the gritty details of the company-government negotiations surrounding the loans. Moreover, virtually no journalistic or academic discussion is devoted to the pivotal debate in Canada about saving Chrysler, one that hinged on the attitudes of Canadians themselves towards the giant corporation and the very notion of saving a U.S. multinational at a time when Canadian nationalism was a serious force in political discourse north of the border.

Between the initial shock of Chrysler's revelations in July 1979 and 1982, there was a steady drumbeat of debate over what should happen to the giant company in both countries. The debate was often driven by political or economic ideology and reflected a broader discussion over the respective roles of the market and the state in society in this difficult period, a discussion that questioned the post-war Keynesian economic approach. This 'discourse of Chrysler's demise,' as it might be called, raged across the continent: pundits, executives, auto workers, politicians, and average North Americans participated in the debate in a host of different forums, from newspapers to talk shows to conversations at work and on the street. The debates over GM's and Chrysler fate in 2009 were very similar and provide an insightful reminder of this discourse.

On one side of the ideological debate was the 'let the market decide' school. One early notion that appeared as a serious option was that a failing Chrysler should simply merge with an existing auto company. Although it had sold virtually all of its foreign holdings, Chrysler still owned stakes in both Peugeot and Mitsubishi, both of whom were bandied about as possible saviours. Neither company, however, was interested.[25] A more serious merger possibility came in the form of a 'Ford-Chrysler' link-up that was pursued by Chrysler officials in early 1980. While plans were developed to consider the possibility of Dodge/Chrysler becoming a division of Ford, the scheme was abandoned when it became clear that Ford was uninterested in such a marriage, owing to its own difficulties in the increasingly challenging automotive environment. When Chrysler's fortunes brightened over 1981–2, the idea of merger was abandoned by company officials.[26]

A far more prevalent idea that emerged from laissez-faire advocates was that the company should simply be left to die. Iacocca's request that Chrysler receive some sort of assistance was met with disdain by many observers. On the political right, the prevailing sentiment was epitomized by David R. Henderson of the conservative Cato Institute:

Should the US government let Chrysler fail? Let's reword the question: Should the government force taxpayers to subsidize a company whose products do not meet the market test? The answer becomes clear: No. Why should taxpayers have to pay to keep a firm in business? As consumers and producers, they have shown that they do not want to keep it going. Consumers are not willing to pay enough for Chrysler's products to cover the company's costs; producers – including suppliers to Chrysler and Chrysler employees – are not willing to sell their goods and services at a cost below Chrysler's projected revenues. Consumers and producers have spoken, and that should be the end of it.[27]

Economist Milton Friedman, the conservative luminary, also felt that Chrysler's arguments about saving the company were 'hogwash.' Friedman argued that saving Chrysler 'would simply preserve unproductive jobs at the expense of productive jobs,' and that the market should be the ultimate arbiter of the giant company's fate.[28]

The kind of dirigisme being pushed by Iacocca was repellant to many American observers who were less ideologically orthodox than Friedman. Even the notion of loans guaranteed by the federal government was considered by many to be anathema. Iacocca recalled that, during the debate over Chrysler's fate, 'everybody was beating on us. Everybody saying, "How dare you violate the altar of free enterprise and ask for a loan guarantee?"... We did not take taxpayer money. We had a guarantee.'[29] Iacocca was incensed not only that critics derided his plan, but that they equated any help as government money given directly to the company. Intervention of any kind to save Chrysler – even loan guarantees, as opposed to loans – was considered un-American. Unsurprisingly, this was the emphasis of GM Chair Thomas Murphy's criticisms of the idea of any type of bailout: 'I do not think,' he stated, 'that is in accordance with what made this country great.'[30]

Pundits feared that 'saving Chrysler to save jobs opens the way for every wheezing conglomerate behemoth to swim, spouting and tail-flapping, up on the beach to gasp for federal aid ... Since there will inevitably be other Chrysler-sized flops, we're open to more social blackmail.'[31] Cities such as Denver passed resolutions opposing any help for Chrysler, rejecting 'the argument that competition should be maintained by such means.'[32] Even some native Michiganders were less than convinced of the utility of keeping Chrysler alive. In the *Washington Post*, Michigan Representative Dave Stockman wrote a piece entitled 'Let Chrysler Go Bankrupt.'[33] Some U.S. government officials, too, were unsympathetic to Chrysler's plight: State Department Assistant Secretary Julius Katz, a key player on the automotive file, felt that if Chrysler's mismanagement led to its downfall, this was simply 'a function of the free market system.'[34]

This reasoning was echoed by those on the left, who also had little sympathy for the company. The only difference between Chrysler and the thousands of small businesses that failed every year in the United States was that Chrysler was a large corporation that had political sway, while all those scattered small companies lacked the clout of the automaker. Writing in the *New Republic*, Stephen Chapman bluntly argued that 'the crucial point is that we have a capitalist economy, and no one at Chrysler suggests that we should have anything else ... If Lee Iacocca wants the opportunities for riches and prestige that go with being a successful capitalist, he should accept the chance of failure that also goes with it. Naturally he would prefer to have his cake and eat it too.' But, Chapman concluded, 'his preference here is a poor basis for public policy. If ever a company deserved to fold, it's Chrysler.'[35] The idea that a Chrysler bailout would amount to corporate welfare was pushed by consumer advocate Ralph Nader as well.[36] Folksingers such as Tom Paxton lampooned the bailout in his song 'I Am Changing My Name to Chrysler,' whose chorus mocked:

> I am changing my name to Chrysler,
> I am going down to Washington DC
> I will tell some power broker,
> 'What you did for Iacocca
> Would be perfectly acceptable to me.'
> I am changing my name to Chrysler,
> I am leaving for that great receiving line.
> When they hand a million grand out,
> I'll be standing with my hand out.

Many Americans on the left were appalled at the corporate welfare the bailout represented, and simply felt the market should decide.

At the other end of the ideological spectrum was the notion of nationalization. In the United States, this idea was quickly dismissed. So too was the argument that the government should at the very least purchase a stake in Chrysler. The UAW proposed that the U.S. government take an equity position in the floundering company as a better response than simple loans or loan guarantees. Partial government ownership would surely save the company, the union reasoned. Such a plan also offered the advantage of more direct input into the company's affairs, perhaps even a tripartite labour-government-management arrangement. However, the UAW suggestion received little serious consideration from the Carter administration.[37] Such state intervention in the economy – especially in the auto sector, the paragon of American industry – remained outside the scope of what was politically acceptable in that period.

In Canada, the notion of buying Chrysler was taken far more seriously. If the company was eventually going to be asking the Canadian government for a bailout package in the hundreds of millions, just to

4.2 Canadians were more accepting than Americans of the idea of state intervention, including nationalization. Patrick Corrigan, *Toronto Star*, 26 April 1980. Reprinted with permission – Torstar Syndication Services.

keep it afloat, why not just buy Chrysler outright? Nationalization in the automotive industry was a dream the many Canadians had had for the sector since even before the 1960s, when Walter Gordon had loudly threatened to create an automobile crown corporation if Canada did not gain production and investment guarantees under the auto pact.[38]

Nationalization was also an idea that had been pushed in the mid-1960s by vocal elements in the Canadian UAW.[39] And the idea was not immediately dismissed by some inside the government. With all of its problems, Chrysler's stock had fallen to the point where the company could be had for less than $400 million – far less, unnamed federal officials noted, than the value of the loans or guarantees that the company could be expected to ask the government for.[40] Here was a golden opportunity to finally achieve the dream of an 'all-Canadian' company, producing all-Canadian cars, with the attendant benefits of R&D as well.

The idea of nationalizing Chrysler gained currency on a number of fronts in Canada. The federal NDP, a long-time supporter of greater Canadian control in the auto sector and an ally of the Canadian UAW, actively pursued the notion and demanded that the federal government take an equity stake in the company in return for any assistance package, at the very least.[41] When the Liberal-friendly *Toronto Star*'s editorial board also wrote in support of the idea, it was clear that nationalizing Chrysler had moved beyond the realm of speculation.[42]

Indeed, the notion of the federal government buying the company outright or at least gaining a stake in the firm was a proposal that the government was seriously considering.[43] According to anonymous federal officials, taking control of Chrysler was a 'last chance' to finally achieve for Canadians a domestic ownership stake in the industry, with all of the accompanying benefits of employment and research and development.[44] Confidential talks with Ottawa indicated to the Canadian UAW that purchasing a share of Chrysler Canada was 'the major option,' since equity participation would be safer than straight-out loans and, from a public relations perspective, would be seen as less of a corporate-welfare measure than loans and be more 'nationalistic.'[45]

Others in Canada, however, thought the idea outlandish. Simon Reisman, who had negotiated the auto pact in 1965 and chaired the recent royal commission on Canada's auto industry, called the notion 'the dumbest idea I've ever heard.' He was deeply sceptical that the federal government could operate an entity such as Chrysler. Larry Grossman, Ontario's minister of industry, laughed at the notion of buying the wounded giant, pointing to the immense competitive challenges the company faced and its huge debt.[46] But the extent of the debate in Canada indicated just how seriously the option was considered.

In the end, pragmatism – with a dash of patriotism – proved more effective in determining a middling outcome than either ends of the ideological spectrum. In the United States, regardless of philosophical beliefs towards government intervention, it was clear that legislators had no stomach for a Chrysler failure. Michigan Governor William Milliken, a Republican, felt that 'there has been a good deal of public debate in recent months concerning the merits and wisdom of extending governmental assistance to Chrysler. Whatever economic theories each of us may subscribe to, the practical solution is that a Chrysler bankruptcy would be many times more costly to the state and federal government than properly drawn aid programs.' Milliken estimated that the total annual loss to Michigan if Chrysler went under was in excess of US$200 million.[47]

At the same time, no one in the United States was suggesting that the government propose direct involvement in Chrysler through an equity position, or even a grant. As Democrat James Blanchard, the Michigan representative who eventually shepherded a bailout bill through the House of Representatives, put it, 'even if you can convince a congressman to abandon his predetermined economic theology, you might as well forget trying to talk him into putting hundreds of millions of dollars in a gift-wrapped package and handing it over to a private corporation.'[48] This pragmatism towards saving the giant company instigated some unlikely bipartisanship: Milliken, a conservative Republican, was strongly in support of saving Chrysler, and worked closely with liberal Democrat Blanchard to see the eventual government bailout through.

Legislators south of the border also heard patriotic calls to save the floundering American giant. American auto workers were particularly effective at generating support for some sort of intervention that played upon nationalism at a time when a symbol of America's economic might was under duress. One UAW flyer made the case that 'we are Americans ... Chrysler needs help,' and that keeping the company going was 'in the best interest of the nation.' Those who supported government assistance argued that the idea of granting loans to companies was decidedly not un-American: the U.S. government made billions in loans every year – sometimes even to foreign firms. The UAW made much of the fact that, in 1979, the U.S. government budgeted US$409 billion in loan guarantees, including US$6.4 billion in loans to foreign governments to help them purchase U.S. arms.[49] When he finally announced the bailout package in 1980, President Jimmy Carter stated that the bailout was necessary 'to avoid the loss of hundreds of thousands of American jobs among automobile workers and to keep a highly competitive automobile industry in our country.'[50] These words would echo those of President Barack Obama a generation later.

In the end, the Canadian government, too, took a middling approach to the Chrysler problem. It rejected the idea of taking control of the company or in acquiring an equity stake in return for its assistance.

Although the federal government had openly speculated about taking an equity position in Massey-Ferguson, a Canadian company that was also in serious trouble during this period, the Liberals passed on taking a share in Chrysler's Canadian operations or even its parent.[51] The government's reasoning reflected the integrated nature of Chrysler and other the Big Three operations. As Industry Minister Herb Gray stated, 'the government did not feel that the solution would rest in taking an equity position in Chrysler Canada. It is not a stand alone company and is dependent on its parent and the United States dealer network for its survival.'[52]

Moreover, taking over Chrysler did not fit the interventionist mould that the Canadian government had shaped for itself in this period. Although this was an era of increasing economic nationalism, taking over the auto industry was not on the agenda. Liberal governments, often with the prodding of the NDP, had intruded dramatically in the economy since the early 1970s through the creation of crown corporations such as Petro-Canada. But the auto industry was not a good candidate for this kind of autarky. Although he had authored the nationalistic 'Gray Report' and had helped to create FIRA, Gray did not see Ottawa taking Detroit's place. The nature of the car business did not fit within the government's conception of its role: 'Equity participation also implies other obligations which, as a government, we do not consider appropriate to take on.'[53]

Instead of letting the company die or taking it over, then, political leaders in both countries determined that state intervention in the form of government loan guarantees was the best solution for the Chrysler crisis. The debate over saving Chrysler, and the level of government involvement necessary to do so, reflected a continental divide over the merits of state intervention in the economy. In the United States, there was a passionate discussion over whether the giant corporation should be allowed to die, in keeping with the social Darwinism of modern capitalism to which many Americans ascribed. In Canada, the debate was much more subdued and reflected Canadians' long-standing acceptance of the merits of state intervention.[54] It also reflected the particularities of the Canadian auto industry, one that had come to be personified by business-government management following the implementation of the 1965 Canada-U.S. auto pact. Canadians did not feel that this kind of intervention was un-Canadian: the government had been rigorously intervening in the auto industry for more than a decade by the time Chrysler came knocking on its door.

Canadian State Responses to the Chrysler Crisis, 1979–81

Interaction between host countries and multinational enterprises is an important issue in international political economy.[55] The relationship between the state and foreign corporations has been characterized by both conflict and cooperation. This is especially true in the manufacturing sector in general and in the strategic automotive industry in particular. In some instances of state-automotive MNE interaction, scholars have recognized that the multifaceted state has agency and works to achieve outcomes that benefit various stakeholders, be they workers or local companies. In other instances, the state acts on behalf of multinational capital, which can be to the detriment of local actors. Clearly, MNEs and states both exercise power and are also constrained by existing political, social, and economic structures and historical factors.[56] As one leading scholar of the relationship between the state and MNEs has argued, these interactions 'reflect a kaleidoscope of power relationships' which emerge from the complex triangular diplomacy between home states, host states, and MNEs.[57]

In addressing state-MNE relations and the question of Canada and the Chrysler bailout, one must first recognize that these relationships were indeed complex. For the Canadian governments, their main goals were to maintain employment and to protect the Canadian taxpayer from the unnecessary exposure which might result from their efforts to maintain employment if Chrysler failed – a distinct possibility. At the same time, both the federal and Ontario governments understood that Chrysler itself was dealing with the U.S. government in attempting to improve its own position by gaining assistance. Chrysler understood, too, that it was bargaining with two different sets of governments. While the company was willing to accept some restrictions on its ability to run its affairs (both in the United States and in Canada), it sought to limit the constraints government placed upon it as the price of aid.

Similarly, the Canadian governments were also constrained: they were bargaining with a foreign corporation which was continentally integrated yet run from Detroit (while Chrysler's Canadian managers had little independence, they often did act as an intermediary between Ottawa and Detroit). In turn, this continental integration provided both challenges and opportunities. Chrysler Canada's integration with its parent firm meant that the company's failure in the United States would inevitably lead to the Canadian subsidiary's demise, and at the same time precluded the idea of Chrysler Canada being bought out or separated from its parent firm. All of these considerations were influenced by the automotive regime that governed the auto industry: the auto pact required Chrysler to maintain content and output levels in Canada, and acted as a production floor for the company. In short, both governments and Chrysler faced constraints within the context of the bailout negotiations and the broader auto trade and politics of Canada and North America.

During the Chrysler crisis, state responses towards the company occurred at two different levels: at the two federal governments, and at the subnational level (provinces and states). As the story of the U.S. government's role in saving Chrysler has been told in detailed elsewhere,[58] this section focuses upon the Canadian story, including the role of the Ontario government. Although the focus here is upon the Canadian state's responses, it is necessary at points to convey the responses of the U.S. federal government (and, to a far lesser degree, U.S. state governments) to understand the broad range of responses initiated by these state apparatuses, and their interactions with the Canadians, in an effort to save the company. As one senior U.S. State Department official put it, 'given the integration of the North American industry and the existence of the automotive agreement, it was only natural for the two governments to consult ... about Chrysler's problems and our respective reactions to them.'[59]

In Ottawa, Joe Clark's minority government had been in power for only a few months following its May 1979 defeat of the Trudeau Liberals. Although the Clark government was ideologically less interested in wholesale state intervention in the economy than the Liberals had been, it took a pragmatic approach towards the Chrysler crisis, one that was predicated upon a Canadian willingness to accept some form of assistance and the fact that Chrysler was slow in approaching the government.

In the weeks after Riccardo's July 1979 announcement of Chrysler's precarious position, little movement was made by the company to include Canadian assistance in the recovery plan that was being slowly developed south of the border.[60] Finally, in August 1979, Canadian Chrysler officials visited Ottawa to begin discussions towards seeking assistance. The Canadians had stated that they would consider assistance only if the US$1.5-billion plan of loan guarantees proposed by Iacocca was accepted by Congress. Publicly, both government and company officials were unwilling to divulge the details of the talks. But the government was determined to show that this was not a form of corporate welfare: it was not, according to Industry Minister Robert de Cotret, 'a bailout plan' but an effort to find 'financial help' for the company. Minister de Cotret had stated unequivocally that Canadian assistance was a non-starter if the company did not secure guarantees from the U.S. government, which brought a sharp rebuke from Liberal industry critic and Windsor MP Herb Gray.[61]

Privately, the government continued to hold discussions with Chrysler Canada. During one meeting with company executives, de Cotret hinted strongly that if the company worked out a project that included conversion of the Windsor engine plant to the production of smaller, more fuel-efficient engines, and perhaps a new truck plant in Quebec, assistance would be forthcoming. He held out the possibility that the government might consider a package that included grants under DREE and further loan guarantees. While incentives of up to $500 million were the maximum that the government would consider, some in the Finance Department argued that $150 million in loan guarantees might be more reasonable. They indicated that they considered this figure a more proportionate response, given the U.S. proposal for US$1.5 billion in loan guarantees. But the government wanted to see a 'leaner package' from the company, and sent the Chrysler people back to rework their figures on the understanding that they would meet again in a few weeks' time.[62]

In November 1979 Chrysler officials presented their 'Chrysler Canadian Product Proposal' to the Clark government. The plan called for Canada to receive exclusive product mandates for a van at the Pillette Road Truck plant and conversion of the existing Windsor engine plant to build a V-6 engine. In return for Chrysler investments of $1.047 billion, the government was expected to give the company a $200-million grant, $25 million for training, and guaranteed loans totalling $491 million. In other words, the government's expected total aid package was $616 million. The Chrysler proposal suggested that failure to accept the plan would result in Chrysler products being 'manufactured in other locations,' the closure of the Windsor engine plant, and the downgrading of the Pillette Road plant to 'a marginal operation.' These threats were accompanied by an unsubtle suggestion that 'the Canadian government indicate, at the earliest possible date, that it is supportive of this proposal.'[63] Although federal officials met again with Iacocca and Chrysler representatives in early December 1979, the government held the line. In the House of Commons, ministers repeated their position that nothing could be announced until matters were settled in the United States.[64]

On this point, the Clark government would not budge. Even a November 1979 meeting between Clark and Carter did not elicit further steps. Canadian officials reiterated their wish to see the company's proposal to the U.S. government before committing to any response, and the prime minister maintained publicly that he would not raise questions about Chrysler with the president. In support, de Cotret stated unequivocally that he 'would not bring this to cabinet before we know what the final decision is in the US.'[65] This position infuriated MP Gray, who felt that with a divided Congress, an end to Canadian dithering might tilt the balance in favour of the loan- guarantee package.[66] It also signalled to the United States – both the government and the company – that the Canadians were willing to hold out for as good a deal as possible.

With the Canadian government publicly announcing that no steps were to be taken until the issue of Chrysler's survival had been clarified in the form of a bailout package passed by the U.S. Congress, attention shifted southward. After months in which the Carter administration remained relatively mute on the issue, the company received a boost when U.S. Treasury Secretary William Miller announced his support for the loan guarantees in a letter to Congress in November 1979. Miller, originally resistant to any deal (as head of Textron he had criticized the Nixon administration's 1971 guarantees for Lockheed), recommended loan guarantees totalling US$1.5 billion. In return, the company would be required to raise US$1.5 billion from private sources, sell assets, and provide a four-year survival plan.[67]

In December 1979 Iacocca went to Ottawa to discuss the company's situation with de Cotret. He was accompanied by Chrysler Canada chief Robert Lander. Even with the Chrysler CEO lobbying in the capital, and with the U.S. package announcement just days away, federal politicians refused to show their hand until the Americans had made a deal with the company. After meeting with Iacocca, cabinet minister Michael Wilson stated that 'we do not want to make a decision relating to any degree of support we might provide for Chrysler Canada until the decision in the United States has been made.' The next day, Clark reiterated the Canadian position – no discussions until the United States had made a deal.[68]

Of course, the opportunity would disappear if Chrysler did not get its deal from the U.S. government, and the Congress was wavering. Bleeding cash and losing customers, on 17 December Iacocca proposed a new plan and desperately pleaded with American lawmakers: if they did not pass the Chrysler bill immediately the company faced destitution. Chrysler was against the wall, and there was no question in Iacocca's mind that if the company did not find some new funds, it meant the demise of America's tenth-largest firm. U.S. Vice-President Walter Mondale concurred. On behalf of the Carter administration, he urged Congress to vote on the bailout legislation.[69] The situation was so bleak that the Ontario government officials thought it 'prudent' to begin preparing contingency plans in the event of a Chrysler failure.[70]

In Ottawa, the Chrysler situation was being watched closely, but there had still been little movement. De Cotret awaited news of congressional acceptance of the parent corporation's aid package; until that time, the federal government would not engage in anything beyond discussions. Indeed, although it was well known that the government was seriously considering the idea, the industry minister had not yet officially broached the idea of aid to his cabinet colleagues. Nor had he initiated discussions with the Ontario government – a necessary partner for any assistance package for Chrysler.[71] In the media, reports circulated that Ottawa would 'not move' until the U.S. deal had been made and until Chrysler Canada's proposals were drastically improved.[72]

De Cotret's hesitation proved somewhat less fatal than that of the Clark government's inability to count. On 13 December 1979 the Conservative minority government fell after losing a vote on a budget motion. Although the Conservatives continued to discuss terms with Chrysler in their capacity as government, Chrysler representatives could not be sure that government policy would not change after the outcome of the election, called for February 1980. The company's already complicated crisis became even more confused with the advent of a Canadian general election campaign at the most sensitive moment of negotiations.[73]

In the uncertainty over the government's approach to the company, Chrysler's fate became an election issue. Gray, the presumptive industry minister if the Liberals were returned to power, made his party's intentions clear following the government's fall and during the campaign: if the Liberals won, there would be no question about aid to Chrysler, though the nature of the government's assistance would depend on what Chrysler was promising in return. Gray had complained about de Cotret's dithering on the issue, and now he took the opportunity to provide an unambiguous statement of the Liberals' position. For their part, the Conservatives remained committed to negotiations.[74]

The Canadian election campaign also meant a delay in any final decision on federal Chrysler assistance for the American government. At
an early January 1980 meeting between U.S. and Canadian officials in
Washington, Treasury Department representatives admitted to their
Canadian counterparts that they considered Chrysler's projections to
be on the optimistic side. While the company foresaw a loss of US$473
million for 1980, Treasury pegged it at US$660 million. Nonetheless,
U.S. officials felt that if Chrysler raised the non-guaranteed amount required by the aid package and cut US$1 billion out of their 1980–3 prod-
uct plan, the deal would pass. They cautioned the Canadians, however,
that if the terms of the agreement were changed, the package being
considered by Ottawa would have to be substantially revised.[75]

Even if the numbers did not mesh, cutting US$1 billion out of Chrys-
ler's capital budget jeopardized the projects the company had mentioned as possibilities for Windsor. A meeting between federal and
Ontario officials in Toronto following the Washington rendezvous left
provincial representatives deeply concerned about the possible adverse
effects of the new plan. But they agreed that nothing could be done
until the U.S. bailout package had been signed into law. No discussions
had yet been held at the ministerial level in Ontario. Provincial deputy
minister of industry L.R. Wilson felt that when a proposal did come
from the federal government, the province would address it on its merits, and did not provide a blanket acceptance of the notion of provincial
assistance.[76]

As the Carter administration haggled over the final aspects of the
bailout bill, Chrysler faced its darkest days. In January 1980 Chrysler
closed its famous Dodge Main plant in Hamtramck, Michigan, the symbolic heart of Walter Chrysler's company. Within weeks the company
announced that its 1979 loss was a spectacular US$1.2 billion – the larg-
est in U.S. corporate history. In Windsor, 5,000 of 12,000 workers were
on indefinite layoff. To avoid running out of money, the company simply stopped paying suppliers. At that moment, by calling in a loan or
asking for payment, the smallest bank or parts supplier could have top-
pled one of the largest industrial enterprises in the world.[77]

Finally, to the immense relief of over 100,000 Chrysler workers on
both sides of the border, on 7 January 1980 President Carter signed
the bill into law. The plan provided US$1.5 billion in loan guarantees
but required the company to secure another US$1.43 billion in private
financing and mandated US$462.5 million in concessions from the
company's employees.[78] The company also sought exemptions from

clean-air standards that would allow it to meet the new requirements two years later than originally expected. This measure was fought by GM and Ford, who felt that Chrysler's management problems should not preclude them from meeting the same requirements that they faced. The company also received favourable tax treatment from the U.S. Internal Revenue Service, allowing it to accelerate the write-off of losses for 1979 and 1980 and thereby giving it immediate access to returns for those years.[79]

The deal was contingent on financing from a number of state governments, particularly that of Michigan. The epicentre of the Chrysler crisis, Michigan, had immediately taken action within days of Riccardo's statement on 31 July. Governor Milliken announced a number of initiatives designed to give the company support. The state government purchased 800 Chrysler vehicles and began looking at ways in which to provide financial support through loans or loan guarantees: ultimately, the state pledged US$185 million in loan guarantees and purchased the US$150-million mortgage on the company's Highland Park headquarters.[80]

The deal was also contingent upon the cooperation of the Canadian government – but which Canadian government would that be? With the Progressive Conservative government distracted by the election, little movement had been made in the Chrysler-government negotiations, though word leaked that a plan to offer Canadian assistance in return for $1.2 billion in new investment, including a V-6 engine plant, was being devised.[81] During the campaign, the Liberals committed to provide loan guarantees to Chrysler, while the Conservatives remained mute on the subject of assistance. On 18 February, the Liberals under Pierre Trudeau won a majority and were returned to power. In the wake of election victory, Liberals reaffirmed their commitment to Chrysler.[82]

With the Liberals' return, the negotiations between Chrysler and the government resumed. In March, Chrysler Canada executives met with senior federal officials including Herb Gray and Mark MacGuigan to pitch a new plan. Under the revised proposal, the government's expected contributions had decreased from the November plan. Instead of grants of $125 million and loan guarantees of $491 million, the figures now being proposed by Chrysler included grants of $150 million and loan guarantees of $400 million.[83] While the company considered these revisions 'a substantial effort on the part of Chrysler to improve employment and reduce the support originally requested from the government,' federal officials remained wary of promising assistance that was more than a proportionate share of the U.S. government's package. A reasonable level of support was considered $400 million in loan guarantees, split 60/40 between the federal and Ontario governments. Such a calculation would result in federal support of $240 million in guarantees, a far cry from what Chrysler was asking.[84] Nonetheless, in return for bringing a significant segment of new production to Canada, the government was committed to providing support. The Ontario government also expressed its commitment to a package that included job targets.[85]

In an April 1980 meeting, Chrysler Canada's Don Lander made his 'final' offer to federal officials. Investment totalling $997 million would be used to produce a new 'mini-van' ($426 million) and a new front-wheel-drive car ($246 million), along with other operations ($325 million). But the conversion of the Windsor engine facility, which had been leaked as a possibility, and a second shift at the Pillette Road Truck plant, were dropped from the proposal. The government was being asked to give the company $100 million in grants and guarantee $300 million in loans. This was still disproportionately large in comparison to the US$1.5-billion request made by Chrysler to the U.S. government. The Canadians, who represented less than one-tenth of Chrysler's worldwide car market, were being asked to guarantee nearly one-quarter of the loans. While federal officials considered this share of the risk 'rich,' they also noted that the government was not expected to supply the loan guarantees until 1984, protecting taxpayers from an early Chrysler failure. In contrast, the U.S. loan guarantees were immediately applicable.[86]

In response to the Chrysler proposals, Gray took the notion of government assistance for the company to the federal cabinet. Although his submission stated that the idea of taking an equity position in the company had 'surface appeal,' it instead presented two options, both centred around loan guarantees. One package was a $200-million loan guarantee based on the April proposal in exchange for $1 billion in investments. The second was a $285-million loan-guarantee package based on the March proposal, resulting in $1.4 billion in investment. Neither option included grants, and both expected loan guarantees to come from Ontario as well. In either scenario, the government expected Chrysler commitments for employment targets, a new product with R&D support, and the promise of future consideration for other investments. Significantly, both options were for much less government assistance than Chrysler officials had asked in either operating plan. Ottawa was committed to seeing a proportional response, one without grants, and which guaranteed minimum investment levels and an expectation of acceptable employment levels for the Canadian operations.[87]

Like their federal counterparts, Ontario policy makers were keen to seek a deal that guaranteed further Chrysler investment and jobs yet protected the taxpayers from the risk of a Chrysler failure. Provincial representatives worked closely with their federal counterparts to work towards a package that was acceptable to the province. A key goal for the Ontario government was 'to tie any financial incentive programs to a commitment for more jobs in Canada.'[88] In early May 1980, with rumours rampant about a deal between the two governments and the company, Larry Grossman revealed that the negotiations hinged on jobs: 'The situation surrounding the job guarantees is ... the prime concern of this government, and one of the prime reasons for the delay, is simply that the job guarantees have not been arrived at which are satisfactory to us, and I believe the federal government, in order to permit a deal to be struck at this time.'[89] Some observers felt that the idea of job guarantees was unrealistic.[90]

While the latest proposals were being considered by cabinet, Gray and Chrysler officials continued their negotiations. Gray stated publicly that the entire package hinged on guaranteeing employment levels. Grossman seconded his federal counterpart's position, saying that until the issue of job guarantees was squared away, there was 'little point' in dealing with any other outstanding issues.[91] In the House of Commons, Gray defended the government against accusations from the NDP that he had bargained away Canadian automotive jobs: 'I am determined, and the government is determined, that this matter will not come to an end in the absence of a fair deal for our country and for Canadian workers.' While 'the NDP seem ready to cave into the Chrysler Corporation,' Gray maintained, 'we are not.'[92]

The tough Canadian negotiations, which went on for days, almost scuttled the entire Chrysler bailout. The negotiations bounced from Ottawa to Toronto to Washington, and even to Winnipeg, where Gray roped in Canadian UAW Director Bob White, who was at the Canadian Labour Congress meetings. White saw the talks as 'raw politics,' especially between Ontario and Ottawa over the size and nature of Ontario's contribution.[93] Ontario, according to Grossman, was working around the clock for a deal – bargaining hard with their federal counterparts and the Chrysler people 'for 16 or 17 hours out of 24.'[94]

In his own efforts, Gray cancelled a planned announcement at the last moment in an effort to extract further guarantees from the company.[95]

In Washington, anxious legislators awaited the outcome of the Canadian negotiations and deferred a final decision on the US$1.5-billion loan-guarantee package until they heard from Ottawa. 'We need that piece of the puzzle,' warned U.S. Treasury Secretary Miller, as the whole bailout enterprise was 'down to really waiting for the Chrysler Canada negotiations.' Without the Canadian segment of aid, the entire package was on hold.[96]

Finally, after weeks of bargaining, Gray made official the government's agreement with the company on 10 May 1980. In return for $200 million in loan guarantees, the company promised to invest $1 billion in its Canadian facilities over the next five years. The loan guarantees themselves were not to be drawn until 1982, thus insulating the government from risk in the early stages of the Chrysler recovery. Publicly, Gray stated that the $200-million figure had been achieved after an 'extensive period' of negotiation, and he assured the House of Commons that the original figure requested had been much higher. Indeed, the initial Chrysler request had been for over $600 million in total aid, then reduced to $550 million, then $400 million, and finally to the present package.[97] Canadian negotiators had been largely successful in achieving loan guarantees which were proportional with the U.S. contribution.

Most important, they had also cut a deal ensuring that the number of Chrysler workers at Windsor increased over the life of the government commitment, and that unemployment levels would not rise. With 8,000 workers on indefinite layoff and an unemployment rate of nearly 16 per cent in Windsor, the key condition of the deal was that Chrysler's Canadian employment returned to its 'historic levels.' As a result, Gray announced that Chrysler's Canadian employment was targeted to reach 9,100 in 1981 and increase over the next three years to 10,100 (1982), 11,300 (1983), and 15,900 (1984). Under the plan, Chrysler's Canadian employment figures were not expected to drop below 15,900 for 1984, 1985, and 1986. Understanding that there might be factors that could alter the employment targets (the company was still in dire financial straits), Gray stated that in return for the loan guarantees, Chrysler had agreed that if the company did not meet these targets, Canadian employment would never be lower than 11 per cent of the U.S. employment for the 1982–6 period, and not lower than 9 per cent of U.S. employment for 1980–1.[98] The Canadian government had succeeded in guaranteeing minimum employment levels from a foreign corporation.

Moreover, the loan guarantees were tied to two main products. The first was the T-115 'van wagon,' which Chrysler Canada had the exclusive product mandate for until the loans were repaid in full. This was a particular coup for the government, since it was expected that the new product, a front-wheel-drive six-passenger mini-van, would generate significant sales. Others were less sanguine. Sam Gindin of the Canadian UAW noted that most assessments of the market for mini-vans saw significantly fewer sales than the 1.2 million vehicles that Lander projected for 1985. Moreover, Gindin thought that Iacocca's constant reference to the project as a 'light truck' suggested some 'very real uncertainty on the part of Chrysler.' He concluded that the project 'is seen as expendable. If Canada doesn't finance it, it may be dropped so Chrysler can concentrate on something else.'[99]

While approximately $400 million was earmarked for the existing Windsor van plant to build the mini-van, another $250 million was to update Windsor's car plant for the forthcoming 'K-Car.' Like the mini-van, this was a low-priced gas-saving front-wheel-drive car expected to generate big sales for a fuel-conscious public. The rest of the $1 billion was marked for improving existing facilities such as the Etobicoke aluminum casting plant. Significantly, Gray revealed that one of the conditions of the deal was that 'none of the facilities of Chrysler Canada can be closed without obtaining the approval of the minister,' and that the Canadian government had the right to appoint a member of Chrysler Canada's board.[100] The UAW felt that the government's stance had established an important principle: the fact that Ottawa had held out strongly for the K-Car meant, according to White, that 'for the first time we have bargained a product line of an auto manufacturer in Canada.'[101]

The Ontario government's contribution was considerably less than that of Ottawa yet symbolically important. Critics of the auto pact, and the auto industry in general, had often pointed to the lack of automotive research and development in Canada. Investment incentives in the 1970s had not been used to leverage R&D, but now Ontario used the Chrysler bailout to do so. In January 1980, as Chrysler teetered on the verge of bankruptcy, Premier Davis met with Iacocca in Boca Raton, Florida, to make the case that Ontario deserved an R&D facility, which the Chrysler boss was deeply reluctant to grant. In the end, Iacocca acquiesced, and as part of the overall Canadian package, the Ontario government pledged $10 million towards the creation of a $20-million Chrysler automotive R&D centre in Windsor by 1982, employing 150 research and engineering staff. This was seen as a 'breakthrough' step for the Canadian industry and reflected the Ontario government's willingness to leverage more than just jobs out of Chrysler.[102]

On the surface, it looked as though the Canadian and Ontario governments had cut themselves a deal. For a minimum outlay, the company promised to invest $1 billion dollars in Canada and to maintain and even boost Canadian employment levels. The Canadian government had only promised loan guarantees, which would cost taxpayers nothing if Chrysler recovered. The Ontario government's $10-million research investment was also secure: if the company failed, the facilities and equipment would become the property of the province. Of course, the governments still ran the risk that the company still might collapse. Nonetheless, with the Canadian aspects of the total Chrysler bailout package in place, the company had commitments to keep it going for the moment, if not for the immediate future. In May 1980 Treasury Secretary Miller asked officials at the Canadian embassy in Washington to convey his appreciation for the Canadian government's cooperation, and particularly expressed his admiration for Gray's 'energetic effort' in helping to put together the final package.[103]

In the two years after the Canadian governments' agreement with Chrysler, the company continued to face adversity. In December 1980 Iacocca asked for a further US$400 million from the U.S. guarantee fund, adding to the US$800 million of initial loan guarantees to the company. Without the infusion of capital, the company would go down – Iacocca admitted that the firm would run out of cash in January 1981, months ahead of his earlier dire predictions of insolvency.[104] The situation was so bad that one parts firm told Canadian government officials in early 1981 that it had 'already cut off Chrysler, written off $300,000 in debts and another $300,000 in inventory, dies and other equipment.'[105] When the company announced its 1980 loss at US$1.7 billion, its credit rating was dropped to just above junk status.

But the company held on, barely. Facing greater than anticipated losses in the last quarter of 1980, Chrysler fought to rework and renegotiate its Canadian government agreements between 1980 and 1981. Initially, the firm proposed changing its plan to cut $400 million out of the May 1980 agreement by revamping the Canadian production plans (including getting rid of K-Car production in Canada, and closing the Windsor spring plant). Gray informed the company that these proposals were 'not acceptable.' Gray's stance on Chrysler's reworked plan, and his insistence that there would be no help without guarantees of future investment by the company in its Canadian facilities, was met with approval by cabinet and by editorialists. In January 1981 Gray again met with Chrysler officials to hammer out a new plan, announced in February, that included cutting back the government's loan-guarantee commitment from $200 million to $150 million, and delaying access to the guarantees until 1983. Total employment figures guaranteed by the company fell, though Canadian employment was to make up a larger percentage of the corporation's entire workforce.[106]

Eventually, in July 1981, Chrysler submitted yet another plan. The new plan promised $681 million in new investments, including LeBaron derivatives to be built at the Windsor Assembly plant, along with the new mini-van, and the K-Car to be built at the Windsor Pillette Road Truck plant. By 1983, Chrysler had not fulfilled some of its original commitments, but it had also made new investments in Canada which were not originally agreed upon by the government and the company.[107] For instance, the K-Car was never built in Canada, and the Windsor spring plant was closed in 1981, but the success of the mini-van led to further production and increased employment at Chrysler's other facilities.

In the end, the government cancelled the loan-guarantee agreement, which Chrysler never used in Canada.[108] The federal government did not get exactly what it wanted out of the corporation, but it did force Chrysler to provide investment; Chrysler did not do exactly what the government wanted, but never got access to the loans and still invested in Canada. The company ended up largely meeting the employment targets that Gray had demanded. Indeed, by 1983, the company's impressive turnaround was starting to take hold. By then, reinvestment and production changes were beginning to have a positive impact, both on Chrysler's Canadian operations and on the broader automotive sector in Canada.

Chrysler and Canadian Reindustrialization, 1982–8

The Chrysler bailout deeply affected the company's performance, its workers, and the role of its Canadian subsidiary within the firm's North American structure and operations. In the first instance, the near death of Chrysler and the bailout allowed the company to make the necessary investments, update its plant and facilities, and rebuild its workforce. Although these steps were painful, and the Chrysler situation represented a general downsizing of the Big Three in the North American marketplace, they did ensure the company's survival, and its eventual recovery.

With the loan guarantees in place, Chrysler began its restructuring. In 1981, following the closure of the St Louis, Missouri, 'B' van plant, all Chrysler van production was centralized at the Pillette Road plant. In 1983 Chrysler invested $321 million in Canadian plants and equipment. This included the seventeen-week shutdown of the car line at the Windsor Assembly plant, which began entirely new production of the Dodge Caravan and Plymouth Voyager mini-vans. It was one of the fastest and most successful plant conversions in Canadian industrial history. By 1986, the company had invested $666 million in its Canadian operations, boosting capacity, employment, and output significantly.[109]

These operational moves had a number of implications. One major impact was upon the company's production mix, which benefited Chrysler Canada immensely. Chrysler's product decisions, namely the move to front-wheel-drive cars such as the economic K-Car, and the development of the mini-van, were pivotal in triggering the Chrysler turnaround. These two vehicles doubled the company's production from just over 900,000 vehicles in 1980 to 1.8 million in 1984, increasing Chrysler's market share in North America substantially by two full percentage points. (See Table 4.1.) Other successes included the LeBaron and its very successful convertible model. Initially, Iacocca had projected sales of 3,000 for what was considered a 'halo' vehicle, yet in its first year the convertible sold 24,000 units.[110]

Most important was the Canadian government's insistence that the new 'van-wagon,' soon known as the Chrysler mini-van, be built in Canada. Furthermore, the government's requirement that Canada have an exclusive product mandate for the mini-van until the Chrysler's loans were paid off ensured that its success meant even more production for Canada. Following the commencement of mini-van production in 1984, one Canadian official visiting Chrysler's facilities in Windsor – called the 'crown jewel' of Chrysler's North American plants by the Canadian company's president[111] – could not help but be 'stunned' at the company's turnaround: 'It's a hell of a lot more fun visiting the New Chrysler with K-Cars, T-115's [mini-vans], and profits than it was seeing the last of the V-8's and the need for loan guarantees. I did not think it could be done, but I saw living proof in the T-115 plant.'[112] By 1984, the company was producing vehicles 'flat out,' 92 per cent of which were exported to the United States.[113] The mini-van's influence spilled over into the Canadian parts sector as well, as Chrysler purchased nearly $800 million in parts in 1983.[114] That year, Iacocca triumphantly an-

4.3 Herb Gray became Chrysler Canada's Mr Fix-It. 1980. Courtesy of Glenbow Museum and Archives.

nounced the repayment of $800 million of Chrysler's U.S. loans – seven years ahead of schedule.[115]

The turnaround was indeed dramatic and pointed to Chrysler Canada's increasingly central place in the company's North American operations following the bailout. Just as important as building key vehicles such as the mini-van, Chrysler's Canadian factories turned out a much bigger share of the company's total North American output. The federal demands for investment dollars and product guarantees ensured that, after 1982, Canada became the heart of Chrysler's operations and built far more vehicles than ever before. In the six-year period between 1976 and 1981, the Canadian share of Chrysler's continental production averaged 14.64 per cent. In the six years between 1982 and 1987, this figure jumped to 21.31 per cent. In the wake of Chrysler's near death, Canada had boosted its production to over one-fifth of all the cars the company built in North America.[116] (See Table 4.1.) Although the auto pact required a 1:1 ratio on production to sales in order for the

Table 4.1
Chrysler North American production, 1973–89

Year	Canada	U.S.	Chrysler	Cdn. %
1973	356,015	1,893,932	2,249,947	15.82
1974	339,777	1,538,670,	1,878,447	18.08
1975	386,614	1,222,596	1,609,210	24.02
1976	329,604	1,775,251	2,104,855	15.66
1977	332,068	1,710,360	2,042,428	16.25
1978	255,500	1,614,348	1,869,848	13.66
1979	184,493	1,224,386	1,408,879	13.09
1980	125,190	778,771	903,307	13.85
1981	154,556	849,741	1,004,297	15.38
1982	245,915	722,902	968,817	25.38
1983	246,610	1,051,846	1,298,456	18.99
1984	363,712	1,463,423	1,827,135	19.90
1985	389,661	1,480,066	1,869,727	20.08
1986	409,789	1,450,148	1,859,937	22.03
1987	386,114	1,439,751	1,795,865	21.50
1988	439,695	1,461,861	1,901,556	23.12
1989	409,411	1,317,923	1,727,334	23.70

Source: Compiled from Ward's Automotive Annual Reports (various years).

company to maintain its duty-free status, Chrysler's Canadian facilities produced much more than its share of North American output. This went well beyond the 1:1 ratio and illustrated the company's willingness to shift more of its production to Canada.[117]

In the wake of the bailout and the demands made by the federal government, Chrysler's Canadian production was pivotal to the company's recovery. Yet Chrysler's reindustrialization led to a further strengthening in the Canadian auto sector as well. Canada's Big Three plants were already producing in excess of the country's North American consumption level because of the auto pact by the late 1970s. But the boost in Chrysler production reinforced this trend. With the Chrysler moves, the northward shift in production, which had slowly been building since the advent of the auto pact in 1965, greatly accelerated after 1982. (See Table 4.2.)

Another significant impact was upon Canadian auto workers. This boom in production meant that Windsor, the heart of Chrysler Canada, and home to the greatest concentration and largest number of auto workers, did not suffer the same fate as similar auto-dependent com-

Table 4.2
North American production, 1973–89

Year	U.S. Total	Canadian Total	N. Am. Total	Cdn. %
1973	12,662,919	1,589,499	14,537,986	12.55
1974	9,983,934	1,563,850	11,898,731	15.66
1975	8,965,413	1,442,076	10,764,113	16.08
1976	11,485,536	1,646,824	13,457,339	14.33
1977	12,699,086	1,764,987	14,744,886	13.89
1978	12,895,286	1,818,378	15,097,791	14.10
1979	11,475,737	1,629,855	13,550,018	14.20
1980	8,010,563	1,369,697	9,870,176	17.09
1981	7,940,781	1,280,499	9,818,398	16.12
1982	6,985,313	1,235,668	8,693,618	17.68
1983	9,225,698	1,502,325	11,013,508	16.28
1984	10,939,058	1,835,074	13,132,135	16.77
1985	11,653,956	1,934,110	14,046,746	16.59
1986	11,335,241	1,854,418	13,530,711	16.35
1987	10,925,605	1,635,151	12,956,014	14.96
1988	11,237,947	1,976,896	13,727,619	17.59
1989	10,875,574	1,965,480	13,482,329	18.07

Source: DesRosiers, Yearbook 2000, 114.

munities, especially in places such as Michigan or Ohio. Of the nearly 14,000 Canadian Chrysler employees, 12,000 of them worked in Windsor. And so, if Canada was to experience the level of deindustrialization experienced in the United States, Windsor was the city in which it would happen. Initially, the prognosis was not good. The city was in the early throes of a bleak decline. In the winter of 1980, Chrysler left thousands of unsold vehicles to rust on the grounds of the Windsor Raceway. In 1981, with temporary layoffs decimating the auto industry in general, and Chrysler in particular, Windsor's unemployment level reached 12 per cent, nearly twice the national rate.[118]

But the Chrysler Canadian reinvestment guarantees and minimum-employment targets helped to reverse the unemployment situation in the city. By 1986, federal politicians were claiming that Windsor's unemployment rate had actually declined to 5 per cent.[119] Though the true figures were higher, it was certain that unemployment had dramatically decreased, especially in the auto sector. By March 1987, Windsor's unemployment rate had declined to 8.2 per cent. A year later, the city's unemployment rate fluctuated between 6 and 8 per cent.[120] Clearly,

Table 4.3
Chrysler employment, 1980–6

Year	Chrysler U.S. employment	Chrysler Canadian Employment	Canadian employment as a % of U.S.
1980	133,811	13,600*	10.08
1981	92,596	10,920	11.79
1982	87,825	11,176	12.72
1983	74,700	12,028	16.10
1984	81,478	12,448	15.27
1985	100,435	12,356	12.30
1986	107,850	12,093	11.21

*approximate
Source: Fortune Annual Survey of Companies (various years); Chrysler Canada, Annual Reports (various years). This table does not include 1987, which marks the amalgamation of AMC into Chrysler. That year, Canadian employment at the company reached 15,677.

Windsor was bouncing back and did not face the debilitating effects faced by Michigan auto-towns such as Flint in the 1980s, and so poignantly portrayed by Michael Moore in his 1989 film *Roger and Me*.

Employment at Chrysler played an important role in this jobs reversal. By January 1984, the company had hired back all of its employees on indefinite layoff, and with the addition of a second shift at the Windsor Assembly plant, it had actually hired 574 new employees as well. This hiring reflected a steady employment improvement between 1981 and 1986, although Chrysler did not reach the yearly figures promised to Herb Gray in its initial May 1980 agreement with the government. For those years, average Chrysler Canada employment was close to 12,000 workers. This was below the company's employment levels in the immediate post-crisis period yet higher than its employment for 1970–6.[121] But Chrysler more than achieved the minimum percentage targets agreed to by the government and the company. Chrysler Canada's workforce increased as a percentage of the U.S. parent's workforce, as expected under the agreement, and reached one-sixth of the company's total by 1983. It levelled off thereafter, but Chrysler Canada's share of the company's total workforce remained disproportionately large for the rest of the decade.

The sheer number of *new* auto workers in the whole automotive sector was even more startling in the post-bailout period. From 1975 to

Table 4.4
Automotive employment in Canada, 1975–87 (thousands)

Year	Motor Vehicle Assembly (SIC 323)	Trucks/ Trailers (SIC 324)	Auto Parts (SIC 325)	Auto Fabric / Accessories (SIC 188)	Total
1975	43.4	14.4	41.2	4.8	103.8
1976	46.6	14.0	46.2	5.6	112.4
1977	50.6	12.6	48.6	6.5	118.3
1978	52.3	13.6	52.1	6.9	124.9
1979	52.6	14.8	49.8	6.6	123.8
1980	43.9	12.9	41.0	6.3	104.1
1981	43.4	12.1	44.7	7.2	107.4
1982	42.7	8.6	41.1	6.3	98.7
1983	44.4	11.5	55.2	4.5	115.6
1984	49.5	12.5	56.9	4.9	123.8
1985	50.4	13.5	60.3	5.1	129.3
1986	49.9	14.1	63.6	5.1	132.7
1987	50.2	17.8	70.6	7.6	146.2

Source: IT&C, Report on the Canadian Automotive Industry (Ottawa, 1989).

1979, the total employment in the automotive industry was just over 116,000 workers, with just over 49,000, on average, in the assembly sector. Between 1980 and 1982, the worst part of the automotive downturn and general recession as well as the height of Chrysler's difficulties, employment declined severely, to an average of 103,000, with 43,000 in assembly. But between 1983 and 1987, the Canadian auto sector not only regained all the employees it had shed at the height of Chrysler's difficulties, but also added a substantial number of new workers. In the four years after 1983, the average number of workers in the sector was 129,000, with 48,800 in assembly. (See Table 4.4.) Good news announcements were the norm, and by virtually every measure, the Canadian auto sector had been strengthened in the wake of the Chrysler crisis.

Counter-intuitively, automotive employment figures – far from being a leading cause of the rust belt's emergence, as in the United States – were actually leading Canada out of recession. In 1980 one-third of all of Windsor's unemployed were in the auto sector. But the Chrysler turnaround was soon felt throughout the industry. By 1984, auto employment had actually surpassed its 1978 level and, by 1986, automotive unemployment was even lower than that of the rest of the manufacturing sector – 6.5 per cent compared to 8.8 per cent.[122] Far from hurting manufacturing in Canada, the automotive sector – led by Chrysler – had helped to soften the general malaise in overall industry.[123]

The stunning recovery of automotive employment in Canada contrasted sharply with the situation in the United States. There, the number of auto employees dropped from over one million in 1978 to just over 700,000 by 1982. Overall, the blue-collar workforce in America's automotive factories shrank by 22 per cent in this period. Michigan automotive cities such as Flint and Detroit were devastated by the job losses and never fully recovered. As one analyst who studied the cross-border industry remarked, 'Canada's industry has outperformed its American counterpart, expanding its share of production and employment beyond the levels reached in 1978.'[124]

Far from emerging as a part of the North American rust belt, Chrysler's Canadian resurgence led to the rebuilding of Canada's automotive heartland. After 1984, General Motors and Ford also followed Chrysler's lead and sourced more and more of their North American production in their Canadian plants. By the late 1980s and early 1990s, the Big Three's Canadian facilities accounted for one-fifth of total North American production, and the Canadian parts sector experienced tremendous growth.[125] In a period when the U.S. automotive industry declined and the American sector lost thousands of jobs, observers marvelled at 'Canada's New Economic Clout.'[126] In negotiating a Chrysler bailout, the Canadian state had helped to create a booming auto sector.

Conclusion: The State, Chrysler, and Canada's Reindustrializing Heartland

There are many factors that help to explain Chrysler's turnaround and the impact of that turnaround upon its Canadian operations. After suffering such a significant decline in the 1978–83 period, the industry experienced the benefits of a resurgence in consumer confidence which, while not inevitable, was expected in the highly cyclical auto sector. This confidence was boosted by a more general economic turnaround that saw a decline in record-high interest rates that benefited car sales significantly. Chrysler's new products were also appealing to consumers; Canada further benefited by producing successful models such as the mini-van in Windsor, helped by a low Canadian dollar that encouraged even more production north of the border.[127] As we shall see in chapter 7, trade policies that limited foreign competition also helped fuel the Chrysler and Big Three rebound: the 1981 'voluntary' export restraints agreed to by the Japanese and the U.S. and Canadian governments provided some relief for domestic carmakers. Thus, there are many reasons that help to explain Chrysler's rebound, and also to explain the increasingly important role of the Big Three Canadian operations in their North American production.[128]

But the willingness of policy makers to directly intervene in the industry was pivotal. Just as the Canadian and Ontario governments had leveraged new automotive investment through incentives in the mid-1970s, their actions in propping up Chrysler through the offer of loan guarantees at the turn of the decade succeeded in maintaining (and eventually boosting) the Canadian sector. Ironically, in the latter case, Chrysler never actually accessed the federal loan guarantees, though a perception existed that government had actually given money to Chrysler. In 1980 one MP even accused Gray of having 'sunk $200 million into saving Chrysler.'[129]

At that point, Chrysler's turnaround was still in the future, and the extent of the revitalization of the Canadian auto sector was yet unimaginable. In fact, in 1980 most observers felt that the North American sector was on its last legs, and pointed to Chrysler's terminal state as obvious evidence for such a position.[130] After all, even with Chrysler's salvation, the Canadian auto sector faced seemingly insurmountable challenges: troubles continued to brew between Canada and the United States over the auto pact and the auto trade between the two countries, organized labour faced concessions, conflict, and disunion, and – perhaps most dauntingly – the great wave of Japanese imports that had destabilized the whole North American automotive firmament had not yet crested.

5 Integration's Bounty, Integration's Bounds: The Unusual Life of the Auto Pact

The auto pact was no ordinary trade treaty. Given the size and stature of the industry it governed and the agreement's ambiguous nature, the APTA captured the public's imagination in unexpected ways and gripped the attention of politicians and policy makers. From its inception in 1965, the auto pact existed on three interconnected planes of being. It existed in the public imagination on both sides of the border, where its perception was shaped by political rhetoric, academic analysis, and its connection to workers and consumers. Less grandly, yet probably more important, was the auto pact's reality, in how it actually operated and shaped the North American auto trade. Finally, the agreement also existed on a plane in between these two places, where the rhetoric and the reality collided in Washington, Ottawa and Toronto, and Detroit, Windsor, Oakville, and Oshawa. Here the imagined pact and its functioning self intersected, pulled, and tugged as various interests, individuals, and governments strove to shape the agreement and its industry.

For most of its existence, this was the auto pact's lot. Living a fitful life, the agreement was always just one step ahead of abrogation, almost loved and often hated, cherished and protected, yet schemed against incessantly. It was an existence infused with emotion, which had not been present in something as abstract as a trade agreement in Canada since the bruising reciprocity election of 1911, and not matched again until the passionate free-trade debates of the later 1980s, culminating in the milestone election of 1988.

Chief among the emotions the auto pact engendered were unhappiness, fear, and anger. There was American unhappiness at auto trade deficits, and then Canadian unhappiness at auto trade deficits, too.

There was Canadian unhappiness at a lack of investment, and American anger at Canadian unwillingness to embrace 'true' free trade under the agreement by ending what the United States saw as the pact's 'transitional' safeguards. There was fear because of the threat of job losses, on both sides of the border, and a fear of economic opportunities lost by parts makers and auto companies. Anger was directed at the pact by Canadian consumers frustrated by the agreement's seeming inability to drive car prices down to their American equal. Unhappiness, fear, and anger on all sides filtered upward through the policy makers to the politicians – and emerged from the politicians themselves, as they worried over the implications of these auto pact-induced emotions upon their electorates.

Here, amidst the sharp-edged battle over the abstractions of a trade agreement, did the Canadian struggle for the auto industry emerge most profoundly and tangibly. The emotional responses created in the fight over the auto pact were transfused into actions and reactions, negotiating positions and policy decisions. All the battles over investment, fair shares, Chrysler's fate, trade balances, and jobs hinged upon this fulcrum. In the struggle for the Canadian auto industry, the auto pact became the proxy battleground where national interest, self-interest, economic interest, and political interest collided.

Free Trade, Fair Trade, or Article of Faith? The Auto Pact in the Public and Political Imagination

Early in Hugh Hood's novel about the auto pact, *The Motor Boys in Ottawa*, confusion surrounds the structure of the rumoured new auto trade agreement between Canada and the United States. It is September 1964, and Charlie Pope, Hood's fictional External Affairs doyen, is holding a hushed conversation with the fictional Andrew Goderich, NDP MP and former Nobel Peace Prize winner, in the Lord Elgin Hotel in Ottawa. Pope hints at dramatic changes in the near future:

'… Oh, but I can tell you a few things that will interest you. Not exactly external affairs and not exactly not internal affairs, if you follow me.'
'Why,' said Andrew, 'you might almost be talking about the automotive industry.'
'So I might.'
'And how are matters proceeding?'
'There ought to be something on the table right after Christmas. Say by mid-January.'

Goderich is sceptical. The new agreement is an unnatural combination of free trade and protectionism. It strikes him as straddling an unholy middle ground in Canadian political terrain, certain to fail: 'It won't work, you know. In trade and politics you can never have everything your own way. In Canada you're either a free trader or a protectionist. You can't be both and you can't be neither.'[1]

That the auto pact was the subject of a popular novel reflects its special place within the Canadian public consciousness. Hood's novel also encapsulates well the confusion and controversy that the new agreement produced in the decades following its creation. The auto pact was debated, discussed, and demonized long before modern globalization rekindled civic society's recent interest in trade agreements. From 1965 onward, editorialists commented often on the agreement's consequences and controversies. Political cartoonists loved it and lampooned it for its easy and suggestive imagery. Canadian auto workers spoke about it reverentially, while some of their American brethren condemned it unequivocally. American politicians simultaneously disdained it and tried to kill it, while their Canadian counterparts fretted over it and, more often, tried to protect it.

The Motor Boys in Ottawa also reflects the fact that the auto pact was asymmetric, both in its structure and in the attention it attracted, an object of intense interest for many Canadians but only an intermittent annoyance for those Americans actually aware of its existence. For instance, when the agreement was the subject of the obscure 1976 Congressional House Committee on Education and Labor's Subcommittee on Labor Standards, only six American congressmen bothered to show up, two of whom were not actually on the committee. But, reflecting Canadians' sensitivity to the agreement, the proceedings met 'under the glare of CBC TV lights,' as one Canadian embassy official taking in the meeting reported back to Ottawa.[2]

The auto pact may have simultaneously been the object of derision and scrutiny, interest and inattention, but what, exactly, did it mean to the public and the politicians? The agreement's ambiguous nature defied easy definition. The auto pact was, on the face of it, a technical trade treaty, yet it aroused colourful description and passionate discourse over its actual meaning. The most prominent debate was whether or not the auto pact actually constituted a free-trade agreement, or something else.

Many observers defined the agreement as free trade, especially in its first few years. In 1965 Conservative MP Alfred Hales denounced the auto pact in a hail of National Policy rhetoric, claiming that Canada had

. . . Home again, home again, jiggety-jig!

5.1 From its inception, the auto agreement was often described as free trade, as in this 18 January 1965 *Globe and Mail* cartoon. Permission granted for reproduction by the *Globe and Mail*.

sacrificed its protectionist 'birthright' on the altar of free trade.[3] *Ward's Automotive Reports* referred to the treaty as the 'US-Canada Free Trade Pact,' as did newspapers such as the *Windsor Star*.[4] Cartoonists did the same (see above). Henry Kissinger's definition was that 'the agreement … provides for free trade between the US and Canada in cars, trucks and original equipment parts,' though he also noted that 'it has safeguards to protect production in Canada.'[5] Even Philip Trezise, the chief American auto pact negotiator, described the agreement as 'a free trade approach' that was 'constructive and sensible.'[6]

Others differed significantly. In the 1967 *Financial Analysts Journal*, Douglas P. Thomas wrote that 'the autopact is a most extraordinary trading agreement. Contrary to popular thought, it does not permit free trade in automobiles and parts between the US and Canada, but it does involve the removal of tariffs if certain conditions are met.'[7] The *Washington Post* called the agreement 'treacherously misleading,' full of 'unpleasant surprises,' nothing like free trade.[8] For his part, Ed Broadbent thought that the reputation of the auto pact as a expression of free trade was a 'myth.'[9] Neil Macdonald, a Canadian government official when the auto pact was created, called it 'a form of controlled free trade.'[10] University of Toronto economist J.H. Dales was much harsher, labelling the agreement a 'national disgrace ... much closer to protectionism than to free trade.' Even worse for Dales was the auto companies' pivotal role in the deal: 'Not since Mussolini has there been such a close liaison between Big Business and the State in the Western world. Shame! Shame! All considerations of dignity and political philosophy have been sold for a ... mess of gross national product.'[11]

By the mid-1970s, a wave of academic appraisals had tried to come to terms with what the agreement was and how it operated. All were considerably less spirited than Professor Dales's analysis, and most concluded that the auto pact was a hybrid of free trade and protectionism, a managed trade treaty that had benefitted the Canadian industry significantly in terms of production and employment.[12] These studies provided good and earnest assessments of the economic impact of the agreement, but they barely penetrated the collective consciousness of ordinary Canadians. Nor did they resolve the perception problem of what the auto pact meant to the wider public.

At the core of the definitional problem was the fact that the agreement's creators had very different perspectives on what it was supposed to achieve. The notion of the auto pact as 'fair share' – the Canadian mantra – largely sprung from the language of the agreement itself. Article I of the treaty stated that the two governments were to seek a number of objectives, including 'enabling the industries of both countries to participate on a fair and equitable basis in the expanding total market of the two countries.' This seemed to conflict with what the Americans focused on, in another part of Article I, 'the development of conditions in which market forces may operate efficiently to attain the most economic pattern of investment, production and trade.' (See appendix B.)

In Herb Gray's view, the two sides had 'approached the negotiation from different philosophical bases, both of which [were] reflected in the Agreement's objectives.' Fair share was an entirely 'Canadian concern,' while market conditions were a 'USA optic.'[13] These differences in understanding permeated any discussion of the pact and its aims and outcomes. A decade and a half after its inception, Canadian policy makers were acutely aware that there was still a 'gap in perception' that had 'existed from the beginning.' The United States entered into the agreement because it wanted free trade; the Canadians because they wanted to ensure the survival of their industry by rationalizing the sector through a conditional, managed trade arrangement.[14] This perception gap was further complicated by the fact that free trade *did* exist under the agreement – for manufacturers, but not for individuals – an issue that became a major sticking point for the Americans after 1965.[15]

Still, others saw the auto pact as a way station *towards* free trade. U.S. Undersecretary of State George Ball, in a Toronto speech a few months after the agreement's signing, saw 'the handling of the automotive problem as a good example of [how] two nations can live together rationally on a single continent,' an exercise that illustrated the benefits of free trade between the two countries.[16] GM executive Archie M. Long testified to congressional inquisitors that his company considered the auto pact as a 'movement toward "free trade" … a workable solution to a difficult trade problem.'[17] American Treasury Secretary George Shultz told the CBC in 1973 that he saw the auto agreement as a 'model for future trade relations' if its protectionist safeguards, which stubbornly persisted in the agreement, could be phased out.[18]

The significant gap in the price of cars between the two countries stubbornly persisted, too. If the auto pact was free trade, or even a step towards free trade, auto prices were the single most important indication of whether this actually was the case. Equalizing car prices (Canadian car prices in the 1960s were much higher) had been heralded by the pact's proponents as one of its greatest potential benefits and had been a major focus of commentary about the agreement following its passage.[19] Car prices connected the operation of the auto pact directly to ordinary Canadians, most of whom drove and purchased automobiles. Many Canadian consumers who bought cars in the 1960s and 1970s were keenly aware of how debates over the auto pact and its evolution could have pocketbook consequences for them.[20]

In the early 1970s persistently higher car prices than those in the United States made Canadians angry, and made the auto pact a target of their anger. What was the point of a 'free trade' agreement if prices remained consistently higher in Canada? In 1972 the average car price difference was about 8 per cent; American sources cited a range of 7.5 to 11.4 per cent in 1973. By 1975, the UAW's Leonard Woodcock claimed that Canadian cars were still about 6.5 per cent more expensive, while the *President's Annual Report* found differences as high as 20 per cent for some makes.[21] There was no question that the supposedly tariff-ending auto pact had made little impact on prices.

Part of this difference was due to exchange-rate fluctuations, but part of it was also the result of a remaining 15 per cent tax on any cars (either new or used) bought by individual Canadians in the United States and brought back across the border.[22] Few Canadians realized that the auto pact's version of 'free trade' did not extend to them individually. The tax had the effect of keeping Canadian prices higher, as the Canadian subsidiaries continued to maintain the price difference which reflected this tax. Indeed, the car assemblers in Canada were 'violently opposed' to any suggestion of the tariff's removal and argued that their industry was 'not yet ready for price parity.'[23]

They also had no interest in seeing Canadians flood across the border to buy new U.S. cars, or U.S. used cars flood across the border into Canada, wreaking havoc with their delicate dealer and distribution networks. Dealers made the same point to the government, telling External Affairs Minister Mitchell Sharp that an 'open border' for used cars 'could do massive harm not just to our dealers and our marketplace but to our Canadian car buyers, too!' Open borders, the dealers told Sharp without the slightest trace of irony, were 'a dimension of free trade we Canadians really don't deserve.'[24]

Canadians thought otherwise and loudly vented their frustrations at elected officials for doing nothing about the price differential. In 1972 Ed Broadbent relayed consumers' outrage to the House of Commons, when he pointed out that GM Canada's president had publicly stated that the government had made no effort to get GM to reduce its prices, even after a 7 per cent reduction in the firm's corporate tax: What was the Canadian government doing to rectify this travesty?[25] IT&C Minister Alastair Gillespie claimed that he had done his best to get the companies to rein in sharp increases and to end the differential between U.S. and Canadian cars, but to little avail. Unsurprisingly, the public was still incensed by car prices and laid the blame at the feet of the government and its faulty auto pact.

The depth of Canadians' feelings was illustrated in 1975 when Trudeau and Gillespie took questions on Hamilton's Channel 11 call-in program, 'Open Line,' and were berated for car prices. Trudeau told irate viewers that that the difference was due to distribution costs (cannily avoiding any mention of the 15 per cent tax), with little effect. The outrage had been brewing for some time. In 1972 *Globe and Mail* reporter Tom Claridge priced similar cars in Buffalo and Toronto, and found that Canadian consumers were paying $275 more for a Chevelle, $300 more for a Torino, $325 more for a Satellite, and $325 more for a Matador. The paper estimated that the Big Three and AMC were making an additional $150 million in profits from this price differential, while the Canadian government was pocketing an extra $70 million in taxes.[26]

Behind the scenes, the Canadian government was scrambling to get some answers that might help defuse the situation. Federal officials badgered the Big Three as to why the gap persisted. The answers weren't entirely satisfactory, since none would 'admit that the price differential is too large,' feeling it was 'less than the higher costs of doing business in Canada.' Chrysler Canada Treasurer C.W. Sanders told IT&C's C.D. Arthur that exchange rates, taxes, duties, warranty differences, distribution costs, and merchandising could all be blamed for more expensive Canadian cars, though, he cheerfully added, 'the purchase of an automobile today requires a smaller portion of a Canadian consumer's income than was the case a few years ago.'[27]

Sanders's reasoning was not the kind that a politician could use with the car-buying public. When ministers were pressed in the House of Commons or a provincial legislature, testimonials that the price gap was steadily narrowing did little to stem Canadians' frustration. The end result was that Canadian consumers remained 'very angry,' and the differential might, according to the *Globe and Mail*, 'enlist Canadian car buyers on the US Government's side in the battle to delete protections' in the auto pact. The *Globe* suggested two paths for the government to alleviate the problem: remove the 15 per cent tariff, and 'launch a combines investigation to see if there was any collusion – which would be illegal – in arriving at that average $300 higher price to Canadians for Canadian made-cars.' The auto pact took on a dark hue in the public's eyes, since it appeared that there was 'a conspiracy against the Canadian car buyer, who probably retains the dim recollection that part of the whole US-Canadian auto pact was to have been the gradual elimination of the price differential.'[28]

The Americans felt as much and began to see the persistent price differential between Canadian and American cars as a symptom of the

"It must be Ottawa's latest move under the Canada-U.S. Auto Pact to give us price parity with the States . . ."

5.2 'It must be Ottawa's latest move under the Canada-US Auto Pact to give us price parity with the States.' *Vancouver Sun*, 13 January 1973. Len Norris, permission granted by Simon Fraser University Special Collections.

inequities in the agreement, and yet another indication that it did not represent true reciprocity. Treasury official John R. Petty summarized the American view when he told Simon Reisman that 'full reciprocity under the agreement is necessary for the viability of the agreement ... the principle visible sign that reciprocity is lacking is that Canadian individuals cannot purchase North American-made cars across the border and drive them back into Canada without payment of the 15% duty.'[29] Ironically, American negotiators became Canadian consumers' greatest allies in the fight against higher car prices. They consistently sought the removal of the 15 per cent tax and saw the manufacturers' 'monopoly' on duty-free entry as a 'real impediment to price parity.'[30] Not until the end of the 1970s did Canadian and American prices reach a rough parity, however.

The price differential was only the tip of the auto pact iceberg for the Americans. Quite a few U.S. legislators saw the agreement as a give-away to Canada that hurt American industry and jobs. On 1 July 1969 (Dominion Day, no less) Democratic Senator Al Gore, Sr, of Tennessee introduced a 'Bill to Repeal the Automotive Parts Trade Act,' claiming that the agreement hurt American workers and was in violation of its own terms because the Canadians had not ended the 'transitional' safe-guards by their supposed 1968 expiry date.[31] Another Democrat, Indi-ana Senator Vance Hartke, disparagingly called the auto pact 'a form of foreign aid' to Canada from the United States.[32] Gore, Hartke, and other senators continuously attacked the agreement in the 1960s and 1970s, criticizing car prices, the safeguards that led to 'unfree trade,' or the trade balance, which in some years benefitted Canada. Since they could not call the Canadian government before them, senators and representatives questioned the carmakers on how this agreement had come to be.

For instance, in 1973 the Senate Finance Committee called on GM's vice-chair, Thomas Murphy, to explain the workings of the agreement and particularly a massive swing that had resulted in Canada's favour-able 1971–2 auto trade balance. As the committee session progressed, Utah Republican Wallace F. Bennett grew increasingly frustrated by Murphy's answers and made little effort to hide his view that the U.S. government had been swindled by both the Canadian government *and* the auto companies.[33] Bennett utterly rejected the notion that GM itself had not had a hand in creating this 'patently lopsided agreement.' In a testy exchange, Bennett pressed Murphy on his company's role in the auto pact's emergence:

> Senator Bennett: 'I cannot believe that the Federal Government, out of the blue, with no pressure – maybe that is too strong a word, but with no urg-ing from the American automobile industry, conceived this Canadian au-tomobile agreement. I think the motivation for the agreement came from the American manufacturers. Do you agree with me or not?'
> Murphy: 'No, sir. I cannot.'
> Senator Bennett: 'Did you oppose it?'
> Murphy: 'No sir. We did not. We did not initiate it nor did we urge its adoption.'

After a long explanation that centred on the difficulties the Canadian industry faced, a situation that would have seen a trade conflict between the two countries and the potential for Canadian higher local-content requirements of '80 or 90 per cent as some of the countries in South America have done,' Murphy repeated that it was the governments 'that sat around the table and negotiated this agreement without inputs from us or urging or initiative on our part.' Bennett was unequivocal: 'Frankly, this is hard for me to believe.' For his part, Murphy was not being entirely honest, for the companies had indeed played a pivotal role in the agreement's conception.[34]

If the car companies were keen to deny any role in the auto pact's provenance, others were more than willing to take credit for its creation. Former Diefenbaker cabinet minister George Hees fancifully told the House of Commons that 'I was the one who started the negotiations and that without such negotiation there would not have been any auto pact.'[35] The *Globe and Mail* credited economist Vincent Bladen, since the pact 'was the reaction' to Bladen's 1961 royal commission on the auto industry.[36] Ontario MPP Bernard Newman held that 'in fact, the pact originally was suggested by the late alderman, Bill Riggs, on the Windsor City Council,' though he did give some credit to Bladen as well.[37] Canadian UAW leader George Burt also took credit for instigating the agreement. Paul Martin, Sr, agreed, saying that 'it was a proposal that had first been made by George Burt of the UAW. True, George later, for reasons best known to himself, criticized the Pact, but the basic idea of a reciprocal arrangement between the two countries, lowering the tariff barriers to permit parts and automobiles to be made, came from the UAW.'[38]

Others saw the agreement's emergence as a product of 'high politics.' During the 1973 Senate hearings, Clifford P. Hansen (R.Wyo.) stated that 'I understand that really the genesis of the agreement resulted from a phone call between – originating in Washington from President Johnson to Lester Pearson when Canada agreed to put troops on Cyprus, and the question raised by the President was what can we do for Canada, and out of that conversation came this auto agreement.'[39] Such a deal may have helped to ease its congressional passage, but the agreement itself emerged because of circumstances far more convoluted and complex than any simple diplomatic quid pro quo, and was far less romantic. The pact emerged as a solution to a trade problem that satisfied in 1964 the necessities of the main actors involved – the Canadian and American governments, the auto industry, and workers. Simon Reisman is traditionally considered to be the 'father' of the trade agreement on the Canadian side, with Philip Trezise, his U.S. counterpart, as its

American progenitor. Henry Ford II also had a direct hand in ensuring the agreement's adoption by the Johnson administration.[40] Yet the auto pact-for-Cyprus exchange was passed down over the years as irrefutable truth, becoming part of the pact's lore.[41]

The auto pact's genesis may have remained foggy for the public and politicians alike, but even more confounding was its actual metrics. In the same 1973 session during which Senator Bennett challenged GM's Murphy over the auto companies' role in the creation of the agreement, he was equally sceptical of the figures and comment proffered by Murphy on the auto trade balance between the two countries. To the surprise of the committee members, Murphy indicated that the United States had a surplus of $100 million. Magically, it seemed, the $1.4-billion U.S. trade-balance shortfall of 1972 that had sparked Bennett's congressional inquiry had become a surplus. Bennett was again incredulous. How could this be?

Murphy's response was that 'both of the [figures] being referred to, Senator,' were 'government figures.' Bennett could not hide his exasperation and frustration with the automotive executive. 'We sit here in this committee,' he lectured Murphy, 'and we have got to have something we can depend on, and I think if you are representing a major company, the automobile industry, cannot give us definitive answers to why one set of figures is a $100 million surplus and the other set of figures is a $1.4 billion deficit, I do not know where to turn to for the information. What is the difference?'[42]

Murphy's long-winded and confusing answer left Bennett unconvinced. Auto pact trade figures were such a statistical maze that policy makers on both sides of the border were often befuddled by the wildly divergent numbers given by each government, and by the auto companies themselves. It did not help that the figures were charged with political import: since one country's surplus was another's deficit, the auto trade numbers became political footballs that were punted back and forth across the border. The very same figures that so incensed senator Bennett were enough to cause the APMA's D.S. Wood to demand that the Canadian government release the exact figures of the auto trade to the public, since Canadian news outlets were using American figures, which gave the impression that the United States was reaping a huge windfall from the auto pact. Wood claimed that the Statistics Canada *and* Department of Commerce figures were both inaccurate. The incorrect figures 'quoted so loosely by US politicians have tended to create an emotional atmosphere in our trade talks that is completely unworthy of both parties.'[43]

In fact, because the auto trade statistics had become such a problem, in 1970 a special intergovernmental statistical committee had been created to hammer out the differences and come to some agreed-upon standards for reporting the numbers. This was no easy task. The problem was that the huge automotive trade had innumerable constituent parts, not all of which were reported in each country, some of which were reported differently, and many of which were valued and counted differently. In the end, confusingly, the 1970 committee determined that each country should use its own import statistics to report imports and the other country's import statistics to report exports.[44]

This 'import-to-import' format helped, but there was still uncertainty. The *President's Report* on the auto agreement used U.S. Bureau of Statistics figures, which reflected actual transaction costs, but these were not the same figures as the U.S. Foreign Trade Series, where imports were valued at prices determined by the Bureau of Customs for duty purposes. These differences stemmed, for example, from the variety of valuations that a car could have over its life: there was the difference between the factory price that the carmakers themselves used versus the wholesale price which the carmakers used to sell to their dealers, which was again different from the final retail price which dealers used to sell to the public. These price differences were significant, sometimes on the order of 15–20 per cent.[45]

Whatever the details of the figures, there was no doubting that the auto trade balance revealed a pitched battle over the broader meaning of the auto pact. The rhetoric surrounding the agreement imparted it with an increasing importance as a symbol of national autonomy or dependence, of economic success or demise, or as an indicator of Canada-U.S. relations. The auto pact's health – especially the trade balance – became a shorthand for the health of the Canadian economy as a whole. North of the border, in a period of intensifying nationalism, the continentalizing auto pact became a lightning rod of controversy.

Even mild-mannered Progressive Conservatives sometimes saw the auto pact as a barometer of Canadian subservience. MP Terry O'Connor argued that the centralization of automotive decision making in the United States under the pact resulted in an 'increasing danger to Canadian independence and autonomy' since decisions were now based on 'continental rather than national considerations.'[46] Windsor NDP Ontario MPP Ted Bounsall was just as damning: the auto pact stripped Canada of any skilled, administrative, technical, or research jobs, leaving Canadian workers 'just one step removed from being hewers of wood and drawers of water.' Canadians had now simply 'become screwers and drivers' in an increasingly complex industry, a sentiment that was echoed by journalist Mark Witten. Witten argued that, in light of the technological changes facing the industry, the auto pact had forever impoverished Canada: 'Given the scarcity of high-technology production ... it's hard to draw any conclusion other than that we are little more than hewers of wood and drawers of water.'[47]

For stauncher economic nationalists such as those found in the NDP splinter group the Waffle, the auto pact was nothing less than a complete sell-out to the Americans and a reflection of Canada's dependent status. A widely distributed 1972 Canadian UAW leaflet, *New Canada*, illustrated how easily the rhetoric of dependency could be employed by disgruntled auto workers. 'Canadians Against the Auto Pact' (a union group based in Oshawa) argued that the agreement not only signalled the economic enslavement of Canada to the United States but also the subordination of the Canadian UAW to the U.S.-based international: 'The UAW has always worked hand-in-glove with US foreign policy – imperialism – in Canada.' The remedy was a made-in-Canada industry, and a made-in-Canada union.[48] On the other side of the border, some U.S. UAW locals were just as vociferous in their hatred of the integrationist agreement, especially in the later 1970s and early 1980s as production flowed northward and their union brothers refused to accept concessions.[49]

At the same time, auto workers were also among the auto pact's most vocal defenders. 'Pact Facts,' a 1969 Canadian UAW publication, pointed to 'the impressive record of the Pact' in creating jobs and argued that 'the UAW can only agree that it has been good for Canada.'[50] In the early 1970s, when the agreement was under attack and rumours of renegotiation swirled, UAW locals such as Oshawa's giant GM Local 222 demanded action to protect the auto pact and pushed for a more militant response, including protests in Ottawa. UAW leader Dennis McDermott's response to these demands was to urge caution since the matter was 'extremely delicate' and needed to be handled through 'diplomatic channels.'[51] McDermott's reply only generated further demands for action, and about 200 Local 222 workers instead went ahead organized a 1971 'Community Committee on the Auto Pact Safeguards' letter-writing campaign and protest.[52]

Others affixed a much more profound meaning to the auto pact than simple bread-and-butter employment issues. Some members of the U.S. Congress saw the agreement as a violation of American foreign policy which threatened Canada-U.S. relations. Powerful senators such as Abraham Ribicoff of Connecticut and Russell B. Long of Louisiana viewed the auto pact as an expression of presidential power run amok. Fellow Senator Vance Hartke was equally grave, calling the pact a 'lopsided agreement which threw open our foreign trade doors in response to only a partial opening on the part of the foreign power.'[53]

For some Canadians, the auto pact was seen as a test of Canada-U.S. relations and a symbol of international cooperation. During negotiations with the United States on the agreement in 1973, Canadian delegation leader Robert Latimer, who would remain lead official on the file for the most of the decade, extravagantly stated to the Americans that the auto pact was 'the touchstone for showing the world whether or not we can get along together.'[54] By the early 1970s, the auto pact had come to represent much more than a simple trade agreement.

All of these imagined auto pacts – this free-trading, managed-trading, trade-balance destroying, car-price-fixing, Cyprus-saving, job-destroying, job-creating, Canada-U.S. relationship-saving agreement – existed in the world of ideas, rhetoric, and, above all, politics. The different interpretations of what the pact actually meant were well removed from the stark realities of a complex and sprawling motor-vehicle industry. But the massive impact of the auto trade upon the livelihoods and lives of so many in North America helps to explain how a relatively pedestrian trade treaty came to be an object of such emotion.

On the Ground: The Intricate Realities of an Unusual Agreement, 1971–80

Far from the rhetorical flights of fancy that accompanied discussion of the agreement was its reality. The emotions generated by the auto pact stemmed from a number of 'facts': the shifting trade patterns and uncertain statistics that underlay the agreement's operations became signposts for the various constituencies as to how they were faring. The most important of these constituencies were the governments, the companies, and the workers. They, along with the public, watched the auto pact trade very closely – any sign of imbalance, of unfairness, or of any other slight was enough to generate fear and recrimination.

In the beginning, things were fine. After 1965, as the two nation's industries were integrated, there was tremendous growth in the sector on both sides of the border in consumption and, more important for those assessing the pact's operation, production. Total production, cross-border trade, and employment all increased dramatically, especially in

Canada. In order to meet the auto pact and Letters of Undertaking safe-guards (a base CVA, the ratio, and the 60 per cent CVA increase equiva-lent to sales), the manufacturers invested heavily in Canada between 1965 and 1968 and rationalized their production to take advantage of economies of scale. Within a decade, cross-border auto trade had ex-ploded: in 1965 total two-way trade was $1.25 billion, and by 1975 it was $13.6 billion.[55] (See appendix E, Table E.3.)

This amazing growth in total trade did not distract the auto pact's constituents from their most important benchmark, the trade balance. The trade balance was the easiest way to understand how each country was doing under the agreement, relatively speaking. Given the oligopo-listic nature of the industry, the auto trade and the resulting balance were largely shaped by production decisions made in Detroit. And, since they needed to meet the auto pact requirements, which included investments of $260 million in Canada by 1968, the Big Three skewed continental production in a particular way in the pact's first few years of existence. According to GM's Murphy, the company had focused 'in Canada on the higher volumes in order to get the advantage of scale and get an increase in the efficiency up there and ship from there the lower volume type of product to take care of one of our Canadian de-mands.'[56] This was also the view of the Canadian government, which thought the agreement 'slanted vehicle manufacturer investment in favour of labour-intensive assembly operation as Canadian producers found such activity could easily cover off their obligations under the agreement.'[57]

As a result, Canada initially gained immensely as its factories be-gan to produce for the whole continent for the first time. Not only did the total trade rise rapidly, but the Canadian auto deficit, which had been a key factor in the auto pact's creation, was quickly reversed as Canadians built significantly more cars than before 1965 for export to the United States. (See Table 5.1.) This shift, however, did not obscure the fact that, even within the Canada-U.S. auto trade, there continued to be a profound imbalance. For most of the period between 1965 and the early 1980s, Canadians maintained a large and growing surplus in cars sent to the United States but experienced an even greater deficit in parts. Since auto parts now came across the border duty-free, the more cars the Big Three and AMC built in Canada, the more parts Canada imported, even as the auto pact required a certain CVA and even as the Canadian parts sector grew.[58] There was fantastic growth in the Cana-dian industry, but this growth could result in massive trade deficits,

Table 5.1
Canada's balance of trade with the U.S. in auto products, 1965–78

Year	Vehicle Balance	Parts Balance	Total Balance
1965	−59	−646	−705
1966	104	−104	−600
1967	275	−802	−527
1968	605	−974	−469
1969	1212	−1270	−58
1970	1193	−980	213
1971	1215	−989	126
1972	1201	−1129	72
1973	978	−1382	−404
1974	876	−1940	−1064
1975	665	−2477	−1813
1976	1488	−2531	−1043
1977	2056	−3127	−1071
1978	2967	−3568	−601

Source: Industry Analysis Branch, Policy Planning, IT&C, 'Re-
Negotiation of the Canada-United States Automotive Products
Agreement,' May 1979, LAC, RG 19, vol. 5348, file 3881-02, pt. 4.

too, both in parts and in the total trade, especially if cars built in Canada
stopped selling well south of the border.

Corporate decision making, then, wasn't the only factor at play in
how the North American auto trade worked. The trade balance was
also directly influenced by the market, especially the American market.
Through their purchases consumers had a hand in determining how
many cars would be made, and when, which further affected the auto
pact's metrics. In the early 1970s, high gas prices pushed American
consumers towards smaller cars, which were not being built in Canada. That hurt the Canadian trade balance. When gas prices levelled off
in the mid-1970s, larger cars and vans became popular, both of which
were assembled in Canada, which helped the balance in Canada's favour, as did the import of popular snowmobiles.[59]

These fluctuations were corroborated by a 1974 IT&C assessment. A
relatively buoyant Canadian industry before 1973 was hurt by three factors: the rapid switch to small cars in the United States (further hurting
Canadian parts makers, who focused more on medium and large car
parts, thus resulting in a greater parts deficit); production and invest-

ment decisions by the Big Three; and an appreciating Canadian dollar.[60] Though they might argue about why and how the trade balance had shifted, all sides could agree that the overall surplus had swung from a Canadian deficit in the 1960s to a Canadian surplus between 1970 and 1972, and after 1973 to a deficit again. A Canadian surplus would return in the 1980s, but in the 1970s these fluctuations were the key point of contention among the auto pact's constituents.

Canadian consumption could also have a profound impact on the auto pact's 'performance.' Because the sales-to-production ratio was based upon production (that is, the companies were required to produce as many vehicles as they sold, as opposed to selling as many as they produced), Canadian sales, which were also dictated by market factors, affected the ratio and Canadian content targets dramatically. For instance, if Canadian sales increased, but those cars were mostly imported models with no Canadian content, the car companies in Canada would require higher Canadian content levels to meet the CVA and 60 per cent targets. Conversely, if there was a slump in U.S. demand for Canadian-made production, yet high Canadian demand for products originating in the United States, the ratio would be difficult to meet since the sales value of Canadian cars might be unexpectedly high in relation to the production value of Canadian made products. (See Tables 5.2 and 5.4.)

In virtually all the years after 1965, the CVA targets were met by the automakers, though there had been some dramatic swings on this front too. The base CVA requirement under the auto pact for all makers was set at just over $600 million, the total contributed during the 1963–4 year. This target was always met by the manufacturers, given that it was set at a 1964 level and remained unchanged. Wages alone usually more than met this requirement. For instance, in 1979 the government calculated the Big Three CVA by source and use, as in Table 5.2.

The 1979 breakdown gives an indication of how each company met its base CVA requirement and the CVA requirements contained in the Letters of Undertaking (which required an increase of 60 per cent of CVA for any increase in the Canadian sales for cars and 50 per cent for commercial vehicles, as seen in Table 5.3). Clearly, the base CVA was easily being met by assembly CVA alone and was essentially the labour costs of putting the vehicles together. But the assembly CVA was also a big chunk of the total CVA produced in a given year, which the Big Three supplemented through parts purchases, used in vehicles either assembled in Canada or exported to the United States. All three compa-

Table 5.2
Big Three CVA, source and use, 1979 (value in $ millions)

Firm	Assembly CVA		In-Vehicle Parts CVA				Parts Exports CVA				Total CVA
			Independent		In House		Independent		In House		
	Value	%	Value	%	Value	%	Value	%	Value	%	
GM	660	26.6	588	22.5	323	12.4	509	19.5	530	20.3	2,612
Ford	385	25.7	140	9.3	25	1.7	647	43.1	303	20.2	1,502
Chrysler	267	36.1	54	7.4	32	4.4	249	33.7	136	18.4	740

Source: Robert Latimer to Herb Gray, 'Options Paper,' 10 November 1980, Annex 13,' LAC, RG 19, vol. 5738, file 3881-01, pt. 3fp.

nies exported more parts (either from independents or from their own captive parts plants) than they used in their Canadian facilities, though Ford and Chrysler more so owing to the size of GM's operations in Canada. Ford, in fact, derived over 60 per cent of its CVA from parts exports, Chrysler over 50 per cent.

This made sense, since the companies could maximize economies of scale to transfer parts made in Canada by their own captive plants to all their facilities, including their Canadian factories. For example, in 1979 GM's St Catharines parts plant built 17,600 axles a week for various different models. About 6,800 axles were shipped for 'domestic' consumption to GM's assembly facilities at Oshawa and Scarborough. But every week, St Catharines trucked 6,300 axles to Lordstown, Ohio, 2,300 axles to St Louis, Missouri, and 2,200 to Warren, Michigan. In other instances, captive parts production was purely 'domestic' or purely for U.S. use: Oshawa built 1.3 million batteries a year (OEM and aftermarket), and also 12,000 instrument clusters every week sold for domestic use; but the Oshawa stamping plant pumped out 60 million pieces in 1979, entirely for U.S. plants.[61]

The examples also illustrate how the Letters of Undertaking requirements were met. This happened largely without fail over the life of the agreement, much to the chagrin of pact opponents such as Vance Hartke, who complained bitterly to President Ford that these obligations, which were in his view to have lapsed in 1968, were still being adhered to by the manufacturers in the 1970s.[62] Big Three CVA increased in the mid-1970s (as larger Canadian cars recovered somewhat in the U.S. market) but declined precipitously by the early 1980s (when the Iranian oil crisis prompted another rush to small cars in the United States) to a share similar to what had been common in the 1960s, around 60 per cent, or just above the mandated requirement.[63] Only Chrysler, in 1974, 1975, and 1979, did not meet its Letters of Undertaking CVA requirements. (See Table 5.3.) Overall, the industry as a whole always met its CVA requirements in the period between 1965 and 1979, though this requirement declined as growth of the Canadian market slowed towards the end of the decade. (See Table 5.4.)

For Canadian policy makers, the declining CVA was a key problem that underlay their concern with the agreement. Because of the deficit and the slow CVA growth, by 1979 officials in the federal government had come to the conclusion that 'the Auto Pact does not provide an adequate framework for the future development of the Canadian industry.' It had become clear to them that 'the scale of balance of pay-

Table 5.3
Big Three CVA, required and produced, and total CVA by model year, 1965–79

Year	General Motors			Ford			Chrysler		
	CVA Required $ mil.	CVA Produced $ mil.	CVA as % of sales	CVA Required $ mil.	CVA Produced $ mil.	CVA as % of sales	CVA Required $ mil.	CVA Produced $ mil.	CVA as % of sales
1965	391.9	436.9	63	259.7	288.3	64	166.2	188.8	72
1966	428.1	506.9	67	290.7	349.2	69	195.1	238.5	77
1967	409.5	459.8	63	295.5	405.6	79	216.5	234.5	68
1968	597.4	567.6	67	403.5	424.5	75	290.7	309.2	74
1969	645.2	699.7	75	420.1	519.7	87	289.8	343.5	83
1970	585.5	687.9	84	371.0	535.6	103	264.8	361.1	97
1971	514.6	674.3	97	409.0	601.7	103	295.4	375.3	88
1972	649.8	818.2	87	464.6	677.1	99	319.9	436.4	93
1973	864.7	979.6	75	575.8	792.5	90	421.8	469.3	73
1974	959.2	1120.5	75	667.4	765.6	73	**489.3**	**451.9**	**59**
1975	1172.8	1318.1	70	774.9	782.8	63	**561.6**	**497.8**	**56**
1976	1370.9	1592.2	72	909.0	939.1	63	687.1	689.4	62
1977	1601.8	1923.2	73	983.1	1148.2	71	734.7	840.4	70
1978	1807.0	2244.2	75	1150.2	1399.9	73	717.5	787.6	68
1979	2365.3	2620.4	66	1380.6	1495.8	64	**770.9**	**740.1**	**59**

Source: Company Reports to IT&C, LAC, RG 19, vol. 5959, file 8705-08-15, file: 'Statistics.'

ments problems are directly tied to the CVA to sales ratio.' That is, 'the closer this ratio is to one, the closer the Canadian value added to sales, the more equitable is domestic production and hence employment and investment flows, and the smaller is the balance of trade deficit.'[64] But this was not happening. Instead, CVA was gradually decreasing from the peak between 1970 and 1972, and consequently the auto trade deficit was getting larger. (See Table 5.4.)

The companies had problems too, as some missed their ratio requirements under the auto pact or came close to doing so. These misses threatened the credibility of the agreement, since the ratio was, in Simon Reisman's words, 'probably the main bargaining lever available for obtaining further production commitments from the motor vehicle companies … one of the few bargaining counters available to the Government.'[65] There were near-misses for GM and Ford in the late 1960s which prompted the companies to ask for changes to the ratio. In both cases, the government declined the request.[66] Chrysler missed its target on commercial vehicles by a huge margin in 1972–3, 1973–4, and again in 1974–5. Chrysler's base ratio was 100.5:100.0 (that is, it needed to produce the dollar value in trucks equal to the value of trucks it sold), but it had hit only 68:100 in 1972–3.[67] Such a significant shortcoming meant that Chrysler Canada was liable for at least $25 million in duties. If Chrysler did not pay, or the government did not collect, there was no point in pretending to 'manage' the trade, and it certainly would not be a 'conditional' trade agreement in any sense. As one Canadian official lamented, 'if Chrysler is forgiven the safeguard penalty it will lead to trouble with the public; if it is not forgiven, there will be trouble with the US.'[68]

Instead, the government negotiated an agreement with Chrysler allowing the company to avoid duties in exchange for building a new truck plant in Windsor. Chrysler Assistant Comptroller Brian T. O'Keefe admitted under congressional scrutiny that 'over a period of years, the result of that new truck production in Canada will be to exceed the requirements sufficiently in the years ahead to offset the under achievement in the prior years.' In exchange for the new factory, the company hoped that the government would 'remit the duties otherwise that would have been imposed.' O'Keefe was at pains to point out that these negotiations were between a private company and the government, and that there were to be 'no public published record of it.'[69] In 1973 Chrysler Canada President Ron Todgham announced the new plant, essential to meet market demands and 'to maintain the required truck

Table 5.4
Total Canadian auto industry CVA, and relationship to trade balance, 1966–79

Year	Cost of Vehicles Sold, millions	Total CVA Required, millions	Total CVA Produced, millions	Diff. Between Cost of Sales and CVA Produced, millions	Total CVA Required as a % of Cost of Sales	Total CVA achieved as a % of Cost of Sales	Trade Imbalance as a Percentage of Total Canada-U.S. Trade
1966	1716	988	1186	530	58	69	−24.7
1967	1738	1002	1200	538	58	69	−15.8
1968	1977	1395	1420	557	71	72	−7.8
1969	2110	1471	1703	407	70	81	−1.4
1970	1891	1341	1743	148	70	92	4.4
1971	1911	1350	1825	86	69	95	3.5
1972	2371	1592	2145	226	66	90	2.5
1973	3200	2056	2522	678	64	79	−2.5
1974	3795	2373	2687	1108	62	71	−7.0
1975	4545	2787	2987	1558	61	66	−11.1
1976	5345	3249	3606	1739	61	67	−3.0
1977	6001	3611	4337	1664	60	72	−3.2
1978	6727	4010	4951	1776	59	74	−1.4
1979	8554	5002	5491	3063	58	64	−11.0

Source: Company Reports to IT&C, LAC, RG 19, vol. 5959, file 8705-08-15, file: 'Statistics Canada'; *1983 Report on the Canadian Automotive Industry* (Ottawa, 1983), 76.

Table 5.5
Big Three ratio required, achieved, cars and trucks, by model year, 1965–78

		General Motors		Ford		Chrysler	
		Ratio Required, Cars:	Ratio Required, Trucks:	Ratio Required, Cars:	Ratio Required, Trucks:	Ratio Required, Cars:	Ratio Required, Trucks:
	Year	97.9	100.1	99.4	108.1	99.6	100.5
	1965	102.5	111.5	101.9	111.5	99.7	101.9
	1966	102.8	112.2	102.8	156.5	112.6	106.6
	1967	98.4	103.3	101.1	208.9	110.9	101.8
	1968	101.2	112.2	106.9	218.3	127.9	106.8
	1969	122.5	122.3	160.1	238.7	143.0	105.0
Ratio	1970	133.6	129.5	220.7	236.4	168.2	102.7
	1971	127.5	103.5	184.1	202.1	137.3	102.2
	1972	126.4	101.2	189.8	162.2	137.6	101.5
	1973	102.2	100.8	171.8	159.5	109.4	**68.6**
	1974	115.1	101.5	142.6	112.4	101.4	**53.8**
Achieved	1975	107.9	101.3	155.0	109.6	117.2	**64.2**
	1976	98.6	114.3	163.4	112.9	126.5	111.1
	1977	118.0	136.3	158.7	112.4	106.0	182.4
	1978	121.9	141.4	154.5	159.0	115.6	195.8

Source: Company Reports to IT&C, LAC, RG 19, vol. 5959, file 8705-08-15, file: 'Statistics.' For brevity's sake, the chart does not include Specialized Commercial Vehicles (SCVs).

production sales ratio' under the auto pact.[70] In this case, the Canadian government indeed put to use the 'lever' that Reisman had envisioned to compel further investment and production by Chrysler.

Then, during the great economic downturn between 1979 and 1983, a number of companies missed their ratio targets. Facing bankruptcy in 1980, Chrysler missed both its truck and car targets, owing to poor sales of the exclusively Canadian-built Cordobas and vans in both Canada and the United States. The long shutdowns at the company's plants for retooling and changeovers also hurt its production considerably. It was not alone: AMC missed its combined car-truck ratio target of 95:100 as well. Under its new alliance with Renault, the company had imported a large number of French-built vehicles duty-free, but it had been hurt by a drop in the market for Jeeps, vehicles built in Canada at AMC's Brampton plant.[71] IT&C Minister Herb Gray warned publicly that 'the safeguards have to be taken very seriously. I would not be inclined to recommend simply waiving the requirement.' In neither instance did the Canadian government require payment of duties, since it was understood that the severity of the recession made for unusual circumstances. But Ottawa did exact demands. In Chrysler's case, the company was given a reprieve on the $225 million in duties it technically owed for missing its ratio as long as it 'lived up' to the terms of its loan-guarantee agreement and made up 'any deficiencies' in the 1980 ratio year by the end of 1985, which it did.[72] In AMC's case, the Brampton plant increased production in 1981 and hired more workers, in the face of sharp protests by AMC workers in Kenosha.[73]

Ford also faced difficulties meeting its ratio requirements in 1980. The company had no problems with the car ratio, but with a recent increase in truck sales, one that reflected an emerging shift towards that segment of the market, the Ontario Truck plant at Oakville did not produce enough vehicles to meet the company's truck ratio. Ford Canada put forward a proposal to the government to combine its truck and bus ratio into single ratio, in exchange for moving the Oakville Car Assembly operation (building LTD cars and vans to that point) onto a double shift building only cars, and agreeing to build fuel-efficient front-wheel-drive vehicles at the plant by 1983.[74]

After some negotiation, a 'contractual agreement' was worked out whereby the government granted Ford a temporary combined 80:100 ratio on buses and trucks. The case provided another example, along with the Chrysler situation, of some flexibility for both parties: Ford avoided paying nearly $20 million in penalties, while the Canadian government managed to get a new production mandate, which included fuel-efficient vehicles (and an additional 1,300 jobs), for Canada.[75] Though it never missed its ratio targets, GM also told Canadian government officials that there had to be 'safeguard flexibility.' If the government did not allow such flexibility, the company made a 'veiled threat' to import cars en masse from Brazil, which it could do under the auto pact.[76]

Meanwhile, the changing auto market and the companies' efforts to remain profitable in the face of regulatory constraint had begun to make something of a mockery of the established ratio classes. By the late 1970s and early 1980s, many consumers in both Canada and the United States remained attracted to larger vehicles, notwithstanding the oil crises and rising price of gasoline. As fuel-economy constraints on autos led to a decrease in passenger-car size, it prompted a consumer shift towards trucks and a new, emerging category of vehicles which defied traditional classification.

Since the auto pact's inception, the Department of National Revenue (DNR) had used seating capacity and primary purpose as the main criteria to classify vehicles. As such, vehicles such as Ford's Bronco (introduced in 1966) or the Chevrolet Suburban (1933) had been classified as Specialized Commercial Vehicles (SCVs), owing to their bench seating and size. But the embrace of these vehicles, coupled with automakers giving them passenger-car amenities starting in the mid-1970s, meant that these vehicles were now being used essentially as passenger cars. When it came to the seating of the vehicles, in some instances dealers – often at customers' behest – simply sent the vehicles back to the factory to be refitted with seats instead of benches, or put them in themselves.[77] Thus was born the modern sport utility vehicle (SUV) in Canada.

In 1979–80 DNR decided that these changes required action to 'obviate certain anomalies which have arisen under the Auto Pact,' namely the fact that vehicles previously classified as SCVs were now being used as passenger cars. When DNR informed the Motor Vehicle Manufacturers Association that it intended to reclassify the vehicles, the announcement was met with fierce resistance. The auto companies claimed that the change would be far too difficult in terms of sales and excise taxes. Perhaps more important, such a change made meeting their ratios under the auto pact much more difficult. If the SUVs under question became 'cars,' this would necessitate a much higher production of cars in Canada (since their sales would become part of that ratio).[78]

The change would indeed cause serious problems for the companies. Shifting GM's Blazer, Jimmy, and Suburban to the automobile category for the 1981 model year meant that the company would miss its car ratio by 3.28 points. For Ford, the situation was much worse if its Bronco was classified as a car. In that case, the company would miss by 5.4 points and thus be on the hook for a $4-million duty payment to offset the failure. Chrysler's situation was less clear, given its near bankruptcy. IT&C officials told DNR that, 'because of the current situation in the automotive industry,' implementation of these criteria could cause considerable problems for all major vehicle manufacturers, and recommended delaying any such move.[79] This suited the carmakers (and their consumers), who were not keen to see some of their most cherished big vehicles pushed into the car category and thus also come under more stringent fuel-economy regulations. Eventually, there were some changes to the classifications, but the case showed that the vehicle manufacturers were not above bending the auto pact's rules.

This kind of chicanery may not have been limited to car classifications. The question of whether the auto companies manipulated the trade balance to avoid political pressure also hung in the air, especially in the early 1970s when U.S. unhappiness with the agreement was high. In 1970 and 1971, just as the auto pact faced its most sustained attacks in the U.S. Congress, the trade balance started to shift in favour of the United States. In 1973 GM's Murphy appeared before Congress to make his announcement that the balance had 'reversed' and the United States had a $100-million surplus. This shift had, according to APMA Chair Borge Reimer, 'greatly reduced the Canada-US controversy on the issue.' Tellingly, Reimer stated that 'it would appear that industry itself has rectified a situation for which there was no apparent political solution.'[80] In Simon Reisman's view, the return to a U.S. surplus 'served to ease some of the pressure from the US for removal of the safeguards,' though they still remained a 'bone of contention.'[81]

The idea that the agreement could be manipulated was not entirely unknown. The fact that virtually all of the auto pact trade was in the form of intra-company transfers made it highly suspect from an accounting point of view. As the UAW's Leonard Woodcock told the U.S. International Trade Commission (ITC) in 1975, 'transnational business operations enable corporations to manipulate production and prices so as to maximize their net gains, regardless of the impact of their policies on labour and governments.' Woodcock urged ITC to 'examine carefully the methods currently employed to measure trade flows under the APTA, and further, the possibility that the auto companies may be motivated to manipulate their internal transfer prices in order to shift accounting profits to the country where total tax payments are minimized by the combined effect of US and Canadian tax laws.' If profits could be manipulated, why couldn't trade balances?

Woodcock argued that 'it hardly seems necessary to point out that if these deliberate price and profit distortions are indeed occurring, the revenue loss to either the US or the Canadian governments must be very considerable.'[82] Woodcock repeated these concerns at congressional hearings a year later, stating that 'the question of the accuracy of valuation of trade with Canada on the basis of manufacturers' transaction prices remains unanswered.' He argued that 'data supplied by multinationals must be suspect, especially when governments create artificial tax incentives to shift profits from one country to another.' Here, Woodcock was talking about the DISC, which gave an incentive to U.S. corporations to show higher profits from domestic production sold abroad. The case of Ford, GM, and Chrysler in Canada bore this out, since their profits during the early 1970s often exceeded that of their parents.[83]

Auto manufacturers, in the UAW chief's view, exaggerated American export figures to Canada by inflating invoice values, which further put in question the very trade balances under scrutiny.[84] When, in 1972, Canadian officials pressed the Big Three about transfer prices and corporate profits in connection with the operation of the DISC, the result was revealing: 'GM would not undertake to report if they change their transfer prices; Chrysler dodged the question; Ford reported that transfer prices were the same in both directions and that a company in their position (with Canadian shareholders) could not use such methods.'[85]

Whether or not the auto companies were manipulating the agreement is impossible to tell. On one level, it would be exceedingly difficult for companies to game such a vast and complex system, on both sides of the border. Production realities, consumer tastes, and external factors such as oil prices or imports made predicting or influencing the North American industry extremely difficult. For instance, in the 1980s, when the trade surplus returned to Canada's favour, Big Three executives told Canadian government officials that this was not planned but was simply a 'bit of good luck,' in that the Canadian factories were building cars that happened to be, at that time, popular in the American market.[86]

Yet, at the same time, the Big Three acted as an oligopoly on many issues, from pricing to dealing with government regulations.[87] They made continental decisions on investment and production, so it is not beyond the realm of possibility that they manipulated the system. Perhaps a 'bit of luck' was partially a consequence of production decisions. After all, if lowering the temperature on the trade balance took the focus off the auto pact and their industry, surely Detroit would be happy if this happened, and might take steps to do so.[88]

In any event, the important point is that companies largely met their requirements, both under the pact and under the Letters of Undertaking, in the latter case even well after 1968. They understood that the Canadian government could intervene and impose duties on them if they missed their targets, and if not, could exact other concessions, as in the cases of Chrysler and Ford. The ratio was the main threat they faced, and the fact that the Big Three hit their targets virtually every year, save for AMC's car miss in 1975 and Chrysler's truck miss in two years, illustrates how seriously committed they were to meeting these safeguard requirements. Indeed, in most years in the period between 1965 and the early 1980s, the companies exceeded the CVA targets by at least 10 per cent, and the ratio significantly. Clearly, the safeguards kept the automakers on their toes.

Even as the automakers strove to meet the demands of a managed-trade regime that was sometimes very difficult to manage, there was acute unhappiness with the auto pact's performance on both sides of the border. The trade balance almost prompted the Americans to abrogate the pact in 1971, while as early as 1974 Canadian officials lamented that 'the concept of fair share of the North American market envisaged in the Agreement is not being achieved and the companies are ignoring the ground rules.'[89] In both Washington and Ottawa, the auto pact's uncertain realities ran headlong into the emotional discourse surrounding the agreement, with often explosive results.

Where Rhetoric and Reality Collide: The Battle over the Auto Pact, 1968–81

The emotional responses caused by the industry's performance under the auto pact, the unhappiness, fear, and uncertainty, manifested themselves practically in the conflict that emerged over the auto pact's operation. The main stakeholders – the governments, the assemblers and parts makers, the workers, and the car-buying public – all channelled these emotions into responses designed to influence the auto trade and the auto pact itself. Whether it was through negotiating, voting, lobbying, opinion making, or protesting, all these actors tried to shape the discourse surrounding the pact, and its actual operation.

Throughout this period, two main shifts drove these reactions. Initially, from 1968 to 1974, the American government was generally unhappy about the agreement and how it functioned, and tried to change it through threats of abrogation and renegotiation. After 1974, the Canadian government and Canadian parts makers became unhappy about the pact's performance and sought their own ways to shape public opinion, largely through studies and reports, and the operation of the agreement, largely through negotiation.[90] Then, after 1980, and especially after 1984, with the near death of Chrysler, the import and transplant question, and the emergence of the free-trade option, the dynamic changed dramatically. The United States was no longer interested in maintaining the auto pact and sought to eradicate the problems it experienced under the treaty as the price of free trade.

During this whole period, there was little disagreement within the Canadian government about Ottawa's position on the agreement. A standing interagency committee, which had its genesis as far back as 1962, coordinated a unified approach between IT&C, the lead department on the automotive file, and Finance and EA, all of which played significant roles on the auto issue: the former owing to its industry expertise, the latter two on account of their concern with the tariff, balance-of-payments, and diplomatic aspects of the agreement. Coordination was helped by a familiarity of old hands scattered throughout the government, civil servants who had been working on automotive issues for years. Robert Latimer (assistant deputy minister, International Trade Relations) and C.D. Arthur (director, Transportation Industries Branch) in IT&C, Reisman (deputy minister) in Finance, and A.E. Ritchie (undersecretary) in EA had all played key roles at one time or another.[91]

Their ministers were also familiar with the agreement and its functioning, since many had been in Pearson's cabinet in 1964–5 when the agreement was consummated. As Trudeau put it in a television interview in 1973, 'it's a Liberal government that did this. The same Minister who negotiated the pact, Mr. Drury, is in the cabinet now, the same deputy minister, Mr. Reisman, who negotiated the auto pact, is a deputy minister now. We're not going to give anything away.'[92] Even changes in government from Liberal to Progressive Conservative had little impact on the auto file, as the Joe Clark interregnum during the Chrysler incident illustrates. For Canadian politicians, the auto file remained largely non-partisan.

On the American side, there was less unanimity on the auto issue. The sprawling American governmental apparatus allowed for stark divisions over the auto pact. Canadian measures in the auto field had been a long-standing thorn in the side of Commerce and Treasury, less so for State. More important, Congress had soured on the agreement since its passage in 1965, especially in the wake of the massive trade shift. These positions were further complicated by changes in government. The Democratic Johnson administration had negotiated and implemented the APTA, supporting it until 1968. Republican Richard Nixon, and especially his tough-talking secretary of the treasury, John Connally, were not so enamoured of the agreement. Things changed again in 1974 with Ford, in 1977 with Carter, and again with Reagan in 1981.

But the Americans *were* consistent and clear on one thing: since the late 1960s, they had sought the ending of the 'transitional' safeguards (both in the pact and in the Letters of Undertaking), removal of the 15 per cent tax on individuals importing cars from the United States, and the inclusion of used cars under the agreement. The safeguards in particular had been a very sore point in Canada-U.S. relations since 1968, when the Letters of Undertaking officially ran their course and should have been put to rest, in the Americans' view. Between 1968 and 1971, the Canadians refused to remove the safeguards permanently, arguing that they were needed to ensure a viable Canadian industry.[93]

The solution for the Nixon administration was to include the auto pact in the series of economic measures which came to be known as the New Economic Policy – the Nixon Shocks, or *shokku*, as the Japanese referred to the package. In response to a worsening American trade position, in August 1971 Nixon stunned the world by removing the U.S. dollar from the gold standard, imposing a 10 per cent surcharge on imports, and creating a number of job and industrial growth policies, such as a Buy America program, a Job Development Tax Credit (JDTC), and the Domestic International Sales Corporation.[94] Unbeknownst to Canadians, abrogating the auto pact was initially also included in the Nixon economic package. This provision was removed only at the last minute, owing to the pleading of State Department officials who felt that ending the pact would profoundly damage the integrated industry and disrupt the operations of the manufacturers, who would be incensed by the move.[95]

But the Canadians quickly got the picture. Following the August *shokku*, word leaked out of Washington about how close the auto pact had come to its demise. In response, Ottawa sought to alleviate American pressure on the auto pact without unduly compromising its position or the health of the Canadian industry. During a December 1971 meeting between Nixon and Trudeau, the Canadians offered to suspend (but not terminate) the CVA and ratio, as long as Canadian employment did not fall below 1970 levels and Canada would 'share fairly in future increases in employment and production in the industry.' But they would not budge on the 15 per cent tax or the used-car prohibition. Finally, the Canadians sought to set up a joint committee to examine issues arising under the agreement, to consider improvements to the pact that were 'of interest to Canada,' and 'to keep developments in investment, production and trade under review.'[96]

Though the U.S. side accepted the principle of suspending the CVA and ratio, it did not accede to the Canadian counter-demands, and the 1971 talks ended without resolution, further frustrating the Americans.

To a very large degree, the Canadian position was helped by the manufacturers, who wished to avoid any disruption to the integrated industry: Kissinger advised Nixon that 'the US companies say that removal
of the safeguards would have little economic effect and have asked that
the US government place a low priority on their removal.'[97] The administration did not press the issue, but the Canada-U.S. relationship over
the auto pact had irretrievably changed. A few months later, Nixon declared an end to any 'special relationship' that existed between the two
countries when he made his only visit to Ottawa, in April 1972.

After 1971 the Americans nonetheless continued to beat the drum
of what they saw as the agreement's unfairness. As part of his stump
speech in support of the Nixon administration's New Economic Policy,
Connally's assistant, Gene Rossides, told a Rochester, New York, audience that the auto pact was a 'patently one-sided' agreement whose
Canadian production guarantees skewed the balance of payments. Rossides wondered, 'Is this fair trade?'[98] Pressure was also being brought
in the backrooms. When Canadian Ambassador Marcel Cadieux met
with Treasury Undersecretary Paul Volker for lunch in March 1973, the
latter warned that 'unless some adjustments to the automotive pact
were made fairly soon, there was serious risk of Congress repudiating
the agreement when it took up the Administration's trade bill.'[99] Con-
veniently leaked news out of Washington that the U.S. Senate Finance
Committee was threatening to abrogate the agreement as the price of
its passage of Nixon's trade bill was forcefully raised in the House of
Commons.[100]

These American threats put Trudeau and his government on the
defensive. Auto workers, ordinary Canadians, and public opinion demanded that Canadian interests be protected and that the safeguards
remain in place. The UAW's Dennis McDermott railed that suspending the safeguards would be an 'obvious surrender' by the government
and a 'betrayal' of auto workers.[101] The *Globe and Mail* was typical in
its opinion that the safeguards were still necessary to ensure 'fairness'
in the agreement.[102] When he was asked during a television interview
about the seemingly intractable economic talks with the United States,
and specifically if the auto pact safeguards were up for negotiation,
Trudeau replied:

Look, the auto pact was brought in by a Liberal government in 1964. It
has brought immense benefit to the people in the auto industry, notably in
Southern Ontario. It is because it has been so good for Canada and Cana-

5.3 By the early 1970s, many Canadians felt that the auto pact was something of a hold-up. Duncan Macpherson, *Toronto Star*. Copyright: Estate of Duncan Macpherson. Reprinted with permission – Torstar Syndication Services.

dians that the Americans are complaining about it now ... we're not going to give anything away. We want to protect Canadian jobs, we want to protect Canadian well-being ... We are prepared to make in some areas some concessions, in return for other concessions from the Americans, because we do want to help them in this short term problem. We are not going to do it if it means disaster for Canadian workers.[103]

Speculation in the press that IT&C Minister Gillespie and new American Treasury Secretary George P. Schultz had come to some arrangement which included the permanent removal of the safeguards prompted Gillespie to reiterate that there was no such arrangement and that Canada would move forward only if 'we can provide for a Canadian share of the market as well as a fair share for existing Canadian jobs as well as future Canadian jobs.'[104]

The tenor of the issue was such that Gillespie was attacked for two days in the House of Commons for stating that one of the CVA safeguards was 'transitional,' a term used repeatedly by American officials to describe the agreement's protectionist provisions. Gillespie backpedalled furiously, telling members that, if anything, the CVA requirement operated at 'far too low a level.'[105] When the threat of abrogation reappeared, Gillespie repeated that he would not accede to any changes to the agreement unless the Americans 'provide some kind of built-in mechanism so we can have our fair share of production.'[106]

American-initiated talks on the auto pact began in this charged atmosphere in August 1973. Despite their public posture, the Canadians proposed that in exchange for ending the safeguards and 15 per cent tariff, a committee could be struck to oversee the agreement to ensure that the trade balance remained within a certain percentage or dollar-figure band of the trade balance. Either country was free to take remedial action if this band was exceeded. At the same time, the oversight committee would ensure that each country maintained an agreed-upon percentage of production. This idea had emerged out of an American interagency committee set up by the State Department, and had been taken on by the Canadians and turned into a proposal. Gillespie raised the idea in March when he visited Schultz, who reacted favourably.[107]

The Canadian proposals were guardedly received by the American delegation. The Americans were chiefly concerned that a 'band' system would not sit well with Congress, which was determined to remove from the agreement any market-distorting measures. Though the Americans understood the Canadian desire for some protection from the vagaries of the market, Congress had expected the end of the 'transitional' safeguards in 1968, and now they would have another set of safeguards. They also wondered how remedial action would take place, and what would constitute the actual size of the band, questions that the Canadians said required more discussion. The Americans were also miffed at new Canadian measures such as FIRA, which seemed to run contrary to the spirit of cooperation. But the U.S. side felt that the proposals were worth considering, and said they would take some time to reflect upon them and report back in 'weeks.'[108]

Finally, six months after their initial talks, the Canadians received word that the United States was interested in holding another round of discussions, in February 1974. The Americans would accept all the Canadian concessions but rejected outright any notion of a band of production, or any idea that the two countries should monitor or manage production outcomes. Though the Canadians were disappointed by the American position, they obtained 'the impression that the Automotive Agreement is not a high priority issue for the US at this stage.'

In fact, the Americans did not want an immediate reply but simply an undertaking that the Canadians would further consider their proposal. Informal talks between the two delegations made it clear that their dialogue provided a basis for 'informing' Senator Russell B. Long, chair of the Senate Finance Committee, that talks were 'in progress' on the more contentious issues of the agreement. Moreover, EA officials did not think that Henry Kissinger would even raise the issue with Mitchell Sharp when the two met later in February; both sides were prepared to see the issue remain 'on the back burner' for some time 'unless it was promoted into a major issue by legislators or the press in either country.'[109]

By then, American pressure to abrogate the treaty or even to force the Canadians to suspend the safeguards had faded considerably. John Connally, the pact's most committed critic inside the administration, had left office in 1972. With Nixon's trade-reform bill pending in Congress, there was no appetite for new negotiations by the American administration. Moreover, as the deficit continued to swing dramatically in favour of the United States, pressure from Congress also lessened. When Treasury Secretary Schultz testified in front of Senator Long's committee regarding the trade bill, he was able to say that the administration was still looking at this issue with an eye to removing the safeguards, but also pointed out that the United States had achieved a sizeable automotive surplus in 1973. This seemed to satisfy Long, who did not pursue the issue further.[110]

Perhaps most important, the utter chaos that accompanied Richard Nixon's spectacular fall from the White House further pushed the auto file to the background. The new president, Gerald Ford, had no interest in provoking conflict over the auto issue, especially since the industry was vital to his home state of Michigan. Ford's views on the auto industry could be 'described in one word,' according to the Canadian consul in Detroit, M.B. Bursey, 'stability.' Bursey had been told by a high-ranking GM official that Ford was a strong supporter of both the industry and the auto pact itself. The consensus in Detroit was that Ford would 'not permit anything to change the intent of the Automotive Pact as it now stands.' The 'loudmouth, bullying approach' of the Nixon-Connally years was 'not Mr. Ford's style,' and there would be no repeat of the 1971 shockwaves into Canada.[111] In 1974 new American Ambassador William Porter made no mention of the agreement in his inaugural Canadian address, causing one Canadian observer to joke that though this was an odd omission, 'perhaps it has been the outstanding irritant for so long that Washington is taking the irritation for granted.'[112]

Ford's ascendency to the presidency and the U.S. trade balance shift to a surplus did not preclude one last congressional investigation into the pact. In July 1975 the Senate Subcommittee on Finance, largely at the urging of pact opponent Vance Hartke, requested that the International Trade Commission begin a wide-ranging investigation into the operation of the agreement by the end of the year, paying particular attention to whether Canada had 'fully complied with the letter and spirit of the Agreement by phasing out the so-called transitional provisions.' Hartke claimed that the agreement had destroyed 100,000 American jobs.[113]

After an exhaustive investigation, including testimony taken in Detroit, ITC reported that contrary to the presidential reports on the agreement, the transitional measures – including the contentious Letters of Undertaking – were still in force. Worse, the ITC report stated that 'when the agreement is examined in its totality, it is manifest that the only true concessions granted in the agreement are those granted by' the United States. For his part, Hartke urged President Ford to renegotiate the agreement immediately with the goal of 'equalizing automotive trade relationships.'[114]

Hartke's protest did little to move the president. The auto pact was not a priority for the Ford administration, which was burdened by automotive regulatory issues surrounding fuel economy and emissions. When Trudeau visited Ford at the White House in 1976, there was no discussion of the automotive agreement.[115] Instead, the president, who considered himself a friend to Canada and to Trudeau, pushed for Canada to be included in the Group of Seven industrialized countries. At the same time, congressional pressure also lessened. In 1976 a report by fifteen Republican congressmen recommended that the provisions of the agreement be left intact. That year, Hartke, one of the auto pact's most vocal and long-standing critics in the Senate, was defeated in his attempt for re-election.

Significantly, throughout this period of American unhappiness with the auto pact, the auto companies remained cautiously protective of the agreement. When pressure in the Nixon administration was greatest to abrogate the treaty, or to force changes to the safeguards, the auto companies gingerly ensured that word reached Kissinger that such moves were a 'low priority' for them.[116] They were keen to see that nothing unexpected happened to the agreement that might disrupt what was proving to be a lucrative trade. From the auto manufacturers' perspective, the agreement worked, and should largely be left alone.

Typical was the view of GM Comptroller Archie M. Long. Long pointed out in his 1975 ITC testimony that the difficulties over the auto pact were between the two governments, 'must be worked out between the two governments,' and had nothing to do with GM. But he went on to say that the safeguards included in the agreement and the Letters of Undertaking were largely moot from the company's point of view. The ratio and minimum-dollar amount of CVA were part of the agreement and so were not subject to interpretation as to their status, transitional or not. The investment requirement of $260 million by the companies was no longer operative, since it had been completed in 1968. But there was, in Long's view, some question as to whether the requirement that there be a 60 per cent CVA increase equal to the growth of the Canadian market was still operative.[117]

Of the threat of the auto pact's cancellation, Long felt that the company's 'actions in both countries were made on the assumption there would be an element of permanency in the Agreement. Cancellation of the Agreement, as some have advocated, would cause considerable harm to the automotive industry on both sides of the border.'[118] Long stated that it was GM's view that the ratio and the CVA requirements 'should be modified to allow for either a cumulative running average, or a several-year period of overall attainment without regard to any given year's performance.' This would give the companies some flexibility in a highly fluctuating marketplace, and also provide them with the lead time required to better meet these safeguards. In short, though GM was amenable to some tinkering, the company was not interested in seeing the agreement cancelled.

As American unhappiness towards the agreement ebbed, Canadian anger rose. By the mid-1970s, a persistently massive Canadian deficit had prompted Canadians to question the benefit of the agreement. This feeling was compounded by the serious economic difficulties Canada faced in the period, marked by Trudeau's imposition of wage and price controls in 1975 to curb inflation. Canadian anxiety about the auto pact's performance mounted as the trade balance reverted to deficit, investment flowed to U.S. factories, and technological changes triggered in the industry by the new regulatory regime threatened to make Canadian facilities obsolete. Now, many Canadians were keen to renegotiate the agreement to ensure a 'fair share' of the North American auto trade.

Ontario Treasurer Darcy McKeough felt that 'in our view, fundamental problems have developed. They threaten the long-term viability of both auto assembly and parts manufacturing in Canada and the economic well-being of this province.' There was a 'widening productivity gap; a declining Canadian share of auto assembly; and serious losses in Canadian parts production.'[119] In Ottawa, the rhetoric was equally strong: the 'lack of "fair shares" [had] been manifested in trade balance; parts production, especially high technology; investment, innovative activity, including R&D; quality of employment; and deficiencies in management functions.' Overall, this had resulted in a 'pressing need to guard against further deterioration of Canadian shares.'[120]

The public was just as unhappy. Auto town mayors, such as Cliff Barwick of St Thomas, Ontario, proposed resolutions decrying the trade imbalance and the 'thousands of jobs' that were disappearing in the industry.[121] The *Globe and Mail* forcefully declared that 'the country that has been sliding further and further onto the losing end' of the auto pact in this decade was 'not the United States. It is Canada.'[122] Canadian unhappiness over the agreement's operation was noticed south of the border, too.[123]

While the emerging narrative in Canada was one of criticism of the auto pact, James Dykes, president of the MVMA, defended the agreement. Though he admitted that there were some problems in the parts sector, the agreement had boosted the 'trade balance, increased employment, and led to a narrowing of the car price differential in the two countries.' Moreover, Canada should not complain about the deficit, given that Canadians bought 8.9 per cent of all cars in North America yet produced 11.2 per cent. For his part, Ontario Industry Minister Larry Grossman felt that 'the auto pact has been good for Canada and Ontario,' but it was not 'a perfect solution' to the problems of the industry.[124]

Canadian displeasure sparked a 'study phase' of the auto industry over the next few years. Canadians engaged a host of experts, royal commissions, and government panels to determine what to do about the agreement. During this period, the auto pact and automotive issues were largely overtaken by governmental concerns over constitutional matters, as the Trudeau Liberals grappled with the emergence of a separatist government in Quebec, the referendum of 1980, and the fight over the constitution and its patriation. A change in government also distracted the Canadians. This suited the Americans too. While there might be a growing displeasure at Canadian investment incentives or duty-remission orders, their own unhappiness with the pact's operation had dissipated with the trade deficit, and they had no interest to reopen negotiations.

The flurry of studies kicked off in November 1976 when Trudeau and Ford agreed to initiate parallel studies of the agreement. The two studies reflected the growing divergence of concerns in the two countries. The American report, *The Impact of Environmental, Energy and Safety Regulations, and of the Emerging Market Factors upon the US Sector of the North American Auto Industry*, was a 275-page tome that, as its title suggests, had little to say about the auto pact or any Canadian concern. The Canadian Automotive Task Force *Review of the North American Auto Industry*, authored by former IT&C official C.D. Arthur, focused on jobs and investment.[125]

After that came the 1977 APMA plan for an 'Automotive Investment Corporation.'[126] The APMA report was followed by yet another task force chaired by Norman H. Bell which reported its findings in 1978 ('A Report by the Task Force on the Canadian Automotive Industry'). The Reisman report was released in 1978, as was the Ontario study, *Canada's Share of the North American Auto Industry: An Ontario Perspective.*[127] The Science Council of Canada commissioned 'The Future of the Canadian Automotive Industry in the Context of the North American Industry' by N.B. Macdonald, while the Canadian Institute for Economic Policy had its own study. A 1979 report commissioned by the Ministry of State for Science and Technology looked at the question of R&D in the sector.[128] Even the separatist government of René Lévesque, outraged at the favouritism shown towards Ontario in automotive policies (*especially* the auto pact), struck a committee to look at the industry's place in Quebec and demanded federal cooperation to ensure that Quebec received its fair share of the sector.[129] The avalanche of studies prompted N.B. Macdonald, himself author of one of the reports, to lament that 'the poor automotive industry tends to be studied to death.'[130]

Meanwhile, the auto pact had been put on the back-burner by the new U.S. administration of Jimmy Carter. At the first meeting between Carter and Trudeau in February 1977, the auto agreement was to be mentioned only 'in passing,' if at all.[131] The next year, publication of the *President's Annual Report* (the twelfth), a document that only a few years earlier had provoked howls of outrage from Congress, caused barely a ripple. So low was the auto pact as a priority that in 1978 Carter's senior domestic advisor, Stu Eizenstat, recommended to the president that 'because the annual preparation of this report is of questionable value, *we would like your approval to... seek the elimination of the requirement in law for such further reports*.' To which Carter replied, simply, 'ok.'[132] The *Report* escaped the chopping block, but its days as a lightning rod of controversy in the Congress were clearly over.

The 1978 Ford Canada incentive for the Windsor engine plant did manage to get the Americans' attention, though. The Ford decision to put its engine plant in Ontario instead of Ohio provoked another series of inconclusive negotiations. Meetings held in August, September, and December 1978 largely covered familiar territory. This time it was the Canadians who were upset about the operation of the agreement, complaining about the trade balance and the lack of a 'fair share' of investment in Canada. The Americans replied, without irony, that Canada was 'focussing too much on the trade deficit' and failed to pay attention to the 'global benefits' deriving from the agreement. The very emergence of the 'fair share' concept itself caused 'serious difficulties' for the U.S. delegation. Canadians might want to see a proportionate balance in employment, investment, R&D, and production, but the Americans were satisfied that there simply be a fair share of the 'expanding market.'[133] There remained basic differences that were not resolved.

Still, in the Canadian view, something needed to be done. The deficit was growing, imports were flooding into Canada, and investment was slowing. The auto pact no longer seemed to be getting Canada its fair share of the sector, prompting Trudeau to warn Carter of the 'mounting public criticism' towards these problems. A 1979 report, written by IT&C officials in reply to the Reisman inquiry, suggested that 'a national consensus has emerged that the Auto Pact has failed to provide an adequate framework for the future development of the Canadian industry.' A number of proposals were offered, including new safeguards to boost Canadian parts production (among them, new Letters of Undertaking and a CVA requirement of 87 per cent), a limitation of investment incentives, and changes to the existing auto pact. Not surprisingly, none of these measures came to pass during the next round of negotiations, held in 1980–1.[134] Reisman's report, as we saw in chapter 3, suggested that Canada abandon the duty-remission schemes being utilized to induce more investment by non-Big Three producers, and shift to a Designated Vehicle Importer plan, which would, in his view, avoid the threat of U.S. countervail looming over the Canadian plans and encourage other foreign makers to set up in Canada. The government was keen to adopt a few of the Reisman recommendations, such as putting a moratorium on further auto pact negotiations, but not all; they were unsure about the DVI scheme and the reaction it might cause both in the United States and under Canada's international-trade obligations.[135]

In 1980, with the auto industry in tatters and little movement on the auto pact with the Americans, the government created yet another task force, this one headed by civil servant Campbell Stuart. Working out of IT&C, Stuart initiated consultations with the assemblers, parts makers, workers, the Ontario government, and others. When the task force met with the APMA and the Aftermarket Parts Advisory Council, both were deeply concerned with the state of the auto pact negotiations and pressed for measures to ensure continued growth in the Canadian parts sector. Some parts makers lamented that their companies were 'a creation of the Pact and that, in its absence, they would die.'

Other parts companies felt that the Canadian government had compromised any chance of getting a new deal from the Americans through its hard bargaining with Chrysler during the bailout negotiations and its willingness to give Ford ratio concessions, some of which would draw American production northward. Without the safeguards, they were vulnerable; the APMA argued that abrogation of the pact might be required, with the introduction of a broad duty-remission scheme in its place.[136] In the end, the 'Options Paper' created by the task force stressed the 'need for change ... once the North American economy comes out of recession, Canada may find itself with an industry which has not kept abreast of the rapid changes now being introduced in the automotive sector and which may therefore assume a diminished role in the new world trading environment.'[137] The latter part of the statement referred to the increasing presence of Japanese imports in North America.

Between the task force, the Resiman Commission report, Ontario's contributions, IT&C's own work, and the various other government initiatives, Ottawa had a host of options. One was to reopen the auto pact in order to change the ratios and the CVA (increasing it dramatically was APMA's preference) or expand coverage of products under the agreement. The task force also explored the dramatic option of abrogation, coming to the conclusion that Canada's industry might survive, but it would suffer, and that 'terminating the Agreement would be worse than the "status quo."' In its place, the task force speculated that greatly expanded duty-remission orders, encouraging (but not forcing)

5.4 By 1981, the industry looked confused and in need of repair. *Globe and Mail*, 19 January 1981. Permission granted for reproduction by the *Globe and Mail*.

Canadian production towards exports by remitting duties for companies that manufactured to a certain level of CVA in parts and vehicle exports, might be the most feasible plan. A comprehensive DRO regime provided a potential basis for the industry going forward and might be welcomed by the Big Three, who could maintain the benefits of an integrated North American industry.[138]

With criticism mounting that the government was doing little to alleviate the troubles in the industry, IT&C Minister Herb Gray plunged into the fray. First, he flew to Washington in June 1980 for preliminary discussions with the Americans and to remind them of the Canadian desire for a fair share under the auto pact. Then he flew to Detroit to meet with Thomas Murphy and Elliot Estes of GM and Gerald Meyers and William Pickett of American Motors to feel out the American car chiefs. The auto men were sceptical about Japanese intentions in North America, believing that they would make only 'token' investments, and Murphy felt that voluntary restraints were the only way to solve the immediate problems of Japanese imports. On the auto pact, the companies both asked for more flexibility in terms of the production-to-sales ratio, with GM even offering to trade lower ratio requirements for increased CVA.[139]

Then, the Canadians requested formal consultations with the Carter administration under Article IV of the agreement and met with American officials, including USTR Reubin Askew. Again, there were discussions about the operation of the agreement, especially Canadian concerns about the trade balance and the slowly declining CVA achieved by the companies. The Canadians pressed for changes to ensure a viable industry in the future, since 'Canadian participation in the North American automotive sector could not be expected to be maintained at historical levels.' These suggestions included some ratio flexibility and increased Canadian content requirements.

Again, the American reaction was 'strongly negative,' with officials questioning the Canadians' pessimism over their industry's operation under the agreement. The United States was 'seriously concerned by any Canadian move to force uneconomic decisions in the name of "fair shares" for Canada at a time when the auto companies are struggling with survival.'[140] The Carter administration had spent most of its past two years barely keeping the U.S. industry afloat by bailing out Chrysler and grappling with the question of Japanese imports. Canada and the auto pact were far down the list of American concerns. When Carter visited Ottawa in the fall of 1979, Canadian officials warned that there would be 'little merit' to raising automotive issues.[141]

The situation changed once more following the presidential election of Ronald Reagan. The new U.S. government was much more concerned with the Japanese import situation and had little interest in reopening an auto pact, which, overall, it felt had been beneficial to Canada. In March 1981 meetings between Herb Gray, new International Trade Minister Ed Lumley, and USTR William Brock and Commerce Secretary Howard Balridge, the Americans 'questioned the usefulness of tackling the Auto Pact when the industry was in such poor shape' and suggested that the two sides focus on a revival of the sector.[142]

The Canadians failed to move the Americans on the auto pact. Soon, both countries became preoccupied with Japanese imports and eventually the question of Japanese investment in North America. The Canadians' inability to incite a response from the Americans to renegotiate the agreement to meet their fair-share needs prompted them to consider different policy measures to generate investment, especially from the Japanese, and to solve the problems of the sector. Some of these measures, such as the duty-remission orders suggested by the Automotive Task Force, might provide the response that the Canadian industry needed in the face of the North American sector's growing internationalization. They also might provoke a far sharper American reaction, as Reisman had warned in his 1978 report. Canadian politicians and policy makers, always striving to achieve their fair share of the North American sector, were willing to take that risk, no matter the consequence.

Conclusion: The Exhausted Auto Pact

By the early 1980s, the auto pact was exhausted. It had been incessantly argued about for nearly two decades, the focus of deliberation, diatribes, and dissension. For all this verbiage and endless assessment, the agreement was likely better known yet less understood by both the public and the politicians alike. Ambiguous, misunderstood, and overstudied, it had become something of an awkward teenager, not entirely comfortable in its own skin and not necessarily welcomed into adult conversation. As the Chrysler crisis and especially the Japanese import wave took centre stage, the agreement receded as the main focus of conflict in the North American industry. When, after 1985, the agreement returned to the spotlight because of the free-trade debate, its meaning and import would again come into question.

The agreement had played an illuminating role in Canada-U.S. relations. For all of the irritation it caused between the two countries, the auto pact was still a useful tool. The United States, Canada, and the industry had avoided more serious conflagrations – countervail threats, industry disruptions, cross-border trade wars – that could have arisen had they not been locked together under the agreement as they were. More surprising was the fact that, throughout countless non-automotive Canada-U.S. issues, the auto pact had remained unlinked to any other cross-border policy disputes. The agreement may have been targeted for destruction, as it was on at least one occasion, but it never became a bargaining chip between the two countries. Finally, the agreement again reflected not only the asymmetry of the Canada-U.S. relationship but also the ability of the junior partner to maintain a semblance of parity, if not equality, with its much larger and more powerful neighbour. As an exemplar of interdependence between the two countries, the auto pact remained unique.

Yet the auto pact was exhausted, too, in that the functioning agreement had been pushed to its limits. The treaty had been stretched to the breaking point by government and industry alike as each tried to game the agreement to better suit its own needs, or to kill it for not living up to expectations. Manipulation of trade figures, exceptions and waivers, flexibility, and shifting classifications had all been visited upon the APTA. It was a surprise that such a tortured arrangement had not simply imploded. Indeed, the auto pact had faced extinction on more than one occasion, saved at moments by circumstance, lethargy, disinterest, distraction, or stubbornness on the part of one of its suitors. Most tellingly, in the early 1970s, when U.S. pressure was greatest to abrogate the pact, the Canadian government had managed to avoid the agreement's demise because of the divergence of views between the Big Three, which wanted the auto pact kept in place, and the U.S. government, which was keen to see it ended. The auto companies' wishes were not the sole reason the auto pact survived, but they did play a pivotal role in its continued existence.

By the early 1980s, it seemed that the agreement had run its course as a policy tool for Canadians to achieve their fair share. The changing dynamics of the North American industry – the increasing presence of offshore imports, and the potential for offshore transplant operations – did not cohere with an agreement created in the mid-1960s for a world that could not imagine Japanese or German cars overwhelming the North American market. But the agreement retained immense symbolic meaning, and still asserted significant sway on the Canada-U.S. auto trade. If it were finally to be laid to rest through some sort of renegotiation, only Simon Reisman, the agreement's maker, could put the auto pact on the table. It just so happened that in 1986 he would be called upon to do just that and the auto pact would, once more, become the focus of national debate.

6 Schism: The Canadian UAW and the End of Auto Worker Internationalism

It is perhaps one of the most famous events in Canadian labour history, celebrated forever on film and in print. For many, the moment that Bob White led the Canadian section of the United Auto Workers out of their international union to create the Canadian Auto Workers remains the singular expression of worker nationalism in Canada. Indeed, the 1980s are known as a decade of Canadian union nationalism, when patriotic auto workers and their allies challenged American corporations, American-based international unions, and the pro-American free-trade agreement of Brian Mulroney. At the head of this fight was White, the most famous labour leader Canada had ever seen and a symbol to many of the powerful nationalism that had pushed Canadian auto workers along this path.[1]

But what if nationalism as a cause of this great outburst is more myth than reality? After all, nationalism had been a powerful force among Canadian auto workers for decades before the 1985 split from the union's American-based international. In fact, there had been epic struggles pitting the nationalistic Canadian leadership and membership against Solidarity House, the UAW's Detroit headquarters, as far back as the 1960s. Sharp fights over the auto pact, over anti-communism within the union, and, most important, over collective bargaining, strikes, and concessions had not succeeded in sundering the international. Why, then, did it take until 1985 to break up the union?

Nationalism certainly played a part, but it was not the deciding factor that led to the Canadian separation from the international. Instead, nationalism was a convenient vehicle that provided a justification for the Canadian leadership to challenge the international union's existing structures, its bargaining methods and philosophy, and its leadership.

The fight was less about flags than it was about fair share – about concessions, wages, and the willingness of the union to fight the corporations. In the end, it wasn't solely nationalism that helps to explain the break with the international UAW: ultimately, it was about Canadian workers' self-interest and power within an integrated North American industry, and their ability to exercise it.[2]

Personalities were also key in this dynamic, however. White clashed with Solidarity House almost from the time he arrived as Canadian director and international vice-president in 1978. A driving personality, White was a gifted orator, determined strategist, and master of media relations. Yet the core of this clash was not White's nationalism or his ego but his vision of the Canadian section's place within the international union. White's vision, accepted to a large degree by Douglas Fraser, international president from 1977 to 1983, but much less so by his successor, Owen Beiber, viewed the union as a form of asymmetrical federalism. Region 7, as the Canadian 'region' was officially called within the union hierarchy, was the Quebec of the UAW – if it was to stay in the union, it had to be able to go its own way on some issues.

In almost every instance in which the Canadian section differed from its U.S. counterpart, White explained his vision as being international if necessary but not necessarily international. As he said upon becoming Canadian director in 1978, 'Quebec should have the right to self-determination,' words that were eerily similar to his own reasoning for the Canadian section's struggle for autonomy with the union's leadership six years later, when the final break with the international was made.[3]

Another factor that helps to explain the break-up is the changing circumstances the union faced after 1965. The integration of the industry profoundly affected the Canadian region's role and power within the North American auto sector. This could be both a bane, as the Chrysler concessions battle showed, or a benefit, as the 1982 and 1984 strikes proved. The former demonstrated that the two sections of the union were going in different philosophical directions, particularly over the question of confronting the corporations. The latter events illustrated beyond doubt to the Canadian UAW leadership that its position was very powerful within North America: the realization that the Big Three found Canada a very profitable place to build cars, and that the Canadian membership could bring the entire North American industry to a standstill, strengthened White's resolve. Ironically, some more militant members of the union were initially ambivalent about the idea of continentalization in the 1960s; this was soon overcome by the realization that going 'national' within an integrated industry could enhance their fair share.

Inside Placer Court, where the Canadian section had built its imposing Toronto headquarters, getting a fair share of the automotive pie meant fighting for parity, having their own contract negotiations, demanding their own terms, and, ultimately, going their own way. The schism between the UAW's cross-border brethren was not inevitable, but it made complete sense within the context of growing Canadian nationalism, the personal conflict between two labour leaders, the circumstances of an integrated auto industry in the period, and the longer-term strategy of the Canadian union's leaders. Fair share was more than just a government motto – it was a compelling mantra for workers too.

The Canadian UAW, Prosperity, and Nationalism, 1965–78

Auto workers hold a special place within the labouring world. In the post-war period, it was their union, the UAW, which brought prosperity to much of the working class and raised living standards for all blue-collar workers in North America. The charismatic Walter Reuther, a beacon of American progressivism and a stalwart of Cold War pragmatism, led the union from 1946 until his death in a 1970 plane crash. Reuther's UAW ushered in an era of union cooperation with the corporate world when the 1950 Treaty of Detroit established the grand bargain between workers and capital. By the 1950s, auto workers and their unions had propelled their members into the middle class, foregoing a direct attack on capitalism in favour of the creature comforts of the new age of consumption.[4]

Canadian workers joined their American brethren in this grand bargain. The UAW's unlikely sit-down victories in Flint, Michigan, leading to the union's recognition by GM, the world's largest and most powerful corporation, were a pivotal moment in North American history, and Canadians played their own part in this story. When Hugh Thompson, an organizer from the fledgling UAW, came to Oshawa in the spring of 1937, he found a willing ally in George Burt. Burt led thousands of Canadian GM workers in their own bitter eighteen-day strike against GM, culminating in the creation of Local 222, which gained a historic first contract with the company. By the end of 1945, after wartime strikes at Chrysler and especially Ford, all of the Big Three had recognized the union in Canada. Burt headed Region 7, the 'Canadian Region' of the union, until 1968, and remained a close ally of Reuther's.[5]

Thus, from its genesis in Canada, the UAW was an international, as were so many other unions in Canada. From the 1940s to the 1960s, Canadian UAW members operated within their local Canadian context and at the same time belonged to a continental labour movement. Before 1965, however, their industry functioned very distinctively from that of the United States, constrained as it was by tariffs, borders, and a small domestic market. Union members understood the branch-plant limits of their industry and either called for greater integration with the United States or fought for greater autonomy for the Canadian auto sector by supporting the creation of an indigenous industry.[6] The union also faced attacks on its administrative structure from within, since much of its membership retained its pre-1945 militancy and often chafed at the international's American leadership, a problem evident in other international unions in post-war Canada.[7]

These internal strains emerged into the open in the 1960s. Auto workers reflected the activism and militancy of the decade, and spurred it along too. Wildcat strikes became common and were a challenge both to the authority of the established capitalist order and to the bureaucratic unions that had institutionalized this order for workers since the 1940s.[8] Such unruliness became an important trait of the growing nationalism that spread throughout the Canadian labour movement in the 1960s, spearheaded by members of the UAW. This outburst of nationalistic labour ferment saw younger workers question the international structure of the union, the 'dependent' status of Canada's auto industry, and the post-war labour compromise which had been so pivotal to the success of the UAW, and of which the union was the leading proponent and beneficiary.

Nationalist rank-and-file auto workers aggressively asserted their views on the structure of the Canadian industry. In response to a 1960 royal commission examining problems in the sector, militant locals called for a 'made-in-Canada' car which would have directly challenged the overwhelming dominance of the Big Three in Canada.[9] Local 444 (Chrysler-Windsor) also condemned any idea of integration outright, since it would give 'the big monopoly Corporations who control US industry the right to choke off Canadian jobs' and bring about Canada's 'deliberate subordination' to a foreign country. It instead recommended that the Canadian government 'fundamentally reappraise' *all* policies towards the United States in order to free Canada from American economic and political domination.[10]

Unsurprisingly, the 1965 adoption of the continentalist auto pact outraged many in the union and became conflated with a hatred for internationalism. Though it provided guarantees for Canadian production, the agreement signalled the end of any notion of an indigenous industry. When it became public that Reuther had quietly met with President Lyndon Johnson to help seal the auto pact, some Canadian UAW members saw Reuther as 'sneaking in the back door of the White House to cut the throats of Canadian workers.'[11] A leaflet distributed to Chrysler workers claimed that Reuther could never adequately represent Canadians: 'When the chips are down Reuther and the International speak for AMERICAN interests FIRST and FOREMOST. Make no mistake about that!' For some, the only solution was for the Canadian union to break from the international completely.[12]

The auto pact remained a flashpoint of conflict for many Canadian auto workers. For its part, the union hierarchy (including the Canadian leadership) supported the agreement – conditional upon dislocation assistance for workers affected by industry rationalization.[13] But some locals continued to challenge the agreement's continentalism, notwithstanding Reuther's willingness to accommodate Canadian desires. The UAW leader lobbied hard for the auto pact, believing that it paved the way for a healthier industry, especially in Canada. Reuther also fought for wage parity for Canadians, which he saw as direct consequence of integration (and to protect U.S. workers from being undermined by lower Canadian wages, too). Organizationally, Reuther pushed through a change within the union's International Executive Board (IEB), the union's top leadership committee in Detroit, automatically making the Canadian director an international vice-president. These moves did not quell the nationalist outcry, however.

Nor did Reuther's hard-line anti-communist approach, another significant divergence between the two sections of the union. The UAW's constitution included a clause forbidding members from being a member of any communist or fascist party. In the 1930s and before, Canadian communists had played key roles in organizing auto workers.[14] Prominent Canadian locals chafed at this restriction and pushed that the constitution be amended to end what they saw as political discrimination. In 1969 Local 444 submitted a resolution to amend the constitution so that it 'would not be applicable to the Canadian Region.'[15] Not until the 1980 constitutional convention did the IEB agree to remove the section, recognizing that the prohibition had made it 'completely impossible to operate' in Canada.[16] This political difference continued to rankle.

After 1968, the Canadian section took steps to distance itself from the international. Based in Windsor, Canadian Director George Burt spent much time at Solidarity House, negating any need for a large Canadian staff or research department. His successor, the 'mod, brash,' Dennis McDermott, recognized that only by distancing the two sections could Canadians develop their own identity and infrastructure. 'After I became the director in 1968,' McDermott recalled, 'every time I arrived in my office in Windsor, I found myself going through the tunnel. Every time I needed something, every time I needed to consult, we had no expertise or virtually no expertise of our own.' McDermott decided to 'cut the umbilical cord.'[17] The union moved to Toronto in 1971. Instead of a stone's throw from Solidarity House, there was now a physical distance between the two headquarters.[18]

The divide grew. In 1969 Canadian locals demanded more Canadian content in *Solidarity*, the UAW newspaper, or a separate Canadian edition. The issue became 'a running sore between the Region and the International Union.'[19] Eventually, in an effort to alleviate tensions over the newspaper and within the union itself over the question of Canadian 'identity,' a Canadian *Solidarity* was published with the reluctant blessing of Detroit.[20] Other steps gave the Canadian region the look of a full-fledged union within the UAW: it acquired its own research specialist, Sam Gindin, affiliated with international labour bodies directly, and established its own educational department.[21]

The tenor of the Canadian UAW's nationalism was also affected by the 1969 emergence of the Waffle, a sharply nationalistic movement of intellectuals, some NDP members, and workers that denounced Canada's dependency on the United States. In 1971 a New Left caucus sympathetic to the Waffle appeared in the union, advocating distinctive Canadian policies, an end to international agreements with the Big Three, and a new constitution for the Canadian UAW.[22] This nationalism quickly spread to other internationals operating in Canada in this period. In 1971 the Communications Workers of America separated from their international, as did the Paperworkers and Brewery Workers in 1974.[23]

Canadian auto workers' most important effort to distance themselves from the international came through the union's raison d'etre, collective bargaining. Starting in 1968, Chrysler workers on both sides of the border had ratified an 'international agreement' negotiated by Solidarity House, while GM and Ford workers in Canada had their own very limited, non-monetary Canadian bargaining. Negotiations for both countries had always been led by Detroit and had almost always occurred in the same year; they were, essentially, the same contract with some local wrinkles. Some significant differences were taken into account in achieving these agreements, not the least of which was the long-standing disparity between wages in Canada and the United States. Americans had always been paid more than Canadians, and as long as Canadians had been in the international union, they had sought wage parity with their American brothers – a cause that seemed particularly just given that members of the same union were doing basically the same jobs on either side of the Detroit River.[24] 'Equal pay for equal work' had finally been achieved through collective bargaining in 1968, and implemented by 1973. It was a significant victory.

But disparities still existed, some of which benefited the Canadian side, others the U.S. The wage-parity formula, for instance, did not take into account currency differences. There was also a difference between benefits on either side of the border owing to the publicly funded Canadian health-care system after 1968.[25] These differences, and the growing nationalism in the Canadian section of the union, pushed McDermott to question the idea of international agreements and the very foundation of the international itself. 'It is my current belief,' McDermott told his union brothers in 1973, 'that unless international unions in Canada can make some fairly drastic accommodations and adjustments to the needs of the current emotions that exist in this country, then the role of international unions is in serious jeopardy. Indeed, their very survival as an effective entity is questionable.' McDermott appropriated the nationalistic rhetoric of the day: 'Genuine international unionism, with Canada as a true partner, is one thing. A US union with a branch-plant mentality and Canada treated as an occasional and patronizing afterthought,' he warned, 'is something else.'[26]

Growing Canadian agitation prompted the UAW to hold a referendum for Canadian Chrysler workers in 1973 asking them if they wished to continue under their international contract. 'The Committee to Gain our Canadian Contract,' composed of nationalistic members in Windsor, implored the membership to vote against continuing the international agreement. Local control, the end of any special provisions in the agreement that related to Canadian workers, and the potential for a better contract were all cited as reasons to vote 'No.' There was no mistaking these nationalistic blandishments, notwithstanding the committee's declaration that 'a "No" vote against the International Agreement is *Not* a vote against our International Union. We need their co-operation, not domination.'[27]

In the end, Canadian Chrysler locals voted strongly in favour (85 per cent) of keeping the international contract, prompting Doug Fraser, then the union's Chrysler chief, to remark that 'our members in Canada recognize the common interest between Chrysler workers on both sides of the border and the necessity for the strongest kind of solidarity ... only by united action can we hope to make progress at the bargaining table.'[28] The 1973 pattern with the U.S. Chrysler agreement had not only resulted in wage parity but also contained a '30-and-Out' retirement clause, a milestone victory thought unachievable by an earlier generation of Canadian UAW workers.[29]

Following the Chrysler referendum, the international worked to diffuse Canadian nationalism on other fronts too. When the UAW launched an anti-dumping complaint with the U.S. Treasury on auto imports in 1975, the union's leadership went to great lengths to ensure that the Canadian section understood that Canadian imports had been added only at the insistence of congressional interests critical of the auto pact. The international supported the Canadian region's call for action on the price differential between Canadian and American cars, one that persisted well after the advent of the auto pact. It also stood 'unequivocally' in solidarity with the Canadian section as it fought against Trudeau's wage and price controls in the mid-1970s, policies that eroded wage parity between the two sections.[30]

During the 1976 International Trade Commission hearings on the auto pact itself, Reuther's successor, Leonard Woodcock, defended the agreement in front of the commission and did not call for the end of the Canadian safeguards, a position that was taken primarily at the behest of the Canadian section. Woodcock admitted that there might be some disagreements across the border over the agreement surrounding the trade balance, as 'our Canadian membership looks at the parts coming in, US membership looks at the cars coming in, and neither, very frankly, have too balanced a reaction.' But 'when we sit down and carefully reason it out, we come to common conclusions.'[31] And both sections had been 'completely' in agreement in their denunciation of location incentives for auto plants, even in the case of the 1978 Ford engine-plant decision that had benefited Canadian workers over their U.S. counterparts in Ohio.[32]

Moreover, as we shall see, when the protectionist backlash against the Japanese emerged in the United States in the late 1970s and early 1980s, the UAW pointedly called for North American content requirements – not solely for the United States. This was important to the Canadian UAW leadership, since many on Capitol Hill were arguing for U.S.-

only rules that would have left the Canadians in dire straits if enacted.[33] Indeed, when it came to the Japanese question, the Canadian UAW was not so nationalistic: Sam Gindin recommended that the union's leadership encourage Herb Gray to push his American counterparts to 'endorse "domestic content" as including Canada.' Gindin understood that 'this would limit Canada's autonomy to act differently than the US' but saw it as necessary, even if it did not relieve anti-Japanese sentiment in the United States.[34]

By the mid-1970s, the Canadian section of the union had experienced one of its greatest periods of growth as the auto industry prospered. Canadian auto worker nationalism had become a driving force within the union, largely kept in check by an accommodating international. Soon, other factors, such as organizational discontent and a quickly shifting North American auto dynamic, strained the union further. When the economy and the auto industry took a sharp downward turn after 1978, these challenges rose to the fore. They would be met by a new Canadian UAW leader, Bob White.

'Our Union Wasn't Formed to March Backward'[35]: Fighting Concessions, 1979–82

The ascendance of Bob White coincided with a period of great difficulty in the industry and economy as a whole. Elected unanimously in 1978, White was only the third Canadian director since 1939, and he represented a different style from that of McDermott. White had joined the union as a teenager in the 1950s, cutting his teeth as a plant organizer between 1965 and 1971 during the booming years of auto pact-fuelled growth. Tough and stubborn yet very likeable, White had organized dozens of plants, overseeing a membership increase from 65,000 to nearly 100,000. In recognition of his leadership abilities, White was brought to Toronto as McDermott's special assistant. He quickly climbed the union hierarchy and by the mid-1970s was leading Big Three negotiations. Bob White was the new face of the Canadian UAW: he knew thousands of members he had personally recruited, members who remained intensely loyal to their leader throughout incredibly trying times.[36]

At the time of White's election in 1978, the union faced daunting challenges. Trudeau's anti-inflation measures meant a sustained attack on the wages of working people, which the UAW protested vociferously. Then came the downturn in the auto sector starting in 1978 and lasting into the early 1980s. North American sales plummeted, imports

Table 6.1
Automotive manufacturing employment in Canada, 1964–87 (thousands)

Year	Vehicle Assembly (SIC 323)	Truck Bodies & Trailers (SIC 324)	Auto Parts/ Accessories (SIC 325)	Auto Fabric & Accessories (SIC 188)	Total
1964	34.3	4.4	30.5	1.3	70.5
1965	39.8	−5.8	35.3	1.9	82.8
1966	40.7	6.3	37.6	2.7	87.3
1967	38.7	6.7	37.7	2.6	85.7
1968	39.6	6.8	37.3	3.1	86.8
1969	42.3	8.2	40.4	4.1	95.0
1970	37.5	8.4	36.4	3.7	86.0
1971	41.0	10.1	41.3	4.3	96.7
1972	41.9	14.2	41.4	5.2	102.7
1973	15.2	14.8	48.8	5.8	84.6
1974	47.1	15.2	45.9	5.7	113.9
1975	43.4	14.4	41.2	4.8	103.8
1976	46.6	14.0	46.2	5.6	112.4
1977	50.6	12.6	48.6	6.5	118.3
1978	52.3	13.6	52.1	6.9	124.9
1979	52.6	14.8	49.8	6.6	123.8
1980	43.9	12.9	41.0	6.3	104.1
1981	43.4	12.1	44.7	7.2	107.4
1982	42.7	8.6	41.1	6.3	98.7
1983	44.4	11.5	55.2	4.5	115.6

Source: IT&C, *Report on the Canadian Automotive Industry* (Ottawa, 1989).

flooded into the market, and the union faced its most layoffs in history. In 1978 Canadian UAW membership peaked at 130,000, largely fuelled by growth in the automotive sector. But by the depths of the crisis, in January 1982, Gindin estimated that there were 18,000 fewer people working in the industry (either on permanent or indefinite layoff) than in 1978.[37]

The biggest challenge White faced as 1979 contract negotiations began was Chrysler. Although GM was the union's target to set the bargaining pattern, Chrysler merited special attention for a number of reasons. First, it teetered on the edge of bankruptcy. Second, its production decisions since 1965 meant a dependence upon Canadian output, much more so than GM or Ford. Third, Chrysler had very strong Canadian sales, nearly a fifth of the market. Overall, Canada accounted for 13.4 per cent of the company's North American sales. Strong sales

resulted in healthy profits, a rarity at Chrysler, where the parent corporation had lost over US$200 million in 1978. Gindin estimated that
Chrysler Canada accounted for 85 per cent of Chrysler's profits in the
1974–8 period and starkly laid out the company's dependence upon
Canada: 'It would be misleading to exaggerate it, but the basic point
involved is worth making – namely, we're a particularly important part
of Chrysler's operations.'[38]

Clearly, 1979 was not going to be a normal bargaining year. In early
August the depth of Chrysler's troubles became painfully evident. Lee
Iacocca had little choice but to ask for a government bailout. Such were
Chrysler's difficulties that Iacocca personally addressed the UAW's
Chrysler master bargaining team – the first time a Big Three CEO had
ever directly spoken to union negotiators. Iacocca called for a two-year
freeze on wages and benefits to save the company $400–500 million. It
was, according to White's eventual successor, Buzz Hargrove, an un-
forgettable speech because 'at the end of that he said "now if all this
fails and you guys don't agree to do this, and the government doesn't
agree to do this, and the parts industry doesn't agree to do this, just
pull the lights on the factory, and the factories will be dark." And at
that time somebody turned off the lights around the podium and he
moved away from the podium. It was a really well-staged presentation
and it had its effect because at the bargaining committee no one asked
any questions.'[39] Despite these dramatics, the union was unmoved.
Both the international and the Canadian UAW rejected this 'initial demand' outright, though they concluded that the concession request
was just the beginning of Chrysler's attempts to 'partner' in saving the
corporation.[40]

At the onset of Chrysler's crisis, the Canadian section had been absolutely clear in its position: protecting existing jobs in Canada. If that
meant that the U.S. government took an equity position in Chrysler
(which the international had proposed), so be it, as long as there was
some help for the company and its workers.[41] Protecting workers'
wages was as important as maintaining jobs. As the union's braintrust
argued, 'no one – not even the corporation – has blamed Chrysler's
problems on labour costs or labour productivity. And no one has suggested that such sacrifice on our part will save the corporation.' Besides, any such questions would not be considered until after GM and
Ford negotiations were concluded.[42]

Publicly, the Canadian UAW was in favour of government help for
Chrysler, a stance that new International President Douglas Fraser was

pushing for. This was, for White and the Canadian UAW, a sometimes difficult position. The union had come out against the Ford engine incentive package in 1978. Now that White was arguing for Ottawa's help, this about-face smacked of hypocrisy to some. The union hierarchy rationalized Chrysler help as necessary for a troubled company, whereas Ford's money was being given to a profitable firm only to benefit the corporation at the expense of workers.[43] White's position was not helped by the unwillingness of federal and provincial officials to state what plans, if any, they had to help Chrysler. White expressed his frustration to the IEB, complaining that both levels of government were reluctant to make any commitments until Washington's first move.[44]

In the fall of 1979, the UAW concluded its collective bargaining with the Big Three. Recognizing the corporation's difficult situation, Chrysler workers on both sides of the border agreed to break their pattern with GM and Ford and take a lesser settlement from the company. Chrysler workers accepted a wage freeze for the first two of a three-year agreement, finally catching up to GM and Ford by 1982. Moreover, the company deferred over $200 million in pension contributions. The $400 million in concessions were the first wage and benefits clawbacks in the UAW's long history. Windsor's Chrysler Local 444 voted 73 per cent in favour of the deal, ratifying it in November 1979, as did the rest of the union.[45]

These unprecedented concessions did not, however, satisfy interests in Washington. As Chrysler foundered and Iacocca struggled to convince Congress to pass the US$1.5-billion loan-guarantee package, it became exceedingly clear that some American politicians wanted further union concessions in exchange for their support. When the Senate Banking Committee proposed that Chrysler workers take a three-year wage freeze before government gave the bailout the go-ahead, White called the suggestion 'utterly asinine and completely unacceptable to Chrysler workers in Canada.' White warned anyone who would listen that 'we just won't accept it in this country.' [46]

Unfortunately for White and the Canadians, the international felt compelled to accept further concessions. When the labyrinthine congressional wrangling was finally over and the Carter administration signed the Chrysler Loan Guarantee Act into law, the union had given up an additional US$239 million in exchange for an Employee Stock Ownership Plan (ESOP) and the promise that by 1982 Chrysler workers would be returned to parity with Ford and GM workers. In January 1980 Fraser informed all U.S. Chrysler workers of the details of the new round of concessions.[47] Fraser's announcement outraged many in the union.[48]

In Canada, concessions were flatly rejected. White was unequivocal: the Canadian UAW would simply not be a party to such a measure. It smacked of interference and extraterritoriality. 'It is just that basic,' argued White, 'you can't have an American Congress making decisions which include Canadians.' Because Canadian Chrysler workers were included in the company's international collective agreement, they were being told to make concessions, something that was anathema to the Canadian UAW leadership.[49] Fraser reluctantly agreed, and argued in the IEB that the union should be 'sensitive' to the Canadian situation. Publicly, Fraser stated that he understood 'the point of view of the Canadian workers perfectly, because what you have is, in their eyes, a foreign government, a foreign Parliament, electing or enacting legislation that abrogates their collective agreement. American workers would feel the same way if a Canadian government were to force concessions on them.'[50]

Inside Solidarity House, however, the Canadian refusal was met with confusion and hostility. For some UAW staff, the Canadian position was incomprehensible – how could Canadians not be included in this? Weren't they part of the international? White 'was getting arguments, including an argument from a [UAW] staff member in the United States who said "Bob, you don't understand, if the US Congress had meant to exempt the Canadians from this legislation, it would have said so." White replied: "You don't understand. We don't care whether the US Congress has the right to exempt us or not exempt us, it's a matter of international unionism here."'[51]

White and the Canadians held firm. The international grudgingly accepted their position but made it absolutely clear that none of the savings realized from the congressionally imposed concessions would be spent in Canada, since 'those sacrifices are being made by US Chrysler workers.' For American Chrysler workers, the additional concessions meant a sacrifice of $2,000 over the three-year life of the contract – $400 more because of the Canadian section's refusal. Further, the Canadians would not participate in the ESOP. Most profoundly, Solidarity House informed Chrysler that in 1982 the union would 'bargain separately in the US and Canada, will reach agreement separately and will ratify separately.' For their intransigence, the American leadership had effectively kicked the Canadians out of the international agreement.[52]

The end of Chrysler's contract internationalism marked a significant moment in the UAW's evolution and the first real step towards the break-up of the union. For some, it indicated that Canadian nationalism, ebbing since the 1973 Chrysler referendum, had returned with a vengeance. White saw it differently. This was not 'a nationalist victory' but 'a difficult decision' that was actually 'an important step in maintaining the relationship within our international union between the Canadian and American workers.'[53]

The Canadian leadership understood that, while many in Canada would be sympathetic to the decision to reject the wage freeze, they would have a 'tough time defending' the position. After all, from the outside it looked as though the Canadians were selling their American brothers down the river, even though, as White argued, this was an American political decision based on aid to Chrysler's U.S. operations.[54] Chrysler Local 444 in Windsor even took out full-page ads in the *Windsor Star* explaining why 'Chrysler Canada Workers Had No Alternative!' Local 444 President Frank LaSorda complained that Canadians were unfairly been targeted as 'whipping boys' by American Chrysler workers.[55]

Despite White's optimistic assessment of the split over concessions, fallout from the Canadian decision poisoned relations between the union's two sections. Lillian Zirwas, steward of Local 889 (Chrysler-Detroit), summed up the feeling of many UAW members when she wrote to White to tell him 'how disappointed the American people are by the decision of the Canadians.'[56] Other rank-and-file American Chrysler workers were equally disappointed, and angry. Workers at the Jefferson Avenue plant in Detroit complained that the Canadians 'should give up what we're giving up' and that the Canadians 'should contribute like we do.'[57]

American disappointment was followed by action. Days after the Canadian decision, the American Chrysler Council and Local 212 (another Detroit-Chrysler local) struck back. Canadian Chrysler employees had worked in Detroit since the 1940s delivering and distributing parts and cars from Canada. Their presence had long rankled the local Detroit UAW leadership. The Americans saw the Canadian stance on concessions as a symptom of ungratefulness and now called for those positions to be held by Americans. They also demanded an end to trips by Canadian Chrysler drivers into Michigan 'in our pursuit of preservation, protection, restoration and acquisition of all jobs that are in the US for American workers.'[58]

More provocatively, Local 212 President Joe Zappa complained that 'American workers did everything it took to keep this company from going bust! Canadian Chrysler workers decided not to share in the necessary sacrifice, with an "I don't give a damn attitude."' Zappa, who was also chairman of the UAW International Bargaining Committee for Chrysler, called on the company to keep 'every job that is humanly possible in America.' He claimed that Chrysler was considering shifting hundreds of jobs across the river to take advantage of the lower Canadian dollar. It was 'inconceivable' to Zappa that Chrysler 'could even think about moving American jobs to any foreign nation. Especially Canada, with what the Canadian workers did to them.'[59]

Coming from a senior union member, Zappa's comments provoked a Canadian backlash. Local 444's Frank LaSorda complained to Fraser that, if Zappa's attacks continued, it would 'lead to division in our relationship with the UAW.' LaSorda thought Zappa should 'quit heckling and tell the workers the truth' – that Chrysler was not bleeding jobs to Canada. Fraser's response to LaSorda was that he would tell Zappa that 'we must never forget, that you cannot divide scarcity, you can only share an abundance.'[60] Though Zappa was silenced, his outburst reflected the steady erosion in cross-border relations between Chrysler locals.

Chrysler concessions also exacerbated the growing tension within the international between White and the American leadership. White himself admitted that the issue no doubt 'strained somewhat my relationship with some of my colleagues.' But to have conceded would have 'seriously ruptured' the relationship and made a mockery of any notion of a Canadian say in the union. White's warm relationship with Fraser, whom he saw as a father figure, changed profoundly: 'I couldn't speak freely with Doug. I had to bargain with him the same as I would with the corporation.'[61] Buzz Hargrove also felt the chill in Detroit as Fraser pressured Solidarity House staff: 'Doug made it very clear to people that if they don't feel comfortable about this, you have one choice, and that is to hand in your resignation.' He thought that Fraser was simply forcing the concessions on the union and would not brook any dissent. There was 'no one who challenged him ... the only one to challenge him was the elected leadership from Canada.'[62]

Following the concession bitterness, both sides sought to calm the waters. The September 1980 IEB meeting was hosted by White in Toronto, and there was little formal discussion of the issue. The union's leadership instead focused on the two-week plant sit-in at Oshawa's

Houdaille company, where White was able to report some positive outcomes and address the question of plant-closing legislation in Ontario and Canada.[63] Within the Chrysler membership, LaSorda reached across the river in a gesture of rapprochement. He told Chrysler Director Marc Stepp that he wanted to put the cross-border 'bad feelings ... to bed so that we can concentrate on the work that needs to be done for the membership.' This, hoped LaSorda, would rebuild a 'good relationship now and in the future.'[64] In the context of an economic downturn with so many layoffs and closures on both sides of the border and the potential election of anti-union Ronald Reagan as president, organizational infighting took a back seat.

Unfortunately, the bad blood created by the Canadian refusal on concessions spoiled any chance of reconciliation. During the Chrysler Council's December 1980 meetings in San Antonio, Texas, the Canadian Chrysler leadership met with Stepp to explore the possibility of returning to an international agreement. The meeting exploded in anger and recriminations when Stepp declared that the Canadians had to 'pay their dues, prove their manhood, and get their self-respect back.' LaSorda's goodwill gesture was completely spoiled, and now the Canadians felt that it was 'highly unlikely' that they would remain under the international agreement.[65]

Iacocca's desperate request for more concessions in December 1980 in order to get a further $400 million of the total $1.5-billion guarantee was the final straw for the Canadians. Unlike the January 1980 congressional request, this time the Canadians could not refuse, since it was coming directly from Chrysler. Still party to Chrysler's international agreement, they could only complain that these concessions were being forced 'indirectly' by the U.S. government. This round of concessions totalled $622 million and included the end of cost-of-living allowances (COLA) for the remainder of the contract, the cancellation of paid holidays, and a delay in pension payments by the corporation. In return, the Canadians were now a part of the ESOP that they had criticized so heavily in January. The company also promised to keep the Windsor Spring plant open for the life of the contract, and indicated that some car production was ensured for the future, since the latest Chrysler survival plan called for only van and mini-van production in Canada.[66]

Forced into further concessions because of their inclusion within the international agreement, the Canadians decided to leave before they were officially kicked out. In November 1981 the Canadian UAW held a referendum on withdrawal from the international agreement. The position of White and the Canadian Council was that 'we cannot be subject to the dictates of another country' or part of an agreement that 'subjects our membership to the dictates of the US Congress.'[67] Chrysler's Canadian workers voted 79 per cent in favour of leaving the international agreement (white-collar workers were less enthusiastic, 52 per cent voting in favour). This did not mean, according to White, the end of the international union, but merely established a Canadian bargaining structure under the international.[68] But for all intents and purposes, Chrysler Canada's withdrawal represented a fundamental break with the union. Canadian workers had been forced to give concessions that their union had wanted to fight.

Chrysler was only the opening round in the concessions battle. In 1981 the already shaky economy went into the deepest recession since the Great Depression as interest rates, unemployment, and bankruptcies soared. Big Three car sales plummeted, while Japanese imports continued to take North American market share. GM suffered its first loss in fifty-nine years and Ford was also losing money. Echoing Iacocca's 1980 pleas for clawbacks, both troubled automakers asked the UAW to reopen contracts and grant concessions. Initially, the union balked, but by the time White attended the December 1981 IEB meeting, the American leadership had decided to push for a reopening of the contracts.[69]

White was the lone voice arguing against reopening the contracts. In an impassioned speech, White told the IEB that the Canadian position was not about nationalism but about fighting the corporation: 'My argument ... is that I think if there ever was a time when the membership needed the leadership of the union to fight back, it is now. They don't need the leadership to fight back when the corporations are not attacking them. They need the leadership to fight back when the goddamn attack is on.'[70] Despite mounting criticism, including a direct threat by GM that no concessions meant fewer jobs, White's dissent was supported by the Canadian locals, who viewed the issue as one of union solidarity, not nationalism. UAW Local 222, GM's largest, unanimously opposed the IEB's recommendation and saw its action as in 'direct opposition of the sworn obligations taken by this same Executive Board on their election to office.' Other Canadian locals voiced similar dismay, stung that the IEB's position had 'severely reduced the credibility of our International Union in the eyes of our local membership.' Both the Ford and GM Canadian councils voted against reopening their contracts, as well.[71]

The Canadian protests were to no avail. At the January 1982 IEB meeting in Chicago, White and the Canadian delegation strenuously lobbied delegates and members in the hotel lobby not to reopen the contracts while IEB members met upstairs. Their pleas achieved nothing. The decision to reopen contracts passed 25–1, with only White casting a dissenting vote.[72]

The willingness of Solidarity House to reopen the contracts marked a stark divergence in the two section's approaches to dealing with the corporations' request, and the whole notion of concessions. White felt that there were 'just too many fundamental differences for us to automatically "piggy back" the decisions of the US workers. We must help them when they need assistance, and vice versa, but we cannot and must not let this cancer of cutbacks flow over into Canada.'[73] Yet these core differences did not mean that he was advocating Canadian secession, at least not yet:

> I have heard the argument from some quarters that we must get out of the International Union, and that we cannot take a different direction within the International Union – I reject both of those arguments. Our International Union is a union representing workers in more than one country. We are not a region – we are a country within the International Union, and if our union is truly international, then the US workers have the right to pursue their course of action in this situation and we have the right to pursue ours – and both groups are entitled to and should expect the support of the leadership of the International Union in the direction they are taking.[74]

The Canadian section's position against concessions was further emphasized at the May 1982 meeting in Winnipeg of the Canadian Labour Congress, where the UAW sponsored a unanimously carried motion pledging all members of the Congress to reject any concession demands from any employer.[75]

White's continuing fight against concessions was a direct challenge to the international, and at the June 1982 IEB meetings Fraser made his displeasure known. Though he thanked White for defending him against some of the 'harsh' personal attacks and 'vindictive rhetoric' emanating from Canada, White's ongoing campaign against concessions was unacceptable. In his speech at Winnipeg, in a *Globe and Mail* opinion piece, and in a *Solidarity Canada* article, White had taken the position that concessions were not only the wrong approach but did

6.1 The *Solidarity Canada* cartoon that further fuelled the battle between White and Fraser at the IEB over concessions. *Solidarity Canada*, Special Edition (February 1982). Permission of Canadian Auto Workers.

not work. Fraser was having none of it: 'The premise that concessions don't save jobs is false. Concessions, Bob, is not a principle. It's a tactic. Sometimes it's good to make concessions; sometimes it's bad to make concessions; sometimes concessions shouldn't be made; sometimes concessions are made and it turns out badly. There are no absolutes here.'[76]

The characterization of concessions by someone in the Canadian staff as 'insanity' had deeply offended Fraser. Were the long list of UAW breakthroughs – paid vacation, paid holidays, COLA, Annual Improvement Factor, pensions, Supplemental Unemployment Benefit (SUB), and wage parity, all achieved by American UAW workers and passed onto the Canadians – insane? The people, Fraser continued, 'who designed this insane policy were smart enough to do all these things called "breakthroughs."' He was at the end of his rope with White and wanted to know 'sooner or later where Bob thinks we can end up.' White did not address Fraser's argument but held firm. This was not about leaving the union, but about concessions, the only fundamental disagreement 'that I have had since I have been on this Board with Doug,' one that he had in his 'guts.'[77]

But, Fraser charged, White's own actions in the battle over concessions had rekindled talk of Canadian secession: White had told *Automotive News* that the IEB felt that 'well, maybe, you didn't belong in the UAW.' White denied the allegation, saying, 'A reporter asked me the question: Does this mean the end of the International Union? I said: "No." I said that I thought that the International Union had to have this kind of flexibility,' but he was not advocating the break-up of the union.[78] Fraser was also particularly offended by a cartoon in the February 1982 issue of *Solidarity Canada* insinuating that Canadian job losses were a direct result of the auto trade deficit with the United States. With American 245,000 auto workers on layoff, Fraser felt that the cartoon didn't 'serve a very constructive purpose or show what I would consider the kind of sensitivity that one country should show to another, which I think we tried to show towards you.'[79]

White countered again that the issue at hand was concessions, and that both the IEB and the corporations had to realize the Canadian reality. The economic differences in Canada, with higher inflation, lower costs, and 'probably a $5.00 an hour labour cost difference because of the devaluation of the Canadian dollar and because of the difference in fringe benefit costs,' meant that neither the corporations nor the international could come to the Canadians 'on the basis of concession and ignore those differences.'[80] Fraser was unconvinced. The international union was now in uncharted territory. With White breaking so publicly with the UAW on concessions,[81] and committing to negotiating on his own with Chrysler in the next round, Fraser had 'no clear idea' of where the union was going. He told White to 'go ahead with your bargaining and good luck to you.' But he was not convinced that White could succeed. 'If you can bargain to conclusion without a strike and without any concessions, than go to it.'[82] White would indeed go to it, and achieve an utterly unexpected outcome.

Breaking the Pattern: The Chrysler and GM Strikes, 1982–4

The growing divergence between the two sections of the union became even more profound with the 1982 contract negotiations. The UAW had opted to open the agreements early at the behest of the Big Three, and against White's recommendation. By October, with concession-laden agreements having been concluded with GM and Ford both in Canada and the United States, White turned his attention to Chrysler.[83] When Chrysler's offer was rejected in the United States, the UAW leadership asked U.S. workers if they wanted to go on strike on 1 November or delay and resume negotiations in January 1983. The Americans decided to suspend bargaining.

White, on the other hand, was inclined to push for a settlement and continued negotiations. His tough stance resulted in a 'great deal of public criticism for our position' from many in government and in the public. Numerous pundits, editorials, and even political cartoonists criticized the union's position, implying that, as White put it, 'we had suicidal tendencies that we did not care about the industry, or the workers in the auto industry in Canada, that we were attempting to drive the industry out of Canada.'[84]

It was the first time Canadians were negotiating a Big Three contract entirely on their own, and without simultaneous negotiations in the United States. White and the Canadian leadership were determined to recoup the estimated $12,000 Chrysler Canada workers had conceded in wages and benefits since 1979.[85] After weeks of negotiations with no movement from the corporation, tensions rose in Windsor. One incident included a wildcat strike and plant takeover that White considered 'actually life threatening.' When the company finally tabled an offer, White called the Chrysler proposal 'one of the most stupid labour relations moves that I have ever seen in my life' since it was 'almost verbatim' the proposal already rejected by nearly 70 per cent of U.S. Chrysler workers.[86]

Feeling he had little choice, in November 1982 White and his 10,000 Canadian Chrysler workers struck, the first Chrysler walkout since 1973.[87] The shutdown threatened to derail Chrysler's entire North American recovery, since the integrated nature of the corporation meant that the firm's plants in Windsor and Etobicoke built for the whole continent. Needing a quick settlement, Iacocca jetted to Toronto and had a meeting with White and federal Industry Minister Ed Lumley, who was asked to help broker a deal.[88] But White refused to budge and told the Chrysler boss that the Canadians needed upfront raises given their past sacrifices. He argued that Chrysler could afford it since Canadian wages were closer to the Japanese level.[89] Iacocca left empty-handed, but the media frenzy surrounding Iacocca and his private jet 'helped the workers' cause and hurt the credibility of the corporation,' in White's view.[90]

Doug Fraser's appearance in Toronto didn't sway White, either. The UAW president tried to convince White that upfront increases would kill the company. The shutdown was hurting U.S. workers, since Chrysler was grinding to a standstill on both sides of the border. As Hargrove, then a special assistant to White, recalled, 'Doug came up ... [and] said "25 cents an hour up front will break Chrysler and put them into bankruptcy."' Caught between workers demanding upfront money and an international president who claimed such an increase would bankrupt Chrysler, Hargrove felt like 'the *Titanic* heading towards an iceberg.'[91]

But White remained adamant: 'We understand the integration of the industry and the effect that a strike has on production in the other country,' but 'the Canadian strike is really what is forcing the corporation to get back to the bargaining table in the US, and hopefully will help the US workers to get a better economic settlement.'[92] White's stubbornness worked. Unable to convince him to give in, Fraser left Toronto and restarted American negotiations well before their scheduled date, in order to bargain simultaneously with the Canadians. For the first time in history, the Canadian section was setting the pace of UAW bargaining.

Not everyone was convinced of White's strategy. The normally labour-friendly *Toronto Star* opined that the strike had all the 'makings of an industrial disaster.'[93] The sensationalist author Richard Rohmer – his book *Ultimatum* depicted Canadians repelling an invasion by the United States – penned 'The Day Chrysler Went Bankrupt,' a grim account imagining what would happen if Chrysler went bust because of a prolonged Canadian strike. In his tale, Rohmer saw a Chrysler bankruptcy followed by GM and Ford closing all their Canadian plants in a pre-emptive strike against Canadian labour militancy. In the end, 'the ramifications for Canada were beyond description ... the economy and society was crippled. It would take years to recover.'[94]

These grim prognostications never came to be. Six weeks into the strike, Chrysler caved. Amazingly, Chrysler's Canadian workers had set the pattern for North America. A breakthrough at the Canadian table led to a U.S. agreement, one that included upfront money. The

6.2 Chrysler Canada workers strike, Windsor, November 1982. Image courtesy of *Windsor Star*.

Canadians won a wage increase of $1.15 an hour coupled with an American upfront increase of 75 cents an hour – and Chrysler did not go bankrupt, as Fraser had warned. The new agreement did not mean immediate wage parity with GM and Ford, but it did go some way towards alleviating the shortfall. White had won, and was completely vindicated in his strategy for taking on the corporation.[95]

American Chrysler workers might have been ecstatic with White and the Canadians, but the international leadership was not so happy. After the strike, White appeared at the December IEB meeting and did not hide his pleasure at the outcome. He told board members, 'I think it broke well for us. It broke well for us on both sides of the border.' As for the differences in strategy with Fraser, White was magnanimous. 'There are many times,' he told his union brothers, 'when we question each other as to where trade unionism is in this day and age because it's such a struggle out there, but I feel very proud of the fact that we were able to do this. I think it's good for our International Union. I think it's good for our Chrysler workers.' In response, Fraser weighed his words carefully: 'Hopefully, we should seize upon this ... to try and get back to where we were in international unity and international solidarity.'[96]

Fraser's hopes illustrated the extent he would go to accommodate White and the Canadians. For their part, even during the most strained moments over the Chrysler concessions battle and strike, the Canadians had remained committed to the international. But for all his efforts to keep White and the Canadians happy, Fraser's 'international solidarity' would be broken forever by yet another strike and, eventually, a clash between White and Fraser's successor, new international president Owen Bieber, who took office in 1983.

Emboldened by his success with Chrysler, on the opening day of 1984 bargaining White threw down the gauntlet. He told reporters that 'this will be an agreement for Canadian workers, negotiated in this hotel with Canadians representing the union and dealing with the corporation.' White declared that 'the pre-1982 days of rubber-stamping a US agreement in Canada are gone. We will no doubt have some priorities that may differ from the US section of our union, but we have to pursue those at the bargaining table.'[97] White's fiery rhetoric was aimed as much at his own international union as it was at the corporation, and was captured by a film crew he had arranged to document the negotiations.

White's confidence also stemmed from his belief that GM's Canadian profits could more than sustain any increases that the union bargained for. At Placer Court, GM Canada's 1983 profits were being called 'astounding' – $675 million. Sam Gindin calculated that the figure was nearly one-fifth of GM's worldwide earnings and represented $19,000 for each hourly GM Canada worker.[98] The company had also recovered quickly from the downturn and actually had 34,000 workers, 4,000 more than at its 1970s peak, an amazing fact considering that Ford and Chrysler had together shed nearly 7,000 jobs in the same period.[99]

Despite his bluster, White decided to wait until after the U.S. strike deadline before making any moves. If the U.S. plants went down because of a strike, the Canadian plants would surely soon follow in any event because of a lack of parts. But if the United States settled, and Canada went on strike, the Canadian UAW would be in the driver's seat. Starting on 14 September, the UAW in the United States conducted a series of rotating strikes at plants across the country, a strategy instituted by Bieber.

The rotating strikes did the trick. GM sweetened its offer, and Bieber accepted. The three-year agreement included provisions for job security, a key demand for the U.S. section of the union. On the financial side, the deal was a stark departure from previous pacts. It included a wage increase of 2.25 per cent in the first year but lump-sum payouts to workers in years two and three, and profit sharing, something that Gindin had referred to as a 'gimmick' during the previous round of Chrysler negotiations since these one-time payments did nothing for the long-term pay of workers. The American membership was not completely convinced either; the agreement was subsequently ratified by only 58 per cent.[100]

When the settlement was reached in the United States on 21 September, White made it clear that this did not mean automatic Canadian acceptance. 'If the corporations have listened to us for the last 18 months,' he warned, 'they will make a proposal across this table that will fit the Canadian situation.'[101] The Canadian situation, in White's view, necessitated additional increases to make up for the shortfall in parity which existed because of the exchange-rate differences between the two countries. He was also dead set against any lump-sum payouts from the corporation.[102]

With no movement from GM, the union's target for the pattern, in late September White announced a 17 October strike date, to the dismay of Solidarity House.[103] White complained that, as the Canadians moved towards a strike deadline, 'interference started from Detroit again.' It was 'very clear that Owen Bieber in his discussions with me was really saying to me that they can't handle a situation of where the Canadians are always going to go a different direction than the Americans.'[104] But White was undeterred. GM's first offer on 5 October was, in White's words, 'a rubber stamp of the US agreement, only worse.' A second proposal one day before the strike deadline was essentially the same, and wildcat strikes broke out at Oshawa.[105] On 17 October, the Canadian UAW struck for a second time in three years.[106]

At Oshawa, Windsor, and St Catharines, where the largest GM Canada facilities operated, picket lines quickly sprang up and the company's production ground to a halt. GM Canada was the sole source of a number of parts and vehicles for the firm. In particular, the St Catharines plant alone produced engines and parts for some of GM's most important vehicles for all of North America. Within a few days of the strike's start, ripples were already being felt across the continent as U.S. workers began to be laid off owing to a lack of Canadian-made parts.[107] Within a week, 60,000 U.S. workers were on layoff owing to the Canadian strike. The integrated nature of the industry threatened to derail GM's recovery and cost the company millions; meanwhile, there was sharp criticism of White and the CAW for calling the strike and threatening to disrupt the entire industry's recovery.[108]

As the strike continued, Bieber and White clashed over the negotiations. Initially, the two men had disagreed over whether the Canadians should even go on strike. Bieber had, according to some accounts, told White to simply conform to the U.S. pattern, while White argued that differences in the exchange rate meant Canadians had to have a different agreement. The two men also clashed over who had the ultimate authority to negotiate with GM during a Canadian strike by an international union – the international president, or the Canadian director. White told one reporter 'flatly' that Bieber had not encouraged the Canadians to fight for the best deal but had actually urged GM to ignore the Canadian demands. It was also 'rumoured' that Bieber considered cutting off strike pay to GM Canada workers to 'bring them and White to heel.'[109] These reports, true or not, unquestionably found their way back to Solidarity House, which no doubt infuriated Bieber.

In the end, after a thirteen-day walkout, the Canadians got what they wanted. Their deal included raises called 'Special Canadian Adjustments,' and no lump sums, a major departure from the U.S. agreement. GM workers voted 87 per cent in favour of the contract, followed by Ford workers, who ratified at 85 per cent. It was another pivotal moment for the Canadian union. White had won again, and he had again broken with his international brothers to do so.

Some saw the victory as one of nationalism. McDermott, now head of the Canadian Labour Congress, told his wife that 'this thing is now over. Get a bottle of champagne. General Motors finally recognized Canada as a sovereign nation.'[110] *Solidarity Canada* trumpeted that 'the bargaining had proved that the UAW in Canada would have to gain a greater degree of independence from the US section in order to pursue its goals and determine its own destiny. The Canadian section had gone through the growing pains. It had come of age.'[111] But, it darkly warned, 'on the horizon loomed the question of the structure of the international union.' The clash between White and Bieber over the GM strike proved the unravelling of the international.

'It's Not the End of the World": Sundering the UAW and Making a National Hero

In the wake of the 1984 GM strike, emotions ran high for Canadian auto workers. Rumours swirled over the direction of the union, now that the Canadians had yet again broken the pattern with their U.S. brethren. During a telling post-strike press conference, White held court with a throng of reporters. Asked whether he was considering taking the Canadians out of the UAW, White vehemently denied that this was his goal. 'I am not advocating the break-up of the international union,' White maintained. 'As a matter of fact, I would prefer to keep the International Union intact.' He had no idea where such a rumour had come from. Hearing earlier on the radio 'that I was getting out of the International union,' White joked, 'I got my pension early.' But one reporter pressed him:

> Q: Where did this report come from? Who do you think picked up the old ball and spread that around?
> A: I don't know. We have a deep throat in our midst I guess. I don't know. I think it came from some speculation of the difficulties that we were going through. And I shared those with the local union leadership at the time.

White did admit that he was 'thinking about the structure, thinking about the future,' and publicly cited the 'fairly serious' problems that he faced during the GM negotiation with Bieber and Solidarity House.[112] He also told reporters that he faced 'high level' pressure to break away from members in the Canadian wing, even though the Canadian-bargained contracts had actually blunted some of the desire for separation among certain locals: Gerry Michaud, Local 199 president (GM-St Catharines), who in 1982 had pushed for a task force to look at the idea of a separate union, was 'less inclined to go that route now.' Local 444 President Ken Gerard told reporters that 'I don't know anything that's so powerful, so urgent or so deep that would lead us to break solidarity with the international union in the US.'[113]

The press conference was another example of White as a master of media relations, a trait that he had already demonstrated during the GM strike. White was being honest when he said that he did not want to take the Canadians out of the union, at least not yet, and that he did not directly know where the rumours came from. But if White wanted to achieve his vision of an asymmetric international, making the Canadian section virtually autonomous or, failing that, to actually take the union out of the international, he had to have two things: an issue to bring his membership onside, and their unanimous support to take on the international.

The question of interference from Solidarity House during the GM strike became the issue White needed. News reports had swirled for weeks of 'rumours' that Bieber was threatening to 'close the tap' on the Canadians' strike pay unless they accepted the U.S. contract. This was false, according to White, and he told reporters that the rumour 'never came from our union in Detroit.'[114] But, wherever the strike-pay rumours originated, they clearly gave impetus to the issue of 'interference' by Solidarity House in Canadian affairs, an issue that White could easily use to provoke his membership.

Indeed, by the time 300 Canadian UAW representatives converged in Toronto to hash out their union's future within the international in December 1984, just a few weeks after the emotional GM strike, the issue of interference had reached a boiling point for many union members. White laid out the allegations of interference with his usual passion and charisma: 'We have reached a stage in our history,' he declared to the Canadian Council, 'where our union's collective bargaining direction in the US is different from ours and we must pursue a program in the interests of our Canadian membership, and do so without interference from anyone in the US, and without any veiled references to strike authorization or strike pay.' But he was willing to take a conciliatory tone, too: 'I want to be fair to Brother Bieber. We were involved in many discussions and he was personally involved with Roger Smith of GM in the final economic framework – but it is exactly that framework which is troublesome.' White feigned ambivalence at the choice facing the union. 'So, what must we do?' he asked. 'Well, I guess we can take the grand step, say this relationship cannot continue and therefore we must discuss complete new structures independent of each other, with close solidarity ties, but the end as we know it, of the International Union. Or we can do as I prefer to do at this stage in our development, change our structure internally to meet the new realities. But change we must – my preference is to pursue the latter course and if that's not possible or acceptable, then a complete new structure must be formed.' Ultimately, however, he needed his brothers' support: 'Whatever we do, whatever direction we decide to go – we must be united, and if we are, in my opinion, our union and our members in both the United States and Canada will be better off in the future.'[115]

Whipped to a frenzy of indignation at the allegations of interference, the council unanimously demanded that bargaining be conducted solely by the Canadian UAW, including the right to call strikes (and receive strike pay) without prior approval from Solidarity House. The notion of interference by the international was the main complaint of the union, which stated that collective bargaining must be 'independently pursued ... without interference from the US,' and that there was to be 'no interference' from 'any officer or representative' of the international unless requested by the Canadian director. The Canadians also sought the right to pursue mergers with other unions, including other Canadian sections of international unions, whether or not parallel mergers were available in the United States. White publicly emphasized that 'we must be able to pursue a program in the interests of our Canadian membership, and do so without interference from anyone in the US.'[116]

The issue of the reported interference from Solidarity House – which White referred to as 'sharp conversations' with Bieber – turned many members uncertain or even opposed to autonomy into full-blown supporters. After hearing White's tales of Detroit interference, Local 444's Gerard had changed his tune: 'I said we'd be crazy to get out of the international union ... before I knew the degree of interference.' The 'details' offered by White about Solidarity House's efforts to impose an early settlement during the GM strike had convinced Gerard – 'when you find out that someone from another country is saying that "we didn't get it in our contract and you shouldn't deserve it," that is not the way it should work.' Bob Longeuay, Local 1973 president (GM-Windsor), was just as adamant. 'We should not,' Longeuay argued, 'under any circumstances, be dictated to by a source outside of this country.'[117]

The Canadian Council's decision sent shockwaves through the union movement and generated headlines across North America. Most observers saw the decision as precipitating a dramatic confrontation with Solidarity House, nothing less than a declaration of secession.[118] In Detroit, the UAW leadership prepared for a showdown, obtaining a legal opinion that it could maintain 'full ownership' of the strike fund in case of a split and, if it came to 'a total war situation,' would have a claim against all Canadian local union properties.[119] From Brussels, former international president Douglas Fraser, while expressing his admiration for the Canadian UAW leader, told reporters that 'if White thinks he's going to get a better deal out of those auto companies than the Canadian UAW has been getting in the last fifteen years, he's crazy.' Fraser also suggested that the UAW might save money by shedding Canada, since its dues did not make up for the costs associated with the Canadian section.[120]

The fight over the Canadian demands came to a head during the blistering 10 December meeting of the IEB in Detroit. Facing Bieber and twenty-five other UAW bosses, White walked into one of the most important meetings in Canadian labour history with only Buzz Hargrove at his side. For six epic hours, White made the Canadian case for more autonomy, while Bieber made the international's in an effort to convince the leadership that there was no 'interference' and that no more autonomy could be granted without breaking the union.[121]

White's nearly two-hour presentation started with the declaration that this dispute was 'not a matter of personalities.' The situation would have been the same 'had it been Doug Fraser or Leonard Woodcock or anybody else in this room who had been International President, so it is not about the question of Owen Bieber.'[122] Despite these protestations, it was clear that the two men had developed an intensely combative relationship.[123] This was followed by a lecture on the Canadian history of unionism, one that prominently featured the 1982 Chrysler strike.

White then laid out his view that this conflict was not about nationalism. The Canadian moves in the past were 'not an attempt to break up our union ... You can play narrow nationalism any time you want to in the International union and you can break it up.' Instead, White was trying to make the UAW 'truly an International Union.' He was asking that the IEB 'clearly recognize and adopt a policy that says that ... the Canadians have a right to pursue that program, up to and including a strike, without interference from anyone outside of Canada. The question of whether the International President or others are involved should be on request of the Canadian director.'[124]

It was, in White's view, simply 'another step in the evolution of our organization,' one that recognized that 'we have the flexibility to pursue collective bargaining priorities that are Canadian labour movement priorities.' Fundamentally, the motion authorizing greater Canadian autonomy meant that 'this International Union is an equal partnership.' If, however, the board could not see the logic of this step, White felt that 'we have an obligation at this stage in our history to talk about a much different structure – talk about two separate UAW's, one in Canada and one in the United States, each structured financially and geographically and Constitutionally sound, with complete autonomy, with close fraternal ties.' This wasn't White's first choice, but he was pragmatic: 'My roots are in this organization, but I also want to say it's not the end of the world. We can recognize our two countries, and have two UAWs with fraternal relationships. It's not the end of the world.'[125]

Bieber's response focused mostly on the question of interference, the details of the GM strike settlement, and how White's request challenged the very being of the union. What rankled him most were insinuations that the IEB would withhold strike pay, where this notion had come from, and who had made such a statement: 'Now, I saw what you said in your news release and you said that never was said, and it wasn't. There never was a time that you and I ever had any discussion relative to any strike benefits being cut off.'[126]

But the suggestion of interference was all over the media: 'It's my name that's in the newspapers here. There are things in here that say that if I hadn't interfered, there might not have been a strike. That is a goddam lie. It's absolutely untrue.' As to where the suggestions of interference had come from, Bieber played coy: 'I don't believe that Bob White would say that and I don't believe he did say it, but that's what's in the newspapers, and I'm not going to continue with that way ... I'm not going to keep on taking a beating on it and I wouldn't ask anyone else to. If the reporters ask me that, I'm going to tell them it's a lie because it is.'[127]

In the sharpest exchange of the meeting, the two leaders' visions of the union, and their animosity over the question of interference, came to a head:

White: I'm not saying the International President can't call the Canadian Director. I'm not saying the International President can't come in on the negotiations. I am saying that before they intervene with the corporation, it ought to be at the request of the Director.
Bieber: Bob, I'm not sure I heard you right: 'Intervene with the corporation?'
White: I mean going to the corporation to talk about a settlement, talking about a formula for a settlement, without being requested to do so by the Director for Canada.
Bieber: Who did that?
White: I'm saying I have to have it clear. It has to be clear. It has to be clear because we have been through so much. It's not a question of whether you did or didn't do it here.
Bieber: The point is, I didn't do it.[128]

Ultimately, Bieber could not countenance what White was asking for. The IEB had to have final say on strike matters or the union could not survive. Granting the Canadians complete control over strike decisions in the face of a UAW constitutional provision giving the board the right to end a strike would simply not work, in Bieber's view.[129]

The exchange had shaken the union to its core, but the IEB was unconvinced by White's argument. Vice-President Don Ephlin, a long-time ally of White's, felt that the meeting marked 'a very sad day' for the union. Though White was always 'a very articulate and logical spokesman,' Elphin was not persuaded. White was not up to 'his usual logical standards.' After some discussion, the board voted to reject White's motion for more autonomy, 24–1. In response, White put forward a second motion, for separation proceedings to begin. The board debated how the split could be done, and whether or not there should be a referendum for the Canadian workers on the question. White was confident that he could 'get a referendum vote tomorrow of 95 percent, if we have to do that. That's immaterial.' He didn't want to do this 'as a divorce, where the family goes through a long an agonizing divorce, but as adults.' Eventually, White's motion to form a committee to look at how to create two separate organizations passed 17–7, with White abstaining. Some on the board could not bring themselves to vote for separation in any form.[130]

Having made the decision to split the union, the meeting became a battle over how to spin the schism in the media and public. Bieber pulled out a pre-written press release that included language denying interference, painted a positive picture of the UAW in general, and stated that the Canadian 'demand' to 'be free to pursue their objectives without accountability to the IEB would destroy the International Union.' It further stated that the IEB 'totally and unconditionally rejects any suggestion that we or the International Union as a whole have been unresponsive to the specific needs and aspiration of our members in Canada.'[131] White was appalled. He simply could not adopt such a statement, since it included 'all the arguments that I made on the opposition side.' He would not vote for it but did think it 'should be adopted by the US members of the IEB.'[132]

Exhausted by the gravity of the meeting, White left the room and headed to his hotel. The battle between White and Bieber was more than just a fight over what was best for the international union. It was a clash of forceful personalities, and a fundamental disagreement over what had happened during the GM strike. For White, the sundering of the union was an 'emotional experience for me because the UAW had been my life ... That night I remember going to the hotel room after it was all over and crying my eyes out because I said what the hell did I do here, but I knew what I did.'[133]

The union had broken irrevocably. News of the split ricocheted across Canada and North America and was seen by many in the media and the general public as the quintessential David taking on the UAW Goliath.[134] During a period of prolonged economic difficulty, when the Canadian economic model was being questioned (the milestone Macdonald royal commission on Canada's economic future had been published earlier that year), White's willingness to break from the international was viewed as courageous and heroic by many Canadians. One union member called it 'guts poker.' Newspaper reports and columnists variously referred to White as a 'hero,' taking on U.S. 'bullies,' and 'Canada's labor superstar.'[135]

At the Canadian Council meeting on 15 December, White was welcomed as a conquering hero, though he cautioned his fellow Canadian unionists that this was a time not for 'faint hearts' but for 'courageous leadership.' He easily pushed forward acceptance of his motion to 'commence the restructuring of the Canadian UAW into a completely autonomous union,' avoiding a referendum on the issue, which he argued was not provided for in the constitution and therefore not necessary. White planned to hold a founding convention of the new union in September 1985, and even told the council that he hoped Brother Bieber would attend.[136]

Reaction to the split was wide-ranging. New Prime Minister Brian Mulroney told reporters that 'if they feel that it's in their interests as Canadian workers to do that, then they ought to do that. Bob White is an outstanding labor leader showing remarkably sane leadership.' CLC leader McDermott felt it was 'a positive move that takes into [account] the sharp differences between Canada and the US.'[137] Cec Taylor, president of United Steelworkers of America Local 1005 (Hamilton), a strong supporter of an independent Canadian union movement, was ecstatic: 'I've been waiting twenty years for this. The people who have to do this first are the UAW. That will make it easier for us at Steelworkers to follow ... Our separation movement will start to grow now.'[138] Victor Reuther, brother of Walter, enthusiastically endorsed the Canadian move.[139]

Others were not so sanguine. Auto analyst Arvid Jouppi was convinced that the split would dissuade investors from Canada because of the uncertainty caused by the new union, and that it would 'retard investment to a degree.' This sentiment was echoed by Detroit executives at Chrysler and GM, who suggested that the new union was 'one more complication in an already complicated business.' Some editorialists in Canada also thought that new union could prove problematic to attracting new investment, and if White and the new CAW were not careful, they would 'kill the chances for expansion in this country.'[140] The *Detroit News* saw White's move as 'petty grandstanding.'[141]

6.3 White's departure from the UAW generated headlines and cartoons across North America. *Toronto Sun*, 13 December 1984. Andy Donato, reprinted with permission, QMI Agency.

Nor were all unionists happy, either. Former Canadian director George Burt, who had led the union from 1939 until 1968 and had on numerous occasions faced demands for greater Canadian autonomy, disagreed with White's decision. Burt felt that White was causing too many problems and that he himself had never been subjected to pressure from Solidarity House – 'they'd advise you. They can't hit you over the head with a club. I never had any trouble with them over the river.' Likewise, the head of the Canadian section of the United Steelworkers of America, Gerald Docquier, viewed the split with 'some apprehension.'[142]

In the spring of 1985 White and the international began their discussions on the separation proceedings. Many questions remained: What about locals that did not want to disaffiliate with UAW to join the new Canadian entity? How would the strike fund be divided, if at all? What about Canadian UAW property, which technically belonged to the international? During initial meetings, the question of the strike fund loomed. White argued that Canada should get 10 per cent of the fund, about C$67 million, which he called 'a fair proposition.' Though the discussions were civil, he got much less – US$36 million (about $45 million Canadian at the time), of which $3.7 million was deducted to pay for outstanding liabilities to the international in terms of real estate, mortgages, and equipment. After some legal wrangling over the timing of the secession, the transfer of funds, and even the question of the new union's name and logo (the UAW was firmly opposed to the Canadians using them), virtually all of the issues had been resolved by the summer of 1985.[143]

The break was complete. In September 1985 the new Canadian Auto Workers held a founding convention, adopted a constitution, and acclaimed White as president. Victor Reuther spoke in favour of the new union.[144] Bieber did not attend the convention but did send his 'best wishes' to White and the new union, though he noted that 'while we wish you Godspeed, our greetings our tempered by a sense of sadness ... until now, there has been more that has united us than divided us. As the power of multinationals grow, so should the unity of workers.' The missive ended by saying, 'Although we disagree with your decision to separate, we, of course, respect it.'[145]

Solidarity House's reaction to the Canadian separation would change following the founding CAW convention. The pleasantries Bieber had extended were cut short in the UAW's next correspondence, given the tone the Canadians had adopted: 'It is unfortunate that so much time at the founding convention of your new Canadian union was devoted to criticism of the strategies and objectives pursued by the UAW in the US.' The UAW was particularly incensed by criticism of its agreement with GM for the new Saturn plant in Tennessee giving management greater flexibility with workers in job classifications and operations. Bieber could not help but take a final parting shot. 'In any case,' he wrote White, 'you have now established your independent, and totally autonomous union. You can no longer make the claim of pressure or interference from the US.' Bieber's bitterness lingered: 'Yankee-baiting won't work forever. We hope your new union and its leadership can soon mature to the point where you can define a program for Canada without attacking the efforts of workers in the United States.'[146]

Conclusion: Explaining the Emergence of the CAW

Despite Bieber's harsh rhetoric, nationalism may have been the vehicle that propelled the Canadians out of the UAW but it was not the main cause. The break-up, according to *Toronto Star* labour reporter and White confidant John Deverell, had 'little to do with flag-waving nationalism,' though White could 'wrap himself handsomely in the Maple Leaf' when he needed to. Instead, Deverell argued that the Canadian section of the union believed that the international simply could not protect its interests properly.[147] Three key developments drove the Canadian shift from support for the international to the eventual decision to break away, each of which had little to do with nationalism.

The first major issue was the change in leadership within the UAW. Charlotte Yates has argued that 'union collective identities and internal organizational structures shape how unions intervene in political debates and conflicts and are therefore critical in fully understanding the strategic choices made by unions.'[148] But the role of individuals within the union is also essential to this equation: the influence of Bob White on the Canadian UAW's internal dynamics, and its public positioning during the early 1980s, is as indisputable as his clash with Bieber. Though some media outlets such as the *Windsor Star* noted the 'divergent' personalities of Bieber and White had 'brought things to a head,' both men repeatedly declared that there was no issue of personalities at play.[149] But Owen Bieber was no Doug Fraser, and White himself admitted that 'the fact that Doug Fraser and I were good friends helped keep our union together in spite of our fundamental difference on the direction of our union.'[150]

To understand just how different White and Bieber were, consider their conflict over White's public and media role as Canadian director. White's media role helps to explain the confusion and conflict over the rumours of interference during the GM strike, an issue that had been used to mobilize the Canadian membership and that hung over the entire issue of Canada's place within the union. Bieber, described as 'cautious, lugubrious' and the 'least colourful' candidate to replace Fraser, operated on the principle that there was only one spokesperson for the UAW – the international president. White's media approach was 'the key problem' for Solidarity House, in that he 'acted outside the usual parameters of US leaders' behaviour, particularly when it came to media relations.'[151] In Bieber's view, White had grandstanded, unfairly exploited the media against Solidarity House, and allowed unsubstantiated rumour to stand uncontested.

White had come to understand the power of the media to get his message out during the Chrysler strike, something he was able to exploit even more effectively in the 1984 GM bargaining. During the latter episode, GM negotiator Rod Andrew chose not to speak to the press, leaving the podium wide open for White, who clearly enjoyed the spotlight. A *Solidarity Canada* article detailed the intense media scrutiny of the negotiations and White's willingness to engage reporters on a daily basis.[152] White himself admitted that 'there was enormous media interest in these negotiations and once again, I never refused an opportunity to discuss publicly the issues in this strike. I did that not just because of my belief in the public's right to know, but also because most of our members want to know what is happening and the quickest way to communicate is through the medium of radio, TV and newspaper.'[153]

White also understood the power of film, especially documentaries that could be used to lasting effect. In 1980 the UAW Canada leadership considered a film project about the Houdaille sit-in.[154] Though that film never materialized, White decided, unbeknownst to Bieber, to allow a documentary film crew to have almost complete access to the Canadian UAW's 1984 negotiations with GM. At the final 1985 meeting discussing the separation settlement, Bieber, who had found out about the film from producer Sturla Gunnarsson, warned White that 'I better know what is in there before anything is run on it. I'll tell you that I'm really shocked that someone would have filmed them and not tell them.'[155] Unfortunately for Bieber, *Final Offer* may have originally been intended to record the bargaining, but, according to *Solidarity Canada*, it ended up portraying 'the union's frustration over the intervention of the US section into the collective bargaining process in Canada.'[156] Another film project documenting the creation of the CAW, *No Looking Back*, declared that 'Bieber's attempt at sabotage of the GM negotiations was the last straw. The Canadians needed full autonomy to ensure that such interferences would never be repeated.'[157]

During the union's divorce proceedings, UAW staff in Detroit blamed White for leaks to the media and attempted to reach an agreement with him that there would be no discussion of the settlement with the press. At the first break-up negotiating meeting in Bal Harbour, Florida, Bieber warned White: 'I hope there is not much of this that gets in the press. I've talked to you about that before.' UAW Secretary Treasurer Ray Majerus also told White that 'I would hope there will be very little conversation about this meeting. It is going to be difficult enough with our colleagues without there being a discussion of this meeting in the press.'[158]

White was, in Solidarity House's view, 'encouraging Canadian press coverage' in an effort to 'take a high profile' and thereby generate 'stories all over the country.' Officials close to Bieber felt that an agreement with White on media strategy was, in any event, probably not possible: 'We know that what he does in the open, and what he does quietly with the press are two different things.' But senior UAW member David Mitchell warned Bieber, 'If we don't set in place some kind of strategy, however, we can be sure Bob will use the media to boost his position, and to hurt our position and the image of the International Union ... we must not let him use the media against the International.'[159] The conflict over White's use of the media reflected the personal difficulties between White and Bieber, which in turn hastened the split in the union.

The second important development was the change in economic circumstances facing Canadian auto workers. More than anything else, the changing dollars and cents realities pushed their militant posture. The cross-border economics of the 1970s had, as the 1983 federal *Report on the Canadian Auto Industry* indicated, given way to a new reality after 1980, one in which 'Canadian economic conditions' were now 'central' to the negotiations.[160] In the 1960s and 1970s, the U.S. side of the union had always negotiated monetary issues and set the pattern for the Canadians. That had been adequate when the economies were largely in tune, or when the U.S. situation lent itself to providing a pattern that the Canadians could agree to. But some economic factors had changed dramatically by the early 1980s.

Ironically, one key factor was wage parity. As part of the wage-parity agreement bargained in 1973, the UAW had agreed to an annual COLA, to be determined by weighing a combined U.S. and Canadian rate. It was expected that inflation rates in the two countries would remain somewhat similar and that the exchange rate would also remain stable. But by 1982, persistently higher inflation rates in Canada and the lower value of the Canadian dollar meant that a separate Canadian COLA would have resulted in a significantly higher increase. In the 1979 collective agreement, Canadian workers actually received about thirteen cents an hour less than if they had had their own rate, while the U.S. workers received about two cents more (owing to the fact that there were only 35,000 Canadian workers under the deal, as opposed to near-ly 430,000 American workers).[161]

This difference added to tensions between the two sections of the union, tensions exacerbated by the divergent approaches each was taking towards bargaining as a whole. Sam Gindin felt that 'even if we assume that the union is moving in the *same* direction and relationships remain "friendly," there is an argument to be made that *rigid* wage parity can't survive.' Gindin felt that there was 'no point in having any illusions about *ending* these tensions – the issue is: can the tensions be reduced to a containable level?'[162] In the 1982 negotiations, the Canadian UAW sought and achieved a 'Canadianized' formula that better reflected the Canadian circumstances, one that Fraser continued to characterize as 'parity of base rates.'[163]

But this was not enough to keep the Canadians onside. Exchange-rate differences and the benefits of national health care meant that Canadian workers' labour costs were far lower than their American counterparts, a factor that White was willing to exploit. During the 1982 negotiations with GM, White realized that 'GM could move some of their products, we knew they could lay off workers and close down certain lines, but it didn't make any sense for a company to work in a country whose labour costs are probably $6.00 an hour less, and move that work to a country whose labour costs are $6.00 an hour more.'[164] The Big Three were aware of this difference, too, and had been slowly moving to take advantage of it. Between 1978, as the Canadian dollar began its descent, and 1984, news reports noted that the 'devaluation has had powerful affects on production decisions' as GM slashed its U.S. workforce by 100,000 jobs while adding 6,000 jobs in Canada.[165]

This was at the heart of the GM strike: whether Canadians should get additional money to reflect their different economic circumstances, and how this money could be bargained for without breaking the union. As White told the Canadian Council in December 1984, after seeing the U.S. settlement at the IEB, he 'was very careful not to criticize the US proposed settlement.' But he was 'also very clear in stating that it did not and would not "fit" in Canada, that our labour costs were vastly different, our priorities and objectives in other areas were different including time off the job and that we intended to pursue those objectives in our Canadian negotiations.'[166] In this case, the Canadian UAW's notion of fair share crashed headlong into the concept of union solidarity.

Third, and perhaps most important, was White's recognition that the integrated nature of the North America auto sector gave the Canadian section tremendous power. This realization could be seen in the 1985 negotiations, the first time that the new CAW bargained a contract. The *Detroit Free Press* wondered whether 'White might use the talks to show he can negotiate a better contract than US union leaders,' given that a Canadian strike 'could close nearly all of Chrysler's US plants.'[167] True to White's word, the Canadian union 'proved their maturity' by bargaining a contract with Chrysler that returned their members to parity with GM and Ford workers following a short strike. The settlement proved, according to White, that 'the companies, contrary to their response when we first made the decision to go our own separate way, have accepted our new national union.'[168] The agreement was symbolic in two ways: it was the first time that the Canadians settled before their U.S. counterparts, and the first time they had done so without any U.S. input.

Perhaps most significantly, the CAW had bargained a contract with an expiry date of 1987, a year before UAW contracts ended in the United States. Bargaining separately at different intervals than the U.S. union gave the Canadians additional leverage in the North American sector. Though they could also be victimized by strikes south of the border, White had slowly come to understand the Canadian section's ability to shut down the continental industry. The agreement reflected the strategic thinking of White and the CAW's leadership, strategic thinking forged during the difficult period between 1979 and 1984. White had learned two key lessons from the Chrysler bailout, the battle over concessions, and the 1982 and 1984 strikes. The first was that the American leadership could not and would not recognize the differing economic realities constraining the Canadians' ability to achieve what they saw as their fair share within internationally bargained agreements. The second was that the integrated nature of the North American industry had made the Canadian section powerful enough to take on the industry, and gain its fair share by itself.

The vulnerability of the integrated North American industry became increasingly evident throughout the 1970s. A 1976 month-long Ford strike in the United States had left 14,000 Canadian Ford workers unemployed owing to lack of parts.[169] A 1979 Teamster's strike effectively paralysed the industry, including the Canadian firms.[170] Even a small plant shutdown could cripple one of the Big Three. In early 1982 Chrysler's mini-van launch threatened to be delayed by the troubles at a small Twinsburg, Ohio, plant that produced metal clamps used in the vehicle.[171] Then the 1982 Canadian Chrysler strike threatened

Chrysler's recovery and prompted both Lee Iacocca and Douglas Fraser to make pilgrimages to Toronto to plead with White to end the Canadian work stoppage. The thirteen-day GM strike shut down all the Canadian plants but also idled over 60,000 GM workers in the United States and cost the company an estimated US$200 million per week.[172]

Of course, strikes on different sides of the border and occasionally at different times had been part of the UAW-industry dynamic since the 1960s and even before. But, by the mid-1980s, circumstances had changed. The industry was even more integrated than it had been in 1970 or even 1975. Though the Big Three had not yet fully embraced lean production techniques and just-in-time (JIT) delivery, the great culling of plants in the 1970s had left the companies dependent upon far fewer facilities, and these plants more often had sole-source production mandates. Quite a few of these facilities were in Canada, such as Chrysler's mini-van plant in Windsor, some assembly lines at GM's giant Oshawa Autoplex, and its parts plant in St Catharines. The great integrationist jigsaw puzzle that represented North American production could be quickly shattered by removing one piece. If a union had control over that piece, it was very powerful.[173]

Such was the nature of the integrated industry. The new CAW's position was quickly recognized by Detroit executives. Chrysler's industrial relations chief Thomas Miner noted that all of Chrysler's pistons were built in Canada. A strike by the new CAW could shut down the whole company. Similarly, Alfred Warren, who served GM in a similar capacity, worried that the company would be 'held hostage' by the new union. John Smith, president of GM Canada, warned the emergent union about the use of its new-found status in North America: 'Future investment decisions must now take into account the change in the Canadian labour environment, including the potential impact of labour action in Canada on production throughout North America.'[174]

Others understood the dynamic as well. The *Globe* editorialized that White and the Canadians needed to be careful, that they could not 'count indefinitely on [their] trump card during negotiations – that a Canadian strike, because the two countries' operations are tied by the auto pact, has a severe impact on the US auto industry.' The paper warned that the spurned American union, 'if it sees its jobs being used as ammunition in a Canadian battle, may be unwilling to continue to support the existence of the auto pact.'[175] The *Oshawa Times* also understood that the new Canadian union 'could in fact hold the North American auto industry to ransom if it wished' and that 'it will now have to make certain that newfound muscles are not flexed to an extent that future expansion plans for this country are scrapped.'[176] The *Detroit News* recognized that the Canadians' power was such that it threatened to destabilize the industry: 'As long as the international could exercise a restraining influence on Canada's more militant labor leaders, this system worked pretty well. Now it could get out of balance.'[177]

After 1985, White spent much of his time fighting against free trade and protecting the auto pact. His nationalist image and media savvy served him well in these battles, as he became a leading spokesperson for the anti-free-trade side. There is no doubt that White came to this nationalist position genuinely. But, at its core, his union's decision to leave the international was not solely borne by nationalism, though it may have helped to birth it. What drove the creation of the CAW was the same impulse that pushed the Canadian state to initiate so many aggressive policies towards the auto sector – the demand for a fair share of North America's auto bounty. This impulse would be tested again as Canadian workers, firms, politicians, and consumers tackled the paradigm-changing question of Japanese imports and investment in Canada.

7 Transplant: 'Foreign' Production, Imports, and the Tumultuous Arrival of the Japanese

Deindustrialization and despair stalked the Canadian auto sector in the early 1980s. According to one observer, the industry was 'under siege.' Economist Ross Perry's book, *The Future of Canada's Auto Industry*, described a bleak landscape: 'Plants had been closed, or were only partially used; workers had been laid off in large umbers or were employed for short periods of time; and the industry's momentum of capital investment established since 1978 appeared to have waned … within the industry itself there was a pervasive gloom about the prospects for recovery.'[1] Total assembly and parts employment, which had reached a 1978 peak of about 125,000 workers, tumbled to less than 100,000 in 1982, with thousands of those workers on temporary layoff. The term 'rust belt,' recently coined to describe the industry's malaise, was sadly and quickly coming into common use, and the decline it described looked to be spreading to Canada's Golden Horseshoe.

Now, in the depths of crisis, the industry faced seemingly intractable foes. The long-term trends sparked by the 1973 OPEC embargo had been rapidly accelerated and profoundly exacerbated by a second oil shock, this one caused by the 1979 Iranian Revolution. If 1973 had marked the beginning of North American consumers' shift towards small cars and fuel economy, the Iranian situation indicated that the shift might be more permanent and greater than anyone could have predicted. The 1979 oil spike exacerbated the overall malaise in the North American economy. High interest rates, high unemployment, and high inflation all collided in the early 1980s to create a perfect storm, one that the auto industry – and Chrysler in particular – barely survived.

Of course, Chrysler's near death, which epitomized so much of Perry's dismal assessment, contrasted dramatically with the spectacu-

lar emergence of the Japanese automakers as a global force. In the proverbial blink of an eye, the tables turned dramatically. Whereas the Big
Three had ruled North America virtually uncontested for much of the
post-war period, Japanese products had for most of that time been derided as cheap and undesirable. As late as 1975 Henry Ford II had fam-
ously declared that 'no car with my name on the hood will ever have
a Jap engine' when it was suggested that he consider putting Honda
engines in some Fords.[2]

Yet the arrival of the Japanese in North America could not be stymied by Henry Ford II or anyone else. The Japanese impact – from the
first imports to the 'voluntary' export restraints to the building of the
first Japanese transplants – has been a focus of many scholars.[3] Most
attention has fallen upon the American side of the story, and rightly
so, considering the scale of the Japanese auto wave that transformed
the United States and its auto sector in the 1970s and 1980s. But there
is another aspect of the Japanese arrival that has been somewhat overlooked: given the industry's integrated nature owing to the auto pact,
the Japanese import and investment tsunami had as profound an impact upon Canada as upon the United States – and provoked as sharp a
response from policy makers.[4]

In fact, the Canadian state's reaction was even more aggressive, and
had to be. The decision by Japan's leading automakers to invest created
an internationalized North American automotive environment, but one
that was entirely geared to the United States. If Canada did not receive
what it saw as its fair share of the billions of Japanese auto investment
dollars pledged in the 1980s, the very existence of the Canadian auto
sector was at stake. Thus, not only did Canadian policy makers follow
in the footsteps of their U.S. counterparts by negotiating 'voluntary'
export restraints in the early 1980s, but they took additional dramatic
steps – steps that pushed the limits of international trade law to the
breaking point – to force the Japanese to invest in Canada. These measures, which included an unprecedented port slowdown of Japanese
cars entering Canada at Vancouver and strident demands for local content regulation (not unlike the demands made by many in the United
States), eventually succeeded in helping to persuade the Japanese to
invest in Canada. The measures also included, as we shall see in the following chapter, controversial duty-remission schemes patterned after
those first created in the early 1960s.

The decisions by Honda and Toyota in 1984 and 1985 to build assembly plants in Canada marked a significant victory for Canadians in the

battle for Japanese automotive foreign direct investment. This victory could be primarily attributed to an adaptive and aggressive Canadian government, the differing philosophies of certain Japanese auto multinationals, and the changing international economic circumstances in the 1980s. In another way, the episode also marked the beginning of the end for creative Canadian policy making in the auto field: ironically, successfully luring the Japanese to Canada eventually resulted in the demise of all these policies and, ultimately, of the auto pact itself.

First Wave: Non-Big Three Production in Post-War Canada

The Japanese transplants that arrived in the 1980s were not the first new entrants into the Canadian car industry in the post-war period. A number of manufacturing efforts, both 'domestic' (that is, American) and 'foreign,' began operations after 1945. The first of these was Studebaker, which started and ended production even before the 1973 shock. Studebaker, like Ford, Chrysler, GM, Hudson, Packard, Reo, and a number of other American firms, initially set up shop in Canada in the initial boom times of the auto industry, opening a plant in Windsor in 1910. Production ceased, however, during the Depression in 1936 and did not restart during the war. In 1947 Studebaker, drawn to the potential of the suburban baby boom and the prosperity of post-war Canada, re-entered the Canadian market, taking over a munitions factory in Hamilton, Ontario.[5]

For the next twenty years, Studebaker's Hamilton factory would follow the roller-coaster fortunes of its parent firm, located in South Bend, Indiana. In good times and bad (including a merger with the Packard Corporation in 1956), Studebaker in Canada continued to produce a few car models and maintained a small but loyal following. By the early 1960s, however, the parent company was on its last legs, a victim of relentless competition in the industry. Determined to keep going, the company's management decided to suspend production in Indiana and just build cars in Canada.[6]

For the first time since the demise of Gray-Dort Motors in 1925, Canada had its own auto company. While it was still wholly American owned and produced cars that were designed in the United States, largely for the American market, Studebaker Canada was, as its advertisements proclaimed, the manufacturer of 'Canada's Own Car.' Between 1964 and 1966 the Hamilton plant produced 45,000 vehicles, nearly three-quarters of which were exported to the United States. The

7.1 In the mid-1960s, Hamilton's Studebaker plant produced for all of North America. March 1964. Courtesy of *Hamilton Spectator*.

plant also had a special deal with the Hamilton police department to build cruisers for the hometown force. Studebaker maintained a popular position in the Canadian market and for a short time was a Canadian success story.

But the realities of the modern car market soon caught up to Hamilton's plucky little factory. Without a full line of cars, Studebaker was not an attractive proposition for many car buyers. Moreover, even though Studebaker had smartly carved out a niche market with its smaller, more economic cars after 1960, GM, Ford, and Chrysler all introduced products in this price and size bracket. And, while the Hamilton plant showed a small profit, the Indiana corporation, which had branched out into other consumer products after killing off its auto production in the United States, was not inclined to maintain such a minor operation. Even with the remission plans and the auto pact, Studebaker could not survive. In a final plea for help, Studebaker President Robert Growcock wrote to Ontario Premier John Robarts, without success.[7] In March 1966, 700 Studebaker Canada employees were thrown out of work when the last Studebaker rolled off the assembly line.

The first new 'foreign' manufacturing entry in the post-war period was Volvo. The Swedish company's 1963 assembly plant in Dartmouth, Nova Scotia, was heralded as the harbinger of a 'New Nova Scotia' which could vault the province to the forefront of the manufacturing age.[8] Volvo Chairman Gunnar Engellau explained that the company had established 'our first overseas factory in Nova Scotia because we like the environment very much. Everybody is so enthusiastic there – and that is important. Your government has given us good co-operation.' Moreover, market factors were also a part of the decision. According to Engellau, 'we have chosen Canada because we have the kind of cars that should give us special standing there – and because, too, I have always had a strong feeling for Canadians.'[9] Increasing Volvo sales in Canada in the late 1950s and early 1960s also helped.

One problem, however, was that the pre-auto pact content regulations for automotive production were unrealistic for an operation as small as the one Volvo envisioned for Canada. In 1963 the most-favoured-nation (MFN) tariff rate was 17.5 per cent for all autos and most parts. In order to gain duty-free access for imported parts, a company producing 10,000 units was required to achieve 40 per cent Commonwealth (essentially Canadian) content, while the rates for companies producing 10,000–20,000 units and more than 20,000 units were 50 per cent and 60 per cent, respectively.[10] But with the added cost of importing most parts from Sweden, it was impossible to reach the 10,000-vehicle target in the first period of production without some special dispensation.

As a result, the company was granted a number of tariff concessions by the Diefenbaker government, since Volvo represented a 'special case' involving the establishment of a new enterprise in Canada. In return for assurances that Volvo would train 500 Canadians as mechanics and hire at least 400 production workers, the company received remission of duties on bodies, engines, and parts. Initially, Volvo was allowed to begin production with virtually no Canadian content but was still allowed to import parts duty-free as it increased Canadian content and slowly adapted to the Canadian market. The Volvo production-based remission plan presaged similar plans enacted by the Canadian government for other foreign makers in the 1970s and 1980s.

When the auto pact was implemented, Volvo was included as a bona fide manufacturer under the agreement. But, because of the company's particular circumstances, the government set its requirements at less than those of the Big Three. Though it needed to maintain its ratio of sales to production and base CVA, with 1963–4 as the reference point,

Volvo was required to increase its CVA by only 40 per cent of the growth in its sales, as opposed to the 60 per cent expectation placed upon the Big Three. Additionally, the company's expected additional investment was only $600,000 (compared to the Big Three's $228 million), to be achieved by 1967–8. Volvo further received significant support from the Nova Scotia government, including infrastructure funding, the direct purchase of facilities, and transportation subsidies.[11] Volvo's special treatment marked an important precedent for later foreign ventures that established plants in Canada.

Even then, the company had a difficult time. At the end of 1965, Volvo informed Ottawa that it could meet its ratio targets only if it engaged in 'uneconomic practices,' and it could not meet its growth targets unless it received some concessions from the government.[12] In response, Ottawa agreed to change Volvo's requirements: instead of 40 per cent Canadian content, the company was allowed to hit a 25 per cent Canadian content target by July 1966, rising annually by 5 per cent, so that the 40 per cent figure would be achieved by 31 July 1969. The government also agreed to allow Volvo to invest its additional $600,000 by the end of July 1969.[13]

The concessions helped little. Though output jumped from 1,000 cars in 1963 to nearly 5,000 in 1968 and over 10,000 in 1973, Volvo's president noted that the Halifax plant was the company's most expensive, and that it would actually be cheaper to import cars directly from Sweden.[14] After reaching a 1975 peak of 13,000 vehicles, production consistently dropped under 10,000. By the end of the 1970s, the plant operated as a very rudimentary assembly venture, produced never more than a few thousand vehicles, and employed only hundreds of workers in the province. After its initial burst of enthusiasm, Volvo itself exhibited a lukewarm attitude towards the plant, providing only limited investment and support for its Canadian offspring. The plant closed in 1998.[15]

Another government-supported venture was the Société de Montage Automobile, a Quebec-backed plant building Renault 12s in Saint-Bruno, Quebec. Established in 1965, the $4-million plant was owned by the General Investment Corporation, a Quebec government agency. SOMA lived a precarious existence, with constant shutdowns and speculation of closure. The firm lost money every year of operation, including $130,000 in 1971, despite government subsidies. It survived by importing components from France but faced difficulties breaking into the U.S. market. In February 1972 the plant was suddenly shuttered but restarted production a month later, its 460 employees turning out 300 cars per week. The head of Renault Canada even stated publicly in 1972 that the plant should be closed, since it would never make any money; each car actually cost $200 more to make than to import the same vehicle from France. By January 1973, his wish came true, and the plant was shuttered permanently.[16]

Far more famous than Studebaker, Volvo, or SOMA was the brief yet spectacular story of the Bricklin. Malcolm Bricklin, the car's colourful promoter, had gained a name for himself by bringing Japanese Subaru cars to America beginning in the late 1960s. In the early 1970s he convinced New Brunswick Premier Richard Hatfield to provide financial support for his gull-winged sports car, the SV-1. Betting that the car could vitalize the province's manufacturing sector, Hatfield lent Bricklin the money and helped him establish plants in Saint John and Minto, and eventually New Brunswick took a majority ownership stake in the firm. With great fanfare and publicity, the cars went into production in 1974. But building a brand new car, particularly a flashy high-maintenance sports car immediately after the 1973 oil crisis and during one of the North American auto industry's most difficult periods, was a challenging undertaking. Nor did it help that the car quickly became known as something of a lemon, or that the company was wracked by poor organization and engineering along with and massive cost overruns. By 1976, the company went bankrupt, with less than 3,000 cars built. Bricklin owed the government $23 million.The catastrophe became something of a punchline and provided a cautionary tale of the perils of government intervention.[17]

Though it remains a largely forgotten episode, the Japanese also established their first North American production beachhead in eastern Canada. Announced in 1966, Canadian Motor Industries, or CMI, was a joint venture, 87 per cent of which was owned by the Toyota, Isuzu, and Mitsui companies and the remainder by two Canadian firms, Clairtone Sound and Westcoast Transmission. The Japanese were establishing a foothold in Canada to help market and distribute their vehicles, with the goal of replicating the North American success of other foreign imports, such as VW's Beetle. The initiative also reflected an effort by the Japanese to build upon their trading relationship with Canada, one in which they imported significant raw materials but hoped one day to export some of their manufactured goods.[18]

As with the Volvo plant, Nova Scotia's Industrial Estates Ltd, the provincial development corporation, had a strong hand in the plant's

7.2 Premier Richard Hatfield and Malcolm Bricklin at the Bricklin launch in New York, 1974. Permission of New Brunswick Archives, RS 417-76-12.

creation and early operation, holding an ownership stake and representation on CMI's board. The government's position in the venture, essentially to help finance the national distribution of Toyotas, was held on the condition that CMI establish a plant in the province to produce cars.[19] CMI also signed a Letter of Intent with the Canadian government that granted the company duty-free entry for every car imported for every three complete knock-down units (CKDs) locally assembled, and required CMI to achieve 40 per cent CVA in the cars that it built in Canada.[20]

In 1967 CMI opened its rudimentary assembly plant at Point Edward, Nova Scotia, just outside Sydney. Initially, the plant bolted together CKD Isuzu Belletts shipped from Japan, and its thirty-five workers turned out about 300 vehicles in the first two years. The passage of new safety and emissions regulations precluded further sale of the Belletts in Canada, and so Toyota 'reluctantly,' in the words of Toyota Chairman Eiji Toyota, stepped in to continue operating the plant.[21] After 1968, the facility assembled Toyota Corollas, eventually reaching 1,300

Corolla vehicles (all sold in Canada) of the company's 58,000 total sold in Canada in 1971.

Notwithstanding efforts by the Nova Scotia government to secure an expansion at the plant, and support from the federal government through the Department of Regional Economic Expansion, the Toyota venture amounted to little. The problems were myriad. Each car assembled actually lost Toyota's Canadian operation about $200, and the more cars the facility built actually meant even higher losses.[22] Nor did it help that the Canadian firm had difficulties communicating with Toyota and Mitsui in Japan, both on the manufacturing side and in terms of the distribution of imported vehicles.[23] Atlantic Canadian Toyota dealers refused to accept 1974 model-year Corollas from the plant owing to poor quality.[24] The firm also had a difficult time meeting the CVA requirements, which, like Volvo, required it to ask for forgiveness from the government or face tariff penalties.[25] Transportation costs, the price of the Toyota CKDs, an inability to maintain a steady flow of parts and materials, and labour woes added to the plant's troubles. CMI lost $1.6 million by 1973, and in 1974 Nova Scotia officials felt that the firm had 'no possibility of reaching a break-even point in the near future' and that losses would continue 'at an ever-increasing rate.'[26]

After considering a number of alternatives, including building the Toyota FJ Land Cruiser at the plant (and then increasing the Canadian price for the vehicle), CMI and Toyota decided to close the facility in 1975. Persistent efforts to keep the Japanese in Nova Scotia, including a meeting in Toyota between Eiji Toyoda himself and the Canadian ambassador, could not convince the Japanese automaker to reconsider the decision. The plant was shuttered in late 1975, leaving sixty-three employees out of jobs and having built only 9,008 vehicles in total. CMI claimed that total losses amounted to $3 million, though this was considered to be not unreasonable since 'the cost of the intangible benefits that accrued to the Company as a result of maintaining a manufacturing presence in Canada were charged against the profits earned in the vehicle importing and distributing business.'[27] In the end, Nova Scotia sold its shares back to CMI, and equipment from the Sydney plant was removed and shipped to a Toyota facility in Ireland, where that government had imposed stringent local content requirements on foreign automakers.[28] Toyota and Japanese auto manufacturing in Canada would not return for another decade, and in much different circumstances.

All of these examples of non-Big Three manufacturing in Canada illustrate some basic premises that are important to understanding the eventual response to the question of Japanese investment in Canada in the 1980s. The ventures reflected the corporate philosophies of the firms that established in Canada – companies such as Volvo were willing to take a chance in Canada, as were individuals such as Malcolm Bricklin. Perhaps just as important, the Canadian state – both federal and provincial – usually took a very active role in supporting these ventures, demonstrating the willingness of Canadian policy makers to intervene to encourage automotive FDI. The examples underline a use of public-policy tools outside the auto pact regime to encourage foreign auto investment, tools that would later be used to greater effect in luring companies such as Honda to Canada, and Toyota back to the country.

The auto pact itself was designed to allow third-country companies to be included in the agreement: Canadian negotiators at the GATT had ensured that this was the case; for the United States, the agreement was bilateral and required a GATT exemption.[29] Though only Volvo was a pact member initially, all of the facilities were either considered for auto pact status or were given auto pact-like conditions for duty-free entry. In this sense, the Canadian government was establishing a precedent that new foreign manufacturers could eventually join the auto pact. This precedent would prove contentious in the future.

Further support beyond tariffs, particularly from provinces such as Nova Scotia, Quebec, and New Brunswick, point to the willingness of state actors to promote automotive manufacturing. These efforts, either to maintain existing production or to diversify regional industrial bases, were not always successful. In many instances, they were hampered by shifting market forces and unforeseen external events.

The next wave of 'transplant' operations would emerge dramatically from these market and external events and corporate philosophies, and would challenge Canadian automotive policy makers in a manner that they could never have anticipated.

Prelude to the Second Wave: The Japanese Import 'Invasion'

Imports, like non-Big Three production in Canada, were not simply a post-1973 phenomenon. After the Second World War, non-U.S. imports (considered 'foreign' by Canadians) always had a significant share of the Canadian market, one that often grew whenever the economy took a downswing. In the post-1945 period, European (and later Japanese) automakers, having recovered from the ravages of war, offered smaller, less costly models than the Big Three, which Canadians sought during periods of economic uncertainty. The British, in particular, could export duty-free to Canada owing to preferential tariff policies initiated in the 1930s, and by the late 1950s imports of British cars to Canada increased dramatically as the post-war boom suffered its first slowdown.

The emergence of these imports, and especially 'compacts,' in the Canadian market created a crisis mentality in the auto industry. In 1960 nearly a third of the 300,000 cars purchased in Canada were imports. The Bladen Commission was appointed a year later, in part to study the trade-balance problems associated with foreign imports of small cars such as British Minis.[30] According to CBC reporter Norman DePoe, the word 'compact' was 'taboo' in Oshawa, while George Burt, the Canadian UAW director, called European imports a 'tremendous problem.'[31]

In an effort to fight imports and protect a slipping trade surplus, the Conservative government of John Diefenbaker took a number of steps. It imposed a 10 per cent surcharge on all imports in 1962. Since the growth of imports had also been further encouraged by a strong Canadian dollar, in 1962 the government devalued the dollar to 92.5 cents. The added taxes, coupled with the removal of excise taxes on Canadian-made cars, had a devastating impact on imports of cars from Europe. Prices on British and German cars were discounted, but with little effect. In 1960 imported cars held 28 per cent of the Canadian market; by the end of 1962, the figure had dropped to 14 per cent, and the 'crisis' temporarily subsided.[32]

By the mid-1960s, the imported car market was slowly starting to recover, and included a few newly popular entrants. Though it had been in production since the 1930s, the VW Beetle captured the imagination of the 'Baby Boom' generation and represented an economic and attitudinal rejection of the Big Three. Along with the Europeans, the Japanese had begun to export to Canada. In 1965 Nissan (then known as Datsun) and Toyota both opened sales offices in the country. Honda began selling motorcycles in Canada in 1969 and followed with the establishment of Canadian Honda Motor Ltd a year later. Many Japanese firms would follow these pioneers and set up their own sales operations in Canada in the 1970s.[33]

These early Japanese forays into the Canadian market were modest but grew quickly. In 1965, the year the auto pact came into effect, the Japanese sold less than 3,000 vehicles in Canada, constituting 0.3 per cent of the market. By 1969, Japanese sales had increased to 39,000 vehicles and 4.2 per cent, and in the next year they hit 70,000 vehicles and 9.1 per cent. In the 1970s, Japanese sales in Canada maintained a steady and significant share of the market. Between 1970 and 1979, annual Japanese penetration in the Canadian market averaged approximately 8.5 per cent of light vehicle sales, with a high of 11.7 per cent in 1971 and a low of 6.6 per cent in 1979. [34] (See Table 7.1.) Import growth was enough to necessitate the construction of a $4.5-million loading terminal at the Fraser River in British Columbia in 1972, allowing easier discharge of autos offloaded from the car-transporting vessel *Canada Maru*. On the other side of the country, the Halifax Autoport was processing more than 40,000 Japanese cars arriving annually after 1973. [35]

The Canadian embrace of Japanese imports tracked that of the United States, but with some significant differences. In the 1970s the Japanese share of the U.S. market was considerably larger than in Canada, averaging almost one-tenth, and increased dramatically towards the end of the decade. The difference could be accounted for by a few factors: lower Canadian gasoline costs, thereby negating some of the demand for smaller, more fuel-efficient cars; Canada's fluctuating and often lower-valued dollar; and a Canadian MFN tariff rate of 15 per cent compared to the U.S. rate of 3 per cent. [36] By 1980, Japanese import penetration into the United States had reached more than one-fifth of the market, an astounding 1.9 million cars. Moreover, the Japanese clearly dominated the U.S. import market, taking 80 per cent, versus about two-thirds in Canada, which still purchased quite a few British and European cars. [37] After the Iranian Revolution sparked another upsurge in world oil prices in 1979, however, Japanese sales in Canada also took a significant chunk of the Canadian market. [38] Between 1981 and 1985, the Japanese never took less than one-sixth of the Canadian market. (See Table 7.1.)

The emergence of the Japanese as serious competitors to the Big Three in the 1970s was the consequence of a number of factors. On the one hand, Japanese productivity was superior to that of the United States, and their labour costs were lower. GM representatives complained to Canadian officials that the Japanese advantage per car was approximately $1,500, with $500 resulting from lower wages rates, $500 from better productivity, and $500 from less regulation in Japanese plants. [39] The Carter administration estimated a difference of at least $1,000 per vehicle. [40] The greatest example of this productivity advantage could be seen with Toyota. The Toyota Production System, or TPS, was a model of lean production. It emphasized just-in-time delivery for minimum inventories, 'autonomation' (automation 'with a human touch'), the

Table 7.1
Japanese auto sales in Canada, 1965–86

| Year | Total Canadian Sales | Japanese Sales | | | |
		Cars	Trucks	Total	Share %
1965	830,995	2,834	0	2,834	0.3
1966	827,431	2,742	0	2,742	0.3
1967	815,307	5,617	684	6,301	0.8
1968	889,453	14,731	1,562	16,293	1.8
1969	917,227	35,963	2,814	38,777	4.2
1970	774,372	65,569	4,562	70,131	9.1
1971	938,720	103,631	6,068	109,699	11.7
1972	1,059,091	106,500	13,121	119,621	11.3
1973	1,219,726	111,467	20,421	131,888	10.8
1974	1,246,887	87,609	18,821	106,430	8.5
1975	1,316,629	95,772	16,759	112,531	8.5
1976	1,291,463	101,558	13,948	115,506	8.9
1977	1,344,959	134,900	15,647	150,547	11.2
1978	1,366,544	113,166	13,413	126,579	9.3
1979	1,396,402	79,879	11,832	91,711	6.6
1980	1,263,807	138,107	21,474	159,581	12.6
1981	1,190,882	207,639	28,442	236,081	19.8
1982	920,403	177,483	33,079	210,562	22.9
1983	1,079,940	177,930	40,078	218,008	20.2
1984	1,283,502	166,632	41,779	208,411	16.2
1985	1,530,410	201,323	49,741	251,064	16.4
1986	1,515,920	202,328	53,009	255,337	16.8

Source: DesRosiers Automotive Ltd, Statistics Canada, and company data as cited in JAMA Canada, 'A Short History,' 17.

kanban card system in the factory, workplace harmony and teamwork with an emphasis on worker flexibility, and, above all, the mantra of kaizen, or 'continuous improvement.'[41] As the 1970s wore on, consumers also saw Japanese vehicles as superior in terms of quality.

Along with productivity, labour, and quality advantages, Japanese cars also had the benefit of having met fuel-efficiency and emission standards early on. Honda, for example, had burst upon the import scene with the Civic, a car whose humble exterior hid the company's 'technological triumph': its Compound Vortex Controlled Combustion (CVCC) was the only engine that could meet Clean Air Act standards without a catalytic converter. By 1975, the company was selling

10,000 Civics a month in the United States, many of these in the all-important California market, the continent's largest.[42] Meanwhile, Big Three efforts to build and market a small car had not been so successful. Following Nader's exposé, GM's Corvair was a public-relations nightmare, though its Vega was more successful; Ford's Pinto was a marketing disaster, owing to its dangerous design; and Chrysler didn't really even have a small car until the poorly designed late 1970s Horizon.[43]

Canadians themselves were of two minds when it came to the onslaught of Japanese imports. Clearly, many Canadian consumers welcomed the reliable and fuel-efficient vehicles. The thousands of imports being snapped up were a testament to how badly the Big Three had fumbled matters in their home markets. Even labour leaders such as Ed Finn, public-relations director for the Canadian Brotherhood of Railway Workers, reasoned that 'Canadians are buying more Japanese cars because of their quality and reliability – because they've lost faith in the American product, whether it's made in Detroit or Windsor.' Finn added a personal view: 'I switched to a foreign import when I got tired of waiting for the Big Three to respond to the demand for a smaller car that didn't have to be recalled every second month; and I guess another million or more Canadians did the same.' Finn felt guilty about owning a four-year-old Honda – but not that guilty. In his view, the UAW was not to blame for the current predicament; the fault rather lay with the management of the Big Three.

Other Canadians were not so welcoming of the mass of Japanese imports and struck a nationalist chord. One concerned citizen complained that the 'people who buy foreign cars are probably the ones who scream when the unemployment rate goes up … If we are to maintain a reasonably sound economic future, we must learn to back our own country first.'[44] Bert Weeks, the mayor of Windsor, poured $500,000 into a 'Buy The Cars Your Neighbours Help Build!' campaign, part of a fifty-city North American effort to get people to buy 'domestic' vehicles.[45] Weeks and the rest of the mayors of Ontario's automotive cities passed resolutions calling for Canadian government measures to 'better control' imports and 'closely monitor' other countries so that Canada was not a victim to 'dumping' or 'other unfair trade practices.'[46]

By the fall of 1980, Canadian policy makers were becoming deeply concerned about the import situation. It was not simply that increased Japanese penetration of the U.S. market meant a possible decrease in output for Canadian plants, which exported more than 80 per cent of their production south. The Carter administration was not keen to apply pressure on the Japanese to reduce their exports. But, with rampant speculation about U.S. unilateral action such as import quotas, or new tariffs, or a 'voluntary restraint agreement' (VRA) with Japan, it looked inevitable that the uncontrolled flow of imports to America was going to end.[47] But what was to stop Japan from diverting cars to Canada if the Americans were able to slow Japanese imports? American protectionism towards Japanese imports could have a devastating effect upon the Canadian market.

In Ottawa, the government considered its rather unpleasant options. Any moves would have to 'correspond fairly closely to any US action,' because of the integrated nature of the Canada-U.S. industry. A surtax on imports could be levied under section 8 of the federal Customs Tariff if it was determined that these imports were causing or threatening serious injury to Canadian producers. This strategy, however, was undermined by the fact that the Canadian industry produced mostly larger cars, while the Japanese exported smaller cars, and the level of Japanese penetration was still below that of the United States. Also, given that Canada did export more than 80 per cent of its production, it would be difficult to argue that Japanese imports were hurting domestic production. A surtax would be 'criticized by importers and consumer groups unless the situation deteriorate[d] significantly,' might be contrary to GATT rules, and would last for only 180 days unless extended by Parliament.[48]

At the same time, the Canadians were constrained by the need to wait for the results of a U.S. International Trade Commission investigation into the effects of the Japanese imports initiated by the UAW and supported by Ford. Under section 201 of the Tariff Act, if it was determined that Japanese imports were causing harm to U.S. producers, the United States could increase its tariff, impose new tariffs or quotas, negotiate an agreement between the two countries, or any combination thereof. Again, since a U.S. tariff could be contrary to GATT, Canadian officials thought that the United States would likely seek a negotiated agreement. The U.S. situation was further complicated by the impending presidential election. President Carter might seek to make the import issue a centrepiece of his campaign, which could affect the outcome of the Japanese-U.S. auto issue and thus spill over into Canada.[49]

In November 1980 the ITC voted not to recommend quota or tariff restrictions on auto imports. The ITC stated that high interest rates, high gas costs, and the generally slow economy were to blame for the woes of the American auto sector, not Japanese imports. In the wake of the

7.3 'I think it's a Japanese car in disguise.' *Calgary Herald*, 15 May 1981. Courtesy of Glenbow Museum and Archives.

decision, however, calls for restrictions actually increased. In response to the ruling, the UAW, Ford, and their congressional allies pushed Carter to seek a negotiated voluntary restriction by the Japanese of their exports to the United States, which Carter was reluctant to do.[50] For its part, the UAW also called for Japanese investment in the United States. Bob White echoed Doug Fraser by pushing IT&C Minister Herb Gray to demand a Japanese commitment to locate assembly and parts production in Canada: 'Offshore producers who want to assemble vehicles and parts in either Canada or the United States must understand that they have to locate facilities on both sides of the border. This is a common market arrangement and neither country can carve out large sections of that market.'[51]

Soon enough, the Canadian concerns came to pass. In September 1980 the Japanese had announced that they would exercise 'prudence and caution' when it came to automotive exports to the United States. Then, following the 1980 U.S. presidential election, Reagan's new USTR, William Brock, phoned Gray to tell him that the United States was about to reach an agreement with the Japanese, while giving him only the barest of details. This would be a Japanese initiative, without any formal U.S. involvement (which would be contrary to U.S. anti-trust regulations and the GATT), and Brock hinted at a 'ball park' import cut of 10 per cent. Reports were also beginning to circulate that Secretary of State Alexander Haig was to take the lead in the discussions.[52]

In an effort to glean more information, Campbell Stuart, head of IT&C's Automotive Task Force, also met with U.S. officials in Washington to get a sense of the direction of the Japanese-American talks. Stuart was told by the Americans that, while no firm details of a U.S.-Japanese agreement had been reached, the Japanese had been warned that something had to be done. He was also told that U.S. producers were to get some regulatory relief through the easing of emission and fuel-economy standards, saving the Big Three up to US$2.5 billion. In turn, Stuart reiterated Canada's need to be kept abreast of any U.S.-Japanese developments, and reminded the Americans that 'Canada is in a very vulnerable position if vehicle exports to the US are restrained.' This already seemed to be happening – the 1980 figures showed that Japanese imports had increased by 43 per cent over 1979, sending a further shudder through the government and the industry.[53]

The Japanese had assured the Canadians through diplomatic channels that, if they imposed restrictions for the United States, they would do so for Canada as well. But, since details were scarce, Ottawa remained concerned as to how the Japanese-U.S. VRA might impact the Canadian market. With the fluid situation in Washington (USTR officials were 'shocked' by Haig's rumoured takeover of the talks), senior Canadian bureaucrats advised Gray that Canada should begin discussions with the Japanese towards their own restriction agreement. A good opening position was to offer the 1980 level of Japanese imports. The Canadian officials recommended that Gray call upon the Japanese ambassador to ensure that there was no diversion to the Canadian market, and that if diversion in fact happened, to tell him that Canada 'would be forced to take prompt action under Canadian law.' They also recommended that a small team be sent to Tokyo to open discreet talks.[54]

Before Gray could begin his Japanese gambit, he had to deal with the concerns of the Canadian industry, united in its condemnation of the import surge. In Ottawa in early April 1981, the MVMA, the APMA, and the UAW all met together with Gray. It was, according to American Motors President W. Pickett, the 'first time all three groups had met with the government in a united approach to a problem.' Ford Canada's Roy Bennett stated unequivocally that all segments of the industry were committed to the same cause: the government must ensure that 'either Japanese exports be restrained or that the Japanese be required to produce vehicles in Canada.' If not, the North American companies would be forced to source overseas to remain competitive.[55]

Bob White seconded Bennett's position and told Gray that the union wanted to see the 15 per cent tariff rate retained, a 10 per cent quota placed on Japanese imports, and the continuation of duty-remission orders which gave the Japanese some incentive to source parts in Canada. At the same time, White proposed that quotas be maintained until the Japanese agreed to 'major commitments to source or invest in Canada proportional to their shares here.' In response, Gray noted all the actions that he had taken, including his discussions with both the Americans and the Japanese. He told the meeting that 'the US situation was coming to a head' and that he would keep everyone informed of developments. In the general discussion that ensued, the industry again argued strongly for Japanese investment in Canada. Gray concluded by indicating that he realized the symbolic importance of such a unified front by the industry and its workers, and assured them that he would convey their sentiments to cabinet.[56]

With the Canadian industry's views in hand, Gray went into action. In March he met with USTR Brock and Commerce Secretary Howard Baldridge to press the Americans to consult with Canada before making any final move regarding imports. Then, in early April, he met with the Japanese ambassador to express plainly the Canadian government's views. Within a week, a Canadian delegation was flying to Tokyo to meet with Japanese officials. The April meetings in Japan were not meant to be negotiations but simply an occasion to reiterate the views that Gray had expressed to the ambassador, particularly the need for coincidental Japan-Canada action if the Japanese came to an understanding on restrictions with the United States. Canadian officials also hoped that the meetings would provide an opportunity to get a sense of where the Japan-U.S. discussions were at. Further meetings with the Japanese in Washington in late April were meant, in Gray's words, to 'bring [the] Americans up to date on our approach in the matter.' When the smoke cleared from this shuttle diplomacy, Canadian officials were still unsure where they stood: though it looked as if the United States and Japan had come to some agreement, 'the modalities [were] still obscure.' It was necessary for further talks with the Japanese, es-

7.4 Actually, the UAW's Bob White was as deeply concerned as the Big Three about foreign sales. By John Larter, *Toronto Star*, 8 August 1980. Reprinted with permission – Torstar Syndication Services.

pecially since Japanese officials at the Ministry of International Trade and Industry (MITI) had essentially admitted that 'undesirable' effects for Canada might flow from any limiting of exports to the American market.[57]

The abrupt announcement of the U.S.-Japanese VRA in the midst of Canada-Japan talks sparked a new round of concern for Canadian policy makers. The 1 May 1981 VRA meant a reduction of Japanese imports by about 8 per cent below 1980 U.S. levels, with an increase of up to

7.5 The Japanese auto import wave, 1981. *Calgary Herald*, 13 May 1981. Courtesy of Glenbow Museum and Archives.

16.5 per cent of the growth of the U.S. market in the second year. This meant a decrease in Japanese imports from 1.9 million vehicles to approximately 1.75 million. A third year was to be negotiated at the end of the second year. At the same time, it was clear that the Japanese had already begun limiting their exports to the United States well before the 1 May formal announcement. This had resulted in some diversion to the Canadian market: in March 1981 Japanese exports to Canada reached a record 24,000 units. This constituted over one-fifth of the Canadian market, was 115 per cent higher than the previous year's figure, and represented an annualized rate of nearly 300,000 vehicles – much higher than any other year and disproportionately large in comparison to the U.S. market. The Japanese boom raised the ire of the MVMA's James Dykes and the UAW's Bob White, who both complained to Gray.[58]

With the U.S.-Japanese deal agreed upon before any clear understanding had been established between Canada and Japan, Gray felt that events were 'overtaking' the Canadians. On 1 May, the day the U.S.

VRA was announced, he called in the Japanese ambassador in Ottawa to reiterate the government's initial points about needing to come to some agreement to avoid diversion of Japanese exports from the United States to Canada. Gray also told the ambassador that he wanted to be able to report that some progress was being made on the issue before Prime Minister Trudeau met with his Japanese counterpart, Zenko Suzuki, upon the latter's visit to Ottawa on 9 May.[59]

A firm response needed to be formulated as quickly as possible to deal with the situation. In early May, Gray brought the outlines of the Canadian strategy before cabinet and asked for authority to push for a rollback of Japanese exports to Canada. In cabinet, it was concluded that such an outcome was likely only if the government 'made clear its resolve to consider unilateral action if necessary.'[60] The opening Canadian position was that the Japanese restrict their exports to the 1980 level of 143,000 vehicles sold in Canada (versus 158,000 cars exported). Failing a negotiated agreement, IT&C officials were committed to a unilateral plan that would see any increase in exports from the 1980 level (including 'captive imports,' such as Chrysler's Japanese exports to Canada) slapped with a 50 per cent surtax. This plan, supported by Chrysler and the UAW, also called for an auto pact exemption, in that cars exported from the United States would not be counted as part of the measure to restrain. The consequences of a unilateral Canadian tariff response, as opposed to a settlement with the Japanese, could be far-reaching: notwithstanding the flood of cars eastward, Canada still had a $1.6-billion trade surplus with Japan, albeit one that was vastly tied to raw exports.[61]

Inside the government, the reaction to Gray's proposal was not entirely enthusiastic. The Finance Department, for instance, was agreeable to the general approach espoused by Gray, but officials wanted to allow imports of up to 18.7 per cent of the Canadian market (which would match the U.S. restrictions), resulting in approximately 170,000 to 175,000 cars, significantly higher than the initial IT&C target of 143,000.[62] The number of cars was significant, since it had a direct impact on the functioning of the auto pact: higher Japanese sales would mean lower domestic (that is, Big Three) sales, which, under the production-to-sales ratios established by the auto pact, would result in lower production. If these sales/production levels were not maintained, the Big Three might shift some of their output to the United States.

Ultimately, Gray acceded to the higher figure and began negotiations with the Japanese in earnest. Following a meeting between Trudeau and Japanese Prime Minister Suzuki, in which the Canadian leader raised the issue, cabinet granted Gray authority to engage the Japanese. After more talks in Tokyo, it was becoming clear that the Japanese were finally 'seized of the nature of the Canadian problem, and [were] willing to grapple with it.'[63]

By late May, it seemed as though a breakthrough had been achieved. The Japanese MITI had agreed to the principle of export restraint, though it had not met most of Gray's specific target figures. Indeed, the targets were much higher than Gray had initially aimed for. The Japanese agreed to introduce a one-year 'weather forecast' system to work with Japanese producers in overseeing exports to Canada. Through this weather forecast, exports for the 1981–2 year would be restricted to a maximum of 174,213 units, or a maximum increase of 10 per cent over the 1980–1 market (though an actual decrease of about 6 per cent for the 1981 calendar year). For 1982–3, MITI agreed to consult with the Canadians to assess the situation further, but ultimately it simply 'noted' the Canadian view that the increase for that year should be no greater than 16.5 per cent of the increase in the Canadian car market in the first year. A third year would also be subject to review, following further discussions between the two countries. Significantly, the agreement did not include trucks, or station wagons, and only covered passenger cars.[64]

Following sharp discussions within cabinet, the agreement was accepted in early June and formalized through a letter from MITI Minister Rokusuke Tanaka. On 4 June, Gray announced that the government had managed to achieve a voluntary export restraint (VER) program not dissimilar to the VRA in the United States. Diversion to the Canadian car industry would not occur, at least not on an uncontrolled scale, and the sales-to-production ratios of the Big Three would not be eroded further, which could threaten Canadian production. By August, Japanese car sellers were already complaining about the adverse effects of the agreement, since the bulk of their imports had to be reduced in the latter half of the restraint year to make up the cutbacks. Owing to the breakdown in the 'voluntary' restraint, smaller sellers such as Subaru and Mazda were particularly hard hit, since they had a smaller share of the Canadian market. They simply could not sell enough cars to meet the demand and stay under the quota.[65]

The reaction to the VER program reflected the difficulties that this restraint represented. Some Canadians saw the 'quotas' as an attack on free choice and an admission that the North American auto industry deserved what it got. A letter to the editor of the *Toronto Star*, written by Colin Kemp-Jackson of Mississauga, was typical in his lament that 'apparently, Canada's bloated, overpaid monolith of inefficiency – laughingly known as the auto industry – can't sell its crummy product unless it is almost literally rammed down our collective throats.' Kemp-Jackson's harangue continued: 'What the auto industry fails to recognize is that this embarrassing display of unqualified panic tells us that Japanese cars must be far superior to domestic ones. The recent antics of the auto industry are the ravings of desperate, frightened men who are running blind from the mirror of their own actions.' These views were echoed by others, who placed the blame for the industry's woes directly on the Big Three and criticized the treatment of the Japanese. Most of those against the VERs identified the Canadian consumer as the biggest loser of the policy, a finding confirmed by a 1985 federal government report which found that the restraints raised prices (Japanese dealers claimed up to $1,500 per car) and hampered choice in the market.[66]

On the other hand, some Canadians did not think that the agreements went far enough. Sam Gindin of the UAW echoed Bob White's views when he argued that 'there is no solution to the problem if we don't force the Japanese to provide a fair share of jobs to Canada.' Constraints were a 'short-term measure' which could be effective only if they were one part of a larger industrial strategy. Municipal politicians in Scarborough, Ontario, also thought that the government should force the import makers to start building their cars in Canada.[67] In this vein, some criticized the VERs as an explicit admission that Canada's American-centric automotive approach had failed: 'Canada must emulate Japan, and bring its industry under Canadian ownership. US ownership has abjectly failed the Canadian people and leaves Canada with a trade deficit in automotive products of $2.6 billion and thousands of destroyed jobs.'[68]

Editorials across the nation reflected this hostile view. Even before the VER announcement, the usually pro-Liberal *Toronto Star* argued that import quotas were 'unwise' and consistently voiced its displeasure at the policy. The North American industry needed instead to focus on building the better cars that the public actually wanted. 'Protecting the auto industry now with quotas that deliver up the public as a captive market,' continued the *Star*, 'would be unfair to the public – and in the long run, could be harmful to the industry itself.' But, when the final agreement was announced, the *Star* considered it a 'fair solution,' in that it did not impose hard quotas but gave 'the ailing domestic auto industry a fair chance to regain its feet, while not unfairly limiting consumers' choice.' The *Montreal Gazette* was against the import restrictions, as was the *Globe and Mail*.[69] Meanwhile, the Automobile Importers Association of Canada released a report which argued that replacing 40,000 imports with domestically produced cars would actually result in a *loss* of 176 Canadian jobs overall.[70]

As the battle over import restraints dragged on, ordinary Canadians seemed to be conflicted over the 'voluntary' quotas. The federal government was deeply concerned that the issue could enflame regional tensions: westerners and Atlantic Canadians were being forced to pay higher prices for cars in order to protect central Canada's industry.[71] Meanwhile, competing polls illustrated an increasing polarization of public opinion. A survey commissioned by the Canadian Association of Japanese Auto Dealers (CAJAD) showed that 98 per cent of Canadians were in favour of 'freedom of choice in automobile buying,' but another poll, by Wilfrid Laurier University, had Canadians almost evenly split on the specific question of quotas, with 52 per cent in favour and 48 per cent against. The polls seemed only to fan the emotions of the debate, with APMA head Patrick Lavelle calling the CAJAD poll 'outrageous propaganda.'[72]

Notwithstanding these strident responses to the VERs, they remained in place for the rest of the decade, during periods of both Liberal and (after 1984) Conservative government.[73] Annual discussions were held between Canadian and Japanese officials over the yearly 'forecast' of how many cars the Japanese would 'restrict themselves' to in the Canadian market. The restraint figure fluctuated somewhat but generally increased over the period between 1981 and 1987, and the Japanese averaged approximately 18 per cent of the Canadian market in these years. More important, the annual meetings between Japan and Canada became a site of contention over the level of Japanese imports and, eventually, the question of Japanese investment in Canada.

Second Wave: The 'Yokohama Squeeze' and Japanese Automotive Investment

The North American protectionist backlash sparked by the wave of Japanese imports did not stop at import restraints. While the quotas remained central to both the United States and Canada's response to the import 'crisis,' demands for local content requirements, increased parts purchases, and direct investment by the Japanese in assembly plants in North America became a growing part of the discourse surrounding the Japanese after 1980. But for Canadian policy makers, this shift in discourse threatened to leave them out of the key solution to the Japanese import problem: direct investment by Japan in establishing assembly and parts operations *in Canada*.

Japanese auto investment in Canada was not beyond the realm of possibility. There had been the Toyota-CMI facility in Nova Scotia, while Hino had set up a CKD operation for its diesel trucks in British Columbia in 1974. As early as 1969, Nobohiku Ushiba, Japan's deputy minister of foreign affairs, proclaimed that 'it may not be too farfetched to think that in the future Japanese industries will come to this country for manufacturing here, or for export to other countries.' Tapping into the ethos of the moment, Ushiba declared that 'in this Apollo age, we don't have to be frightened by the wide distances between Saskatchewan and Japan.' A 1975 MITI study suggested that Japan would have to increase its overseas investment by thirteen times, to $90 billion, in order to maintain its economic growth, though this investment was to be largely focused on commodity production.[74] For all these positive signs, automotive investment had not materialized for Canada and, ominously for Canadians, seemed to be heading to the United States instead.

In the spring of 1980, reports out of Tokyo that Japanese automakers were considering building plants in the United States prompted the Canadian government to complain in earnest about the lack of Japanese auto investment north of the border. Herb Gray warned that 'Canada means business when it comes to getting a fair share of auto investment,' and the country would do whatever it took to ensure that Canada was not shut out of any Japanese investment.[75] Gray's successor as IT&C minister, Ed Lumley, was just as keen to 'encourage' the Japanese to set up operations in Canada. Canadian assemblers, the parts industry, and labour were also in favour of direct Japanese investment in Canada. Industry-UAW meetings since the onset of the import controversy had resulted in a continued unified call for the Japanese to build (with Canadian content) where they sold. White even went to Japan to try to convince industry leaders there that 'Canada and the Canadian UAW should have their own relationship with Japan, separate from the US,' one that included production.[76]

James Dykes of the MVMA felt that 'the Japanese should recognize the principle that automotive companies participating in the Canadian market should invest, provide employment and create value within

7.6 The battle between the United States and Canada over Japanese auto investment was often no-holds-barred. Patrick Corrigan, *Toronto Star*, 12 July 1986. Reprinted with permission – Torstar Syndication Services.

Canada commensurate with the benefit received.'[77] When he visited Ottawa in May 1980, Japanese Prime Minister Masayoshi Ohira was told in no uncertain terms that 'in any consideration of overseas investment by the Japanese vehicle manufacturing industry, the importance of the Canadian market [should] be taken fully into account.' After USTR Reubin Askew went to Japan to demand investment in the United States, Gray called the Japanese ambassador to warn him of Canada's 'strong interest in ensuring that we obtain our fair share of automotive investment and in the sourcing of parts in North America.'[78]

As with the quotas, the investment issue was quickly becoming an urgent concern. The United States was already getting some Japanese investment and banging the drum for more. While Gray was busy warning the Japanese to start investing 'or else,' the Carter administration made it clear to the Japanese that they needed to increase their investment in the United States and to allow American products access to Japan. UAW President Doug Fraser had also travelled to Japan in 1980 to persuade the Japanese to start building in the United States. In response to these entreaties, Honda committed itself to car production in Ohio to supplement its motorcycle plant, Nissan announced a truck plant, and Toyota began actively studying potential sites for investment.[79]

Despite these initial investment announcements, many Americans were still demanding harsher measures against the Japanese. As early as December 1980, the UAW asked president-elect Reagan to enact a North American content requirement designed to curtail Japanese exports.[80] Both the Carter and Reagan administrations sought to temper the anti-Japanese backlash by maintaining the VRAs, but Congress became a focal point for additional trade measures. A number of trade-restriction bills emerged, and in December 1982 the House of Representatives narrowly passed a bill requiring an upward scale of local content; if a company sold 100,000 cars in America, it required 10 per cent local content, a figure that increased up to 90 per cent if a company sold 900,000 cars. House Speaker Tip O'Neill called the measure 'a symbol to the nations of the world, especially Japan. We're sick and tired of the way the Japanese Government has been treating Americans, tracking our American industry and stealing it.' Though the bill did not make it through the Senate, it signalled the depth of U.S. politicians' displeasure over Japanese imports.[81]

Importantly, the U.S. domestic content legislation being considered in Congress excluded Canada, even though the two industries were integrated. This caused deep concern in Ottawa, where officials realized that growing U.S. protectionism through content requirements towards the Japanese could be even more damaging to Canada than voluntary restraints.[82] Auto workers realized this, too, and Solidarity House called for North American content, not U.S. content.[83] The congressional threat of content requirements could be devastating – and not just for the Japanese.

The Japanese quickly got the message and promptly took action to avoid further and more damaging American measures. By 1982, two of the Japanese Big Three exporters, Nissan and Honda, had either confirmed plans to begin production in the United States or had actually started production there. Honda, which had a long-standing policy of building where the firm sold its products, opened the first Japanese assembly plant in the United States in Marysville, Ohio, in 1982. The company also wanted to boost its sales figures, which were limited by a small quota figure under the VRA, and was in any event already at full capacity at its Japanese plants. Nissan, Japan's second-largest producer, opened its first American plant in Tennessee in 1982. Toyota, Japan's automotive leader, remained officially uncommitted to American production, but that could quickly change.[84]

In Canada, what little previous Japanese auto investment existed had ended quietly. CMI had ceased production in 1975, abandoning its Nova Scotia plant. Even with the quotas in full swing, the Japanese seemed to have forgotten Canada and were focused upon satisfying the demands of the giant American market. When Ontario Industry Minister Larry Grossman visited Japan in 1979, he impressed upon his hosts the need for auto investment in Canada. Though he realized that the Japanese were sure to build 'a great number' of assembly plants in the United States, he hoped 'a couple' might be built in Ontario. More likely, though, he realized that the Japanese were not interested in assembling vehicles in Canada, but that at least it 'would be fair and equitable to do a great deal of auto parts purchasing from Canada.'[85]

In the face of this seeming Japanese indifference, a harder line, one that included calls for Canadian content in exchange for the right to sell in Canada, was quickly becoming part of the Canadian discourse with the Japanese. In advance of his March 1982 trip to Japan, Lumley met with the assemblers, parts makers, and the UAW, who stood united for some sort of content requirement for the Japanese. The industry/labour group proposed that, by 1984, Japanese automakers selling 10,000 or more vehicles in Canada should face Canadian-content requirements similar to those already faced by other manufacturers. Though Lumley could not confirm that the government had a specific target in mind, he did concede that 'I don't think anybody's against the general principle of content.'[86]

Lumley's sabre-rattling on content did little to move the Japanese. He returned from his visit to Japan with no agreement but more than ever committed to 'do something to dramatically emphasize our sincere desire to ensure the long-term viability of our automotive industry.'[87] To make matters worse for Lumley and the Canadian industry, Japanese imports seemed to be rising in Canada: there might have been 'voluntary' restraint agreements, but these did not cover light trucks, which had surged in 1982 to over 30,000 vehicles, pushing the total Japanese imports well over the 'forecast' target of 177,000 vehicles. (See Table 7.1.)

The Japanese trip was not a total loss, however. The excursion provided Lumley with a stroke of inspiration as to what to do about the Japanese unwillingness to invest in Canada. A dramatic move that pushed the limits of international trade rules, Lumley's idea was a show of grit that might just make the Japanese finally pay heed to the Canadian demands. As he later recalled, 'On one of my trips to Japan, I learned about some boatloads of European vehicles sitting in the harbour in Tokyo. They had been sitting there for a considerable period because they did not meet a regulatory standard. That's when the light went on. We could do something similar to help make our point. We would demonstrate our resolve by slowing down the delivery of Japanese vehicles to Canada.'[88] And that's exactly what Lumley did.

Upon returning to Canada, he proposed to cabinet that inspection of Japanese vehicle imports be slowed to a regulatory crawl. After all, as he told his cabinet colleagues, 'Canada was not taken seriously at the bargaining table because our own market was too open, particularly in terms of applying existing non-tariff barriers against countries which practice similar measures against Canadian exports.' Though his proposal 'to rigidly enforce customs procedures at the Port of Vancouver for Japanese cars represented a non-tariff barrier' (to which he was 'philosophically opposed'), Lumley felt that Canada had little choice. It was a risky strategy, but if the Japanese could do it, why couldn't Canada? The stakes were high: Lumley was convinced the future of the Canadian auto industry hung in the balance.[89]

What one observer called the 'Yokohama Squeeze' was put into action on Lumley's orders in April 1982. Though the Japanese protested the scheme, Lumley held firm, and by late April he had ordered that 'stronger enforcement action be taken by Canada Customs at the point of entry.'[90] At the Port of Vancouver, customs manager Vincent Castonguay explained that he was now 'going by the book and examining 10 per cent of the cars coming in, instead of less than 1 per cent, which was the previous practice.' With the recession in full swing and imports of other goods down, Castonguay happily had the manpower to do the inspections 'properly.' At Fraser Wharves Ltd, where import leader Toyota landed its cars, shipments of 1,400 to 1,500 cars were soon taking about twenty days to process instead of only one or two days, and ships were backing up outside the port.[91] Along with nearly 200,000 vehicles, the Yokohama Squeeze was being imported into Canada.

The port slowdown quickly had the desired effect. By July 1982, there were between 10,000 and 16,000 cars backed up in Vancouver, and Japanese dealers across the country were apoplectic. For Toyota Canada President Yukiyasu Togo, the move smacked of unfairness. His company was operating legally under international trade rules, and his dealers were angry with the delays. Other Toyota and Datsun executives claimed that their dealers had to lay off staff and faced bankruptcy because of the month-long postponements in receiving car shipments. The newly established Canadian Association of Japanese Automobile

7.7 Offloading thousands of cars at Fraser Wharves, Vancouver, where the 'Yokohama Squeeze' port slowdown had its greatest impact. Image courtesy of Fraser Wharves.

Dealers met with Lumley in Ottawa to air its complaints just days before his next round of talks with the Japanese. But Lumley held firm. There would be no let-up on the port slowdown unless the Japanese did something to help the Canadian car sector beyond limiting their exports.[92]

In the midst of the slowdown, Canadian fears about Japanese investment in the United States sharpened considerably. In the spring of 1983, GM and Toyota announced that they were taking joint ownership of an abandoned California car plant to produce low-cost vehicles for the American market. The GM-Toyota joint venture brought home the reality that full-scale Japanese investment in the United States had arrived. Unlike the Honda facility in Ohio, which was a small operation expected to have an annual production of 50,000 units, the Fremont GM-Toyota venture aimed at 200,000 vehicles. More significantly, Honda was a much smaller player in Japan, while the move by industry leader (and traditionally much more cautious) Toyota to build in the American market signified that the Japanese Big Three were indeed committed to producing in North America. Although the announcement was accompanied by a Japanese promise to continue limiting exports to both Canada and the United States, the New United Motor Manufacturing Inc. (NUMMI) joint venture illustrated the obvious possibility that Canada stood a good chance of being left out of an expected wave of Japanese investment upon the continent.[93]

The Japanese remained seemingly impervious to the Canadian measures. The quotas and the port slowdown had not produced any commitment to Canadian assembly by Japanese manufacturers. Frustrated by a lack of movement on the file, Lumley took the next step. In late 1982 he had established an Automotive Task Force which included Robert White of the UAW, Patrick Lavelle of the APMA, and the heads of the Canadian Big Three. All had been calling for harsh measures against the Japanese, including significant content requirements. When the task force published its report in 1983, the document called for just such a step, which Lumley now happily embraced.[94]

According to the Japanese Automotive Manufacturers Association of Canada (JAMA Canada), created in response to Lumley's moves, the task force's recommendations were totally unfair: 'Such overtly protectionist measures would not only have been contrary to GATT, but would also have resulted in higher prices for consumers, reduced competition and jeopardized a positive trade relationship with Japan.' Nonetheless, along with the port slowdown, the task force's report did have some impact, as JAMA itself later admitted: 'The provocative nature of the report did succeed in getting the attention of Japanese automakers and the Japanese government, and opened the door for bilateral discussions and negotiations.'[95]

There was a measure of public support for the bold demands being made by Lumley and his allies. The *Globe and Mail* seconded the task force's recommendations and opined that the call for content was fair: 'Japanese automakers may sell as many cars as they wish here – indeed, can take over the whole market if they are good enough – as long as their cars have 60 per cent Canadian content.' Moreover, the need for investment in Canada was urgent, especially given the emerging Japanese moves in the United States: 'The principle is that they participate in the industry here, not merely knock it off at long range. It is a principle Japan has already begun to recognize in the United States.'[96] Others were not so supportive: the *Toronto Star* argued that government should focus on ensuring that the Canadian sector was not merely 'assemblers and salesmen of cars' and push for a stronger parts industry and more R&D instead of focusing on 'neutralizing' foreign competition.[97]

The 1983 Speech from the Throne, which set out Canadian policy for the upcoming parliamentary session, signalled a further hardening of the Canadian position, one that built upon the task force's report. The speech promised that the government would seek a 'Japan-Canada auto pact' aimed at gaining 'additional production facilities and parts procurement' in Canada.[98] The throne speech was followed by a January 1984 trip to Japan by Lumley to talk to Japanese automakers about the benefits of investing in Canada: 'Japanese auto companies have made large investments in many countries throughout the world, including several billion dollars in the US, and we are actively seeking our fair share of Japanese investment and sourcing in Canada.'[99] After his trip Lumley reported back to cabinet that he expected 'a minimum of $250 million in investment commitments would be made' over the next six months. He also told his colleagues that 'the Japanese were extremely fearful of the prospect of content legislation in Canada, and were extremely anxious to accommodate Canadian concerns in a fair way.'[100] Nonetheless, in February, in one of his final meetings before announcing his retirement as prime minister, Trudeau met with White and a delegation of UAW representatives who lobbied heavily for content regulations and presented him with a petition in support of the idea bearing more than 100,000 signatures.[101]

As the deadline for the extension of the VERs loomed in March 1984, Lumley and new International Trade Minister Gerald Regan (Lumley had switched to the regional industrial expansion portfolio) further pushed the issue. Regan told the Japanese that restraints would remain until they promised to invest in Canada, and threatened to demand a further quota cut. While Regan pressed for an extension of the quotas, Lumley sought out promises of investment. On one of a series of trips to Japan, Lumley indicated that he was 'looking for early results from our discussions and will be pressing hard for further Japanese investment and sourcing in Canada,' and he hinted that a significant investment was in the works.[102]

In the face of all of these measures, a trickle of Japanese auto investment was starting to appear. In 1981, during a meeting of the Canada-Japan Businessman's Committee meeting and at the height of the export-restraint discussions, Toyota had expressed interest in building aluminum wheels in British Columbia. The Japanese had already shown interest in British Columbia as an investment site, given its geographic location. In 1966 Titan Steel and Wire had built a $2-million facility in North Surrey, British Columbia. The plant was the first Japanese-Canadian joint venture, co-owned by the Mitsui conglomer-

7.8 A thorn in their side: Ed Lumley with Nissan President Yutaka Kume, 1984. Image courtesy of the Japanese Automotive Manufacturers Association of Canada.

ate, Kobe Steel Works, and Hercules Steel of Vancouver.[103] In the early 1980s, the idea of developing more Japanese investment in the province was rekindled, in part to weather the criticism that Japanese companies faced over the imports issue.

Toyota decided to consider a British Columbia site after holding secret negotiations with Premier Bill Bennett. Taking advantage of Alcan's nearby Kitimat smelter and a Canadian government promise that the company could deduct the duty on incoming cars equivalent to the value of the wheels sold to Japan, Toyota decided to go ahead with the project. Though the figures were not large in terms either of the wheels produced (an estimated volume of 240,000 wheels valued at about $8.4 million) or the duty that could be saved under the remission order (it amounted to only hundreds of thousands of dollars), Canadian Auto Parts Toyota Inc. (CAPTIN) marked an important step in Japanese investment in Canada.[104]

Not surprisingly, the Japanese claimed that the wheel plant's construction was threatened by Lumley's port slowdown. In October 1982 Toyota Canada president Yukiyasu Togo decried the 'harassment' that the customs slowdown at Vancouver represented, and hinted that it might scuttle the plant. 'This kind of negative situation is discouraging the top management of Toyota,' Togo told reporters. Toyota was 'being asked to invest money in Canada but the Canadian Government is pressuring them.' The company had 'very mixed feelings' about the plant and the overall situation in Canada because of the port slowdown. At the same time, Togo was cognizant of the need for government support for the venture: 'A wheel plant itself doesn't pay. We expect a loss unless we get help from the Government, such as the duty-free importation of tools.'[105]

Despite Togo's comments, he announced that the plant would go ahead in November 1982. Though all parties denied that the port slowdown had anything to do with the final decision, Togo did say that 'I hope this will be helpful to change the (Canadian) Government's attitude toward the import of Japanese cars.'[106] The plant was a small investment, but Toyota hinted that it could be a stepping stone to further production. Toyota Chairman Eiji Toyoda himself stated that, if the venture was a 'success, we will be thinking of the next step. We would probably be considering other types of parts.'[107] Canadian policy makers were hopeful that the Japanese giant was thinking of more than just parts.

Yet it was not the Japanese industry leader Toyota but Honda, Japan's third-largest carmaker, which first made the historic decision to locate an assembly plant in Canada. In keeping with the firm's philosophy to produce where the company sold its products, Honda had considered a Canadian plant in 1979, when it had made inquiries to the federal government about the auto pact. This initial effort had come to naught, but Honda kept the possibility open, especially after the opening of its Ohio facility. In June 1984 the firm announced that it would build a $100-million plant in Alliston, Ontario, employing about 350 workers to produce approximately 40,000 vehicles. The company was expected to achieve a CVA of 20 per cent by 1990. No government grants were accepted by Honda in making the decision, though Ontario expedited Ontario Municipal Board approvals for the site and provided $11 million in infrastructure reimbursements to the local municipality for building roads and water supplies to the plant.[108]

During its negotiations with Ottawa, and in a Memorandum of Understanding (MOU) between the government and the company, Honda laid out a number of undertakings that augured well for the future. The company stated confidentially that it eventually intended 'to achieve full Auto Pact status,' indicated that 'production would be doubled by adding a second shift' as demand warranted, and promised to boost parts purchases and assist the Canadian parts industry to further develop its technology and capabilities. In return, the government granted normal duty remission for its machinery imports and agreed that Honda's production from Alliston would not count against the company's VER quota. Though the 20 per cent in-car CVA might arouse criticism for being too low, Lumley pointed out that it was comparable to Chrysler's (19 per cent) and Ford's (17 per cent), though not as high as GM's (31 per cent).[109] The Honda MOU was a significant step forward in achieving Japanese investment in Canada, though it also included the promise of a production-based duty-remission order that threatened American reprisals, as we shall see in the following chapter.

The Honda announcement, while welcomed by International Trade Minister Gerald Regan, did not mean the end of export restraints, though it did expedite negotiations on the 1984–5 quota figures. As Regan told reporters, 'if I hadn't seen the Japanese as recognizing the need to have investment in Canada and to become part of the Canadian automotive community, then I don't think there's any way I would have gone above 153,000' in coming to the final figure of 166,000 cars for the year, an increase of about 13,000 cars or 8.5 per cent. The pressure remained on the Japanese to boost their investment, as Regan warned that 'I'm interested in seeing what more they are able to commit to Lumley in ongoing discussions.'[110] Bob White also stated that, while he welcomed the Honda plant, 'the Japanese multinationals still have a long way to go. It still shows we need legislated Canadian content.'[111]

Despite Honda's move, Toyota still remained silent on any investment plans. As the leading importer in Canada, Toyota had borne much of the brunt of Canadian policies. Having Honda beat Toyota to both the American and Canadian markets undoubtedly played upon the company's anxieties. Even the decision to open the parts facility in British Columbia had only led to more pressure from the Canadians, pressure that had not abated with the election of Brian Mulroney's Progressive Conservative government. At the opening of the CAPTIN plant in British Columbia, new Industry Minister Sinclair Stevens referred 'pointedly' to the recently opened NUMMI plant in California, and hinted that he expected more Toyota investment: 'I hope this will not be the only opening I attend on behalf of Japanese investment in

Canada.'[112] Meanwhile, new International Trade Minister James Kelleher had been given authority by cabinet to remind the Japanese during negotiations that 'pending the announcement of a major investment by a Japanese automotive firm,' restraints would be maintained. The Tory government also made preparations to follow in Lumley's footsteps for another port slowdown, at least as a warning to the Japanese.[113]

The ongoing quota battles, port slowdowns, and demands by Canadian politicians for further investment finally seemed to make a difference. In July 1985 the Toyota board decided to build plants in both the United States and Canada, a decision that reflected Toyota's cautious and even-handed approach. While the United States would get an $800-million, 200,000-car-a-year plant with 3,000 workers to build the Camry, the Canadian plant was proportionately more modest. The Canadian facility, at a yet to be determined site, was initially a $150-million investment employing 1,000 workers to build 50,000 Corollas annually, though it was still unclear as to what level of Canadian content might be achieved by the company, or if Toyota could or wished to gain admission to the auto pact. At the same time, it quickly became evident that the plant might be rapidly expanded: Sinclair Stevens reported from Ottawa that Eiji Toyoda had hinted that the new Canadian plant might also get a coveted stamping facility that would boost employment and provide a customer for Canadian steel production. The plant's investment quickly escalated to $300 million as Toyota confirmed the stamping plant and a paint shop, increasing potential employment to 2,000 workers.[114]

The company's announcement set off a spirited competition between provinces over the plant's location. When it became clear that the company was focused on Ontario, dozens of towns jockeyed to become the site of the new facility.[115] Eventually, Toyota settled upon Cambridge. According to the company's official history, 'one of the principal reasons for deciding to build the Canadian plant in Cambridge was the particularly enthusiastic invitation Toyota had received there. The invitation had been tied in with efforts made by the local authorities to promote industry in the area ... the local authorities even exceeded Toyota's expectations by actively cooperating in building access roads to the plant.'[116]

A federal-provincial government support package of $80 million, consisting of a $15-million grant, $35 million in interest-free loans, and $31 million in infrastructure improvements, had also been promised the company. A Memorandum of Understanding between Toyota and the federal government, similar to the Honda MOU, included 'duty remission programs and an effort to increase Canadian value added.' Additionally, Ottawa agreed in the MOU to allow Toyota to import additional vehicles beyond its quota, in exchange for the investment. Cambridge's proximity to Toyota's largest Canadian market, to the bulk of the Canadian parts industry, and to the U.S. market also swayed the company's decision.[117] Construction was begun in May 1986, and the first Corolla rolled off the assembly line in December 1988. In the end, the initial investment by Toyota was over $400 million, and though the plant initially had 500 employees it quickly ramped up to over 1,000.[118]

The Honda and Toyota plants spurred further Japanese investment and production in Canada. Days after Toyota had announced its Cambridge facility, Honda 'hurriedly called a press conference' to announce that it was expanding its own Alliston plant, and Nissan hinted it might build a new parts facility or an assembly plant in Canada.[119] The initial forays by Honda and Toyota were soon joined by a $500-million Suzuki-GM joint venture at Ingersoll, Ontario, which began production in April 1989, building small cars for the Canadian market and creating 2,000 jobs.[120] Canadian Auto Manufacturing Inc. (CAMI), as the joint venture was officially called, was helped along by federal and provincial offers of $39 million and $42.5 million respectively, and the promise of duty remissions on parts, machinery, and imported vehicles, subject to the joint-venture company achieving auto pact status. As with Toyota, which had also publicly stated its intention to achieve auto pact status, GM/Suzuki pushed for exceptions to the quota in exchange for their investments.[121]

By the mid-1980s, it was clear beyond doubt that Canadian efforts to force Japanese investment into Canada had been successful. Between the VRAs, the port slowdown, the content threats, and the inducements offered to get Japanese investment, Canadian officials had exhibited a willingness to push the limits of automotive policy making. In doing so, they had avoided Ottawa's worst fear: that Canada would be left behind as the North American sector internationalized, leaving the industry orphaned and impoverished. Instead, by 1986, Canada could look forward to Honda, Toyota, and Suzuki creating a vibrant Japanese assembly sector in Ontario alongside the Big Three, one with the potential to become part of the auto pact along with the 'domestics.' As we shall see, however, circumstances would change again with the beginning of negotiations for free trade with the United States.

Conclusion: Lessons from the Flood

The issue of Japanese automotive imports and FDI can tell us a number of things about the changing dynamics of the North American auto industry in the 1970s and 1980s, particularly from the Canadian point of view. First, Canadian policy makers had no choice but to take an aggressive stance with the Japanese on both imports and FDI. This was a consequence of both the Japanese focus upon the U.S. market and the constraints imposed upon Canada because of its integrated continental auto industry. In the case of imports, the threat of trade diversion from the American market with the onset of the Japanese-U.S. VRA prompted Canada to seek a similar agreement with the Japanese. Japan-U.S. bilateralism on the automotive issue necessarily affected Canada and required some Canadian response, one that turned out to be largely bipartisan (the Conservative government of Brian Mulroney followed Liberal tactics closely after coming to power in 1984). Because of this activist Canadian approach to the problem, the Japanese belatedly recognized the implication of trade diversion and acceded – in a limited way – to Canadian demands to ensure that Canada was included in a 'voluntary' restraint agreement which encompassed all of North America. This provided some protection for the Canadian industry, just as occurred with the VRAs in the United States.[122]

In the case of Japanese automotive FDI, a strong Canadian response to Japanese efforts to alleviate U.S. protectionism was even more necessary. At a most basic level, Ottawa and Queen's Park faced the threat that the Japanese would simply ignore Canada and pour billions of investment dollars into the United States. If the Japanese did not build in Canada, it might mean the end of the Canadian sector. With the huge decline in Big Three market share after 1980, it was essential for Canada to carve out a stake in this, the only growing sector of the industry. Not only could these U.S.-based Japanese plants symbolize lost opportunities for the Canadian sector, they threatened the viability of the Canadian industry in different ways.

At the very least, just like the flood of Japanese imports, American-built Japanese cars could erode the auto pact significantly – the sale en masse of non-Big Three cars in Canada lowered the number of Big Three cars that were required to be built in Canada, a problem that the Canadian industry (particularly the parts industry) was already facing. A continued flood of Japanese cars might cause the U.S. Big Three to reduce their production in Canada dramatically. Without a corresponding uptake in Japanese production (as was happening in the United States with the investment announcements before 1983), the Canadian industry would be impoverished. Moreover, while Canadians might be able to use port slowdowns and quotas to slow 'offshore' vehicles, it would be extremely difficult to justify trade actions against American-built Japanese cars.

It should be recognized that the Canadians exhibited some real chutzpah here: while Canada could make a case that it deserved some share of production from the U.S.-owned auto industry, which had been in Canada for decades and effectively wiped out any indigenous Canadian sector, the Japanese were true 'foreigners.' Did Canada really 'deserve' a fair share of Japanese investment? After all, the United States was fighting for the same investment, and it was U.S.-owned companies that were entirely bearing the brunt of the loss of market share to the Japanese. But the Canadians were well versed in auto-investment battles, as we have already seen with the $68-million federal-provincial incentive package provided to Ford for the Windsor engine plant.

Canadian politicians and policy makers were willing to play hardball. Again, the 1981 quotas, the 1982 port slowdown, the 1983 task force report, and the constant demands by for investment all indicated how willing Canadians were to force the issue. In the end, they framed the question as one of fairness, about corporate citizenship and about ensuring that the Japanese (or any maker, for that matter) produced where they sold. The Canadian case is another example of the evolving relations between multinationals and home and host nations in the battle over auto investment, one in which the Canadian state was successful in leveraging investment and production.[123]

The second-wave transplant story also tells us much about the evolving strategies of Japanese automotive multinationals in the period. Japanese companies were not solely responding to the aggressive Canadian measures when they decided to build in Canada. Though the tactics used by the Canadians likely helped make the Japanese notice Canada, there were other considerations. For one, each company had its own approach that dictated the nature of its decision to invest in Canada. Honda was always seen as something of a maverick company, whose 'outside the box' strategy had led to stunning successes in a very short period of time – from the astounding jump from motorcycles to cars, to the CVCC engine, to its decision to be first to build in North America. In this context, it made sense for Honda to be the first company to establish production in Canada.

Toyota's decision, on the other hand, reflected its conservative and even-handed approach. Toyota waited until it had established that the Toyota Production System could be successfully implemented in North America through the NUMMI-GM joint venture. It also tested the Canadian waters through its CAPTIN wheel plant in British Columbia. Only when these ventures proved successful, by which time the company was also well aware of the Canadian concerns through the government's port slowdown, did Toyota make the decision to go through with investment in *both* Canada and the United States. Similarly, Nissan, which has always had a much smaller market share in Canada than either Honda or Toyota, has declined to produce in the Canadian market. Its corporate policy has remained constant: the company will come to Canada only when its market share reaches a level to make the move economically worthwhile.[124]

Along with each Japanese firm's own strategies, these companies were further influenced by the dynamics of the North American situation and the shifting realities of the global economy. For instance, Honda recognized early that it could boost its quota-imposed market share by building in North America, which was quickly becoming the biggest market for the company – including Japan. Since cars produced in the United States were not part of the quota, American-built Hondas gave the company an advantage over its other Japanese rivals, who remained hemmed in by the VRAs. As early as 1987, Honda was able to surpass both Toyota and Nissan in the U.S. market on the strength of its American-built cars, and despite the VRA-imposed limit.[125] Toyota recognized this strategy and eventually followed suit. With plants in both Canada and the United States, the companies could circumvent the restraints imposed by each country. At the same time, the establishment of Japanese plants in North America made sense for other economic reasons. By the mid-1980s, a slowdown in the Japanese economy and the increasing value of the yen made North American production even more attractive.

The battle over Japanese auto investment also reaffirms the ongoing story of Canadian attitudes towards FDI in North America. For Canada, this was yet another ironic moment. As we have seen, for much of the 1960s and 1970s, Canadian economic nationalists, including many in the Liberal Party, had railed against foreign control of the economy. Herb Gray himself had been responsible for a famous 1972 report, *Foreign Direct Investment in Canada*, which called upon limits to foreign investment, and the Liberals had in 1972 created the protectionist Foreign

Investment Review Agency to screen foreign capital.[126] Yet here were Gray, Lumley, and the Liberals again demanding, cajoling, and using every trick in the book to get as much foreign investment as possible into Canada. Clearly, for these Canadian policy makers, automotive FDI – either Japanese or American – was not the same as other types of foreign investment.

Finally, there are the long-term consequences of Japanese investment in Canada. While the original motivations of the Japanese to decide to spread some of their investment north of the border were, almost assuredly, in part a consequence of Canada's disruptive tactics, whatever reluctance they may have had was soon replaced by a new-found confidence in their Canadian facilities. The modest Japanese investments in the mid-1980s were quickly expanded by the 1990s, spurred by the high quality of Canadian workers and the benefits of Canada's location. For instance, Honda's Canadian workers were sent to Marysville for their initial training, but from the mid-1990s, many new Honda vehicles launched in North America have been first produced in Alliston before going into production in the United States.

Of course, there were many who argued that the Canadian actions were simply not worth it, and that Canadian policy makers should have just let the Japanese import as many cars as the market demanded, or that Canadians should not have cajoled them into building auto plants here. In particular, the VERs were seen as a sop to the Big Three which cost consumers billions. Incentives provided to the Japanese to locate their plants in Canada came under attack as a form of corporate welfare, a long-standing complaint against subsidies of any kind.[127] The bidding wars over the Japanese plants were also criticized for fanning the flames of regionalism. Some critics argued that the massive incentives to lure manufacturing jobs did little to alleviate high unemployment.[128] But many in the industry disagreed with these criticisms, just as they do now. Even the indigenous Canadian parts industry, the most vulnerable branch of the sector, welcomed the flood of Japanese investment. In 1986 APMA's Patrick Lavelle commented upon the arrival of the Japanese: 'I think the whole thing is absolutely sensational. It's like a wish come true for Canadian auto parts suppliers.'[129]

Ultimately, the success of Canadian efforts to force the Japanese to set up plants in Canada emerged as a result of both the constraints and the opportunities inherent in the integrated North American industry. The continental industry posed threats to the Canadian sector, but it also provided unique openings that Canadian policy makers took advantage of. With the Japanese established in Canada, Canadians had weathered yet another storm. But the greatest challenge to the industry – and to the auto pact that underlay these constraints and opportunities – awaited. Few could have foreseen that the aggressive policies initiated by the Canadians would eventually lead to the demise of the auto pact.

8 Rebirth or Requiem? Duty Remissions, Free Trade, and the Death of the Auto Pact

In the two decades following the auto pact's creation, the Canadian and North American auto industries were fundamentally transformed. Successive waves of paradigmatic change had buffeted the industry: oil shortages and regulatory revolutions, investment battles and near bankruptcy, diplomatic struggles and labour schisms, foreign imports and transplant fights. Throughout, Canadian politicians, policy makers, and workers had utilized a host of strategies to garner what they saw as their fair share of the industry's bounty. The most recent battle over the Japanese import wave had seen the use of 'voluntary' export restraints, border bottlenecks, and content threats. All of these had led to a commitment by the Japanese to invest in Canada.

Policy makers had also used one other measure to lure offshore producers to Canada, a scheme that had first been used decades before, had almost sparked a trade war, and eventually had led to the creation of the auto pact itself. Duty remissions, which Simon Reisman had pioneered in the early 1960s but which he had warned against in his 1978 royal commission, re-emerged in the 1970s as a way of cajoling 'foreign' firms selling in Canada to contribute jobs and investment. The resuscitated remission plans were first used as a carrot to boost parts exports by companies like Volkswagen, and later to help induce Japanese manufacturers to assemble cars in Canada. Pivotally, these renewed duty remissions could be applied to exports to the United States, a practice that smacked of trade distortion and subsidy to those south of the border.

American anger over the remission programs coincided with the industry's greatest regime change yet, the 1989 comprehensive Free Trade Agreement between Canada and the United States. The FTA's automotive provisions were not a direct consequence of duty-remission programs. But these schemes were the proverbial straw that broke the camel's back, and they help to explain how Canadian auto policies became a target of renewed American indignation and intransigence before and during the free-trade negotiations. Having been unable to end the auto pact safeguards and investment incentives through diplomacy, having watched the Canadian sector grow as the U.S. sector shrank, having seen a restructuring Chrysler essentially held hostage by Canadian governments and workers alike, having witnessed Canadian auto unionists gain their own fair share, even at the expense of their American brethren, and having seen Canadians cajole Japanese plants to their country through questionable tactics, Washington finally compelled an end to creative Canadian automotive policy making by holding out its own carrot.

That carrot was free trade. In the end, the auto pact's essential death with the emergence of the FTA reflected both the triumphant success and the ultimate failure of Canadian automotive policy. Success because, by the 1980s, Canadians had achieved a goal first imagined in the 1960s and reimagined again in the 1970s: a strong, continentally and then multinationally oriented auto sector with tens of thousands of jobs and a vibrant and growing indigenous parts sector. But the death of the auto pact, and the birth of the FTA, also represented failure: the price for admission into any free-trade agreement with the United States was nothing less than the destruction of the auto pact itself, and an abrupt end to the diverse, creative, and aggressive policies that had shaped the Canadian automotive struggle for more than two decades. This was a price that Canadian policy makers willingly accepted. After free trade, only the blunt tools of direct subsidies and, eventually, direct government ownership remained as policy options.

Back to the Future: The Return of Duty-Remission Orders, 1978–85

Canadian automotive policy seemed to have come full circle by the late 1970s. During this period the federal government initiated a series of duty-remission orders for various auto companies operating in Canada, most notably with Volkswagen in 1978. These measures were a replay of the government devices developed in the early 1960s to spur parts investment and production and to alleviate the growing Canadian auto trade deficit with the United States. The plans, instituted in 1962 and 1963, worked simply and effectively: companies that boosted their auto-parts exports to the United States beyond a base year would be remitted any duties on parts imports to Canada. The plans worked well enough to prompt a legal challenge from a radiator company in Wisconsin that claimed to have lost business in the United States because of a sourcing decision. Attempting to avoid further conflict over the Canadian remission plans led directly to the negotiations that produced the auto pact.[1]

In the decades that followed, as we have seen, the auto pact was not an entirely satisfactory resolution to automotive problems for either nation. Clashes between the two countries focused on the operation of the agreement, usually either around the trade balance or the persistence of Canadian 'transitional' safeguards. But the difficulties never amounted to direct action. Despite endless conflict, negotiation, and speculation, the auto pact was never changed, seemingly having been 'cast in concrete for all time.'[2] With Canadian automotive remission plans – what the Americans referred to as subsidies –apparently having been ended by the auto pact regime, there was only one episode, involving the Michelin tire corporation and its plant in Nova Scotia, where the issue of subsidies in the auto industry became a cause for conflict. The 1972 Michelin subsidy case illustrated the willingness of the United States to punish Canadians over their policies in an area of trade that not coincidentally happened to be in automotive parts. The Michelin countervail also reflected a doctrinaire American view of subsidies or any other 'trade distorting' practice, one that could be easily provoked.[3]

Of course, the Michelin case was not the only instance of cross-border conflict over automotive investment and trade. By the late 1970s and early 1980s, Canadians had become much more aggressive in courting and cajoling foreign automotive investment. The investment incentives and port blockade tactics had resulted in some success in getting greater Big Three investment and in at least getting offshore producers to begin considering investing in Canada. But the federal government determined that, in order to speed the latter process along, a renewal of remissions could help to convince foreign firms, especially the Japanese, to build and source in Canada. By 1980, the Canadian approach, according to Paul Heimbecker, chief of EA's U.S. division, had 'entirely shifted from a pre-occupation with the operation of the Auto Pact and more broadly the need to obtain a "fair share" of the benefits of the North American automotive industry for Canada to the problems posed by third country suppliers, especially Japan, to North America.'[4]

Duty-remission programs were used by Canadian policy makers to gain sales for parts makers and to achieve greater foreign investment. Like incentives, they had an uneven record. They also could have great political ramifications. Legally, they existed in a kind of no man's land: duty-remission orders were not specified in the illustrative list of export subsidies which appeared in the GATT subsidies and countervailing duties agreement, yet there was no question they could be seen as trade distorting. Though it never came to a final determination, the Americans had all but concluded that the Canadian 1962–4 remissions were subsidies and therefore subject to countervailing duty.[5]

Despite this chequered past, efforts to resuscitate a duty-remission program were considered by the Canadian government as early as 1971. With the growth of offshore imports from Germany and Japan, the APMA pushed the government to create a new program which would give it access to some of the cars that were flooding into the country: by 1971, 22 per cent of the cars sold in Canada were overseas imports, effectively shutting one-fifth of the market to parts makers. A program that granted these companies remission of the duties they paid on these vehicles if they purchased some of their parts from Canadian firms could significantly help the Canadian parts sector. Volkswagen (VW), enjoying tremendous success with its Beetle, was seen as a particularly good candidate for such a scheme.[6]

The idea of a VW DRO ran into trouble from the outset. IT&C officials were concerned that it would hurt the Big Three and lead to difficulties with the United States, which was wary of any new Canadian unilateralism in the auto sector, especially measures that looked like the pre-auto pact programs. At the same time, the auto pact itself was under serious strain, owing to the Canadian trade surplus. Any new provocation might derail the already delicate negotiations between the two countries. Although IT&C Minister Jean-Luc Pepin visited VW in the spring of 1971, the idea was put on the back-burner.[7]

Nonetheless, the problem remained. VW was exporting thousands of cars to Canada, and Canadian parts makers were not getting any of the action that these exports represented. After 1973, when VW's exports jumped again following the oil embargo, there was a new initiative to do something. Increased production costs, a decline in the German mark, and the fact that VW was no longer a 'niche' importer spurred the notion of an assembly plant in Canada, along the lines of Volvo's Halifax plant. Talks between the company and the Quebec government aimed at having VW take over the SOMA plant in Saint-Bruno, which had ended its assembly of Renault cars in 1973, did not proceed beyond the discussion stage.[8] By 1974, VW's sales in Canada had reached 23,000 units. In comparison, the Nova Scotia Volvo plant was producing on average of 13,000 vehicles a year. So, again in 1975, the company met with Canadian officials to consider the possibility of establishing a Canadian plant. And again, after 'long and searching discussions,' the company held off.[9]

The dynamic changed dramatically when VW announced its intention to build an assembly plant in Pennsylvania in 1976.[10] VW's decision meant that Canadian parts makers faced an even greater challenge: now VWs could flood into Canada from the United States along with the wave of imports from Germany. Further, U.S. parts makers had a chance at supplying VW in Pennsylvania, again leaving Canadian parts makers out of the loop. But the situation might be turned to Canadian benefit. If there was little chance for a VW assembly plant in Canada now that the company had made its Pennsylvania decision, the concept of boosting parts exports from Canada, in exchange for duty-free entry of VW vehicles, remained in play. The idea was again broached by an interdepartmental committee in the spring of 1977. With the U.S. VW plant soon coming on line, government officials recommended some sort of expanded 'Automobile Components Remission order' to boost exports to the plant.[11]

In the late summer of 1977, IT&C Minister Jean Chrétien met with Bruno Rubess, the president of VW Canada. Sensing a renewed opportunity for a mutually beneficial remission plan, VW proposed that it export $32 million in parts from Canada to its new plant in Pennsylvania under a DRO. But VW wished to get a sense from Chrétien about the government's view before making any investment decisions. Chrétien remained cagey – he wanted more from VW, and noted that $14 million of VW's 'offer' included Michelin tires already exported from Canada.[12] The deal had to be worth it: the Americans had heard rumours about the possibility of the plan, and warned Ottawa that the DRO was a 'gimmick' that opened the door to possible countervail.[13]

Even before any VW-specific plan was worked out, the federal government had adroitly amended an existing 1975 duty-remission scheme. Under the old plan, a company gained credits only for the value of the actual Canadian-made part that was installed in the imported vehicle coming back to Canada. With the newly revised 1977 DRO, a company would gain credit for *any* Canadian parts exports to countries other than the United States, which did not necessarily include parts in the vehicles imported into Canada. This opened the door to much greater parts sales by Canadian firms, and thus greater duty-free imports by VW. In December 1977 cabinet approved the expanded remission scheme. Then, in August 1978, the government came to an agreement with VW. It expanded the previous duty-remission program in place for third-country imports that itself had been amended in December. Significantly, the new VW DRO was further modified by allowing credits to the U.S. VW plant in Pennsylvania.[14]

This changed the dynamic again, dramatically so since the United States was now the target of expanded exports. While normally VW cars would be charged a 15 per cent tariff under the MFN rules, the DRO allowed the company a rebate on any duties it paid, equivalent to the value of CVA in parts purchased and shipped to Pennsylvania. By selling Canadian-made parts to its U.S. assembly operations, VW could import fully assembled cars into Canada (from Germany or the United States) with reduced tariffs. Sam Gindin estimated that VW would likely save about $3 million on the plan, or nearly $800 per car imported.[15]

The impact of the new program was quickly obvious. Even before the official agreement had been signed, VW boosted its Canadian sourcing. The APMA's Patrick Lavelle said in May 1978 that VW had already increased its parts purchases from $2 million to $28 million in less than two years.[16] Much of the newly sourced Canadian VW parts were intended to go to the assembly plant in Pennsylvania, which produced fuel-efficient Rabbit cars. The 1978 tally of VW's purchases was $25 million, increasing to nearly $40 million in 1979.[17]

Though the APMA may have been thrilled at the prospect of huge sales to VW, the United States was deeply unhappy with the plan, and expressed its displeasure early and often. In its view, the program was essentially a replica of the 1962–4 schemes which had caused so much difficulty and had directly led to the auto pact negotiations. American diplomats saw the new DRO as an 'artificial stimulus' of 'questionable GATT legality' and warned that it would 'adversely antagonize' some members of Congress who were only now getting past their dislike of the auto pact.[18]

The Americans felt as though Canada was unilaterally changing the auto pact by adding VW through a DRO back door, a charge that would be repeated on numerous occasions in the future with respect to Japanese assemblers. For their part, the Canadians maintained that the VW deal had nothing to do with the auto pact, and was only barely related to the Reisman recommendations, which were nominally still under consideration by the government. In the Canadian view, there was a 'Volkswagen-specific' basis for the arrangement.[19] But the Canadians did not help matters by expanding the program to include a number of other offshore producers. By the fall of 1979, similar DROs had been negotiated with Fiat, Mercedes Benz, BMW, and Nissan. Parts purchases by these companies were expected to total $10 million within the first year of the deals, and $20 million a year in the next two model years.[20]

During the 1980 consultations between IT&C Minister Herb Grey and USTR Reubin Askew, the new DROs became an emerging issue. Publicly, Askew told reporters of his 'concern' about the DROs, and was non-committal as to whether a countervailing duty could be used against them. During the talks, the Canadians had defended the DROs by pointing out that there now were, and would soon be, a number of new assembly plants only on the U.S. side of the border, as with VW. IT&C's Robert Latimer wondered whether the United States would want these companies 'to be discriminated against by not being able to count their parts purchases in Canada for their US plants under the duty remission scheme.' The Canadians further argued that these programs were very minor, from $1 million to $10 million per year. Duties remitted were a miniscule $750,000 annually.[21]

But the Americans warned that, though the GATT did not specifically forbid remissions, a case against DROs could be made using 'other arguments,' and that the GATT list was 'illustrative' rather than exhaustive. After two U.S. parts producers launched complaints that they could not take advantage of the scheme (they did not have subsidiaries in Canada), the Americans felt that a case could now be made that the DROs were discriminatory. Latimer's response to the suggestion that the DROs should be held up to GATT scrutiny was firm. He told the Americans to 'go ahead' and do so. By November 1980, the Canadians had reiterated that they would not 'give up the duty remission program available to offshore producers in return for American concessions' on the auto pact negotiations.[22] Ottawa was digging in its heels on the remission programs.

The U.S. government was not alone in its critique of the DRO program. GM criticized the plan heavily. GM Canada's president, F. Alan Smith, was 'astounded' that the government would embark on such a scheme to help foreign firms, when domestic companies such as GM constituted the vast bulk of the parts industry. 'The duty remission program,' Smith argued, 'would appear to hurt the very manufacturers which are intended to be helped' by the auto pact.[23] In his royal commission report, Simon Reisman also considered the remissions imprudent and warned of brewing American unhappiness towards the program.[24]

Meanwhile, the success of the program was such that, by the spring of 1979, VW was seriously interested in expanding its presence in Canada. What ensued was the development of a new type of remission, one oriented towards inducing VW *production* in Canada as opposed to simply parts *exports* purchased from Canadian sources. The 1978 Reisman report had laid out the possibility of a 'Designated Vehicle Importer' classification for companies that boosted their Canadian parts purchases. This had piqued the company's interest in developing some kind of further arrangement in Canada. Consequently, VW launched a study in November 1978 to examine the possibility of boosting the productivity (and profitability) of its North American operations. This included considering a potential VW Canadian parts facility, spurred by the increasing exchange costs associated with importing German parts for its Rabbit plant in Pennsylvania that accounted for 40 per cent of the car's content.

In February 1979 VW officials met with Canadian representatives to pitch a plan to boost VW's presence in Canada and ease its tariff burden. In exchange for duty-free entry for its vehicles, the company would build a parts plant somewhere in the country with, of course, some federal or provincial financial assistance. As long as VW generated CVA equivalent to 75 per cent of its sales in Canada, and actually produced 35 per cent of that CVA at its parts plant, VW would be remitted 100 per cent of the duties it faced on its car imports. The company estimated that such a deal could generate up to $145 million, $65 million of which would be achieved at the new plant. The Canadian deficit with VW would also be cut from $155 million to $25 million. The proposed VW plant would mean 500 direct jobs, 1,000 jobs at other parts makers, and even more indirect employment. Canadian officials were impressed. New IT&C Minister Jack Horner thought the plan, a production-based duty-remission program, 'a very interesting concept' that he was 'prepared to pursue' in cabinet.[25]

The VW plan looked feasible in the abstract but could be easily felled on a number of counts. First, there was the location of the plant, necessitating the usual political tug-of-war between provinces, and even within provinces. Second, and more important, was the American reaction. The United States had not liked the VW remission order for exports, and it would likely look askance at a remission plan designed to boost exports *and* VW parts production in Canada. Finally, there was the reaction of the car manufacturers. Like the U.S. government, the Big Three had always been very wary of any duty-remission scheme which helped offshore producers, even if it also helped Canadian parts producers.[26]

The location of the plant presented a dilemma for both the company and the federal government. VW was committed to a central Ontario site, which made the most sense in terms of distribution, production, and transportation (both vis-à-vis the Canadian market and proximity to the Pennsylvania plant). The company had targeted Barrie as the best candidate for the facility, with Cambridge an alternative. But federal officials had other ideas. In order to qualify for DREE money, VW was being pushed to consider sites outside central Ontario. For domestic political reasons, Montreal was one area that was being promoted. There was also Sydney/Halifax, Winnipeg, and Windsor. All of these areas fell under DREE parameters as better suited to meet federal needs and to qualify for DREE grants that would not provoke hostility from the Americans.

In August 1981 federal officials flew to Wolfsburg, Germany, to propose the alternative sites to company officials. But VW officials were reluctant: though they agreed to examine the Montreal and Windsor locales, they emphasized to the Canadians that, if cabinet did not make a final decision on the whole duty-remission project by the end of the month, the company would terminate its plans for Canadian parts production. VW officials told the Canadians that the project needed to be started by 1 October at the latest if it was to deliver parts to the U.S. assembly facility in time for the introduction of the new 1983 models.[27]

The Canadians and VW returned to their negotiations over the possible parts plant/duty-free entry plan in the summer of 1981. This time, the Canadians ensured that the United States was kept aware of their negotiations with VW. This was, in part, in response to the initial meetings between Trudeau and Reagan (and between Gray and Brock), where the two had pledged to inform each other on 'matters of potential interest in the automotive sector.' In July 1981 Canadian officials including Robert Latimer and Campbell Stuart flew to Washington to inform their U.S. counterparts of the proposed VW agreement, including the CVA requirements, penalty provisions for missing these targets, transitional removal of VW's previous DRO levels, and even the potential locations of the parts plant. The Canadians emphasized that the VW duty-free entry plant would benefit the United States, particularly since it hinged on utilizing the Pennsylvania plant for optimal efficiency. They also stressed that they saw this as an arrangement where 'normal Auto Pact conditions' were not practical, which explained the special arrangement with VW.[28]

Initially, the American reaction to the Canadian VW proposal was cautiously subdued. The Americans said little during the July meeting in Washington, but they later hinted that they were not pleased with the plan, particularly the CVA requirements. Deputy USTR David MacDonald made a point of saying that 'the law of supply and demand cannot be repealed.'[29] Following the meeting, he hardened his outlook further, telling the Canadians that, although the initial 'lack of reaction' during the meetings 'might be interpreted as US Government acquiescence to the plan,' this was decidedly not the case.[30]

In fact, the United States objected strongly to the VW deal. It was, in MacDonald's view, an attempt to modify the auto pact unilaterally to benefit one company. Although he sympathized with the Canadian concerns about the direction of the auto industry in North America, the United States was 'not presently engaged in a renegotiation of the terms of the Automotive Products Agreement, nor has it acquiesced in any suggested modifications of the implementation of the Agreement.' The VW plan, which required the company to meet increased CVA requirements in return for duty-free entry, 'could be viewed as attempts to modify unilaterally the auto pact.' Accordingly, MacDonald invoked section 205(B) of the U.S.-implementing Automotive Products Trade Act of 1965, which required the president to report to Congress in the event that a manufacturer had undertaken 'by reason of governmental action' to boost its CVA. He also called for consultations between the two governments under the auto pact's terms.[31]

In response, the Canadians held that the American objections were not salient. The VW arrangement was 'separate from the [Auto] Agreement and clearly falls outside its coverage since VW will not be assembling vehicles in Canada,' but parts. Instead, the Canadians argued that the VW agreement needed to be cast in a wider context, taking into account the fundamental changes taking place in the world automotive industry. These changes helped to explain the Canadian rationale for the VW agreement, which would, in the Canadians' view, also tremendously help the American VW plant in Pennsylvania.[32]

For now the two sides agreed to disagree. In the meantime, the Canadian-VW negotiations were coming to a head over the location of the facility. The company was determined to put the plant at its preferred

site in Barrie. Federal officials, especially from DREE, were equally determined to convince the company to consider a site outside Ontario,
particularly in Montreal. In the light of the recent political and constitutional battles between the province's separatist government and the
federal Liberals, the VW decision could have significant economic and
political implications. In late August, DREE officials again pushed VW
to consider the Montreal site, and complained that the twenty days the
company had allotted for a site inspection was 'ridiculous' given that
VW traditionally took four months to consider a plant site. DREE officials felt that VW was unfairly biased towards Barrie. The only way
around the problem, they concluded, was a direct appeal to the chairman of the company. DREE considered this strategy as 'calling VW's
bluff' on the site location.[33]

VW did not fall for the Canadian play. The company held firm, and
in September 1981 Gray informed VW that cabinet had approved an
agreement. The firm would build its parts plant in Barrie with an investment of over $100 million, hiring 500 workers. The duty-free access
provisions of the agreement were slightly different from the ones VW
had initially proposed. The CVA overall requirement was pegged at
64 per cent, with 25 per cent CVA coming from in-house production at
the Barrie plant. This was a drop from 75 per cent and 35 per cent. By
1987, the final 'in-house' and overall CVA was to be 30 per cent and 85
per cent respectively. If the company did not meet these targets, it was
liable 'for full duties and taxes' on all of its imports during the model
year in which the failure occurred. Also, while there was no federal
money for the plant, there was a $10-million grant from Ontario.[34]

When the company announced its decision in October 1981, the
reaction was predictable. Quebec politicians were outraged at what
they saw as the inequitable distribution of manufacturing in the auto
industry. Ontario was unfairly getting the lion's share of new investments. This was not just a matter of location or Ontario's long-standing ties to the industry. Quebec Minster of Industry Rodrigue Biron
claimed that the closeness between Ottawa and Ontario was responsible for Quebec losing out on the VW plant: 'We feel there is also a direct linkage between the Ontario Government and the Department of
Industry Trade and Commerce which merely cements the *status quo* in
such key industries.' Even the decision to locate a diesel engine plant
by another German manufacturer, KHD AG, in Quebec did not satisfy
the provincial government.[35] Eventually, the Barrie VW plant opened
in 1985.[36]

The success of the VW duty-remission scheme led to further and more ambitious programs. As we saw in the previous chapter, by the early 1980s, the intense Canadian concern over Japanese imports and the Japanese decision to build transplant operations in the United States had prompted dramatic Canadian responses, including VERs, content threats, and port slowdowns. These sticks had been accompanied by carrots – namely, remission programs. As with VW, the Japanese DROs had initially been export-based programs for countries other than the United States but had then been revised to grant remissions of up to 70 per cent of duties and, significantly, could include the United States as a destination for exports from Canada. For instance, in 1980, the federal government created an export-based DRO for Honda which excluded exports to the United States. But in 1985 the Honda DRO was revised to allow credit for export anywhere in the world, including the United States, echoing VW's DRO history.[37]

In adopting this approach, policy makers in Brian Mulroney's government followed the path first taken by the Liberals with VW. Changing the export-based DROs in 1985 allowed the Japanese to source from Canadian parts firms and then send these purchases to their facilities in the United States, in exchange for duty remission. Canadian officials were deeply concerned that the growing Japanese assembly and parts production in the United States, accelerated by American protectionism and an increasing yen, would mean that the Canadian parts industry would face 'an increasingly contracting market.' This was especially likely given that the Japanese imported virtually all of their high-value parts, such as engines and transmissions, from Japan.[38] Thus, export-based remissions were only part of the solution.

The other obvious remedy was to bring the Japanese into Canada, and perhaps even incorporate them into the auto pact at some point in the future, which technically could be done given the multilateral Canadian provisions of the agreement. As one Canadian official argued in 1985, 'the issue that is upper most in the Canadian government's mind at this particular time is that of Japanese access to the Canadian market ... The Auto Pact could be extended to include overseas vehicle manufacturers which presently export to Canada rather than producing in this country.'[39] Whether or not Ottawa believed that the Japanese could be included in the auto pact or even eventually meet auto pact production requirements was secondary to its desire to get Japanese investment into Canada, and DROs were an important part of this plan.[40]

In order to help facilitate Japanese production in Canada, in 1985 the government established a new type of production-based remission order. These new DROs provided a 100 per cent rebate on imports for companies that invested directly in production facilities in Canada. When Ottawa made its agreements with Honda and Toyota (and later, the Korean maker, Hyundai), it followed the VW DRO by granting remissions based upon the amount of production investment each company promised to make in Canada. By 1986, Honda and Toyota had signed Memorandums of Understanding towards this goal with the Canadian government. The 'CVA/Cost of Sales ratio undertakings' established with the companies were 'minimal at the outset and [were] well below the Big Three's performance.' For instance, Sam Gindin expected Honda's total CVA (including parts purchases) to be at 23 per cent, far below the Big Three average, which had been 65 per cent in 1981 and had been increasing since.[41]

Nonetheless, these MOUs held out the possibility that the companies could, in time, be granted auto pact status. Federal officials reported that the companies had publicly 'committed themselves to achieving eventual auto pact status' but also remained cagey, and in their promises to the government 'refused to commit to a date.' They also resisted committing to the specific auto pact requirement of a 60 per cent CVA in cost of sales, which was the level agreed to by the Canadian government and the Big Three in the original 1965 Letters of Undertaking.[42] Though there is some debate as to how much of a role these production-based remission plans had in enticing the Japanese to Canada, there is no questioning their political impact on Canada-U.S. trade relations.[43]

American reaction to the new production-based remission programs was scathing. Though the United States did not immediately take direct action in response, the policy caused serious consternation in Washington and Detroit, especially since the DROs could be a way eventually to grant the Japanese auto pact status. It seemed that the Canadians were again unilaterally attempting to modify the auto pact and its membership. Officials in DRIE warned cabinet that the United States was already examining the Japanese DROs through an ITC section 332 'Fact Finding' mission: 'Once the US Administration becomes fully aware of the potential for increases in Canadian parts shipped under the remission programs to Toyota and Honda plants in the US, further investigations will almost certainly be taken.'[44] The remission plans put Canadian auto policy – and the auto pact itself – back into the crosshairs of U.S. industry and government as it had not been since the mid-1970s.

Typical was the view of U.S. MVMA President Thomas Hanna. Hanna testified to Congress that Canada's 'two-tiered automotive policy' was causing severe problems in the industry. The influx of foreign makers into Canada who were producing outside the auto agreement raised 'a serious question as to whether the principles of the pact are being met today.'[45] The American parts industry felt similarly. In September 1986 Julian C. Morris, president of the Automotive Parts and Accessories Association (APAA), told another congressional committee that 'duty-free access for OE shipments under the US-Canada Auto Pact has become a selling point to lure Japanese suppliers to Canada. This abuse by unintended third party beneficiaries demands our re-evaluation of the Pact.'[46]

APAA Vice-President Robert W. McMinn echoed Morris and warned that the auto pact now represented 'another opening for abuse,' since it could be used to launch Japanese original equipment into the United States duty-free, and thus needed to be reviewed. McMinn also took a shot at Canadian investment incentives, saying that 'Canada has so much bounty to give that our states complain that even their best packages are only half of the Canadian loaf.' As for the Canadian remission programs, McMinn thought them so effective that he urged the Congress to adopt the APAA's Parts Purchase Incentive Plan, 'tailored after Canada's duty remission program.'[47]

Far less accommodating was the state of Michigan, which had the harshest reaction. Governor James Blanchard, who had led the Chrysler bailout as a representative from the state, wanted the remission programs killed outright. The DROs were a '9% benefit' that would compel Japanese assemblers and parts makers to invest in Canada, according to Mark Santucci, Blanchard's trade adviser in Lansing.[48] The state was willing to back its displeasure through action: in 1986 Michigan started the process of filing a 301 Trade Act complaint against the duty-remission programs in an effort to kill them.[49]

On the Canadian side of the border, reaction to the DROs was more ambiguous and was tied up with the larger question of Japanese and Korean sales and investment in Canada. The Canadian Big Three were deeply unhappy about the remissions, a stance they had maintained since GM Canada's president had attacked the VW remission in 1980. Along with the MVMA, they had, in the government's eyes, 'mounted an attack in the media on the government's Asian investment program.' Two 'difficult' meetings with Mulroney had not assuaged them.[50]

The APMA complained that the new entrants operated under different rules, maintaining a lower level of content as well as 'a lower level of commitment to the Canadian economy in terms of investment and employment.' Since the Japanese were not yet required to hit the 60 per cent CVA or ratio targets, or the 50 per cent North American content for export to the United States (they simply paid the 2.5 per cent duty), they continued to import major components such as engines or transmissions for their vehicles assembled in North America. The association was in favour of 'a mechanism whereby offshore participants must be brought under the auto pact.'[51]

Bob White and the CAW felt similarly. In March 1986 White demanded an expansion of quotas to include the Koreans, and again reiterated his view that quotas were only part of the solution – the companies that had announced investments in Canada should be subject to restraints 'until the facilities are in fact in place and until they achieve a level of Canadian content that *exceeds* sixty percent.' White pointed to the 1986 *Report of the Automotive Industries Human Resource Task Force*, an industry-parts-labour group, which restated the 1983 task force's recommendations that new entrants should meet auto pact requirements.[52] Along with the APMA and MVMA, White wrote to Mulroney laying out these concerns and pushed again for higher content requirements by the Japanese and the continuation of restraints.[53]

As to the specific issue of the DROs, the CAW was lukewarm. Sam Gindin argued that transplant firms should pay full duty unless they met the auto pact safeguards. But the 'reality' was that the program attracted only a few hundred jobs to Canada, and in the case of the export-based DROs amounted to probably less than $1 million in subsidies, in Gindin's estimate. Moreover, since the program had infuriated the Americans, who argued that the DROs violated 'the spirit' of the auto pact, it was not worth the risk: 'The benefit is minimal and the potential cost in terms of US retaliation is high.' Gindin was convinced that the remission policy was '*not* the turf on which to take on the US,' though he did not think that the union should lead any charge against the remissions, either.[54]

The union's views were, surprisingly, echoed by economist and free-trade supporter Ron Wonnacott. In March 1987 Wonnacott, writing of the export DROs, warned that 'the rebates have a symbolic significance which perhaps exceeds their importance in dollars.' The DROs added to U.S.-Canadian trade difficulties, and 'unless the Canadian government withdraws the rebates and undertakes not to reintroduce them, it is not clear that the strains can be contained.' Ominously, he described the scheme as 'a ticking time bomb, which threatens to explode several years down the road.' Other academics also recognized the American unhappiness about the DROs, and their implication for Canada-U.S. relations.[55]

The end result of the DROs was that they provoked the United States in a way that had not occurred since congressional attacks on the auto pact in the mid-1970s. The reappearance of a massive Canadian trade surplus, the Canadian approach to the Chrysler bailout, and the Canadian decision to negotiate its own 'voluntary' import restraints with the Japanese had all added strains to the Canada-U.S. auto relationship since 1980, yet none had incited this kind of reaction. From the U.S. point of view, there was something unseemly about the Canadian DROs. Americans might not necessarily like what had happened under the auto pact, but at least that had been agreed to fair and square. These DRO programs left the impression that the Canadians were bending the rules in the middle of the game. The American solution was to rewrite the rulebook by holding out the opportunity for free trade, a dramatic gesture that the Canadians willingly acceded to, given their own recent conversion to reciprocity.

An Idea That Didn't Go Away: Debating Free Trade and the Auto Sector, 1984–7

Free trade with the United States has a long, complex, and emotional history in Canada. From the creation of John A. Macdonald's 1879 National Policy to the 1988 federal election, the issue was something of a 'third rail' in Canadian politics – those who dared to grasp for reciprocity usually paid a price, as elections in 1891 and 1911 illustrated. Yet it remained an idea that always beckoned, tempting politicians, especially in the Liberal Party, as a grand panacea for Canadian economic problems. In the post-war period, the notion of free trade was seriously considered in the 1940s, though it was abandoned by Mackenzie King at the last moment, and again in the 1950s. During the long interregnum of Walter Gordon economic nationalism, the idea of Canada-U.S. free trade seemed remote, though it remained, if not prominent, at least always in the background.[56]

As economic malaise settled over Canada by the end of the 1970s and early 1980s, the issue of free trade began to re-emerge forcefully. Canadians faced inflation, high unemployment, and sluggish productivity.

Meanwhile, U.S. protectionism had increased sharply in the period, in no small part owing to the wave of Japanese and other foreign imports in the auto sector. Protectionism and the demand for U.S. content requirements in motor vehicles had scared Canadians, as had the voluntary restraint agreements negotiated by the United States. Similarly, the failure of any significant breakthroughs at the GATT multilateral trade negotiations, and a growing realization by Canadian policy makers that Canada needed guaranteed access to the U.S. market, began to shift attitudes towards free trade.[57]

During Pierre Trudeau's last government, Liberals led this shift. The recognition that economic policy required a major overhaul convinced many politicians and policy makers that free trade with the United States provided a legitimate option for Canada. In 1982 the Senate Standing Committee on Foreign Affairs released a report calling for free trade, while External Affairs released a paper in August 1983 supporting free trade in selected areas. The Trudeau government quietly launched a 1984 initiative to negotiate free trade in selected areas of the cross-border economy: steel, agricultural machinery, and government procurement around urban mass transit. Though the negotiations did not result in any agreements, the U.S. administration was heartened by the efforts, which laid 'the foundations for subsequent freer trade arrangements' and could 'set an historic example for the world in the future.' This new interest in reciprocity was a sharp contrast to the protectionist tone of the early 1970s.[58]

The greatest spur towards free trade came from another Liberal initiative. In 1983 Trudeau had appointed his former cabinet minister, Donald S. Macdonald, to lead the Royal Commission on Canada's Economic Prospects and Social Union. One of the most extensive royal commissions in Canadian history, the Macdonald Commission ultimately recommended that Canada take a 'leap of faith' and pursue a comprehensive free-trade agreement with the United States. The report and its recommendations garnered widespread attention and became a cudgel in the hands of free-trade supporters. Here was a former member of Trudeau's government – the same government that had instituted protectionist measures such as FIRA, the Canada Development Corporation (CDC), Petro-Canada, and the NEP – now advocating free trade. By 1985, the Macdonald Commission, along with a host of other scholarly studies, had laid the academic and political groundwork for a renewal of the free-trade debate in Canada.[59]

After his election in 1984, Prime Minister Brian Mulroney and his Progressive Conservative government eventually embraced the idea, and promoted it forcefully. Mulroney's conversion to free trade was – if not difficult given his party's historical attachment to protectionism – at least very good timing. U.S. President Ronald Reagan, elected to a second term in 1984, had been advocating free trade since the 1960s. Upon announcing his candidacy for president in November 1979, Reagan had called for a free-trade area from 'the Arctic Circle to Tierra del Fuego.'[60] The two men hit it off personally, which also helped. After initial discussions on the issue, including a March 1985 meeting between the two leaders in Quebec City dubbed the 'Shamrock Summit,' Mulroney formally requested talks towards an agreement in September 1985. In December, Reagan was granted fast-track authority by Congress to get a deal by October 1987, and negotiations began in May 1986. The endeavour promised to be one of the most politically charged in Canadian history.[61]

This was especially true for the auto industry. At the outset, questions were raised as to what would happen to the sector and the auto pact under free trade. By the mid-1980s, at the start of FTA negotiations, the Canadian industry was booming. Chrysler had recovered spectacularly, and GM's and Ford's plants were running full-out building cars that were popular in the U.S. market. The trade balance had shifted to an enormous Canadian surplus, as the Big Three moved more production northwards to take advantage of the lower Canadian dollar, better productivity and quality, and additional lower labour costs because of national health care. Massive investment in new plants in Canada, by the Big Three, AMC, and the Japanese, meant that Canada was producing a growing share of North American output.[62] In 1986 auto employment was at an all-time high of 132,000, while U.S. employment had dropped by 164,000 jobs since its 1978 peak. Canadian parts makers, such as Magna, Woodbridge, and AG Simpson, flourished and even started getting major business from the Japanese in North America.[63] On the face of it, things seemed extremely positive. 'The beauty of the auto pact,' one GM Canada executive remarked without irony, was that 'both sides have won.'[64]

But there were worries, too. All the new plants coming on line meant that by the late 1980s there was unquestionably going to be overcapacity in the industry. Honda, Toyota, the GM-Suzuki joint venture, and a recently announced Hyundai plant in Quebec added another 480,000 cars

Table 8.1
Canada in the North American auto trade, 1973–91

Year	N. American Total	Canadian Total	Cdn. % of U.S.	Canada Prod. to Sales Ratio	Canada-U.S. Auto Balance (millions Can.)
1973	14,537,986	1,589,499	12.55	129.6	−402
1974	11,898,731	1,563,850	15.66	125.2	−1192
1975	10,764,113	1,442,076	16.08	109.5	−1821
1976	13,457,339	1,646,824	14.33	127.5	−996
1977	14,744,886	1,764,987	13.89	131.2	−1092
1978	15,097,791	1,818,378	14.10	133.1	−589
1979	13,550,018	1,629,855	14.20	116.7	−3088
1980	9,870,176	1,369,697	17.09	108.4	−2045
1981	9,818,398	1,280,499	16.12	107.5	−1737
1982	8,693,618	1,235,668	17.68	134.2	2853
1983	11,013,508	1,502,325	16.28	139.0	3286
1984	13,132,135	1,835,074	16.77	143.0	5935
1985	14,046,746	1,934,110	16.59	126.4	5499
1986	13,530,711	1,854,418	16.35	122.3	5170
1987	12,956,014	1,635,151	14.96	107.0	3903
1988	13,727,619	1,976,896	17.59	126.5	3973
1989	13,482,329	1,965,480	18.07	132.5	6870
1990	12,550,533	1,946,542	19.89	148.1	8535
1991	11,688,754	1,887,537	21.42	146.7	7754

Source: DesRosiers, Automotive Yearbook 2000, 112.

to Canadian production, while U.S. transplants added another 1.5 million. This astounding two-million-car boost to capacity was equivalent of Ford's entire North American output. Clearly, older plants, including some in Canada, would eventually need to be phased out. Bob White warned Mulroney that this shakedown would probably come as soon as 1987, even before some of the new transplants were in operation.[65]

There were other worries. The Big Three had still not effectively responded to Japanese competition and quality, which was slowly eroding their customer base in North America and threatened the long-term stability of the Detroit automakers.[66] Much of the Canadian industry's recent production growth had stemmed from exchange rates, but Canadians could not count on a cheap dollar forever. Another concern stemmed from GM's awarding of the Saturn plant to Tennessee: even with a Canadian labour advantage of $7.50 an hour, the decision showed that the institutional barriers that the auto pact safeguards had been designed to overcome remained strongly in place. GM's choice of location for Saturn was plainly not a matter of simple economics.[67]

Clearly, political considerations still mattered, and though the auto pact may have been lauded by Canadians, there were serious and growing grumblings in the United States over how Canada had achieved all its new capacity, especially the Japanese capacity. In Washington, the DROs had become a particular flashpoint for unhappiness. John Dingell, the powerful Democratic congressman from Michigan and key supporter of the U.S. auto industry, had targeted the programs as a trade-distorting subsidy and violation of the 'spirit of' the auto pact. He told USTR Clayton Yeutter that the FTA negotiations provided 'the quickest opportunity to address US concerns over the Canadian duty-remission programs.'[68] Even if he did not expressly state that the auto pact was his direct target, Dingell was keen to use the looming FTA negotiations to challenge Canadian automotive policy.

Following Mulroney's announcement in September 1985 that the Canadian government would pursue a comprehensive agreement with the United States, free trade sparked a passionate and fully engaged debate in Canada which that galvanized ordinary people from coast to coast. At the centre of this debate was the auto pact. The agreement's studied ambiguity, the confusion over its structure, and the willingness of free-trade advocates and detractors alike to cite it, to bend it to suit their purposes, and to hold it up as an example of either the benefits of free trade or its perils made the agreement a lightning rod of controversy in an already electric discourse. While it is not possible to convey the extent of the debate here in its entirety, two examples will suffice to illustrate the intensity surrounding the auto pact's place in the free-trade debate.

The first example is the question of whether or not the pact was, or should be, in fact, part of the free-trade talks. By the 1980s, the pact had come to be seen as sacrosanct by workers, parts makers, and many ordinary people and politicians, especially in Ontario. As such, the announcement that the federal government would embark on free- trade negotiations immediately provoked fear that the auto pact would be bargained away. After all, the agreement and its Canadian safeguards had been the target of attacks by the Americans since the early 1970s. Ontario Premier David Peterson put the view succinctly. In a Liberal Party advertisement in the *Windsor Star*, he pledged that 'there can be no deal unless it's the right deal ... If our auto pact is gutted – No Deal. Canada's auto industry cannot be a bargaining chip and that is my bottom line.'[69]

In an effort to allay those fears, Mulroney and his government told Canadians that the auto pact was not a part of the negotiations. As early as May 1985, Trade Minister James Kelleher reiterated to reporters that the agreement was not on the table, and that 'I think we would prefer that the auto pact be left intact.'[70] David Peterson agreed, and hoped that this would be the case, though USTR William Brock, following his meeting with the premier, told reporters that 'everything has to be on the table ... We both have to bare our souls to each other.'[71] Publicly, during his June 1986 televised address to the country on the agreement, Mulroney boasted about the success of the auto pact and claimed that it would not be part of the negotiations.[72] Privately, in meetings with Bob White in January and June 1986, Mulroney restated that the agreement was not part of the negotiations.[73] White had his doubts, having long held that it was unrealistic that the United States would exclude the agreement from the talks.[74]

Unsurprisingly, as the contentious negotiations progressed, a number of leaked documents began to appear and it became increasingly apparent that the automotive sector and presumably the auto pact were both indeed part of the negotiations. In early October 1986 a leaked report from the U.S. Department of Commerce seemed to support Simon Reisman's insistence that auto issues had not yet been raised in the negotiations, though it hinted at the Americans' deep displeasure with the DROs, which they saw as threatening the viability of the auto pact. For now, however, the report stated that renegotiation of the auto pact was not in the American's best interests, at least not yet.[75]

More incriminating was the External Affairs memo revealed by Ed Broadbent in late October 1986. The document stated baldly that it was 'time to review the auto pact in light of the experience and changed circumstances of the last 22 years.' Moreover, there was a 'widespread belief' by the public that the safeguards were still central to the functioning of the auto pact; this was a 'misconception' and 'an obstacle to necessary change in automotive trade rules.' The recommendation was to 'stress the importance of examining the safeguard issue in depth,' a proposal that was enough to prompt Broadbent to attack Mulroney and the government in blistering terms for its 'broken promise' regarding the APTA and 'the dangerous incompetence of the negotiating team.'[76]

The incident provoked a firestorm. One conservative Windsor councillor asked Mulroney to make a 'strong an unequivocal' statement that the auto pact was not 'up for grabs' in an effort to disarm the Liberal and NDP members in Windsor who were exploiting the issue 'for their own political advantage.' In both Windsor and St Thomas, city councils expressed 'concern over the latest developments with regard to the potential destruction of the Autopact,' or had 'grave concerns regarding the Federal Government's consideration to abandon the safeguards negotiated in the 1965 Auto Pact.'[77] Again, the federal government reassured Canadians that the auto pact was not, in fact, being put on the table by the negotiating team, but that they needed to be prepared if this happened.

Then, in January 1987, chief U.S. negotiator Peter Murphy told a Canada-U.S. trade conference in Washington that the auto pact should be a part of 'freer trade' negotiations, and specifically pointed to the duty-remission programs and safeguards as something that helped to explain 'why there's pressure in Congress' over the auto trade.[78] The remarks prompted a stern rebuke from his Canadian counterpart. Reisman told reporters that 'I don't know if Peter Murphy is being foolish in daring to get up on a platform with eight or nine hundred businessmen and ad-libbing, whether he's being foolish or whether he's being a knave.'[79] Nonetheless, Murphy's comments prompted a request from Windsor MPs Howard McCurdy and Steven Langdon that Mulroney 'give clear and unequivocal direction to our Canadian negotiating team that the Auto Pact will – under no circumstances – be on the free trade table.'[80]

Another leaked memo in June 1987, this time written by William Merkin, an American FTA negotiator, put to rest any doubt that the auto pact was indeed part of the talks, at least in the U.S. view. Merkin's memo stated that, under the FTA, the auto pact would be 'no more than a shell,' since tariffs on autos – the only penalty for missing the safeguards – would be erased. Just as significantly, the memo outlined that 'there are two reasons automakers operating in Canada consider the Autopact advantageous: 1) duty remission program; and 2) multilateral implementation by Canada. If the US can get at these two things, the pact becomes no more than a shell ... Looked at from this angle, it will not be necessary to completely remove the Autopact.'[81] Only a few days before, Reisman had told reporters, 'If it ain't broke, why fix it?'[82]

Larry Buganto, head of the APMA, was 'shocked' at the revelations, saying that 'removal of the tariffs would render the auto pact toothless and ineffective.' Notwithstanding Trade Minister Pat Carney's protestations otherwise, it was clear that changes to the auto trade under the FTA meant changes to the auto pact. Though Carney claimed that the auto group, beyond 'informative exchanges' in November 1986, had

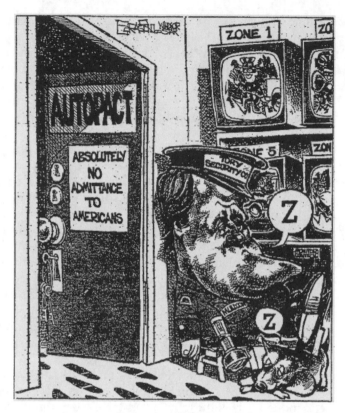

8.1 The auto pact became a flashpoint of the free-trade negotiations and of the controversy generated by Mulroney's willingness to fight for the agreement. *Windsor Star*, 18 October 1987. Permission of Mike Graston.

not even met, one letter to the editor accused the Mulroney government of 'deliberate lying to the Canadian people that the auto pact was not up for sale.'[83] The issue of the whether the auto pact was on the table reflected the emotional intensity surrounding the agreement.

A second example can be seen in the great rhetorical battle between the government and the newly formed Canadian Auto Workers over the auto pact's meaning and place within the free-trade talks. This war of words, especially between Simon Reisman and Bob White, played out on the pages of national newspapers, in the broadcast media, and, eventually, on the hustings. The combatants were larger-than-life personalities: Reisman was perhaps the most famous and powerful civil servant of his era; White, coming off his titanic battle and split with the UAW, was at the height of his power and influence. A grudge match waged to convince Canadians of their respective points, the 'air war' pitted two master media showmen against one another, with sometimes explosive results.

The Reisman-White debate hinged on three key issues. The first was the government's use of the auto pact as an example of free trade. In a *Globe and Mail* interview in May 1986, Reisman complained that the auto union was 'out there praising to the skies the automotive pact, treating it as a piece of religion, sacred and untouchable, worrying about maybe this will be talked about.' But, he wondered, 'have you ever heard one of them get up and say Simon Reisman led the negotiations and negotiated that pact?' In Reisman's view, the auto pact was a model of free trade which illustrated 'the fruits ... of what freer trade is supposed to bring you. The province of Ontario and, for that matter, a good part of Canada is living off this, is benefiting from this. Now how in the world can the leader of the UAW get up on his hind legs and say we've got it, we won it, don't touch it, but nobody else can have it in their sectors?'

White's response was to ask in the *Globe and Mail*: 'Is Mr. Reisman giving us a new definition of free trade that rejects leaving decisions totally to corporations and includes *safeguards* for Canada to ensure commitments to Canada? Is Mr. Reisman confirming that the Auto Pact has worked so well that it will definitely not be eroded by his bargaining team?' Reisman fired back that 'history appears to be repeating itself,' and that White and the UAW were beginning 'with the assumption that things will work out badly.'[84]

The following month, on 16 June, Mulroney gave a televised speech to the nation in which he prominently linked the auto pact to the free-trade idea, saying that 'everyone agrees it's been good for the country.' White responded in a column in the *Financial Post*, arguing that 'Simon Reisman, who should know better, has strangely argued that the Pact represents free trade. And the prime minister has followed Reisman's line.' Instead, White argued that the two men were 'wrong in how they characterize the Pact,' since, as he wrote to the *Globe*, it 'included safeguards for Canada and so was in fact not at all an example of free trade.' The *Globe*, however, did not include this sentence in its printed version of White's letter.[85]

Reisman persisted in his campaign to equate the auto pact with free trade, releasing a statement saying in October 1987 as the negotiations came to a head that 'the Auto Pact provides a model, not in form but in results, of the success that might be achieved through a free trade agreement covering other manufactured goods sectors.'[86] Somewhat disingenuously, given its protectionist measures, the auto-pact-as-free-trade theme also appeared in government literature on the agreement.[87]

Another issue was the government's claim that the union had not supported the auto pact. This was an attempt to discredit the union and put it on the defensive over the agreement. During his 16 June address, Mulroney had stated that when it was created the auto pact 'was roundly criticized by some prominent politicians and union leaders.' Similarly, in the *Globe* interview, Reisman said that the UAW had originally opposed the auto agreement. This prompted a sharp response from White, who replied that 'Reisman has either been misquoted or has suffered an uncharacteristic memory lapse.' White also wrote directly to Reisman, telling him that 'you know, or should know, that the UAW *did* support the auto pact from its inception.'[88]

Both men were partially correct. In 1964–5 George Burt and Walter Reuther had supported the auto pact, though both had voiced misgivings and had threatened to withdraw support if governments did not provide adequate adjustment assistance for workers affected by the agreement's dislocation.[89] Eventually, the union became a strong supporter of the agreement, a position the UAW reaffirmed in 1970 when the auto pact was threatened by renegotiation. The union released a statement that the agreement had been 'of great economic value to both countries' and that 'the outcome of the present discussions must be a continuation of the agreement.'[90] By the time of the FTA negotiations, the CAW was the most vocal supporter of the auto pact.

Finally, and most important, the antagonists fought over the impact that the FTA would have on the auto pact and the industry. After meeting with the prime minister, White wrote to him to reaffirm his position that the auto pact should not be included in the FTA negotiations, and warned him 'of the dangers of such a road.' To put the pact on the negotiating table 'would be giving up a fundamental tool that provides Canada with some security and flexibility in dealing with an uncertain future and we simply can't, on the basis of present optimism, risk such an irreversible step.'[91] The union leader was consistent in his claim that entering into a negotiation with the United States would inevitably lead to putting the auto pact 'up for negotiation,' wherein the agreement 'and the important safeguards it provides could be lost.'[92]

On this point, White was not the only one worried about what would happen to the sector under a free-trade negotiation. Canadian parts makers were deeply concerned that Canada would lose the auto pact. This was one of the few policy advantages Canada had in the auto trade, in their view. The United States, on the other hand, already had Foreign Trade Zones, which gave breaks to offshore companies. There was also the possibility that 'one side of the border' producers, based in the United States, might circumvent export restraints. For instance, the cars built by the GM/Toyota NUMMI plant in California would not be considered offshore imports, though they would certainly have an impact on the market and therefore production in Canada.[93] The parts makers therefore felt that 'another trade vehicle or negotiated instrument – a strengthened auto pact, not free trade – was necessary to ensure a stronger outlet for Canadian parts.'[94] Even individual firms were speaking out about free trade: Magna's Frank Stronach was against the agreement, and eventually ran and lost as a Liberal anti-free-trade candidate in the election of 1988.[95]

Like Bob White, APMA president Patrick Lavelle was a staunch opponent of the idea of a free-trade agreement with the United States. When the Macdonald Commission's report had been released, Lavelle called it a 'facile attempt to justify Donald Macdonald's cry for a leap of faith. The underlying assumption is that we should throw ourselves off the cliff and hope someone will catch us.'[96] He held that 'we are living in an environment where major trade relationships are managed and arranged – not left to laissez-faire free trade.' In 1986 Lavelle was appointed by Ontario's Peterson to the post of deputy minister of industry trade and technology, a key position as the agreement headed into negotiations.[97] Soon, he would discover just what Macdonald's leap of faith meant for the Canadian industry.

'No More Than a Shell': Negotiating the FTA's Automotive Provisions, 1986–8

Inside the federal government's Trade Negotiations Office (TNO), perched high above downtown Ottawa, the auto sector was proving to be an 'early and enduring concern,' according to more than one senior negotiator. Reisman's history with the auto pact, the symbolic and political status of the agreement, and the overwhelming importance of the auto trade (by 1986 a third of Canada-U.S. trade was automotive, making it the largest component of the largest trade relationship in the world) all made the issue fraught with challenges.[98]

The auto-industry study commissioned by the TNO, one of dozens Reisman and his team had prepared for the negotiations, recognized that negotiating free trade presented an opening for the United States to settle old scores on the auto pact: the Americans 'may be expected to take a more aggressive position against Canadian initiatives either to increase the safeguards as proposed in the 1983 Task Force Report ... or any other measures to extend benefits to increase automotive production in Canada.' The study also warned that 'there are potential costs and risks and no discernible benefits from rolling the Automotive Agreement into a more comprehensive trade arrangement,' and that if the automotive sector became 'an element in the discussion of a comprehensive trade agreement' the United States would seek removal of the safeguards. There was also the question of the DROs, which the Americans saw as 'little more than subsidies to Canadian auto parts producers.' The obvious threat was that these programs 'could get caught up in "levelling the playing field."'[99]

Another early TNO discussion paper on autos was dismissive of the importance of the agreement. It emphasized that 'the bottom line is that the APTA, which never applied to certain aspects of the industry, is becoming daily more irrelevant with the coming on stream of production controlled by non-North American companies, and imposes no real constraints or obligations on the existing participants.' Since the safeguards were being significantly surpassed, and 'GM, Ford and Chrysler unanimously agree that sourcing decisions are currently made on the basis of quality, reliability and cost competitiveness, not CVA,' they were essentially irrelevant.[100]

Instead, as a 'desirable outcome,' the TNO study proposed that tariffs be removed over a five-year period, replaced with a 50 per cent North American rule-of-origin requirement. The paper also warned that the USTR 'did not yet know about the confidential commitments to the Japanese and Korean firms building assembly plants,' which had the potential to 'dramatically expand the amount of trade' coming from Canada and cause further friction. EA officials were not so convinced, however, and felt that this initial approach was 'shallow' and did 'not warrant detailed comment and study at this time.' Yet the TNO study did point to important issues in the auto negotiations – and became famous as the leaked evidence of Canadian willingness to bargain the auto pact and its safeguards as part of the FTA negotiations revealed by Broadbent.[101]

By September 1986, there had yet to be substantive talks on auto issues between the two sides. Another major assessment of the auto trade, this time from DRIE, considered the place of the APTA within the free-trade talks and was also less than enamoured of the auto pact. 'There appears to be,' DRIE officials stated, 'a tendency in examining the ability of the auto pact to deal with critical automotive issues to view it without fault or to dissect it to examine its structural weaknesses.' But a 'better focus' from the government's point of view might be 'a second round of rationalization given the recent trend to internationalization in the industry.' The result would be to consider the issue as 'not whether the auto pact is sacrosanct but rather what is required to foster and preserve the benefits of rationalization.'

In fact, the DRIE memo pointed out that duties had never been applied to companies for missing safeguards, and the decreasing tariff rates, coupled with the 'significant loophole' ability of the manufacturers to simply opt out of the ratio requirement by paying duties, meant that the auto pact's days as an effective policy might be numbered. Overall, the thrust of the recommendation was that cabinet should seek to maximize parts investment over assembly, given the impending overcapacity of the latter.[102] Some Canadian policy makers were clearly no longer attached to the auto pact as the key industrial strategy of the government.

Despite all the discussion, there was little actual movement on the auto field over the next few months. By April 1987, reports circulated that the Canadians had not received any substantial proposals regarding autos, and Ottawa had not made any decision on its own about automotive policy, either in terms of the ongoing assessment of the auto pact's status or as a part of the FTA negotiations.[103] In July, American Big Three executives told Yeutter that they wanted a 50 per cent rule of origin, based on a more flexible corporate average as opposed to in-product content. This would allow some vehicles and parts to enter the United States (or Canada) without having any North American content, giving the Big Three a significant advantage on imports from their offshore subsidiaries. Not long after this, Industry Minister Michel Côté announced that he was putting off a government strategy paper on the auto industry, likely until after the October deadline for FTA talks required by the U.S. fast-track authority.[104]

In May, government officials considered the implications of bilateralization of the auto pact. Such a move would mean the end of duty-free imports from third countries by the Canadian-based makers who were bona fide manufacturers under the auto pact, thereby restricting auto pact benefits to Canada and the United States. But bilateralization would also create major problems: U.S. makers would have a difficult time meeting selling their captive offshore products, which would in turn reduce the sales ratio and therefore the production ratio of the auto pact safeguards. Volvo Canada would not be able to import parts duty-free and would have to be 'grandfathered' under bilateralization. Canada would need to obtain a waiver at the GATT, as the United States had done in 1965. GM, with its Suzuki plant in Ingersoll being built, would be opposed. In the end, it was argued that, if a FTA was negotiated with a commensurate removal of auto tariffs, bilateralization would not be an issue. If an FTA was not negotiated, it was 'difficult to see any net benefit to Canada unless bilateralization is used as a coinage to achieve bigger gains in other areas.'[105]

The Canadian industry took a directly opposite approach. Instead of bilateralization, it reaffirmed its desire to see auto pact status extended to the new manufacturers in Canada during meetings with Côté and senior External Affairs officials in April and June 1987. The industry representatives, from the MVMA, APMA, and CAW, underlined their view that the auto pact standards were essential, should be 'enforced,' and served as 'standards of corporate behaviour' for all auto producers. They sought to 'send a signal' to the negotiating teams. It was a rare example of unanimity from the industry, save for the offshore producers, of course.[106] It also reflected a willingness of the Canadian Big Three subsidiaries to assert their continued support of the auto pact.

In August, Trade Minister Pat Carney's officials laid out a number of options for her to consider as the auto talks headed into their final phase. As part of their analysis, EA officials reminded the minister that the Letter of Undertaking commitments signed by the Big Three in 1964 for an increase beyond 60 CVA to match any increase in sales were 'outside the agreement' and were therefore 'not negotiable.' But the U.S. standard for duty-free entry under the auto pact of 50 per cent North American content was 'more effective and better defined.' This was a standard that the Big Three were observing closely, and the Japanese were 'setting up' to 'recognize these conditions' and 'plan accordingly.' The figure was also considerably higher than the 35 per cent rule of origin that was under discussion by the FTA negotiators.[107]

Another option, which had the backing of the Big Three in the United States, was a new 50 per cent corporate standard, one that was not on a product-by-product basis. Also considered was the 60 per cent CVA standard as laid out by the 1965 Letters of Undertaking (which the auto companies had generally hit), an increased 80 per cent North American standard, as proposed by the APMA, MVMA, and CAW, and a 70 per cent North American standard, suggested by the Sectoral Advisory Group on International Trade (SAGIT). The latter represented a compromise between the U.S. Big Three proposal and that of the Canadian industry. If none of these options were workable, officials felt that in the last resort 'the existing US conditions under the Auto Pact might well be used, if necessary, as the common standard governing duty free automotive trade between Canada and the United States.'[108]

As the intense negotiations continued, things took a bleak turn in September. Talks became more difficult. Yeutter told senior administration officials in Washington that the Canadians were 'getting very nervous.' At one pivotal movement, Reisman and his team walked away from the negotiating table over dispute settlement and subsidies. Yeutter knew that dispute settlement was 'their primary negotiating objective,' since Carney had 'tried an end run on dispute settlement just as the Prime Minister did' at a Venice international meeting. But Yeutter was confident that Murphy and the Americans could get a deal done, even 'under difficult circumstances as their chief negotiator has a volatile personality.'[109]

With the talks at an impasse, Canada's New York consul general reported that, according to senior GM officials, the Big Three and the state of Michigan were working on a joint statement outlining their desire for the end of duty remissions, 50 per cent content on a direct processing basis, and recognition of the auto pact but with its membership frozen and 'with value added to be on a North American basis.' That is, the auto pact would remain in place for the Big Three (and significantly, not the Japanese), but the 50 per cent rule would essentially supersede the safeguard requirements.[110]

Talks restarted a few days later and, after a frenzy of last-minute discussions, a draft accord was reached by the 3 October deadline. The broad strokes of a comprehensive Canada-U.S. trade deal included a dispute-settlement mechanism, a reduction of tariffs to zero, some exemptions for certain Canadian industries such as culture, and a host of changes that touched upon virtually every sector of the economy, from the trade in services to investment and energy.[111] In the White House, President Reagan called Prime Minister Mulroney in Ottawa to congratulate him on the accomplishment.[112]

Even after the October release of the draft agreement, negotiations continued on a number of contentious auto issues. One major sticking point was GM's Ingersoll joint-venture with Suzuki, CAMI. The FTA froze out any firm that was not on the auto pact list if it did not meet pact requirements by 1 January 1989. This made it nearly impossible for Honda, Toyota, and Hyundai to be a part of the auto pact list, since their operations were not close to meeting the agreement's requirements. Neither was CAMI, but GM was insistent that the plant, which had only been announced in 1986 and was not yet complete, be part of the auto pact, even if it did not begin production by the deadline.

GM had made an agreement with the Canadian government in June 1987 which explicitly required CAMI to 'meet the terms of the Auto Pact over a specific period commencing August 1, 1986.' George Peapples, GM Canada's president, told Reisman that CAMI's situation was 'entirely distinct' from that of the other Japanese and Korean companies, since it had made a 'legal obligation' that predated the FTA: though GM had fought stringently to freeze the other transplants out of the auto pact forever, 'it is our position that CAMI is and has been an auto pact participant.' Peapples also informed Finance Minister Michael Wilson that his parent firm had brought the same issue to the attention of the USTR. Eventually, CAMI was given auto pact status owing to GM's pressure.[113]

In the end, when the final text was initialled in December 1987, it was clear that if the auto pact itself had not been on the table, Canadian auto policy certainly was. The actual text of Chapter 10 of the FTA, 'Trade in Automotive Goods,' was surprisingly brief. At the outset, it stated that both parties would 'endeavour to administer' the APTA 'in the best interests of employment and production in both countries.' Language in the draft agreement that called for Canada and the United States to 'ensure that the industry in both countries should prosper in the future' had been expunged.[114] After that, the first items in the chapter laid out the prohibition of export- and production-based remissions, immediately for the former, and for the latter at 'such earlier date specified in existing agreements between Canada and the recipient of the waiver' or by 1996. Next was the explanation of Canada's phase-out on the prohibition of imports of used cars, followed by the creation of a 'blue-ribbon panel' to examine the auto trade in the future.[115] A new more stringent 50 per cent rule of origin, one that included only the direct costs of manufacturing, was the final substantive section, with the bulk of the chapter devoted to definitions and annexes which included lists of auto pact companies, companies with export-remission waivers, and companies with production-based waivers. (See Appendix D.)

Simple on the surface, Chapter 10 reflected a labyrinth of consequence. The auto pact remained, so it seemed, unaltered, though it
was now a part of the FTA. In public, Reisman stated that 'we hon-
oured our pledge that we would retain the auto pact and only entertain suggestions that would make things better.'[116] Privately, officials
in EA maintained that 'yes, the government did say that it felt that the
Auto Pact had been working well, and that Canada would not raise it
at the bargaining table during the negotiations. We didn't.' Instead, 'the
government said that if the Americans made some proposals which offered the potential for improvements in terms of opportunities for more
production and employment in Canada, we would listen to them.' The
Americans 'did have some ideas which we found to be a sound basis
for discussion.' The end result was an 'Auto Pact plus – because the
Auto Pact is very much a part of the Free Trade Agreement.'[117]

The very fact that the auto pact and its safeguards continued to exist,
at least ostensibly, rankled many Americans. In Washington, Commerce
Department officials explained to Michigan's John Dingell, chair of the
House Committee on Energy and Commerce, that American negotiators had 'sought the elimination' of the auto pact safeguards. But the
Canadians 'made it clear that the matter was not negotiable, and if the
US insisted, there would be no FTA.' This was, according to the administration, 'a credible threat given the political situation in the Province
of Ontario where most of the automobile industry is located.'[118]

In fact, though it was still intact, the auto pact had essentially been
rendered a shell, as Canadian diplomats privately admitted. By the
end of the 'transition period,' one External Affairs official remarked,
'all Canada-US automotive trade will be governed by the provisions
of the FTA.' Though '*the Auto Pact remains in place*,' and third-country
duty-free entry was still subject to those companies meeting the ratio,
'backed by the declining tariff,' there was no real consequence for auto
pact firms missing the now peripheral safeguards.[119] Only the new 50
per cent North American content rules really mattered; third-party imports, though growing, constituted a paltry $300 million out of the total
North American two-way auto trade in 1986 of $46 billion.[120]

Just as important, from the U.S. point of view, the DROs had been
effectively killed. As the USTR proudly reported when the draft deal
had been sealed, the remissions, 'all of which distort trade and investment patterns,' faced either immediate (export-based) or phased (production-based) elimination, over six years. But the latter's slow death
did not appease some Americans. Dingell wanted to know why there

8.2 Killing the goose that laid the golden eggs? *Toronto Star*, 5 June 1986. Reprinted with permission – Torstar Syndication Services.

was such a long phase-out for the production-based remissions. The administration's response was that the export-based programs were renewable on an annual basis, and could be terminated by 1 January 1989. The production-based remissions, on the other hand, were '*multi-year* contracts. Canadian negotiators insisted that these contractual obligations, made in return for investment already in place or started, be allowed to run their course. Whether one accepts their rationale is not the issue. Rather, the immediate termination of one program was negotiable, the other was not.'[121]

Dingell could not find much solace in the rule-of-origin changes, either. Though the American parts industry (and Canadian parts makers, too) had argued for a 60 per cent rule of origin, the Canadians had agreed to a 50 per cent rule. The new rule was stricter than the auto pact rules in that the new content regulation was based solely on the production costs, and did not allow profits, marketing, or distribution costs, as under the auto pact rules. This made it tougher for the Japanese to export across the border from Canada, but not impossible. It was a major disappointment for Dingell, who argued that the Japanese could still export Canadian-assembled cars with Japanese-built engines or transmissions, something that a 60 per cent rule would have made very difficult to achieve.[122] In any event, if the Japanese did not hit the 50 per cent content requirement, the U.S. tariff of 2.5 per cent was not so onerous.

The agreement's negotiators must have considered it a measure of success that, across industry and governments on both sides of the border, few were completely satisfied with the outcome. Most pleased were the U.S. Big Three. Thomas Hanna, head of the American MVMA, testified to the Senate Finance Committee that the FTA was 'a good and solid agreement for this industry, and one that we believe advances United States national industries as well.' Hanna felt the FTA preserved duty-free status under the auto pact but also offered 'the possibility of free trading rights for the new companies establishing plants in North America.'[123] He focused on three key issues for his industry. The first was duty remission, where there was 'the potential for a major trade distortion.' Hanna was pleased that the FTA settled the issue: though the FTA did not 'wipe out the whole program immediately as we had hoped,' it did secure a commitment to 'shut it down completely' as the individual commitments to each company expired.

Second, Hanna noted that, on the rule of origin, the original negotiating figure had been 35 per cent, which had been raised at the insistence of the MVMA to 50 per cent, ensuring that 'the benefits of the agreement go to companies and products which can fairly be considered American or Canadian.' Third, Hanna spoke of the auto pact safeguards. While the Canadian government 'made them a permanent feature of their automotive policy,' the MVMA had not understood them to be so. In any event, since auto pact members now so far exceeded these requirements, 'we can project into the future [that] they will have no practical effect on our companies' operations.' Hanna said the MVMA 'told that to our negotiators and said that, if the Canadians insisted that there could be no free trade agreement without keeping the Auto Pact intact, we could accept that.'[124] The upshot was that the retention of the auto pact and its safeguards would have virtually no impact in the future.

Michigan politicians were nowhere near as pleased as the automakers. The state's Marc Santucci was very unhappy that the auto pact stayed in place, that the remissions were only being phased out over time, and that there was a 50 per cent rule of origin as opposed to a 60 per cent rule. He was scathing in his assessment: 'The US accomplishment of goals is more perceived than real. Canada's accomplishments are more real than we perceive. The response of our policy makers was to cave in on nearly every issue that was in dispute.'[125] Michigan Senator Don Riegle, Jr, was also very upset about the continuation of the production-based duty-remission plans. Riegle reminded the USTR that it had requested copies of the Japanese-Canadian MOUs in January 1988, but that the Canadians refused to give them to the Americans. The continuation of the DROs was 'more damaging than it would appear,' since it would affect future sourcing decisions for a long time to come.[126]

American parts makers were also displeased. APAA Vice-President Linda J. Hoffman felt that 'what the administration accepted is a lop-sided agreement that sanctions long-standing Canadian protectionism and unfairly favors Canadian parts and car production at the expense of US manufacturing and jobs.' As to auto pact safeguards, the agreement would 'codify these protectionist and one-sided rules long opposed by our government.' Hoffman declared that 'by combining the Canadian content rules and the duty-free ride accorded other country's suppliers, it is possible to envision cars built in Canada, without a dime's worth of US content,' though this was highly unlikely. Hoffman told senators flatly that she thought the auto provisions of the FTA should be renegotiated to get rid of any 'trade distorting' aspects, including the auto pact.[127]

UAW economist Steve Beckman was especially upset that auto pact was retained: the UAW had 'serious problems with the auto sections of the agreement.' The retention of the safeguards 'puts a tremendous impetus on the North American companies to close US rather than Canadian plants so that the companies will continue to meet the Canadian safeguards and thereby qualify for the duty free benefit of importing into Canada.' The rule of origin was not high enough, the DROs stayed in place until 1996, and the GM-Suzuki transplant was provided 'special treatment' allowing it to become a member of the auto pact, even though it was not going to produce any cars until 1989, thus giving GM a huge advantage through its Japanese subsidiary. Beckman claimed that 'the agreement is not, in fact a free trade agreement – it is misrepresented – it is in fact a standstill agreement which permits excessive Canadian intervention in the economy to remain and prevents the US from taking necessary intervention in the economy by making it illegal under the agreement.'[128] Solidarity House, which had spent the better part of two decades defending the auto pact, felt no need to do so following White's breakaway.

Yet, on the Canadian side of the border, stakeholders were equally concerned. Bob White maintained that, with tariffs phased out over ten years, there was no penalty for missing the safeguards – it was 'like having a speed limit with no fine or penalty to enforce it.' Moreover, 'our hands are tied in terms of any future trade-related auto policy. This is particularly dangerous.' Extending the auto pact to include the Japanese was White's main lobbying goal, but instead the negotiators froze the list. The 50 per cent content rule wasn't enough, either, since it made it easier for the Japanese to export from Canada with significant overseas parts, and gave the Big Three a green light to increase their own offshore sourcing, duty-free. Overall, White felt that 'it is unforgiveable to surrender the policy footholds we have, to lose the vital instruments of future policy, and to leave the future to the uncertainties of market forces and unilateral corporate decisions.'[129]

Ontario Premier David Peterson was equally scathing in his assessment. Since the FTA did not include sanctions for missing the safeguards under the auto pact, then Ontario was 'obviously against' the agreement. His minister of industry, trade, and technology, Monte Kwinter, was far more colourful in his view of the deal: 'My position is that we were promised a Cadillac, when we got the bill it was for a Rolls Royce, and they delivered a Chevette.' Joking aside, Kwinter and the Ontario government was 'totally opposed to what they have done with the auto pact ... We feel they have gutted it.' Ontario NDP leader Bob Rae felt that the FTA was a deal 'which no Canadian government in its right mind would sign and no Ontario government could conceivably go along with.'[130]

The Japanese, though they did not make any public statements about the agreement, could not have been pleased with the outcome. One confidential report written for the Ontario government made the case that the FTA discriminated against Japanese producers in a number of ways, and that they could 'not afford to accept these without a response,' likely at the GATT.[131] The fact that the Canadians had acceded to freezing the auto pact list, and had gone as far as to state (in a foot-note to the FTA) that any company on the auto pact list would cease to be included if it was taken over by another manufacturer (a clause clearly aimed at the Japanese without specifically naming them), indi-cated how badly Japan had fared in the negotiations.[132]

Of course, the two federal governments were pleased that an agree-ment had been achieved. In the White House, though there were still a few hurdles to having the agreement passed in Congress, Reagan looked to the future, declaring that the agreement 'great as it is ... only the beginning.' The Great Communicator continued, as only he could: 'We will, together with our new partner in peace and freedom, Canada, carry the banner of free trade to Mexico, to the Caribbean, and all of Latin America, and from there on around the world.'[133] For his part, Mulroney faced one more round of titanic free-trade debates, which he won during the bruising election campaign of 1988. By then, the FTA's impact on the auto pact and the North American auto trade was only beginning to come into focus. It would be more than a decade before the fate of the former would finally be clear.

Conclusion: The Auto Pact's Death and the End of Creative Policy Making, 1989–2001

In negotiating a free-trade agreement with the United States, Canadian politicians and policy makers faced difficult choices when it came to the automotive sector. On the one hand, they wished to keep the original auto pact signatories happy. These companies had invested billions of dollars in the Canadian industry in the post-war period and were the core of the sector. The Big Three had virtually always adhered to the auto pact safeguard requirements since 1965, and by the mid-1980s had embarked on another round of investment which had led to a reindus-trialization of the sector after the difficulties experienced between 1979 and 1983.

On the other hand, Canadian policy makers wanted to lure new for-eign automotive investment into the country, given the increasing in-ternationalization of the North American industry. Once they did so, Ottawa wished to keep these new auto producers happy and, to that end, offered them remissions and incentives, some of which infuriated the Big Three – both the Canadian subsidiaries and their American par-ents.[134] The conflict between these two impulses came to a head during the FTA negotiations, which forced Ottawa to decide which sector of the industry – Big Three or offshore –would benefit most from the new arrangements being worked out with Washington.

The end result largely favoured the American producers in Canada. Though the Canadians gained some concessions in terms of timing (the long phase-out of tariffs and production-based DROs), and the 50 per cent rule or origin (as opposed to 60 per cent), what resulted rendered the auto pact essentially obsolete when it came to automotive trade between Canada and the United States. Yes, the auto pact still mattered for third-country trade, but this was a pittance and made very little difference for the U.S. manufacturers. And, while free trade did not hurt Canadian parts makers too much – a low dollar meant that the industry flourished in the 1990s – it signalled to the Japanese producers in Canada that theirs was a second-class status.

As Lorraine Eden and Maureen Molot have shown, during the FTA negotiations the Japanese manufacturers remained outsiders in the bargaining process and did not lobby to protect their position. The FTA meant that 'the Asian transplants clearly lost ... once they realized that the FTA had enshrined the two-tier character of the Canadian assembly industry, they expressed their concerns to the Canadian government.'[135] The Japanese manufacturers had faced export restraints, port blockades, and content threats; they had finally been induced to produce in Canada through remissions and promises of auto pact status. But, after the FTA negotiations, they were legally frozen out of the auto pact (while Suzuki, because of its joint venture with GM, was allowed in), and their remission programs were to be eradicated entirely by 1996. And, although Honda and Toyota could gain some benefit from the 50 per cent threshold in the FTA (which upset quite a few in the United States), eventually that threshold was replaced by a 62.5 per cent rule of origin when the North American Free Trade Agreement was implemented in 1993. The 62.5 per cent marker made it significantly more difficult for the Japanese to export into the United States duty-free.[136] At the same time, the United States tightened its customs surveillance considerably following the FTA, reflecting the continuingly inhospitable American approach to Japanese exports from Canada.[137]

This attitude was exemplified by the Honda engine case in the early 1990s. During this incident, the United States claimed that engines in Honda cars assembled in and coming from Canada did not meet the 50 per cent rule of origin, and slapped tariffs amounting to millions of dollars on the vehicles, prompting a low-grade diplomatic contretemps between the two countries. Canada held that the engines – ironically, built in the United States – met the rule of origin as part of the Canadian-assembled vehicle, while the United States felt they did not. Eventually, the issue was resolved, but it indicated the residual level of American unhappiness towards Japanese assembly in Canada, and towards Canadian policy making in the auto field, especially the still-operative production-remission plans.[138]

In assessing the overall Canadian strategy in this period, it makes sense to ask if the remissions were simply a bargaining chip for the free-trade talks. After all, the expanded export and production remission plans appeared at almost the same time that the Canadian government decided to launch its free-trade initiative. Were they set up to simply get the Japanese to Canada, and then to be used in the FTA negotiations to avoid further erosion of the auto pact? At a meeting between MVMA, APMA, and CAW representatives and Industry Minister Michel Côté in September 1985, Grant Wilson of the APMA privately told Sam Gindin that the remission program 'wasn't worth the potential costs of the US reaction and that we could save it as a bargaining chip to surrender down the road.' Gindin wasn't convinced, given that the remission was mobilizing U.S. displeasure towards Canadian auto policy in general – including the auto pact.[139] If this was indeed the case, it was a cagey and highly risky strategy by the Canadians. But such a tactic did echo the 1962–4 push for remissions (accompanied by the threat of higher content) and, at the same time, strengthened continentalism. Though the circumstances were not exactly identical, there were similarities, especially given the presence of Simon Reisman during each period.

Indeed, Reisman's role in both negotiations was pivotal. In 1964 Reisman had been able to negotiate the hybrid protectionist-free trade auto pact, an agreement that had over its life become sacrosanct in the eyes of many of its supporters. Two decades later, as only Nixon could go to China, only Reisman could put the auto pact on the free-trade negotiating table. Only Reisman, the progenitor of the auto pact and so many of the creative auto policies utilized by the Canadian state, could have signed off on the effective demise of the auto pact and those policies. Though a 'volatile' negotiator, his presence reassured many Canadians that the FTA could be as beneficial as the auto pact. Reisman's stature as the father of the auto pact gave him an authority and credibility in the free-trade negotiations which allowed him to cement a deal that effectively ended the auto pact as a functioning managed-trade regime. The FTA provisions superseded those of the auto pact, save for a minor part of the North American auto trade. It was, in the view of Neil Macdonald, clear that 'when we read the fine print ... Canada gave way to American demands.'[140]

Eventually, the Japanese exacted their revenge. In 1998, as soon as the last production-based duty-remission orders had been phased out as required by the FTA, the Japanese (along with the European Union) launched a complaint at the WTO against the auto pact's remaining measures. Given that all North American manufacturers were bound by the NAFTA rules, the Japanese complaint rested on the privileged status accorded under the APTA to auto pact members, which allowed them to import into Canada duty-free (and avoid a 6.1 per cent MFN tariff). This meant that the auto pact discriminated against some manufacturers in Canada, contrary to Canada's assurance in 1964 at the GATT that the agreement would be multilateral in nature. Freezing the auto pact list in 1989 put Canada in violation of its own promises under the agreement, especially since by the 1990s the Japanese were effectively meeting the auto pact requirements. In 2001 the WTO ruled in favour of the Japanese, and Canada was forced to give up the last vestiges of its auto pact.[141]

The WTO decision signalled the death knell of creative Canadian policy making in the auto field. With the official end of the auto pact, the eradication of both export- and production-based duty-remission orders, and the seeming impossibility of measures such as port slowdowns or even voluntary restraint agreements in this rigorously new rules-based trading world, there was little left in the government's policy cupboard when it came to shaping the Canadian auto sector. What remained were direct subsidies by governments such as loans or investment incentives and, unlikely though it might have seemed in the 1990s and 2000s, direct government ownership of the industry.

Both of these measures came to play important roles in the Canadian government's automotive strategy after 2001. In the case of direct support, the success of governments such as Ontario's in luring new automotive investment to the province was a direct consequence of its willingness to provide multinational corporations with millions and billions in taxpayer funds to support new plants and facilities. In the case of direct ownership, both Canada and Ontario – not to mention the U.S. federal government – reluctantly embraced partial nationalization as the only effective response to the auto industry's meltdown in 2008–9. Like the 1980 Chrysler bailout a generation before, the Canadian decision to take minority ownership stakes in both General Motors and Chrysler was as much a consequence of the country's economic dependence upon this dominant industry as it was a recognition that the state had few tools left at its disposal when it came to automotive policy making. The coming of free trade, and the end of the auto pact, had rendered a once creatively activist state little more than a bailout fund for institutions seemingly too big or important to fail.

Conclusion
One in Six: The Ratio of Survival

Half a century ago, a very simple idea about the Canadian auto sector started to take hold in the political and public imagination. The auto industry's importance to the Canadian economy and body politic could be summarized by a basic equation, an easy-to-remember ratio that varied only slightly in the decades to follow. Whether accurate or not, the notion that such a sprawling and complex industrial sector could be boiled down to a simple rubric made it very appealing. It gave politicians and policy makers a convenient rhetorical hammer by which to drive home the industry's importance and, perhaps more significant, justify their actions in the automotive field. It is not that the ratio wasn't true, because it essentially was; then, as today, the production of automobiles remains without question the largest and most important economic sector in North America.

It began innocuously enough. In a 1960 CBC television report on the problems in the industry, journalist Norman DePoe claimed that 'one business in seven' in Canada was automotive or auto-related.[1] A few years later, a young economics student at the University of Windsor ran an input-output analysis of employment in Ontario and came up with the startling result that one in six jobs in the province was connected in some way to the automotive sector. That student, Dennis DesRosiers, was hired by the provincial government as an auto analyst in the early 1970s, and his figure was used in a 1974 budget statement.[2]

By the mid-1970s, 'one in six' had become a mantra repeated almost as often as 'fair share.' Ontario Treasurer Darcy McKeough stated in the legislature in 1976 that the auto industry supported either 'directly or indirectly, one in every six jobs in this province.' In a 1976 *Canadian Business* article, journalist Mark Witten wrote that 'the auto industry is

Ontario's largest employer. Directly or indirectly it accounts for one out of six jobs in the province.' In 1978 Ontario NDP leader Michael Cassidy also cited the figure, which had been prominently mentioned in the Ontario government report, *Canada's Share of the North American Auto Industry: An Ontario Perspective*.[3] Similarly, a 1979 *Saturday Night* article noted that 'the auto industry is directly or indirectly responsible for one out of every six jobs in Ontario; it's the one indispensible industry.'[4]

The ratio had its cross-border variations, too. The 1977 *Review of the North American Auto Industry*, written by C.D. Arthur, stated that 'nearly one out of every six persons in North America, either directly or indirectly, owes their livelihood at least in part to the fortunes of the motor vehicle.'[5] Indeed, in the United States, the same figure proliferated, so much so that during the bleak Chrysler bailout period the Carter administration questioned its veracity. Even though Neil Goldscmidt, Carter's secretary of transportation, told the president that 'the industry estimates that as many as 14 million jobs, or about one in six in the US, are related to the motor vehicle industry as a whole,' White House officials felt that, upon closer inspection, one in six was 'a political statement, not a policy or analytic statement.' The real figure, 'though not inconsiderable,' was really 'a far cry' from one in six workers. In the depths of the auto crisis of 1980, this was not merely an academic exercise.[6] At that point, politicians, journalists, and the industry itself were all using the figure.[7]

By 1985, Ontario Premier David Peterson was telling reporters that 'one in five' people in Ontario were in some way employed by the auto industry.[8] During the 1987 Ontario provincial election and in the midst of the free-trade debate, one of Peterson's Windsor candidates ran radio ads declaring that 'one in six jobs in Ontario depends on the auto industry.'[9] The figure has persisted, even after decades of change and downsizing in the sector: in 2009 Stephen Beatty, managing director of Toyota Canada, told a University of Guelph audience that 'one in six workers in Canada derives some portion of his or her livelihood from the auto sector.'[10]

The long-standing use of the one-in-six ratio is important because it reflects, in a very representative way, the central and underlying argument of this book. The sheer number of jobs and the relative importance of the auto industry within the Canadian economy became the driving paradigm that explains Canadian state action in the auto sector. More than any other 'fact,' the level of automotive employment, itself a consequence of the level of production and investment in the

Canadian sector and the health of the trade balance and the auto pact, pushed politicians, policy makers, and workers to initiate and engage in a host of creative and aggressive policies and actions to ensure that Canada and its workers received what was seen as their fair share of the sector's bounty. One in six was, and remains, the corollary of the fair-share mantra.

If one steps back for a moment, however, this idea seems highly unusual as a justification for state action. Where did this sense of automotive entitlement originate? Canadians did have a market that foreign automakers sold into, but it was one of the smallest in the industrialized world. Further, Canada had no ownership or control over any auto-assembling firm, and the Canadian-owned parts sector was, until the late 1980s, only a minor player in the industry. Why did Canadians *deserve* such a share of the North American auto sector, even given the one-in-six ratio? A 1980 Canadian government 'Options Paper' put it this way: 'The objective can be broadly stated as being to achieve a "fair" (more "fair") (greater) share of North American automotive activity and, in order to maintain this level of activity, to cooperate with the US in achieving for the North American industry a "fair" share of world automotive activity. "Fair" share in the Canada/US context can most logically be expressed as a percentage based on the Canadian share of the North American market for North American vehicles.'[11] This attitude, and the actions that accompanied it, reflected an engrained imperative by governments to play a role in the Canadian economy.[12]

But Canadians were not just looking for a fair share – they were looking for even more than that. By the 1980s, Canadian auto factories were producing nearly two million cars a year, while Canadians were buying only three-quarters that many. In other words, Canadians were enjoying a share of automotive production far greater than they 'deserved.' More than anything else, this disproportionate production-to-sales ratio demonstrates the success of Canadian policy makers in pushing the fair-share mantra to its limits, especially given that the Canadian market and industry was integrated into that of the world's largest market and largest car-producing nation, the United States.

Indeed, the connectedness of the North American auto industry was both Canada's greatest strength and its most daunting threat in this period. Integration allowed Canadians a certain leeway that was not possible in a solely national market. Whether through investment incentives, regulatory variations, or union break-ups, integration provided Canadians with opportunities that would not normally have appeared within a normal national or non-continentalized industry. At the same time, what were initially threats that emerged because Canada's industry was continentally integrated, such as the Chrysler crisis or the issue of Japanese investment, became, in time, strengths.

All of this hinged upon the integration introduced by the auto pact. The agreement legitimized Canadians' claims for a fair share of the industry and created opportunities for Canadian policy making that were not present in other areas of trade or diplomacy. Achieving that fair share brought out ingenious and sometimes daring public policies and political manoeuvres, such as the Ford incentive, Lumley's Yokohama Squeeze, or the duty-remission orders, all of which were designed to accrue a greater share of the industry for Canadians. In the short term these measures undoubtedly worked in bringing investment or production to the Canadian sector, and in the long-term they established Canada as a legitimate North American and global force in automotive production, though most of the policies themselves were ultimately dismantled.

Other factors helped Canadians achieve their fair share. Strong personalities played a role in this dynamic: determined and aggressive Canadian politicians and policy makers, from Simon Resiman to Ed Lumley to Herb Gray to Bill Davis, pushed the fair-share mantra, each in their own way but all with the overriding goal of building a vibrant auto sector in Canada. A state is only as activist as its key actors, and a policy only as strong as the personalities behind it; as we have seen in incidents from investment to the Chrysler bailout to the Japanese transplants, in the Canadian automotive field Ottawa (and Queen's Park) were blessed with an abundance of riches.

It helped, too, that Canadians could count on a close-knit bureaucracy in Ottawa, a willingness to cooperate with provinces in most instances, and a laser-like focus when it came to negotiating with other states, firms, associations, and especially the United States. Bargaining with a hegemon is a daunting task, yet Canadian politicians and policy makers were extremely capable in this regard. In numerous instances, from the auto pact to the stillborn efforts to prohibit incentives and the free-trade negotiations, Canadian diplomats and civil servants exhibited preparedness, daring, and a willingness to stand dangerously close to the twitching and grunting elephant that was the United States. Canadians had to focus in a way that the United States did not, given how high the stakes were for the former. And in most instances, the Canadians proved effective negotiators.[13]

Differing governmental structures also played a role in determining the outcomes of the auto trade, usually in Canada's favour. The parliamentary system, with its fused executive and legislative, the high level of cooperation between its core agencies, and the closeness between senior bureaucrats and elected officials, made strategy development and tactical execution far less difficult than in Washington. In the American capital, the division of powers, jurisdictional competition, and the sprawling nature of the giant U.S. bureaucracy slowed American responses and hindered aggressive bargaining. Moreover, Canada remained low on Washington's list of priorities, a position that undoubtedly helped Canadians at some points though it hindered them at others.

But, eventually, American policy makers saw the immense leeway Canadians exhibited in the auto trade – and particularly under the auto pact – as simply too much. The agreement itself had always been viewed as an intractable problem by elements of the U.S. government, and by the mid-1980s its staunchest American defenders – the auto companies themselves – realized that Canadian auto-policy efforts were in fact benefiting offshore producers to their detriment. When it became a subject for negotiation during the FTA talks, the Big Three saw no reason to further defend the auto agreement beyond maintaining it as a shadow of its former self.

Indeed, the success of the auto pact for Canadians in part helps to explain its demise and the subsequent emergence of the free-trade agreement. By the time the idea of free trade was being negotiated, the industry was in its best shape. Most of the investment promises that the Canadian Big Three had made to Herb Gray in 1981 were being fulfilled. AMC had committed $8 million to convert its Brampton plant from Jeep production to cars, and eventually in 1984 it announced a new plant worth nearly $800 million in Brampton to build new cars.[14] As promised, Ford's St Thomas plant was converted at a cost of $73 million to produce EXP and LN7 front-wheel vehicles, Oakville had added a second shift to produce only cars, and the $40 million Essex Aluminum plant had opened, not to mention the booming success of the Essex Engine plant.[15] GM Canada spent $3 billion to upgrade its facilities in Windsor, Oshawa, and St Catharines.[16] By mid-decade, the Japanese were coming on strong, too, with Honda doubling its plant size, Toyota adding to its facility, and GM's Suzuki plant rounding out the 'foreign' transplants operating in Canada to a tune of nearly $1 billion in new investments.

The greatest fears of the Canadian industry – that it would be left behind as the Big Three retooled for the next generation of vehicles, and that offshore producers would not establish plants in Canada – had been avoided. The state had played an indispensible role in this achievement. In 1981 the chairman of the federal government's automotive task force, Campbell Stuart, triumphantly enumerated the different forms of 'Government Assistance to the Automotive Industry' to his minister, Herb Gray. The long list included $200 in million loan guarantees for Chrysler, a $10-million grant from the Ontario government to Chrysler for an R&D centre, the $68-million federal-provincial grant for the Ford Essex Engine plant, 'flexibility' under the auto pact, and two duty-remission programs (the general order and the expanded order) that had provided 'a major incentive to foreign vehicle producers to source parts in Canada,' resulting in exports of over $88 million under these programs in 1980.[17] By mid-decade, Canadian policy makers could add to this list voluntary export restraints, port slowdowns, and additional production based on duty-remission orders, all of which had helped convince the Japanese to come to Canada. It was an impressive record, one that reflected an aggressive state interventionism and a willingness to push the limits of public policy. In a 1984 speech Bob White summed up perfectly Canadian state attitudes towards the industry: 'The importance of this industry,' he told his union brothers, 'meant that we couldn't simply leave its survival to the dictates of the market.'[18]

Autonomous State, however, is not solely concerned with the specific impact of state action by policy makers. In examining the breadth of the auto sector in this period, I offer six other concluding arguments – matching the notion of one in six jobs being dependent on the auto sector – that stem from the thematic explorations in this book. The activist state permeates many of these subarguments, which in turn add to the overall thrust of my analysis. Each emerges, in whole or in part, from the preceding chapters, and each attempts to ask questions, add new understandings, or break from previous conceptions of the theme considered.

Geography and Federalism

On looking closely at a political map of North America, one is struck by just how prominently southern Ontario juts into the Midwestern U.S. automotive heartland on one side and into one of its greatest regional markets, the northeast, on the other. The historical factors that shaped the initial geography of the North American auto industry, and Canada's place within it, are beyond the scope of this book. Briefly, however, it is important to note that southern Ontario became Canada's automotive heartland through its good fortune to be located near the burgeoning Midwestern carriage trade (with its southern Ontario counterpart), just across the river in Detroit. Risk, as exhibited by earlier entrepreneurs such as Ford Canada's Gordon M. McGregor, played a role, as did, of course the protectionist policies of John A. Macdonald, which created Canada's original branch-plant industry.[19]

Geographers on both sides of the border have been prolific and astute analysts of the post-war auto sector. James Rubenstein's extensive and detailed overviews of the American sector are indispensible assessments of the integral aspects of modern production and consumption. John Holmes has taken a more political, Marxian approach to his expansive assessment of the Canadian industry's evolution, especially its largely non-union parts industry. Both have illustrated the centrality of location and space to the industry's development on either side of the continental divide, and the essential links drawing them together.[20] Geography is key to any understanding of how the Canadian auto sector evolved, though this is not a story of geographic determinism. Two themes in particular are important to understanding the intersections and interactions between geography and the auto industry.

First, the success of the industry, and the ability of Canadian policy makers to utilize the wide range of approaches they did, was in part a consequence of the concentration of the sector in the great automotive-producing cluster that stretched northeastward from Windsor. Cluster theory has played a prominent role in explaining the success of some regional industries in Canada and beyond, and the Canadian automotive sector has been the focus of a number of these assessments.[21] The concentration of automotive assembly and parts production in southwestern Ontario focused policy makers, both at Ottawa and at Queen's Park, in terms of creating a coherent industrial policy for the region, and certainly in keeping elected officials attuned to the political power that this populous region represented.

Yet the influence of the Ontario cluster did not mean that other regions were abandoned when it came to support for automotive industrial development. Federal efforts to stretch the auto sector outward from Ontario, often in the name of regional development, proliferated in the 1970s and 1980s. When Honda announced in 1985 that its Canadian plant would be located in southern Ontario, British Columbia NDP MP Ian Waddell complained that 'while we welcome the Honda plant ... for Ontario workers, the Minister must appreciate that western Canadians would like some of that, too.' Waddell's argument was partially inspired by the logic that Toyota already had a wheel plant in British Columbia. Moreover, British Columbia was not far from California, the world's largest car market, where the GM-Toyota joint venture NUMMI had recently been announced. In response to these demands, IT&C Minister Ed Lumley replied that the nature of the industry, focused as it was on a just-in-time model, called 'for suppliers to be within a 75-mile radius of an assembly facility.' In any event, Lumley argued, the federal government had provided 'almost one-half of the financial assistance to get that Toyota plant' to locate in British Columbia – while it had given no direct cash for Honda's Ontario facility.[22]

The federal government also made titanic efforts to maintain or secure additional assembly capacity in Quebec, often in the face of severe corporate reluctance. The late-1970s DREE offer to GM, federal support to maintain the GM plant in Sainte-Thérèse, and massive federal funding for Hyundai's short-lived Quebec facility are prominent examples of Ottawa's attempts to diversify the industry outside its southern Ontario stronghold, for political as much as economic reasons. In the first instance, GM kept Sainte-Thérèse open until 2002 only because of federal money, and notwithstanding the labour and quality difficulties company officials complained of. Hyundai's 1989 plant, also supported by massive federal funding (and Quebec money as well), survived for four years before being shut owing to poor quality and a declining market for the firm's vehicles.

This is not to say that the demise of these Quebec operations was inevitable, nor either to assert a type of geographic inevitability to success in the auto sector. After all, Studebaker's Hamilton plant, located in the heart of Ontario's automotive cluster, was nominally a success while it was in operation in the mid-1960s. Studebaker production ended because of reasons that had little to do with geography or productivity. Similarly, other ventures, from Volvo to Bricklin to Toyota's stillborn efforts in Nova Scotia, did not necessarily fail because of their locations, but nor were they helped. Even in the 1970s, before just-in-time and lean production techniques were starting to reshape the industry, location did matter. Though transportation costs in the industry had declined spectacularly since the 1960s, Volvo, for instance, still needed government support to pay for shipping its cars from the Nova Scotia plant to the central Canadian marketplace.[23]

But Volvo ultimately did not close because of its location – it closed because the plant had become too small and costly to run within the corporation's global operations, and especially because it made little sense to maintain a Volvo plant after Ford took over the company in 1998 and could import Volvos duty-free under the auto pact. Obviously, other factors that shaped corporate decision making as to whether to keep a plant open could easily overwhelm geographic considerations. However, as the industry moved towards a leaner production model, as it exploited economies of scale and required just-in-time delivery from parts and other suppliers, it is clear that these outposts could not compete as effectively.[24] Geography played some role in the success of the Canadian industry, but it was only one factor among many.

Federalism is, in many ways, a product of geography. The geography of the auto sector had a second main consequence upon federalism that was driven as much by geographic concentration as anything else. From the battles over investment to the heated debate over bailing out Chrysler or the regional implications of voluntary export restraints – which drove up prices of Japanese cars bought in British Columbia and Alberta in order to protect jobs in Ontario – the auto sector strained federal relations as much as it witnessed the growth of a strong Ottawa-Ontario axis designed to procure a slice of the continental auto pie.

In chapter 1, this book addressed how the auto pact fundamentally altered the federal-provincial dynamic within the auto field and marked the emergence of subnational governments as key players in industrial policy directed at the auto sector. Before 1965, the Ontario government was largely absent from questions surrounding the automotive industry, which it considered a tariff issue outside its jurisdiction. From 1965 onward, provincial (or U.S. state) governments such as Ontario's were players in the automotive field in a manner that they had never been before, and were central actors in automotive decision making. This was especially true on the paramount issue of automotive investment. As a result of this altered dynamic, Ottawa and Ontario began to work together to ensure the health of the Canadian auto sector. The auto pact created a new strain of interstate cooperation, largely focused on intergovernmental relations between the federal state and the Ontario government.[25]

This broader argument about the evolution of the auto industry points to another development that emerges in the examination of the federalism of the Canadian auto industry: the emergence of this new strain of asymmetric interstate cooperation after 1965 created an extensive federal-provincial bureaucracy centred around the auto industry.

The auto pact sparked its own Quiet Revolution in the growth, sophistication, and necessity of both federal and provincial apparatuses for dealing with the auto industry. The 1960s witnessed the emergence of a federal Department of Industry (1963), accompanied by growth in the Ontario Ministry of Economic Development and Trade in the 1970s. By and large, these growing Ottawa and Ontario state automotive apparatuses worked in cooperation to address questions within the automotive field, from nurturing the auto pact, to cross-border competitions for auto investment, to periodic crises within the industry, such as the Chrysler bailout.[26] The historic development of this automotive bureaucracy at both the federal and Ontario level remains central to understanding the successes in attracting investment to Canada's automotive heartland in the period before the government-orchestrated bankruptcies of General Motors and Chrysler in 2009.[27] It also helps to explain the close Ottawa-Ontario cooperation in successfully navigating the 2009 crisis, cooperation that resulted in a direct federal and Ontario ownership stake in these two giant firms.

Yet it is important to note that the nature of this automotive federalism had limits. Federal-Ontario auto cooperation did not necessarily lead to agreement in other areas of Queen's Park's dealings with Ottawa. There was, according to Bill Davis, 'no horse trading' on issues with Ottawa.[28] Linkage did not exist within federal-provincial automotive diplomacy, and there was no quid pro quo between provinces and the federal government in the 1970s, 1980s, and beyond.[29]

Just as important, the federation still experienced strains over automotive issues. Ottawa's close dealing with Ontario upset Quebec, which aspired to its own auto sector. Nor was Quebec alone. Other provinces often felt neglected, too, given the size and scale of Ontario's sector and the looming influence in their view of Ontario in determining the fates of their own auto ventures. When Toyota-fronted CMI closed its doors in Nova Scotia in 1975, provincial officials noted with some frustration that 'the officials of CMI in Toronto are completely negative about continuing this facility as they can import vehicles from Japan at a fixed cost which is cheaper than the assembled vehicle in Sydney.'[30] Malcolm Bricklin's venture in New Brunswick never received, in his view, adequate support from Ottawa. Similarly, when Volvo shuttered its plant in 1998, local reporters noted that the executives came to the press conference 'with their Ontario public relations experts in tow.'[31] More recently, some western observers complained that Ontario's auto plants were granted unfair exemptions under the federal government's plans to cut greenhouse gas emissions, and there was a decidedly regional bias in opinion against the 2009 federal-Ontario bailouts of GM and Chrysler.[32]

Geography and federalism are central to any understanding both of the evolution of the auto sector and of the growth and nature of state activism in this field. Although intergovernmental willingness to work together on auto files generally prevailed, there was not always happy cooperation between Ottawa and the provinces. Moreover, automotive cooperative federalism between Ontario and Ottawa could spur unhappiness across the federation. Geography shaped state responses to the auto sector and automotive federalism, but it did not necessarily shape its outcomes.

Economic Integration and Harmonization

Transnational and regional economic integration has long been stalked by a fear that regulatory harmonization will lead to a 'race to the bottom' of environmental and other standards. In North America, this fear reached a crescendo following the inclusion of Mexico in the 1993 NAFTA.[33] The integration of the Canadian and American auto industries, long before either the 1989 FTA or NAFTA came into place, provides an opportunity to test this concern. After all, the auto sector is particularly salient given the intense regulation of cars and their wide-ranging environmental externalities, from smog to acid rain to global warming. In the case of the 1965 auto pact and its integrative effects upon harmonization and regulation, one example stands above all others – that of emissions regulations. In this instance, if the fears of a 'race to the bottom' were to be realized, it stands to reason that in an industry as integrated and tightly regulated as the automotive one, and with an issue as high profile and consequential as automobile emissions, Canadian emission standards would necessarily follow those of the United States.

But this was not the case. The 'interim' 1975 Canadian emission standards lasted until 1988. Not only did Canada not follow U.S. standards, it maintained a *less stringent* standard for automobile emissions for more than a decade following the introduction of emission regulations. This development prompts a number of questions. Most important, why was the Canadian government able and willing to sacrifice environmental standards when it came to automobiles?

The political economist Stan Luger has applied a Marxist analysis to the relations of the auto industry and the U.S. government and has made a convincing case that 'big auto' was able to delay meeting emissions, safety, and fuel-economy standards because its allies on Capitol Hill protected the automakers from the harshest aspects of regulation.[34] Was the Canadian government simply doing the auto industry's wishes in maintaining a lower emission standard than that of the United States? The evidence is not convincing in this case. GM, the Canadian market leader and the country's largest corporation (and employer), pushed to have the higher standards, in contrast to Ford and Chrysler, but was rebuffed by the government. It was not the auto industry that pushed government to decide in favour of lower standards. The government's constant refrain in the matter was that Canadian consumers would not want to pay for the pollution-control devices, and this became the most cited concern in the 1970s, along with fuel-economy questions. In this sense, the government saw itself as protecting the interest of Canadians – but reasoned that their economic interest was more pressing than their environmental interest.

Does the government's decision make sense given the Canadian circumstances within the North American context? On the one hand, perhaps the federal government should be commended for being cautious in the face of the uncertainty surrounding the standards in the United States. After all, EPA delayed implementation of the original 1975/6 standards on a number of occasions in the 1970s, in response to the auto industry's pleas and the volatile political and economic circumstances of the period. It would have been foolish to plough ahead with Canadian regulations that matched the original U.S. standards, and then have to reverse course when the United States delayed implementation. This was a key factor in the 1971 cabinet decision to publish the Canadian standards only as proposals, and was also a factor in the Canadian decision to maintain the lower standards in the mid-1970s. In the context of the regulatory and political battles between Detroit and Washington, this could be seen as prudent.

But, on the other hand, Canada missed a golden opportunity to strike a blow against air pollution. Canada could have simply followed the U.S. standard, or gone to California standards, as Environment Minister Jack Davis implored the federal cabinet to do in 1974.[35] The California standard was completely feasible: the automakers were already meeting it and California represented approximately 10 per cent of the North American auto market. If Canada had made the decision to adopt the California model, it would have become only another destination for California-standard cars, and the emission standards in North America would have been streamlined to two from three.

Should the automakers themselves be blamed for the lower stand-ards, since they could have just used U.S. standards in Canada?[36] The Canadian automakers responded to a market situation shaped by reg-ulation. If there was no need to meet the higher standards, why would automakers implement costly, emission-saving technologies? Ford Canada's Roy Bennett had anticipated this strategy in 1972. With the weaker Canadian legislation, 'you would not need a unique engine. You just wouldn't put on some of the additions that are very costly and tend to further reduce vehicle performance.'[37] After Canada an-nounced in 1973 that it would not meet the U.S. standards, GM de-cided to reverse its earlier decision to equip all Canadian cars with catalytic converters, citing a competitive disadvantage (Ford and Chrysler said they would meet the lower Canadian standards with-out catalytic converters).[38] Because of Canada's 1978 decision not to increase standards to match the 1980–1 U.S. standards, Canadian cars did not require more advanced, three-way catalytic converters. And the automakers were in no rush to install them, given the fuel-econo-my questions.[39]

What was the environmental cost of the Canadian decisions to re-tain lower emission standards? Pollution, and the health and economic costs caused by automotive emissions, is difficult to ascertain in the best of times – for instance, pollution deniers in the 1960s could always claim that heightened carbon monoxide levels in people were caused by smoking, and not cars. But it is clear that the Canadian regulations had environmental, political, and economic consequences. One specific ex-ample can be shown in the case of three-way catalytic converters: while the United States required three-way catalytic converters for the 1981 model year, Canada did not require them until 1987. The earlier use of three-way catalytic converters might have reduced emissions such as nitrous oxide (N_2O), a key GHG, by Canadian autos in the 1970s and 1980s. A 1999 Natural Resources Canada study indicated that the use of three-way catalytic converters, which can heat up more quickly than other converters and thus cut emissions, had reduced nitrous oxide emissions considerably in the 1990s. If Canadians had put three-way converters on their cars earlier, this would likely have helped in the battle against N_2O.[40]

Then there is the case of acid rain and auto emissions. When the House of Commons Subcommittee on Acid Rain realized in 1981 that 'motor vehicles in Canada emit three times as much nitrogen oxides per vehicle mile as vehicles in the United States,' it was 'appalled.' In a landmark report, *Still Waters: The Chilling Reality of Acid Rain*, the committee recommended that the Canadian standard be harmonized with the U.S. standard, and that the legislative authority to regulate emissions be moved from the Motor Vehicle Safety Act (under DOT's purview) to the Clean Air Act (under the responsibility of Environment Canada).[41] The report forced Canadians to realize that they were laggards in the emissions battle: in an editorial titled 'It Came from the Tailpipe,' the *Globe and Mail* opined that the Canadian regulation 'isn't a standard; it's a blank check' for environmental damage.[42]

The Canadian Coalition on Acid Rain, Canada's largest 1980s anti-pollution group, was stymied in its efforts to fight acid rain because of the lower Canadian vehicle-emission standards. For his part, Commons Acid Rain Committee Chair Ron Irwin complained that Canada's lobbying efforts in Washington were continually hampered by the fact that every time the Canadians raised the issue of sulphur dioxide emissions, American politicians kept 'throwing at us' the lower Canadian NO_X car standard. 'The whole question of auto emission standards is a vulnerable spot in negotiations for bilateral acid rain controls,' echoed Environment Canada's Martin Rivers.[43]

What about the Canadian public? Much like Americans, Canadians responded to automobile pollution only after it reached critical proportions. When smog became an issue in the 1960s and early 1970s in the United States (and to a lesser degree in Canada), motivated citizens, environmental groups, and governments pushed to address the problem. Likewise, in March 1985, by which time the acid-rain issue had become a visible, prevailing environmental matter for Canadians, Brian Mulroney followed through with a campaign promise to finally bring Canadian auto-emission standards to the U.S. level by 1988 as part of his wider acid-rain efforts.[44]

Canadian arguments against stricter auto-emission standards in the 1970s foreshadowed the same discourse employed to challenge the need for lower emissions of GHGs in the 1990s and more recently. The arguments against meeting Canada's obligations under the Kyoto Protocol – that the problem is a 'myth,' that Canada cannot do it economically, that consumers will not want to spend the money, that Canada's emissions are not as much of a problem as other countries', that we need a 'made-in-Canada' approach – are not new or original. Nor is the seemingly timid policy response to this pressing environmental problem. Sadly, by examining the case of auto-emissions policy, we can see that this is, in many ways, the same story all over again.

Economic Nationalism, Foreign Investment, and Multinationals

Economic nationalism in Canada in the period under examination had very well-defined limits when it came to the auto sector. While Canadian policy makers paid lip service to the notion, in the auto field they struggled mightily to gain any FDI they could – be it American, Japanese, German, or Korean. Given that automotive investment constituted in some years the greatest single component of inward foreign monies, this was not an insignificant exception to the prevailing view in this period.

But the issue of foreign investment tells us about more than just the contradictory Canadian attitude towards FDI; it can tell us much about the evolving nature of foreign multinationals in North America. Given the continental integration of the auto sector, multinationals found themselves operating in a unique environment in the period after 1965, one that altered the home-host country dynamic significantly. In few other instances did the actions of an MNE in a host country have such a direct and immediate impact upon the home country: when host and home countries are merged in a single entity, as they were under the integrationist auto pact, the lines between what was foreign or domestic policy – for either country – blurred beyond recognition. In the 1960s and 1970s, this was the situation faced by the Big Three.

One implication of this continental dynamic for multinationals was the growing divergence, in the case of the Big Three, between the home country's goals and their own. This was clear when it came to the operation of the auto pact, which the Big Three supported even in the face of U.S. governmental unhappiness. This divergence continued with the creation of the FTA. Both the federal government in Washington and the Michigan state government were not entirely happy with the outcome of the negotiations, which reflected the Canadian ability to find, in their view, a beneficial space between corporations and their home countries. Following the FTA, Michigan official Mark Santucci complained that 'the Big three are very happy with the agreement, and they should be. It is a good agreement for the companies; it is not a good agreement for production and investment in the US because it codifies certain Canadian protectionist measures.' Santucci felt that 'we have a problem here in the US in that, as our economy becomes more global, we no longer have companies speaking for the best interests of the country. They are speaking for their own best interests and rightly so.'[45]

The Big Three became adept at utilizing this situation to their benefit, especially given their unique advantage of having subsidiary operations in Canada which could play a role in shaping outcomes or passing along vital information to 'host' governments, even when those governments' decisions had a direct impact upon 'home' operations. For instance, in 1972, in the wake of serious efforts by the Nixon administration to cancel or alter the auto pact, information about Treasury motives in Canada-U.S. trade flowed from Chrysler to its Canadian subsidiary, and finally to the government in Ottawa, long before Canada-U.S. talks on the issue began. John Connally, the tough Texan treasury secretary who sought changes to the agreement, told Chrysler officials that he could live with the 15 per cent tax on U.S. cars imported by Canadian individuals and the prohibition on used cars under the agreement if the Canadians would move on the CVA ratio and letters of commitment.[46] Though this did not happen, it reflected the unusual dynamic present in the North American industry.

The integration of the North American sector also affected offshore multinationals operating in the continental industry. In the 1980s, Japanese and German moves to establish facilities in the United States had direct impacts upon Canada, and vice versa, and these firms were forced to govern themselves accordingly. This situation was not present in other home-host relations for offshore producers in countries such as Brazil or Mexico, where only one nation's industry and government(s) were directly affected. German firms, as in the case of VW and its operations in North America, had to deal with both the U.S. and state governments, and at the same time Canadian and provincial governments whose industries were directly affected by these decisions. Similarly, Japanese firms (and their own government, in the case of MITI) had no choice but to deal with Canadian concerns when it came to American imports and production, given the direct impact upon the Canadian marketplace and industry.

This continental reality profoundly affected the behaviour of both multinationals and state actors: continentalism liberated the multinationals to pursue more efficient and profitable operations; at the same time, the auto pact and the insistence of Canadian governments forced these firms to act in ways that often challenged their best interests. Conversely, in some instances, integration helped Canadian policy makers to achieve their fair-share goals; in others, it hindered them. But it unquestionably forced Ottawa and Queen's Park to act more audaciously, and required a diplomacy towards both other governments and MNEs which was, in the words of one historian of the period, 'self-assured, deliberate, and very conscious of its responsibilities.'[47] This attitude, in part, helps to explain the next theme, the question of deindustrialization in North America and Canada.

Deindustrialization and Worker Nationalism

Historians and other social scientists have examined deindustrialization largely in the context of the hardship that accompanied the emergence of what has been termed the 'rust belt' in the 1970s and 1980s. In the United States, and to a lesser extent in Canada, this emerging deindustrialization literature focuses on responses to plant shutdowns and the impact of factory closings upon communities on both sides of the border.[48] Older, more traditional Canadian political-economy views of deindustrialization, such as those of Robert Laxer and Daniel Drache, posit that Canada's branch-plant manufacturing sector existed at the mercy of U.S.-based multinational corporations and invoke the language of dependency in assessing the causes of deindustrialization. In this dependent dynamic, companies were only too willing to retreat to the 'home market' when their businesses were threatened, thus leaving Canadian workers exposed to the brutal dictates of a foreign corporation.[49]

Yet, as Steven High has astutely pointed out in his *Industrial Sunset: The Making of North America's Rust Belt, 1969–1984*, there is a disconnect between images of deindustrialization (assumed to have spread across North America) and the reality of industrial dislocation. This is particularly true of the auto sector in Canada. In fact, not a single car-assembly factory in Canada closed down between 1969 and 1984, the period usually seen as witnessing the first great wave of deindustrialization that swept the continent. Indeed, some new automotive plants actually opened in Canada during this period, and overall automotive employment *increased* by the mid-1980s, leading a resurgence in the manufacturing sector.[50] Why was that? Why did the deindustrialization that swept North America in the 1970s and 1980s not tarnish Canada's automotive industrial heartland?

High's explanation is that, in the face of this great wave of disruption, Canadian workers 'were able to marshal nationalist claims as rhetorical weapons against plant shutdowns and lobbying tools.' As a result, 'Canadian politicians were convinced to legislate advance notice of layoffs, severance pay, pension reinsurance, job placement assistance, and preferential hiring rights.' In High's view, nationalistic worker agency was the key in mitigating the harshest excesses of mass layoffs and plant closings which occurred in the United States: 'By literally wrapping themselves in the Canadian flag, industrial workers won important legislative victories that forced companies to soften the blow of displacement.' For High, then, worker activism built on a greater sense of Canadian nationalism and community was key to saving jobs, especially after plant- closure announcements.[51]

This book approaches the question of deindustrialization from a public-policy perspective, focusing on the industrial and economic development measures taken by the state to ensure a strong auto sector. It shows how Canadian state action in the automotive sector in the 1970s and 1980s largely avoided deindustrialization by encouraging investment and bailing out Chrysler, and how these measures explained the resurgence of the Canadian auto sector. In explaining the break-up of the UAW, the book makes the case that it was not nationalism that drove Canadian workers to challenge corporations or to leave the international union, but more pragmatic economic reasons.

The 'visible hand' of state intervention provides an essential element in helping to explain why Canada largely avoided deindustrialization.[52] Between 1965 and 1984, this preventative, interventionist approach was framed by the continentalist auto pact, which mandated minimum production and content targets as a requirement for duty-free trade within North America. Moreover, this state interventionist approach also forcefully emerged during the Chrysler bailout negotiations in the late 1970s: Canadian governments – both Liberal and Conservative – bargained effectively with Chrysler executives and achieved investment for the Canadian auto sector and thus job protection for Canadian workers as a condition of loan guarantees to help stave off the company's bankruptcy.

The Canadian Chrysler bailout is reflective of the complex dynamics and particular historical circumstances that surround government-MNE bargaining. Most obviously, the state and its main actors, politicians and civil servants, sought to achieve outcomes most beneficial to their stakeholders and to their own position. In the case of both federal Progressive Conservative and Liberal governments, and the Ontario Progressive Conservative government, these goals included maintaining employment in Windsor and Ontario. This was a particularly sensitive issue for Liberal Herb Gray, who was minister of industry during the 1980–1 Chrysler negotiations and who was a long-time MP from Windsor.[53] Voters in Windsor and southern Ontario expected some form of government intervention or action from Gray and his colleagues to mitigate the job losses faced by Chrysler workers. Thus, a Chrysler failure would be catastrophic for the community and would have political consequences that political actors – both Liberal and Progressive Conservative – hoped to avoid. Canadian politicians did not need to be 'convinced' to act to protect worker interests. For Gray, bargaining hard was a way to protect jobs in his hometown and, of course, to secure political support. But it was more than part of a po-litical calculus: it simply made good public-policy sense. 'My mandate is based on jobs,' Gray stated flatly to newspaper reporters at the height of the Chrysler negotiations.[54] He meant it.

Most important, state actions in the case of Chrysler must be framed within the context of the auto pact. This agreement had created a dy-namic in which the state played a fundamental role in the management of the Canadian auto industry, one that remained interventionist and designed to ensure that this industrial policy resulted in jobs and in-vestment for Canadians. As such, the Canadian state's Chrysler inter-vention was well in keeping with the federal government's approach in the auto sector: by the mid-1970s, governments in Canada had become accustomed to achieving a say in automotive investment under the aus-pices of the auto pact – the requirement that Chrysler build a new plant in Windsor in the mid-1970s to make up for its auto pact shortfalls is only the most obvious example.[55]

Of course, the competitive dynamic between the government and the Big Three over the direction of the industry was not always so one-sid-ed. For instance, in the case of the Chrysler bailout, the state's demands were not entirely acceded to. Chrysler did not meet every expectation that it had agreed to with the federal and provincial governments: the company asked for more money after the initial negotiation; it ended engine production in Windsor in 1980, and had to shift 350 jobs to the van plant; instead of building the popular K-Car in Canada, it made an agreement to build a diesel-engine plant, which it ultimately reneged upon; Chrysler even received a duty remission of approximately $250 million for 1981 and 1982, when it did not meet its auto pact require-ments; and on more than one occasion, it sought to change the terms of its loan- guarantee agreement with the Canadian government.[56] Clearly, though Chrysler initially came to the negotiations seeking aid, the company continuously sought to improve its position, even after it had struck an agreement with the federal and Ontario governments for assistance.

Yet, on balance, government intervention in the case of Chrysler was highly successful. Without the loan guarantees, it is likely that Chrysler would have collapsed. The conditions exacted by the government in return for the loan guarantees – particularly the product mandates and minimum worker levels – were essential in boosting the company's fortunes in Canada and helping to stave off the emergence of a rust belt in southern Ontario. Moreover, in a period during which the government was willing to intervene in the economy on a massive scale, the Chrysler intervention remains conservative by comparison, and the benefits significant. In the 1970s, the federal government bailed out companies such as Massey Ferguson and Dome Petroleum, created crown corporations such as Petro-Canada, and purchased outright firms in the aeronautics industry such as de Havilland and Canadair.[57] Comparably, the Canadian governments' commitments to Chrysler did not result in any real financial outlays by the federal government, since Chrysler never actually utilized the loan guarantees.

Ultimately, the state's role in the Chrysler bailout helped to prevent the deindustrialization of southern Ontario. The Canadian governments' Chrysler response was framed by the auto pact regime and reflected a long-standing willingness to intervene in the auto sector to protect jobs and investment. It was also framed by a more receptive Canadian attitude towards state intervention in the economy which initially contrasted with that found in the United States, though eventually political parties on both sides of the Canada-U.S. border all agreed to a bailout.[58] Finally, the Canadian government's willingness to utilize its position within the triangular diplomacy between the home government, the host government, and Chrysler allowed it to achieve the best possible outcome, given the circumstances. Instead of signalling the emergence of a Canadian rust belt, the Chrysler bailout, and the public policies pursued by Canadian state actors during this incident, marked the beginnings of a two-decade boom in Canada's strategic auto sector.

Canada-U.S. Relations

The auto industry is a particularly apt sector for an examination of two key themes in post-war Canada-U.S. relations: the nature of the relationship between the two countries, and the notion of policy linkage between issues within Ottawa's and Washington's diplomacy. Was the integrated North American auto trade, and the auto pact that underlay it, reflective of any 'special relationship' between Canada and the United States? Not in any official view. In 1975 Henry Kissinger and Canadian Foreign Affairs Minister Allan MacEachen 'publicly agreed that the "special relationship" no longer existed,' and the term was not henceforth used by either government. By the time of the February 1977 meeting between Carter and Trudeau, the very notion of a 'special relationship' was now *verboten* in the White House, where Carter was cautioned: *'Don't* refer to a "special relationship" between the US and Canada; to some Canadians this implies a historic paternalism on our part.'[59] Indeed, when State Department officials noticed that two notes had gone from Carter to Trudeau using the words 'special relationship,' they told the White House that while this term was once 'understood to refer to a specific policy of the US Government that accorded Canada preferential treatment, particularly in economic matters,' it no longer applied.[60]

Yet it is clear that after 1965 the auto trade was special within the North American regime and had a unique place within Canada-U.S. diplomacy. It was in the auto industry, after all, that the first significant attempt was made to create something approximating free trade in the continent's most important economic sector. As such, the auto industry, and the auto pact that governed it, became a powerful symbol of continental cooperation. Henry Ford II captured the specialness of the continentalized auto trade in a 1966 speech to the Toronto Board of Trade at the Royal York hotel. 'As the Canadian nation approaches its centennial,' Ford told his audience, he was aware of the 'great debate' in Canada over how to achieve its political and economic prosperity, 'whether through North American partnership or through a multilateral approach, whether industry-by-industry or on a broad front.' The auto magnate could 'think of no better illustration ... than the automotive trade agreement between Canada and the US ... My country had the good sense to recognize that it could help itself by helping Canada to solve its automotive trade problems, and together the two governments worked out the terms of the agreement.'[61]

Yet, for all this lofty rhetoric, the auto trade also became a flashpoint for sharp conflict, as we have seen. Automotive issues reflected both the larger reality that Canada-U.S. diplomacy was based on consensus but punctuated by intermittent conflict, and the nature of the interdependence between the two countries. As to the former, the auto pact itself had been born out of sharp conflicts over unilateral Canadian measures in the auto field. But, after 1965, automotive diplomacy was characterized by a grudging consensus on either side that not much could be done to change the dynamic, even in the face of sharp periodic unhappiness in each country over the auto trade.

As to the latter, the auto industry reflected one of the greatest examples of interdependence at work: Canada's ability to leverage its 'fair share' from the North American sector was a classic example of a junior partner achieving aims beyond its 'realist' stature within international (in this case bilateral) relations. This Canadian ability stemmed, as we have seen, as much from the caginess of its negotiators as it did from the willingness of multinationals to play along because the shape of the continentalized sector was useful and profitable for them. The United States, for its part, may have rued the original auto pact deal – itself a long-standing example of interdependence – but it was unable to assert its prerogative over this seemingly intractable situation.

Perhaps most surprisingly, though it was so often a target of either government's diplomatic focus, for most of its existence the auto pact was never a victim of issue linkage. That is to say, a number of issues could have easily been linked to the automotive sector over the period; the United States, especially, which had a higher level of dissatisfaction with the agreement, as its congressional critics could attest, could have made such linkages. Yet this never happened. From Nixon and his economic policies to Reagan and his difficulties over the National Energy Program, cruise missiles, steel imports, or acid rain, the auto pact was never successfully tied to another issue. Problems in the auto sector did not result in spillovers into other sensitive areas, such as Canada-U.S. energy relations in 1970s, though there was some idea that free-trade auto negotiations were in *response* to previous Canadian measures.

Indeed, when in March 1981 USTR William Brock hinted to Herb Gray that auto pact negotiations could be linked to energy issues, the exchange prompted a stern warning from American Deputy Chief of Mission Richard J. Smith in Ottawa, one that deserves to be quoted at length:

> A central tenet of US-Canadian relations has traditionally been that progress in one area must never be linked to or made contingent upon progress on some other unrelated issue. Thus, I am seriously concerned about occasional suggestions, such as that in the referenced letter, that may be considering creating linkages and seeking quid pro quos in one

area for progress achieved in another. That way lies disaster in this relationship. It is no more acceptable to us for Canada to ask for changes in their energy policy on the basis that we would be more forthcoming in auto talks, than it would be for us if Canada had said that would renew NORAD only if we agreed to give them a larger share of the East Cost fisheries resource ... I strongly recommend that we resist the temptation that always exists to link unlike issues in this relationship ... It is clearly not in our interest to initiate a pattern of specific quid pro quo type linkage between issues.[62]

The unwillingness to link other issues to the automotive trade was not only a consequence of diplomatic necessity. It also sprang from the unique nature of the auto industry, integrated as it was along continental lines. Domestic actors – in this case the Big Three – played a key role in ensuring that the auto pact was not sacrificed on the altar of some other cross-border issue. The most prominent instance of this was, of course, the 1971 Nixon Shocks, but the fact that the auto agreement remained essentially undisturbed until the mid-1980s is a reflection of its fundamental role in shaping a significant economic and political force in American life, the auto sector.

This reality corroborates findings by political scientists such as Brian Bow, who have explored the question of linkage in Canada-U.S. relations. Domestic political actors played an increasingly larger role in framing U.S. foreign policy after the mid-1960s, not coincidentally a period that also witnessed the passage of the 1965 auto pact. This development was not only illustrated by the auto trade, it was in part a consequence *of* the auto pact. The integration of the automotive industry – the most important domestic sector in each country and, for both Canada and the United States, the most important trade category – reordered the two countries' relations in a manner that helped to fracture the post-war Canada-U.S. network which had governed cross-border relations since the 1940s.[63] The other implication of that development – the increasing role of U.S. domestic (and some non-state Canadian) actors in the course of Canada-U.S. relations – was that as much as it eroded traditional Canada-U.S. diplomatic channels, it also provided new opportunities for policy makers, especially on the Canadian side in the case of the auto trade. The direct links that Canadian politicians made with automakers in Detroit, and the willingness to negotiate directly with these non-state actors, could result in outcomes beneficial to Canada. The 1978 Ford investment and the Chrysler bailout are two prominent examples where Canadian involvement with U.S. domestic actors *facilitated* outcomes, as opposed to hindering matters.[64]

Of course, Washington became increasingly unhappy with Canadian activities in the auto field by the mid-1980s. At this point, so did Detroit, which saw measures such as Ottawa's use of duty-remission orders to induce offshore investment into Canada – investment that could have a direct impact upon American jobs and production levels – as detrimental to the Big Three. This development represented a sea change in Canada-U.S. automotive diplomacy, one that again emphasized the role of non-state domestic actors in the United States in shaping diplomatic outcomes. But this time the willingness of Detroit to seek concessions from Canada in some areas of the auto trade (such as remissions) was directly linked to its overall stance in the free-trade negotiations – as was Washington's. In this sense, the auto trade example ultimately departs from Bow's view of a generalized lack of linkage by providing an instance where linkage was specifically invoked between Canadian automotive policies and the free-trade negotiations.

Free Trade and the End of Automotive Policy Making

The integrated Canada-U.S. auto industry between 1965 and the 1980s was not classic free trade but a form of managed trade. Yet it paved the way for free trade and, in some ways, presaged post-Cold War corporate globalization. This was paradoxical, given the fair-trade nature of the agreement. After all, the auto pact's existence and operation actually emphasized the difficulty of free trade for Canadians: Alastair Gillespie's comments in the 1975 Economic Council of Canada publication, *An Outline of a New Trade Strategy for Canada*, illustrated this problem. Though the *Outline* pushed the idea of freer trade with the United States, Gillespie was convinced that the auto pact proved how poorly Canada might fare under a comprehensive continental trade agreement. 'The auto trade,' Gillespie felt, 'has only been kept in relative balance because the agreement is conditional. If it were not for the conditional factors in the Auto-Pact, political pressures, rather than economic ones, would have forced more investment in the US.' The *Outline* appeared to have 'little appreciation that political pressures, e.g. Labour Unions or State pressures, could play a disruptive role in any kind of free trade agreement. Nor does there seem to be any acknowledgement that incentives by States (the Regional Expansive type of incentive) as applied to the tire and rubber industry, for example, could bedevil any free trade arrangement between Canada and the US.'[65]

Of course, free trade was eventually consummated, and the auto pact and auto trade played a key role in that process. This is further deeply ironic, given the fair-share measures contained in the agreement and the initial rationale for those measures. In 1964 Simon Reisman himself told U.S. negotiators that safeguards were necessary if the Canadian industry were to survive. There could be no free trade in the auto sector, Reisman declared – Canada could not simply 'just remove tariffs and let the ball roll where it would.' Such a step would be a 'colossal gamble' for Canada, one that the country was not willing to take.[66]

What resulted was the creation of a managed North American industry, which is still today predicated on constraints such as content requirements and rules-of-origin as much as it is on liberalized duty-free access for cars. In this sense, though it was not a free-trade agreement, the auto pact, and the larger Canada-U.S. auto trade that resulted, did act as a precursor to free trade. The evolution of Canadian policy making in the trade field is reflected in the significant shift between the type of state-managed trade that existed under the auto pact in the 1960s and 1970s and the rules-based trade that prevailed under the FTA and NAFTA in the 1980s and 1990s. In the 1960s, the Canadian body politic embraced autarky and greater economic nationalism; by 1985, the body politic was increasingly open to freer trade. This was in part a consequence of the success of the auto trade, which allowed politicians and policy makers – including Simon Reisman – to argue that the auto pact had proved, in result if not in form, that free trade was a leap of faith worth taking.

The nature of the North American auto sector in the post-1965 period acted as a precursor to free trade in another distinct manner: it raised the status and power of corporations vis-à-vis states. In the mid-1960s, the Canadian state had utilized the unique nature of the auto sector, where 90 per cent of the industry was owned by Detroit, to propose a hybrid, protectionist-tariff-free intergovernmental agreement which granted the Big Three considerable responsibility in playing a role in managing that industry. Significantly, the auto pact essentially erased borders for the corporations and freed them from the limits of national markets and national production. Canadians gained the benefits of the continentalized economy, but in liberating these corporate entities from the shackles of national constraint, they were elevated to an even more powerful economic and political position, equal in many ways to that of government, notwithstanding the safeguards that were supposed to keep them in check.

As Canadian policy makers grappled with this development, which was further complicated by the entrance of the Japanese in North America, Canadian officials summarized the auto-industry dynamic by telling Brian Mulroney's cabinet in 1986 that

> to all intents and purpose, decision on the major course of direction of the North American industries will be made by the US and Japanese governments and in boardrooms in Detroit and Tokyo. Canada's influence on this process is limited. Yet, the Canadian government must deal with two critical issues: the need to preserve the benefits of rationalized automotive production and trade in North America and the need to manage increasing volumes of imported automotive products from Asia and other offshore sources. Thus, the decision to maintain the present policy framework or to adopt a revised one, should be based on a clear understanding of Canada's political and industrial ability to influence the direct of this important sector of the Canadian economy.[67]

Eventually, this dynamic led Canadian policy makers to the conclusion that the best way to influence the sector in the future was by attaching the auto pact to a comprehensive free-trade agreement which would require them to surrender their more creative automotive policies and which, in time, would render the auto pact essentially obsolete.

This is the ultimate lesson that the evolution of the Canadian auto industry from the 1973 OPEC embargo to the creation of the free-trade agreement in the mid-1980s teaches us. Canadian state planners exhibited creativity and daring in bending the circumstances they confronted in the auto sector and in the Canada-U.S. relationship to their benefit. They utilized innovative and forceful measures to gain Canada a fair share of a continental and then multinational industry in North America that faced severe disruption, rationalization, and uncertainty. These measures illustrated what an activist state could do in a context of national, continental, and international constraints. The great irony of this activism is that its successes eventually led to the demise of any creative Canadian policy making in the auto field. This, in the end, was a choice Canadians made. They willingly sacrificed a vibrant auto policy to achieve what they saw as an even greater policy goal: comprehensive free trade with the United States.

Appendix A
The Evolution of Canadian Automotive Tariffs since 1936 / Canadian Duty-Remission/Tariff Plans in the Auto Sector

Automotive tariff rates, 1936–96

1936 MFN Auto Tariff, 17.5%
1936 Tariff Revision

Item:	MFN Tariff	Gen. Tariff	Brit. Pref.
438a (finished autos)	17.5%	27.5%	0
438b (products of parts makers)	17.5%	30%	0
438c (products of automakers)	17.5% if made in Canada, free if not made in Canada and carmakers' production is: 40% Commonwealth content if less than 10,000 cars 50% Commonwealth content if 10,000–20,000 cars 60% Commonwealth content if over 20,000 cars	25%	0
438d (parts of commercial vehicles)	17.5% if made in Canada, free if not made in Canada and commercial vehicle makers' production is: 40% Commonwealth content (no scale)	27.5%	0
438f (parts not included in above)	25%	35%	0

1967 MFN Auto Tariff (GATT Kennedy Round), 15%
1982 MFN Auto Tariff (GATT Tokyo Round), 12.6%
1987 MFN Auto Tariff (GATT Uruguay Round) 9.2%
1996 MFN Auto Tariff, 6.1%

Duty-Remission/Tariff Plans

1962 Duty-Remission Plan (see chapter 1)

1963 Duty-Remission Plan (see chapter 1)

1965 Canada-U.S. Automotive Products Trade Agreement (see appendix B)

1978 Duty-Remission Plan (Volkswagen and others, exports to third countries only, see chapter 8)

1980–1 Duty-Remission Plan (expanded to include exports to United States, see chapter 8)

1985 Duty-Remission Plan (production-based remissions; Toyota, Honda, CAMI, see chapter 8)

1989 Free Trade Agreement (Canada-U.S. tariff reduced to zero by 1998, subject to 50% rule of origin, see chapter 8)

Appendix B
Text of the Automotive Products Trade Agreement, 1965 / Sample Letter of Undertaking

The Automotive Products Trade Agreement

The Government of the United States and the Government of Canada,

Determined to strengthen economic relations between their two countries;

Recognizing that this can best be achieved through the stimulation of economic growth and through the expansion of markets available to producers in both countries within the framework of the established policy of both countries of promoting multilateral trade;

Recognizing that an expansion of trade can best be achieved through the reduction or elimination of tariff and all other barriers to trade operating to impede or distort the full and efficient development of each country's trade and industrial potential;

Recognizing the important place that the automotive industry occupies in the industrial economies of the two countries and the interests of industry, labour and consumers in sustaining high growth in the automotive industry;

Agree as follows:

Article I

The Governments of the United States and Canada, pursuant to the above principles, shall seek the early achievement of the following objectives:

a) The creation of a broader market for automotive products within which the full benefits of specialization and large-scale production can be achieved;

b) The liberalization of United States and Canadian automotive trade in respect to tariff barriers and other factors tending to impede it, with a view to enabling the industries of both countries to participate on a fair and equitable basis in the expanding total market of the two countries;

c) The development of conditions in which market forces may operate efficiently to attain the most economic patter of investment, production and
trade.

It shall be the policy of each Government to avoid actions which would frus-
trate the achievements of these objectives.

Article II

a) The Government of Canada, not later than the entry into force of the legislation contemplated in paragraph b) of this Article, shall accord duty-free
treatment to imports of the products of the United States described in Annex
A.
b) The Government of the United States, during the session of the United
States Congress commencing on January 4, 1965, shall seek enactment of
legislation authorizing duty-free treatment of import of the products of
Canada described in Annex B. In seeking such legislation, the Government
of the United States shall also seek authority permitting the implementation
of such duty-free treatment retroactively to the earliest date administrative-
ly possible following the date upon which the Government of Canada has
according duty-free treatment. Promptly after the entry into force of such
legislation, the Government of the United States shall accord duty-free treatment to the products of Canada described in Annex B.

Article III

The commitments made by the two Governments in this Agreement shall not
preclude action by either Government consistent with its obligations under
Part II of the General Agreement on Tariffs and Trade.

Article IV

a) At any time, at the request of either Governments, the two Governments
shall consult with respect to any matter relating to this Agreement.
b) Without limiting the foregoing, the two Governments shall, at the request of
either Government, shall consult with respect to any problems which may
arise concerning automotive producers in the United States which do not at
present have facilities in Canada for the manufacture of motor vehicles, and
with respect to the implications for the operation of this Agreement of new
automotive producers being established in Canada.
c) No later than January 1, 1968, the two Governments shall jointly undertake a comprehensive review of the progress made towards achieving the
objectives set forth in Article I. During this review the Governments shall

consider such further steps as may be necessary or desirable for the full achievement of these objectives.

Article V

Access to the United States and Canadian markets provided for under this Agreement may by agreement be accorded on similar terms to other countries.

Article VI

This Agreement shall enter into force provisionally on the date of signature and definitively on the date upon which notes are exchanged between the two Governments giving notice that appropriate action in their respective legislatures has been completed.

Article VII

This Agreement shall be of unlimited duration. Each Government shall however have the right to terminate this agreement twelve months from the date on which that Government gives written notice to the other Government of its intention to terminate the Agreement.

In witness thereof the representatives of the two Governments have signed this Agreement.

Done in duplicate at Johnson City, Texas, this 16th day of January, 1965, English and French, the two texts being equally authentic.

For the Government of the United States of America:
L.B. Johnson   D. Rusk

For the Government of Canada:
L. B. Pearson   P. Martin

Annex A
1.
1) Automobiles; when imported by a manufacturer of automobiles.
2) All parts, accessories and parts thereof, except tires and tubes, when imported for use as original equipment in automobiles to be produced in Canada by a manufacturer of automobiles.
3) Buses, when imported by a manufacturer of buses.
4) Al parts, and accessories and parts thereof, except tires and tubes, when imported for use as original equipment in buses to be produced in Canada by a manufacturer of automobiles.

5) Specified commercial vehicles, when imported by a specified manufacturer of commercial vehicles.

6) All parts, accessories and parts thereof, except tires and tubes, and any machines or other articles required under Canadian tariff item 438a to be valued separately under the tariff items regularly applicable thereto, when imported for use as original equipment in specified commercial vehicles to be produced in Canada by a manufacturer of specified commercial vehicles.

2.

1) "Automobile" means a four-wheeled passenger automobile having a capacity for not more than ten persons;

2) "Base year" means the period of twelve months commencing on the 1st day of August, 1963 and ending on the 31st^t day of July, 1964;

3) "Bus" means a passenger motor vehicle having a seating capacity for more than ten persons, or a chassis thereof, but does not include any of the following vehicle or chassis therefore, namely an electric trackless trolley bus, amphibious vehicle, tracked or half-tracked vehicle or motor vehicle designed primarily for off-highway use;

4) "Canadian value added" has the meaning assigned by regulation made under section 273 of the *Canadian Customs Act*;

5) "Manufacturer" vehicles has the meaning assigned by regulation made under section 273 of the *Canadian Customs Act*;
   i) produced vehicles of that class in Canada in each of the four consecutive three month's periods in the base year, and
   ii) produced vehicles of that class in Canada in the period of twelve months ending on the 31st day of July in which the importation was made

A) The ratio of the net sales value of which the net sales value of all vehicles of that class sold for consumption in Canada by the manufacturer in that period is equal to or higher than the ratio of the net sales value of all vehicles of that class produced in Canada by the manufacturer in the base year to the net sells of all vehicles in that class sold for consumption in Canada by the manufacturer in the base year, and is not in any case lower than seventy-five to one hundred, and

The Canadian value added of which is equal to or greater than the Canadian value added of all vehicles of that class produced in Canada by the manufacturer in the base year;

6) "Net sales value" has the meaning assigned by regulation made under section 273 of the *Canadian Customs Act*;

7) "Specified commercial vehicle" means a motor truck, motor truck chassis, ambulance or chassis therefor, or hearse of chassis therefor, but does not include:

    a) any following vehicle or chassis designed primarily therefor, namely a bus, electric trackless trolley bus, golf of invalid carrier, straddle carrier, amphibious vehicle, tracked or half-tracked vehicle or motor vehicle designed primarily for off-highway use or motor vehicle specially constructed and equipped to perform special services or functions, such as, but not limited to, a fire engine, mobile crane, wrecker, concrete mixer or mobile clinic, or

    b) any machine or other article required under Canadian Tariff item 438a to be valued separately under the tariff item regularly applicable thereto.

3) The Government of Canada may designate a manufacturer for not falling with the categories set out above as being entitled to the benefit of duty-free treatment in respect of the goods described in this Annex.

Annex B

1) Motor vehicles for the transport of persons or articles as provided for in items 962.05 and 692.10 of the *Tariff Schedules of the United States* and chassis therefor, but not including electric trolley buses, three-wheeled vehicles, or trailers accompanying truck tractors, or chassis therefor.

2) Fabricated components, not including trailers, tires, or tubes for tires, for use as original equipment in manufacture of the motor vehicles of the kinds described in paragraph 1) above.

3) Articles of the kinds described in paragraphs 1) and 2) above include such articles whether finished or unfinished but do not include any article produced with the use of materials imported into Canada which are products of any foreign country (except materials produced within the customs territory of the United States), if the aggregate value of such imported materials when landed at the Canadian port of entry, exclusive of any landing cost and Canadian duty, was –

    a) with regard to the kinds described in paragraph 1), not including chassis, more than 60 percent until January 1, 1969, and thereafter more than 50 percent of the appraised custom value of the article imported into the customs territory of the United States, and

    b) with regard to chassis of the kinds described in paragraph 1) and articles of the kinds described in paragraph 2), more than 50 percent of the appraised customs value of the article imported into the customs territory of the United States.

Sample Letter of Undertaking, Ford Motor Company of Canada

Ford Motor Company of Canada, Ltd.
Oakville, Ontario
14 January, 1965

Dear Mr. Minister:

We are writing with respect to the agreement between the governments of Canada and the United States concerning production and trade in automotive products.

Ford Motor Co. of Canada, Ltd., welcomes the agreement and supports its objectives. In this regard, our company notes that the Governments of Canada and the United States have agreed "that any expansion of trade can best be achieved through the reduction or elimination of tariff and all other barriers to trade operating to impede or distort the full and efficient development of each country's trade and industrial potential." In addition, we note that the Governments of Canada and the United States shall seek the early achievement of the following objectives:

a) The creation of a broader market for automotive products within which the full benefits of specialization and large-scale production can be achieved;

b) The liberalization of United States and Canadian automotive trade with respect to tariff barriers and other factors tending to impede it, with a view to enabling the industries of both countries to participate on a fair and equitable basis in the expanding total market of the two countries; and

c) The development of conditions in which market forces may operate effectively to attain the most economic patter of investment, production, and trade.

Our company also notes that the right to import motor vehicles and original equipment parts into Canada under the agreement is available to vehicle manufacturers in Canada who meet the conditions stipulated in the Motor Vehicles Tariff Order of 1965. These conditions are, in brief, that vehicle manufacturers shall maintain in each model year their production of motor vehicles in Canada in the same ratio to sales of motor vehicles for consumption in Canada and the same dollar value of Canadian value added in the production of motor vehicles in Canada, as in the period August 1, 1963 to July 31, 1964.

We understand that –

i) in ascertaining whether Ford qualifies as a motor vehicle manufacturer and whether the requirements of paragraphs 1 and 2, below, are satisfied, production of automotive vehicles in Canada by Ford Motor Co. of Canada, Ltd. ("an associated person") will be taken into account, whether sold in Canada or exported;

ii) in determining whether the requirements of paragraphs 1 and 2, below, are satisfied, export sales of original equipment parts by Ford Motor Co. of Canada, Ltd., and by any associated person in Canada (as well as production of automotive vehicles in Canada by Ford Motor Co. of Canada, Ltd., and by any associated person, whether sold in Canada or exported), and purchases of original equipment parts by any affiliated Ford company outside of Canada from Canadian vendors, will be taken into account. An "affiliated Ford company" is one that controls, or is controlled by, or is under common control with, Ford Motor Co. of Canada, Ltd.

iii) for *the* purpose of computing the ratios referred to in paragraph 2 1) e) ii) A) of the order in council of the definition of manufacturer, the numerators of the fractions will consist of the net sales value of all passenger automobiles (or specified commercial vehicles or buses) produced by the motor vehicle manufacturer in Canada, including those sold in Canada and those sold in export, and the denominators of the fractions will consist of the net sales values of all passenger automobiles (or of specified commercial vehicles or buses) sold by the motor vehicles manufacturer for consumption in Canada, including imported passenger cars (or specified commercial vehicles or buses) but excluding passenger cars (or specified commercial vehicles or buses) that are produced by the motor vehicle manufacturer in Canada and sold in export.

The undertakings in this letter are based on the definition of "Canadian value added" in your present regulations.

We understand that in the computation of Canadian value added for vehicle assembly in Canada, section 2 A0 I) of the regulations would prevent us from including the cost of parts produced in Canada that are exported from Canada and subsequently imported into Canada as components of original equipment parts; this provision reduces the incentive to source in Canada parts that would be incorporated in US engines and other original equipment parts. Accordingly, we request that you give careful consideration to the revision of this clause.

In addition to meeting these stipulated conditions in order to contribute to meeting the objectives of the agreement, Ford Motor Co. of Canada, Ltd., undertakes:

1. To increase in each model year over the preceding motel year Canadian value added in the production of vehicles and original equipment parts by an amount equal to 60 percent of the growth in the market for automobiles sold by our company for consumption in Canada and by an amount equal to 50 percent of the growth in the market for commercial vehicles speci-

fied in Tariff Item 950 sold by our company for consumption in Canada, it being understood that in the event of a decline in the market a decrease in Canadian value added based on the above percentage is acceptable. For this purpose, growth or decline in the market shall be measured as the difference between the cost to our company of vehicles sold in Canada during the current model year and the cost to our company of vehicles sold in Canada during the preceding model year net of Federal sales taxes in both cases.

We understand that in the event that the total passenger car and /or total truck sales of our company in any model year fall below the total passenger car and /or total truck sales of our company during the base period, Canadian value added requirements would be reduced below the base period amendments for the purpose of this section, and for the conditions stipulated in the Motor Vehicles Tariff Order of 1965.

We believe that the definition of growth is unfair because it includes as growth the difference between the cost of the vehicles produced in Canada and the cost to us of identical imported vehicles. In the event that we rationalize our vehicle production in Canada so as to concentrate our production in Canada on high volume models for the North American market with other models being imported, the difference in cost as defined above would result in substantial growth even though there was no change in the number and models of vehicles sold in Canada. We request your careful consideration of a change in the definition that would eliminate this inequity. This inequity is compounded by the fact that Ford Motor Co. of Canada, Ltd., is compelled by the Canadian anti-dumping law to import vehicles at dealer price, and we request that your Government also give careful consideration to a change in the antidumping law in respect of vehicles imported under the Motor Vehicles Tariff Order of 1965.

2. To increase Canadian value added over and above the current amount that we achieved in the period August 1, 1963 to July 31, 1964, and that which we undertake to achieve in 1) above, by and amount of $74.2 million during the period August 1, 1967 to July 31, 1968.

The undertakings given in this letter are to be adjusted to the extent necessary for conditions not under the control of the Ford Motor Co. of Canada, Ltd., or of any affiliated Ford company, such as acts of God, fire, earthquake, strikes at any plant owned by Ford or by any of our suppliers, and war.

The Ford Motor Co. of Canada, Ltd., also agrees to report to the Minister of Industry, every 3 months beginning April 1, 1965, such information as the Minister of Industry requires pertaining to progress achieved by our company as well as plans to fulfill our obligations under this letter. In addition, Ford Motor Co. of Canada. Ltd., understands that the Government will conduct an audit each year with respect to the matters described in this letter.

We understand that before the end of the model year 1968 we will need to discuss together the prospects for the Canadian automotive industry and our company's program.

Yours sincerely,

Ford Motor Co. of Canada, Ltd.,
by K.E. Scott, President.

Appendix C
Memorandum of Understanding between Honda Canada and the Canadian Government, May 1984

Memorandum of Understanding

Memorandum of Understanding

THIS MEMORANDUM OF UNDERSTANDING signed this day of May, 1984,
BETWEEN
HER MAJESTY THE QUEEN in right of Canada as represented by the Minister
of Regional Industrial Expansion (the "Crown")
AND
HONDA CANADA INC., a Company incorporated under the laws of Canada
(the "Company")
WHEREAS:

The company has made a proposal to the Crown entitled "Proposal for the
Establishment of an Automobile Assembly Plant in Ontario" ("The Proposal)
which is dated April 3, 1984.

NOW THEREFORE this Memorandum of Understanding reflects the conclusions of the discussions between the two parties during the period of January 3rd, 1984 and this day and the understandings reached in respect of The
Proposal submitted.

A. Subject to the requirements of points B3 to 7 being satisfied, the Company
proposes, on the basis and subject to the conditions set out in The Proposal,
to proceed either in its own right or through a Canadian subsidiary (the
"Producer"):

1. To establish an automobile manufacturing facility in Canada which, based
on current estimates and planning of the Company, will involve and investment of $100 million, will commence production in 1987 and will reach
one-shift output of 40,000 units per year by 1989. The Canadian Value Added of such production will be approximately twenty percent of the cost of
production. The manufacturing facility will employ about 350 people by
1989.

2. To undertake, in addition to the base plan described above, the following

initiatives which will improve the potential for further increasing Canadian content:

a) By developing an automotive parts supplier development program:

(i) by establishing a parts purchasing department at the manufacturing facility to deal with the procurement of Canadian made parts and supplementary material, subject to suppliers meeting quality, cost and related requirements;

(ii) by assisting Canadian parts manufacturers who supply the Producer, the Company or its parent company in further developing their technology and capabilities.

b) By conducting testing programs in Canada relating to the suitability of its automobiles to the Canadian environment, e.g. cold weather, durability, etc.

B. If the Company or the Producer proceeds with the activities described in points A1 and A2, the Crown would:

3. Not object if the relevant Japanese Government does not include the Canadian production (on a one shift basis as outlines in The Proposal) and original equipment parts, accessories and parts thereof imported for use in such production for any year after 1985 in any voluntary export restraint agreement that may be in place in respect to the export of Japanese automobiles or original equipment parts, accessories or parts thereof to Canada in any such year after 1985.

4. Treat the automobile production (on a one shift basis as outlined in The Proposal) of the Company or the Producer as automobile manufactured in Canada and not as non-Canadian manufactured automobiles in the event that changes are made in the Canadian regime governing the entry and sales of automobiles.

5. As soon as practicable, amend the Honda Remission Order 1980, effective the date construction of the manufacturing facility commences, to provide for a reduction in the Value For Duty of Automobiles imported by the Company fully equivalent to the Canadian Value Added in automotive parts, accessories and parts thereof exported by or on behalf of the Company or the Producer.

6. Extend to the Company or the Producer the benefits of the Machinery Program on Remission of Duty under Tariff item 42700–1.

7. Entertain an application for establishment assistance for the manufacturing facility by the Company or the Producer pursuant to the Industrial and Regional Development Program (IRDP) as long as the application is in respect of a manufacturing facility to be located in any tier other than Tier I and provided the Producer's or the Company's project as set out in such application meets all other IRDP criteria.

C. If the activities described in points A1 and 2 are successfully completed and points B3 to 7 are satisfied, then the Company or the Producer will consider expanded activities as set out in The Proposal provided the Company and the Producer are satisfied that all the development contemplated by the first two paragraphs in Section IV of The Proposal have been achieved. Specifically, such activities will include:

a) increasing the base plan production volume of the manufacturing facility with the addition of a second shift;

b) expanding the production capacity of the facility, if market demand exceeds the capacity of the two shift operation;

c) increasing the Company's or the Producer's parts procurement and parts production;

d) expanding the Company's or the Producers R&D activities to cover a broader range of test and development programs in Canada.

D. Upon the Company signing this Memorandum of Understanding, the Crown shall consider, taking into account the terms and conditions accorded other manufacturers, the introduction of an Order in Council, which would allow a reduction in the duty payable on automobiles and/or original equipment parts, accessories or parts thereof imported for use in the production of automobiles by the Company or the Producer, effective the date production at the manufacturing facility comments, taking into account partially or wholly the total Canadian Value Added generated by or on behalf of the Company and/or the Producer.

E. This Memorandum of Understanding will continue to be in effect until replaced by a further exchange of notes.

F. This Memorandum of Understanding does not create any legal or equitable rights or obligations between the parties but merely serves to document the areas on which discussions have been held and general understandings have been reached.

G. Any public announcements or press releases regarding the project will be mutually agreed to by the parties.

H. The Crown and the Company agree to keep this Memorandum of Understanding and its subject matter confidential and not to make any disclosure thereof to third parties unless the prior written consent of the other party is first obtained.

HER MAJESTY THE QUEEN

Per: _____

HONDA CANADA INC.

Per: _____

Source: Privy Council Office, Serial no. 413-84MC, 'Executive Summary, Honda Investment, Minister of Regional Industrial Expansion, May 29,1984.'

Appendix D
Canada-U.S. Free Trade Agreement, 1 January 1989, Chapter 10, Trade in Automotive Goods

Article 1001: Existing Arrangement

Each Party shall endeavour to administer the *Agreement Concerning Automotive Products between the Government of Canada and the Government of the United States of America* that entered into force definitively on September 16, 1966 in the best interests of employment and production in both countries.

Article 1002: Waiver of Customs Duties

1. Neither Party shall grant a waiver of otherwise applicable customs duties to a recipient other than those recipients listed in Annex 1002.1, nor shall either Party expand the extent or application of, or extend the duration of, any waiver granted to any such recipient with respect to:

a) automotive goods imported into its territory from any country where such waiver is conditioned, explicitly or implicitly, upon the fulfillment of performance requirements applicable to any goods; or

b) any goods imported from any country where such waiver is conditioned, explicitly or implicitly, upon the fulfillment of performance requirements applicable to automotive goods.

2. Waivers of customs duties granted to the recipients listed in Part Two of Annex 1002.1, where the amount of duty waived depends on exports, shall:

a) after January 1, 1989 exclude exports to the territory of the other Party in calculating the duty waived; and

b) terminate on or before January 1, 1998.

3. Waivers of customs duties granted to the recipients listed in Part Three of Annex 1002.1, where the amount of duty waived depends on Canadian value added contained in production in Canada, shall terminate not later than:

a) January 1, 1996; or

b) such earlier date specified in existing agreements between Canada and the recipient of the waiver.

4. Whenever the other Party can show that a waiver or combination of waivers of customs duties granted with respect to automotive goods for commercial use by a designated person has an adverse impact on the commercial interests of a person of the other Party, or of a person owned or controlled by a person of the other Party that is located in the territory of the Party granting the waiver of customs duties, or on the other Party's economy, the Party granting the waiver either shall cease to grant it or shall make it generally available to any importer. The provisions of this paragraph shall not apply to the waivers of customs duties to those recipients listed in Part One of Annex 1002.1 in accordance with the headnote to that Part or to the waivers of customs duties referred to in paragraphs 2 and 3 for the periods during which such waiver of customs duties may be conditioned upon the fulfillment of performance requirements set forth in paragraphs 2 and 3.

Article 1003: Import Restrictions
Canada shall phase out the import restriction on used automobiles set out in tariff item 99215–1 of Schedule C to the *Customs Tariff*, or its successor, in five annual stages commencing on January 1, 1989 in accordance with the following schedule:
a) in the first year, used automobiles that are eight years old or older;
b) in the second year, used automobiles that are six years old or older;
c) in the third year, used automobiles that are four years old or older;
d) in the fourth year, used automobiles that are two years old or older; and
e) in the fifth year and thereafter, no restrictions.

Article 1004: Select Panel
The Parties recognize the continued importance of automotive trade and production for the respective economies of the two countries and the need to ensure that the industry in both countries should prosper in the future. As the worldwide industry is evolving very rapidly, the Parties shall establish a select panel consisting of a group of informed persons to assess the state of the North American industry and to propose public policy measures and private initiatives to improve its competitiveness in domestic and foreign markets. The Parties shall also cooperate in the Uruguay Round of multilateral trade negotiations to create new export opportunities for North American automotive goods.

Article 1005: Relationship to Other Chapters
1. Chapter Three (Rules of Origin for Goods) applies to:
a) automotive goods imported into the territory of the United States of America; and

b) automotive goods imported into the territory of Canada under this Agreement.

2. In determining whether a vehicle originates in the territory of either Party or both Parties under paragraph 4 of Section XVII of Annex 301.2, instead of a calculation based on each vehicle, the manufacturer may elect to average its calculation over a 12-month period on the same class of vehicles or sister vehicles (station wagons and other body styles in the same car line), assembled in the same plant.

3. The provisions of Article 405 apply to the waiver of customs duties affecting automotive goods except where otherwise provided in this Chapter.

4. The list of recipients in Annex 1002.1 and the definition "class of vehicles" may be modified by agreement between the Parties.

Article 1006: Definitions

For purposes of this Chapter:

automotive goods means motor vehicles and those goods used or intended for use in motor vehicles;

Canadian manufacturer means a person who manufactures automotive goods within the territory of Canada;

class of vehicles means any one of the following

a) minicompact automobiles – less than 85 cubic feet of passenger and luggage volume,

b) subcompact automobiles – between 85 and 100 cubic feet of passenger and luggage volume,

c) compact automobiles – between 100 and 110 cubic feet of passenger and luggage volume,

d) midsize automobiles – between 110 and 120 cubic feet of passenger and luggage volume,

e) large automobiles – 120 or more cubic feet of passenger and luggage volume,

f) trucks, or

g) buses,

NOTE: A vehicle that may have more than one possible use (e.g., vans, jeeps) would be defined as either an automobile or truck based on whether it is designed and marketed principally for the transport of passengers or the transport of cargo;

comparable arrangement means arrangements whereby waivers of customs duties are granted to Canadian manufacturers upon the fulfillment of conditions comparable to those described in the agreement referred to in Article 1001;

customs duty has the same meaning as in Article 410;

performance requirements has the same meaning as in Article 410;

used automobiles means used or second-hand automobiles and used or second-hand motor vehicles of all kinds that are manufactured prior to the calendar year in which importation into the territory of Canada is sought to be made; and

waiver of customs duties has the same meaning as in Article 410.

Annex 1002.1

Part One: Waivers of Customs Duties

The following Canadian manufacturers have qualified under the agreement referred to in Article 1001 and comparable arrangements or, on the basis of available information and projections, may be reasonably expected to qualify by the 1989 model year. The final list of those companies covered by the list below that so qualify will be provided by Canada to the United States of America within 90 days after the end of the 1989 model year.

AMI Stego Limited ...

... Wiltsie Truck Bodies Ltd.

Part Two: Export-Based Waivers of Customs Duties

The following Canadian manufacturers have qualified for export-based waivers of customs duties or, on the basis of available information and projections, may be reasonably expected to qualify by the date of entry into force of this Agreement. Canada shall provide the United States of America with the final list of those companies on this list that have qualified as of the date of entry into force of this Agreement.

BMW Canada Inc.
Fiat Canada
Honda Canada Inc.
Hyundai Auto Canada Inc.
Jaguar Canada Inc.
Mazda Canada Inc.
Mercedes-Benz of Canada Inc.
Nissan Automobile Company (Canada) Ltd.
Peugeot Canada Ltée/Ltd.
Saab-Scania Canada Inc.
Subaru Auto Canada Limited
Toyota Canada Inc.
Volkswagen Canada Inc.

Part Three: Production-Based Waivers of Customs Duties

The following Canadian manufacturers have qualified for production-based waivers of customs duties or, on the basis of available information and projections, may be reasonably expected to qualify by the date of entry into force of this Agreement. The final list of those companies covered by the list below that so qualify will be provided by Canada to the United States of America within 90 days after the end of the 1989 model year.

CAMI Automotive Inc. 2
Honda Canada Inc./Honda of Canada Mfg., Inc.
Hyundai Auto Canada Inc.
Toyota Motor Manufacturing Canada Inc.

Appendix E
Automotive Statistics, 1960–99

Table E.1
North American vehicle production summary, 1960–99 (in units)

Year	U.S. Total	Canadian Total	Mexican Total	N. America Total	Cdn. % of U.S.	Cdn. % N. America
1960	7,894,220	395,855	49,807	8,339,882	05.01	04.74
1961	6,643,822	390,459	62,563	7,096,844	05.87	05.50
1962	8,189,402	508,667	66,637	8,764,716	06.21	05.80
1963	9,100,585	632,172	69,135	9,801,892	06.94	06.44
1964	9,245,678	669,549	90,752	10,005,979	07.24	06.69
1965	11,114,213	853,931	97,395	12,056,539	07.68	07.08
1966	10,363,254	896,119	114,521	11,373,894	08.64	07.87
1967	8,992,269	939,635	126,991	10,058,895	10.44	09.34
1968	10,793,744	1,178,186	146,781	12,118,701	10.91	09.72
1969	10,182,562	1,350,481	165,811	11,698,854	13.26	11.54
1970	8,262,657	1,189,461	189,986	9,642,104	14.39	12.33
1971	10,649,666	1,373,108	211,393	12,234,167	12.89	11.22
1972	11,297,509	1,471,392	229,791	12,998,692	13.02	11.31
1973	12,662,919	1,589,499	285,568	14,537,986	12.55	10.93
1974	9,983,934	1,563,850	350,947	11,898,731	15.66	13.14
1975	8,965,413	1,442,076	356,642	10,764,113	16.08	13.39
1976	11,485,536	1,646,824	324,979	13,457,339	14.33	12.23
1977	12,699,086	1,764,987	280,813	14,744,886	13.89	11.97
1978	12,895,286	1,818,378	384,127	15,097,791	14.10	12.04
1979	11,475,737	1,629,855	444,426	13,550,018	14.20	12.02
1980	8,010,563	1,369,697	490,006	9,870,176	17.09	13.87
1981	7,940,781	1,280,499	597,118	9,818,398	16.12	13.04
1982	6,985,313	1,235,668	472,637	8,693,618	17.68	14.21
1983	9,225,698	1,502,325	285,485	11,013,508	16.28	13.64
1984	10,939,058	1,835,074	357,998	13,132,135	16.77	13.97
1985	11,653,956	1,934,110	458,680	14,046,746	16.59	13.76
1986	11,335,241	1,854,418	341,052	13,530,711	16.35	13.70
1987	10,925,605	1,635,151	395,258	12,956,014	14.96	12.62
1988	11,237,947	1,976,896	512,776	13,727,619	17.59	14.40
1989	10,875,574	1,965,480	641,275	13,482,329	18.07	14.57

Table E.1   (*Concluded*)

Year	U.S. Total	Canadian Total	Mexican Total	N. America Total	Cdn. % of U.S.	Cdn. % N. America
1990	9,783,433	1,946,542	820,558	12,550,533	19.89	15.50
1991	8,811,808	1,887,537	989,373	11,688,754	21.42	16.14
1992	9,731,478	1,950,646	1,080,863	12,762,987	20.04	15.28
1993	10,891,740	2,242,186	1,080,687	14,221,613	20.58	15.76
1994	12,249,990	2,320,403	1,109,338	15,679,731	18.94	14.79
1995	11,974,616	2,407,155	934,733	15,316,504	20.10	15.71
1996	11,831,225	2,397,166	1,222,711	15,451,102	20.26	15.51
1997	12,149,987	2,622,278	1,356,360	16,128,625	21.58	16.25
1998	12,001,864	2,570,321	1,459,891	16,032,076	21.41	16.03
1999	13,024,010	3,048,693	1,532,623	17,605,326	23.40	17.31

Source: *DesRosiers Automotive Yearbook 2000* (Richmond Hill, Ont.: DesRosiers Automotive Consultants 2000), 112.

Table E.2
North American production-to-sales ratios of vehicles, 1960–99

Calendar Year	U.S. Total	Canada Total	Mexico Total	N. America
1960	104.3	75.7	91.0	102.4
1961	97.1	76.3	101.5	95.7
1962	100.4	86.9	104.0	99.5
1963	101.7	96.5	91.5	101.3
1964	97.8	92.2	97.2	97.4
1965	102.3	102.8	101.1	102.3
1966	97.3	108.3	101.2	98.1
1967	91.1	115.2	100.9	93.1
1968	94.5	132.5	100.7	97.3
1969	88.9	147.2	100.3	93.3
1970	81.9	153.6	102.3	87.2
1971	87.6	146.0	103.0	92.0
1972	85.1	138.1	99.5	89.2
1973	88.1	129.6	110.2	91.6
1974	87.9	125.2	106.3	92.0
1975	84.1	109.5	103.1	87.4
1976	89.7	127.5	107.1	93.4
1977	88.6	131.2	97.1	92.3
1978	86.5	133.1	106.4	90.7
1979	83.0	116.7	104.5	86.6
1980	71.3	108.4	105.5	76.1
1981	74.4	107.5	104.6	79.2
1982	68.6	134.2	101.3	75.1
1983	77.5	139.0	104.6	83.1
1984	77.2	143.0	108.4	83.2
1985	74.9	126.4	117.1	80.3
1986	71.1	122.3	131.8	76.4
1987	72.4	107.0	159.4	76.8
1988	71.6	126.5	150.0	78.0
1989	72.7	132.5	143.8	79.9
1990	69.2	148.1	150.6	78.4
1991	70.3	146.7	153.9	80.8
1992	74.2	158.9	152.9	84.8
1993	77.0	188.7	179.2	89.1
1994	79.7	184.9	185.7	91.9
1995	79.5	207.1	503.3	93.3
1996	76.9	199.8	348.8	91.2
1997	78.7	184.6	272.5	92.9
1998	75.4	180.5	226.9	89.2
1999	75.0	198.2	230.2	91.2

Source: *DesRosiers Automotive Yearbook 2000* (Richmond Hill, Ont.: DesRosiers Automotive Consultants 2000), 113.

Table E.3
Canadian automotive industry, trade with U.S., 1960–99 (C$ millions)

Year	Vehicle Export	Parts Export	Total Export	Vehicle Import	Parts Import	Total Import	Vehicle Bal.	Parts Bal.	Total Bal.
1960	0	4	4	90	317	407	−90	−313	−403
1961	0	9	9	71	327	398	−71	−318	−389
1962	3	13	16	78	441	519	−75	−428	−504
1963	4	36	40	49	555	604	−46	−518	−564
1964	26	79	105	67	655	723	−41	−576	−617
1965	90	147	237	170	852	1022	−80	−705	−785
1966	493	361	854	409	1103	1511	84	−741	−657
1967	1105	494	1600	807	1310	2117	298	−816	−518
1968	1686	758	2444	1093	1818	2910	593	−1060	−466
1969	2367	950	3317	1154	2344	3498	1213	−1394	−181
1970	2127	1142	3269	934	2131	3065	1193	−989	204
1971	2536	1504	4040	1321	2521	3842	1215	−1017	198
1972	2752	1801	4553	1551	2957	4508	1201	−1156	45
1973	3060	2240	5300	2082	3620	5702	978	−1380	−402
1974	3408	2027	5435	2517	4110	6627	891	−2083	−1192
1975	3790	2113	5903	3125	4599	7724	665	−2485	−1821
1976	4774	3105	7879	3287	5588	8875	1487	−2483	−996
1977	5996	3865	9861	3952	7001	10953	2044	−3136	−1092
1978	7048	4945	11993	4360	8222	12582	2688	−3277	−589
1979	6709	4723	11432	5699	8821	14520	1010	−4098	−3088
1980	6670	3636	10306	4605	7746	12351	2065	−4110	−2045
1981	8287	4437	12724	5066	9395	14461	3221	−4958	−1737
1982	11116	5308	16424	3748	9823	13571	7368	−4515	2853
1983	13410	7475	20885	6015	11584	17599	7395	−4109	3286
1984	18965	10885	29850	8124	15791	23915	10841	−4906	5935
1985	21699	12104	33803	10552	17752	28304	11147	−5648	5499
1986	22232	12525	34484	11452	17862	29314	10780	−5610	5170
1987	20343	12240	32583	11973	16707	28680	8370	−4467	3903
1988	23689	12272	35961	11681	20307	31988	12008	−8035	3973
1989	23515	12051	35566	10856	17840	28696	12659	−5789	6870
1990	24153	10697	34850	9621	16694	26315	14532	−5997	8535
1991	24025	9340	33365	9909	15702	25611	14116	−6362	7754
1992	27709	10812	38521	9869	18853	28722	17847	−8041	9799
1993	35245	11448	46693	12152	19964	32116	23093	−8516	14577
1994	43229	13193	56422	15717	23739	39456	27152	−10546	16966
1995	47021	13212	60233	16009	26056	42065	31012	−12844	18168
1996	46979	14825	61804	16865	26283	43148	30114	−11458	18656
1997	50686	16208	66894	20347	29949	50295	30339	−13741	16599
1998	57040	18922	75962	21146	34658	55803	35894	−15735	20159
1999	70239	22248	92487	22757	39941	62698	47482	−17693	29789

Source: DesRosiers Automotive Yearbook 2000 (Richmond Hill, Ont.: DesRosiers Automotive Consultants 2000), 190.

Table E.4
Canadian automotive industry, trade with all countries, 1960–99 (C$ millions)

Year	Vehicle Export	Parts Export	Total Export	Vehicle Import	Parts Import	Total Import	Vehicle Bal.	Parts Bal.	Total Bal.
1960	28	24	52	247	332	579	−219	−308	−528
1961	21	29	50	183	343	527	−163	−314	−477
1962	29	34	62	179	463	642	−150	−430	−580
1963	37	60	97	117	575	692	−80	−516	−595
1964	82	105	187	164	673	836	−82	−567	−649
1965	183	182	364	285	868	1154	−103	−687	−789
1966	603	402	1005	507	1124	1631	96	−722	−626
1967	1205	541	1745	912	1346	2259	293	−806	−513
1968	1833	816	2650	1269	1849	3118	564	−1033	−469
1969	2488	1035	3523	1398	2399	3797	1091	−1364	−273
1970	2268	1244	3512	1174	2280	3454	1094	−1036	58
1971	2650	1593	4243	1695	2681	4376	955	−1088	−133
1972	2869	1892	4761	2015	3190	5205	854	−1298	−444
1973	3186	2364	5550	2459	3889	6348	727	−1525	−798
1974	3612	2174	5786	2967	4440	7407	645	−2266	−1621
1975	4211	2298	6509	3535	4887	8422	676	−2589	−1913
1976	5201	3284	8485	3809	5898	9707	1392	−2614	−1222
1977	6610	4067	10677	4544	7346	11890	2066	−3279	−1213
1978	7759	5269	13028	5254	8630	13884	2505	−3361	−856
1979	7267	5179	12446	6426	9388	15814	841	−4209	−3368
1980	7304	4087	11391	5764	8309	14073	1450	−4222	−2682
1981	8943	5038	13981	6665	9924	16589	2278	−4886	−2608
1982	11556	5738	17294	5161	10317	15478	6395	−4579	1816
1983	13691	7747	21438	7641	12325	19966	6050	−4578	1472
1984	19311	11189	30500	10300	17326	27626	9011	−6137	2874
1985	21915	12456	34371	13659	19418	33077	8256	−6962	1294
1986	22454	12712	35166	15406	19843	35249	7048	−7131	−83
1987	20530	12654	33184	16053	18799	34852	4470	−6145	−1668
1988	23992	12651	36643	15617	22180	37797	8375	−9529	−2254
1989	23882	12499	36381	14866	20558	35424	9016	−8059	957
1990	24395	11201	35596	13725	19850	33575	10670	−8649	2021
1991	24273	9909	34182	14886	19196	34082	9387	−9287	100
1992	27956	11289	39245	14842	22468	37310	13114	−11179	1935
1993	36006	12454	48460	16483	23375	39858	19523	−10921	8601
1994	44173	14278	58450	19808	28008	47815	24365	−13730	10635
1995	48468	14664	63132	20110	30266	50376	28358	−15602	12756
1996	47932	15937	63869	21071	30394	51465	26861	−14457	12404
1997	51446	17768	69214	26228	34211	60439	25218	−16443	8775
1998	57674	19990	77665	27294	39358	66652	30382	−19369	11013
1999	71061	23334	94395	30230	45579	75809	40832	−22246	18586

Source: *DesRosiers Automotive Yearbook 2000* (Richmond Hill, Ont.: DesRosiers Automotive Consultants 2000), 189.

Notes

Abbreviations Used in Notes

AO   Archives of Ontario
BHL   Bentley Historical Library
DFAIT   Department of Foreign Affairs and International Trade
FP   *Financial Post*
G&M   *Globe and Mail*
GFL   Gerald R. Ford Presidential Library
JCL   Jimmy Carter Presidential Library
LAC   Library and Archives Canada
NSARM   Nova Scotia Archives and Records Management
NYT   *New York Times*
OBP   Owen Bieber Papers
PCO   Privy Council Office
RRL   Ronald Reagan Presidential Library
SGP   Sam Gindin Papers
TS   *Toronto Star*
WA   *Ward's Automotive Reports*
WHCF   White House Central Files
WRL   Walter P. Reuther Library
WS   *Windsor Star*

Introduction: The Ripples of 1973

1 For an overview of the embargo and its impact globally and in North America, see Parra, *Oil Politics*; Yergin, *The Prize*; Fossum, *Oil, The State and Federalism*.
2 The literature on the car's impact upon society is extensive. A very small

sampling includes: Flink, *The Automobile Age*; Volti, 'A Century of Automobility'; Davies, '"Reckless Walking Must be Discouraged"'; Norton, *Fighting Traffic*; McShane, *Down the Asphalt Path*.

3 In explaining the persistently different outcomes between the two countries on a host of automotive matters, even after the auto pact, one analyst wrote that the differences 'result from tailoring policies to accommodate different relative evaluations of political outputs in the two countries, and from the companies' sensitivity to these differences. Fundamental differences in the economic endowments and physical attributes of the two countries and in the economic characteristics of their electorates result in predictable differences in the relative assessment by their governments of the importance of reducing regional job disparities, altering income distribution, generating new jobs, protecting intellectual property rights, and other dimensions of domestic policy performance.' Acheson, 'Power Steering the Canadian Automotive Industry,' 238.

4 For a very good brief view of American approaches to the Japanese, see Smitka, 'Foreign Policy and the US Automotive Industry.'

5 Clarke's brilliant *Trust and Power* explores this issue and illustrates the difficulties Detroit faced in meeting consumers' expectations.

6 Luger, *Corporate Power*, 3.

7 Shapiro, *Engines of Growth*.

8 For a view on Mexico, see Bennett and Sharpe, *Transnational Corporations versus the State*.

9 On transborder studies, see Penfold, 'Ontario at the Great Lakes Border/land,' 5. See also Bukowczyk et al., *Permeable Border*.

10 Fahrni, 'Reflections on the Place of Quebec in Historical Writing on Canada.'

11 High, *Industrial Sunset*.

12 See, for instance, overviews such as Thompson and Randall, *Ambivalent Allies*; and Hillmer and Granatstein, *Partners Nevertheless*.

13 Muirhead, *Dancing around the Elephant*. See also Bothwell, *Alliance and Illusion*.

14 Bow, *The Politics of Linkage Power*.

15 Hart, *A Trading Nation*.

16 Weintrub and Sands, eds. *The North American Auto Industry under NAFTA*; Molot, ed., *Driving Continentally*.

1 Industrial Revolutions: A New Automotive Landscape Emerges

1 Motor Vehicle Manufacturers' Association, *Annual 1971* (Toronto, 1972), various pages. On the development of the Canadian industry before 1945,

see: White, *Making Cars in Canada*; Ankli and Frederickson, 'The Influence of American Manufacturers on the Canadian Automobile Industry'; Davis, 'Dependent Development'; Anastakis, 'From Independence to Integration'; Roberts, *In the Shadow of Detroit*.

2 Dominion Bureau of Statistics figures cited in Sun Life Assurance, *The Canadian Automotive Industry*, 3. On the pre-war conflict over the auto tariff, see Traves, *The State and Enterprise*. See also Anastakis, 'Cars, Conflict and Cooperation.'

3 For the post-war labour issues surrounding the auto industry, see: Yates, *From Plant to Politics*; Gindin, *The Canadian Auto Workers*; Wells, 'The Impact of the Postwar Compromise on Canadian Unionism'; and Wells, 'Origins of Canada's Wagner Model of Industrial Relations.'

4 On the operation of the post-war auto industry, and post-war automotive statistics, see *Royal Commission on the Automobile Industry* (hereafter Bladen Commission), *Report*, 101–4.

5 James Easton, 'Automotive Industry: Export Answers for Import Problems,' *Saturday Night*, 6 August, 1960, 9–12.

6 On the problems of the late 1950s Canadian auto sector, see Bladen Commission, *Report*, various pages.

7 On the Canadian UAW's approach towards the auto industry in this period, see Anastakis, 'Between Nationalism and Continentalism.'

8 On the Bladen Commission and the duty-remission schemes, see Macdonald, 'A Comment: The Bladen Plan for Increased Protection for the Automotive Industry,' and Johnson, 'The Bladen Plan'; Anastakis, *Auto Pact*, chapter 1.

9 Canada, *Debates*, 16 May 1963, 7 (Speech from the Throne).

10 On the duty-remission program, see Johnson, 'The New Tariff Policy for the Automotive Industry'; Wonnacott, 'Canadian Automotive Protection'; Baxter, 'Ottawa's Car Formula "Clever," but What Will the World Say? We've Bent the Rules Somewhat,' *Financial Post* (hereafter *FP*), 2 November 1963.

11 In Canada the auto pact's implementing legislation was the 1965 Motor Vehicles Tariff Order; in the United States, the Automotive Products Trade Agreement, 1965. See Anastakis, *Auto Pact*.

12 CVA meant any expenditure in Canada, such as labour or parts purchases. The yearly base Canadian value-added requirement for the total industry was approximately $600 million.

13 As a result, between 1965 and 1975, the Big Three and the Canadian state developed a sometimes uneasy relationship in managing the sector's performance. See Anastakis, *Auto Pact*, particularly chapter 5.

14 Volvo was a good example of this. The firm established a plant in Canada

in 1963 and was part of the auto pact, though with special terms because of difficulties meeting its content and production requirements. See chapter 7 for more detail, and Anastakis, 'Building a "New Nova Scotia.'"

15 On the auto pact at the GATT, and its demise at the hands of the WTO, see Anastakis, 'The Advent of an International Trade Agreement' and 'Requiem for a Trade Agreement.'

16 For a more detailed explanation of the auto pact's impact, see Anastakis, *Auto Pact*, chapter 5, especially 128–31. At the time of the agreement, it was estimated that Canadian plants were approximately 18 per cent less productive than their U.S. counterparts in the pre-auto pact period, while Simon Reisman in his royal commission report estimated the difference at 30–35 per cent. This difference was quickly made up by the end of the decade. 'Canadian Production May Skyrocket as a Result of Auto Pact,' *Globe and Mail* (hereafter *G&M*), 16 January 1965; Reisman, *The Canadian Automotive Industry*, 36.

17 DesRosiers, *DesRosiers Automotive Yearbook 2000*, 114.

18 'New Plants and Expanded Facilities Announced as a Result of Automotive Programs,' vol. 12, Department of Industry, 10 January 1967, Department of Foreign Affairs and International Trade (DFAIT), file 37-7-1-USA-2.

19 According to Chris Roberts, 'labour productivity in the Canadian industry surpassed US levels between 1968 and 1973.' See Roberts, 'Harnessing Competition?' 508.

20 For an overview of the Canadian parts industry, see Tabachnick, 'The Impacts of Lean Production and Continental Economic Integration.' For a view of the role of labour in innovation within the sector, see Rutherford and Holmes, '"We Simply Have to Do That Stuff for Our Survival."'

21 The 1964 Statistics Canada 'List of Establishments Classified to This Industry' included about 150 parts makers, 118 of which were in Ontario. It did not include tool-and-die makers or moulders. Statistics Canada, Catalogue 42–210, *Motor Vehicle Parts and Accessories Manufacturers* (Ottawa, 1964), 13–14. For an assessment of the tool-and-die and moulder industries, see Holmes, Rutherford, and Fitzgibbon, 'Innovation in the Auto Parts Industry.'

22 'Commonwealth' content reflected the imperial focus (and age) of Canada's tariff structure. One of Bladen's recommendations was to rename it 'Canadian' content. See Anastakis, *Auto Pact*, 20–2.

23 Ibid.

24 Ibid., 34–5.

25 'Study Impact on Small Firms,' *G&M*, 19 January 1965; Robert Rice, 'Parts

Makers Back Auto Plan, But Warn of Danger to Jobs,' and 'Parts Plan May Doom Small Firms,' *G&M*, 20 and 26 January 1965.

26 Roberts, 'Harnessing Competition, 510–11; see also chapter 5.

27 Detroit Consulate to director, Policy Planning Branch, Trade and Commerce, 'Comments on Auto Trade Difficulties,' 24 March 1972, DFAIT, 37-7-1-USA-2, vol. 31.

28 For a good, brief overview of the impact of the auto pact on the parts sector, see Holmes, 'Industrial Reorganization, Capital Restructuring and Locational Change.' The figure of sixty firms is cited at 268n.24. See also 'Most Auto Parts Makers Are Rubbing Their Hands in Glee at High Market Prospects,' *FP*, 2 April 1966. Examples of firms that failed in the decade after the auto pact include Canadian Acme Screw and Gear (Windsor), Coulters (Oshawa), and Eltra (Point Edward).

29 V.C. German, president, Pilkington Glass, to Mitchell Sharp, 17 July 1972, DFAIT, 37-7-1-USA-2, vol. 31.

30 Mexico embassy to Ottawa, 'Canadian Auto Parts Exports,' 17 October 1972, DFAIT, 37-7-1-USA-2, vol. 31.

31 J.H. Stone to J.F. Grandy, 'Auto Trade – Detroit,' 30 March 1972, DFAIT, 37-7-1-USA-2, vol. 31.

32 Ken Romain, 'GM Chairman Thinks Auto Pact Should Include Sales Tax, Duty Cuts,' *G&M*, 26 September 1973.

33 Gordon Pitts, 'The Blueprint Boys,' *G&M*, 24 June 2005.

34 Stronach later said of the auto pact: 'We could already make whatever they needed. Now, we could go after the automakers' business without having to worry about tariffs.' Stronach's partner Pabst, who was from Detroit, 'scrambled down there right away and got familiar with the buyers down there. I knew dammed well if we didn't get at least one part from each automaker, and do a good job, we couldn't grow. We had to get at least one part or two parts.' Lilley, *Magna Cum Laude*, 32; Margot Gibb-Clark, 'Magna's Main Man,' *G&M*, 31 October 1986.

35 'Stock Prices Show Increases in North American Markets,' *G&M*, 23 November 1968.

36 'Companies in the News,' *G&M*, 30 July 1969, 26 September 1970, 21 June 1972.

37 For 'Magna's Corporate Constitution,' see Lilley, *Magna Cum Laude*, 79; Anderson and Holmes, 'New Models of Industrial Organization.' On Magna's relationship with its workers, see Lewchuk and Wells, 'When Corporations Substitute for Adversarial Unions.'

38 On Magna's structure and operations, see Anderson and Holmes, 'High-Skill, Low-Wage Manufacturing in North America'; 'Magna International,'

G&M, 25 May 1970; Margot Gibb-Clark, 'Magna's Main Man,' *G&M*, 31 October 1986; Lilley, *Magna Cum Laude*, 56.

39 David Climenhaga, 'Linamar: Analysts' Praise for Profits, Incentives, Plastics,' *G&M*, 3 August 1987; Harvey Enchin, 'Limamar Marches to a Different Tune,' *G&M*, 12 October 1991; Vik Kirsch, 'Let's Be Frank: *Mercury* Reporter Vik Kirsch Sits Down with Linamar Founder Frank Hassenfratz,' *Guelph Mercury*, 5 June 2008.

40 See http://www.atsautomation.com/profile/news/founder.asp (accessed 3 December 2010).

41 On ABC, see http://www.abcgroupinc.com/en/default.htm (accessed 10 December 2010); Ken Romain, 'Woodbridge Foam Succeeding after Spin-Off from Monsanto,' *G&M*, 17 September 1984.

42 The company was restructured in 2002 after it lost business from its two main customers, Chrysler and GM, and could not keep up with the shift from metal to plastic bumpers. Greg Keenan, 'Simpson Auto Plan Passed,' *G&M*, 13 November 2002; Wilfrid List, 'Houdaille's Oshawa Plant Bought by Canadian Firm," *G&M*, 30 September 1980; 'A.G. Simpson to Take over Comco Aug. 1,' *G&M*, 7 July 1982; http://www.agsautomotive.com/heritage.cfm (accessed 3 December 2010).

43 See http://www.wescast.com/en/heritage (accessed 6 December 2010).

44 Reisman, *The Canadian Automotive Industry*, 79. These figures differ slightly from Table 1.2 since they do not include some categories of parts.

45 Reisman estimated that 'independent' parts production (that is, the non-motor-vehicle manufacturers' share of production) at over 80 per cent in 1964, declining to 54 per cent in 1978, a consequence of the massive growth of Big Three parts production in Canada. Reisman, *The Canadian Automotive Industry*, 86 (Table 3.12). When the Canadian government questioned the executives of the nine largest independent American parts firms in 1978, virtually all were in favour of the auto pact and made a corporate effort to aim 'for 10% of their North American sales, investment and employment in Canada,' with many of them exporting 'more than one-half of their Canadian production back to the United States.' W.G. Huxtable, Detroit consul general, to External Affairs (A.R.A. Gherson), 'Meeting of Minister of Finance with U.S. and Canadian Auto Parts Executives,' 31 July 1978, Library and Archives Canada (LAC), Department of Finance, RG 19, vol. 5348, file 3881–01, pt. 2.

46 Statistics Canada, Catalogue 42–210, *Motor Vehicle Parts and Accessories Manufacturers*, various years, various pages.

47 'Though it was in 1972, Chrysler officials told Canadian government representatives that 'there was no prejudice against Canadian suppliers of vehi-

cles or parts and no disadvantage to quoting from Canada. They knew of no incidents where border delays had given trouble.' Canadian Automotive Activities,' *WA*, 14 January 1974, 15; 'Consultations with Automotive Producers: DISC and Canada-US Price Differentials, May 3, 1972,' 16 May 1972, DFAIT, 37-7-1-USA-2, vol. 31.

48 'Canadian Automotive Activities,' *Ward's Automotive Reports* (hereafter *WA*), 3 April 1973, 159.

49 'Life in the Fast Lane,' *Report on Business Magazine*, December 1986, 104.

50 Patrick Lavelle to E. Goldenberg, 19 May 1978, and W.G. Huxtable, Detroit consul general, to External Affairs (A.R.A. Gherson), 'Meeting of Minister of Finance with U.S. and Canadian Auto Parts Executives,' 31 July 1978, LAC, RG 19, vol. 5348, file 3881–01, pt. 2; author's interview with P. Lavelle, 29 August 2008.

51 Reisman, *The Canadian Automotive Industry*, 234; for an overview of the parts sector in the post-1980 period, see Tabachnick, 'The Impacts of Lean Production and Continental Economic Integration.'

52 By the early 1990s, for instance, North American-built Toyota Corollas – including those made at its Cambridge, Ont., facility – boasted 718 suppliers, of which 173 were Canadian, though many of these suppliers did low value-added work. See, for instance, Rutherford, 'Re-embedding, Japanese Investment and the Restructuring Buyer-Supplier Relations'; Timothy Pritchard, 'Canadian Makers Playing a Bigger Part in the Industry,' *G&M*, 19 May 1992.

53 For a more detailed explanation of the federal government's emerging auto mandarinate, see Anastakis, *Auto Pact*, 35. From 1963 onward, there would be close interdepartmental cooperation among government officials on the auto issue, though the core of this group worked out of the industry department. Drury, the minister of defence production, became the first minister of industry. He was Finance Minister Walter Gordon's brother-in-law. N.B. Macdonald, director of the Mechanical Transport Branch, was listed in the organizational charts of both industry and defence production, as were a number of other industrial sector branches. *McGraw-Hill Directory and Almanac of Canada*, 210–19; C.M. Drury, 'The Canadian Department of Industry,' *Addresses of the Empire Club of Canada*.

54 On the impact of the car on post-war Ontario, see, for example, Bloomfield, 'No Parking Here to Corner'; Van Nostrand, 'The Queen Elizabeth Way'; Penfold, '"Are We to Go Literally to the Hot Dogs?"'; Robinson, 'The Dundas and Ancaster Highway Disputes in Ontario, 1967–68'; Stevens, 'Cars and Cottages.'

55 Government of Ontario, *Legislature of Ontario, Debates* (hereafter Ontario, *Debates*), 18 April 1963, 2552 (Robert Macaulay, Riverdale).

56 In responding to Frost, Todgham wrote: 'Premier, during these recent years which form the basis of your criticism, our company has paid out in wages, salaries, and benefits an average of 16 million dollars more each year to sustain local employment and to maintain a high level of prosperity in this area, that was paid during the period prior to our expansion.' R. Todgham (president of Chrysler Canada) to Frost, 6 March 1958. Archives of Ontario (AO), Premiers' Records, RG 3–25, Leslie Frost Papers, box 7, file 12-G.

57 Frost to Todgham, 10 March 1958, AO, RG 3–25, Leslie Frost Papers, box 7, file 12-G.

58 Wood to Frost, 12 May 1960, acknowledged by R.A. Farrell, executive officer to the premier, 17 May 1960, AO, RG 3–25, Leslie Frost Papers, box 7, file 12-G.

59 William Gent (president, Gent Advertising) to Frost, 12 July 1960, and Frost to Gent, 14 July 1960, AO, RG 3–25, Leslie Frost Papers, box 7, file 12-G.

60 Ontario, *Debates*, 22 February 1963, 998 (Richard Sutton, York-Scarborough).

61 Chritchlow, *Studebaker*, 131–40; Studebaker Corporation, *Annual Report for 1962*, 16 October 1962, Historical Collections, Baker Library, Harvard Business School.

62 'Studebaker Auto Making Ended Except in Canada,' 'Studebaker Corporation Traces Its Origin Back to 1852 and an Oak-Sided Wagon,' *New York Times* (*NYT*), 10 December 1963; 'Canada Applauds Studebaker Move,' *NYT*, 16 December 1963.

63 'A Special Report on Canadian Automobile Manufacturing: Studebaker,' by Gordon Grundy, president, Automotive Division, 13 December 1963, DFAIT, 73–7–USA–2, vol. 1; Critchlow, *Studebaker*, 182.

64 Interview with William Davis, 7 August 2008; Robert Growcock (president of Studebaker Canada) to Robarts, 17 March 1966, AO, RG 3–26, John P. Robarts Papers, box 350, file January 1966–December 1966.

65 On Davis, see Hoy, *Davis*. There has been surprisingly little written on Davis in the last two decades. On the relationship between Ontario and the federal government in the post-war period, see Bryden, *'A Justifiable Obsession.'*

66 Trudeau wrote back that 'my colleague, the Minister of Industry, Trade and Commerce [Jean Luc-Pepin], welcomes this offer and I would suggest that you let him know the names of your reps who might meet with federal

officials to discuss matters relating to the auto, so that specific arrangements can be made for appropriate consultations.' William Davis to Pierre
Trudeau, 14 October 1971, and Trudeau to Davis, 5 November 1971, LAC,
RG 19, vol. 5624, file 87053–4, pt. 1, Representations, 1964–1971; author's
interview with P. Lavelle, 29 August 2008.
67 Throne Speech as quoted by Windsor NDP MPP Ted Bounsall, in Ontario,
   Debates, 16 March 1972, 497; Ken Romain, 'Davis Opposes Dropping 15%
   Tax on Vehicles Imported from the US,' *G&M*, 30 May 1973.
68 Author's interviews with L.R. Wilson and P. Lavelle, 27 June 2006 and
   29 August 2008.
69 According to Wilson, 'the emergence of a policy function in MIT began under Fleck and I was the first executive director of it. They focused on autos
   and the GATT.' Fleck eventually became secretary to the cabinet in 1974
   and was deputy minister of industry from 1976 to 1978. The province also
   hired former federal civil servants who had worked on automotive issues
   such as Robert Latimer and Rodney de C. Gray. Author's interviews with
   Dennis DesRosiers, 1 August 2006; L.R. Wilson, 27 June and 19 September
   2006; and Michael Dube and Felix Pilorusso, 14 August 2003.
70 Ontario, *Debates*, 10 December 1975, 1488, and 9 November 1976, 4551
   (Claude Bennett, Ottawa). On Davis's meetings with the Big Three, see
   Ontario, *Debates*, 13 April 1978, 1475 (Claude Bennett, Ottawa).
71 Ontario, *Debates*, 2 April 1976, 1130 (Budget); Ministry of Treasury, Economics and Intergovernmental Affairs (Ontario), *Canada's Share of the North
   American Automotive Industry*.
72 On BILD, see Wolfe, 'Harnessing the Region,' 136. In 1980 the Economic
   Development Fund had given fourteen Ontario parts companies more
   than $7 million in the form of grants and loans. Frank Miller to Allan
   MacEachen, 12 March 1980, LAC, RG 19, vol. 5738, file 3881–01, pt. 3.
73 Frank S. Miller to Larry Grossman, 14 July 1981, AO, RG 9–2, Acc. 222206,
   box 7, deputy minister, file: 'Policy and Priorities Division Executive Director Brock A. Smith.'
74 Author's interview with Wilson, 27 June 2006. For an insightful view of
   this episode, see Weaver, *The Suicidal Corporation*, 34–8.
75 On the sometimes difficult intergovernmental negotiations, see 'Chrysler,'
   A.S. Rubinoff to Ian A. Stewart, 10 April 1980, LAC, RG 19, vol. 5959, file
   8705–04–2, pt. 7; 'Chrysler Canada,' J.D. Girvin to L.R. Wilson, 10 April
   1980, AO, RG 9–2, Acc. 22206, box, deputy minister, file: 'Chrysler – 1979.'
76 William Davis to Pierre Trudeau, 30 July 1980, LAC, MG 28 I119, CAW Papers, vol. 8, file 298; Pierre Trudeau to William Davis, 11 September 1980,
   LAC, RG 19, vol. 5958, file 8705–02, pt. 21.

77 Rodrique Tremblay to Robert de Cotret, 13 August 1979. The original letter has been translated from French. Department of Industry Access to Information and Privacy Act request (ATIP), file 4954-1, vol. 2, May 1974–December 1979, at 469.
78 This development also shows that, while continentalism has pushed Ontario to become more of a 'region state' within North America, and loosened the bonds of federalism, there are instances where federal-Ontario cooperation has increased. See, for instance, Courchene with Telmer, *From Heartland to North American Region State.*
79 Ontario, *Debates,* 24 March 1980, 146 (Larry Grossman, St Andrew-St Patrick).
80 For example, Frank Miller to Allan MacEachen, 12 March 1980, and MacEachen to Miller, n.d., LAC, RG 19, vol. 5738, file 3881–01, pt. 3.
81 For a good overview of this changing dynamic, see Muirhead, 'Ottawa, the Provinces and the Evolution of Canadian Trade Policy since 1963,' 30.
82 Emphasis added. Ottawa to Washington, 'Ontario Interest in CDA/USA Relations,' 28 August 1973, and Washington to Ottawa, 'Ontario Interest in CDA/USA Relations,' 29 August 1973, DFAIT 37-7-1-USA-2, vol. 32.

2 The New Big Three: Canadian Safety, Emissions, and Fuel Economy in a Continental Industry

1 Robert Marshall, 'A Nation Driven: Canadians and Their cars, Till Death Do Them Part,' *Maclean's,* 16 May 1977, 59–61.
2 'Milestones for US Motor Vehicle Production and Sales,' *Ward's Automotive Yearbook* (Detroit, Mich., 1982), 8.
3 On the battle between safety and styling in Detroit, see Eastman, *Styling vs. Safety;* and Gartman, *Auto Opium.* James Easton, 'Automotive Industry: Export Answers for Import Problems,' *Saturday Night,* 6 August 1960, 9–12 at 10.
4 Joseph Beric, Trudeau's Ottawa mechanic, remembered that 'he would come in with the car, followed by his chauffeur in another car and his bodyguards. The bodyguards would hang around, but Mr. Trudeau would take off his jacket and work with me. He knew quite a bit about mechanics and wanted to know more. He understood motors and cars. He liked to help.' Dave Brown, 'Mechanic Remembers Trudeau and His Car,' http://www.motormedics.ca/history.htm (accessed 4 September 2010).
5 Flink, 'Three Stages of American Automobile Consciousness.'
6 Keats, *The Insolent Chariots;* Nader, *Unsafe at Any Speed;* Jacobs, *The Life and Death of Great American Cities.* For a view of the battles between GM and Nader, see Whiteside, *The Investigation of Ralph Nader.*

7 Lower, *Canadians in the Making*, 424.
8 On Canadian's 'love-hate relationship with the car,' see Ruffilli, 'The Car in Canadian Culture,' iii. On battles against 'honky-tonk' roadside culture and expressways, see: Penfold, '"Are We to Go Literally to the Hot Dogs?"'; Mohl, 'Stop the Road'; Nowlan, *The Bad Trip*; Robinson, 'Modernism at a Crossroad.'
9 See, for example, Norton, *Fighting Traffic*.
10 On early battles over traffic, see Norton, 'Street Rivals,' and Davies, '"Reckless Walking Must be Discouraged."' On the issue of styling versus safety, see Eastman, *Styling vs. Safety*; Dummitt, 'A Crash Course in Manhood.'
11 Between 1950 and 1970, over 70,000 Canadians were killed in motor-vehicle accidents. The number of vehicles on Canadian roads had tripled from 3.1 million in 1952 to 9.4 million in 1972. Historical Statistics of Canada, http://www.statcan.ca/english/freepub/11-516-XIE/sectiont/T271_284.csv (accessed 4 March 2008). Roy Shields, 'There ARE Ways to Cut the Bloody Road Toll,' *Toronto Star* (hereafter *TS*), 2 January 1965; Rex Tasker and Patricia Burwash, *Every Second Car*, National Film Board of Canada, 1964.
12 Shields, 'There ARE Ways to Cut the Bloody Road Toll'; and editorial, 'How to Get Safer Cars,' *TS*, 2 June 1965; Una Abrahamson, 'Of Consuming Interest,' *Chatelaine*, April 1971, 16–18; Ronald Cohen, 'The Case for Wearing Your Seat Belt,' *Canadian Consumer*, February 1975, 24–7.
13 Emphasis in original. Howard Grafftey et al., 'Traffic Accident Deaths and Injuries in Canada,' 2 July 1965, LAC, Department of Transport (hereafter RG 12), file S1500–21–1, vol. 2. The MP group included the NDP's Stanley Knowles and the Liberals' John Matheson.
14 Nader successfully sued GM; for other views of the safety issue, see Lee, 'The Ford Pinto Case'; and Tedlow and Hundt, 'Cars and Carnage.'
15 'Committee to Invite Car Critic to Ottawa,' *G&M*, 6 May 1966.
16 Eventually, Edmonston gained even more fame as Quebec's first-ever elected NDP member, in 1990. Bellemare, 'End Users,' 397. On groups such as the APA, see Goldstein, 'Public Interest Groups and Public Policy,' which mentions the group and Edmonston.
17 Cabinet Conclusions, 15 December 1966, LAC, Records of the Office of the Privy Council (hereafter RG 2), Series A-5-a, vol. 6321.
18 The federal government, under its 'trade and commerce' power, regulates standards for new vehicles. Provinces regulate vehicles after they have been purchased, as both Ontario and British Columbia have chosen to do in the past (for example, in the case of automobile-emissions standards). Cabinet Conclusions, 3 October 1967, LAC, RG 2, Privy Council Office,

Series A-5-a, vol. 6323; 'Federal Legislation on Motor Vehicle Safety Standards,' 13 February 1969; and 'Federal-Provincial Ministerial Meeting on
Traffic Safety, Quebec City, 14 January 1969,' LAC, RG 12, file S1500-21-1,
vol. 2 (box 6); D.G. Campbell, 'This Man Wants to Make Driving Safer,' *TS*,
5 February 1974.

19 Cabinet Conclusions, 3 October 1969, LAC, RG 2, Privy Council Office,
Series A-5-a, vol. 6340; 'Timetable for Regulations under Motor Vehicle
Safety Act,' Gilles Sicotte to O.G. Stoner, 29 April 1970, LAC, RG 12, file
S1500-21-1, vol. 3 (box 6).

20 Initially, there were only two minor variations from the U.S. rules: Canada
allowed convex external rear-view mirrors (versus flat mirrors in the
United States) and a different type of bulb for headlights. 'Points Raised at
Motor Vehicle Manufacturers Meeting June 18 and 19, 1970,' M. Barber to
H. Young, 25 June 1970, LAC, RG 12, file S1500-21-1, vol. 1 (box 6); 'Motor
Vehicle Safety Act and Regulations,' O.G. Stoner to D. Jamieson, 15 July
1970, LAC, RG 12, file S1500-21-1, vol. 3 (box 6); John Burns, 'Ottawa Considering Limiting Noise through Motor Vehicle Safety Standards,' *G&M*,
22 August 1970.

21 The Big Three provided very detailed suggestions for revision for the new
rules, virtually all of which the government followed. For instance, GM
suggested clarifying definitions (what was a 'chassis'? or did the United
States include Puerto Rico and other U.S. territories?), streamlining compliance, and how the Canadian legislation dealt with revisions to the U.S.
regulations. W.A. Woodcock (director of engineering, GM) to G.D. Campbell (MOT), 29 June 1970, LAC, RG 12, file S1500-21-1, vol. 1 (box 6); J.E. Elliot (Chrysler Canada) to D. Jamieson, 18 September 1970, LAC, RG 12, file
3340-3-31, vol. 4 (box 7); James Dykes (MVMA) to D.G. Campbell (MOT), 9
July 1970, LAC, RG 12, file S1500-21-1, vol. 2 (box 6).

22 SOMA and Toyota are discussed in more detail in chapter 7. About 161
vehicles did not meet the safety standards. D.W.C. McEwan to file, 'Telephone Call of Bill Gamblin, Road and Motor Vehicle Traffic Safety Branch,
Transport Canada,' 19 April 1974, LAC, Department of Industry (hereafter
RG 20), file 4956-2-2.

23 Government officials speculated that the real reason that SOMA threatened the plant closure was poor sales. G.D. Campbell to O.G. Stoner, 'Temporary Shut-down SOMA/Renault Production at St. Bruno,' 25 January
1970, LAC, RG 12, file 3340-3-31, vol. 2 (box 7); O.G. Stoner to the minister,
'RE: Impact of Proposed Motor Vehicle Safety Standards on SOMA,' 10
April 1972, LAC, RG 12, file 3340-3-31, vol. 2 (box 7).

24 'Canadian Automotive Activities,' *WA*, 18 December 1972, 407.

25 'Consumers Are Warned They Must Pay Costs,' *G&M*, 20 January 1971.

26 D.W.C. McEwan to C.D. Arthur, 'New Program to Achieve 1979 Canadian Road Safety Goals,' 1 October 1974, and 'Draft Memorandum to Cabinet: New Program to Achieve 1979 Canadian Road Safety Goals,' September 1974. Both RG 20, file 4956-2-2.

27 The issue of seat-belt *use*, as opposed to mandatory seat-belt equipment, did generate significant opposition in the early 1970s. When Ontario announced regulation enforcing seat-belt use in 1974, some Ontarians were incredulous. One writer to the *Toronto Star* complained that 'Big Brother has finally arrived. He has just told me that he intends to make it law that I wear my seat belt while driving my car. This is preposterous. Clearly this is a human rights issue, and has no place in a free society. It could only have been born in the minds of dictators.' Thomas White to editor, 13 March 1974. Later in the decade, the installation of air bags generated a similar heated discussion.

28 The auto companies were also in support of mandatory seat-belt usage laws in Canada, though this was a provincial jurisdiction. Robert Williamson, 'Davis Cites Safety Figures, Will Enforce Seatbelt Use,' *G&M*, 6 March 1974; Robert Catherwood, 'Fasten the Seat Belt – or You May Lose Money,' *FP*, 27 November 1971; 'Canadian Automotive Activities,' *WA*, 24 April 1972, 135; D.G. Campbell to O.G. Stoner, 'Motor Vehicle Safety Regulations,' 11 December 1974, LAC, RG 12, file S1500-21-1, vol. 6 (box 6); S.C. Wilson to the minister, 'Motor Vehicle Safety Regulations,' 7 June 1976, LAC, RG 12, file S1500-21-2, vol. 7 to vol. 8, box 7A; William Tucker, 'The Wreck of the Auto Industry,' *Harper's*, November 1980, 47–60 at 57.

29 W.L. Higgitt (president, Consumer Safety Council of Canada) to Herb Gray, 1 April 1975, LAC, RG 20, file 4956-2-2.

30 Name withheld (ATIP) to Herb Gray, 12 April 1981, LAC, RG 20, file 4956-2-2.

31 The two countries had different bumper standards after 1975, for instance, with the Canadian standard being less stringent (and therefore less costly). The U.S. standard required that vehicles meet a 'low corner impact requirement,' which the Canadians felt had 'little or no safety benefit.' Canadian companies were given an exemption for export on the U.S.-destined cars with different standards. D.G. Campbell to the minister, 27 January 1975, LAC, RG 12, file S1500-21-1, vol. 6 (box 6); S.D. Cameron to the minister, 'Motor Vehicle Safety Regulations,' 8 November 1975, LAC, RG 12, file S1500-21-2, vol. 8 (box 7A).

32 See, for instance, 'US Transportation Secretary Adams Decisions on Air Bags and 1981–84 Fuel Economy Goals,' 24 June 1977, LAC, RG 12, file S1500-21-2, vol. 10 (box 7A).

33 McCarthy, *Auto Mania*.

34 For a fascinating view of this battle, see Dewey, '"The Anti-Trust Case of the Century."'

35 HCs also include Volatile Organic Compounds, or VOCs, leading greenhouse gas emissions (GHGs).

36 For a more detailed explanation of auto pollutants, see Environment Canada's 'Criteria Air Contaminants and Related Pollutants' website, http://www.ec.gc.ca/cleanair-airpur/Criteria_Air_Contaminants-WS7C43740B-1_En.htm (accessed 6 March 2008).

37 On Pollution Probe, see O'Connor, 'Toronto the Green,' and Chant, *Pollution Probe*; 'Carbon Monoxide Study,' and 'Carbon Monoxide in Blood Rose after Car Ride,' *G&M*, 9 and 10 October 1970.

38 Richard J. Doyle, 'The Real Cost of Driving Is Blowing in the Wind,' *G&M*, 26 June 1972.

39 Editorial, 'Clean Automobile Exhausts by 1975,' *TS*, 28 July 1972. Written by staff reporter Philip Sykes, the series ran from 25 to 28 July 1972.

40 Clair Balfour, 'The Blanket over the Heart of a Beautiful Metropolis Is Air Pollution,' *G&M*, 14 February 1970.

41 MP Francis Cyril complained in 1972 that 'anyone trying to take a walk, even in Ottawa which I consider to be a relatively unpolluted city, finds himself plagued with exhaust fumes, the waste products of lead fuels used in internal combustion motors. They are inescapable.' Canada, *Debates*, 13 March 1972, 773 (Francis Cyril, Ottawa West). In Hamilton, environmental group CHOP (Clear Hamilton of Pollution) was founded in 1970; Reg Vickers, 'Alberta: Attackers Zero in on the Car,' *G&M*, 12 December 1970; and, of course, Greenpeace was founded in Vancouver in 1970.

42 Environment Canada, *The Clean Air Act, Annual Report, 1974–1975* (Ottawa, 1975), 6–7.

43 To All CLC members, locals, etc., 'Our Environment,' 21 December 1970, Walter Reuther Library (hereafter WRL), UAW-Ford Collection, box 14, file 7.

44 Poll numbers as cited in Read, 'Addressing "a Quiet Horror,"' 208; the Liberal Party policy cited is from O.G. Stoner to minister, 'Memorandum to the Minister: Re: 1975 Automobile Exhaust Emission Standards,' 22 June 1973, RG 12, box 94, file 156-14-4, vol. 2.

45 Richard M. Clee, 'Air Pollution,' letter to the editor, *G&M*, 28 September 1970; Stephen Duncan, 'Our Costly Cleanup: But First, We Need Priorities,' *FP*, 3 March 1973.

46 McCarthy writes that the Clean Air Act 'was not only the toughest environmental law ever passed in the United States, it may well have been the most anti-business piece of legislation ever passed by Congress.'

McCarthy, *Auto Mania*, 173. For other views, see Carter, 'The Responses of the American Automobile Industry to Environmental Protection'; and Doyle, *Taken for a Ride.*

47 Although these three substances are caused by the burning of fossil fuels, they are not generated in the same way. CO and HCs are the result of the incomplete burning of fuel, that is, they are leftovers of a not entirely efficient process of combustion. NO_x, on the other hand, results from the heating of air during the process of combustion. Steps that decrease CO and NCs may actually lead to increased NO_x, making NO_x reductions far more difficult to achieve. Margolis, 'The Politics of Auto Emissions,' 5.

48 The Canadian Clean Air Act did not directly address the control of air pollution from mobiles sources. Environment Canada, *The Clean Air Act, Annual Report, 1974–1975,* 1, 33.

49 Lyndon Watkins, 'Car Exhaust Rules Likely in Two Months,' *G&M*, 23 April 1970; John Davidson, 'Auto-Pollution Rules by Fall,' *FP*, 24 June 1972.

50 J.F. Grandy (ITC) to O.G. Stoner, 30 August 1971, LAC, RG 12, box 94, file 156-14-4, vol. 2, (either pt. 1, 1 July 1971–30 June 1973, or pt. 2, from 1 July 1973). Unless otherwise noted, all citations in this section are from this collection and files. Editorial, 'Industry Will if It Must," *G&M*, 27 August 1970.

51 J. Austin (EMR) to O.G. Stoner, 16 September 1971.

52 'Proposed Government Objectives for Emissions from Motor Vehicles for 1973, 1975 and 1976,' W. Le Clerc to O.G. Stoner, 19 November 1971; J. Austin (EMR) to O.G. Stoner, 16 September 1971.

53 Cabinet Conclusions, 2 December 1971, RG 2, Privy Council Office, Series A-5-a, vol. 6381; 'Memorandum to the Cabinet: Proposed Government Objectives for Emissions from New Motor Vehicles for 1973, 1975 and 1976,' 22 October 1971.

54 The Canadian Clean Air Act did not include legislative authority to regulate emissions from automobiles, since air pollution remained a provincial responsibility, though it set factory standards for emissions control. Further, the act delineated a leadership role for the federal government, given that 'certain tasks can and should be handled at the federal level either because of constitutional considerations or because the federal government is in the best position to manage the task.' Environment Canada, *The Clean Air Act, Annual Report, 1974–1975,* 1.

55 'Ottawa Plans Cuts in Exhaust Emissions,' *G&M*, 16 December 1971; Gordon McGregor, 'Vehicles Fume Less, Drivers More as Muscle Car Becomes Has Been,' *G&M*, 4 March 1972.

56 J.E. Elliot to D. Jamieson, 'Proposed Amendments, Motor Vehicle Exhaust Regulations,' 24 February 1972, LAC, RG 12, box 6, file: 'Motor Vehicle Safety Regulations: Correspondence from the Automotive Industries,' 1 October 1970–30 September 1972.

57 Gordon felt that, since the emission-control equipment was an 'add on,' 'production line problems should be minimal.' R. Illing to O.G. Stoner, 19 October 1972; Ken Romain, 'Canadian Car Makers Seek Less Stringent Emission Controls,' G&M, 11 January 1973.

58 'Canadian Automotive Activities,' WA, 4 June 1973; O.G. Stoner, 'Memorandum to Minister: Re: Proposed Government Objectives for Emissions from New Motor Vehicles for 1975 and 1976 Model Years,' 23 February 1973.

59 O.G. Stoner, 'Memorandum to the Minister: Re: Proposed Government Objectives for Emission from New Motor Vehicles for 1975 and 1976 Model Years,' 5 February 1973.

60 'Emission Standards Set Back to '76: New EPA-Industry Controversy Erupts by Setting of Stringent Interim Standards,' WA, 16 April 1973; McCarthy, Auto Mania, 186–7; 'US Agency Backs Down on Car Curbs,' G&M, 6 June 1973.

61 Jean Marchand to Jack Davis (Environment), Alastair Gillespie (ITC), Marc Lalonde (Health), Donald Macdonald (EMR), Jeanne Sauvé (Science and Technology), and Herb Gray (Consumer and Corporate Affairs), 25 June 1973.

62 'Memorandum to the Minister: The 1975/6 Automobile Emission Standards,' J.F. Shaw (deputy minister, Environment Canada) to J. Davis, 14 June 1973; S.O. Winthrop to G. Campbell, 27 June 1973; Jack Davis to Jean Marchand, 29 June 1973; G.W. Taylor (Environment), Automobile Emission Trends in Canada, 1960–1985 (Ottawa, 1973).

63 Ibid.; Jack Davis to Jean Marchand, 29 June 1973; S.O. Winthrop to G. Campbell, 27 June 1973.

64 O.G. Stoner to J. Marchand, 'Memorandum to the Minister: Briefing Note on Canadian Automobile Exhaust Emission Standards with Six Cabinet Colleagues Most Directly Concerned with This Decision,' 17 July 1973.

65 Environment Canada, The Clean Air Act, Annual Report, 1974–1975, 35.

66 'Press Release: Ministers of Transport and Environment Announce 1975 Automobile Exhaust Emission Standards, 19 July, 1973,' LAC, RG 12, box 6, file S1500-21-2, vol. 5, 1 September 1973–31 May 1974.

67 In June 1973 British Columbia NDP MP Randolph Harding asked Davis 'why he now refuses to adopt the more stringent automobile emission standards to be implemented in the United States by 1976 and which were

also planned for Canada at the same time?' Davis replied that the decision had not yet been made. Canada, *Debates*, 15 June 1973, 4799 (Randolph Harding, Kootenay West).

68 'Canadian Automotive Activities,' *WA*, 22 July 1973; 'Canada Won't Compel Cars to Fit Costly Fume Control,' *TS*, 20 July 1973.

69 Ontario Energy Minister Darcy McKeough stated of the new regulations: 'We don't think they're necessary. I don't want to be in the position of saying it's okay to break the law, but I think that's what people are doing.' 'Ontario to Ignore Auto Emission Rule,' *G&M*, 16 November 1973.

70 Because engines tended to run colder, and thus burn gasoline less completely, Canadian cars produced higher levels of CO and unburned HCs. Jeff Carruthers, 'Canadian '75 Car-Emission Rules as Strict as in US, Davis Says,' *G&M*, 22 March 1973.

71 GM had announced it would install the converters in March 1974, then reversed course owing to the government decision. The battle over unleaded gasoline was another cleavage between EMR and Environment, with the former invested in the views of the petroleum industry, which was against converting their refineries towards production of unleaded gasoline. Eventually, however, unleaded gasoline became the norm by the end of the 1970s. 'Canadian Automotive Activities,' *WA*, 18 March 1974, 87; Ken Romain, 'GM Backs away from Catalytic Converters, Offers 1975 Options,' *G&M*, 29 August 1974.

72 Jean Marchand to various ministers, 12 December 1973.

73 Jack Davis to J. Marchand, 24 January 1974, including 'Rationale for Canadian Exhaust Emission Standards for New Motor Vehicles: 1976 and Beyond,' and 'Draft Press Release: Ministers of Transport and Environment Announce Program for Future Automobile Emission Reductions.'

74 'Memorandum to the Minister: Re: 1976 Automobile Exhaust Emission Standards,' O.G. Stoner to J. Marchand, 6 February 1974; J. Marchand to J. Davis, 6 February 1974.

75 In making the case that the 1977 standards should remain unchanged, Marchand argued that 'the extension would not be deleterious' for air quality, that the U.S. position remained unclear, that catalytic converters were still not proven technologies, and that the delay gave the automakers more time to refine existing emission technologies. J. Marchand to various ministers, 25 November 1974.

76 Glenn Schleede to Jim Cavanaugh, 'Auto Emissions,' 6 May 1975. Gerald R. Ford Presidential Library (hereafter GFL), James M. Cannon Papers, box 4, File Auto Emissions, 1–15 May 1975; James T. Lynn, 'Memorandum for

the President: Automobile Emission Standards,' 16 May 1975, GFL, James
M. Cannon Papers, box 4, File Auto Emissions, 16–31 May 1975.

77 'Press Release: Ministers of Transport and Environment Announce Automobile Exhaust Emission Standards for 1978–80,' LAC, RG 12, box 7A, file
S1500-12-2, vol. 8, 11 January 1975–30 June 1976.

78 'Environment Canada Conclusions: Ambient Air Quality and Emissions,'
8 May 1978.

79 In terms of the cost to consumers, GM told government officials that the
savings to Canadian car buyers for the 1981 model year were over $250
million, and quoted a cost of $700 per vehicle to meet the U.S. standards.
D.W.C. McEwan to Gordon D. Campbell, 26 August 1981, RG 20, file
4956-2-3; B.J. Giroux to Otto Lang, '1981 to 1985 Exhaust Emission Levels
for Light Duty Motor Vehicles,' 5 July 1978; 'Discussion Paper: 1981–1985
Light Duty Vehicle Emission Levels,' 28 June 1978; 'Car Fume Standards
Unchanged till 1985,' *G&M*, 22 July 1976.

80 Of course, in 1979 EPA granted a number of car companies (including
Chrysler, GM, and Toyota) a waiver allowing them to miss, and increase
to 7 from 3.4, the CO standard. See Environmental Protection Agency,
'Revised Motor Vehicle Exhaust Emission Standards for Carbon Monoxide
(CO) for 1981 and 1982 Model Year Light Duty Vehicles,' *United States Fed-
eral Register*, 13 September 1979, 53408.

81 This figure is in U.S. gallons, versus imperial gallons, which were still in
use in Canada in 1977 (1 U.S. gallon = 1.2 imperial/Canadian gallon). After 1976, when Canada switched to metric, the fuel-economy figures were
also cited in litres per 100 km. For consistency, unless otherwise noted, figures cited are in mpg using U.S. gallons.

82 For overviews of the geopolitics of oil, see Yergin, *The Prize*; Philip, *The
Political Economy of International Oil*.

83 Anderson, 'Levittown Is Burning!' and a 2008 Canadian Centre for Archi-
tecture exhibit, '1973: Sorry, Out of Gas,' illustrated some responses to the
embargo.

84 See Pitts, Willenborg, and Sherrell, 'Consumer Adaptation to Gasoline
Price Increases.' They argue that American consumers (the study focused
on South Carolina) adapted to changing gas prices and scarcity by driving less and buying more fuel-efficient cars. Other views on the impact of
gasoline prices include Greenlees, 'Gasoline Prices and Purchases of New
Automobiles.'

85 MVMA, *Motor Vehicle Facts and Figures*, 1974.

86 Wayne Cheveldayoff, 'Oil Exports to US to Be Cut by a Third,' *G&M*,
21 November 1975. For an overview of the Canadian industry, see Gray,

The Great Canadian Oil Patch. On the role of the Canadian oil industry and lobbying during the crises, see Berry, 'The Oil Lobby and the Energy Crisis'; and Toner and Doern, 'The Two Energy Crises and Canadian Oil and Gas Interest Groups.'

87 Editorial, 'Thirstier Than Ever,' *G&M*, 21 September 1973.

88 In a March 1974 poll, only 7 per cent and 6 per cent of Canadians saw the crisis or gas prices as a concern, respectively. The Canadian Institute of Public Opinion results can be found at http://www.library.carleton.ca/ ssdata/surveys/doc/gllp-74-mar364-doc (accessed 21 February 2008).

89 John Doig, 'The Big Car Is Alive and Well in Canada,' *TS*, 28 June 1974; 'Remember the Energy Crisis? Some Good Came of It,' *TS*, 18 May 1974; Automotive Task Force, *Review of the North American Automotive Industry*, 205.

90 For a good view of this, see William Tucker, 'The Wreck of the Auto Industry,' *Harper's*, November 1980, 47–60.

91 Ken Romain, 'Auto Firms' Cost Called Frightening,' *G&M*, 7 May 1974.

92 Ken Romain, 'Ford Canada Cars Will Have Catalysts as Standard Fitting,' *G&M*, 5 September 1975.

93 'Move to Compact Cars Is Seen by Riccardo,' *G&M*, 6 August 1975.

94 But such an ad war could be tricky – in the United States, the Big Three all ran afoul of the Federal Trade Commission for false advertising by providing 'deceptive claims' about the fuel economy of their vehicles. 'Auto Mileage Claims Described as Deceptive,' *G&M*, 1 August 1974.

95 Ken Romain, 'Smaller Cars Get Favorable Reaction,' *G&M*, 5 November 1977.

96 See Luger, 'Government Policy toward the Automobile Industry,' 425.

97 D.S. Macdonald to J. Marchand, 9 January 1974; Herb Gray to J. Marchand, 11 January 1974; Alastair Gillespie to J. Marchand, 24 January 1974.

98 Conversions meant that, for example, the 1980 fuel-economy standards were 20 mpg (U.S.), 24 mpg (imp.), and 12 litres/per 100 km.

99 Of course, a cost-benefit analysis showed that missing the fines could prove far more profitable than meeting the legislation's requirements. For instance, in 1985 when it became clear that GM and Ford might miss the 27.5 mpg target, they faced fines of $400 million and $80 million respectively. These figures paled in comparison to the estimated $8 billion (GM) and $3 billion (Ford) that the companies stood to profit on selling larger vehicles. Luger, 'Government Policy towards the Automobile Industry,' 430. On the response of Detroit to the CAFE rules, see Halberstam, *The Reckoning*; and Rae, *The American Automobile Industry*.

100 C. Fincer to file, 'Meeting with Representatives of MVMA and Auto Companies, MOT, IT&C, on Conservation and Motor Vehicles, May 7 1975,' 3 June 1975; MOT, 'Discussion Paper: Motor Vehicle Fuel Economy Programs,' 28 November 1977, LAC, RG 12, file S1500-23-1, vol. 2 (box 9).

101 Michael Benedict, 'Ottawa Eases Mileage Rules for 1980 Cars,' *TS*, 25 February 1976; 'Car Excise Tax Urged for All but Compacts,' *G&M*, 26 February 1976; Record of Cabinet Decision (685–75RD), 'Meeting of December 18, 1975: Need for Immediate Federal Action for Energy Conservation,' LAC, RG 12, file S1500-23-1, vol. 2 (box 9); Cabinet Minutes, 'Need for Immediate Federal Action for Energy Conservation,' 18 December 1975, LAC, RG 2, Cabinet Conclusions, Series A-5-a, vol. 6457.

102 Vehicle-consumption standards were self-certified by the manufacturers, since the Canadian government did not have extensive testing facilities. CAFC standards were determined by the total number of sales of model types and established fuel-consumptions numbers for the model types, divided by the total sales of a particular manufacturer or importer. Cabinet Minutes, 'Need for Immediate Federal Action for Energy Conservation,' 18 December 1975, LAC, RG 2, Cabinet Conclusions, Series A-5-a, vol. 6457.

103 The 1971 Motor Vehicle Safety Act required manufacturers to affix a label on each individual car certifying it had passed safety standards.

104 On the constitutional question, see R.E. Williams (MOT) to I. Efford (EMR), 'Whether Energy Consumption Standards and Labelling Requirements Can Be Validly Enacted by the Parliament of Canada,' 20 May 1977; W.G. Nelson to G.D. Campbell, 'Whether Fuel Consumption Standards Can be Validly Enacted by Parliament,' 4 October 1977. Both in LAC, RG 12, file S1500-23-1, vol. 2 (box 9).

105 M.A. McHattie, 'Record of Meeting DTS/Justice,' 8 December 1980, LAC, RG 12, file S1500-23-1, vol. 3 (box 9).

106 S.D. Cameron to D. Cuthbertson, 'Motor Vehicle Fuel Efficiency Legislation,' 3 November 1977; EMR, 'Memorandum to Cabinet: Energy Conservation Legislation,' 2 November 1977; GM Canada press release, untitled, 1 November 1977. All documents in LAC, RG 12, file S1500-23-1, vol. 2 (box 9). Jeff Carruthers, 'Higher Prices, Savings Seen Curbing Oil Needs and Delaying Shortfall,' *G&M*, 24 August 1974.

107 Canadians also complained that EPA's fuel-economy listings, which were the basis for most advertising, were faulty at best and incorrect at worst. See, for example, Bruce Simpson, 'Gas Mileage,' letter to the editor, *G&M*, 5 December 1973.

108 Ken Romain, 'Auto Dealers Contend Federal Mileage Ratings Are Unattainable for the Majority of Drivers,' *G&M*, 6 December 1977.
109 S.D. Cameron to D. Cuthbertson, 'Motor Vehicle Fuel Efficiency Legislation,' 3 November 1977; EMR, 'Memorandum to Cabinet: Energy Conservation Legislation,' 2 November 1977. All documents in RG 12, file S1500-23-1, vol. 2 (box 9).
110 S.D. Cameron to D. Cuthbertson, 'Motor Vehicle Fuel Economy Legislation,' 25 November 1977, LAC, RG 12, file S1500-23-1, vol. 2 (box 9).
111 Complaints in the United States about the mileage figures prompted EPA to revise its testing methods in 1978 and to report only city mileage. The Canadians did not follow their U.S. counterparts. Hugh Winsor, 'Almost Half of 1977 Cars Don't Meet Planned Mileage Standard, Ottawa Says,' *G&M*, 31 March 1977; EMR, 'Memorandum to Cabinet: Energy Conservation Legislation,' 2 November 1977, RG 12, file S1500-23-1, vol. 2 (box 9); Sylvia Stead, 'Cars' Fuel Consumption Compared: Gas-Guzzlers Detected at CNE,' *G&M*, 25 August 1978; Sylvia Stead, 'US Using More Realistic Gas Mileage Claims but Canadian Government Won't Follow Suit,' *G&M*, 16 November 1978.
112 'Memorandum to Cabinet: Motor Vehicle Fuel Economy Programs,' 28 November 1978; Record of Cabinet Decisions, 'Motor Vehicle Fuel Economy Programs (635–77RD),' 19 January 1978, LAC, RG 12, file S1500-23-1, vol. 2 (box 9).
113 'General Motors of Canada Emissions and Fuel Economy Status Report,' February 1977, LAC, RG 20, file 4956-1 at 1507.
114 The Transport-EMR fight over fuel economy became increasingly bitter after 1978. One EMR official complained in 1978 that 'a number of us in the department have had some difficulties in reaching a close working relationship with' MOT, and that 'Transport frustrated various attempts to cooperate with EMR on significant policy issues.' There were also problems with drafting the actual legislation, particularly with adapting the U.S. standards and procedures into the Canadian legislation. See, for example, R.J. Grroux (MOT) to Charles H. Smith (EMR), 3 April 1978; N.G. Mulder to R.Y.J Giroux, 'Fleet Average Performance Standards,' 11 May 1978; M.A. McHattie to G.D. Campbell, 26 January 1979. All LAC, RG 12, file S1500-23-1, vol. 2 (box 9).
115 It should be noted that the Clark government fell on its 1979 budget, which included an eighteen-cent fuel tax, ostensibly a conservation measure as much as it was an attempt to generate additional revenue.
116 MOT Press Release, 'Fuel Consumption Objectives,' 17 June 1980, LAC, RG 12, file S1500-23-1, vol. 5 (box 9).

117 James G. Dykes to Jean-Luc Pepin, 3 October 1980, LAC, RG 12, file
     S1500-23-1, vol. 5 (box 9).
118 Jean-Luc Pepin to Marc Lalonde, 10 October 1980, LAC, RG 12, file S1500-
     23-1, vol. 3 (box 9).
119 R.J. Giroux to the minister, 'Motor Vehicle Fuel Consumption Standards
     Bill,' 14 May 1981, LAC, RG 12, file S1500-23-1, vol. 4 (box 9).
120 Ibid.
121 According to MOT's website: 'In 1982, the Motor Vehicle Fuel Consump-
     tion Standards Act (MVFCSA) was presented to Parliament to reinforce
     federal support for an effective fuel efficiency program in Canada.
     Among other things this Act would regulate minimum CAFC standards
     for specified fleets of motor vehicles, with financial penalties for non-
     compliance. The MVSFCA was not proclaimed because the motor vehicle
     industry agreed to comply voluntarily with the requirements of the Act.'
     http://www.tc.gc.ca/eng/mediaroom/releases-nat-2007-07-h215e-2339
     .htm (accessed 22 December 2010).
122 Minister of Transport, 'Discussion Paper: Motor Vehicles Fuel Consump-
     tion Standards Legislation,' 24 March 1981, LAC, RG 12, file S1500-23-1,
     vol. 4 (box 9).
123 Ken Romain, 'Mileage for 1975 Cars Claimed 13.8% Higher,' *G&M*, 22 Oc-
     tober 1974; 'Fuel Economy Rises 12.8% in 1976 Cars,' *G&M*, 23 September
     1975.
124 Ken Romain, 'Steadfast Core of Car Buyers Still Prefers Family-Size Car
     to Smaller Compact Model,' 2 October 1979, and 'Domestic Auto Makers
     See No Stampede to Small Cars,' *G&M*, 14 December 1979.
125 Olewiler, 'North American Integration and the Environment.'
126 Many scholars have erroneously assumed a harmonization of auto-
     emissions policy between Canada and the United States: In 'Canada's
     Voluntary Agreement on Vehicle Greenhouse Gas Emissions,' Lutsey
     and Sperling write: 'Historically, Canadian automobile emission and fuel
     efficiency characteristics were harmonized with comparably light duty
     vehicle standards set by the US.' In a paper for the Fraser Institute, Ross
     McKitrick wrote that 'Canada has effectively followed the US federal
     motor-vehicle emission standards since they were first enacted in the
     1960s.' See McKitrick's paper, 'Air Pollution Policy in Canada: Improving
     on Success,' at http://www.fraserinstitute.org/Commerce.Web/product_
     files/AirPollutionPolicyinCan.pdf (accessed 6 February 2008). In *Business
     and Environmental Politics in Canada*, Douglas Macdonald of the University
     of Toronto writes: 'Since Canadian motor-vehicle manufacturers function
     in an integrated North American market, Canadian regulations of their
     product design has always closely followed US policy' (103–4).

127 Canada, *Debates*, 9 December 1974, 2069 (Flora MacDonald, Kingston and the Islands).
128 Harrison, *Passing the Buck*, 81.
129 On the 'diminished' Canadian environmental involvement in comparison to that of the United States in this period, see Van Nijnatten, 'Participation and Environmental Policy in Canada and the United States.' On the California mobilization against emissions, see Dewey, '"The Anti-Trust Case of the Century."'
130 'Buyers Resist Move to Smaller Vehicles,' *G&M*, 9 September 1978; Ken Romain, 'Auto Trend Is to Smaller, More Efficient Engines,' *G&M*, 11 November 1978; Ken Romain, 'Market Comeback Being Made by Large North American Cars,' *G&M*, 9 February 1979.

3 Fair Share: The Battle over 'Domestic' Automotive Investment in North America

1 Henry A. Kissinger, 'Memorandum for the President: US-Canadian Relations – Status and Near-Term Prospects,' 5 March 1975, GFL, NSA, Country Files, Canada, box 2.
2 Government figures showed that in the 1970s employment in the auto sector was 30 per cent higher than in the rest of the economy, and that the parts industry had come within 10 per cent of the productivity level of its U.S. counterpart, while Canadian assembly operations actually exceeded those in the United States by approximately 20 per cent. 'Canadian Automotive Industry: Situation Report,' 18 June 1979, LAC, RG 19, vol. 5348, file 38810-02, pt. 4. On the trade deficit, a *G&M* editorial, remarking on the 1977 $1.09-billion auto trade deficit with the United States, declared that 'Canadians have a right to expect that the federal Government, which is a partner to the pact, will do more about it than take evasive action in the House.' 'Auto Pact Imbalance,' 6 April 1978.
3 Ontario Treasurer Darcy McKeough felt that 'what this imbalance means, and our studies show, is that Canada is not now receiving its fair share of jobs, production and investment form the North American auto industry.' As quoted in Ronald Anderson, 'The Auto Deficit,' *G&M*, 18 April 1978.
4 'Memorandum to Ministers: The Automotive Industry: Situation Report,' 17 May 1977. DFAIT, file 37-7-1-USA-2, vol. 37.
5 In a 1979 assessment of the agreement, IT&C held that 'no adverse balance of payments problems were envisaged for the US particularly as automotive investment by the Big Four [including AMC] in Canada would come out of the retained earnings of their Canadian subsidiaries, avoiding cash flows out of the US.' Industry Analysis Branch, Policy Planning,

IT&C, 'Re-Negotiation of the Canada-United States Automotive Products Agreement,' May 1979, LAC, RG 19, vol. 5348, file 3881-02, pt. 4, 6.

6 Canada, *Report of the Royal Commission on Canada's Economic Prospects*.

7 See for instance, Azzi, *Walter Gordon and the Rise of Canadian Nationalism*; on Gordon's views on the auto pact, see Anastakis, *Auto Pact*, 100–1.

8 Azzi, '"It Was Walter's View."'

9 Gordon's own work includes his autobiography, *A Political Memoir*, and numerous books such as *Troubled Canada: The Need for New Domestic Policies*, *A Choice for Canada: Independence or Colonial Status*, and *Storm Signals: New Economic Policies for Canada*. Other works on Gordon include: Axworthy, 'Innovation and the Party System'; Douglas Fetherling, 'The Lion in Winter,' *Saturday Night* (May 1983); John Hutcheson, 'Walter Gordon,' *Canadian Forum* (May 1987); and Smith, *Gentle Patriot*.

10 Other academics, such as A.E. Safarian, saw MNEs and foreign investment as having positive benefits for Canada. See his *Foreign Ownership of Canadian Industry*.

11 See Vernon's classic *Sovereignty at Bay* and his article 'US Direct Investment in Canada'; Wilkins's books included (with Frank Ernest Hill) *American Business Abroad* and two mammoth contributions, *The Emergence of Multinational Enterprise* and *The Making of Multinational Enterprise*.

12 Surveys indicated that the proportion of the population who viewed U.S. investment in Canada as a 'bad thing' increased from 36 per cent in 1969 to 55 per cent in 1973. Murray and Leduc, 'Public Opinion and Foreign Policy Options in Canada,' 489. In their analysis comparing newspaper coverage of economic issues in 1971–2 and 1980–2, Cohn and Bailey found that 'in 1972, most newspapers (and especially *Le Devoir* and the *Financial Post*) were inclined to argue that Canada should do something about the large degree of US investment and ownership in the Canadian economy.' 'Newspaper Coverage of Canadian-US Economic Relations,' 7.

13 For more on this issue, see Anastakis, 'Between Nationalism and Continentalism.'

14 Smith, *Gentle Patriot*, 291–2; Azzi, '"It Was Walter's View,"' 113–14.

15 On Trudeau, the Third Option, and economic nationalism in the Liberal Party in this period, see Bothwell, *Alliance and Illusion*, especially chapter 18. On the Gray Report, see McMillan, 'After the Gray Report.'

16 Henry A. Kissinger, 'Memorandum for the President.'

17 Of the $24-billion U.S. foreign investment in Canada in 1972, $10 billion was in manufacturing, of which automotive would have been the largest sector. See 'Table G227–243, Foreign direct investment in Canada, 1926 to 1974,' *Historical Statistics of Canada*, http://www.statcan.gc.ca/cgi-bin/af-fdr.cgi?l=eng&loc=G227_243b-eng.csv (accessed 27 December 2010).

18 United States, *Seventh Annual Report of the President to the Congress on the Operation of the Automotive Products Trade Act of 1965* (Washington, 1973), 22.

19 R.E. Latimer to Robert de Cotret, 'Canadian Automotive Industry: Situation Report,' 18 June 1979, LAC, RG 19, vol. 5348, file 3881-02, pt. 4.

20 Reisman, *The Canadian Automotive Industry*, 157.

21 Sam Gindin to Dennis McDermott and Robert White, 'Investment in Canadian Auto Industry, 1971 to Present,' 23 January 1975, LAC, Canadian Auto Workers Union Collection (MG 28 I 119) (hereafter CAW), vol. 10, file 4; 'Collective Bargaining Program 1976,' n.d., 34–13, WRL File, UAW Ford Collection, pt. 2, box 34, file: 'Canada, Negotiations, 1976'; see also 'Canadian UAW Council, "We Deserve Our Fair Share,"' *Solidarity Canada*, 5, no. 5 (1978): 8.

22 Lyndon Watkins, 'Pint-Size Ford Pinto Coming in September,' *G&M*, 15 May 1970.

23 This issue is discussed in more detail in chapter 5. Sam Gindin to Dennis McDermott, 'Safeguards,' 9 January 1975, LAC, CAW Papers, vol. 10, file 3.

24 J.J. Shepherd, 'Slam the Brakes on the Auto Pact's Vicious Circle?' *G&M*, 21 November 1978. Shepherd was the author of a Science Council of Canada Report, *The Canada-US Auto Pact: A Technological Perspective* (Ottawa, 1978).

25 Campbell Stuart (chairman, Automotive Task Force), 'US-Canada Automotive Consultations,' 13 February 1981, LAC, RG 19, vol. 3881–02, pt. 13, 7.

26 Editorial, 'We Deserve a Better Share of Jobs,' *TS*, 29 June 1977.

27 'Spending to Reach Record $1.8 billion,' *G&M*, 9 September 1976; Ken Romain, 'Makers of Auto Parts Told to Use Initiative, Imagination, Ingenuity,' *G&M*, 26 April 1978.

28 'Chrysler Undertaking Major Spending Plan,' *G&M*, 3 May 1978.

29 Lyndon Watkins, 'Export Target for Autos, Parts Is $250 Million,' *G&M*, 23 April 1970; Lyndon Watkins, 'New President of Auto Parts Makers Forecasts Large Investment in New Plant,' *G&M*, 2 April 1970.

30 Ontario, *Debates*, 7 March 1972, 160 (David Lewis, York South).

31 Ontario, *Debates*, 24 April 1978, 1835 (William Davis, Brampton).

32 Canada, *Debates*, 4 May 1978, 5144.

33 On Broadbent, see Steed, *Ed Broadbent*; Isabella Bardoel, 'Perfect Day for a Picnic … plus a Serving of Politics,' *G&M*, 10 July 1978.

34 Editorials, 'We Deserve Better Share of Jobs,' and 'Canada Short-Changed in Auto Pact,' *TS*, 29 June and 27 July 1977.

35 Bogdan Kipling, 'Canada Could Lose out to US in the Great Car Race,' *TS*, 6 March 1978.

36 Ronald Anderson, 'A Risky Game,' *G&M*, 10 May 1978.

37 Ken Romain, 'Ontario Auto Market Study Finds Canada Is Not Getting Fair Share,' *G&M*, 28 April 1978.

38 Although Ottawa 'did not accept the figures' in the Ontario report, particularly when it came to employment, intergovernment sniping over the perceived benefits, or shortcomings in this case, of the pact did not help matters. Canada, *Debates*, 21 November 1978, 1312 (Jack Horner, Crowfoot); Ontario, Ministry of Treasury, Economics and Intergovernmental Affairs, *Canada's Share of the North American Automotive* Industry, 20, 12.

39 Automotive Task Force, *Report* (Ottawa, 1978); Ken Romain, 'Better Terms for Investing in Auto Industry Are Urged,' *G&M*, 12 September 1978. This report is not to be confused with the April 1977 Automotive Task Force report, *Review of the North American Automotive Industry* (Ottawa, 1977), also known as the Arthur report, after its primary author, C.D. Arthur.

40 David Blaikie, 'Auto Pact "Sellout" Is Hinted by NDP,' *TS*, 17 June 1978; 'Liberals Cop out on Auto Pact,' *Solidarity Canada*, 5 no. 5 (1978): 9.

41 Reisman, *The Canadian Automotive Industry*, 32, 173–202, 237.

42 Ibid., 207–8.

43 These remission programs are dealt with in more detail in chapter 8. See also Reisman, *The Canadian Automotive Industry*, 156, 192–3; Ken Romain, 'Reisman Urges Auto Parts Development,' *G&M*, 24 November 1978; Lawrence Martin, 'US Official Agrees with Reisman in Opposing Pact Renegotiation,' *G&M*, 28 November 1978.

44 Michael Valpy, 'Defending What Comes Naturally,' *Maclean's*, 4 December 1978, 46–7; Mel Watkins, 'The Auto Pact, Donald Creighton, and Some Good Late Winter Reads,' *This Magazine*, December 1978, 38–40; Editorial, 'Mandarin, Heal Thyself,' *G&M*, 24 November 1978; Editorials, 'Get Those Auto Industry Jobs,' and 'Reisman Auto Study Termed Merely Band-Aid Measure,' *TS*, 24 November 1978.

45 Patrick Lavelle to Pierre Trudeau, 27 November 1978, LAC, RG 19, vol. 5348, file 3881-05, pt. 1 Reisman inquiry; Ken Romain, 'Parts Manufacturers Are Critical of Report,' *G&M*, 28 November 1978; Ronald Anderson, 'An Idea Scorned,' *G&M*, 1 December 1978.

46 The federal response, which largely downplayed the report and ignored most of Reisman's proposals, can be seen below. For the Ontario reaction, see Ontario Industry Minister Larry Grossman's remarks in which he disagreed with much of the report, particularly Reisman's views on incentives. Ontario, *Debates*, 24 November 1978, 5275–9 (Larry Grossman, St Andrew-St Paul).

47 'Auto Pact Report Evades "Fair Share" Issue,' *Solidarity Canada*, 5, no. 9 (1978): 7; UAW Auto Tariff Committee, 'UAW Statement to Reisman Commission,' 23 October 1978, LAC, CAW Papers, vol. 306, file 2.

48 Terrance Wills, 'Foreign Car Makers Welcome Proposal for Duty-Free Entry,' *TS*, 24 November 1978.

49 Canada, *Debates*, 1 June 1978, 5990 (Derek Blackburn, Brant).

50 Financial support would eventually be given to Chrysler, as we shall see, in the form of loan guarantees when governments helped bail the company out in 1980–1. 'Automotive Adjustment Program,' 25 May 1978, DFAIT, file 37-7-1-USA-2, vol. 37.

51 On regional development in the period, see Savoie, *Regional Economic Development*, and McGee, *Getting It Right*. In 1982 the federal government created the Department of Regional Industrial Expansion (DRIE), even more specifically tailoring policies to distribute industrial activity across the country.

52 T.K. Shoyama to the minister, 'DREE Grant to General Motors of Canada Ltd.,' 20 December 1977, LAC, RG 19, vol. 5347, file 3881-01, pt. 1.

53 Ibid.; Ken Romain, 'GM Adds Two More Plants to Its Expansion Proposals,' *G&M*, 12 October 1978.

54 The *Globe and Mail* did not question the fairness of this notion from the American point of view, given that the companies were American-owned and headquartered. Editorial, 'Still More Car Payments,' *G&M*, 13 October 1978.

55 'GM of Canada Backs off on $400 Million Parts Plant,' *WA*, 26 June 1978, 207; 'Canadian Gas Sales Up; GM Boosts Industry Output,' *WA*, 28 August 1978, 279.

56 'Possible GM Aluminum Parts Foundry in Canada: Incentives Aspects,' J.R. McKinney to Johnstone, 9 July 1979, DFAIT, file 37-7-1-USA-2, vol. 39, 16 December 1978–31 July 1979.

57 'DREE Offer to GM,' Ottawa to Washington embassy, 13 August 1979, DFAIT, file 37-7-1-USA-2, vol. 40, 1 August 1979–15 November 1980.

58 P. Slyfield, 'Meeting of Interdepartmental Committee on Automotive Policy,' 17 August 1979, DFAIT, File 37-7-1-USA-2, vol. 44.

59 'Automotive Industry Issues,' 19 October 1979, LAC, RG 19, vol. 5959, file 8705-03, pt. 3.

60 Ottawa to Washington, 'GM Investment In Canada,' 25 October 1979, LAC, RG 19, vol. 5738, file 3881-01, pt. 3.

61 On the GM announcement, see Ontario, *Debates*, 11 October 1979, 3293–4 (Larry Grossman, St Andrew-St Paul); J.R. Rinehart (president, GM Canada) to Herb Gray, 4 May 1981, LAC, RG 19, vol 5738, file 3881-02, pt. 14; Canada, *Debates*, 18 October 1979, 329 (Joe Clark, Peace River).

62 The Ontario government also committed $600,000 in loans to the companies. Cabinet decision, sponsoring minister, IT&C, 'Assistance to Canadian Automotive Parts Manufacturers – Accurcast Die Casting Ltd., A Subsidi-

ary of CAE, and H.E. Vannatter Ltd.,' 17 April 1980, LAC, RG 20, file 4954-1, vol. 2, May 1974–December 1979, 787.

63 Canada, *Debates*, 8 November 1979, 1082 (Joe Clark, Peace River).

64 'Canada May Be Site of New Ford Plant,' *G&M*, 24 January 1978.

65 Ken Romain, 'Makers of Auto Parts Told to Use Initiative, Imagination, Ingenuity,' *G&M*, 26 April 1978.

66 In the mid-1970s, Ohio had successfully attracted a US$50-million transmission plant by offering direct financial incentives. State officials had made it clear to Ford that similar incentives were on the table for the engine plant.

67 Canadian tax rates were lower, making the cost of the Windsor plant over its lifetime less than Ohio. 'Canadian Car Plants Down; Decision Expected; Growth Seen,' *WA*, 11 July 1978, 359.

68 Cabinet Minutes, 12 February 1978, and 'Memorandum to Cabinet: Ford – The V6 Engine Program,' 21 June 1978. Privy Council Office (PCO), ATIP request.

69 Quoted in editorial, 'Auto Pact Imbalance,' *G&M*, 6 April 1978. In the Ontario legislature, Davis said that the province would 'much prefer to have it done [an investment] in the spirit of the auto pact rather than by having some major capital appropriation made to any of the big four.' Ontario, *Debates*, 3 April 1978, 1111 (William Davis, Brampton).

70 Peter Mosher, 'Ontario Gives Ottawa New Offer to Get Grant from Ford,' *G&M*, 29 June 1978.

71 Indeed, according to Horner, Ontario's initial reaction had been a flat refusal to participate, and the federal government had had to 'cajole' Ontario to put up its share of the money for the plant. 'Deal at the Calgary Stampede Won Ford Over, Horner Says,' *G&M*, 5 August 1978; Canada, *Debates*, 9 November, 1978, 952 (Jack Horner, Crowfoot). For more detail on the Ontario-federal negotiations over the deal, see Lleyton-Brown, 'A Mug's Game?'

72 Author's interview with William Davis, 7 August 2008.

73 'Deal at the Calgary Stampede Won Ford over, Horner Says,' *G&M*, 5 August 1978; author's interview with L.R. Wilson, 27 June 2006.

74 Author's interview with William Davis, 7 August 2008.

75 Cabinet Minutes, 22 June 1978. PCO.

76 Cabinet Minutes, 5 July 1978, PCO; see also the statement of John Rhodes (Sault Ste Marie), Ontario minister of industry and tourism, in Ontario, *Debates*, 23 June 1978, 3897.

77 Cabinet Minutes, 29 June, 5 July 1978; Record of Cabinet Decisions, 29 June, 5 July, 9 August 1978; Ad hoc Cabinet Committee of Ministers on the

Ford – V6 Program Minutes, 6 July 1978; Memorandum to Cabinet, 'Ford of Canada Grant,' 9 August 1978, PCO; 'Deal at the Calgary Stampede Won Ford over, Horner Says,' *G&M* 5 August 1978.

78 Thomas, *Capital beyond Borders*, 115.

79 Canada, *Debates*, 26 June 1978, 6711 (Ed Broadbent, Oshawa); 'Canada: Car, Truck Sales Strong, Leader Charges Blackmail,' *WA*, 17 July 1978, 232.

80 'New Financing Plan for Ford Plant,' *Windsor Star* (*WS*), 29 June 1978; Ontario, *Debates*, 23 June 1978, 3963 (Michael Cassidy, Ottawa Centre).

81 'Collective Bargaining Program 1976,' n.d., WRL, UAW Ford Collection, pt. 2, box 34, file 34-13: 'Canada, Negotiations, 1976.'

82 Emphasis in original. Editorial, 'Ford Has a 'Better Idea,' a $75-Million Better Idea,' *Solidarity Canada*, 5, no. 5 (1978): 2.

83 Director's Report, Canadian UAW Council, 16 and 17 September 1978, WRL, UAW Ford Collection, pt. 2, box 53, file 53-16.

84 Douglas Fraser to Robert Strauss (USTR), 28 August 1978, LAC, CAW Papers, vol. 298, pt. 1 of 2, file 13, 'Auto Tariff Committee Correspondence.'

85 Peter Mosher and Stan Oziewicz, 'Ford Ignores US Pressure, Plans New Plant in Ontario; $68 Million Grant Beats Ohio,' *G&M*, 4 August 1978; 'Ford Picks Windsor Plant Site; GM of Canada Starts '79s,' *WA*, 4 August 1978, 379; Barbara Yaffe, 'Windsor Location Is First Choice for Plant, Ford Spokesman Says,' *G&M*, 5 August 1978; Rick Haliechuk and Joe Hall, 'US Protest Ignored: New Ford Plant Means 7,800 jobs,' *TS*, 4 August 1978.

86 And the VW offer, which will be discussed in more detail in chapter 8.

87 'Canada-US Auto Pact,' D.S. McPhail to Allan Gotlieb, 28 July 1978, DFAIT, file 37-7-1-USA-2, vol. 37, 1 May 1977–31 July 1978.

88 Lawrence Martin, 'US Opposes Canadian Aid to Car Makers,' *G&M*, 2 August 1978.

89 The plant was originally scheduled to open in 1983 but in fact opened in 1981. Bill Shields, 'Ford Plant: It's Official,' *WS*, 15 August 1978; Ontario, *Debates*, 16 June 1981, 1639 (Larry Grossman, St Andrew-St Paul).

90 J.R. McKinney to D.S. McPhail, 'Canada-US Auto Discussions,' 3 August 1978, DFAIT, file 37-7-1-USA-2, vol. 38.

91 Ibid.

92 Weaver, *The Suicidal Corporation*, 34. For a fascinating insider's account of the decision, see 33–9.

93 Ibid., 36.

94 Author's interview with William Davis, 7 August 2008.

95 Weaver, *The Suicidal Corporation*, 38.

96 Though it did not establish the engine-testing plant, Ford did build a new, $40-million aluminum components plant at Essex, which opened in 1981.

Memorandum to Cabinet, 'Ford Motor Company Engine Test Facility,'
29 August 1978, Special Operating Committee of Cabinet, Minutes, 30
August 1978; Cabinet Minutes, 30 August 1978; Record of Cabinet Decision, 30 August 1978, PCO; 'Ford of Canada Grant,' A.E. Gotleib to the
minister (J. Horner), 29 August 1978; 'Ford of Canada Grant,' 4 September
1978, DFAIT, file 37-7-1-USA-2, vol. 38.

97 Editorial, 'Maybe Canadians Should Buy up Chrysler,' *TS*, 18 August 1978.
98 Thomas, *Capital beyond Borders*. For another view of the changes to the
automotive investment regime, see Lleyton-Brown, 'A Mug's Game?'
99 A 1 March 1976 full-page ad in the *Wall Street Journal* proclaimed to
VW that 'Baltimore Wants You So Much, We'll Let You Write Your Own
Terms. We're Confident that We Can Work Something Out.'
100 For a critical view of the VW incentive, see Ron Chernow, 'The Rabbit
That Ate Pennsylvania: Governor Shapp Builds Volkswagen a $70–Mil-
lion Hutch,' *Mother Jones*, 111, no. 1 (1978), 19–24.
101 On VW in America, see David Kiley, *Getting the Bugs Out*.
102 'Canada/USA Automotive Consultations: Investment Incentives: Application of Principles and Criteria in the US Discussion Paper to US Incentive Programs,' April 1979, DFAIT, file 37-7-1-USA-2, vol. 39.
103 Herb Gray to Donald Jamieson (secretary of state for external affairs),
19 April 1978, DFAIT, file 37-7-1-USA-2, vol. 37. Gray also wrote to IT&C
and finance ministers Horner and Chrétien to ask what the government
planned to do to 'ensure that Canada gets and keeps its fair share of automotive employment, investment and production.'
104 Senator John Glenn to President Jimmy Carter, 10 August 1978, Jimmy
Carter Presidential Library (hereafter JCL), White House Central Files
(WHCF), file CO 28, 1 May 1978–31 December 1978.
105 Robert D. Niehaus, 'The Canada-Ford Deal: A Case Study in Government
Business Incentives' (Washington, 1978); 'Congressmen Fight Canadian
Subsidies Luring Auto Plants," *TS*, 6 November 1978.
106 A.E. Gotleib to the minister, 'Canada-US Auto Trade,' 5 September 1978,
DFAIT, file 37-7-1-USA-2, vol. 38.
107 In his *Suicidal Corporation*, Paul Weaver, a former Ford communications
executive during the 1978 Lima-Windsor battle, was withering in his criticism of how the decision had come about: 'There was nothing wrong or
awkward about the fact that Henry Ford had made the ultimate decision
in Dearborn, or that the talking points were drafted in the US, or that we
thought Canadian plant-siting incentives were acceptable international
economic policy. So why did we speak as if these were embarrassing?
Why were we telling lies for no apparent benefit to ourselves? It seemed
to me that we were lying irrationally. I was mystified' (39).

108 Edward Cowan, 'Canada's Offer to Ford Draws Criticism in US,' *NYT*, 2 August 1978.

109 Robert S. Strauss to Senator John Glenn, 13 September 1978, JCL, WHCF, file CO 28, 1 May 1978–31 December 1978.

110 Editorial, 'Don't Let Carter Take Our Jobs Away,' *TS*, 3 August 1978.

111 'Nothing Urgent Seen in Auto Plant Meeting,' *G&M*, 3 August 1978.

112 D.S. McPhail to Allan Gotlieb, 'Auto Pact,' 8 June 1978, 'Memorandum to Ministers: The Automotive Industry: Situation Report,' 17 May 1977, DFAIT, file 37-7-1-USA-2, vol. 37.

113 Editorial, 'Car Wars,' *G&M*, 4 August 1978.

114 Jeff Carruthers, 'Ford Deal Talks Call for an End to Bidding War,' *G&M*, 5 August 1978.

115 'Memorandum to Ministers: Canada-US Auto Consultations,' 9 August 1978, LAC, RG 19, vol. 5958, file 8705-02, pt. 2.

116 Peter Mosher and Stan Oziewicz, 'Ford Ignores US Pressure, Plans New Plant in Ontario; $68 Million Grant Beats Ohio,' *G&M*, 4 August 1978.

117 J.R. McKinney to D.S. McPhail, 'Canada/USA Automotive Consultations: Senior Level Meeting, December 8, 1978'; Washington to Ottawa, 'Automotive Consultations: Senior Level Meeting,' 11 December 1978. Both DFAIT, file 37-7-1-USA-2, vol. 37.

118 Ibid.

119 'Memorandum to Minister of the Board of Economic Development Ministers: Policy for the Canadian Automotive Industry,' 12 February 1979; W.C. Hood to the minister, 'Policy for the Canadian Automotive Industry, Cabinet Document 62–79MC(E), 62-79-CR,' 19 February 1979. Both LAC, RG 19, vol. 5348, file 3881-02, pt. 3.

120 'Reference Notes for an Address by the Honourable Jack H. Horner, Windsor Chamber of Commerce, March 14, 1979,' LAC, RG 19, vol. 5738, file 3881-01, pt. 3; Press Release, 'Board of Economic Development Ministers Outlines Policy for Development of Canadian Automotive Industry,' 14 March 1979, LAC, RG 20, file 4956-1, vol. 2; Ken Romain, 'Horner Outlines Ottawa's Auto Strategy; No Renegotiation Will Be Sought of Canada-US Auto Pact at Present,' *G&M*, 15 March 1979.

121 Washington to Ottawa, 'Prime Minister's Presidential Briefing,' 2 March 1979, DFAIT, file 37-7-1-USA-2, vol. 39.

122 Washington to Ottawa, 'Premier Davis Visit: Auto Industry,' 7 March 1979, DFAIT, file 37-7-1-USA-2, vol. 39.

123 Text of Fred Bergsten speech, November 1978, DFAIT, file 37-7-1-USA-2, vol. 38.

124 P. Syfield to A. Gherson, 27 April 1979; 'Canada/USA Automotive Con-

sultations: Investment Incentives: Application of Principles and Criteria in the US Discussion Paper to US Incentive Programs,' April 1979. Both in DFAIT, file 37-7-1-USA-2, vol. 39.

125 'Minutes of Automotive Incentive Meeting, May 3–4, 1979, Washington, DC,' RG 19, vol. 5348, file 3881-02, pt. 4; 'Automotive Investment Incentives: Meeting with USA,' Washington Embassy to Ottawa, 7 May 1979, DFAIT, file 37-7-1-USA-2, vol. 39.

126 The OECD guidelines required member countries to make incentives as transparent as possible, and to keep such incentives to a minimum. The text of the Declaration can be seen at http://www.oecd.org/document/53/0,3343,en_2649_34887_1933109_119672_1_1_1,00.html; the GATT subsidies codes are at http://www.wto.org/english/docs_e/legal_e/gatt47_01_e.htm (both accessed 12 November 2010).

127 Warren Clarke to A.R.A. Gherson, 27 June 1979, LAC, RG 19, vol. 5348, file 3881-02, pt. 4.

128 'Minutes of Automotive Incentive Meeting, May 3–4, 1979, Washington, DC,' LAC, RG 19, vol. 5348, file 3881-02, pt. 4; 'Automotive Investment Incentives: Meeting with USA,' Washington embassy to Ottawa, 7 May 1979, DFAIT, file 37-7-1-USA-2, vol. 39.

129 'Report to the Senior Interdepartmental Committee on Automotive Policy: Canada/USA Working Group on Investment Incentives in the North American Auto Sector,' 12 June 1979, LAC, RG 19, vol. 5348, file 3881-02, pt. 4.

130 'Automotive Investment Incentives: Canada/USA Working Group Meeting,' External Affairs, Ottawa, to Washington embassy, 31 July 1979, DFAIT, file 37-7-1-USA-2, vol. 39.

131 Ibid.; 'Joint Canada/United States Working Group on Containment of Investment Incentives in North American Auto Sector,' 20 July 1979, LAC, RG 19, vol. 5738, file 3881-01, pt. 3.

132 'Automotive Industry Issues,' 19 October 1979, LAC, RG 19, vol. 5959, file 8705-03, pt. 3.

133 R. Verspoor to W.R. Hines, 'Meeting of the Interdepartmental Committee on Automotive Policy, 11:00 a.m., October 10, 1979,' 9 October 1979, LAC, RG 19, vol. 5959, file 8705-03, pt. 3.

134 Thomas, *Competing for Capital*, 1–2. This kind of criticism of the Ford deal emerged as early as 1979, when Budd Automotive of Canada announced the layoffs of 1,200 workers owing to Ford's decision to phase out the frames the company built. With the demands for lighter vehicles, Ford had moved to unitized body construction, negating the need for separate frames. Critics, such as Ontario NDP leader Michael Cassidy, felt that

Ford could not justify taking $68 million on the one hand to build new plants in Windsor while, on the other hand, cutting jobs in Kitchener. '1,175 Face Layoff after Ford Move,' *G&M*, 17 January 1979.

135 Thomas, *Competing for Capital*, 33–7. See also Thomas, 'Capital Mobility and Trade Policy.'

136 The European Union's success in curtailing investment incentives began with the 1971 adoption of the 'First Resolution on General Regional Aid Systems.' In 1997 the EU implemented its Multi-Sectoral Framework on Regional Aid for Large Inward Investment. Within its own borders, Canada has also faced a problem of competing provincial incentives for relocation of plants, and in 1994, as part of the Agreement on Internal Trade, provinces agreed to a code of conduct to prohibit the practice. The success of the code in doing so, however, has been uncertain. See Kenneth P. Thomas, 'The Code of Conduct on Incentives and the Regulation of Investment Attraction,' unpublished paper presented to the Association of Canadian Studies in the United States Conference, Toronto, 18 November 2007.

137 Molot, 'Location Incentives and Inter-State Competition for FDI.'

138 Hawley, *Dollars and Borders*.

139 'Automotive Industry Issues,' 19 October 1979, LAC, RG 19, vol. 5959, file 8705-03, pt. 3.

140 'New Financing Plan for Ford Plant,' *WS*, 29 June 1978.

141 Though it should be pointed out that the Canadian operations did not yet really have the capability or capacity to take on significant R&D.

142 Industry Analysis Branch, Policy Planning, IT&C, 'Re-Negotiation of the Canada-United States Automotive Products Agreement,' May 1979, LAC, RG 19, vol. 5348, file 3881-02, pt. 4, 16.

143 Hurter and Staley, 'Opportunities for Canadian Research and Development,' A–7.

144 Ontario, *Debates*, 24 April 1978, 1839 (William Davis, Brampton); author's interview with William Davis, 7 August 2008. As we shall see, the demands for an R&D centre that the Ontario government extracted from Chrysler as the price of its support for the bailout in 1980–1 further reflected this ongoing concern.

145 'Canadian Automotive Industry: Situation Report,' 18 June 1979, LAC, RG 19, vol. 5348, file 3881-02, pt. 4.

146 Ibid.

147 For example, Mark Witten, 'Why the Auto Pact Is Obsolete: The Coming Technological Revolution Will Make Our Biggest Trade Agreement about as Practical as a Horse and Buggy,' *Canadian Business*, February 1979, 33–6, 96; P. Best, 'Canadian Auto R&D in Slow Lane,' *FP*, 5 April 1980.

4 Nadir: Saving Chrysler and Debating State Intervention in the Auto Sector

1 In April 1980 the Ontario government put aside ordinary debate to address Chrysler and the crisis in the industry. Ontario, *Debates*, 10 April 1980, 665–89 (various) and 6 October 1980, 3119 (David Cooke, Windsor).
2 See, for instance, Moritz and Seaman, *Going for Broke*.
3 Rae, *The American Automobile Industry*.
4 For a spirited view of the auto battles between the United States and Japan, see Halberstam's *The Reckoning*. Other saw the industry's woes as a consequence not of corporate mismanagement but rather of consumers' continued attraction to bigger vehicles and unrealistic government expectations on the industry. See, for instance, William Tucker, 'The Wreck of the Auto Industry,' *Harper's*, November 1980, 47–60.
5 Puckett (Capital Markets Section) to Chairman Burns, 'Economic Position of Chrysler,' 22 November 1974, GFL, Arthur Burns Papers, 1969–78, box B13, Federal Reserve Board Subject File: 'Chrysler.'
6 Chrysler Corporation, 'Analysis of Chrysler Corporation's Situation and Proposal for Government Assistance, September 15, 1979,' Bentley Historical Library (BHL), University of Michigan, William Milliken Papers, box 713, file: 'Chrysler Corporation.'
7 John Riccado to President Carter, 25 May 1979, JCL, WHCF, box BE 12, file BE 3-15, 1 June 1979–31 July 1979.
8 'Statement by John Riccardo, Chairman of the Board, Chrysler Corporation,' 31 July 1979, WRL, UAW-Chrysler Collection, box 11, file: 'Bailout.' Emphasis in original. Riccardo had complained about government regulations to a Canadian audience in a 15 November 1973 speech to the Empire Club. 'The Promise of Progress in Government-Industry Relations,' *The Empire Club of Canada Speeches, 1973–4* (Toronto, 1974), 106–16.
9 Richard Conrad, 'Surging Sales Iacocca's Target,' *TS*, 13 March 1979.
10 Moritz and Seaman, *Going for Broke*, 13; Irwin Ross, 'Chrysler on the Brink,' *Fortune*, 9 February 1980, 39; Harry Anderson, 'Can Chrysler Be Saved?' *Newsweek*, 13 August 1979, 58. Unlike the Japanese, who had built new plants and facilities from scratch from the ashes of war in the 1950s and 1960s, the U.S. and Canadian Big Three facilities were far older facilities which had by and large not had a complete overhaul since the transition from wartime production in the 1945–50 period.
11 Harry Anderson, 'Can Chrysler Be Saved?' *Newsweek*, 13 August 1979, 55.
12 'Report of UAW Director for Canada and International Vice President, Robert White,' 8 and 9 September 1979, LAC, CAW Papers, vol. 296, file 4.

13 Writing in the *New Republic,* Stephen Chapman argued that 'in the early 1970s, when GM and Ford were beginning to go after the subcompact market with the Vega and Pinto, Chrysler decided to stick with big cars, traditionally the most profitable segment of the market. In fact Chrysler introduced a restyled line of full-sized cars practically on the eve of the embargo, and in the recession that followed suffered crippling losses.' 'On the Hill: Welfare Chrysler,' *New Republic,* 4 and 11 August 1979, 19.

14 See, for example, 'Does Chrysler Want to Stay in the Business Just to Build America's Gas Guzzlers?' *Newsweek,* 13 August 1979.

15 James Daw, 'Chrysler Keeps Blanket on Aid Hunt,' *TS,* 7 September 1979.

16 Hyde, *Riding the Roller Coaster,* 197–200, 230. All figures in Canadian dollars, unless otherwise specified.

17 On the troubles at Chrysler in the United Kingdom, see Young and Hood, *Chrysler UK,* 163–6.

18 Moritz and Seaman, *Going for Broke,* 160–3; Tom Nicholson, 'A Bath at Both Ends,' *Newsweek,* 31 December 1979, 54.

19 'Statement by John Riccardo, Chairman of the Board, Chrysler Corporation,' 31 July 1979, WRL, UAW-Chrysler Collection, box 11, file: 'Bailout'; Harry Anderson, 'Can Chrysler Be Saved?' *Newsweek,* 13 August 1979, 52.

20 Chrysler Corporation, 'Analysis of Chrysler Corporation's Situation and Proposal for Government Assistance, September 15, 1979,' 29, BHL, William Milliken Papers, box 713, file: 'Chrysler Corporation.'

21 '400,000 Jobs Tied to Chrysler's Survival,' *TS,* 12 September 1979.

22 For background material on Chrysler Canada, see James Mays's series of articles in *Canadian Classics,* December 2000, January–July 2001.

23 Economic Development Division, Department of Finance, 'The Future of Chrysler Canada: Macroeconomic and Sectoral Effects,' 29 January 1980, LAC, RG 19, vol. 5959, file 8705-04-02, pt. 5. In 1976 Chrysler Canada actually surpassed Ford Canada in sales for the first time in over four decades. See also Bill Shields, 'Chrysler and Its Impact,' *WS,* 18 August 1979.

24 These include: Stuart, *Bailout;* Moritz and Seaman, *Going for Broke;* Jefferys, *Management and Managed.*

25 Ross, 'Chrysler on the Brink,' 42.

26 Chrysler Corporate Strategic Planning, 'Confidential: Ford-Chrysler Link-Up, Potential Operating Synergies and Estimated Financial Effects,' 23 March 1980, WRL, D. Fraser Papers, box 52, file 52-6; 'Ford to Chrysler: No Thanks,' *Newsweek,* 20 April 1981, 84.

27 David R. Henderson, 'A Step toward Feudalism: The Chrysler Bailout,' Cato Policy Analysis, 15 June 1980.

28 Milton Friedman, 'Chrysler: Are Jobs the Issue?" *Newsweek*, 10 September 1979, 66.

29 Tom Nicholson and James C. Jones, 'Iacocca's "Little Miracle,"' *Newsweek*, 3 August 1981, 64.

30 The Carter administration had turned down a 1978 request for loan guarantees for AMC, stating that 'such a situation cannot be addressed on an ad hoc or case-by-case basis. We believe that before we respond in detail to AMC's and similar requests, we must develop a rational framework for determining which major corporations have a reasonable case for requesting Federal assistance and the requirements upon which such aid should be predicated.' Perhaps this explains why Senator William Proxmire of Wisconsin appeared opposite Michigan Senator Don Riegle, Jr, arguing against a bailout in duelling interviews in 'Should Taxpayers Bail out Chrysler?' *US News and World Report*, 10 December 1979. See also White House staff to John Bradermas (AMC), 13 July 1978, JCL, WHCF, box BE-11, file BE 3-15, 1 January 1978–31 August 1978; Anthony Whittingham, 'A Giant's Fragile Kingdom,' *Maclean's*, 20 August 1979.

31 Nicholas Von Hoffman, 'Too Bad about Chrysler, but ...' *TS*, 4 September 1979.

32 'A Resolution Opposing Federal Aid for the Chrysler Corporation: City of Denver,' 4 September 1979, JCL, Name Files: 'Chrysler.'

33 David Stockman, 'Let Chrysler Go Bankrupt,' *Washington Post*, 9 December 1979.

34 Washington to Ottawa, 'Auto Talks,' 23 August 1979, LAC, RG 19, vol. 5959, file 8705-03, pt. 3.

35 Stephen Chapman, 'Chrysler Will Die for Its Own Sins: No-Fault Capitalism,' *New Republic*, 17 November 1979, 11.

36 Milton Friedman, 'Chrysler: Are Jobs the Issue?' *Newsweek*, 10 September 1979, 66.

37 'UAW Proposal regarding a Government Position in Chrysler,' 3 August 1979, WRL, UAW-Chrysler Collection, box 11, file 29.

38 Anastakis, *Auto Pact*, 69–70. On Walter Gordon and economic nationalism in this period, see Azzi, *Walter Gordon and the Rise of Canadian Nationalism*.

39 On the idea of a 'made in Canada Car' and Canadian UAW demands for a crown corporation in the auto industry, see Anastakis, 'Between Nationalism and Continentalism,' 109.

40 James Daw, 'Could Chrysler Corp. Put Canada in the Driver's Seat?' *TS*, 26 April 1980.

41 See, for instance, Canada, *Debates*, 5 December 1979, 2031 (Ed Broadbent, Oshawa).

42 Editorials, 'Canada Should Buy Chrysler' and 'Solution Is To Buy out Chrysler,' *TS*, 16 March and 6 April 1979. The *Star* had also suggested such a path even before the Chrysler crisis. See editorial, 'Maybe Canadians Should Buy up Chrysler,' 18 August 1978. The *Globe and Mail's* editorialists, in contrast, argued that 'there is no earthly reason why the Government of Canada should invest in Chrysler Canada Ltd,' and that there should be no bailout, either. Editorial, 'No Hand for Chrysler,' 30 August 1970.

43 'Minister Reported urging Ottawa Buy up Chrysler,' *TS*, 25 March 1979.

44 James Daw, 'Could Chrysler Corp. Put Canada in the Driver's Seat?' *TS*, 26 April 1980. The Ontario Liberal Party proposed nationalizing Chrysler Canada during the 1981 provincial campaign, as well. Kirk Makin, 'Voters Are Urged to "Dump Liberals" for Shifting Policies on Auto Industry,' *G&M*, 17 March 1980.

45 Sam Gindin to Robert White and Basil Hargrove, 'Chrysler Canada (Confidential),' 15 August 1979, LAC, CAW Papers, vol. 245, file 8.

46 Bill Shields, 'Talk of Nationalizing Chrysler Is "Absolutely Silly,"' *WS*, 26 March 1979.

47 Milliken to Blanchard, 1 November 1979, BHL, Milliken Papers, box 713, file: 'Chrysler.'

48 James Blanchard as told to Jennifer Holmes, 'How Chrysler Went to Washington and Blanchard Went to Bat,' *Detroit Magazine* (*Detroit Free Press*), 25 May 1980.

49 'We Are Americans … Chrysler Needs Help,' n.d., WRL, UAW-Chrysler Collection, box 11, file: 'Bailout.'

50 Eduardo Porter, 'Auto Bailout Seems Unlikely,' *NYT*, 14 April 2006.

51 Carol Goar, 'Ottawa May Buy a Stake in Massey,' *TS*, 8 October 1980.

52 Canada, *Debates*, 13 May 1980, 1019 (Herb Gray, Windsor).

53 Canada, *Debates*, 13 May, 1980 1019 (Herb Gray, Windsor).

54 The classic expression of this acceptance is found in Aitken, 'Defensive Expansionism.'

55 Classic treatments of U.S. multinationals include Vernon, *Sovereignty at Bay*, and Wilkins, *The Maturing of Multinational Enterprise*.

56 For examples of automotive MNE-state interaction, see Bennett and Sharpe, *Transnational Corporations versus the State*, and Shapiro, *Engines of Growth*.

57 Studer-Noguez, *Ford and the Global Strategies of Multinationals*, 2.

58 See, for instance: Ingrassia and Whilte, *Comeback*; Stuart, *Bailout*; Hyde, *Riding the Roller Coaster*.

59 It is also important to realize that the state responses towards the Chrysler crisis took place within the context of ongoing and often heated negotia-

tions about the auto pact, as will be seen in the following chapter. However, during this period, there was no real linkage between the ongoing talks regarding the operation of the auto agreement and the Chrysler debacle. 'Auto Talks,' Canadian embassy, Washington, to Ottawa, 23 August 1979, LAC, RG 19, vol. 5959, file 8705-03, pt. 3.

60 Anthony Whittingham, 'A Giant's Fragile Kingdom,' *Maclean's*, 20 August 1979.

61 'Chrysler Asks Aid to Save 15,000 Jobs,' *TS*, 11 August 1979; 'Chrysler Asks Help from Ottawa,' *TS*, 25 August 1979; James Daw, 'Washington Must Move First on Chrysler, de Cotret Says,' *TS*, 26 November 1979.

62 'Chrysler Consultations,' G.L. Reuber to the minister, 9 November 1979, and W.R. Hines to R.K. Joyce, 16 November 1979, LAC, RG 19, vol. 5958, file 8705-02, pt. 18; 'Ottawa Still Ponders Chrysler Canadian Aid,' *TS*, 2 November 1979.

63 'Chrysler Canadian Product Proposal,' 29 November 1979, AO, RG 9–2, Acc. 22206, box: 'DM,' file: 'Chrysler – 1979.'

64 Canada, *Debates*, 4 December 1979, 1983–4 (Herb Gray, Windsor).

65 'Automotive Industry Issues,' 19 October 1979, LAC, RG 19, vol. 5959, file 8705-03, pt. 3; Canada, *Debates*, 6 November 1979, 994; James Daw, 'Washington Must Move First to Aid Chrysler, de Cotret Says,' *TS*, 26 November 1979.

66 Canada, *Debates*, 6 December 1979, 2073 (Herb Gray, Windsor).

67 According to James Blanchard, he was 'sandbagged' by Secretary Miller and the administration, who did not provide support for the bill until the last moment. Jennifer Holmes, 'How Chrysler Went to Washington and Blanchard Went to Bat,' *Detroit Magazine* (*Detroit Free Press*), 25 May 1980, 16; James Daw, 'US Treasury Recommends Chrysler Loan Guarantee,' *TS*, 1 December 1979; Tom Nicholson, 'Chrysler's Big Boost,' *Newsweek*, 12 November 1979, 86.

68 Canada, *Debates*, 4 December 1979, 1983, and 5 December 1979, 2031 (Joe Clark, Peace River).

69 'Chrysler Corporation's 1980–85 Operating Plan, December 17, 1979,' LAC, RG 19, vol. 5959, file 8705-04-02, pt. 5; 'Help Us before It's Too Late, Chrysler's Iacocca Pleads,' *TS*, 17 December 1979; 'Will the Bailout Leak?' *Newsweek*, 31 December 1979.

70 'Chrysler Corporation Contingency Planning,' Industry Sector Policy Branch, 19 December 1979, AO, RG 9–2, Acc. 22206, box: 'DM,' file: 'Chrysler –1979.'

71 'Chrysler Canada,' W.R. Hines to R.K. Joyce, 20 December 1979, LAC, RG 19, vol. 5958, file 8705-02, pt. 18.

72 P. Best, 'Chrysler Connects with Ottawa on Big Bail-Out,' *FP*, 8 December 1979.
73 P. Best, 'Election Slows Ottawa Boost for Chrysler,' *FP*, 29 December 1979.
74 James Daw, 'Conditional Aid to Chrysler Urged by Gray,' *TS*, 18 December 1979. The Chrysler bailout became a significant issue during the 1980 U.S. elections, as well, though that issue is beyond the scope of this book.
75 Canadian embassy, Washington, to Ottawa, 4 January 1980, LAC, RG 19, vol. 5958, file 8705-02, pt. 18.
76 'Meetings on Chrysler Situation,' B.A. Sulzenko to staff, 7 January 1980, LAC, RG 19, vol. 5959, file 8705-04-02, pt. 5.
77 'Chrysler's $1.1 Billion Loss Biggest Ever in US,' *TS*, 8 February 1980; Irwin Ross, 'Chrysler on the Brink,' *Fortune*, 9 February 1981.
78 The impact of the concessions on the union is addressed in more detail in chapter 6. Chrysler Corporation, 'Status of Chrysler Corporation Negotiations to Complete the Requirements of the Loan Guarantee Act,' 1 April 1980, WRL, UAW-Chrysler Collection, box 11, file: 'Bailout.'
79 Howard Paster to Douglas Fraser, 'Extraordinary Costs from Disproportionate Burden Faced on Smaller Automobile Companies by Government Regulation,' 23 June 1979, WRL, D. Fraser Papers, box 51, file 51-9.
80 Michigan even considered measures such as the creation of a state lottery whose proceeds would go to the beleaguered company. Bill Lukens (Michigan Department of Commerce), 'Program for Governor Milliken's Involvement in Federal-Chrysler Issues,' 8 August 1979, 'News Conference Transcript, Gov. William G. Milliken, August 10, 1979,' BHL, Milliken Papers, box 7B, file: 'Chrysler'; Tom Nicholson, 'Chrysler's Big Boost,' *Newsweek*, 12 November 1979, 86.
81 James Daw, 'Ottawa Aid Concerns Chrysler Boss More Than Workers Tiff,' *TS*, 10 January 1980.
82 'Chrysler Aid Guaranteed, MacGuigan promises,' *TS*, 8 March 1980.
83 'Chrysler Canada Ltd. 1980–85 Operating and Financing Plan: Revised Government Assistance Request, March 31, 1980,' LAC, RG 19, vol. 5959, file 8705-04-02, pt. 7.
84 The plan dropped the front-wheel-drive car and promised to invest $962 million, as opposed to the previous figure of $1.047 billion. 'Discussion Paper, Assistance to Chrysler Canada Ltd.,' 9 March 1980, LAC, RG 19, vol. 5959, file 8705-04-02, pt. 6.
85 Ontario Minister of Industry and Tourism Larry Grossman stated that 'we have taken a hard line with Chrysler simply because the end result of any financial contribution we made to that company has to be to anchor jobs into the community … any net layout of taxpayers' dollars, be it by way

of loan or grant, is absolutely tied to the maintenance of jobs – if anything, increase of jobs.' Ontario *Debates*, 24 March 1980, 146 (Larry Grossman, St Andrew-St Paul). 'Chrysler Aid "Weeks" Away, Gray Says' and 'Chrysler Aid Guaranteed, MacGuigan Promises,' *TS*, 7 and 8 March 1980.

86 A.S. Rubinoff to Ian A. Stewart, 'Chrysler Canada Ltd. 1980–85 Operating and Financing Plan: Trimmed Down Operating and Financial Alternative, April 9, 1980,' and 'Chrysler,' 10 April 1980, LAC, RG 19, vol. 5959, file 8705-04-2, pt. 7; 'Chrysler Canada,' J.D. Girvin to L.R. Wilson, 10 April 1980, AO, RG 9–2, Acc. 22206, box: 'DM,' file: 'Chrysler – 1979.'

87 Minister of industry to Cabinet Committee on Economic Development, 'Assistance to Chrysler Canada Ltd.,' 15 April 1980. LAC, RG 19, vol. 5959, file 8795-04-02, pt. 7.

88 Cabinet Submission (IT&C), 'Program to Assist the Ontario Automotive Industry,' April 1980 AO, RG 9–2, Acc. 22206, box 5, file: 'Policy Committee.'

89 Ontario, *Debates*, 2 May 1980, 1394 (Larry Grossman, St Andrew-St Paul).

90 The *Globe and Mail* questioned whether expecting job guarantees, given Chrysler's troubles, was a 'flight from reality.' Editorial, 'Without a Warranty,' 8 May 1980.

91 'Progress Seen in Negotiations on Chrysler Aid,' *G&M*, 3 May 1980.

92 Canada, *Debates*, 1 May 1980, 599 (Herb Gray, Windsor).

93 'Report of UAW Director for Canada and International Vice President, Robert White,' 21 and 22 June 1980, 17, LAC, CAW Papers, vol. 296, file: 'National Director's Reports.'

94 In his autobiography, *Hard Bargains*, White recalled a Chrysler official grumbling during the talks with Gray's officials that 'it sure is different in Canada. In the States the union and Chrysler are lined up against the government. Over here the government lines up with the goddamned union' (168). See also Ontario *Debates*, 2 May 1980, 1394 (Larry Grossman, St Andrew-St Paul).

95 'Cabinet Delays Making Chrysler Decision on Aid,' *G&M*, 9 May 1980.

96 Richard Conrad, 'Chrysler Aid Hinges on Job Guarantees, Herb Gray States,' *TS*, 2 May 1980; 'Next Move up to Chrysler,' *TS*, 3 May 1980.

97 'Chrysler,' A.S. Rubinoff to Ian A. Stewart, 10 April 1980, LAC, RG 19, vol. 5959, file 8705-04-2, pt. 7.

98 Gray announced the package on 10 May publicly, and on 13 May in the Commons. Canada, *Debates*, 13 May 1980, 1018–19 (Herb Gray, Windsor); 'Chrysler Deal Pays off by 1984 with More Jobs,' *TS*, 12 May 1980; Mary Kate Rowan and Jane Jankovic, 'Chrysler Rescued with $1.7 Billion in Loans, Grants,' *G&M*, 12 May 1980; John Hay, 'Chrysler Gets the Big Boost,' *Maclean's*, 19 May 1980; deputy minister to Herb Gray, Ed Lumley,

and Charles Lapointe, 'Employment Projections – Canadian Automotive Industry and Windsor Area,' 11 July 1980, LAC, RG 20, file 4956-1, vol. 2.

99 Sam Gindin to Robert White and Basil Hargrove, 'The Chrysler Proposal,' 11 March 1980, LAC, CAW, vol. 254, file 9.

100 Canada, *Debates*, 13 May 1980, 1019 (Herb Gray, Windsor).

101 'Canada Gets K Car, UAW Wins Important Principle,' *Solidarity Canada*, February 1981, 2.

102 The Research and Development Centre did eventually open, but not until 1996. Interview with William Davis, 7 August 2008; Ontario, *Debates*, 12 May 1980, 1761–2 (Larry Grossman, St Andrew-St Paul); D. Dowling, 'Why Grossman Played Tough in Chrysler Cliff-Hanger,' *FP*, 24 May 1980.

103 At the White House, President Carter's signing ceremony included no Canadian representatives; Ambassador Peter Towe was on the initial guest list but was subsequently dropped. 'Assistance to Chrysler,' Canadian embassy, Washington, to Ottawa, 13 May 1980, LAC, RG 19, vol. 5959, file 8705-04-02, pt. 7.

104 At the depths of Chrysler's troubles, and with less than $2.5 million cash on hand, Iacocca presented to his Board of Directors the minivan plan, which called for expenditures of $700 million. Iacocca was convinced that 'mothers are sick and tired with driving a station wagon – too big, not the right kind of space; the mini-van is to be driven like a car, not like a truck or a station wagon,' and that the project was the company's salvation. Jean de Grandpré, the Canadian representative on the Chrysler board, remembered speaking with Iacocca after the presentation: 'What are the jails in Michigan like? The jails in Montreal are not so nice. If this doesn't work out, we might have a good idea of what those jails are like.' Author's interview with Jean de Grandpré, 14 August 2006; Chrysler Corporation, 'Speech Prepared for Lee A. Iacocca, at a Press Conference, Highland Park,' 17 December 1980, WRL, D. Fraser Collection, box 15, file 18: 'Chrysler, 1978–81'; 'Chrysler to Request $400 Million Backing,' *TS*, 20 December 1980.

105 Mel Cappe to file, 'Meeting with Automotive Parts Manufacturing Association, January 15, 1981,' 26 January 1981, LAC, RG 19, vol. 5738, file 3881-02, pt. 13, 2.

106 Instead of the employment figures cited above, the company promised to maintain employment of 9,300 (1981–3), 11,100 (1984), and 12,300 (1985) workers. As a percentage of the company's overall workforce, this was to be 8 per cent (1981–3), 9 per cent (1984), and 13 per cent (1984). The final employment figures are listed in Table 3. The federal government also reworked its assistance to the company when Chrysler reneged in late 1982

on a promise to build a diesel-engine plant, with Massey-Ferguson, in Windsor. 'Amended and Restated Agreement to Provide Loan Insurance among Her Majesty the Queen in Right of Canada, Acting through the Ministry of Industry, Trade and Commerce, and Chrysler Canada Ltd., and Chrysler Corporation, dated as of February 17, 1981'; Press Release, 'New Agreement between Chrysler Canada Ltd. and Canadian Government,' 17 February 1981. Both in LAC, RG 20, file 4956-1, vol. 5. See also Ken Romain, 'Chrysler Plans Spending Cuts,' G&M, 13 January 1981.

107 Chrysler Canada, '1980–1985 Operating and Financing Plan,' 12 February 1981, LAC, RG 20, file 4956-1, vol. 5; editorial, 'Wise Caution on Chrysler,' TS, 9 February 1981; Gillian Mackay, 'A Second Time round for Chrysler,' Maclean's, 2 March 1981; 'Chrysler Corporation 1982–85 Financing Plan, July 15, 1981,' WRL, D. Fraser Collection, box 52, file 52-3.

108 Nicholas Hunter, 'Chrysler Set to Repay US, Unit Still Seeks Guarantees,' G&M, 14 July 1983.

109 Chrysler Canada, Annual Reports, 1983–6. In the summer of 1982, the company announced that the Windsor engine plant would be reopened, backed by loan guarantees totalling US$105 million from both the federal and Ontario governments (this was not part of the original loan-guarantee negotiations). However, the plan was scrapped in December 1982. 'A Chrysler Reopening in Canada,' NYT, 13 August 1982; Ian Austen, 'Chrysler Imperils the Bailout Deal,' Maclean's, 10 January 1983.

110 Hyde, Riding the Roller Coaster, 255.

111 M.J. Closs, in Cowan, ed., The North American Automobile Industry, 8.

112 Ian A.J. Henderson (Ministry of Finance) to R.F. Kilborn (Chrysler Canada), 10 July 1984, LAC, RG 19, vol. 5853, file 3015-15-C558.

113 Under the new production mandate, Chrysler Canada ended production of all passenger cars and retooled its main Windsor plant for mini-van production. 'Corporate Finance Division: Chrysler Canada Interview Notes, July 5, 1984,' LAC, RG 19, vol. 5853, file 3015-15-C558.

114 Chrysler Canada, Annual Report, 1983.

115 James Daw, 'Jubilant Chrysler to Repay $800 Million 7 Years Ahead of Time,' TS, 14 July 1983.

116 This was prior to Chrysler's purchase of AMC's Brampton plant in 1987.

117 Because of retooling and the shift to the production of mini-vans, which were classified as 'trucks,' and the end of car production, Chrysler did not meet its auto pact requirements in 1982 and 1983. These duties were forgiven by the federal government owing to the unique circumstances the company faced, and the fact that its overall output was much greater after 1984. See chapter 5.

118 Heiz, LaRochelle-Côté, Bordt, and Das, *Labour Markets, Business Activity and Population Growth and Mobility in Canadian CMAs*, 24.

119 'Gray Greets Wilson with Other Figures,' *WS*, 24 October 1986.

120 Statistics Canada, CANSIM II Series, vol. 2067457, Table 2820090, 'Labour force estimates, by census metropolitan area.'

121 Chrysler Canada, *Annual Corporate Reports* (various years).

122 Côté, 'The Canadian Auto Industry, 1978–1986,' 14.

123 See ibid., 'Unemployment Rates in Canada, 1978–1986,' 13.

124 Ibid., 16.

125 'North American Vehicle Production Summary, 1960–1999,' DesRosiers, *Yearbook 2000*, 112.

126 Andrew H. Malcolm, 'Canada's New Economic Clout,' *New York Times Magazine*, 17 February 1985.

127 As one Chrysler executive told a Canadian government representative in explaining the differences between employment levels in Canada and the United States, 'it was "simply luck of the draw" in terms of product mix. The two assembly plants in Canada were producing vehicles which the market wanted. Thus, even in a "sea of problems," the Canadian operation was "flat out" and employment levels were much higher than those in the US.' 'Corporate Finance Division: Chrysler Canada Interview Notes, July 5, 1984,' LAC, RG 19, vol. 5853, file 3015-15-C558.

128 While the acceleration of Canadian production was no doubt partially a 'product luck of the draw,' such as the mini-van, Detroit Big Three executives undoubtedly understood the value of sourcing more of their assembly in Canada. With a depreciating dollar in decline after 1976, lower health-care costs owing to universal Medicare in Canada, and the Canadian plants' better production and quality results (Canadian plants have consistently placed well in the industry's J.D. Power annual results for productivity), it made sense to build a larger share of the company's output in Canada.

129 Canada, *Debates*, 24 November 1980, 4987 (Girve Fretz, Erie).

130 Steve Olson, 'Prospects for the Automobile: Sputtering toward the Twenty-First Century,' *The Futurist*, February 1980, 27–34; John Deverell, 'Our Car Industry: Dinosaur or Dynamo?' *TS*, 24 December 1982.

5 Integration's Bounty, Integration's Bounds: The Unusual Life of the Auto Pact

1 Hood, *The Motor Boys in Ottawa*, 36–7.

2 Washington to Ottawa, 'Canada-USA Automotive Agreement, Congres-

sional Hearings,' 14 April 1976, LAC, RG 19, vol. 5347, file 3881-01, pt. 1.

3 Canada, *Debates*, 5 May 1966, 4759 (Alfred Hales, Wellington South).

4 See, for example, 'GM's Chairman Comments on Air Bags, Output Outlook, Canadian Pact, Imported Steel,' *WA*, 6 March 1972, 74; 'Close up on You, Canada and Free Trade, *WS*, 11 January 1965.

5 Henry Kissinger, 'Meeting with Prime Minister Pierre Elliott Trudeau of Canada, December 4, 1974,' December 1974, GFL, WHCF, CO 28, box 11, file: 'Canada,' 12 January 1974–31 December 1974.

6 'Memo for the President: Canada-American Free Trade in Autos and Parts,' Trezise to Wilson, 25 November 1964, Lyndon Baines Johnson Presidential Library (LBJL), Henry H. Wilson Papers, box 1.

7 Douglas P. Thomas, 'The Canada-US Auto Trade Agreement,' *Financial Analysts Journal*, 23, no. 4 (1967): 113–17 at 113.

8 Editorial, 'Free Trade for Whom?' *Washington Post*, 17 January 1965.

9 Ed Broadbent, 'Auto Pact: Dropping Safeguards Would Be a Sell-out,' *G&M*, 10 December 1971.

10 N.B. Macdonald, speech to Science Council of Canada, 'Opportunities in Canadian Transportation Conference,' 17–18 May 1979, LAC, RG 20, file 4954-1, vol. 1, 100.

11 J.H. Dales, 'Closer to Protectionism? Auto Deal National Disgrace: Professor,' *G&M*, 19 January 1965; Dales, *The Protective Tariff in Canada's Development*, 23–8. After 1965, Dales would be often cited by pact opponents, especially the Automotive Service Industries Association (ASIA), an independent American parts-lobby group.

12 See, for instance: Emerson, *Production, Location and the Automotive Agreement*; Beigie, 'The Automotive Agreement of 1965'; Arnold, 'The Impact of the Automotive Trade Agreement between Canada and the United States'; Cowan, 'Effects of the United States-Canadian Automotive Agreement on Canada's Manufacturing, Trade and Price Posture'; Helmers, *The United States-Canadian Automobile Agreement*; Neisser, 'The Impact of the Canada-United States Automotive Agreement on Canada's Motor Vehicle Industry'; Wonnacott and Wonnacott, 'The Automotive Agreement of 1965.'

13 Herb Gray to various ministers, 'Automotive: International Issues,' 11 June 1980, LAC, RG 20, file 4956-1, vol. 2, February 1977–28 August 1980.

14 Industry Analysis Branch, Policy Planning, IT&C, 'Re-Negotiation of the Canada-United States Automotive Products Agreement,' May 1979, LAC, RG 19, vol. 5348, file 3881-02, pt. 4, 6.

15 At one point during Canada-U.S. negotiations, the two sides started talking about 'formal reciprocity' versus 'optical reciprocity,' the latter being

the mere illusion of free trade that existed under the agreement given the fact that individuals could not trade across the border duty-free, though companies could. 'Cabinet Committee on Economic Policy: Trade Discussions with the United States: Automotive Products Trade Agreement,' 15 December 1971, LAC, RG 19, vol. 5390, file 8705-08-16.

16 George Ball, 'The United States and Canada: Common Aims and Common Responsibilities' (Speech to the Canadian and Empire Clubs, 22 March 1965), *Department of State Bulletin*, 52, no. 1347 (19 April 1965): 573–4.

17 ITC, 'General Motors Corporation Statement on the Automotive Products Trade Act of 1965,' 11 December 1975, LAC, RG 19, vol. 5959, file 8705-08-16, pt. 13.

18 'CBC News Item, Wednesday, May 9, 1973, 10 p.m.,' DFAIT, 37-7-1-USA-2, vol. 32.

19 See, for example, editorial, 'Not an Answer, but an Opening: Prices Will Tell ...,' *G&M*, 19 January 1965; editorial, 'Auto Deal: What's in It for Consumers?' *TS*, 20 January 1965.

20 See, for instance, Bruce MacDonald, 'Auto Firms to Face Heavy Pressure for Price Cuts,' and 'Disparity Wide, Auto Price Cuts: Start in 1966?' *G&M*, 19 January 1965 and 16 March 1965. In the mid-2000s, when the Canadian dollar reached parity with the U.S. greenback, there was a minor consumer revolt in Canada over the difference, which carmakers tried to diffuse by lowering some of their prices.

21 A.E. Ritchie to minister, 'Canada-USA Automotive Products Agreement, Possible Question in the House,' 26 April 1972, DFAIT, 37-7-1-USA-2, vol. 31; *Eighth Annual Report of the President to the Congress on the Operation of the Automotive Products Trade Act of 1965* (Washington, 1974), 8; Leonard Woodcock, 'Statement to the ITC, 11 December 1975,' 3–4. The latter two documents are found in LAC, CAW Papers, vol. 173, box 3. See also *Ninth Annual President's Report* (1975), Tables 6, 7, 8.

22 The tariff existed for all imported cars, including those from Europe and Japan.

23 R. Grey to the minister, 'Cabinet Agenda – Automotive Agreement,' 14 January 1972, LAC, RG 19, vol. 5390, file 8705-08-16.

24 James H. Clare, Federation of Automobile Dealer Associations of Canada, to Mitchell Sharp, 15 June 1973, DFAIT, 37-7-1-USA-2, vol. 32.

25 Canada, *Debates*, 26 January 1973 (Ed Broadbent, Oshawa).

26 Tom Claridge, 'Made Here, Cars Cheaper in Buffalo,' and 'Car Makers Reap an Estimated $150 Million Extra Profit by Charging 10% More in Canada,' *G&M*, 26 April 1972; editorial, 'For You, a Special Price,' *G&M*, 29 July 1975.

27　C.W. Sanders (Chrysler) to C.D. Arthur, 3 May 1972, 'Consultations with Automotive Producers: DISC and Canada-US Price Differentials, May 3, 1972,' 16 May 1972, DFAIT, 37-7-1-USA-2, vol. 31.

28　The price issue was also forcefully debated in the Ontario legislature. In 1975 NDP leader David Lewis said that 'the single most glaring omission in the pact is the higher price in Canada' of cars. Ontario, *Debates*, 10 December 1975, 1488 (David Lewis, York South). See also Canada, *Debates*, 11 May 1972, 2191–3 (Jean-Luc Pepin, Ottawa).

29　Washington to Ottawa (S.S. Reisman only), 23 December 1971, LAC, RG 19, vol. 5390, file 8705-08-16.

30　'Cabinet Committee on Economic Policy: Trade Discussions with the United States: Automotive Products Trade Agreement,' 15 December 1971, LAC, RG 19, vol. 5390, file 8705-08-16.

31　United States, *Congressional Record* (Washington, 1969), 7403 (Senate).

32　Editorial, 'Much Noise, Few Facts,' *G&M*, 24 March 1973.

33　This view was held by more than a few American officials, one of whom complained: 'We knew about the Canadian plan to blackjack the companies, but we expected the companies to be harder bargainers. They didn't have to give away so much. It must have been profitable for them.' Quoted in Keohane and Nye, *Power and Interdependence*, 207.

34　Though Murphy himself may not have played a role in the auto pact's creation, Henry Ford II certainly did. At the height of the 1964 auto pact negotiations, Ford told President Johnson and senior White House officials that countervailing duties were the least desirable outcome of the Canada-U.S. impasse, and that the new agreement should be given a chance. See Henry Ford II to L. Johnson, 16 September 1964; Brubeck to Bundy, 23 September 1964; Bundy to record (White House), 24 September 1964. All found in LBJL, NSF, Country File, Canada, box 164: 'Canada Memos'; United States Senate, *Report of Proceedings: Hearings Held before the Subcommittee on International Trade of the Committee on Finance, 27 February, 1973* (Washington 1973), 205–6. On the role of the auto companies in the agreement's creation, see Anastakis, *Auto Pact*, chapter 3.

35　Canada, *Debates*, 4 November 1974, 1004 (George Hees, Prince Edward-Hastings).

36　Editorial, 'MP Must,' *G&M*, 29 August 1973.

37　Ontario, *Debates*, 2 April 1976, 976 (Bernard Newman, Windsor Walkerville).

38　Stursburg, *Lester Pearson and the American Dilemma*, 227. The reality is that the idea for a sectoral trade agreement had existed for some time. See, for instance, the plan put forth by the Universities of Manitoba and Minnesota in *The Mid-Continent and the Peace*.

39 United States Senate, *Report of Proceedings: Hearings Held before the Subcommittee on International Trade of the Committee on Finance, 27 February, 1973* (Washington, 1973), 211.

40 According to Reisman, 'it is not clear who was the real driver in finding the qualified free trade solution. I have always been prepared to give Phil Trezise all the credit and he has always insisted that I must share the blame.' In separate interviews both men agreed that each had played a key role in developing the idea. Reisman, 'The Relevance of the Auto Pact for Other Sectoral Trade Agreements,' 77. Also, author's interviews with Simon Reisman and Philip Trezise, 19 December 1997 and 24 December 1999; and Anastakis, *Auto Pact*, especially chapter 3.

41 See, for example, economist Carl Beigie's statement in the clip 'Americans Disenchanted with Auto Pact,' 1 April 1987, http://www.archives.cbc.ca/economy_business/trade_agreements/topics/326/ (accessed 14 December 2010); also, Dobell, 'Negotiating with the United States,' 20–1.

42 United States Senate, *Report of Proceedings: Hearings Held before the Subcommittee on International Trade of the Committee on Finance, 27 February, 1973*, 196–7.

43 Ken Romain, 'Release of Actual Figures on Canadian-US Auto Pact Requested,' *G&M*, 26 April 1973.

44 U.S. Department of Commerce, Bureaus of Statistics, and Statistics Canada, *The Reconciliation of US-Canada Trade Statistics 1970, A Report by the US-Canadian Trade Statistics Committee* (Washington and Ottawa, 1970).

45 *Eighth Annual Report of the President* (1974), 18.

46 Canada, *Debates*, 17 January 1973 (Terry O'Connor, Halton).

47 Ontario, *Debates*, 16 March 1972, 499 (Ted Bounsall, Windsor); Mark Witten, 'Why the Auto Pact Is Obsolete: The Coming Technological Revolution May Make Our Biggest Trade Agreement about as Practical as a Horse and Buggy,' *Canadian Business*, February 1979, 33–6, 96 at 36.

48 '*New Canada* Special Supplement: The Auto Pact Is Destroying Canada's Auto Industry; May 1972,' 3, LAC, Alfred Dales Papers, vol. 4.

49 See chapter 6.

50 'Brief on the Canadian-United States Automotive Products Agreement,' 10 December 1969, CAW Archives and Library, Briefing Files.

51 Beverly C. McCloskey (Local 222) to Dennis McDermott, 19 October 1971; Dennis McDermott to Abe Taylor (Local 222), 12 November 1971; William Rutherford (Local 222) to Dennis McDermott, 25 November 1971. All in LAC, CAW Papers, vol. 3, file 19.

52 Abe Taylor to various, 13 December 1971, LAC, CAW Papers, vol. 13, file 9.

53 On congressional reaction to the auto pact, see Anastakis, 'Continental Auto Politics'; Senator Vance Hartke to President G. Ford, 29 January 1976, GFL, L. William Seidman Papers, box 47, file: 'Senator Vance Hartke.'

54 'Notes on Meeting on Canada-US Automotive Agreement, August 23–24, 1973,' 29 August 1973, DFAIT, 37-7-1-USA-2, vol. 32.

55 The impact on the ground was equally dramatic: by 1977, nearly 100 new parts and vehicle plants had been built in Canada, with another 170 facilities expanded or updated since 1965. The consequent growth in the parts sector was astounding. In 1965 parts production in Canada was $690 million; by 1977, it was $4.393 billion, much of that exported to the United States. For the growth of the sector, see Anastakis, *Auto Pact*, chapter 5; Industry Analysis Branch, Policy Planning, IT&C, 'Re-Negotiation of the Canada-United States Automotive Products Agreement,' May 1979, LAC, RG 19, vol. 5348, file 3881-02, pt. 4, 8; DesRosiers, *Automotive Yearbook, 2000*, 190.

56 United States Senate, *Report of Proceedings: Hearings Held before the Subcommittee on International Trade of the Committee on Finance, 27 February, 1973*, 205–6.

57 Industry Analysis Branch, Policy Planning, IT&C, 'Re-Negotiation of the Canada-United States Automotive Products Agreement,' May 1979, LAC, RG 19, vol. 5348, file 3881-02, pt. 4.

58 The agreement's Canadian regulations allowed for duty-free third-country importation into Canada: the UAW's Woodcock complained that in 1976 Ford was importing engines from Brazil to Canada, resulting in 700 layoffs in Lima, Ohio, where the engines were previously made; 700 transmissions a day were being imported from France instead of Cincinnati for St Thomas vehicles, with a loss of another 850 jobs; and so on. This loophole would play a growing role for Big Three operations under the auto pact in the 1980s. Washington to Ottawa, 'Canada-USA Automotive Agreement, Congressional Hearings,' 14 April 1976, LAC, RG 19, vol. 5347, file 3881-01, pt. 1.

59 In 1971 the U.S. Department of Labor told the UAW that, of the 1970 deficit of $237 million, $130 million could be attributed to snowmobiles, which had had suddenly become popular. Carol Coburn to Leonard Woodcock, 21 June 1971, WRL, UAW-Ford, box 73, file 37.

60 G.E. Shannon to deputy minister, 'Automotive Agreement,' 25 July 1974, DFAIT, 37-7-1-USA-2, vol. 33.

61 John Bolin to Irv Bluestone, 'Canadian Plants – Shipments to US GM Plants,' 16 April 1979, WRL, UAW-GM, box 172, file 30.

62 In 1986 the Canadian government obtained legal opinions on the Letters

of Undertaking from the departments of finance and regional industrial expansion, both of which found it 'unlikely' that the letters could be considered legally binding. Senator Vance Hartke to President G. Ford, 29 January 1976, GFL, L. William Seidman Papers, box 47, file: 'Senator Vance Hartke'; memorandum to cabinet (DRIE), 'Automotive Issues and Policy Instruments,' 10 September 1986, 45, PCO.

63 Though this roughly 60 per cent CVA was of an immensely larger automotive output, the decline was enough to prompt Canadian officials to complain to the Reagan administration. Campbell Stuart to file, 'Meeting of Ministers Gray and Lumley with US Special Trade Representative Brock and Secretary of Commerce Balridge,' 13 March 1981, LAC, RG 19, vol. 5738, file 3881-02, pt. 14.

64 Industry Analysis Branch, Policy Planning, IT&C, 'Re-Negotiation of the Canada-United States Automotive Products Agreement,' May 1979, LAC, RG 19, vol. 5348, file 3881-02, pt. 4, 25–6.

65 Reisman to Drury, 9 August 1967, LAC, RG 20, file: 'Automotive Correspondence,' vol. 1793.

66 See Anastakis, *Auto Pact*, 142–3. In 1973 International Harvester missed on the ratio, leaving the company liable for $10 million in duties on vehicles and parts imported during the 1971–2 period. Because it faced unusual circumstances and was not a major importer, an order-in-council was required to grant tariff relief for the company. International Harvester's base year ratio was 101:100, but it had achieved only 89:100 in 1971–2. C. Oliver to R. Grey, 'Failure to Meet Manufacturers' Requirements under the Automotive Products Agreement,' 23 May 1973; R. Grey to S.S. Reisman, 'Canada-United States Automotive Products Agreement,' 12 September 1973. Both are from LAC, RG 19, vol. 5390, file 8705-08-16.

67 Ibid.

68 P.A. MacDougall (executive assistant, Economic and Scientific Affairs) to deputy minister, 'Automotive Pact,' 26 August 1974; and 'Senior Interdepartmental Committee on the Automotive Agreement: Summary of Meeting August 21, 1974.' Both in DFAIT, 37-7-1-USA-2, vol. 33.

69 Sam Gindin to Frank LaSorda (Local 444), 'Request for Data on Truck Industry, Chrysler and Auto Pact,' 15 June 1977. The document included testimony from the 1975 ITC hearings by Brian T. O'Keefe of Chrysler regarding the Chrysler truck plant and the auto pact. LAC, CAW, vol. 148, file 14.

70 GM also came extremely close to missing its target in 1973–4 on trucks. Ken Romain, 'Chrysler to Build Small Truck Assembly Plant in Windsor,' *G&M*, 14 December 1973.

71 In 1975 AMC just missed its passenger-vehicle ratio, but the miss was not significant enough to prompt remedial action by the government. Campbell Stuart (chairman, Automotive Task Force), 'U.S.-Canada Automotive Consultations,' 13 February 1981, LAC, RG 19, vol. 5738, file 3881-02, pt. 13, 2.

72 As for AMC and its situation with Renault's recent takeover, Bob White told Gray that 'the Canadian government does have significant negotiating leverage given FIRA's intervention, the monies owed by the corporation for violating the Auto Pact, and the on-going safeguards,' and should thus demand increased jobs and investment from the company. Bob White to Herb Gray, 26 June 1981, Sam Gindin Papers (SGP), vol. 1981; Jim Travers, 'Chrysler Facing Breach in Pact,' and no author, 'Autopact Standards Must Be Met,' WS, 2 April and 13 November 1980; press release, 'New Agreement between Chrysler Canada Ltd. and Canadian Government,' 17 February 1981, LAC, RG 20, file 4956-1, vol. 5, March 1981–June 1981.

73 The AMC local in Kenosha went as far as to get an opinion on the legality of the alleged transfer of work from Kenosha to Brampton. Sam Gindin to Bob White, 'AMC,' 1 June 1981; Max N. Berry (lawyer) to Gene R. Sylvester (UAW Local 72), 'Memorandum: The Transfer of Automotive Employment and Production from the US to Canada under the US-Canadian Automotive Products Agreement of 1965,' 24 April 1981. Both in SGP, vol. 1981.

74 Frank Swift to David Levin, 'Ford Motor Company of Canada, Ltd.: Variation in Ratio Requirements under APTA,' 10 December 1980; Herb Gray to Roy F. Bennett, 'Re: Ratio Flexibility for the Oakville Assembly Plant,' 22 December 1980; press release, 'New Front Wheel Drive to Be Assembled in Canada as a Result of Limited Conditional Adjustments to Ford Moto Company Ratio Requirements, 5 January 1981. All in LAC, RG 19, vol, 5738, file 3881-02, pt. 13. The U.S. government was aware of the plan and did not object. Ottawa to Washington, 'Ratio Flexibility: Ford Motor Co. of Canada Ltd.,' 22 December 1980, DFAIT, 37-7-1-USA-2, vol. 41; P. Best, 'Ford Drives for Relaxed Auto Pact,' FP, 19 April 1980.

75 Ibid.

76 Sam Gindin of the UAW was opposed to the idea of flexibility under the auto pact, arguing that it gave the manufacturers too much leeway in production decisions and therefore might have a negative impact on jobs. At a 1980 meeting with the government, the MVMA pushed for a five-year average on ratio. Sam Gindin to Robert White et al., 'Auto Pact and Auto Industry,' 25 August 1980, LAC, CAW Papers, vol. 298, file 10; T. MacDonald to file, 'Meeting with MVMA, August 28, 1980,' 5 September 1980,

LAC, RG 19, vol. 5958, file 8795-02, pt. 21; Roy Culpeper to file, 'Meeting of the Motor Vehicle Manufacturer's Association, Toronto, Jan. 12, 1981,' 13 January 1981, LAC, RG 19, vol. 5738, file 3881-02, pt. 13.

77 Author's interview with Dennis DesRosiers, 1 August 2006.

78 Furthermore, since specialized vehicles and trucks had a higher fuel-economy standard under the CAFE regulations, moving them to the car category would give them trouble from the regulatory side. A.T. Wickham (DNR) to I.R. Craig (IT&C), n.d., LAC, RG 20, file 4956-1, vol. 2.

79 D. McEwan for I.R. Craig to A.T. Wickham, 14 February 1980, LAC, RG 20, file 4956-1, vol. 2.

80 Ken Romain, 'Possible Standoff Brightens Auto Pact Outlook,' G&M, 26 October 1973.

81 Reisman, The Canadian Auotomotive Industry, 44.

82 Leonard Woodcock, 'Statement to the ITC,' 11 December 1975, 6, LAC, CAW, vol. 173, file 3.

83 According to the 1976 ITC report, Ford's and Chrysler's Canadian operations were more profitable than their U.S. operations, 'both in [their ratio of net profit to net sales and in [their] ratio of net profit to shareholders' equity.' GM Canada's profits were much higher as a percent of shareholders' equity than its parent. United States International Trade Commission, Report on the United States-Canadian Automobile Agreement: Its History, Terms and Impact (Washington, 1976), 172–5.

84 Washington to Ottawa, telex, 'Canada-USA Automotive Agreement, Congressional Hearings,' 14 April 1976, LAC, RG 19, vol. 5347, file 3881-01, pt. 1.

85 In the 1990s, Ford Motor of Canada was taken to court by its Canadian shareholders over the issue of transfer pricing. In 2004 the Ontario Court of Appeal found that the transfer pricing system was 'not realistic.' 'Consultations with Automotive Producers: DISC and Canada-US Price Differentials, May 3, 1972,' 16 May 1972, DFAIT, 37-7-1-USA-2, vol. 31.

86 Jenna MacKay-Alie to Iain Henderson, 'Interviews with Canadian Automotive Manufacturers: Policy Considerations,' 11 July 1984, LAC, RG 19, vol. 5849, file 3015-03-1.

87 See, for instance, the Big Three's actions in response to emissions regulations, in McCarthy, Auto Mania; see also their actions towards regulation in general in Luger, Corporate Power, American Democracy and the Automobile Industry.

88 As with so many issues with the auto trade, in the absence and inaccessibility of corporate records, this can never be determined.

89 P.A. MacDougall (executive assistant, Economic and Scientific Affairs) to

deputy minister, 'Automotive Pact,' 26 August 1974; and 'Senior Interdepartmental Committee on the Automotive Agreement: Summary of Meeting August 21, 1974.' Both in DFAIT, 37-7-1-USA-2, vol. 33.

90 Another view of the auto pact negotiations between Canada and the United States in this period can be found in Muirhead, *Dancing around the Elephant*, especially 84–90 and 124–5.

91 This is not to say that the departments always agreed. In some instances there was serious interagency conflict and sniping, though Canadians usually came to a reasonable accommodation. For an example of interagency conflict, see the criticisms levelled at IT&C by Finance officials over the former's strategy paper in the spring of 1980, which was called 'a glib and rather naïve presentation of a limited set of policy options,' particularly around the 'fair share' notion. C. Miles and M. Cappe to Frank Swiftt, 'IT&C Auto Papers,' 3 April 1980, LAC, RG 19, vol. 5958, file 8795-02, pt. 18.

92 Ottawa to Washington, 'CDA-USA Trade Relations' (transcript of television interview), 26 April 1972, DFAIT, 37-7-1-USA-2, vol. 31.

93 See Anastakis, *Auto Pact*, 153–66.

94 On the Nixon Shocks and administration's relations with Canada in this period, see Bothwell, 'Thanks for the Fish'; and Muirhead, 'From Special Relationship to Third Option.'

95 For different views on this incident, see Bothwell, 'Thanks for the Fish,' 319–20; Anastakis, *Auto Pact*, 165; Muirhead, *Dancing around the Elephant*, 114–15.

96 Trudeau also sought an exemption for the Canadian sector from the Buy America and DISC provisions of Nixon's New Economic Policy, an end to 'certain disparities' under the agreement when it came to all-terrain and special-purpose vehicles, and an extension of duty-free coverage for other items (such as window glass). 'Prime Minister's Meeting with President of the United States, Washington, December 6, 1971: Automotive Products Agreement,' 2 December 1971; memorandum to cabinet, 'Canada-United States Automotive Products Agreement,' 10 December 1971; cabinet document 1346–71, 'Cabinet Committee on Economic Policy: Trade Discussions with the United States: Automotive Products Trade Agreement,' 15 December 1971. All in LAC, RG 19, vol. 5390, file 8705-08-16.

97 'Memorandum for the President: Visit of Canadian Prime Minister Trudeau,' Kissinger to Nixon, 4 December, 1971, NARA, Nixon Presidential Files, National Security Council Files, VIP Visits, box 912.

98 Washington to Ottawa, 'USA Economic Policy,' 25 April 1972, DFAIT, 37-7-1-USA-2, vol. 31

99 Washington to Ottawa, 'Conversation with Volcker, 2 March 1973, DFAIT, 37-7-1-USA-2, vol. 32.

100 A.R.A. Gherson to file, 'Visit to Washington of Ed Broadbent, MP, April 24–25,' DFAIT, 37-7-1-USA-2, vol. 32.

101 Dennis McDermott to Mitchell Sharp and Jean-Luc Pepin, 1 December 1971, LAC, CAW Papers, vol. 3, file 19.

102 Editorial, 'Auto Pact Safeguards Still Needed,' G&M, 1 March 1973.

103 From Ottawa to Washington embassy, 'CDA-USA Trade Relations' (transcript of television interview), 26 April 1972, DFAIT, 37-7-1-USA-2, vol. 31.

104 M. Cadieux, note to file, 'Mr. Gillespie's Talks with Mr. Shultz and Mr. Dent, March 29, 1973' (also sent to J.F. Grandy, IT&C), DFAIT, 37-7-1-USA-2, vol. 32; Terrance Wills, 'Gillespie Claims Job Protection Vital in Any Auto Pact Change,' G&M, 18 April 1973.

105 John Rolfe, 'Opposition Continues to Demand an Auto Pact Policy Commitment,' G&M, 2 March 1973.

106 Terrance Wills, 'Gillespie Claims Job Protection Vital in Any Auto Pact Change,' G&M, 18 April 1973.

107 Eliminating the 15 per cent tariff was to be done in stages and would require Ottawa to be granted a waiver at the GATT. 'Memorandum to Cabinet: Canada-United States Automotive Agreement,' 12 July 1973, LAC, RG 19, vol. 5390, file 8705-08-16; Washington to Ottawa, telex, 'CDA/USA Auto Pact,' 21 March 1973, DFAIT, 37-7-1-USA-2, vol. 32.

108 'Notes on Meeting on Canada-US Automotive Agreement, August 23–24, 1973,' 29 August 1973, DFAIT, 37-7-1-USA-2, vol. 32.

109 John C. Leary (U.S. embassy, Ottawa) to Roger A. Bull (EA), 31 January 1974; S.S. Reisman to the minister, 'Note on the Discussions in Washington, February 4–5, 1974 on the Automotive Agreement,' 8 February 1974; A.E. Ritchie to Mitchell Sharp, 'Memorandum for the Minister: Meeting with Dr. Kissinger, Automotive Agreement,' 8 February 1974; G.E. Shannon (deputy director, Commercial Policy Decision, EA), to deputy minister, 'Automotive Agreement,' 7 February 1974. All in DFAIT, 37-7-1-USA-2, vol. 33.

110 Washington to Ottawa, 'Senate Finance Committee Hearings on Trade: Canada/USA Automotive Agreement,' 4 March 1974, DFAIT, 37-7-1-USA-2, vol. 33.

111 Canadian Consulate, Detroit, to undersecretary of state for external affairs, 'President Gerald R. Ford,' 7 August 1974, DFAIT, 37-7-1-USA-2, vol. 33.

112 Geoffrey Stevens, 'Canada-US Relations,' G&M, 27 September 1974.

113 R.K. Joyce to T.K. Shoyama, 'US Actions re: Automobiles,' 13 August
     1975, LAC, RG 19, vol.5959, file 8705-08-16, pt. 9; United States Interna-
     tional Trade Commission, *Report on the United States-Canadian Automobile
     Agreement: Its History, Terms and Impact*, 9.
114 Senator Vance Hartke to President G. Ford, 29 January 1976, GFL, L. Wil-
     liam Seidman Papers, box 47, file: 'Senator Vance Hartke'; John Picton,
     'US Call for Major Overhaul of Auto Pact Likely after Critical Study,'
     G&M, 26 January 1976.
115 See, for example, Brent Scowcroft, 'Memorandum for the President: US-
     Canadian Relations,' 7 January 1976, GFL, NSA, Presidential Country
     Files for Europe and Canada, box 2, file: 'Canada and Memorandum of
     Conversation, President Ford and Prime Minister Trudeau,' 16 June 1976;
     ibid., box 3, file: 'Canada.'
116 'Memorandum for the President: Visit of Canadian Prime Minister Tru-
     deau,' Kissinger to Nixon, 4 December 1971, NARA, Nixon Presidential
     Files, National Security Council Files, VIP Visits, box 912.
117 ITC, 'General Motors Corporation Statement on the Automotive Products
     Trade Act of 1965,' 11 December 1975, LAC, RG 19, vol. 5959, file 8705-08-
     16, pt. 9, 13–14; Ken Romain, 'US Car Industry Defends Auto Pact at ITC
     Hearings,' *G&M*, 12 December 1975.
118 Ibid.
119 McKeough's 1978 speech in Chatham, where he declared that Canada
     needed a fair share of investment, was even looked upon favourably
     by the UAW. Ontario, *Debates*, 2 April 1976, 1130 (Darcy McKeough,
     Chatham-Kent); 'McKeough Sounds off on Auto Pact,' *Solidarity Canada*,
     5, no. 4 (1978): 12.
120 Campbell Stuart (chairman, Auto Task Force), 'Options Paper,' 9 October
     1980, LAC, RG 19, vol. 5959, file 8705-03, pt. 3, 1.
121 Cliff Barwick, 'To All Heads of Councils in the Cities of Ontario,' 24 June
     1977, LAC, RG 19, vol. 5959, file 8705-08-16, pt. 9.
122 Editorial, 'Car Wars,' *G&M*, 4 August 1978.
123 'Canada Set to Review US Auto Pact,' *Washington Post*, 6 March 1980.
124 Roger Croft, 'Auto Pact Criticism Wrong, Car Industry Spokesman Says,'
     TS, 14 December 1977; Ontario, *Debates*, 12 June 1979, 2867 (Larry Gross-
     man, St Andrew-St Paul).
125 United States Department of Commerce (Charles R. Weaver), *Impact of
     Environmental, Energy and Safety Regulations, and of the Emerging Market
     Factors upon the US Sector of the North American Auto Industry*; C.D. Arthur
     and Associates, *Canadian Automotive Task Force Review of the North Ameri-
     can Auto Industry* (Ottawa, 1977).
126 This government-owned entity would replace the Auto Adjustment As-

sistance Board, which had ceased operations after 1972, having given out approximately $125 million in loans, according to the APMA. It would provide direct loans to auto-parts manufacturers for tooling, expansion, and R&D, with an eye towards improving efficiency and performance and boosting innovation. The idea never materialized. APMA, 'The Automotive Investment Corporation: A Program for Investment and Job Creation in the Independent Automotive Parts Industry,' 1977, various pages.

127 Ontario, *Canada's Share of the North American Auto Industry* (Toronto, 1978); Ken Romain, 'Ontario Auto Market Study Finds Canada Is Not Getting Fair Share,' *G&M*, 28 April 1978.

128 Hurter and Staley, 'Opportunities for Canadian Research and Development Directed toward the Needs of the North American Auto Market.'

129 René Lévesque et al. to Joe Clark, 3 June 1979, LAC, RG 20, file 4954-1, vol. 2, May 1974–December 1979, 476.

130 N.B. Macdonald, speech to Science Council of Canada, 'Opportunities in Canadian Transportation Conference,' 17–18 May 1979, LAC, RG 20, file 4954-1, vol. 1, 100.

131 Robert Hunter to Zbigniew Brzesinksi, 'Meeting with Ivan Head on February 21–23 Visit of Prime Minister Trudeau,' 10 February 1977, JCL, WHCF, box CO 14, file CO 28, 20 January 1977–20 January 1981.

132 Emphasis in original. Stu Eizenstat, 'Annual Report on the Operation of the Automotive Products Trade Act of 1965,' 21 November 1977, JCL, WHCF, Subject Files, box TA-30, file TA 5, 1 October 1977–31 December 1977.

133 'Summary of Meeting with USA Officials on Performance and Future of Canada-USA Automotive Trade,' 21 September 1978, and 'Canada-US Auto Industry Consultations, Friday December 8, 1978, Washington, DC,' LAC, RG 19, vol. 5958, file 8705-02, fp2.

134 Industry Analysis Branch, Policy Planning, IT&C, 'Re-Negotiation of the Canada-United States Automotive Products Agreement,' May 1979, LAC, RG 19, vol. 5348, file 3881-02, pt. 4, 17.

135 Pierre Trudeau to Jimmy Carter, 1978, LAC, RG 19, vol. 5348, file 3881-05, pt. 1; Reisman, *The Canadian Automotive Industry*; 'Detailed Response by the Federal Government to the Recommendations of the Reisman Commission of Inquiry into the Canadian Automotive Industry,' March 1979, LAC, RG 20, file 4956-1, vol. 2, February 1977–28 August 1980.

136 Roy Culpepper to file, 'Meeting with Aftermarket Parts Advisory Council, Toronto, December 17, 1980,' 18 December 1980; Mel Cappe to file, 'Meeting with Automotive Parts Manufacturing Association, January 15, 1981,' 26 January 1981; Campbell Stuart to file, 'Meeting of the APMA

Board of Directors with the Hon. Herb Bray, 26 January, 1981,' 28 January 1981. All in LAC, RG 19, vol. 5738, file 3881-02, pt. 13.

137 This view was presaged by the *G&M* in its editorial 'Stuck in the Slow Lane,' 18 April 1980; Campbell Stuart (chairman, Auto Task Force), 'Options Paper,' 9 October 1980, LAC, RG 19, vol 5959, file 8705-03, pt. 3, 4. The task force caused some internal bickering within IT&C, since some officials felt it was overstepping its bounds. In September 1980 D.W.C. McEwan, the chief of the Motor Vehicles Division, complained to Vehicle Directorate Director I.R. Craig that, if the task force continued to take on work that McEwan thought was beyond its purview, 'the need for a MVD and a Vehicle Directorate could be redundant.' D.W.C. McEwan to I.R. Craig, 'Automotive,' 2 September 1980, LAC, RG 20, file 4956-1, vol. 3, August 1980–December 1980.

138 Campbell Stuart, 'Abrogation Scenario,' 4 February 1981, LAC, RG 19, vol. 5738, file 3881-02, pt. 13, 2.

139 Bill Shields, 'Gray to Seek "Fair Share" in Autopact Negotiations,' *WS*, 24 June 1980; director general, Transportation Industries Branch (M. Brennan), to file, 'Summary of Discussions between Hon. Herb Gray & Executives of American Motors & GM-Detroit, June 23, 1980,' 3 July 1980, LAC, RG 20, file 4954-1, vol. 2, May 1974–December 1979, 774; H. Solomon, 'Gray Idles Motor on Auto Pact Talks,' *FP*, 5 July 1980.

140 External Affairs to Washington, 'CDA/USA Auto Consults, NAmerican Aspects,' 2 July 1980; Campbell Stuart to Canadian delegation, 'USA Automotive Consultations,' 7 August 1980; Campbell Stuart (chairman, Automotive Task Force), 'US-Canada Automotive Consultations,' 13 February 1981. All in LAC, RG 19, vol. 5738, file 3881-02, pt. 13, 3. See also M.S. Wodinsky, 'Automotive Issues: Auto Pact,' March 1981, LAC, RG 19, vol. 5738, file 3881-02, pt. 14; Herb Gray to various ministers, 'Automotive: International Issues,' 11 June 1980, LAC, RG 20, file 4956-1, vol. 2, February 1977–28 August 1980.

141 'Automotive Industry Issues,' 19 October 1979, LAC, RG 19, vol. 5959, file 8705-03, pt. 3.

142 Campbell Stuart to file, 'Meeting of Ministers Gray and Lumley with U.S. Special Trade Representative Brock and Secretary of Commerce Baldridge,' 13 March 1981, LAC, RG 19, vol. 5738, file 3881-02, pt. 14.

6 Schism: The Canadian UAW and the End of Auto Worker Internationalism

1 The focus on the nationalism of White and the CAW can be seen in articles such as High, '"I'll Wrap the F*#@ Canadian Flag around Me,"' and

in films such as Sturla Gunnarson's *Final Offer* (NFB, 1985) and Laszlo Barna's *No Looking Back* (CAW, 1988).

2 For other views on the union and its evolution, see: Roberts, 'Harnessing Competition?'; Duff, 'The Transformation of the Canadian Labour Movement from International to National Union Dominance'; Gindin, *The Canadian Auto Workers*; Holmes, *The Break-Up of an International Labour Union*; Yates, 'Public Policy and Canadian and American Autoworkers'; Yates, *From Plant to Politics*.

3 For a view of White's vision of the union, see his ghost-written autobiography, *Hard Bargains*, especially chapter 12. White's statement that 'I'm hopeful that we can work out a relationship with Quebec which means that we establish a different structure in our country where Quebec is part of that country' reflected his embrace of asymmetrical federalism, but he also understood Quebecers' decision to elect the separatist René Lévesque: 'Had I been in Quebec at that time, I would have voted for him.' The Canadian UAW created a Quebec Council and publicly called for an accommodation for Quebec's political distinctiveness. 'Interview with Bob White, UAW Canadian Director,' *Solidarity Canada*, 5, no. 4 (1978): 6–7.

4 On the union in this period, see Barnard, *American Vanguard*; Lichtentstein, *Walter Reuther*. Also see Sugiman, *Labour's Dilemma*.

5 GM, however, did not recognize Local 222 until 1942. Burt was not always an ally of Reuther's but became so in the 1940s and 1950s. Wells, 'The Impact of the Postwar Compromise on Canadian Unionism'; Abella, ed., *On Strike*.

6 Goldenburg and Bairstow, *Domination or Independence?* For the UAW in this period, see Anastakis, 'Between Nationalism and Continentalism.'

7 Yates argues that 'the particular collective identity and organizational structure of the Canadian UAW, combined with the survival of a left-wing opposition, prevented the full demobilization of the union once the regulatory system had become entrenched.' Yates, *From Plant to Politics*, 19. On post-war international unions operating in Canada, see Abella, 'The Role of the Unions'; Crispo, *International Unionism*; Dawes, *The Relative Decline of International Unionism in Canada since 1970*.

8 Palmer, *Canada's 1960s*, especially chapter 7.

9 'UAW Proposes Probe of Jobless Causes,' *G&M*, 4 April 1960; 'How Canadians Can Get a Made-in-Canada Car They Want and Can Afford,' 5 July 1960, LAC, Royal Commission on the Automobile Industry, RG 33/45, vol. 4, file 33, UAW, 2, 4, 7, 8; George Burt to Vincent Bladen, 1 November 1960, LAC, RG, 33/45, no. 18, file 33a, Confidential Correspondence, UAW.

10 'Submission of Local 444 UAW-AFL-CIO to the Royal Commission on the

Automotive and Parts Industries,' October 1960, LAC, RG 33/45, no. 29, Local 444.

11 Knowlton Nash, 'Claim Canada Provides "Grant": One Word Could Kill Our Auto Export Plan,' and Clive Baxter, 'And It May Blast Canada-US Labor Apart,' *FP*, 13 June 1964.

12 George Burt to Walter Reuther, 29 June 1964, and leaflet, 'R*E*B*E*L, The Other Side of the Story: UAW International Treason,' by Trevelyn Brown, WRL, Walter P. Reuther Papers, box 49.

13 For a good discussion of the 'precariousness' of the Canadian UAW's position on the auto pact in this period, see also Roy, 'Support Pending,' 124.

14 Manley, 'Communists and Autoworkers'; Abella, *Nationalism, Communism, and Canadian Labour*.

15 'Resolution #1,' submitted by Local 444, 1969, LAC, CAW Papers, vol. 8, file 4; Dennis McDermott to Walter Reuther, 18 February 1970, LAC, CAW Papers, vol. 8, file 7.

16 'Pre-Convention IEB Meeting,' 31 May 1980, WRL, International Executive Board Papers (IEB), box 24.

17 Wilfrid List, 'UAW's Mod, Aggressive McDermott Stresses Union's Social Focus,' *G&M*, 17 April 1970, as quoted in Barna, *No Looking Back*.

18 *Solidarity Canada* later called it 'a move out of the shadow of Detroit.' 'The UAW-Canada: A Proud History,' Special Issue of *Solidarity Canada*, fall 1985, 30.

19 'On Increasing Canadian Content in *Solidarity*,' 14 January 1969, LAC, CAW Papers, vol. 8, file 6.

20 In his statement inaugurating the new Canadian paper, UAW International President Leonard Woodcock admitted that the Canadian situation reflected 'special problems,' which was 'why … the Canadian section of our own Union has the right of autonomous decision on Canadian matters.' Leonard Woodcock, 'Your New Paper," *Solidarity Canada*, 1, no. 1 (1973): 1.

21 'Call Spurs Greater Identity on Canadian Side of UAW,' *Solidarity Canada*, 1, no. 1 (1973): 1.

22 McDermott pushed the Waffle out of the union and helped to do so in the NDP as well. See Palmer, *Canada's 1960s*, 294. On the Waffle, see R. Hackett, 'Pie in the Sky: A History of the Ontario Waffle,' *Canadian Dimension*, 15 (October/November, 1980): 1–72; Bullen, 'The Ontario Waffle and the Struggle for an Independent Socialist Canada'; Yates, *From Plant to Politics*, 150.

23 'Call Spurs Greater Identity on Canadian side of UAW,' *Solidarity Canada*, 1, no. 1 (1973): 1; Roberts, 'Harnessing Competition?' 555–7.

24 Some saw wage parity as creating greater problems of inequality and productivity, however. See John Crispo, 'Wage Parity Gains Costly for Other Canadians: Economist,' *TS*, 16 November 1973. On the Chrysler agreement, see Blake, 'Multinational Corporation, International Union and International Collective Bargaining.'

25 When it came to national health care, the UAW in the United States had pushed for the idea but had been unsuccessful. In 1975 Woodcock stated that 'some labour costs are lower because Canada has a good national health insurance program, which we ... unfortunately do not' have. Leonard Woodcock, 'Statement to the ITC, 11 December, 1975,' LAC, CAW Papers, vol. 173, file 3.

26 Wilfrid List, 'UAW Director Leading Move by Canada's International Union Leaders for More Autonomy,' *G&M*, 28 February 1973; 'Call Spurs Greater Identity on Canadian Side of UAW,' *Solidarity Canada*, 1, no. 1 (1973): 1.

27 Committee to Regain Our Canadian Contract, 'For a Canadian Contract,' n.d., WRL, UAW-Chrysler Collection, box 20, file 17.

28 UAW press release, 'Canadian Chrysler Workers Vote to Continue under an International Agreement,' 14 May 1973, WRL, UAW-Chrysler Collection, box 20, folder 17.

29 Wilfrid List, 'Thirty-and-Out Remains a Dream for Most Auto Workers,' *G&M*, 25 July 1973; 'UAW/Chrysler Reach Tentative Agreement,' *WA*, 24 September 1973, 307; 'Chrysler Canada Workers: "Love That 1973 Pattern!"' *Solidarity Canada*, 1, no. 3 (1973): 1.

30 Douglas Fraser to 'All Chrysler Local Union Leadership in Local 444, Canada,' and 'IEB Statement on US-Canadian Auto Trade,' 24 September 1975, WRL, UAW-Chrysler Collection, box 20, file 16; National Ford Council, 'Statement on US-Canadian Solidarity, 19–20 August 1976, 34–12, WRL, UAW Ford Collection, pt. 2, box 34, file: 'Canada, Negotiations, 1976'; Bogdan Kipling, 'UAW Claims Canada Hurting US Auto Market, Unemployment,' *Ottawa Citizen*, 20 August 1975, 16; 'Canadian Cars Included in US Dumping Probe,' *TS*, 10 September 1975.

31 Leonard Woodcock, 'Statement to the ITC, 11 December, 1975'; and Leonard Woodcock to Will E. Leonard, Jr (chairman, ITC), 9 January 1976. Both in LAC, CAW Papers, vol. 173, file 3.

32 Robert White to Auto Tariff Committee, 19 October 1978, and Douglas Fraser to Robert Strauss (USTR), 28 August 1978, LAC, CAW Papers, vol., 298, pt. 1 of 2, file 13, 'Auto Tariff Committee Correspondence.'

33 'UAW to President-Elect Ronald Reagan,' 22 December 1980, WRL, Douglas Fraser Papers, box 54, folder 25.

34 Sam Gindin to Robert White and Basil Hargrove, 'Ford-UAW Joint Presentation on Import Restrictions,' 4 March 1981, SGP, binder 1981.

35 UAW Canada's Phil Bennett, as quoted in Wilfrid List, 'Canadian Conflict over Concessions: Car Union Won't Drive Backward,' *G&M*, 16 April 1982.

36 'Elected Unanimously: White Heads up Canadian UAW,' and 'Robert "Bob" White,' *Solidarity Canada*, 5, no. 3 (1978): 6, 7. See White, *Hard Bargains*, chapter 6.

37 'State of Our Union, 1978,' n.d., LAC, CAW Papers, vol. 255, file 3; Sam Gindin to Basil Hargrove, Robert White, and Robert Nickerson, 'UAW Lay-Offs,' 12 January 1982, SGP, binder 1982.

38 Hyde, *Riding the Roller Coaster*; Sam Gindin to Robert White and Basil Hargrove, 'Chrysler Canada – General Notes,' 17 July 1979, LAC, CAW Papers, vol. 254, file 8; Gordon Legge, 'How Chrysler Canada Roared Past Ford,' *TS*, 7 January 1976.

39 As quoted in Barna, *No Looking Back*.

40 The union called a special meeting to discuss Iacocca's plea on 9 August, where it rejected the plan and decided that it would wait until an agreement was made with Ford and GM. Sam Gindin, 'The Crisis at Chrysler – Confidential,' 8 August 1979, LAC, CAW Papers, vol. 254, file 9, 1, 5–6; 'Report of UAW Director for Canada and International Vice President, Robert White,' 8 and 9 September 1979, LAC, CAW Papers, vol. 296, file 4; 'International UAW Chrysler Council Response to Chrysler Corporation's Proposal of August 3, 1979,' 9 August 1979, WRL, UAW-Chrysler Collection, box 11, folder 29.

41 As noted in chapter 4, there were some discussions about the possibility of the federal and Ontario governments taking an equity position in Chrysler Canada as well. Sam Gindin made the case that partial government ownership or a loan bailout was a 'step towards socialism' which could placate critics in the union movement and the NDP who saw these options as either a form of business unionism or a full-scale capitulation to capitalism. Sam Gindin, 'The Crisis at Chrysler – Confidential,' 8 August 1979, LAC, CAW Papers, vol. 254, file 9, 1, 5–6; 'UAW Proposal regarding a Government Equity Position in Chrysler,' 3 August 1979, WRL, UAW-Chrysler Collection, box 11, folder 29.

42 Sam Gindin to Robert White, Basil Hargrove, and Robert Nickerson, 'Notes for Government Meetings on Chrysler (Confidential),' 20 August 1979, LAC, CAW Papers, vol. 254, file 8.

43 Director's report, Canadian UAW Council, 16 and 17 September 1978, WRL, UAW Ford Collection, pt. 2, box 53, file 53-16.

44 'Proceedings of Special Session, IEB UAW,' 30 August 1979, WRL, IEB Papers, box 23, file 30, August 1979.

45 John Deverell, 'How Ford and GM Workers Won Royal Deal,' *TS*, 7 November 1979.

46 At one point, the union's main antagonist on the issue, Senator Richard Luger (R-Indiana), had demanded an additional US$800 million in concessions, which the UAW negotiated down to over $400 million. In the words of the union's point person on the congressional negotiations, Lugar 'adopted the position which, at the various times, constituted the worst possible treatment of the workers.' Howard Paster to Douglas Fraser, Marc Stepp, and Dallas Sells, 'Senator Lugar and the Chrysler Negotiation,' 10 January 1980, WRL, Douglas Fraser Papers, box 51, folder 51–7; UAW press release, 'Canadian UAW Turns Down Wage-Freeze for Chrysler Workers,' 3 December 1979, LAC, CAW Papers, vol. 254, file 8.

47 Douglas Fraser, 'To All Members at Chrysler-US,' 8 January 1980, WRL, UAW-Chrysler, box 11, folder: 'Bailout.'

48 Some more militant members of the UAW insisted that workers 'fight Fraser's sell out' and that 'the Chrysler Council must reject any concession and demand a policy to defend both jobs and wages.' Revolutionary Autoworkers Committee, 'Fight the Bailout Scheme,' n.d. WRL, Douglas Fraser Papers, box 51, folder 51–7; Statement of the Workers League, 'No Concessions to Chrysler! No Talks with Reagan! Build a Labor Party!' n.d., WRL, Fraser Papers, box 15, folder 18; R. Milkman, 'The Anti-Concessions Movement in the UAW: Interview with Doug Stevens,' *Socialist Review*, 65 (September/October, 1982): 19–42.

49 'Canada's Position on the Chrysler Concessions,' *Solidarity Canada*, December/January 1979/80), 5–6.

50 Fraser said in a later IEB meeting, 'I felt that this was a voluntary association, but we rationalized a way so that the Canadians would not have to make the concessions, as did the Americans. As Marc [Stepp] knows, and as I think Bob knows, much to the chagrin of the committee, whom I argued with, I had an argument with Marc, but I thought there we were being sensitive to the Canadian problems though we really didn't have any right to do it.' 'Proceedings of Regular Session, IEB,' 7–9 June 1982 (hereafter Proceedings, 1982), 45; and 'Why Chrysler Canada Workers Could Not Agree to U.S. Government Demands for Further Contract Concessions,' Local 444 *News*, 11 January 1980. Both in WRL, UAW-Chrysler, box 11, folder: 'Bailout.'

51 Mark Lett, 'Split in Solidarity House,' *Detroit News*, 8 January 1980, as quoted in Barna, *No Looking Back*. See also White, *Hard Bargains*, 163.

52 UAW press release, 'UAW and Chrysler Corp. Reach Tentative Agreement on Modification of Current Contracts Covering U.S. Chrysler Workers,' 5 January 1980; and Douglas Fraser, Marc Stepp, and Joe Zappa to William

M. O'Brien (vice-president employment and industrial relations, Chrysler), 5 January 1980. Both in LAC, CAW Papers, vol. 254, file 17. See also Douglas Fraser, 'To All Members at Chrysler-US,' 8 January 1980, WRL, UAW-Chrysler, box 11, folder: 'Bailout.'

53 John Deverell, 'Face to Face on the Split,' *TS*, 8 December 1984.

54 Sam Gindin to Robert White, Basil Hargrove, and Robert Nickerson, 'Chrysler & the Wage Freeze in the US,' 11 December 1979, LAC, CAW Papers, vol. 254, file 8.

55 Advertisement, Local 444, 'Chrysler Canada Workers Had No Alternative!' *WS*, 15 January 1980; editorials, 'UAW Communications Breakdown' and 'UAW: Canadian Wing Flies Solo,' *WS*, 5 and 14 January 1980.

56 Lilian Zirwas to Robert White, 12 February 1980, LAC, CAW Papers, vol. 256, file 9.

57 Paul Delean, 'UAW Members in U.S. Glare across Border: These People Are Mad …,' *WS*, 16 January 1980.

58 Local 212 to National UAW Council, 8 January 1980, LAC, CAW Papers, vol. 254, file 8; Jim O'Neil to Marc Stepp, 'Local 212's Central Transportation Unit Claiming That Canadian Jobs at 21st Street (Jefferson Terminal) Should Belong to Them Instead of Local 444,' 18 April 1980, WRL, UAW-Chrysler, box 20, file 12; James Daw, 'Ottawa Aid Concerns Chrysler Boss More Than Workers' Tiff,' *TS*, 10 January 1980; 'New Crack Developing within UAW,' *G&M*, 10 January 1980.

59 Joe Zappa, 'USA Workers Betrayed,' *Voice of Local 212*, 2, no. 2 (1980): 1; Edwin G. Pipp, 'Zappa Says Chrysler Used Union,' *Detroit Free Press*, 18 March 1980.

60 LaSorda's son, Tom, would go on to become Chrysler's CEO in 2007, leaving the company in 2009 when it came out of bankruptcy proceedings. Frank LaSorda to Douglas Fraser, 31 March 1980, and Fraser to LaSorda, 11 April 1980, WRL, UAW-Chrysler, box 20, file 12.

61 John Deverell, 'Face to Face on the Split,' *TS*, 8 December 1984.

62 As quoted in Barna, *No Looking Back*.

63 On the Houdaille and other plant sit-ins in this period, see High, *Industrial Sunset*, 181–91; Robert White to IEB members, 22 September 1980, 'Proceedings of the Regular Session of the IEB,' 22–25 September 1980, WRL, UAW, IEB, box 24.

64 Frank LaSorda to Marc Stepp, 24 October 1980, LAC, CAW Papers, vol. 255, file 7.

65 Andrew Marocko to Robert White, 'Report on UAW Chrysler International Council Meeting at San Antonio, 1–5 December, 1980,' 19 December 1980; and Jim O'Neill to Robert White, 'Meeting with Marc Stepp and Canadian

Chrysler Council Delegates regarding the Chrysler International Agreement on December 1, 1980 in San Antonio, Texas,' 22 December 1980. Both in LAC, CAW Papers, vol. 255, file 7.

66 Chrysler had backpedalled on its promise to build the K-Car in Canada, and until the Canadian government protested (at the behest of the UAW), it intended to build only vans and the new mini-vans in Canada. This would likely have put the company in violation of the auto pact, though it had already missed its targets for 1979–81. 'National and Area Staff Reports to the Canadian UAW Council,' 13 and 14 June 1981, LAC, CAW Papers, vol. 296, file 1; 'Attention Canadian UAW Chrysler Workers: Referendum Vote,' n.d., WRL, UAW-Chrysler, box 20, file 10.

67 'Attention Canadian UAW Chrysler Workers: Referendum Vote,' n.d., WRL, UAW-Chrysler, box 20, file 10.

68 News from the UAW (press release), 'Canadian Chrysler Workers Vote to Withdraw from International Contract and Negotiate a Separate Pact in 1982,' 18 November 1981, WRL, UAW-Ford Collection, box 49, file 4; and 'National and Area Staff Reports to UAW Council,' 30 and 31 January 1982, 56. Both in LAC, CAW Papers, vol. 296. Also, 'Chrysler Canada to Negotiate Own Pact,' *G&M*, 19 November 1981.

69 'UAW Authorizes Talks on Chrysler Concessions,' *G&M*, 23 December 1980; John Deverell, 'Auto Workers: A Union Divided,' *TS*, 20 December 1981.

70 'Proceedings of Regular Session of the IEB,' 8–10 December 1981, WRL, IEB, box 25, 30, 84.

71 Ted O'Connor and Ted Murphy (Local 222) to 'All Local Presidents, Secretaries, Chairpersons, etc.,' 6 January 1982, and Jack Tubman (Local 397) to Douglas Fraser, 14 January 1982, WRL, IEB, box 25; 'Report of UAW Director and International Vice President Robert White,' 30 and 31 January 1982, LAC, CAW Papers, box 296; David Crane, 'Pressure Is Mounting on Canadian UAW Members,' *TS*, 13 February 1982; Neil Loutit, 'No Concessions Mean Fewer Jobs: GM Exec,' *TS*, 23 March 1982; Robert Stephens, 'Canadian UAW Defies US Leaders to Oppose Wage, Benefit Cutbacks,' *G&M*, 1 February 1982.

72 'IEB Meeting, Palmer House Hotel, Chicago, Illinois,' 7 January 1982, WRL, IEB, box 25, 21.

73 'Report of UAW Director and International Vice President Robert White,' 30 and 31 January 1982, LAC, CAW Papers, box 296, 24.

74 Ibid.

75 'Resolution for May, 1982 Convention, Concessions,' 8 March 1982, SGP, binder 1982; 'Labor to Hold Line against Wage Cutbacks,' *G&M*, 15 December 1981.

76 Proceedings, 1982, 42, 44, 47; 'Why Concessions Won't Work,' *Solidarity Canada*, Special Edition, February 1982, 6–7.

77 Proceedings, 1982, 51–5.

78 Ibid., 55.

79 Ibid., 60.

80 Proceedings, 1982, 58.

81 John Deverell, 'High-Paid Canadian Autoworkers Won't Be Driven into Concessions,' *TS*, 15 July 1982.

82 Proceedings, 1982, 62.

83 The Canadian GM contract was different from the U.S. contract in that it had wage increases but scrapped some paid personal holidays, which White was criticized for. Wilfrid List, 'GM, UAW Get Tentative Pact,' *G&M*, 15 September 1982.

84 'Canadian UAW Council, Report of UAW Director for Canada and International Vice President, Robert White,' 27–28 November 1982, LAC, CAW Papers, vol. 296 (hereafter, November Report), 12.

85 Sam Gindin to Robert White, 'Chrysler Negotiations,' 15 October 1982, CAW Archives and Library, binder: 'Chrysler Negotiations, 1985.'

86 Wilfrid List, 'Wildcat Strike Shuts Chrysler Plant,' *G&M*, 7 October 1982; 'Proceedings of Regular Session of IEB,' 13–15 December 1982, WRL, IEB, box 26, 27.

87 John Deverell, 'Chrysler's Future at Stake as 10,000 Walk Out,' *TS*, 5 November 1982; 'Canadian UAW Strikes Chrysler, US Bargainers Return to Table,' *Labor Notes*, 23 November 1982, 3.

88 Author's interview with Ed Lumley, 28 May 2008.

89 Sam Gindin to Robert White, 'Labour Costs, Chrysler,' 22 October 1982, SGP, binder 1982.

90 November Report, 33.

91 Wilfrid List, 'Chrysler Salary Offer Rejected by Union, Called "Insignificant,"' *G&M*, 7 December 1982; Barna, *No Looking Back*.

92 November Report, 38.

93 Editorial, 'Chrysler's Too High Stakes,' *TS*, 7 November 1982.

94 Richard Rohmer, 'The Day Chrysler Went Bankrupt,' *TS*, 30 November 1982.

95 After a one-year deal between the Canadian workers and the company (the U.S. side signed a two-year deal), wage parity was eventually achieved in the 1983 round of negotiations. John Deverell, 'Chrysler's $1-Plus Offer May Mean Union Victory,' *TS*, 10 December 1982; Ian Austen, 'The UAW's Double Victory,' *Maclean's*, 19 September 1983, 41–2; Sam Gindin to Claude Ducharme, 'Concessions,' 6 June 1984, SGP, binder 1984; White, *Hard Bargains*, 237–9.

96 'Proceedings of Regular Session of IEB,' 13–15 December 1982, 29–30, WRL, IEB, box 26.

97 'The Inside Story of the 1984 Auto Talks,' *Solidarity Canada*, spring 1985, 2–5 at 3.

98 Ford and Chrysler Canada also had recorded profits in 1983. Sam Gindin to Robert White, Basil Hargrove, et al., 'GM Canada Profits,' 20 February 1984, SGP, binder 1984.

99 Sam Gindin to front office et al., 'Employment, Big Three,' 29 February 1984, SGP, binder 1984.

100 Sam Gindin to Robert White, 'Chrysler Negotiations,' 20 July 1983, CAW Archives and Library, binder: 'Chrysler Negotiations, 1985.'

101 'The Inside Story of the 1984 Auto Talks,' *Solidarity Canada*, spring 1985, 2.

102 John Deverell, 'GM Canada Set to Bargain,' *TS*, 29 September 1984.

103 'GM Is Canada Strike Target,' *NYT*, 30 September 1984.

104 As quoted in Barna, *No Looking Back*.

105 John Deverell, 'GM Oshawa Workers Jump Gun on Noon Strike Deadline,' *TS*, 17 October 1984; 'Canadian UAW Council, Report of UAW Director for Canada and International Vice President, Robert White,' 1–2 December 1984, 19, CAW Archives and Library.

106 John Deverell, 'Canadian Auto Strike Is Really a Political Battle,' *TS*, 25 October 1984.

107 Cathryn Motherwell, 'Strike Ripples Bring First Layoffs,' *G&M*, 20 October 1984.

108 Editorial, 'An Untimely Auto Strike,' *TS*, 18 October 1984; 'GM Strikes a Deal in Canada,' *Time*, 5 November 1984; James Daw, 'Strike Could Cost GM $200 Million a Week,' *TS*, 23 October 1984.

109 John Deverell, 'Face to Face on the Split,' *TS*, 8 December 1984.

110 As quoted in Barna, *No Looking Back*; for a view of the strike and settlement, see Benedict, 'The 1984 GM Agreement in Canada.'

111 'The Inside Story of the 1984 Auto Talks,' *Solidarity Canada*, spring 1985, 5.

112 'UAW Vice President Bob White – Press Conference,' 1 November 1984, WRL, Owen Bieber Papers, vol. 10, file 2, 1, 6; John Deverell, 'White Considers Setting up Separate Canadian Auto Union,' *TS*, 1 November 1984; Lorne Slotnick, 'UAW Head Denies Split by Canada from Union,' *G&M*, 2 November 1984; Brian McAndrew, 'High-Level Pressure Exist to Split UAW, Canadian Chief Says,' *TS*, 2 November 1984; White, *Hard Bargains*, 279–80.

113 Mike Pettapiece, 'Made-in-Canada Pacts Blunt UAW Separation Talk,' *Hamilton Spectator*, 2 November 1984.

114 'UAW Vice President Bob White – Press Conference,' 1 November 1984, WRL, Owen Bieber Papers, vol. 10, file 2, 1; Marty Beneteau, 'White

Denies UAW Split, but …,' *WS*, 2 November 1984; Peter Howell, 'Rift in UAW Played Down,' *Toronto Sun*, 2 November 1984.

115 Canadian UAW Council, 'Report of UAW Director for Canada and International Vice President, Robert White,' 1–2 December 1984, 22, 33–4, 38, CAW Archives and Library.

116 'UAW Canada Press Release,' 1 December 1984, WRL, Owen Bieber Papers, vol. 10, file 2.

117 Ann M. Job, 'UAW Faces Showdown in Canada,' *Detroit News*, 2 December 1984; Marty Beneteau, 'Local Union Chieftains Back Pullout,' *WS*, 3 December 1984; John Deverell, 'Auto Workers Threaten Split,' *TS*, 2 December 1984.

118 The headline of the *NYT* front-page article by John Holusha read 'UAW in Canada Threatens to Split,' while that of the *Detroit Free Press* read 'UAW Canada Threatening to Secede' (Gerald Volgenau), both 2 December 1984. The *Oshawa Times* saw the demand as an 'ultimatum.' Suzanne Steele, 'Canadian UAW to Demand Independence from Detroit,' 3 December 1984.

119 Leonard Page to Jordan Rossen, 'Division of UAW Assets/Canadian Split,' 5 December 1984, WRL, Owen Bieber Papers, vol. 32, file 1.

120 'Secession from UAW May Have Adverse Impact on Canadian Workers, Former President Warns,' *Daily Labor Report*, no. 244, 19 December 1984.

121 The following section comes from 'Proceedings of Executive Session of IEB,' 10 December, 1984,' a 159-page verbatim transcript of this historic meeting. WRL, Owen Bieber Papers, vol. 32, file 1 (hereafter IEB Proceedings, 10 December). See also White, *Hard Bargains*, 286–90. White had wanted to bring both Bob Nickerson and Hargrove into the meeting, which Bieber refused, allowing only one. The two men flipped a coin, and Hargrove won. White, *Hard Bargains*, 287.

122 IEB Proceedings, 10 December, 42–3.

123 See White's *Hard Bargains* (for instance, the introduction and 263–6) and Sturla Gunnarson's film *Final Offer*.

124 IEB Proceedings, 10 December, 42–3.

125 Ibid., 43–5, 47–8, 130.

126 Ibid., 58.

127 Ibid., 126.

128 Ibid., 70–1.

129 Ibid., 78.

130 Ibid., 81. On the issue of the Canadian membership's support for the White secession initiative, Doug Fraser agreed: 'If Owen had pressed Bob into a referendum on this, Bob would have won by about 85 percent.'

'Secession from UAW May Have Adverse Impact on Canadian Workers, Former President Warns,' *Daily Labor Report*, no. 244, 19 December 1984.
131 Press release, 11 December 1984, WRL, Owen Bieber Papers, vol. 32, file 1.
132 IEB Proceedings, 10 December, 155–7.
133 As quoted in Barna, *No Looking Back*.
134 Lorne Slotnick, 'Canadian UAW Splits from US Parent Union,' *G&M*, 11 December 1984; Suzanne Steel, 'White Announces UAW Split,' *Oshawa Times*, 12 December 1984.
135 Others were much less charitable: the *Toronto Sun* mocked White as a 'mini-Napoleon' and 'Mighty Mouse,' and asked: 'Does Canadian UAW Director Robert White live on the planet Earth? Does he give a damn about jobs for his men?' Editorial, 'Mighty Mouse,' 14 December 1984; Marty Beneteau, 'Local Union Chieftains Back Pullout,' and 'Our Labor "Hero" Taking on US "Bullies,"' *WS*, 3 and 8 December 1984; Gerald Volgeneau, 'Canada's Labor Superstar,' *Detroit Free Press*, 26 November 1984.
136 'Special Canadian UAW Council, Report of Robert White,' 15 December 1984, and Robert White, 'To All Canadian UAW Members,' 10 January 1985, WRL, Owen Bieber Papers, vol. 10, file 2.
137 'PM, Labor Hail Union Split from US Parent,' *TS*, 11 December 1984.
138 Ibid.
139 Doug Williamson, 'Victor Reuther Endorses Canadian UAW's Parting,' *WS*, 12 December 1984.
140 The executive was Thomas Miner, Chrysler vice-president of industrial relations. 'PM, Labor Hail Union Split from US Parent,' *TS*, 11 December 1984; Wilfred List, 'Auto Makers Concerned by UAW Split,' *G&M*, 12 December 1984; editorial, 'Canadian UAW Group on Destructive Path,' *Sarnia Observer*, 4 December 1984.
141 Editorial, 'The UAW Divorce,' *Detroit News*, 12 December 1984.
142 Doug Williamson, 'Victor Reuther Endorses Canadian UAW's Parting,' *WS*, 12 December 1984; Lorne Slotnick, 'UAW Break with US Parent Saddens Steelworkers' Chief,' *G&M*, 13 December 1984.
143 It would be more than a year before the Canadians could officially break from the international, since this required a constitutional amendment by the UAW, finally achieved at its June 1986 convention in Anaheim, California. A few locals also voted to stay in the UAW. Jordan Rossen to Dick Shomemaker, 'Confidential and Privileged: Canadian Situation,' 25 January 1985; 'Special Committee on Canadian Separation,' 20 February 1985; Lennox A. MacLean to Robert White, 'Re: UAW Canada and Mechanisms for Withdrawal of Canadian Membership, Bargaining Rights and Assets from UAW International,' 25 April 1985; Dick Shoemaker to Owen Bieber

and Ray Marjerus, 'Canadian Separation,' 18 July 1985. All in WRL, Owen Bieber Papers, vol. 32, file 1. Also, 'UAW Local Votes to Keep US Links,' *TS*, 24 January 1985.

144 'UAW-Canada: The Foundation Is in Place,' *Solidarity Canada*, winter 1986, 2–5.

145 Owen Bieber and Ray Majerus to Robert White, 4 September 1984, WRL, Owen Bieber Papers, vol. 10, file 2.

146 It is unclear if this letter was sent. 'To Bob White,' 30 September 1985, WRL, Owen Bieber Papers, vol. 12, file 2.

147 John Deverell, 'Face to Face on the Split,' *TS*, 8 December 1984.

148 Yates, *From Plant to Politics*, 5.

149 Speculation in the late 1970s that White could succeed Fraser may have added an extra dimension to the two men's relationship. Doug Fraser felt that White was 'just outstanding' as a leader and his Canadian citizenship did not make a shot at the top job 'insurmountable.' The UAW would give White time to gain American citizenship and acclimatize himself with U.S. issues, if the union elected him. Editorial, 'UAW: True North Autonomy,' *WS*, 4 December 1984; 'Canadian in Position for Top Job,' *G&M*, 12 July 1979.

150 Canadian UAW Council, 'Report of UAW Director for Canada and International Vice President, Robert White,' 1–2 December 1984, 32, CAW Archives and Library.

151 'AW Board Chooses President,' *Labor Notes*, 23 November 1982, 3; Cross, '"We Can Tell Them All to Go to Hell,"' 54.

152 'The Inside Story of the 1984 Auto Talks,' *Solidarity Canada*, spring 1985, 4.

153 After the December IEB meeting, White had 'never seen such a huge press conference in all my life, it was so immense it was scary … in the next week I did 100 interviews.' White, *Hard Bargains*, 290; 'Canadian UAW Council, Report of UAW Director for Canada and International Vice President, Robert White,' 1–2 December, 1984, 23–4, CAW Archives and Library.

154 Wendy Cuthbertson to Robert White, 'Suggested Houdaille Film Project,' 12 September 1980, WRL, IEB, box 24.

155 Dick Shoemaker, 'UAW-Canada, August 27, 1985,' WRL, Owen Bieber Papers, vol. 36, file 1.

156 'The Inside Story of the 1984 Auto Talks,' *Solidarity Canada*, spring 1985, 4.

157 As quoted in Barna, *No Looking Back*.

158 'Special Committee on Canadian Separation,' 20 February 1985, WRL, Owen Bieber Papers, vol. 32, file 1.

159 David Mitchell to Owen Bieber, 'February 20 Meeting of Committee on

Canadian Withdrawal,' 29 January 1985, WRL, Owen Bieber Papers, vol. 32, file 1.

160 Department of Industry, *1983 Report on the Canadian Automobile Industry* (Ottawa, 1984), 34.

161 Sam Gindin to Robert White, 'Combined COLA and 1982 Negotiations,' 30 March 1982; and Sam Gindin to Robert White, 'Combined COLA,' 3 May 1982. Both in SGP, binder 1982.

162 Sam Gindin to Robert White, 'Combined COLA and 1982 Negotiations,' 30 March 1982; Sam Gindin to Robert White, 'Combined COLA,' 3 May 1982; and Sam Gindin to Sheldon Friedman, 'Canada-U.S. Union Tensions,' 4 May 1982. All in SGP, binder 1982.

163 Sam Gindin to Robert White, 'Confidential: COLA-Canadian Formula,' 30 July 1982, SGP, binder 1982; 'Proceedings of Regular Session of IEB,' 20–22 September 1982, WRL, IEB, box 26.

164 Canadian UAW Council, 'Report of UAW Director for Canada and International Vice President, Robert White,' 27–28 November 1982, LAC, CAW Papers, vol. 296, 23.

165 John Deverell, 'Face to Face on the Split,' *TS*, 8 December 1984. For another view of auto workers' earnings, see Ktaz and Meltz, 'Profit Sharing and Auto Workers' Earnings.'

166 Canadian UAW Council, 'Report of UAW Director for Canada and International Vice President, Robert White,' 1–2 December 1984, 18, CAW Archives and Library.

167 Ann M. Job, 'Does Trouble Loom for Bargainers?' *Detroit Free Press*, 11 August 1985.

168 The agreement between the UAW-Canada (not yet officially the CAW) and Chrysler was capped by a private meeting between White and Iacocca in New York City. 'Made-in-Canada Agreement Returns Chrysler Workers to Parity,' *Solidarity Canada*, winter 1986, 23; Hal Quinn, 'Chrysler under Siege,' *Maclean's*, 28 October 1985, 54.

169 Wilfrid List, 'No Guideline Hurdles Seen in Ford Pact,' *G&M*, 7 October 1976.

170 Edward Clifford, 'Canadian Firms Feel US Lockout Impact,' *G&M*, 27 March 1979; 'Chrysler Hit by US Truckers' Lockout,' *G&M*, 5 April 1979.

171 Susan Riley, 'Chrysler Fights another Battle,' *Maclean's*, 14 November 1982, 50.

172 Jennifer Hunter, 'Canadian Strike Would Hurt Chrysler's US Production,' *G&M*, 4 November 1982.

173 On the slow shift in Big Three production processes after 1970, see Rubenstein, *Making and Selling Cars*, especially 3–55.

174 Wilfred List, 'Auto Makers Concerned by UAW Split,' *G&M*, 12 December 1984.
175 Editorial, 'When Brothers Fall Out,' *G&M*, 12 December 1984.
176 Editorial, 'A New Union Treads Warily,' *Oshawa Times*, 14 December 1984.
177 Editorial, 'The UAW Divorce,' *Detroit News*, 12 December 1984.

7 Transplant: 'Foreign' Production, Imports, and the Tumultuous Arrival of the Japanese

1 Perry, *The Future of Canada's Auto Industry*, preface. Perry's study remains one of the few non-government examinations of the Canadian industry in this period.
2 Johnson, *Six Men Who Built the Modern Auto Industry*, 13.
3 For views on the Japanese in North America and the Japan-U.S. automotive relationship, see Yanarella, *The Politics of Industrial Recruitment*; Perrucci, *Japanese Auto Transplants in the Heartland*; Kawahara, *The Origin of Competitive Strength*; Halberstam, *The Reckoning*. On the Canadian relationship with Japanese business, see Wright, *Japanese Business in Canada*.
4 For another view of the import issue, see Langdon, *The Politics of Japanese-Canadian Economic Relations, 1952–83*, 48–52. See also Mordue, 'Government, Foreign Direct Investment, and the Canadian Automotive Industry, 1977–1987.'
5 On Studebaker, see Chritchlow, *Studebaker*; Studebaker Corporation, *Annual Report for 1962*, 16 October 1962, Historical Collections, Baker Library, Harvard Business School. On the Canadian plant, see also Paul Cronkwright, 'Studebaker Canada, 1910–1966,' http://www.thehamilton-chaptersdc.ca (accessed 3 April 2009).
6 'Studebaker Auto Making Ended Except in Canada,' and 'Studebaker Corporation Traces Its Origin Back to 1852 and an Oak-Sided Wagon,' *NYT*, 10 December 1963; 'Canada Applauds Studebaker Move,' *NYT*, 16 December 1963.
7 Robert Growcock (Studebaker Canada) to John P. Robarts, 17 March 1966, AO, RG 3–26, John P. Robarts Papers, box 350, file: January 1966–December 1966.
8 On Volvo in Halifax, see Anastakis, 'Building a "New Nova Scotia"'; Volvo Research Group, 'The Volvo Story in Nova Scotia,' *New Maritimes: A Regional Magazine of Culture and Politics*, 7, no. 5 (1989): 14–23; Sandberg, 'Missing the Road.' On Volvo itself, see Christian Berggren, *The Volvo Experience*; Gyllenhammar, *People at Work*; Lindholm and Norstedt, *The Volvo Report*.

9　'Enthusiasm and Workers,' *Halifax Chronicle-Herald*, 22 February 1963.

10　In August 1945 order-in-council P.C. 5623 modified the 40 per cent content bracket by raising the level to 15,000 units. This was intended to ease the way for Nash (later American) Motors, which planned to begin production in Canada. The order remained in effect until the 1965 tariff changes.

11　Anastakis, 'Building a "New Nova Scotia,"' 6.

12　Robert Joyce to Rodney de C. Gray and Hugh Keenleyside, 2 November 1965, LAC, RG 19, vol. 4620, file 8705-01, pt. 2, January 1965–June 1966.

13　C.M. Drury to K.O. Kohler (Volvo Canada), 23 February 1966, LAC, RG 19, vol. 4844, file 8705-02, pt. 8, 'Auto Agreement,' 1965–8.

14　'Canadian Automotive Activities,' *WA*, 16 October 1972, 325.

15　See Anastakis, 'Building a "New Nova Scotia,"' 27–30.

16　The facility was thereafter the subject of numerous rumours that it would be reopened by either Toyota or Datsun, which never happened. The Quebec government also wooed VW to try to get it to build cars in the plant, but the company refused. 'Canadian Automotive Activities,' *WA*, 14 February 1972, 56, and 16 July 1972, 223; 'Quebec Government Woos Volkswagonwerk,' *WA*, 4 December 1972, 387; 'Canadian Automotive Activities,' *WA*, 12 January 1973, 31.

17　On Bricklin, see Dimitry Anastakis, 'Hubris, Nepotism and Failure: The Bricklin Car Company and the Question of Inevitability,' *BEH Online*, http://www.h-net.org/~business/bhcweb/publications/BEHonline/2010/anastakis.pdf (accessed 15 December 2010).

18　Peter Rasky, 'They Sing Their Company Song: Canada and the New Japan,' *TS*, 28 December 1966.

19　Nova Scotia held a 6 per cent share in the firm, with $1.4 million in CMI debentures. R.S. Brookfield to Industrial Estates Limited Directors, 'Re: CMI,' 29 November 1972, Nova Scotia Archives and Records Management (NSARM), RG 55, vol. 10, file: 'IEL, Canadian Motor Industries, 1973–76.' All NSARM citations below are to this collection.

20　A CKD meant that there was virtually no value added to the basic assembly of the car. Yoshihiko Toura (overseas operations manager, Toyota) to D.W. Salsman (IEL), 19 August 1975, NSARM.

21　Eiji Toyoda to Premier Gerald Regan, 8 August 1975, NSARM.

22　Patrick Fellows, 'Imports Punching Away,' *TS*, 1 April 1967; John Saunders, 'Car Making Isn't Big Business for Little Three,' *TS*, 20 August 1969; Lyndon Watkins, 'Nova Scotia Government Seeks Expansion of Japanese Automotive Output in Province,' *G&M*, 19 February 1972; 'Canadian Automotive Activities,' *WA*, 19 February 1972, 73.

23 'Minutes of the Board of Directors of Canadian Motor Industries,' 19 December 1973. NSARM.

24 Narufumi Yano (president, Toyota-CMI) to George Mitchell (minister of development), 20 November 1975, NSARM.

25 Paradoxically, the more efficient the plant became in terms of labour meant that it needed to boost its Canadian-made parts, which became difficult since there were so few Japanese suppliers in Canada or Canadian firms that could supply CMI. T. Mitsui, CMI, to D.W. McEwan, 11 February 1974, NSARM.

26 Dean W. Salsman to G.M. Mitchell, 5 March 1974, and 2 August 1974, NSARM; Corporate Planning Department, 'Sydney Plant,' 25 July 1974, NSARM.

27 A scheme to bring Magna into the plant to produce parts also failed. Yoshihiko Toura to D.W. Salsman, 4 April 1975, NSARM; Canadian Motor Industries press release, 3 July 1975, NSARM; Ambassador Ross Campbell to George Mitchell, 'CMI-Toyota/Mitsui Meeting with Mr. Eiji Toyoda on Thursday, October 2, 1975,' 2 October 1975, NSARM; 'Efforts to Save CMI Pt. Edward Plant Fail,' *Halifax Chronicle-Herald*, 19 November 1975.

28 D.W. Salsman to G.M. Mitchell, 19 November 1975, NSARM.

29 See Anastakis, 'The Advent of an International Trade Agreement.'

30 Bladen, *Report of the Royal Commission on the Automotive Industry*; Ralph Young, 'Imported Cars Taking Almost 30% of Market,' *FP*, 6 August 1960.

31 See DePoe's report in 'Before the Auto Pact,' CBC Newsmagazine television report, 2 October 1960, http://www.archives.cbc.ca/economy_business/trade_agreements/topics/326/ (accessed 17 August 2010).

32 The monthly sales of imported cars reached nearly 10,000 in July 1961. By August 1962, that number had fallen to less than 4,000. John Saywell, ed., *Canadian Annual Review for 1962* (Toronto, 1963), 221–2.

33 On the VW Beetle's image and impact, see Frank, *The Conquest of Cool*. Hino trucks began sales in 1974; Subaru started in Canada in 1976; Suzuki was established in 1979. Japanese Automotive Manufacturers Association (JAMA) Canada, 'A Short History of the Japanese Auto Industry in Canada,' 9–10. The JAMA document can be seen at http://www.jama.ca/industry/history/ (accessed 5 December 2010).

34 Figures from DesRosiers Automotive Consultants, cited in JAMA Canada, 'A Short History of the Japanese Auto Industry in Canada,' 17; Terry McGrath, 'Imports Speed toward Canada for the Year of the Little Car,' *G&M*, 22 March 1969.

35 'Canadian Automotive Activities,' *WA*, 27 March 1972, 109, and 29 January 1973, 39.

36 The Canadian GATT tariff schedules meant that by 1982 the duty for off-shore imports (non-auto pact) was 12.6 per cent, to be reduced to 9.1 per cent by 1987. Of course, the the auto pact exceptions meant that companies included as bona fide auto pact manufacturers could import duty-free from offshore.

37 In the United States, unlike in Canada where the U.S. companies were considered to be 'domestic,' Canadian cars were sometimes seen as imports, too. In 1972 the UAW filed a petition with the U.S. Tariff Commission to investigate whether Japanese and Canadian imports had reached such proportion as to cause or threaten to cause unemployment in the sector. Washington to Ottawa, 'Adjustment Assistance Petition re: Autos from Cda and Jap,' 21 December 1972, DFAIT, 37-7-1-USA-2, vol. 31; MVMA, *Annual Report* (Detroit, Mich., 1983).

38 Ken Romain, 'Imported Cars Stage Startling Comeback,' *G&M*, 29 February 1980; 'Canada: Import Sales up 67%; Chrysler No. 2; Volvo Prices Rise,' *WA*, 17 March 1980, 38.

39 W.V. Turner (Auto Task Force) to file, 'GM Meeting-Japanese Imports,' 2 February 1981, LAC, RG 19, vol. 5740, file 3881-09, pt. 1.

40 Bob Leone to George Eads (Council of Economic Advisors), 'Auto Import Issues,' 12 November 1980, JCL, Council of Economic Advisors Papers, box 3, file: 'Auto Imports' (1).

41 On the Japanese industry, see Shimokawa, *The Japanese Automobile Industry*, particularly chapters 2 and 3. One of the best insights into Toyota and its production system is by its creator, Taiichi Ohno, *Toyota Production System*. See also Womack, Jones, and Roos, *The Machine That Changed the World*; and Reingold, *Toyota*, 41–65. The *kanban* system was used by Toyota to better synchronize production with demand by ensuring that inventories were as sensitive as possible to production needs. For example, workers signalled their need for more parts through the card system.

42 Shook, *Honda*, 23 and 37.

43 On the Corvair, see Nader, *Unsafe at Any Speed*; on the Pinto, see Birsch and Fiedler, eds., *The Ford Pinto Case*.

44 Ed Finn, 'Swing to Foreign Cars Is Blamed on the Automakers,' *TS*, 12 May 1981; E. Smith, Mississauga, letter to the editor, *TS*, 16 May 1980.

45 The UAW distributed over 100,000 'Buy a Car Your Neighbour Built' flyers by 1982. 'Buy a Car Your Neighbour Built,' *Solidarity Canada*, spring 1982, 13; Bert Weeks to Herb Gray, 4 July 1980, LAC, RG 20, file 4956-1, vol. 2, February 1977–28 August 1980.

46 W.J. Dawson (regional clerk, Niagara) to Herb Gray, 4 May 1981, LAC, RG 20, file 4956-1, vol. 5, March 1981–June 1981.

47 The Carter administration estimated that the restriction would drive up the price of Japanese cars, costing consumers $1 to $2 billion, and reduce the fuel economy of the American car fleet. Reubin Askew (USTR), 'Memorandum to the President: Automobile Imports,' 14 March 1980, JCL, Office of Staff Secretary, Handwriting File, box 116, file: 22 January 1979 (1); editorial, 'The Right Way to Help Detroit,' *NYT*, 27 May 1980; Peter Behr, 'Big Japanese Auto Import Cut Predicted,' *Washington Post*, 18 September 1980.

48 Robert K. Joyce to Allan MacEachen, 'Restrictions on Motor Vehicle Imports from Japan,' 4 November 1980, LAC, RG 19, vol. 5740, file 3881-09, pt. 1.

49 Hyman Solomon, 'US Look at Auto Imports Includes Us,' *FP*, 18 October 1980; Clyde M. Farnsworth, 'Auto Workers Union Asks U.S. to Curb Foreign Car Imports,' *NYT*, 12 June 1980; 'Canadian/Japan Automotive Trade: Possible Action Against Automotive Imports from Japan,' November 1980, LAC, RG 19, vol. 5740, file 3881-09, pt. 1.

50 Agis Salpukas, 'Ford Urges 15% Limit on Car Imports in U.S.,' *NYT*, 1 July 1980; Stu Eisenstat, 'Draft Memorandum for the President: S.J. Res. 193 – A Resolution Authorizing the President to Negotiate Import Restraints on Foreign Automobiles and Trucks,' n.d., JCL, Council of Economic Advisors Papers, box 3, file: 'Auto Imports' (1); C. Miles to file, 'US ITC Ruling,' 12 November 1980, LAC, RG 19, vol. 5740, file 3881-09, pt. 1.

51 'Report of UAW Director for Canada and International Vice President, Robert White,' 21 and 22 June 1980, 12–13, LAC, CAW Papers, vol. 296, folder: 'National Director's Reports.'

52 Al McDonald, 'Memorandum to the President: Japanese Automotive Imports,' 18 September 1980, JCL, Office of Staff Secretary, Handwriting File, box 116, file: 18 September 1980 (2); Ian Stewart to Allan MacEachen, 'Possible Restrictions on Exports of Automobiles from Japan,' 24 March, 1981, LAC, RG 19, vol. 5738, file 3881-02, pt. 14; Peter Bahr and Jane Seaberry, 'Haig Taking Charge of Talks with Japan on Auto Curb,' *Washington Post*, 25 March 1981.

53 Washington to Ottawa, 'USA Automotive Policy,' 25 March 1981, and 'Report of Meeting, Washington D.C., 25 March, 1981.' Both in LAC, RG 19, vol. 5740, file 3881-09, pt. 1; Ken Romain, 'Import Cars Raise Sales 43% in '80,' *G&M*, 14 January 1981.

54 A.L. Halliday and Robert Johnstone to Herb Gray, 'Restrictions on Motor Vehicle Imports from Japan,' 26 March 1981, and Ian Stewart to Minister MacEachern, 'Possible Restrictions on Motor Vehicles From Japan,' 2 April 1981. Both in LAC, RG 19, vol. 5740, file 3881-09, pt. 1.

55 The idea of the Big Three importing to Canada from overseas was

broached by Ford in August 1982, when the company proposed importing 50,000 vehicles from Toyo Kogyo (Mazda), in which it had a 25 per cent ownership share. The company claimed that it was losing money on every Ford Lynx and Escort built and sold in Canada and could make up some of these losses through Japanese imports, as long as there was 'no interference' from the Canadian government. Ford did not end up importing the vehicles. A.L. Halliday to file, 'Ford Motor Company: "Laser" Proposal,' 4 August 1982, DFAIT, 37-7-1-USA-2, vol. 43.

56 'Report of Meeting, April 3, 1981,' 'Expected Attendance,' 'MVMA Brief,' 'APMA Policy Position on Japanese Imports, April 3, 1981,' and 'The UAW's Position on Japanese Imports.' All in LAC, RG 19, vol. 5740, file 3881-09, pt. 1.

57 Campbell Stuart to file, 'Meeting of Ministers Gray and Lumley with US Special Trade Representative Brock and Secretary of Commerce Balridge,' 13 March 1981, LAC, RG 19, vol. 5738, file 3881-02, pt. 14. Also: 'Memorandum to Ministers: Imports of Automobiles from Japan,' 21 April 1981; 'Memorandum to Ministers: Restriction on Motor Vehicle Imports from Japan,' 1 April 1981; and Tokyo to Ottawa, 'Cda/Jpn Auto Talks,' 20 April 1981. All in LAC, RG 19, vol. 5740, file 3881-09, pt. 1. See, too, Lawrence Martin, 'Gray Discusses Car Import Policy,' G&M, 11 April 1981.

58 M. Cappe to N.R. Daniels, 'Japanese Automotive Imports,' 1 May 1981, and R.K. Joyce to A.S. Rubino, 'Imports of Automobiles from Japan: Recommendation in the Memorandum,' 1 May 1981. Both in LAC, RG 19, vol. 5740, file 3881-09, pt. 2. Also, James Dykes to Herb Gray, 4 February 1981, and Robert White to Herb Gray, 15 October 1981, LAC, CAW Papers, vol. 298, file 8.

59 ITC, 'Memorandum to Cabinet: Automobile Imports from Japan,' 4 May 1981, LAC, RG 19, vol. 5740, file 3881-09, pt. 2.

60 Cabinet Minutes, 7 May 1981; Record of Cabinet Decision, 7 May 1981, ATIP request, PCO.

61 ITC, 'Memorandum to Cabinet: Automobile Imports from Japan,' 4 May 1981, LAC, RG 19, vol. 5740, file 3881-09, pt. 2.

62 Ian Stewart to McEachen, 'Imports of Autos from Japan,' n.d., LAC, RG 19, vol. 5740, file 3881-09, pt. 2.

63 Ottawa to Tokyo embassy, 'Japan: Auto Imports,' 7 May 1981, and Ian A. Stewart to A. MacEchern, 12 May 1981. Both in LAC, RG 19, vol. 5740, file 3881-09, pt. 2.

64 Michiaki Suma, ambassador of Japan, to Herb Gray, 4 June 1981, and ITC News Release, 'Japanese Auto Exports to Canada,' 4 June 1981. Both in LAC, RG 19, vol. 5740, file 3881-09, pt. 2. Also, Ken Romain, 'Imports Take

31.7% Share of Car Sales,' *G&M*, 13 August 1981; 'Car Quotas Cut Sales of Imports,' *G&M*, 16 February 1982; Perry, *The Future of Canada's Auto Industry*, 16.

65 Determined to seal the deal quickly, on 2 June Gray pressed cabinet to decide on the agreement without submitting a full analysis of the VER, a position that brought a sharp rebuke from Trudeau, who wondered why 'ministers should be asked to make a snap decision in the absence of the analysis requested by Cabinet on the impact of such restraints upon inflation, the consumer, differing regional interests, international relations, and so forth.' Trudeau also pointed out that the VER would be 'a clear form of protection for the industry' that might require government to take a similar position in other sectors. Cabinet Committee on Priorities and Planning Minutes, 2 June 1981, Record of Cabinet Decision, 4 June 1981, PCO.

66 Colin Kemp-Jackson, 'Japanese Cars "Must Be Superior,"' letter to the editor, 6 June 1981; P.G. Belgrave, 'Don't Blame Imports for Auto Makers' Woes,' letter to the editor, *TS*, 29 June 1982; Arthur Donner, 'Car Import Quotas Impose a Heavy Cost on Consumers,' *TS*, 14 December 1984; 'Car Quotas Hurt Consumers; Little Guy Hit Hardest,' *G&M*, 25 January 1985; 'Dealers Assail Auto Quotas,' *G&M*, 15 June 1985; Robert Attrell (CAJAD) to Ed Lumley, 28 May 1982, AO, RG 9–2, Acc. 2205, box 2, file: 'Auto Industry.'

67 Sam Gindin, 'Force Japanese to Provide Jobs, Union Argues,' letter to the editor, 6 June, 1981; Gus Harris, 'Each Import Bought Means Lost Jobs,' *TS*, 3 August 1982; 'Japanese Import Agreement: We're Critical, but an Important First Step,' *Solidarity Canada*, May 1981, 2.

68 Edward Carrigan, 'Japanese Offer Worthy Example,' letter to the editor, *TS*, 2 April 1982.

69 Editorials, 'Car Import Quotas Unwise,' 'Unwise to Curb Imports,' 'Reject Car Import Quotas,' 'Fair Solution on Car Imports,' *TS*, 8 August and 24 October 1980, 4 April and 30 May 1981. Also, editorial, 'Car Quotas Should Go,' Montreal *Gazette*, 5 July 1985.

70 E. John Mackie (Automobile Importers of Canada) to Herb Gray, 23 June 1980 (including 'The Imported Automobile Industry in Canada: An Assessment of Key Aspects of Its Impact on the Canadian Economy and the Canadian Consumer'), LAC, RG 20, file 4956-1, vol. 2, February 1977–28 August 1980.

71 Minister of IT&C, 'Memorandum to Cabinet: 'Automobile Imports from Japan,' 2 June 1981, 17–18, PCO.

72 Edward Clifford, 'Groups Use Polls in Dispute over Japanese Auto Quotas,' *G&M*, 23 May 1984.

73 See Cabinet Minutes, 9 February and 25 May 1983; Minister of State for International Trade, 'Memorandum to Cabinet: Motor Vehicle Imports from Japan,' 31 March 1983; Minister of Regional Industrial Expansion and Minister for International Trade, 'Executive Summary: Canada-Japan Automotive Trade and Investment,' 8 March 1984; and Record of Cabinet Decision, 27 June 1985. All in PCO.

74 Japanese Automotive Manufacturers Association (JAMA) Canada, 'A Short History of the Japanese Auto Industry in Canada', 10; Canadian Press, 'Japanese "May Build Factories in Canada,"' TS, 20 August 1969; Lyndon Watkins, 'Gains Made in Japanese Talks Tied to Canada's Importance as a Raw Material Source,' G&M, 5 July 1975.

75 'Toyota, Nissan Weigh Plans for US Plants,' G&M, 11 March 1980; 'Gray Wants Japan to Make Car Deals,' G&M, 5 June 1980.

76 Interview, Solidarity Canada, May 1981, 5.

77 James Dykes, 'Imports Inarguably Damaging,' letter to the editor, TS, 11 May 1983.

78 Herb Gray to various ministers, 'Automotive: International Issues,' 11 June 1980, LAC, RG 20, file 4956-1, vol. 2, February 1977–28 August 1980.

79 For a view of the Japanese-U.S. auto relationship prior to the OPEC embargo, see Duncan, US-Japan Automobile Diplomacy; Reuben O'D. Askew to President Jimmy Carter, 'Automobile Trade and Japan,' 17 April 1980, JCL, WHCF, file: BE 3-145, 1 January 1980–31 March 1980; 'Statement of Norman D. Lean, Toyota, before the Joint Economic Committee on the Current and Future Health of the American Automobile Industry,' 19 March 1980, LAC. RG 20, file 4956-1, vol. 2, February 1977–28 August 1980.

80 'UAW to President-Elect Ronald Reagan,' 22 December 1980, WRL, Douglas Fraser Papers, box 54, folder 25.

81 John King and Jennifer Hunter, 'US House Vote Removes Threat to the Auto Pact,' G&M, 16 December 1982.

82 For example, J. Gero, 'Memorandum for the Minister of State (International Trade): USA Automotive Domestic Content Legislation,' 23 February 1983; and Neil M. Clegg, 'Inter-Departmental Working Group on Automotive Issues,' 7 February 1983. Both in DFAIT, 37-7-1-USA-2, vol. 43.

83 Sam Gindin, however, argued that a separate U.S. content requirement would 'leave the door open for us to argue (with a better chance of winning) a similar law. In fact, not only do we have a very clear precedent, but ours would in some ways be more modest – they're asking for 90% while we'd ask for only 85%.' Sam Gindin to Robert White, 'US Content Legislation,' 17 December 1981, SGP, vol. 1981.

84 Shook, Honda; Shimokawa, The Japanese Automobile Industry, 15. For a over-

view of the Japanese companies in 1980, see 'Rapid Internationalization of the Auto Industry,' *Oriental Economist*, 36, no. 6 (1980): 21–9. On the differences in philosophy and business approaches practised by the various Japanese automakers, see Tate, *Driving Production Home*. On Japanese auto investment in the United States, see Rubenstein, 'The Impact of Japanese Investment in the United States.'

85 Ontario, *Debates*, 8 June 1979, 2130 (Larry Grossman, St Andrew-St Paul).
86 David Stewart-Patterson, 'Car Makers, UAW Forge Industry Protection Plan,' and 'Lumley Will Aim for Tougher Restrictions on Japanese Auto Imports during Talks,' *G&M*, 5 and 11 March 1982.
87 Author's interview with Ed Lumley, 28 May 2008; JAMA Canada, 'A Short History of the Japanese Auto Industry in Canada,' 20.
88 JAMA Canada, 'A Short History of the Japanese Auto Industry in Canada,' 20.
89 Lumley commented on the backlash to the 'Yokohama Squeeze': 'No question it was not a tactic without risk and I took my lumps in Parliament, in the public and especially in the media. But at the end of the day I was convinced we were doing the right thing, and fortunately for me, our Prime Minister, Cabinet and caucus colleagues were fully supportive.' JAMA Canada, 'A Short History of the Japanese Auto Industry in Canada,' 21; Cabinet Committee on Economic and Regional Development Minutes, 9 March and 6 April 1982, PCO.
90 Cabinet Committee on Economic and Regional Development Minutes, 27 April 1982, 5; and Cabinet Minutes, 29 April 1982. Both in PCO.
91 Albert Sigurdson, 'Slow Inspections Hurt Toyota,' *G&M*, 23 June 1982; 'Toyota, Datsun Dealers Hurt by Customs Pressure Tactics,' *G&M*, 13 July 1982.
92 Ibid.; JAMA Canada, 'A Short History of the Japanese Auto Industry in Canada,' 10.
93 On NUMMI, see Reingold, *Toyota*, 84–99; 'Tokyo Promises to Extend Limits on Car Exports to Canada, US,' *G&M*, 16 February 1983.
94 Notably, the position of the Big Three in Canada differed from that of their parent companies in that they wished to see any new offshore transplant operations in Canada be part of the auto pact, and even formalize and increase the 60 per cent Canadian content rule. This was, in Bob White's view, 'the most significant aspect of the Auto Taskforce, and the one that surprised the most people.' Canada, *Report of the Automotive Task Force* (Ottawa, 1983); James Daw, 'Auto Task Force to Make a Case for Protection,' *TS*, 30 November 1982; Bob White to Brian Mulroney, 2 January 1986, SGP, vol. 1986, pt. 2; author's interview with Ed Lumley, 28 May 2008;

'Canadian Content Could Mean 80,000 Jobs: Task Force,' *Solidarity Canada*, summer 1983, 26.

95 JAMA Canada, 'A Short History of the Japanese Auto Industry in Canada,' 11; Nicholas Hunter, 'Japanese Car Dealers Lobby against Report Urging Content Rules,' *G&M*, 20 May 1983.

96 Editorial, 'A Broader Auto Pact,' *G&M*, 24 May 1983.

97 Editorials, 'Questionable Auto Pact Idea' and 'Risky Approach on Autos?' *TS*, 25 May and 6 November 1983.

98 Canada, *Debates*, 7 December 1983, 3 (Speech from the Throne); Jennifer Lewington, 'Auto Pact with Japan a Priority,' *G&M*, 8 December 1983.

99 David Stewart-Patterson, 'Lumley Seeks Auto Pact in Tokyo,' *G&M*, 7 January 1984.

100 Cabinet Minutes, 19 January 1984, PCO.

101 'Delegation from UAW, Meeting with Prime Minister Trudeau, 27 February, 1984,' CAW Archives and Library, binder: 'Meeting with PM re Content Presentation, Feb. 1984.'

102 '$200 Million Japanese Auto Investment Seen,' *TS*, 14 January 1984; David Steward-Patterson, 'Japanese Auto Quotas Tied to Investment in Canada,' *G&M*, 17 March 1984.

103 Peter Rasky, 'They Sing Their Company Song: Canada and the New Japan,' *TS*, 28 December 1966.

104 Campbell Stuart to E.A. Oestreicher (Finance), 'Toyota/Duty Remission,' 24 December 1981, LAC, RG 19, vol. 5740, file 3881-09, pt. 2; 'Japanese plant in B.C. Possible,' *G&M*, 9 May 1981; 'Toyota Talks on B.C. Plant Are Confirmed,' *G&M*, 5 May 1982.

105 Jennifer Hunter, 'Details Being Finalized for B.C. Toyota Plant,' *G&M*, 8 October 1982.

106 Eventually, the company did get a $5-million interest-free loan from the federal and provincial governments to support the plant. Albert Sigurdson, 'Toyota to Start Construction Next Spring of a $23-Million Plant,' *G&M*, 13 November 1982; John Schreiner, 'Ottawa Wants More from Japanese Automakers,' *FP*, 13 April 1985.

107 Toyota Motor Corporation, *A History of the First Fifty Years*, 350; Albert Sigurdson, 'Toyota Head Warns Quotas Hurt Industry,' *G&M*, 12 December 1983.

108 According to former premier William Davis, the company was mainly concerned about building a plant on pristine agricultural land. It did not ask for direct funding, and Honda's arrival was not a significant issue within the Ontario cabinet. Author's interview with William Davis, 7 August 2008; Minister of Regional Industrial Expansion and Minister

for International Trade, 'Executive Summary: Canada-Japan Automotive Trade and Investment,' 8 March 1984, PCO; Shook, *Honda*, 52–3, 99; '"We Try to Produce Where Market Is,'" Honda Chief says,' *FP*, 20 July 1987; Sam Gindin to Auto Tariff Committee, 'Honda Facility,' 6 June 1984, SGP, vol. 1984; Yanarella and Green, 'Canadian Recruitment of East Asia Automobile Transplants,' 369.

109 The government also promised to amend the Honda duty-remission order to provide a tariff reduction for its car imports 'fully equivalent' to the CVA exported by the company. Minister of Regional Industrial Expansion, 'Executive Summary: Honda Investment,' 29 May 1984; and 'Memorandum of Understanding between Her Majesty the Queen in Right of Canada and Honda Canada Inc,' May 1984. Both in PCO.

110 David Stewart-Patterson, 'New Car Quota Not the Last: Regan,' *G&M*, 13 June 1984.

111 'Honda Will Open Assembly Plant in Alliston,' *Solidarity Canada*, summer 1984, 25.

112 John Schreiner, 'Ottawa Wants More from Japanese Automakers,' *FP*, 13 April 1985.

113 Though most of it is redacted, the 19 June 1985 Memorandum to Cabinet, 'Canada/Japan Automotive Regime' (PCO), states in its communications plan: '*Major Theme*: No public announcement is recommended of a Cabinet decision to impede customs clearance of Japanese vehicles. Communication of a decision to prepare amending legislation can be deferred until it becomes necessary as an additional bargaining lever with the Japanese.' Ministers were further instructed, in response to possible criticism of a slowdown, to reply that 'customs officers and transport inspectors are merely doing their job and following correct procedures.' Record of Cabinet Decision, 27 June 1985, PCO.

114 As to whether the Canadian policies towards the Japanese had influenced the decision, the *G&M* report included the statement that 'the investment can also be seen as a response to the Canadian Government's pressure on Japan to maintain voluntary export restrictions on car shipments to Canada.' Christopher Waddell, 'Toyota Plans $150 Million Plant,' *G&M*, 24 July 1985; James Daw, 'Canada May Capture More Auto Plants,' *TS*, 3 September 1985; Brian Milner, 'Toyota's Auto-Pact Role Questioned,' *G&M*, 29 October 1985.

115 B.C. Trade Minister Don Phillips vowed, 'I will do anything necessary to have the plant in B.C. It's a number one priority,' while his Quebec counterpart, Bernard Landry, wrote directly to Prime Minister Mulroney to demand that the plant be put into Quebec. Andrew Cohen, 'Toyota

Driving into "Obscene" Bidding War,' *FP*, 3 August 1985; Michael Doyle and Brian Dunn, 'We'll Outbid Ontario in Toyota Deal: Race for Car Plant,' *Montreal Gazette*, 25 July 1985; Alan Capon, 'Belleville, Trenton Chase Planned Toyota Auto Plant,' *Kingston Whig-Standard*, 31 July 1985; 'Chatham Beats Drum for Toyota Car Plant,' *G&M*, 3 August 1985.

116 Toyota Motor Corporation, *A History of the First Fifty Years*, 343; 'Toyota to Construct Auto Plant in Ontario, Not Quebec: Report,' *Ottawa Citizen*, 4 December 1985; Brian Milner, '$300 Million Toyota Plant to Be Built Near Cambridge,' *G&M*, 12 December 1985.

117 Toyota asked for an additional 5,000 vehicles beyond its quota as part of its MOU. Memorandum to Cabinet, 'Overview of Current Automotive Issues,' 23 May 1986, 47; and Cabinet Committee on Economic and Regional Development, Minutes, 28 May 1986, 21. Both in PCO. Also, Mordue, 'Government, Foreign Direct Investment, and the Canadian Automotive Industry, 1977–1987,' 258; and Yanarella and Green, 'Canadian Recruitment of East Asia Automobile Transplants,' 370.

118 Toyota Motor Corporation, *A History of the First Fifty Years*, 337.

119 Brian Milner, 'Honda to Expand Its Investment Plans,' *G&M*, 18 December 1985; Robert English, 'Nissan Looking at Canadian Parts Plant,' *FP*, 14 December 1985; James Daw, 'Nissan Eyes Major Plant in Canada,' *TS*, 18 February 1986; Brian Milner, 'Nissan Is Seeking Canadian Presence, *G&M*, 24 September 1986.

120 'Ingersoll Likely to Get New Car Plant, Sources Say,' *TS*, 7 August 1986.

121 In 1986 GM requested an extra 50,000 Suzuki imports as part of its CAMI investment. Nissan, which had proposed a $200-million transaxle plant to the government, asked for 30,000 additional cars if the facility came to fruition, and even tiny Subaru indicated to the government that it had plans for a 10,000-unit plant in Canada. Memorandum to Cabinet (minister of DRIE), 'Overview of Current Automotive Issues,' 23 May 1986, 25, 33, 47; and Cabinet Committee on Economic and Regional Development, Minutes, 28 May 1986, 23, 28. Both in PCO. Also, Yanarella and Green, 'Canadian Recruitment of East Asia Automobile Transplants,' 371.

122 The Canadians continued to play hardball even after Japanese investment began to appear. In April 1986 Susuma Yanagisawa, chairman of JAMA Canada, complained that 'the government has been telling us that if we invest in Canada they will lift the restrictions. Well, the investment is on the way but still the restrictions are there.' 'Japan Seeks End of Car Import Curb,' *Ottawa Citizen*, 24 April 1986.

123 For examples of automotive MNE-state interaction, see Bennett and

Sharpe, *Transnational Corporations versus the State*; and Shapiro, *Engines of Growth*.

124 Rob Ferguson and Tony van Alphen, 'Nissan Closer to an Ontario Plant; Japan Auto Maker No Longer Waiting until It Has 10% Market Share; Minister Reports on Positive Meetings with Top Auto Makers,' *TS*, 4 May 2005.

125 According to news reports, 'Honda's pioneering plant in Marysville has given it a major competitive advantage over some of its larger Japanese competitors by allowing it to supplement imports from Japan – which are restrained by quotas – with US production. Because of this, Honda became the top-selling Japanese car company in the United States in 1986, with 693,515 cars sold, compared with 637,985 for Toyota and 546,151 for Nissan. Both Toyota and Nissan outranked Honda in sales in 1985.' 'Honda Plan to Spend $450 Million Is Company's Largest Move in US,' *G&M*, 10 January 1987.

126 Canada, *Foreign Direct Investment in Canada*.

127 Bob English, 'Japanese Factories: Who Benefits from New Car Plants?' and editorial, 'Are We Getting Value for Money?' *FP*, 2 and 5 November 1985.

128 Yanarella and Green argue in 'Canadian Recruitment of East Asia Automobile Transplants,' 376, that 'one of the ironies of the Canadian strategy of auto recruitment is that it yielded so little direct employment benefit to the communities.'

129 Ashley Ford, 'Automakers Drive to Canadianize Production,' *Asia Pacific Business*, 2, no. 1 (1986): 20.

8 Rebirth or Requiem? Duty Remissions, Free Trade, and the Death of the Auto Pact

1 On the 1962–4 remission plans, see Anastakis, *Auto Pact*, chapter 1.

2 Keeley, 'Cast in Concrete for All Time?'

3 Tires and tubes were not included in the auto pact. The Canadian and Nova Scotia governments had given Michelin nearly $50 million in loans and grants to establish a tire factory in the province, which the United States challenged as an unfair subsidy. On the Michelin case, see Bickerton, *Nova Scotia, Ottawa and the Politics of Regional Development*; Lea and Volpe, 'Conflict over Industrial Incentive Policies.'

4 Paul Heimbecker to J.R. McKinney, 'Automotive Consultations with USA,' 17 June 1980, DFAIT, 37-7-1-USA-2, vol. 40.

5 See Anastakis, *Auto Pact*, 80.

6 C.D. Arthur to R.Y. Grey, 29 March 1971, 'Automotive-Third Country Duty Remission'; R.K. Joyce to R. Grey, 5 April 1971, 'Mr. Pepin's Visit to Germany'; and R. Grey to the minister, 7 April 1971. All in LAC, RG 19, vol. 5347, file 3881-01, pt. 1.

7 Ibid.

8 'VW Assembly in Canada Is Ruled Out,' *G&M*, 10 January 1973.

9 'Volkswagen,' R.K. Joyce to T. Shoyama, 31 July 1975, LAC, RG 19, vol. 5347, file 3881-01, pt. 1.

10 See, for instance, 'Why VW Must Build Autos in the US,' *Business Week*, 16 February 1976, 46–51. The plant closed in 1988, having assembled about 1.5 million cars. VW never matched its late 1960s and early 1970s successes and was eventually largely squeezed out of the small car market by the Japanese and the Koreans. John Housha, 'Volkswagen to Shut U.S. Plant,' *NYT*, 21 November 1987.

11 Alan Gotlieb to the minister, 20 May 1977; and 'Memorandum to Ministers: The Automotive Industry: Situation Report,' 17 May 1977. Both in DFAIT, 37-7-1-USA-2, vol. 37.

12 A.B. Wilson to file, 28 July 1977, DFAIT, 37-7-1-USA-2, vol. 37.

13 Washington embassy to Ottawa, telex, 16 August 1977, DFAIT, 37-7-1-USA-2, vol. 37.

14 The Volkswagen remission order can be seen in Canada, *Gazette*, pt. 2, 112:17 (23 August 1978), 1627; 'Automotive Industry Issues,' 19 October 1979, LAC, RG 19, vol. 5959, file 8705-03, pt. 3; William C. Hood to the minister, 'Automotive Issues,' 18 June 1979, LAC, RG 19, vol. 5348, file 3881-02, pt. 4.

15 VW was not a member of the auto pact, which meant that its cars built in the United States (or Germany) were still subject to duties. The DRO meant that VW was to achieve a sliding scale of CVA of 12 per cent (1978–9), 18 per cent (1979–80), and 24 per cent (1980–1) for all VW's imported vehicles into Canada. If the company exceeded the threshold, it would get all of its duties back, 75 per cent of its duties back if it was over 50 per cent of the threshold, and 40 per cent of its duties back if it was below the annual target. 'Canadian Output Drops; AMC Lays Off; VW Signs Pact,' *WA*, 10 July 1978, 223; Ken Romain, 'Ottawa and VW Sign Duty Remission Pact,' *G&M*, 27 June 1978; Sam Gindin to Auto Tariff Committee, 'Duty Remission Order,' 31 March 1980, LAC, CAW Papers, vol. 298, file 10.

16 Ken Romain, 'Official Alleges Federal Auto Pact Figures on Employment in Canada Are Inaccurate,' *G&M*, 5 May 1978.

17 'Automotive Industry Issues,' 19 October 1979, LAC, RG 19, vol. 5959, file 8705-03, pt. 3.

18 Washington to Ottawa, 'Canadian Duty Remission Scheme,' 3 March 1978, DFAIT, 37-7-1-USA-2, vol. 37.
19 'Record of Interdepartmental Meeting of May 30, 1979: Volkswagen Conditional Duty Free Access to Canadian Automobile Market,' LAC, RG 19, vol. 5348, file 3881-02, pt. 1.
20 In 1985 BMW negotiated a new DRO that boosted its parts purchase from $8.4 million in 1984 to nearly $40 million in 1985. 'BMW to Quintuple Canadian Purchases,' Ottawa Citizen, 8 October 1985; William C. Hood to the Minister (John Crosbie), 'Expanded Automotive Components Remission Scheme-Remission Orders for Parts Exports to Countries Other Than the US,' June 1979, LAC, RG 19, vol. 5348, file 3881-02, pt. 1; 'Automotive Industry Issues,' 19 October 1979, LAC, RG 19, vol. 5959, file 8705-03, pt. 3.
21 Transcript, press conference, 1 April 1980; and Campbell Stuart to Canadian delegation, 'USA Automotive Consultations,' 7 August 1980. Both in DFAIT, 37-7-1-USA-2, vol. 40.
22 External Affairs to Washington, 'CDA/USA Auto Consults, NAmerican Aspects,' 2 July 1980; Campbell Stuart to Canadian delegation, 'USA Automotive Consultations,' 7 August 1980; and Lucie Edwards to file, 'The Emerging Approach to Consultations on the Auto Pact,' 17 November 1980. All in DFAIT, 37-7-1-USA-2, vol. 40.
23 Ken Romain, 'GM President Cites Negative Effect of Auto Parts Duty Remission Plan,' G&M, 12 March 1980.
24 Reisman, The Canadian Automotive Industry, 192.
25 M.A. Cohen to Jack Horner, 'Conditional Duty Free Entry – Volkswagen Canada Limited,' 22 March 1979; and Jack Horner to Bruno Rubess (VW Canada), 22 March 1979. Both in LAC, RG 19, vol. 5348, file 3881-01, pt. 2, v. 3.
26 'Record of Interdepartmental Meeting of May 30, 1979: Volkswagen Conditional Duty Free Access to Canadian Automobile Market,' 30 May 1979, LAC, RG 19, vol. 5348, file 3881-02, pt. 1.
27 'Report on Visit of Canadian Team to Volkswagenwerk, August 10, 11, 1981,' 13 August 1981, DFAIT, 37-7-1-USA-2, vol. 43.
28 T. MacDonald to M. Wodinsky, 'Report on Consultations with U.S. on Volkswagen,' 5 August 1981, DFAIT, 37-7-1-USA-2, vol. 43.
29 'Volkswagen Parts Facility in Canada,' M. Wodinsky to file, 4 August 1981, DFAIT, 37-7-1-USA-2, vol. 43.
30 David R. MacDonald to Robert Latimer, 12 August 1981, DFAIT, 37-7-1-USA-2, vol. 43.
31 Ibid.
32 Robert Latimer to David R. MacDonald, 14 August 1981; and 'Memoran-

dum: Volkswagen Parts Facility in Canada,' M.S. Wodinsky, 3 September 1981. Both in DFAIT, 37-7-1-USA-2, vol. 43.

33 Pierre de Bane to Pierre Trudeau, 'Confidential: Briefing Notes: Canadian Government-Volkswagen Relations,' 30 August 1981, DFAIT, 37-7-1-USA-2, vol. 43.

34 However, the company agreed to a sliding-scale increase in CVA of 1.25 per cent in- house and 5 per cent overall for each of the first three years, with overall CVA increasing by 6 per cent in the fourth year. 'Volkswagen Duty Free Entry,' Ottawa to Washington, telex, 21 September 1981, DFAIT, 37-7-1-USA-2, vol. 43; 'Robert Gibbens, 'VW Immovable over Plant Site,' *G&M*, 14 October 1981; 'VW Hopes Canadian Plant Will Offset Losses,' *G&M*, 2 November 1981.

35 Robert Gibbens, 'Klockner-Humboldt Will Build Plant to Produce Diesel Engines in Quebec,' and 'Biron Seeks Aid to Lessen Ontario Auto Monopoly,' *G&M*, 15 September and 21 November 1981.

36 In August 1982 VW Canada announced the delay of the plant. It eventually opened in 1985, much smaller than originally envisioned, with less than 200 workers building components for Golfs and aluminum wheels. The company's investment was also much smaller, $40 million, as was the Ontario government grant for the facility. 'VW Puts off Canada Parts Unit,' *NYT*, 28 August 1982; Jennifer Hunter, 'Ontario Eager to See Plant Start,' *G&M*, 28 August 1982; Robert English, 'VW Plant Pins Hopes on Longer Prospect,' *FP*, 27 April 1985; Mordue, 'Government, Foreign Direct Investment and the Canadian Automotive Industry, 1977–1987,' 269n.452.

37 The original export-based Honda remission order was passed by order-in-council on 31 July 1980: Canada, *Gazette*, pt. II, 114:15 (31 July 1980), 2756. As part of its May 1984 MOU with the federal government, Ottawa stated that it would, 'as soon as practicable, amend the Honda Remission Order 1980, effective the date construction of the manufacturing facility commences, to provide for a reduction in the Value For Duty of Automobiles imported by the Company fully equivalent to the Canadian Value Added in auto parts ... exported by or on behalf of the Company or Producer.' See Annexes. The general remission order was revoked on 13 March 1985 and replaced by an order 'respecting individual companies.' The revocation order and the new individual remission orders can be seen in Canada, *Gazette*, pt. II, 119:7 (3 April 1985), 1653–81; Mordue, 'Government, Foreign Direct Investment and the Canadian Automotive Industry, 1977–1987,' 267–8. See also Wonnacott, *The United States and Canada*, 79–82.

38 This practice was also being followed by the Big Three and VW, all of whom imported high-cost engines and parts from their offshore captive

facilities – GM from its affiliate Isuzu, Chrysler from Mitsubishi, Ford from Mazda, and VW from its plant in Brazil. Memorandum to Cabinet (DRIE), 'Automotive Issues and Policy Instruments,' 10 September 1986, 37, PCO.

39 Jenna MacKay-Alie to Iain Henderson, 'Canada-US Automotive Products Trade Agreement,' 28 March 1985, LAC, RG 19, vol. 5849, file 3015-03, pt. 1.

40 As one memo to cabinet pointed out, 'new vehicle assemblers locating in Canada are not eligible to join the Auto Pact per se, but can apply for duty remission under various existing programs. Canada can export vehicles duty-free to the US as long as the vehicles have at least 50% American content.' Memorandum to Cabinet (DRIE), 'Overview of Current Automotive Issues,' 23 May 1986, 15, PCO.

41 Sam Gindin to Bob White, 'Japanese Investment in Canada,' 18 September 1985, SGP, vol. 1985.

42 The Japanese reluctance to commit to auto pact status was understandable, since they would have had to pay only a low U.S. duty of 2.5 per cent if they did not meet the 50 per cent content requirement under the pact to export to the United States. On the other hand, if they qualified as bona fide manufacturers in Canada under the requirements of the agreement, they would be able to import duty-free from Japan, thus avoiding a 9.2 per cent duty, and then resell into the United States. In the meantime, the MOUs and duty remissions allowed them to avoid paying some of these duties. J.L. MacNeil and Paul S.H. Lau (EA) to deputy minister, 'Bilateralization of the Auto Pact,' 14 May 1987; and Paul S.H. Lau to deputy minister, 'Auto Pact Safeguards and Conditions,' 10 August 1987. Both in DFAIT, 37-7-1-USA-2, vol. 44. Also, Memorandum to cabinet (DRIE), 'Automotive Issues and Policy Instruments,' 10 September 1986, 47, PCO.

43 Mordue makes the case that the production-based DROs were of 'secondary consequence' to the decision-making process of the Japanese. Mordue, 'Government, Foreign Direct Investment and the Canadian Automotive Industry, 1977–1987,' 269–71.

44 Memorandum to Cabinet (DRIE), 'Automotive Issues and Policy Instruments,' 10 September 1986, 29, PCO.

45 Brian Milner, 'Nissan Is Seeking Canadian Presence,' G&M, 24 September 1986.

46 U.S. Senate, Hearing before the Subcommittee on Employment and Productivity: United States-Japan Auto Relations (Washington, 1986), 69 (25 September 1986).

47 U.S. Joint Economic Committee, Hearing before the Subcommittee on Trade, Productivity, and Economic Growth (Washington, 1986), 104-5, 150–76 (24 April 1986).

48 U.S. Senate, *Hearings before the Committee on Finance, United States-Canada Free Trade Agreement – 1988* (Washington, 1989), 23 (15 and 21 April 1988).

49 There was also speculation that the U.S. Cast Metals Federation would launch a trade challenge against the auto pact in 1986. On the Michigan 301 challenge, see statement by Michigan official Mark Santucci in ibid., 18. On the Cast Metals challenge, see James Kelleher (EA) to Robert White, 8 April 1986, DFAIT, 37-7-1-USA-2, vol. 44.

50 Memorandum to Cabinet (DRIE), 'Automotive Issues and Policy Instruments,' 10 September 1986, 5, PCO.

51 'Statement by Larry G. Buganto, Chairman of the Board, APMA,' 26 June 1987, DFAIT, 37-7-1-USA-2, vol. 44.

52 Emphasis added. Bob White to James Kelleher, EA, 17 March 1986, SGP, vol. 1986, pt. 2; Brian Milner, 'CAW Seeks Strict Content Rules for New Plants,' *G&M*, 14 April 1987. On reaction to the task force's report, see Wonnacott, 'The Canadian Content Proposals of the Task Force on the Automobile Industry.'

53 Robert White, Patrick Lavelle, and Norman Clark to Brian Mulroney, 'The Canadian Auto Industry: Complacency vs. Reality,' 17 December 1985, SGP, vol. 1985.

54 Sam Gindin to Rob White et al., 'Meeting with Cote,' and 'Duty Remission and US Retaliation,' 15 September and 27 August 1986, SGP, vol. 1986, pt. 2.

55 Wonnacott, *The Quest for Free Trade*, 82; When the FTA was threatened with defeat, trade expert Gilbert R. Winham warned of the consequences that the DROs could bring to the auto pact and Canadian auto policy. 'The auto pact is running on empty: Without the new free-trade deal, the old one will be in jeopardy,' *G&M*, 15 November 1988.

56 On free trade in the post-war period, see Anastakis, 'Multilateralism, Nationalism, and Bilateral Free Trade'; Cuff and Granatstein, 'The Rise and Fall of American Free Trade, 1947–1948.' Studies on free trade that appeared in the period include: Lea, *A Canada-US Free Trade Arrangement*; Beigie, *US-Canadian Free Trade*; Wonnacott and Wonnacott, *Free Trade between the United States and Canada*.

57 For an overview of trade developments in this period, see Hart, *A Trading Nation*.

58 Not everyone in the government was keen on the prospect of free trade with the United States. According to one EA official writing in 1982, reciprocity 'seems to be in vogue in the USA' yet was 'of concern to all nations' as the Americans envisioned it. In providing suggested notes for a prime ministerial press conference on the issue, E.R. Johnston, deputy

director of the U.S. General Relations Division, wrote that 'reciprocity is a very uncertain basis for policy. The concept is insensitive to the size of a country, to its political and social organization, to its economic structure, and to established and agreed global trading patterns.' E.R. Johnston, 'Notes for Prime Minister's Press Conference,' 11 February 1982, DFAIT, 37-7-1-USA-2, vol. 43. Also, Standing Senate Committee on Foreign Affairs, *Canada-United States Relations, Vol. III* (Ottawa, 1982); Department of External Affairs, *Canadian Trade Policy in the 1980s*. See, too, Ottawa to secretary of state, Washington, 'Your Meeting with Allan MacEachen, April 1–2,' 24 March 1984; and Department of State Briefing Paper, 'US-Canadian Economic Issues,' 20 September 1984. Both in Ronald Reagan Presidential Library (RRL), Peter Sommer Files, box 90552, file; 'Canada 1984 (February–May) and (September 15–24).'

59 On the Macdonald Commission, see Inwood, *Continentalizing Canada*. On free-trade studies in the period, see Wilkinson, 'Canada-US Free Trade and Some Options'; Harris and Cox, *Trade, Industrial Policy, and Canadian Manufacturing*; Lipsey and Smith, *Taking the Initiative*.

60 White House, Office of the Press Secretary, 'Remarks by the President in Briefing on Canada-US Free Trade,' 2 November 1987, RRL, Dan Crippen Papers, Series I, Subject Files: 'Canada,' box 2, file: 'Canada Free Trade' (1).

61 For views on Mulroney and free trade, see: Hart, *A Trading Nation*; Hart, 'Free Trade and Brian Mulroney's Economic Legacy'; Tomlin, 'Leaving the Past Behind.' For a brief chronology and backgrounder of the events, see White House, Office of the Press Secretary, 'Fact Sheet: US-Canada Free Trade Agreement,' 2 January 1988, RRL, Dan Crippen Papers, Series I, Subject Files: 'Canada,' box 2, file: 'Canada Free Trade' (1).

62 A 1986 cabinet memo also listed the $760-million AMC plant in Brampton, $1.2 billion in GM investments, and Chrysler and Ford projects. Toyota and Honda were investing another $600 million, along with the GM-Suzuki plant of between $500–600 million. Memorandum to Cabinet, 'Overview of Current Automotive Issues,' 23 May 1986, 19, 21, PCO.

63 GM's 1986 announced expansions for building trucks in Oshawa sparked over $200 million in parts investments, with another $350 million alone for Stelco in Hamilton. Sam Gindin to Lorna Moses, 'GM Expansion – Oshawa,' 1 April 1986, SGP, vol. 1986, pt. 2.

64 On the consumption side, Hazledine and Wigington argued in 'Canadian Auto Policy,' 493, that (less taxes and tariffs) Canadian cars by the mid-1980s were actually less expensive than U.S. vehicles, largely owing to lower production costs based on the lower Canadian dollar. As a result, 'Canadian auto consumers could lose from the introduction of free trade,'

as Canadian prices inevitably rose to meet those of their U.S. counterparts. Also, James Daw, 'Auto Boom: Were the Doomsayers Wrong?' 'Thousands of Jobs at Stake as GM Gears up for Car Wars,' and 'Our Car Parts Makers' Fast Test from Japan,' *TS*, 23 June 1984, 12 April and 28 August 1986; Keith Spicer, 'There Are Signs of Hope in Automobile Industry's Recovery,' *TS*, 26 July 1984; Sam Gindin to Robert White et al., 'Auto-Canada-US,' 19 March 1986, SGP, vol. 1986, pt. 2.

65 Sam Gindin estimated that the overcapacity was the equivalent of twelve to fifteen plants. Sam Gindin to All Staff, 'Attached Tables,' 20 March 1986; and Bob White to Brian Mulroney, 2 January 1986. Both in SGP, vol. 1986, pt. 2.

66 Neil Macdonald, 'Autos at Peril,' *Policy Options*, 3 April 1985, 21–4.

67 James Daw, 'Would 125,000 Auto Jobs Survive Free Trade?' and 'Japanese, Korean Car Plants a Mixed Blessing for Canada,' *TS*, 11 May 1985 and 27 August 1986.

68 'US to Oppose Duty Remission for Autos,' *G&M*, 22 August 1986.

69 According to Patrick Lavelle, there was only one meeting between Reisman and Peterson at Queen's Park over free trade, which was also attended by Tom D'Aquino of the pro-free trade Business Council on National Issues. The meeting did not end well, with Peterson and Reisman shouting at one another over the auto pact. Author's interview with P. Lavelle, 29 August 2008. Also, *Windsor Star* ad of 29 August 1987, as quoted in Ontario, *Debates*, 5 November 1987, 77 (David Cook, Windsor-Riverside).

70 James Daw, 'Would 125,000 Auto Jobs Survive Free Trade?' *TS*, 11 May 1985.

71 Alan Christie, 'Trade Talks Must Include Auto Pact, Social Programs, US Official Says,' *TS*, 24 October 1985.

72 'PM Appeals for Support on Free Trade Deal with US: Only Way to Fight Protectionism, He Tells Nation in TV Address,' *TS*, 17 June 1986.

73 Bob White to Brian Mulroney, 2 January 1986, SGP, vol. 1986, pt. 2.

74 John Deverell, 'Free Trade Talks Risky, White Says,' *TS*, 29 October 1985;

75 James Daw, 'US Report Urges Washington to Avoid Major Auto Pact Revision,' *TS*, 1 October 1986.

76 Another leak, of an Ontario government report on the negotiations, accused Canadian negotiator Charles Stedman and his colleagues of having 'little, if, any inclination to fight the Americans' to keep the agreement off the table, and of actually seeming keen to discuss it. Ed Broadbent, Steve Langdon, and Howard McCurdy to Brian Mulroney, 7 November 1986 (with attachment), SGP, vol. 1986, pt. 2; editorial, 'Another Sell-Out?' *TS*, 10 January 1987.

77 Tom Porter to Brian Mulroney, 12 November 1986, 'Petition Presented to Windsor City Council Meeting, November 10, 1986'; and P.J. Leack (city clerk, Windsor) to Brian Mulroney, 'Re: Auto Pact with the United States,' 4 December 1986. Both in DFAIT, 37-7-1-USA-2, vol. 44.

78 'Murphy: What He Said,' *FP*, 19 January 1987.

79 'War of Words over Free Trade: US Backs off Autopact,' *WS*, 16 January 1987.

80 Howard McCurdy and Steven Langdon to Brian Mulroney, 13 January 1987, DFAIT, 37-7-1-USA-2, vol. 44.

81 'Auto Pact to Be Gutted, US Memo Says,' *WS*, 22 June 1987. See also online CBC archives at http://www.archives.cbc.ca/economy_business/trade_agreements/topics/326/ ('Canada Fights for Auto Pact,' 22 June 1987; accessed 14 December 2010).

82 Hart, Dymond, and Robertson, *Decision at Midnight*, 167.

83 Editorial, 'The Auto Pact Is *So* on the Table,' and Pat Carney, letter to the editor, 'The Auto Pact Is Not on the Negotiating Table,' *TS*, 23 and 27 June 1987; 'Statement by Larry G. Buganto, Chairman of the Board, APMA,' 26 June 1987, DFAIT, 37-7-1-USA-2, vol. 44; John D. Clout, letter to the editor, 'Pursuit of Free Trade Has Been Costly,' *TS*, 28 December 1986.

84 Bruce Little and Christopher Waddell, 'Reisman Takes a Hard Line,' *G&M*, 5 May 1986; Bob White, 'UAW on Free Trade,' letter to the editor, *G&M*, 8 May 1986 (original: Bob White to the editor, *G&M*, 5 May 1986, SGP, vol. 1986, pt. 2); Simon Reisman, 'A Reply to the UAW,' letter to the editor, *G&M*, 15 May 1986.

85 In the letter, White had called the *Globe* a part of 'the pro free-trade business press'; the *Globe* did support the initiative. Robert White, 'Auto Pact Protects, Free Trade Does Not,' *FP*, 26 July 1986; Robert White, 'Auto Pact Safeguards,' letter to the editor, *G&M*, 31 July 1986 (original: Robert White to the editor, *G&M*, 29 July 1986, SGP, vol. 1986, pt. 2).

86 During a 1997 interview with the author, Reisman was specifically asked: Isn't the auto pact really a managed trade regime, as opposed to free trade? His response was essentially that if it looks like a duck, walks like a duck, and talks like a duck, it must be a duck. In his ever so gentle manner, he asked me if the auto pact reduced tariffs and trade barriers (I responded yes); he asked if it created a continental market in autos and auto parts (I said yes); and he asked me if it led to rationalization and efficiency in the auto industry (which, I, of course, replied yes); thus, the answer to my question was obvious: the auto pact, in Simon Reisman's view, was free trade. When I protested that the archival record had him stating explicitly that Canada could not agree to unrestricted free trade in autos, he was

dismissive. Of course, Reisman, as the 'father' of Canadian free trade, had a legacy to protect, which helps to explain his unwillingness to label the agreement anything but free trade. Author's interview with Simon Reisman, 19 December 1997. Also see editorial, 'The Auto Pact Myth,' *TS*, 10 December 1987.

87 Canada, *The Canada-US Free Trade Agreement: Overview*, 2.

88 Cuttingly, he told Reisman that 'your incorrect and misleading comments on an issue you've historically been so close to are hardly a positive contribution to such a national debate.' White also pointed out that the 'prominent politicians' who had criticized the auto pact were Progressive Conservatives. Robert White to Simon Reisman, 5 May 1986; and Sam Gindin to Robert White, 'History of the CAW Position on Auto Pact,' 24 June 1986. Both in SGP, vol. 1986, pt. 2.

89 See Anastakis, 'Between Nationalism and Continentalism.'

90 Bob White to the editor, *G&M*, 5 May 1986, SGP, vol. 1986, pt. 2; IEB, 'US-Canadian Automotive Products Agreement, Adopted 6 May, 1970,' LAC, CAW Papers, vol. 289, file 4.

91 Sam Gindin was pessimistic that any 'erosion' of the auto pact could be avoided: 'Canada faces the hardball reality that having asked for free trade talks, and given the profile of auto, if we refuse to talk about it the Americans can remind us of their right to unilaterally end [the auto pact] in 12 months. That would put the Pact and modifications on the table.' Sam Gindin to Bob White, 'Oshawa and the Auto Pact,' 10 June 1986; and Bob White to Brian Mulroney, 2 January 1986. Both in SGP, vol. 1986, pt. 2.

92 Bob White, 'The Dangers of Free Trade,' *Solidarity Canada*, winter 1986, 3. See also the UAW pamphlet 'Free Trade Could Cost US Canada,' n.d., WRL, Owen Bieber Papers, file 2.2.

93 Percy T. Eastman, director general, United States Relations Bureau, 'Bilateral Automotive Meetings with US Officials, November 15,' 3 November 1983, DFAIT, 37-7-1-USA-2, vol. 40.

94 'Statement by Larry G. Buganto, Chairman of the Board, APMA,' 26 June 1987, DFAIT, 37-7-1-USA-2, vol. 44.

95 Lilley, *Magna Cum Laude*, 119–24.

96 Judy Steed, 'Free Trade or Free for All?' *TS*, 13 September 1986.

97 Regina Hickl-Szabo, 'Free-Trade Opponent Awarded Trade Post,' *G&M*, 4 January 1986.

98 Hart, *A Trading Nation*, 202; see also Ritchie, *Wrestling with the Elephant*, 130–1n.32.

99 The report, written by Grey, Clark, Shih and Associates, was released to the public in May 1986 in redacted form after an Access to Information

request. Subsequently, it was republished in its entirety in Cameron, ed., *The Free Trade Papers*, 155–63.

100 'Discussion Paper: Canada-US Trade Negotiations: Automotive Trade,' 30 June 1986, DFAIT, 37-7-1-USA-2, vol. 44.

101 Ibid.; J.M. Weekes, 'Memorandum for the Deputy Minister for International Trade: Canada-US Trade Negotiations: Automobile Trade Discussion Paper,' 3 July 1986, DFAIT, 37-7-1-USA-2, vol. 44.

102 Memorandum to Cabinet (DRIE), 'Automotive Issues and Policy Instruments,' 10 September 1986, 7, PCO.

103 Brian Milner, 'New Automotive Policy Likely Won't Be Created before Trade Deadline,' *G&M*, 14 April 1987.

104 The government's auto strategy paper was again put off by Côté's successor, Robert de Cotret, in February 1988. De Cotret argued that the FTA had dealt with many issues related to the automotive industry. Paul McKeague, 'Tory Auto Policy Still Months Away,' *WS*, 23 February 1988; James Daw, 'Car Giants Propose 50% Rule for Free Trade,' and 'Ottawa Puts off Strategy Paper on Auto Pact,' *TS*, 14 and 15 July 1987; T.A. Bernes (EA), 'Canada-US Trade Negotiations: Automotive Trade,' 27 October 1986, DFAIT, 37-7-1-USA-2, vol. 44.

105 J.L. MacNeil and Paul S.H. Lau (EA) to deputy minister, 'Bilateralization of the Auto Pact,' 14 May 1987, DFAIT, 37-7-1-USA-2, vol. 44.

106 Anthony T. Eyton and G.E. Shannon to Pat Carney, 'Memorandum: Meeting with Automotive Industry Group – June 9 1987,' 12 June 1987, DFAIT, 37-7-1-USA-2, vol. 44. Donald S. Macdonald, chair of the royal commission, urged that the auto pact be included in the negotiations, since the Canadian industry was in good shape but would be in a more difficult position later on.

107 Paul S.H. Lau to deputy minister, 'Auto Pact Safeguards and Conditions,' 10 August 1987, DFAIT, 37-7-1-USA-2, vol. 44.

108 Ibid.

109 Clayton Yeutter to George Schultz, Howard Baker, and Frank Carlucci, 9 September 1987, RRL, Dan Crippen Papers, Series I, Subject Files: 'Canada,' box 2, file: 'Canada Free Trade' (1). For more views on the negotiations, see Doern and Tomlin, *Faith and Fear*; and Ritchie, *Wrestling with the Elephant*.

110 Consul general, New York, to Ottawa, 'CDA-USA Trade Negos – Autos,' 29 September 1987; and Paul S.H. Lau to deputy minister, 'Auto Pact Safeguards and Conditions,' 10 August 1987. Both in DFAIT, 37-7-1-USA-2, vol. 44.

111 A copy of the initial text of the agreement can be found in 'Agreed Text,' 4

October 1987, RRL, Dan Crippen Papers, Series I, Subject Files: 'Canada,' box 2, file: 'Canada Free Trade' (4). On the agreement and its negotiation, see: Hart, Dymond, and Robertson, *Decision at Midnight*; Macdonald, *Free Trade*; Winham and DeBoer-Ashworth, 'Asymmetry in Negotiation the Canada-US Free Trade Agreement, 1985–7'; Kreinin, ed., *Building a Partnership*.

112 'Recommended Telephone Call,' and 'Talking Points,' 4 October 1987, RRL, Dan Crippen Papers, Series I, Subject Files: 'Canada,' box 2, file: 'Canada Free Trade' (4).

113 G.A. Peapples to Simon Reisman and Michael Wilson, 20 and 21 October 1987, DFAIT, 37-7-1-USA-2, vol. 44; Clayton Yeutter to Donald J. Pease, n.d., RRL, Dan Crippen Papers, Series I, Subject Files: 'Canada,' box 2, file: 'Canada Free Trade' (4).

114 'Agreed Text,' 4 October 1987, RRL, Dan Crippen Papers, Series I, Subject Files: 'Canada,' box 2, file: 'Canada Free Trade' (4).

115 When the 'blue ribbon' panel was finally established in 1989, its Canadian membership complained of a lack of U.S. interest and funding. Former Ontario cabinet minister Darcy McKeough, head of the Canadian side, told reporters that the situation was 'very embarrassing' for the U.S. delegation. Eventually the panel did begin meeting, and recommended in 1990 that the North American content requirement of the FTA's auto provisions be raised from 50 per cent to 60 per cent. Madelaine Drohan, 'Dearth of US Government Financing Stalls Joint Free-Trade Auto Panel,' *G&M*, 10 April 1990; James Rusk, 'Free-Trade Panel Offers 60% Solution,' *G&M*, 4 August, 1990.

116 Quoted in 'Trade Deal Offers No Security for Canada's Auto Industry,' *TS*, 13 July 1988.

117 Percy T. Eastham to deputy minister, 'Canada/USA Free Trade Agreement – Automotive Trade,' 16 October 1987; and Paul S.H. Lau to deputy minister, 'Auto Pact Safeguards and Conditions,' 10 August 1987. Both in DFAIT, 37-7-1-USA-2, vol. 44.

118 Secretary of commerce (William Verity, Jr) to John Dingell, n.d., RRL, Dan Crippen Papers, Series I, Subject Files: 'Canada,' box 2, file: 'Canada Free Trade' (1).

119 Percy T. Eastham to deputy minister, 'Canada/USA Free Trade Agreement – Automotive Trade,' 16 October 1987, DFAIT, 37-7-1-USA-2, vol. 44.

120 The $46-billion figure is cited in press release, USTR, 'Background on the US-Canada Economic Relationship,' 4 October 1987, RRL, Dan Crippen Papers, Series I, Subject Files: 'Canada,' box 2, file: 'Canada Free Trade' (1).

121 Secretary of commerce (William Verity, Jr) to John Dingell, n.d.; and press release, USTR, 'Background on the US-Canada Economic Relationship,' 4 October 1987. Both in RRL, Dan Crippen Papers, Series I, Subject Files: 'Canada,' box 2, file: 'Canada Free Trade' (1).

122 John Dingell to James Baker III, 25 May 1988, RRL, Dan Crippen Papers, Series I, Subject Files: 'Canada,' box 2, file: 'Canada Free Trade' (4).

123 U.S. Senate, *Hearings before the Committee on Finance, United States-Canada Free Trade Agreement – 1988* (Washington, 1989), 13–14 (15 and 21 April 1988).

124 Ibid.

125 Ibid., 17.

126 Ibid., 20–1.

127 Ibid., 19.

128 Ibid., 11–12.

129 As early as 1986, Gindin had presciently warned White about the impact of a 50 per cent North American rule: 'In terms of "fairness" why would we accept 50% content – half the content imported – as an adequate goal[?] GM, Ford and Chrysler, which entered the 1980s with over 90% content on average for North America, would be allowed to devastate jobs in the US as they fall to 50% content.' Sam Gindin to Robert White and Buzz Hargrove, 'Meeting with Cote,' 15 September 1986, SGP, vol. 1986, pt. 2; Linda McQuaig, 'Agreement Pulls Auto Pact Teeth, Union Leader Says,' *G&M*, 6 October 1987; Bob White, 'The Deal Undermines Canada's Auto Industry,' *TS*, 19 October 1987.

130 Robert Sheppard, 'Peterson Says He Needs "a Lot of Persuading,"' *G&M*, 6 October 1987; Ontario, *Debates*, 5 November 1987, 77 (Monte Kwinter).

131 Duncan McMonagle and Robert Sheppard, 'Japan Has Basis for Complaint about Deal's Terms, Study Says,' *G&M*, 19 February 1988.

132 This was pointed out by J. Krikorian in her 'Canada and the WTO: Multilevel Governance, Public Policy-Making and the WTO Auto Pact Case,' http://www.wto.org/english/res_e/booksp_e/casestudies_e/case9_e.htm#auto (accessed 13 December 2010).

133 White House, Office of the Press Secretary, 'Remarks by the President in Briefing on Canada-US Free Trade,' 2 November 1987, RRL, Dan Crippen Papers, Series I, Subject Files: 'Canada,' box 2, file: 'Canada Free Trade' (1).

134 This dynamic is well analysed in Eden and Molot, 'Insiders, Outsiders and Host Country Bargains.'

135 Ibid., 376.

136 The Japanese claimed that the 60 per cent rule was not a problem, but that

they simply needed time to achieve that level of content. Ken Romain, 'Japanese May Raise Canadian Parts Use: 60% Level Okay, Car Maker Says,' *G&M*, 26 October 1990.

137 'Trade Deal Offers No Security for Canada's Auto Industry,' *TS*, 13 July 1988.

138 Cantin and Lowenfeld, 'Rules of Origin, the Canada-US FTA and the Honda Case.'

139 Sam Gindin to Robert White and Buzz Hargrove, 'Meeting with Cote,' 15 September 1986, SGP, vol. 1986, pt. 2.

140 Neil Macdonald, 'Will the Free Trade Agreement Drive a Gaping Hole through the Auto Pact?' *Policy Options*, January/February 1989, 10–17 at 10.

141 On this complex issues, see Anastakis, 'Requiem for a Trade Agreement.'

Conclusion: One in Six: The Ratio of Survival

1 'Before the auto pact,' CBC Newsmagazine television report, 2 October 1960, http://www.archives.cbc.ca/economy_business/trade_agree-ments/topics/326/ (accessed 17 August 2010).

2 DesRosiers relates the story as such: 'My first auto sector paper was written as a first year econometrics student at the University of Windsor ... The one interesting aspect of the paper was the use of the phase "one in six jobs in Ontario are tied directly or indirectly to the automotive sector."... And here we are 40 years later and this phrase is still used over and over again to describe the importance of the industry. This paper was the first to use it and now you know the origin of this phrase. The second time the phrase was used was when as a young buck economist working in the Ontario Treasury I was part of a team of economists who published a budget paper (1974) which updated my work and verified the math and that paper is usually considered the source of the quote but in reality it was from the very first article I every wrote on this sector.' Dennis DesRosiers, correspondence with author, 16 September 2009. Author's personal papers.

3 Ontario, *Debates*, 2 April 1976, 1130 (Darcy McKeough, Chatham) and 2 May 1978, 2132 (Michael Cassidy, Ottawa Centre); Ontario, *Canada's Share of the North American Auto Industry*, 1.

4 Mark Witten, 'Why the Auto Pact Is Obsolete: The Coming Technological Revolution May Make Our Biggest Trade Agreement about as Practical as a Horse and Buggy,' *Canadian Business*, February 1979, 33–6, 96; 'Carting away Our Jobs: The Case of the Auto Pact,' *Saturday Night*, March 1979, 74.

5 C.D. Arthur and Associates, Automotive Task Force, *Review of the North American Automotive Industry*, 2.

6 Neil Goldschmidt, 'Memorandum for the President: Automobile Imports,' 14 March 1980, JCL, Office of Staff Secretary, Handwriting File, box 116, file: 22 January 1979 (1); Dan Saks to George Eads, 'Indirect Auto Employment in the US Economy,' 23 June 1980, JCL, Council of Economic Advisors, box 4, file: 'Auto Imports,' 4.

7 To mention just a few examples, conservative icon George Will cited the figure in a *Newsweek* column, while the Ford Motor Company went one better and stated in a 1977 internal report that auto-related employment in the United States was 16.1 million, or about 19 per cent of total U.S. employment – 'roughly 1 person out of every 5 working Americans.' When he introduced a sales-tax rebate in 1979, Ontario Treasurer Frank Miller claimed that 'all of you are aware of the importance of the auto industry to this province. Accounting for one of every six jobs in Ontario, the industry is a vital and critical part of our industrial structure.' A year later, he repeated the ratio in 'spelling out the case for a fair share of North American auto production in Canada' to federal Finance Minister Allan MacEachen. George F. Will, 'The Case for Automakers,' *Newsweek*, 2 March 1981, 88; Ford Motor Company, 'Selected Background Date on the US Automobile Industry,' 1 April 1977, JCL, WHCF, box BE-12, file 3-15, 1 August 1979–22 August 1979; 'Statement by the Honourable Frank S. Miller, Treasurer of Ontario: Announcing the Temporary Ontario Tax Rebate Program for 1979 Model Year Motor Vehicles,' 31 January 1980, LAC, RG 20, file 4954-1, vol. 2, 837; Frank Miller to Allan MacEachen, 12 March, 1980, LAC, RG 19, vol. 5738, file 3881-01, pt. 3.

8 Alan Christie, 'Trade Talks Must Include Auto Pact, Social Programs, US Official Says,' *TS*, 24 October 1985.

9 As quoted in Ontario, *Debates*, 9 November 1987, 124 (D.S. Cooke, Windsor).

10 During its 2009 bankruptcy, General Motors of Canada's restructuring plan repeated the one-in-seven figure. In the 2000s, there were approximately 150,000 jobs directly related to auto manufacture in Canada. There were also hundreds of thousands of jobs in the retail, aftermarket, and repair segments of the industry, and thousands more that indirectly existed to support all this employment. The actual figure is difficult to determine. 'Toyota's Managing Director at U of G,' *Guelph Mercury*, 11 March 2009, http://www.news.guelphmercury.com/News/article/450846 (accessed 14 December 2010).

11 Robert Latimer to Herb Gray, 'Options Paper,' 10 November 1980, LAC,

RG 19, vol. 5738, file 3881-01, pt. 3. The Canadian share of the North American market rarely accounted for more than 10 per cent.

12 See Atkinson and Coleman, *The State, Business and Industrial Change in Canada*.

13 On this point, see Dobell, 'Negotiating with the United States.' See also Muirhead, *Dancing around the Elephant*, and Donaghy, *Tolerant Allies*, for examples of Canadian negotiations with the United States in this period.

14 The federal and Ontario governments provided $60.5 million in funding for the new plants, to be repaid over seven years by a 1 per cent royalty on every car produced. Since AMC would be down for retooling, the federal government also waived any penalties to meet auto pact requirements. Maurice C. Fertey (president AMC Canada) to Herb Gray, 4 May 1981, LAC, RG 20, file 4956-1, vol. 5, March 1981–June 1981; James Daw, 'More Auto Spending Coming after AMC, Lumley Says,' *TS*, 12 June 1984.

15 Roy F. Bennett (president, Ford Canada) to Campbell Stuart, 4 May 1981, LAC, RG 20, file 4956-1, vol. 5, March 1981–June 1981.

16 J.R. Rinehart (president GM Canada) to Herb Gray, 4 May 1981, LAC, RG 20, file 4956-1, vol. 5, March 1981–June 1981.

17 Campbell Stuart to Herb Gray, 'Restructuring of the Canadian Automotive Industry,' 9 April 1981, LAC, RG 20, file 4956-1, vol. 5, March 1981–June 1981.

18 'Automotive Day, 1984: Notes for a Speech by Robert White,' 28 August 1984, binder 1984, SGP.

19 Of course, it has also been argued that this geography was also responsible for the indigenous Canadian auto industry's demise by the 1920s. See, for example, Roberts, *In the Shadow of Detroit*; Anastakis, 'From Independence to Integration.'

20 Rubenstein, *Making and Selling Cars*; Rubenstein and Klier, *Who Really Made Your Car?* For some of Holmes's prolific work, see chapter 1.

21 See, for instance, the work of David A. Wolfe: 'Networking among Regions' and 'The Role of Cooperative Industrial Policy in Canada and Ontario.' See also Barnes and Gertler, eds. *Towards a New Industrial Geography*; and Mordue, 'Government, Foreign Direct Investment and the Canadian Automotive Industry, 1977–1987,' especially 20–3.

22 Canada, *Debates*, 4 June 1984, 4324–5 (Ian Waddell, Vancouver-Kingsway; Ed Lumley, Stormont-Dundas).

23 Between 1955 and 1963, the cost of transporting finished autos fell by 40–50 per cent, according to James Rubenstein. See his 'The Changing Distribution of US Automobile Assembly Plants,' 14.

24 See, for instance, Anastakis, 'Building a "New Nova Scotia."'

25 This dynamic was also present in Quebec, where a much smaller auto sector than Ontario's existed.

26 Another element also comes into view as a consequence of the emerging 'automotive bureaucracy.' The creation and expansion of federal and provincial state capacities to address the post-1965 dynamic was, at the same time, accompanied by a corresponding growth in the auto industry's own apparatus within the new auto pact framework. In the post-war period, especially after 1965, lobby groups such as the MVMA or the APMA became more sophisticated and expanded their efforts to lobby both the federal and Ontario governments. The emergence of this growing 'automotive lobby' is another consequence of the evolution of the federalism of the auto industry.

27 In 2006 *Foreign Direct Investment* magazine awarded Ontario Premier Dalton McGuinty the title of 'Personality of the Year' for bringing $7 billion in new automotive investment to Ontario in 2003–6.

28 Author's interview with William Davis, 7 August 2008.

29 Difficulties between Conservative Ottawa and Liberal Ontario over a range of issues persisted even as the two governments worked together in 2009 to orchestrate the single-largest non-wartime expenditure of government funds in Canadian history in bailing out GM and Chrysler.

30 D.W. Salsman to G.M. Mitchell, 19 November 1975, NASRM, RG 55, vol. 10, file IEL, Canadian Motor Industries, 1973–6, 1.

31 Roger Taylor, 'Volvo Plant Closure Shocking but Not Unexpected,' *Halifax Chronicle-Herald*, 15 September 1998.

32 See, for instance, the *G&M*-CTV poll by the Strategic Council, 'State of Canadian Public Opinion on Government Assistance for the Auto Sector,' 17 March 2009. Fifty-six per cent of Ontarians supported government support for the industry, while 62 per cent of westerners and Quebecers were opposed.

33 See, for instance, Bhagwati and Srinivasan, 'Trade and the Environment,' Klevorick, 'Reflections on the Race to the Bottom,' and Wilson, 'Capital Mobility and Environmental Standards.'

34 Luger, *Corporate Power, American Democracy, and the Automobile Industry.*

35 Ironically, in the wake of the recent debate surrounding global warming, Quebec and Manitoba have pledged to go to California standards.

36 Some cars sold in Canada did have the new technologies and were thus meeting the higher U.S. standards. DOT officials estimated that about 60 per cent of the vehicles on the road in 1978 were specifically of Canadian design, the remainder having U.S. emission standards (this included about 55 per cent of GM's, 31 per cent of Ford's, and 96 per cent of Chrysler's

cars). 'Discussion Paper: 1981–1985 Light Duty Vehicle Emission Levels,'
28 June 1978, LAC, RG 12, vol. 2, file S1500-23-1 (box 9).

37 Gordon McGregor, 'Bennett Questions Cost-Benefit Ratio of Tougher 1975
Auto Emission Standards,' *G&M*, 15 September 1972.

38 Eventually, Ford put converters on all its cars, yet a myth of catalytic converters cutting fuel economy, which had sprung up in part from the government's decision, persisted. Some Canadians were disconnecting any
emission-control devices in the belief that doing so would improve their
fuel economy. This was not the case, however, since catalytic converters actually had been shown to improve mileage. 'Discussion Paper: 1981–1985
Light Duty Vehicle Emission Levels,' 28 June 1978, LAC, RG 12, vol. 2, file
S1500-23-1 (box 9); Ellen Roseman, 'About 40 Per Cent of Cars Stopped
Fail Pollution Tests,' *G&M*, 28 February 1980; Mariana Strauss, '40 to 50
Per Cent of Ontario Vehicles Pollute Too Much,' *G&M*, 30 December 1980.

39 Ken Romain, 'Auto Trend Is to Smaller, More Efficient Engines,' *G&M*, 11
November 1978.

40 The update showed that three-way catalytic converters had reduced emissions of N_2O by two megatonnes in the 1990s from the expected output.
Natural Resources Canada, *Canada's Emission's Outlook: An Update* (Ottawa, 1999), 23. This report can be found at http://www.nrcan.gc.ca/es/
ceo/outlook.pdf (accessed 22 March 2008).

41 This eventually happened in 1999 when automotive emissions were
moved to the Canadian Environmental Protection Act (CEPA). Canada,
Subcommittee on Acid Rain, Commons Standing Committee on Forestry
and Fisheries, *Still Waters: The Chilling Reality of Acid Rain*.

42 Editorial, 'It Came from the Tailpipe,' *G&M*, 9 December 1981.

43 Michael Keating, 'Canada in a Bind over Dirty Car Exhausts,' *G&M*, 9 July
1983.

44 On Canadian auto emissions and acid rain, see Schmandt, Clarkson, and
Roderick, eds., *Acid Rain and Friendly Neighbors*, 143–4; Allison, 'Fortuitous
Consequence.'

45 United States Senate, *Hearings before the Committee on Finance, United States-
Canada Free Trade Agreement – 1988*, 15 and 21 April 1988 (Washington,
1989), 17.

46 P.D. Lee to file, 'Auto Pact-Canada/USA Trade Talks, Michelin,' 21 April
1972, DFAIT, 37-7-1-USA-2, vol. 31.

47 Muirhead, *Dancing around the Elephant*, 9.

48 Examples of deindustrialization historiography which focus on workers
and community responses include: High, *Industrial Sunset*; Dudley, *The
End of the Line*; Sobel and Meurer, *Working at Inglis*; and Mellon, *After the*

Smoke Clears. Some early deindustrialization work in the United States focused more upon industrial policy than community responses. For example, see Reich and Donahue, *New Deals*; and Podgursky, 'A National Industrial Policy.' A significant early book that looked at both community responses and industrial policy more broadly is Bluestone and Harrison, *The Deindustrialization of America*.

49 For these views, see, in particular: Laxer, *(Canada) Ltd.*; and Drache, *The Deindustrialization of Canada and Its Implications for Labour*.

50 Sociologist Michael Del Balso argues that Canada did not, in fact, deindustrialize in the post-war period, and if anything, 'Canada's manufacturing base has generally grown.' See his 'Is Canada: De-Industrializing?' ii.

51 High, *Industrial Sunset*, 11–12, 194. Although he notes that 300,000 auto workers lost their jobs in North America in 1978–82, High does not focus on the auto industry.

52 On the state as the 'visible hand' in Canadian economic development, see Bliss, 'Canada in the Age of the Visible Hand.' In this context, the term refers to state intervention, as opposed to managerial capitalism as expounded by business historian Alfred D. Chandler in *The Visible Hand*.

53 L.R. Wilson, Ontario deputy minister of industry at the time, saw the influence of these Liberal cabinet ministers as key in ensuring that the issue was a priority for the government, and helping to secure the package. Author's interview with L.R. Wilson, 27 June 2006. Along with Gray, Liberal cabinet ministers Eugene Whelan and Mark MacGuigan also hailed from Windsor-area ridings.

54 Richard Conrad, 'Chrysler Aid Hinges on Job Guarantees, Herb Gray States,' *TS*, 2 May 1980.

55 'Secret: Production to Sales Ratios, Specified Commercial Vehicles,' LAC, RG 19, vol. 5959, file 8705-08-15, box 241; Bill Shields, 'New Plant for Chrysler,' *WS*, 13 December 1973; Local 444, Windsor, Ont., 'Auto Pact–Industrial Policy,' in *Recognizing Pillette: Its History, Its Pride, Its Determination, Its People*.

56 Canada, *Debates*, 18 January 1983 (Herb Gray, Windsor). The May 1980 agreement was supplemented by a February 1981 MOU and another change in the agreement in January 1983.

57 Bob Hepburn, 'Ottawa Bails out Dome,' *TS*, 26 June 1982.

58 In the United States, Carter administration Treasury Secretary William Miller initially rejected any federal assistance, while in the Congress Senator William Proxmire (D.Wisconsin) argued against the bailout. Michigan Democratic Representative James Blanchard needed all of his political skills to shepherd the agreement through Congress. In Canada, in contrast, both the Liberals and Progressive Conservatives were committed to some

form of bailout at the outset. On Blanchard, see Holmes, 'How Chrysler Went to Washington and Blanchard Went to Bat,' *Detroit Magazine* (*Detroit Free Press*), 25 May 1980.

59 C. Arthur Borg (State) to Zbigniew Brzesinksi, 'Visit of Prime Minister Trudeau,' JCL, WHCF, box CO 14, file CO 28, 20 January 1977–20 January 1981.

60 The notion of a special relationship between the two countries has been a long-standing aspect of writing on Canada-U.S. relations. For instance, John Kirton and Robert Bothwell have written: 'On July 12, 1965, the heads of government of the United States and Canada issued a document, subtitled "Principles For Partnership," which provided the clearest and most comprehensive statement to date of the special relationship which had governed their countries' interaction throughout the post-World War II period.' 'A Proud and Powerful Country,' 108; David Anderson for C. Arthur Borg (State) to Zbigniew Brzesinksi, 'Characterizations of the US-Canadian Relationship,' n.d., JCL, WHCF, box CO 14, file CO 28, 1 June 1977–30 September 1981.

61 'Henry Ford II Speech,' April 1966, WRL, UAW-Ford, box 14, file 22.

62 American embassy, Ottawa, to secretary of state, Washington, 'Linkage: A Small Ominous Cloud on an Otherwise Bright Horizon,' 16 March 1981, RRL, Executive Secretariat: NSC Country Files, box 12, Canada (6 March 1981–21 June 1981).

63 On Bow's view of the role of domestic actors in reshaping the Canada-U.S. diplomatic relationship, see *The Politics of Linkage*, 14–15.

64 This example provides a contrast to Bow's examination of the Canada-U.S. conflict over Trudeau's National Energy Program, where 'the fragmentation of the American system created opportunities for interest groups adversely affected by Canadian policy to pressure policy-makers for more effectively bargaining.' Bow, *The Politics of Linkage*, 170.

65 Alastair Gillespie to file, 'Re: Impressions and Comments on "An Outline of a New Trade Strategy for Canada" Published by the Economic Council of Canada, Summer 1975,' 4 September 1975, LAC, OG Stoner Papers, MG 31, E100, vol. 7, Working Files (3 of 4).

66 During the auto pact negotiations, Reisman told Walter Gordon that the United States would likely not propose outright free trade in the sector: 'Such a proposition is so obviously unbalanced in favour of the US that we doubt that the US would seriously put up a proposition as crude and obvious as this.' Anastakis, *Auto Pact*, 68, 64.

67 Memorandum to Cabinet (DRIE), 'Automotive Issues and Policy Instruments,' 10 September 1986, 49, PCO.

Bibliography

Archival Sources: Canada

Government of Canada Records
Department of External Affairs
Ministry of Finance
Ministry of Industry
Ministry of Transport
Privy Council Records

Department of Foreign Affairs and International Trade
File 37-7-1-USA-2: Foreign Trade – Tariff Negotiations – Canada – and Canada
   with other countries – USA – Auto Pact; vols. 36–44

Library and Archives of Canada

MANUSCRIPT RECORDS
Edgar Benson Papers
Walter Gordon Papers
Simon Reisman Papers
O.G. Stoner Papers

OTHER
Royal Commission on the Automotive Industry (Bladen Commission)
Royal Commission on Canada's Economic Prospects (Gordon Commission)
Royal Commission of Inquiry into the Canadian Automotive Industry (Reis-
   man Commission)
United Automobile Workers, Canadian Section (Canadian Auto Workers)

Privy Council Office
Cabinet Records

Archives of Ontario
Economic Development and Trade
Leslie Frost Papers
John P. Robarts Papers
Treasury

New Brunswick Provincial Archives
Department of Commerce and Development
Department of Economic Development and Tourism
Premier's Office Files, Richard Hatfield

Nova Scotia Archives and Records Management
Trade and Commerce
Trade and Industry

Other Archives and Institutions
Canadian Auto Workers Union Library and Archives, Toronto
Dennis DesRosiers Papers, DesRosiers Automotive Consultants, Richmond
    Hill, Ont.
Sam Gindin Papers, Toronto
Greig Mordue Papers, Cambridge, Ont.
Ford Motor Company of Canada, Oakville, Ont.

Archival Sources: United States

National Archives of the United States of America (Washington, D.C.)

NARA, ARCHIVES II, COLLEGE PARK, MD.
Bureau of Export Administration
Records of the Department of Commerce
Records of the Department of State
Records of the Department of the Treasury

NIXON PRESIDENTIAL FILES
National Security Council Files
White House Central Files
White House Confidential Files

WHITE HOUSE STAFF PAPERS
Peter Flanigan
Peter Peterson

Lyndon Baines Johnson Presidential Library (University of Texas, Austin, Texas)

ADMINISTRATION RECORDS
National Security Files
White House Central Files
White House Confidential Files

WHITE HOUSE STAFF OFFICE FILES
Mike Manatos
Bill Moyers
Henry Hall Wilson

PERSONAL PAPERS
George Ball Papers
Francis M. Bator Papers
Henry H. Fowler Papers

Gerald R. Ford Presidential Library (Ann Arbor, Mich.)

ADMINISTRATION RECORDS
National Security Files
White House Central Files
White House Confidential Files
White House Name Files

WHITE HOUSE STAFF OFFICE FILES
Arthur Burns Papers
James M. Cannon Papers
Judith R. Hope Papers
Stephen G. McConahey Papers
Glenn R. Schleede
L. William Seidman Papers

OTHER
Congressional Relations Office – Max L. Friedersdorf Papers

Jimmy Carter Presidential Library (Atlanta, Ga.)

ADMINISTRATION RECORDS
Handwriting Files
National Security Files
Presidential Papers: President's Office Files
White House Central Files

WHITE HOUSE STAFF FILES
Kathryn Bernick Files
Stu Eizenstat Files
Ray Jenkins Files

OTHER
Office of Congressional Liaison
Council of Economic Advisors
Alfred E. Kahn Papers
Al McDonald Papers

Ronald Reagan Presidential Library (Simi Valley, Calif.)

ADMINISTRATION RECORDS
National Security Files
Presidential Handwriting Files
White House Central Files
White House Confidential Files

WHITE HOUSE STAFF OFFICE FILES
Howard Baker Files
Tyrus Cobb Files
Dan L. Crippen Files
Tony R. Dolan Files
John G. Roberts Files
Peter R. Sommer Files

Benson Ford Research Center (Ann Arbor, Mich.)
Ford Motor Company, Corporate Records
Frank Hill Research Papers
Allan Nevins Research Papers
Mira Wilkins Research papers

Bentley Historical Library (Ann Arbor, Mich.)
James Blanchard Papers
Frederic Donner Papers
William D. Ford Papers
Robert Grant Papers
Martha Wright Griffiths Papers
Phillip Hart Papers
Arvid Jouppi Papers
George S. May Papers
William G. Milliken Papers
George Romney Papers

National Automotive Research Centre, Detroit Public Library (Detroit, Mich.)
Bricklin Papers

Walter P. Reuther Library: Archives of Labor and Urban Affairs (Wayne State University, Detroit, Mich.)

UNITED AUTO WORKERS COLLECTION
Canadian Regional Office Collection
Chrysler Department Collection
International Executive Board Collection
Toronto Sub Regional Office Collection
Owen Bieber Papers
George Burt Papers
Douglas Fraser Papers
Walter P. Reuther Papers
Leonard Woodcock Papers

Secondary Sources

Government Publications: Canada

Arthur, C.D., and Associates, Canadian Automotive Task Force. *Review of the North American Automotive Industry*. Ottawa: Queen's Printer 1977.
Automotive Task Force. *Report*. Ottawa: Queen's Printer 1977.
Bladen, Vincent. *Royal Commission on the Automotive Industry. Report*. Ottawa: Queen's Printer 1961.
Brecher, Irving, and Simon Reisman. *Royal Commission on Canadian Economic*

Prospects: Canada-United States Economic Relations. Ottawa: Queen's Printer 1957.

Canada. *The Canada-US Free Trade Agreement: Overview.* Ottawa: Queen's Printer 1987.

– *Debates of the House of Commons.* Ottawa: Queen's Printer, various years.

– *Foreign Direct Investment in Canada.* Ottawa: Queen's Printer 1972.

– *Report of the Automotive Task Force.* Ottawa: Queen's Printer 1983.

– *Report on the Canadian Automotive Industry.* Ottawa: Queen's Printer 1983.

– *Report of the Royal Commission on Canada's Economic Prospects.* Ottawa: Queen's Printer 1958.

– *Report of the Royal Commission on the Economic Union and Development Prospects for Canada, Vol. 1.* Ottawa: Minister of Supply and Services 1985.

Canada. Subcommittee on Acid Rain, Commons Standing Committee on Forestry and Fisheries. *Still Waters: The Chilling Reality of Acid Rain.* Ottawa: Queen's Printer 1981.

Department of External Affairs. *Canadian Trade Policy in the 1980's – A Discussion Paper.* Ottawa: Queen's Printer 1983.

– *External Affairs.* Ottawa: Queen's Printer, various years.

Department of Foreign Affairs and International Trade. *Documents on Canadian External Relations.* Ottawa: Queen's Printer, various years.

Department of Regional Industrial Expansion. *Report on the Canadian Automotive Industry.* Ottawa: Queen's Printer 1983.

Environment Canada. *The Clean Air Act, Annual Report, 1974–1975.* Ottawa: Queen's Printer 1975.

Gordon, Walter. *Royal Commission on Canadian Economic Prospects: Final Report.* Ottawa: Queen's Printer 1957.

Heiz, Andrew, Sébastian LaRochelle-Côté, Michael Bordt, and Sudip Pas. *Labour Markets, Business Growth, Population Growth and Mobility in Canadian CMAs.* Ottawa: Statistics Canada 2005.

Industry Canada. *1983 Report on the Canadian Automobile Industry.* Ottawa: Minister of Supply and Services 1984.

Industry Canada. Automotive Branch. *Automotive Industry: Overview and Prospects.* Ottawa: Minister of Supply and Services 1995.

– *Statistical Review of the Canadian Automotive Industry.* Ottawa: Minister of Supply and Services 1990.

Industry, Science and Technology Canada. *Report on the Canadian Automotive Industry.* Ottawa: Queen's Printer 1989.

Reisman, Simon. *The Canadian Automotive Industry: Performance and Proposals.*

Report of the Royal Commission Inquiry into the Canadian Automotive Industry. Ottawa: Ministry of Supply and Services 1978.

Standing Senate Committee on Foreign Affairs. *Canada-United States Relations, Vol. III*. Ottawa: Queen's Printer 1982.

Sun Life Assurance Co. of Canada. *The Canadian Automotive Industry*. Ottawa: Queen's Printer 1956.

Taylor, G.W. *Automobile Emission Trends in Canada 1960–1985*. Ottawa: Queen's Printer 1973.

Woods, J.D., and Gordon Ltd. *Royal Commission on Canadian Economic Prospects: The Canadian Agricultural Machinery Industry*. Ottawa: Queen's Printer 1956.

Young, John H. *Royal Commission on Canadian Economic Prospects: Canadian Commercial Policy*. Ottawa: Queen's Printer 1957.

Government Publications: Province of Ontario

Ministry of Treasury, Economics and Intergovernmental Affairs. *Canada's Share of the North American Automotive Industry: An Ontario Perspective*. Toronto: Queen's Printer of Ontario 1978.

Government Publications: United States

Environmental Protection Agency. 'Revised Motor Vehicle Exhaust Emission Standards for Carbon Monoxide (CO) for 1981 and 1982 Model Year Light Duty Vehicles.' *United States Federal Register*, 1979.

House of Representatives. *Special Report on the Joint Review of the United States Canada Automotive Products Trade Agreement*. Document no. 379, 4 September 1968. Washington, D.C.: Government Printing Office 1968.

Senate Finance Committee. *Canadian Automobile Agreement: Annual Reports of the President to the Congress on the Implementation of the Automotive Products Trade Agreement*. Washington, D.C.: Government Printing Office, various years.

– *Canadian Automobile Agreement: Hearing before the Committee on Finance, United States Senate*. Washington, D.C.: Government Printing Office 1968.

– *Canadian Automobile Agreement: United States International Trade Commission Report on the US-Canadian Automotive Agreement: Its History, Terms and Impact*. Washington, D.C.: Government Printing Office 1976.

– *Hearings before the Committee on Finance, United States-Canada Free Trade*

Agreement –1988, United States Senate, April 15, 21, 1988. Washington, D.C.: Government Printing Office 1989.

– *Report of Proceedings: Hearings Held before the Sub-Committee of International Trade on the Committee of Finance.* Washington, D.C.: Government Printing Office, 27 February 1976.

– *United States-Canada Automobile Agreement: Hearings before the Committee on Finance, United States Senate, on H.R. 9042, September 14, 15, 16, 20 and 21, 1965.* Washington, D.C.: Government Printing Office 1965.

Senate Foreign Relations Committee. *Automotive Products Agreement between the United States and Canada: Hearing before a Subcommittee of the Committee on Foreign Relations, 10 February, 1965.* Washington, D.C.: Government Printing Office 1965.

Senate Subcommittee on Employment and Productivity. *Hearings Held before the Sub-Committee on Employment and Productivity: United States-Japan Auto Relations.* Washington, D.C.: Government Printing Office, 25 September 1986.

United States. *Congressional Record, Senate and House of Representatives.* Washington, D.C.: Government Printing Office, various years.

– *Department of State Bulletin.* Washington, D.C.: Government Printing Office, various years.

– *Seventh Annual Report of the President to the Congress on the Operation of the Automotive Product Trades Act of 1965.* Washington, D.C.: Government Printing Office 1973.

– *Eighth Annual Report of the President to the Congress on the Operation of the Automotive Product Trades Act of 1965.* Washington, D.C.: Government Printing Office 1974.

– *The Foreign Relations of the United States.* Washington, D.C.: United States Government Printing Office, various years.

United States, Department of Commerce (Charles R. Weaver). *Impact of Environmental, Energy, and Safety Regulations and of the Emerging Market Factors upon the US Sector of the North American Auto Industry.* Washington, D.C.: Government Printing Office 1977.

United States Department of Commerce, Bureau of Statistics, and Statistics Canada. *The Reconciliation of US-Canada Trade Statistics 1970: A Report by the US-Canada Trade Statistics Committee.* Washington, D.C., and Ottawa: Government Printing Office 1970.

United States Federal Register. Washington, D.C.: Government Printing Office, various years.

United States International Trade Commission. *Report on the Canadian-United States Automobile Agreement: Its History, Terms, and Impact.* Washington, D.C.: Government Printing Office 1976.

United States Joint Economic Committee. *Hearing before the Sub-Committee on Trade, Productivity, and Economic Growth*. Washington, D.C.: Government Printing Office, 24 April 1986.

Non-Governmental Organization Publications

General Agreement on Tariffs and Trade. *Basic Instruments and Selected Documents*. Geneva, various years.

Books, Journal Articles, and Theses

Abella, Irving. *Nationalism, Communism, and Canadian Labour: The CIO, The Communist Party, and the Canadian Congress of Labour, 1935–1956*. Toronto: University of Toronto Press 1973.
– 'The Role of Unions.' In Norman Hillmer, ed. *Partners Nevertheless: Canadian-American Relations in the Twentieth Century*. Toronto: Copp Clark Pitman 1989. 271–84.
Acheson, Keith. *On Strike: Six Key Labour Struggles in Canada 1919–1949*. Toronto: James Lorimer and Company 1974.
– 'Power-Steering the Canadian Automotive Industry: The 1965 Canada-USA Auto Pact and Political Exchange.' *Journal of Economic Behaviour and Organization*, 11 (1989): 237–51.
Afza, Talat. 'The US-Canadian Auto Pact of 1965: A Case Study of Sectoral Trade Liberalisation.' PhD thesis, Wayne State University, 1988.
Aitken, H.G.J. 'Defensive Expansionism: The State and Economic Growth in Canada.' In W.T. Easterbrook and M.H. Watkins, eds., *Approaches to Canadian Economic History*. Montreal and Kingston: McGill-Queen's University Press 1967. 183–221.
Alexander, W.E. *An Econometric Model of Canadian-U.S. Trade in Automotive Products, 1965–1971*. Ottawa: Bank of Canada.
Allison, Juliann Emmons. 'Fortuitous Consequences: The Domestic Politics of the 1991 Canada-United States Agreement on Air Quality.' *Policy Studies Journal*, 27, no. 2, (1999): 347–59.
Anastakis, Dimitry. 'The Advent of an International Trade Agreement: The Auto Pact at the GATT, 1964–65.' *International Journal*, 58, no. 4 (2000): 583–602.
– *Auto Pact: Creating a Borderless North American Auto Industry, 1960–71*. Toronto: University of Toronto Press 2005.
– 'Between Nationalism and Continentalism: State Auto Industry Intervention and the Canadian UAW, 1960–1970.' *Labour/Le Travail*, 53 (spring 2004): 87–124.

- 'Building a "New 'Nova Scotia": State Intervention, the Auto Industry, and the Case of Volvo in Halifax, 1963–1996.' *Acadiensis*, 34, no. 1 (2004): 3–30.
- 'Cars, Conflict, and Cooperation: The Federalism of the Canadian Auto Industry.' In Dimitry Anastakis and P.E. Bryden, eds., *Framing Canadian Federalism: Historical Essays in Honour of John T. Saywell*. Toronto: University of Toronto Press 2009. 185–210.
- 'Continental Auto Politics: The Implementation of the 1965 Auto Pact in Canada and the United States.' *Michigan Historical Review*, 27, no. 2 (2001): 131–58.
- 'From Independence to Integration: The Corporate Evolution of the Ford Motor Company of Canada, 1904–2004.' *Business History Review*, 78, no. 2 (2004): 213–53.
- 'Multilateralism, Nationalism, and Bilateral Free Trade: Competing Visions of Canadian Economic and Trade Policy, 1945–1970.' In Magda Fahrni and Robert Rutherdale, eds., *Creating Postwar Canada: Community, Diversity, and Dissent, 1945–1975*. Vancouver: UBC Press 2007. 137–61.
- 'Requiem for a Trade Agreement: The Auto Pact at the WTO, 1999–2000.' *Canadian Business Law Journal*, 34, no. 3 (2000): 313–35.
- Anderson, David. 'Levittown Is Burning! The 1979 Levittown, Pennsylvania, Gastown Riot, and the Decline of the Blue-Collar American Dream.' *Labor*, 2, no. 3 (2005): 47–65.
- Anderson, Malcolm, and John Holmes. 'High-Skill, Low-Wage Manufacturing in North America: A Case Study from the Automotive Parts Industry.' *Regional Studies*, 29, no. 7 (1995): 655–71.
- 'New Models of Industrial Organization: The Case of Magna International.' *Regional Studies*, 29, no. 7 (1995): 655–71.
- Ankli, Robert, and Fred Fredickerson. 'The Influence of American Manufacturers on the Canadian Automotive Industry.' *Business and Economic History*, 9 (1981): 101–16.
- Arnold, Samuel. 'The Impact of the Automotive Trade Agreement between Canada and the United States.' MA thesis, McGill University, 1969.
- Atkinson, Michael, and William Coleman. *The State, Business and Industrial Change in Canada*. Toronto: University of Toronto Press 1989.
- Automotive Parts and Manufacturers Association. 'The Automotive Investment Corporation: A Program for Investment and Job Creation in the Independent Automotive Parts Industry.' Toronto: APMA 1977.
- Axworthy, Tom. 'Innovation and the Party System: An Examination of Walter L. Gordon and the Liberal Party.' MA thesis, Queen's University, 1970.
- Azzi, Stephen. '"It Was Walter's View": Lester Pearson, the Liberal Party and

Economic Nationalism.' In Norman Hillmer, ed., *Pearson: The Unlikely Gladiator*. Montreal and Kingston: McGill-Queen's University Press 1999. 104–16.

– *Walter Gordon and the Rise of Canadian Nationalism*. Montreal and Kingston: McGill-Queen's University Press 1999.

Ball, George. *The Discipline of Power: Essentials of a Modern World Structure*. Boston and Toronto: Little, Brown and Company 1968.

– 'Overview of Canadian-U.S. Relations.' In Edward R. Fried and Philip H. Trezise, eds., *U.S.-Canadian Economic Relations: Next Steps?* Washington, D.C.: Brookings Institution 1984. 2–27.

Barnard, John. *American Vanguard: United Auto Workers during the Reuther Years, 1935–1970*. Detroit: Wayne State University Press 2004.

Barnes, Trevor J., and Meric S. Gertler, eds. *Towards a New Industrial Geography: Regions, Institutions and Regulations*. New York: Routledge 1999.

Barry, Donald. 'Eisenhower, St. Laurent and Free Trade, 1953.' *International Perspectives*. March/April 1987, 8–11.

Beck, J. Murray. *Pendulum of Power: Canada's Federal Elections*. Scarborough, Ont.: Prentice-Hall of Canada 1968.

Behrman, Jack N. 'International Sectoral Integration: An Alternative Approach to Freer Trade.' *Journal of World Trade Law*, 6, no. 3 (1972): 269–83.

Beigie, Carl. 'The Automotive Agreement of 1965: A Case Study in Canadian-American Economic Affairs.' In Richard Preston, ed., *The Influence of the United States on Canadian Development: Eleven Case Studies*. Durham, N.C.: Duke University Press 1972. 113–23.

– *The Canada-U.S. Automotive Agreement*. Montreal: Canadian-American Committee 1970.

Bellemare, Guy. 'End Users: Actors in the Industrial Relations System.' *British Journal of Industrial Relations*, 38, no. 3 (2007): 383–405.

Benedict, Daniel. 'The 1984 GM Agreement in Canada: Significance and Consequences.' *Relations Industrielles/Industrial Relations*, 40, no. 1 (1985): 27–47.

Bennett, Douglas C., and Kenneth E. Sharpe. *Transnational Corporations versus the State: The Political Economy of the Mexican Auto Industry*. Princeton, N.J.: Princeton University Press 1985.

Berger, Carl. *The Writing of Canadian History*. Oxford: Oxford University Press 1976.

Berggren, Christian. *The Volvo Experience: Alternatives to Lean Production in Sweden*. Ithica, N.Y.: Macmillan 1993.

Berry, Glyn. 'The Oil Lobby and the Energy Crisis.' *Canadian Public Administration*, 17, no. 4 (1974): 600–35.

Bhagwati, Jagdish, and T.N. Srinivasan. 'Trade and the Environment: Does Environmental Diversity Detract from the Case for Free Trade?' In Jagdish Bhagwati and Robert Hudec, eds., *Fair Trade and Harmonization: Prerequisites for Free Trade?* Cambridge, Mass.: MIT Press 1996. 159–223.

Bickerton, James. *Nova Scotia, Ottawa and the Politics of Regional Development.* Toronto: University of Toronto Press 1990.

Birsch, Douglas, and John Fiedler, eds. *The Ford Pinto Case: A Study in Ethics, Business, and Technology.* Albany, N.Y.: SUNY Press 1994.

Bladen, Vincent. *Bladen on Bladen.* Toronto: University of Toronto Press 1978.

Blake, David. 'Multinational Corporation, International Union, and International Collective Bargaining: A Case Study of the Political, Economic, and Social Implications of the 1967 UAW-Chrysler Agreement.' In H. Günter, ed., *Transnational Industrial Relations: The Impact of Multinational Corporations and Economic Regionalism on Industrial Relations.* New York: Macmillan 1972. 137–72.

Blanchette, Arthur. *Canadian Foreign Policy, 1955–1965: Selected Speeches and Documents.* Toronto: McClelland and Stewart 1977.

– *Canadian Foreign Policy, 1966–1976: Selected Speeches and Documents.* Toronto: Gage 1980.

Bliss, Michael. 'Canada in the Age of the Invisible Hand.' In Tom Kent, ed., *In Pursuit of the Public Good: Essays in Honours of Allan J. MacEachen.* Montreal and Kingston: McGill-Queen's University Press 1997. 21–34.

– *Northern Enterprise: Five Centuries of Canadian Business.* Toronto: McClelland and Stewart 1987.

Bloomfield, Gerald. 'No Parking Here to Corner: London Reshaped by the Automobile 1911–61.' *Urban History Review,* 18, no. 2 (1989): 139–158.

Bluestone, Barry, and Bennett Harrison. *The Deindustrialization of America: Plant Closings, Community Abandonment and the Dismantling of Basic Industry.* New York: Basic Books 1982.

Boland, F.J., ed. *Fourth Seminar on Canadian-American Relations at Assumption University of Windsor, November 8 ,9, 10, 1962.* Windsor, Ont.: Assumption University 1962.

Bothwell, Robert. *Alliance and Illusions: Canada and the World, 1945–1984.* Vancouver: UBC Press 2007.

– 'Thanks for the Fish: Nixon, Kissinger, and Canada.' In Frederick Lovegal and Andrew Preston, eds., *Nixon in the World: American Foreign Relations 1969–73.* London: Oxford University Press 2008. 309–28.

Bothwell, Robert, Ian Drummond, and John English. *Canada since 1945: Power, Politics, and Provincialism.* Toronto: University of Toronto 1989.

Bow, Brian. *The Politics of Linkage: Power, Interdependence, and Ideas in Canada-US Relations.* Vancouver: UBC Press 2009.

Brands, H.W. *The Foreign Policies of Lyndon Johnson: Beyond Vietnam.* College Station: Texas A&M University Press 1999.

Bruce, R.B., and David W. Slater. *War Finance and Reconstruction: The Role of Canada's Department of Finance, 1939–1946*. Ottawa, 1995.

Bryce, R.B. *Maturing in Hard Times: Canada's Department of Finance through the Great Depression*. Montreal and Kingston: McGill-Queen's University Press 1986.

Bryden, P.E. *'A Justifiable Obsession': Conservative Ontario's Relations with Ottawa, 1943–1985*. Toronto: University of Toronto Press, forthcoming.

Bukowczyk, John, Nora Faires, David Smith, and Randy Widdis. *Permeable Border: The Great Lakes Basin as Transnational Region, 1650–1990*. Calgary, Alta.: University of Calgary Press 2005.

Bullen, John. 'The Ontario Waffle and the Struggle for an Independent Socialist Canada: Conflict within the NDP.' *Canadian Historical Review*, 64, no. 2 (1983): 188–215.

Canadian-American Committee. *Toward a More Realistic Appraisal of the Automotive Agreement*. Washington, D.C.: National Planning Association 1970.

Canadian Automobile Chamber of Commerce. *Facts and Figures of the Automobile Industry*. Toronto: Canadian Automobile Chamber of Commerce 1934–57.

Canadian Who's Who. Toronto: Who's Who Canadian Publications, various years.

Carter, Roberta. 'The Responses of the American Automobile Industry to Environmental Protection: A Regulatory Experience.' PhD thesis, University of Colorado at Boulder, 1979.

Cantin, Frédéric, and Andreas Lowenfeld. 'Rules of Origins: The Canada-US FTA and the Honda Case.' *American Journal of International Law*, 87, no. 3 (1993): 375–90.

Chandler, Alfred. *The Visible Hand: The Managerial Revolution in American Business*. Cambridge, Mass.: Harvard University Press 1977.

Chant, Donald. *Pollution Probe*. Toronto: New Press 1970.

Chritchlow, Donald. *Studebaker: The Life and Death of an American Corporation*. Bloomington: Indiana University Press 1996.

Clarke, Sally. *Trust and Power: Consumer, the Modern Corporation, and the Making of the United States Automobile Market*. Cambridge, Mass.: Cambridge University Press 2007.

Clement, Wallace. *Continental Corporate Power: Economic Elite Linkages between Canada and the United States*. Toronto: McClelland and Stewart 1977.

Cohen, Andrew, and J.L. Granatstein. *Trudeau's Shadow: The Life and Legacy of Pierre Elliott Trudeau*. Toronto: Random House Canada 1998.

Cohen, Warren I., and Nancy Berkhopf Tucker, eds. *Lyndon Johnson Confronts the World: American Foreign Policy, 1963–1968*. New York: Cambridge University Press 1994.

Cohn, Theodore, and Inge Bailey. 'Newspaper Coverage of Canadian-US Economic Relations: 1972 and 1982.' *Canadian Journal of Communications*, 13, no. 3 (1988): 1–15.

Conrad, Margaret. *George Nowlan: Maritime Conservative in National Politics.* Toronto: University of Toronto Press 1986.

Côté, Michael. 'The Canadian Auto Industry, 1978–1986.' *Labour Perspectives*, 2, no. 1 (August 1989).

Courchene, Thomas J., and Colin R. Telmer. *From Heartland to North American Region State: The Social, Fiscal and Federal Evolution of Ontario.* Toronto: University of Toronto Press 1998.

Cowan, Ralph. 'Effects of the United States-Canadian Automotive Agreement On Canada's Manufacturing, Trade and Price Posture.' PhD thesis, University of Michigan, 1972.

– ed. *The North American Automobile Industry: Shaping a Dynamic Global Posture.* Windsor, Ont.: University of Windsor Press 1983.

Creighton, Donald. *John A. Macdonald: The Old Chieftain.* Toronto: Macmillan 1955.

Crispo, John. *International Unionism: A Study in Canadian-American Relations.* Toronto: McGraw-Hill 1967.

Cross, Victoria. '"We Can Tell Them All to Go To Hell": The CAW, Multinationals, and the Auto Pact.' In Maureen Irish, ed., *The Auto Pact: Labour, Investment and the WTO*. Frederick, Md.: Kluwer Law International 2004. 53–69.

Cuff, R.D., and J.L. Granatstein. *American Dollars – Canadian Prosperity: Canadian-American Economic Relations, 1945–1950.* Toronto: Samuel-Stevens 1978.

– *Canadian-American Relations in Wartime: From the Great War to the Cold War.* Toronto: Hakkert 1975.

– 'The Rise and Fall of American Free Trade, 1947–1948.' *Canadian Historical Review*, 58, no. 4 (1977): 459–82.

Dales, J.H. *The Protective Tariff on Canada's Development: Eight Essays on Trade and Tariffs When Factors Move with Special Reference to Canadian Protectionism, 1870–1955.* Toronto: University of Toronto Press 1966.

Dallek, Robert. *Flawed Giant: Lyndon Johnson and His Times, 1961–1973.* New York: Oxford University Press 1998.

Davies, Stephen. '"Reckless Walking Should be Encouraged": The Automobile and the Shaping of Urban Canada to 1930.' *Urban History Review*, 18, no. 2 (1989): 123–38.

Davis, Donald F. 'Dependent Motorization: Canada and the Automobile to the 1930s.' In Douglas McCalla, ed., *The Development of Canadian Capitalism: Essays in Business History*. Toronto: Copp Clarke Pitman 1990. 191–218.

Dawes, Colin. *The Relative Decline of International Unionism in Canada since 1970*. Kingston, Ont.: Industrial Relations Centre, Queen's University, 1987.

Del Baso, Michael. 'Is Canada De-Industrializing? The Industrial Restructuring of the Manufacturing Sector, 1961–1995.' PhD thesis, McGill University, 1997.

DesRosiers, Dennis. *DesRosiers Automotive Yearbook 2000*. Richmond Hill, Ont.: DesRosiers Automotive Consultants 2000.

Dewey, Scott. '"The Anti-Trust Case of the Century": Kenneth F. Hahn and the Fight against Smog.' *Southern California Quarterly*, 81 (fall 1999): 341–76.

Diefenbaker, John. *One Canada: Memoirs of the Right Honourable John G. Diefenbaker, Vols. I–II*. Toronto: Macmillan 1976.

Dobell, Peter. 'Negotiating with the United States.' *International Journal*, 36, no. 1 (1980–1): 17–38.

Doern, Bruce, and Brian Tomlin. *Faith and Fear: The Free Trade Story*. Toronto: Stoddart 1991.

Donaghy, Greg. 'A Continental Philosophy: Canada, the United States and the Negotiation of the Auto Pact, 1963–1965.' *International Journal*, 52, no. 3 (1998): 441–64.

– *Tolerant Allies: Canada and the United States, 1963–1968*. Montreal and Kingston: McGill-Queen's University Press 2002.

Doran, Charles F. 'Coping with the "Shock Factor" in Canada-U.S. Commercial Relations.' In Earl Fry and Lee Radebaugh, eds., *Canada-U.S. Economic Relations in the 'Conservative' Era of Mulroney and Reagan*. Provo, Utah: Brigham Young University 1984.

– *Forgotten Partnership: U.S.-Canada Relations Today*. Baltimore: Johns Hopkins University Press 1984.

Doyle, Jack. *Taken for a Ride: Detroit's Big Three and the Politics of Pollution*. New York: Four Walls, Eight Windows, 2000.

Drache, Daniel. *The Deindustrialization of Canada and Its Implications for Labour*. Ottawa: Canadian Centre for Policy Alternatives 1989.

Dudley, Kathryn. *The End of the Line: Lost Jobs and New Lives in Postindustrial America*. Chicago: Chicago University Press 1997.

Duff, Lenore. 'The Transformation of the Canadian Labour Movement from International to National Dominance: Tracing the Roots of Breakaways.' PhD thesis, York University, 2002.

Dummitt, Christopher. 'A Crash Course in Manhood: Men, Cars and Risk in Postwar Vancouver.' In Dimitry Anastakis, ed., *The Sixties: Passion, Politics, and Style*. Montreal and Kingston : McGill-Queen's University Press 2008. 71–98.

Duncan, William Chandler. *US-Japan Automobile Diplomacy: A Study in Economic Confrontation.* Cambridge, Mass.: Ballinger Publishing Company 1973.

Dykes, James G. *Background on the Canada-United States Automotive Products Trade Agreement.* Toronto: Motor Vehicle Manufacturers Association 1979.

– *Canada's Automotive Industry.* Toronto: McGraw-Hill of Canada 1970.

Eastman, Joel. *Styling versus Safety: The Development of Automotive Safety 1900–1966.* Philadelphia: University Press of America 1984.

Eden, Lorraine, and Maureen Appel Molot. *Continentalizing the North American Auto Industry.* Ottawa: Centre for Trade Policy and Law 1992.

– 'Insiders, Outsiders, and Host Country Bargains.' *Journal of International Management,* 8 (2002): 359–88.

Edwards, Charles E. *Dynamics of the United States Automobile Industry.* Columbia: University of South Carolina Press 1965.

Emerson, David L. *Production, Location and the Automotive Agreement.* Ottawa: Economic Council of Canada 1975.

Empire Club of Canada. *Addresses of the Empire Club of Canada.* Toronto: T.H. Best Printing Co., various years.

English, H. Edward. 'Foreign Investment in Manufacturing.' In H. Edward English, ed., *Canada-United States Relations.* New York: Preager Publishers 1976. 77–98.

– *International Economic Integration and National Policy Diversity.* Ottawa: Carleton University Press 1990.

– *The Political Economy of International Economic Integration.* Ottawa: Carleton University Press 1972.

English, John. *Lester Pearson: His Life and World.* Toronto: MHR 1978.

– *The Worldly Years: The Life of Lester Pearson, 1949–1972.* Toronto: Knopf 1992.

Fahrni, Magda. 'Reflections on the Place of Quebec in Historical Writing on Canada.' In Christopher Dummitt and Michael Dawson, eds., *Contesting Clio's Craft: New Directions and Debates in Canadian History.* London: Institute for the Study of Americas 2009. 1–20.

Feldman, Elliot J., and Lily Gardner Feldman. 'The Special Relationship between Canada and the United States.' *Jerusalem Journal of International Relations,* 4, no. 4 (1980): 56–85.

Finlayson, Jock A. 'Canada, Congress and U.S. Foreign Economic Policy.' In Denis Stairs and Gilbert R. Winham, eds., *The Politics of Canada's Economic Relationship with the United States.* Toronto: University of Toronto Press 1985. 127–78.

– 'Canadian International Economic Policy: Context, Issues and a Review of

Some Recent Literature.' In Denis Stairs and Gilbert R. Winham, research coordinators, *Canada and the International Political/Economic Environment*. Toronto: University of Toronto Press 1985. 9–84.

Fleming, Donald. *So Very Near: The Political Memoirs of the Hon. Donald M. Fleming*. Toronto: McClelland and Stewart 1985.

Flink, James. *The Automobile Age*. Cambridge, Mass.: MIT Press 1998.

– 'Three Stages of American Automobile Consciousness.' *American Quarterly*, 24, no. 4 (1972): 451–73.

Flynn, David Michael. 'The Rationalization of the United States and Canadian Automotive Industry, 1960–1975.' PhD thesis, University of Massachusetts, 1979.

Ford Motor Company of Canada. *Some General Aspects of the Canadian Customs Tariff, the National Economy, and the Automobile Industry in Canada*. Windsor, Ont.: 1938.

Fossum, John-Erik. *Oil, the State, and Federalism: The Rise and Demise of Petro-Canada as a Statist Impulse*. Toronto: University of Toronto Press 1997.

Fox, Annette Baker, et al., eds. *Canada and the United States: Transnational and Transgovernmental Relations*. New York: Columbia University Press 1976.

Frank, Thomas. *The Conquest of Cool: Business Culture, Counterculture and the Rise of Hip Consumerism*. Chicago: University of Chicago Press 1997.

Frayne, A., A. Chumack, and R. MacDonald, *Perspectives on the Automobile in Canada*. Ottawa: Transport Canada 1977.

Free Trade and the Auto Pact: Proceedings of the Seminar at the Centre for Canadian-American Studies, Windsor, Ontario. Windsor, Ont.: University of Windsor Press 1988.

Fry, Earl H. 'Canada's Investment Policies: An American Perspective.' In Peter Karl Kresl, ed., *Seen from the South*. Provo, Utah: Brigham Young University Press 1989. 37–74.

– *The Politics of International Investment*. Toronto: McGraw-Hill 1983.

Gartman, David. *Auto Opium: A Social History of American Automobile Design*. New York: Routledge 1994.

Ghent, Jocelyn. 'Canada, the United States and the Cuban Missile Crisis.' *Pacific Historical Review*, 58, no. 2 (1979): 159–84.

– 'Did He Fall or Was He Pushed? The Kennedy Administration and the Collapse of the Diefenbaker Government.' *International History Review*, 1, no. 2 (1979): 246–70.

Gindin, Sam. 'Breaking Away: The Formation of the Canadian Auto Workers.' *Studies in Political Economy* , 29 (summer 1989): 63–89.

– *The Canadian Auto Workers: The Birth and Transformation of a Union*. Toronto: James Lorimer and Company 1995.

Globerman, Steven, and Michael Walker, eds. *Assessing NAFTA: A Trinational Analysis*. Vancouver: Fraser Institute 1993.

Goldenberg, Shirley, and Frances Bairstow. *Domination or Independence? The Problem of Canadian Autonomy in Labour-Management Relations*. Montreal: Industrial Relations Centre 1965.

Goldstein, Jonah. 'Public Interest Groups and Public Policy: The Case of the Consumers Association of Canada.' *Canadian Journal of Political Science*, 12, no. 1 (1979): 137–55.

Gordon, Walter L. *A Choice for Canada*. Toronto: McClelland and Stewart 1966.

– *A Political Memoir*. Toronto: McClelland and Stewart 1977.

– *Storm Signals: New Economic Policies for Canada*. Toronto: McClelland and Stewart 1975.

– *Troubled Canada: The Need for New Domestic Policies*. Toronto: McClelland and Stewart 1961.

– *What Is Happening to Canada?* Toronto: McClelland and Stewart 1978.

Gore, Albert. *The Eye of the Storm: A People's Politics for the Seventies*. New York: Herder and Herder 1970.

– *Let the Glory Out: My South and Its Politics*. New York: Viking Press 1972.

Grady, Patrick Michael. 'The Canadian Exemption from the United States Interest Equalization Tax.' PhD thesis, University of Toronto, 1973.

Granatstein, J.L. *Canada, 1957–1967: The Years of Uncertainty and Innovation*. Toronto: McClelland and Stewart 1986.

– 'Cooperation and Conflict: The Course of Canadian-American Relations since 1945.' In Charles F. Doran and John H. Sigler, eds., *Canada and the United States: Enduring Friendship, Permanent Stress*. Englewood Cliffs, N.J.: Prentice-Hall 1985. 45–68.

– 'Free Trade between Canada and the United States: The Issue That Will Not Go Away.' In Denis Stairs and Gilbert R. Winham, eds., *The Politics of Canada's Economic Relationship with the United States*. Toronto: University of Toronto Press 1985. 11–54.

– *The Ottawa Men: The Civil Service Mandarins, 1935– 1957*. Oxford: Oxford University Press 1982.

– *Pirouette: Pierre Trudeau and Canadian Foreign Policy*. Toronto: University of Toronto Press 1990.

– 'When Push Comes to Shove: Canada and the United States.' In Thomas G. Patterson, ed., *Kennedy's Quest for Victory: American Foreign Policy 1961–1963*. New York: Oxford University Press 1989. 86–104.

Granatstein, J.L., and Robert Bothwell, eds. *Canadian Foreign Policy: Historical Readings*. Toronto: Copp Clarke Pitman 1986.

Grant, George M. *Lament for a Nation: The Defeat of Canadian Nationalism*. Toronto: McClelland and Stewart 1965.

Gray, Earle. *The Great Canadian Oil Patch: The Petroleum Era from Birth to Perk*. Edmonton: June Warren Publishing 2004.

Greenlees, Robert. 'Gasoline Prices and Purchases of Automobiles.' *Southern Economic Journal*, 47, no. 1 (1980): 167–78.

Grey, Clark, Shih, and Associates. 'The Auto Pact: What the Government Held Back.' In Duncan Cameron, ed., *The Free Trade Papers*. Toronto: James Lorimer and Company 1986. 155–63.

Grey, Rodney de C. *Trade Policy in the 1980s: An Agenda for Canada-U.S. Relations*. Calgary, Alta.: C.D. Howe Institute 1981.

Gwyn, Richard. *The 49th Paradox*. Toronto: McClelland and Stewart 1985.

– *Nationalism without Walls: The Unbearable Lightness of Being Canadian*. Toronto: McClelland and Stewart 1995.

Gyllenhammar, Pehr G. *People at Work*. Don Mills, Ont.: Addison-Wesley Educational Publishers 1977.

Halberstam, David. *The Reckoning*. New York: Morrow 1986.

Harris, Richard, and David Cox. *Trade, Industrial Policy, and Canadian Manufacturing*. Toronto: Ontario Economic Council 1984.

Harrison, Kathryn. *Passing the Buck: Federalism and Canadian Environmental Policy*. Vancouver: University of British Columbia Press 1996.

Hart, Michael. 'Almost but Not Quite: The 1947–1948 Bilateral Canada-US Negotiations.' *American Review of Canadian Studies*, 19, no. 1 (spring 1989). 25–58.

– 'Canada at the GATT: Twenty Years of Canadian Tradecraft, 1947–1967.' *International Journal*, 52, no. 4 (1997): 581–608.

– *Decision at Midnight: Inside the Free Trade Negotiations*. Vancouver: UBC Press 1995.

– *Fifty Years of Canadian Tradecraft: Canada at the GATT, 1947–1997*. Ottawa: Centre for Trade Policy and Law 1998.

– 'Free Trade and Brian Mulroney's Economic Legacy.' In Raymond Blake, ed., *Brian Mulroney: Transforming the Nation*. Montreal and Kingston: McGill-Queen's University Press 2007. 61–79.

– 'GATT Article XXIV and Canada-United States Trade Negotiations.' *Review of International Business Law*, 1 (1987): 317–55.

– *A Trading Nation: Canadian Trade Policy from Colonialism to Globalization*. Vancouver: UBC Press 2003.

Hawley, James. *Dollars and Borders: US Government Attempts to Restrict Capital Outflows 1960–1980*. New York: M.E. Sharpe 1987.

Hazledine, Tim, and Ian Wigington. 'Canadian Auto Policy.' *Canadian Public Policy*, 13, no. 4 (1987): 490–501.

Heeney, A.D.P., and Livingston T. Merchant. *Canada and the United States: Principles for Partnership*. Ottawa: Queen's Printer 1965.

Helmers, Henrik O. *Explorations into Trade Liberalization: The Case of the U.S.-Canadian Automotive Aftermarket.* Toronto: Gage Educational Publishing 1970.
– *The United States-Canadian Automobile Agreement: A Study in Industrial Adjustment.* Ann Arbor: University of Michigan Press 1967.
Henderson, David. *A Step toward Feudalism: The Chrysler Bailout.* Washington, D.C.: Cato Institute 1980.
High, Steven. '"I'll Wrap the F*#@ Canadian Flag around Me": A Nationalist Response to Plant Shutdowns, 1969–84.' *Journal of the Canadian Historical Association*, 12, no. 1 (2001): 199–226.
– *Industrial Sunset: The Making of North America's Rust Belt, 1969–1984.* Toronto: University of Toronto Press 2003.
Hillmer, Norman, and J.L. Granatstein. *Partners Nevertheless: Canadian-American Relations in the Twentieth Century.* Toronto: Copp Clarke Pitman 1989.
– *Pearson: Unlikely Gladiator.* Montreal and Kingston: McGill-Queen's University Press 1999.
Holmes, John. *The Break-Up of an International Labour Union: Uneven Development in the North American Auto Industry and the Schism in the UAW.* Montreal and Kingston: McGill-Queen's University Press 1990.
– *Divergent Paths: Restructuring Industrial Relations in the North American Auto Industry.* Montreal and Kingston: McGill-Queen's University Press 1992.
– 'Industrial Reorganization, Capital Restructuring and Locational Change: An Analysis of the Canadian Automobile Industry in the 1960s.' *Economic Geography*, 59 (1983): 251–71.
Holmes, John W. *Life with Uncle: The Canadian-American Relationship.* Toronto: University of Toronto Press 1981.
– 'Merchant-Heeney Revisited: A Sentimental Overview.' In Laure McKinsey and Kim Richard Nossal, eds., *America's Alliances and Canadian-American Relations.* Toronto: Summerhill 1988. 180–99.
Hood, Hugh. *The Motor Boys in Ottawa: A Novel.* Toronto: Stoddart 1986.
Hoy, Claire. *Bill Davis: A Biography.* Toronto: Methuen 1985.
Hurter, Donald, and Jeffrey Staley. 'Opportunities for Canadian Research and Development Directed towards the Need of the North American Auto Market.' Ottawa: Arthur D. Little of Canada 1979.
Hyde, Charles. *Riding the Roller Coaster: A History of the Chrysler Corporation.* Detroit: Wayne State University Press 2003.
Iacocca, Lee. *Iacocca: an Autobiography.* Toronto: Bantam Books 1986.
Ingrassia, Paul, and Joseph Whilte. *Comeback: The Fall and Rise of the American Automobile Industry.* New York: Simon and Schuster 1995.
Inwood, Gregory. *Continentalizing Canada: The Politics and Legacy of the Macdonald Royal Commission.* Toronto: University of Toronto Press 2005.

Jackson, John. 'The Puzzle of the GATT.' *World Trade Law Journal*, 1 (1967): 131–61.

Jacobs, Jane. *The Life and Death of Great American Cities*. New York: Random House of Canada 1961.

Jefferys, Steve. *Management and Managed: 50 Years of Crisis at Chrysler*. New York: CUP Archive 1986.

Johnson, Harry. 'The Bladen Plan for Increased Protection of the Canadian Automotive Industry.' *Canadian Journal of Economics and Political Science*, 29 (May 1963): 212–38.

– 'The New Tariff Policy for the Automotive Industry.' *Business Quarterly*, 29, no. 1 (1964): 43–57.

Johnson, Jon R. 'The Effect of the Canadian-U.S. Free Trade Agreement on the Auto Pact.' In Maureen Appel Molot, ed., *Driving Continentally: National Policies and the North American Auto Policy*. Ottawa: Carleton University Press 1993. 255–84.

Johnson, Richard. *Six Men Who Built the Modern Auto Industry*. Detroit: Motorbooks International 2005.

Kawahara, Akira. *The Origin of Competitive Strength: Fifty Years of the Auto Industry in Japan and the US*. New York: Springer 1998.

Keats, John. *The Insolent Chariots*. New York: Lippincott 1958.

Keeley, James F. 'Cast in Concrete for All Time? The Negotiation of the Auto Pact.' *Canadian Journal of Political Science*, 16, no. 2 (1983): 281–98.

– 'Constraints on Canadian International Economic Policy.' PhD thesis, Stanford University, 1980.

Kent, Tom. *A Public Purpose: An Experience of Liberal Opposition and Canadian Government*. Montreal and Kingston: McGill-Queen's University Press 1988.

Keohane, Robert O., and Joseph S. Nye. *Power and Interdependence: World Politics in Transition*. New York: HarperCollins Publishers 1989.

Kiley, David. *The Rise, Fall, and Comeback of Volkswagen in America*. New York: John Wiley and Sons 2002.

Kirton, John, and Robert Bothwell. 'The Consequences of Integration: The Case of the Defence Production Sharing Agreements.' In W. Andrew Axline, ed., *Continental Community? Independence and Integration in North America*. Toronto: McClelland and Stewart 1974. 116–36.

– 'The Politics of Bilateral Management: The Case of the Automotive Trade.' *International Journal*, 36 (1980–1): 39–69.

– 'A Proud and Powerful Country: American Attitudes toward Canada, 1963–1976.' *Queen's Quarterly*, 92, no. 1 (1985): 108–26.

Klevorick, Alvin. 'Reflections on the Race to the Bottom.' In Jagdish Bhagwati and Robert Hudec, eds., *Fair Trade and Harmonization: Prerequisites for Free Trade?* Cambridge, Mass.: MIT Press 1996. 459–68.

Kreinin, Mordechai, ed. *Building a Partnership: The Canada-United States Free Trade Agreement.* East Lansing, Mich.: MSU Press 2000.

Kronish, Rich, and Kenneth S. Mericle, eds. *The Political Economy of the Latin American Motor Vehicle Industry.* Cambridge, Mass.: MIT Press 1984.

Krugman, Paul. *The Age of Diminished Expectations: U.S. Economic Policy in the 1990s.* Cambridge, Mass.: MIT Press 1990.

Ktaz, Harry, and Noah Meltz. 'Profit Sharing and Auto Workers' Earnings: The United States and Canada.' *Relations Industrielles/Industrial Relations*, 46, no. 3 (1991): 515–30.

Kumar, Pradeep. *Change, but in What Direction? Divergent Union Responses to Work Restructuring in the Integrated North American Auto Industry.* Montreal and Kingston: McGill-Queen's University Press 1993.

– *Continuity and Change: Evolving Human Resource Policies and Practices in the Canadian Automobile Industry.* Montreal and Kingston: McGill-Queen's University Press 1996.

Langdon, Frank. *The Politics of Japanese-Canadian Economic Relations 1952–83.* Vancouver: UBC Press 1983.

Lavelle, Patrick J., and Robert White. *An Automotive Strategy for Canada.* Ottawa: Ministry of Supply and Services 1983.

Laxer, Robert, ed. *(Canada) Ltd.: The Political Economy of Dependency.* Toronto: McClelland and Stewart 1973.

Lea, Sperry. *A Canada-US Free Trade Arrangement: Survey of Possible Characteristics.* Montreal: Canadian-American Committee 1963.

Lea, Sperry, and John Volpe. 'Conflict over Industrial Incentive Policies: Canada-United States Relations.' *Proceedings of the Academy of Political Science*, 32, no. 2 (1976): 137–48.

Leach, Richard. 'Canada and the United States: A Special Relationship.' *Current History*, 12, no. 426 (1977): 145–9.

Lee, Matthew. 'The Ford Pinto Case and the Development of Auto Safety Regulations, 1893–1978.' *Business and Economic History*, 27, no. 2 (1998): 390–401.

Levitt, Kari. *Silent Surrender: The Multinational Corporation in Canada.* Toronto: MAC 1970.

Lewchuk, Wayne, and Don Wells. 'When Corporations Substitute for Adversial Unions: Labour Markets and Human Resource Management at Magna.' *Relations Industrielles/Industrial Relations*, 64, no. 4 (2006): 639–65.

Lleyton-Brown, David. '"A Mug's Game": Automotive Incentives in Canada and the United States.' *International Journal*, 35, no. 1 (1979–80): 170–84.

Leyton-Brown, David, and John Gerard Ruggie. 'The North American Political Economy in the Global Context: An Analytical Framework.' *International Journal*, 42 (winter, 1986–7): 3–24.

Lichtentstein, Nelson. *Walter Reuther: The Most Dangerous Man in Detroit*. Chicago: University of Illinois Press 1997.

Lilley, Wayne. *Magna Cum Laude: How Frank Stronach Became Canada's Best-Paid Man*. Toronto: McClelland and Stewart 2008.

Lindholm, Ralph, and Jan-Peder Norstedt. *The Volvo Report*. Stockholm: Swedish Employers' Confederation 1975.

Lipsey, Richard. 'Canada and the United States: The Economic Dimension.' In Charles F. Doran and John H. Sigler, eds., *Canada and the United States: Enduring Friendship, Persistent Stress*. Englewood Cliffs, N.J.: Prentice-Hall 1985. 69–108.

Lipsey, Richard, and Murray Smith. *Taking the Initiative: Canada's Trade Options in a Turbulent World*. Toronto: C.D. Howe Institute 1985.

Litvak, I.A., C.J. Maule, and R.D. Robinson. *Dual Loyalty: Canadian-US Business Arrangements*. Toronto: McGraw-Hill 1971.

Local 444. 'Auto Pact-Industrial Policy.' *Pillette Road Truck Assembly Plant, 1975–2003*. Windsor, Ont.: Local 444, 2003.

Lower, Arthur. *Canadians in the Making: A Social History of Canada*. Toronto: Longmans, Green 1958.

Luger, Stan. *Corporate Power, American Democracy, and the Automobile Industry*. Cambridge, Mass.: Cambridge University Press 2000.

– 'Government Policy toward the Automobile Industry: Social Constraints, Economic Conditions, and Interest-Group Power.' *Journal of Policy History*, 4, no. 4 (1992): 418–34.

Lumsden, Ian, ed. *Close the 49th Parallel Etc.: The Americanization of Canada*. Toronto: University of Toronto Press 1970.

Lutsey, Nicholas, and Daniel Sperling. 'Canada's Voluntary Agreement on Greenhouse Gas Emissions: When the Details Matter.' *Transportation Research Part D*, 12 (2007): 474–87.

Lyon, Peyton. 'The Canadian Perspective.' In H. Edward English, ed. *Canada-United States Relations*. New York: Preager Publishers 1976. 14–26.

Macdonald, Douglas. *Business and Environmental Politics in Canada*. Toronto: University of Toronto Press 2007.

Macdonald, L. Ian. *Free Trade: Risks and Rewards*. Montreal and Kingston: McGill-Queen's University Press 2000.

Macdonald, N.B. 'A Comment: The Bladen Plan for Increased Protection for the Automotive Industry.' *Canadian Journal of Economics and Political Science*, 29, no. 4 (1963): 505–15.

Mackenzie, Kenneth C. *Tariff-Making and Trade Policy in the US and Canada: A Comparative Study*. New York: Praeger 1969.

Mahant, E.E. *Free Trade in American-Canadian Relations*. Melbourne: Krieger 1993.

Mahant, E.E., and G.S. Mount. *An Introduction to Canadian-American Relations*. Toronto: Meuthen 1984.

Manley, John. 'Communists and Autoworkers: The Struggle for Industrial Unionism in the Canadian Automobile Industry, 1925–1936.' *Labour/Le Travail*, 17 (spring 1986): 105–33.

Margolis, Howard. 'The Politics of Auto Emissions.' *The Public Interest*, 49 (fall 1977): 3–21.

Martin, Lawrence. *The Presidents and the Prime Ministers, Washington and Ottawa Face to Face: The Myth of Bilateral Bliss, 1867–1982*. Toronto: Doubleday Canada 1982.

Martin, Paul. *A Very Public Life. Vol. II, So Many Worlds*. Toronto: Deneau 1985.

Masson, Francis, and H. Edward English. *Invisible Trade Barriers between Canada and the United States*. Washington, D.C.: National Planning Association 1963.

Masson, Francis, and J.B. Whitley. *Barriers to Trade between Canada and the United States*. Montreal: Canadian-American Committee 1960.

Mathias, Philip. *Forced Growth: Five Studies of Government Involvement in the Development of Canada*. Toronto: James, Lewis and Samuel 1971.

Matusow, Allan J. *Nixon's Economy: Booms, Busts, Dollars and Votes*. Lawrence: University of Kansas Press 1998.

Maxcy, George. *The Multinational Automobile Industry*. New York: St Martin's Press 1981.

McCall, Christina, and Stephen Clarkson. *Trudeau and Our Times, Vols. I and II*. Toronto: McClelland and Stewart 1990, 1994.

McCalla, Douglas, ed. *The Development of Canadian Capitalism*. Toronto: Copp Clark Pitman 1990.

McCarthy, Tom. *Auto Mania: Cars, Consumers, and the Environment*. New Haven, Conn., and London: Yale University Press 2007.

McDiarmid, O.J. *Commercial Policy in the Canadian Economy*. Cambridge, Mass.: Harvard University Press 1946.

– 'Some Aspects of the Canadian Automobile Industry.' *Canadian Journal of Economics and Political Science*, 6, no. 2 (1940): 258–74.

McGee, Harley. *Getting It Right: Regional Economic Development in Canada*. Montreal and Kingston: McGill-Queen's University Press 1992.

McGraw-Hill Directory of and Almanac of Canada. Toronto: McGraw-Hill Co. of Canada 1967.

McMillan, Charles. 'After the Gray Report: Tortured Evolution of Foreign Investment Policy.' *McGill Law Journal*, 20 (1974): 213–60.

McShane, Clay. *Down the Asphalt Path: The Automobile and the American City*. New York: Columbia University Press 1995.

Mellon, Steve. *After the Smoke Clears: Struggling to Get by in Rustbelt America*. Pittsburgh: University of Pittsburgh Press 2006.

Metzger, Stanley. 'The United States-Canada Automotive Products Agreement of 1965.' *World Trade Law Journal*, 1, no. 1 (1967): 104–9.

Milkman, Ruth. 'The Anti-Concessions Movement in the UAW: Interview with Doug Stevens.' *Socialist Review*, 65 (September/October 1982): 19–42.

Mohl, Raymond. 'Stop the Road: Freeway Revolts in American Cities.' *Journal of Urban History*, 30, no. 4 (2004): 674–706.

Molot, Maureen Appel, ed. *Driving Continentally: National Policies and the North American Auto Industry*. Ottawa: Carleton University Press 1993.

– 'Location Incentives and Inter-State Competition for the FDI: Bidding Wars in the Automotive Industry.' In Lorraine Eden and Wendy Dobson, eds., *Governance, Multinationals and Growth*. Northhampton, Mass.: Edward Elgar Publishing 2005. 297–324.

Molot, Maureen Appel, and Lorraine Eden. 'The NAFTA's Automotive Provisions: The Next Stage of Managed Trade.' *C.D. Howe Institute Commentary*, no. 53 (November 1993): 1–24.

Mordue, Grieg. 'Government, Foreign Direct Investment and the Canadian Automotive Industry, 1977–1987.' PhD thesis, University of Strathclyde, 2007.

Morici, Peter, Arthur J.R. Smith, and Sperry Lea. *Canadian Industrial Policy*. Washington, D.C.: National Planning Association 1982.

– 'Canadian-U.S. Trade Relations.' In Pater Karl Kresl, ed., *Seen From the South*. Provo, Utah: Brigham Young University Press 1989. 75–132.

Moritz, Michael, and Barrett Seaman. *Going for Broke: The Chrysler Story*. Garden City, N.Y.: Doubleday, 1981.

– *Going for Broke: Lee Iacocca's Battle to Save Chrysler*. Garden City, N.Y.: Doubleday 1983.

Moroz, Andrew R. *Canada-United States Automotive Trade and Trade Policy Issues*. London, Ont.: Department of Economics, University of Western Ontario, 1983.

Muirhead, Bruce. *Dancing around the Elephant: Creating a Prosperous Canada in an Age of American Dominance*. Toronto: University of Toronto Press 2007.

– 'Ottawa, the Provinces, and the Evolution of Canadian Trade Policy since 1963.' In Dimitry Anastakis and P.E. Bryden, eds., *Framing Canadian Federal-*

ism: Historical Essays in Honour of John T. Saywell. Toronto: University of
Toronto Press 2009. 211–30.

– 'From Special Relationship to Third Option: Canada, US, and the Nixon
Shock.' *American Review of Canadian Studies*, 34, no. 3 (2004): 439–62.

Murray, J. Alex, and Lawrence Leduc. 'Public Opinion and Foreign Policy
Options in Canada.' *Public Opinion Quarterly*, 40, no. 4 (1976–7): 488–96.

Nader, Ralph. *Unsafe at Any Speed.* New York: Grossman 1965.

Nash, Knowlton. *Kennedy and Diefenbaker: The Feud That Helped Topple a Government.* Toronto: McClelland and Stewart 1990.

Neisser, Albert C. 'The Impact of the Canada-United States Automotive Agreement on Canada's Motor Vehicle Industry: A Study of Economies of Scale.'
PhD thesis, University of Michigan, 1966.

Nijnatten, Debora. 'Participation and Environmental Policy in Canada and the
US: Trends over Time.' *Policy Studies Journal*, 27, no. 2 (1999): 267–87.

Norrie, Kenneth, and Douglas Owram. *History of the Canadian Economy.* 2nd ed.
Toronto: Harcourt Brace and Company 1996.

Norton, Peter. *Fighting Traffic: The Dawn of the Motor Age in the American City.*
Boston: MIT Press 2008.

– 'Street Rivals: Jaywalking and the Invention of the Motorized Street.' *Technology and History*, 48, no. 2 (2007): 331–59.

Nossal, Kim Richard. 'Economic Nationalism and Continental Integration: As-
sumptions, Arguments and Advocacies.' In Denis Stairs and Gilbert R. Winham, eds., *The Politics of Canada's Economic Relationship with the United States.*
Toronto: University of Toronto Press 1985. 55–94.

Nowlan, David. *The Bad Trip: The Untold Story of the Spadina Expressway.* Toronto:
New Press 1970.

O'Connor, Ryan Ernest. 'Toronto the Green: Pollution Probe and the Rise of
the Canadian Environmental Movement.' PhD thesis, University of Western
Ontario, 2010.

Olewiler, Nancy. 'North American Integration and the Environment.' In Richard
Harris, ed., *North American Linkages: Opportunities and Challenges for Canada.*
Calgary: University of Alberta Press 2003. 575–610.

Ohno, Taiichi. *Toyota Production System: Beyond Large Scale Production.* New York:
Productivity Press 1988.

Owram, Douglas. *The Government Generation: Canadian Intellectuals and the State,
1900–1945.* Toronto: University of Toronto Press 1986.

Palmer, Bryan. *Canada's 1960s: The Ironies of Identity in a Rebellious Era.* Toronto:
University of Toronto Press 2009.

Parra, Francisco. *Oil Politics: A Modern History of Petroleum.* New York: I.B. Tauris
2004.

Patterson, Thomas G., ed. *Kennedy's Quest for Victory: American Foreign Policy 1961–1963*. New York: Oxford University Press 1989.

Pearson, Lester B. *Democracy in World Politics*. Toronto: S.J. Reynolds Saunders and Co. 1955.

– *Mike: The Memoirs of the Right Honourable Lester B. Pearson. Volume 3, 1957–1968*. Toronto: University of Toronto Press 1975.

Penfold, Steve. 'Are We to Go Literally to the Hot Dogs? Parking Lots, Drive-Ins, and the Critique of Progress in Toronto's Suburbs, 1965–1975.' *Urban History Review*, 33, no. 1 (2004): 8–23.

– 'Ontario at the Great Lakes Border/land: An Historical Perspective.' *State of the Federation Paper*. Toronto, November 2010.

Perrucci, Robert. *Japanese Auto Transplants in the Heartland: Corporatism and Community*. New York: Transaction Publishers 1994.

Perry, Ross. *The Future of Canada's Auto Industry: The Big Three and the Japanese Challenge*. Toronto: James Lorimer and Company 1982.

Philip, George. *The Political Economy of International Oil*. Edinburgh: Edinburgh University Press 1994.

Pitts, Robert, John Willionbourg, and Daniel Sherrell. 'Consumer Adaptation to Gasoline Price Increases.' *Journal of Consumer Research* , 8, no. 3 (1981): 322–30.

Podgursky, Mike. 'A National Industrial Policy.' *Labour Studies Journal*, 9, no. 2 (1984): 231–6.

Powell, James. *A History of the Canadian Dollar*. Ottawa: Bank of Canada 1999.

Rae, John B. *The American Automobile Industry*. Boston: Twayne Publishers 1984.

Read, Jennifer. 'Addressing "a Quiet Horror": The Evolution of Ontario Pollution Control Policy in the International Great Lakes, 1909–1972.' PhD thesis, University of Western Ontario, 1999.

Regenstrief, Peter. *The Diefenbaker Interlude: Parties and Voting in Canada, an Interpretation*. Toronto: Longmans 1965.

Reich, Robert, and John Donahue. *New Deals: The Chrysler Revival and the American System*. New York: Times Books 1985.

Reingold, Edward. *People, Ideas and the Challenge of the New*. New York: Penguin 1999.

Reisman, Simon. 'The Issue of Free Trade.' In Edward R. Fried and Philip H. Trezise, eds., *U.S.-Canadian Relations: Next Steps?* Washington, D.C.: Brookings Institution 1984. 50–1.

– 'The Relevance of the Auto Pact for Other Sectoral Arrangements.' *Canada-United States Law Journal*, 10 (1985): 75–84.

Ritchie, Charles. *Storm Signals: More Undiplomatic Diaries, 1962–1971*. Toronto: Macmillan of Canada 1983.

– *Wrestling with the Elephant: The Inside Story of Canada-US Trade Wars.* Toronto: MacFarlane, Walter, and Ross 1997.

Roberts, Chris. 'Harnessing Competition? The UAW and Competitiveness in the Canadian Auto Industry 1945–1990.' PhD thesis, York University, 2002.

Roberts, David. *In the Shadow of Detroit: Gordon M. Macgregor, Ford of Canada and Motoropolis.* Detroit: Wayne State University Press 2006.

Robertson, Heather. *Driving Force: The McLaughlin Family and the Age of the Car.* Toronto: McClelland and Stewart 1995.

Robinson, Danielle. 'The Dundas and Ancaster Highway Disputes in Ontario, 1967–68.' *Ontario History*, 100, no. 1 (2008): 55–79.

– 'Modernism at a Crossroad: The Spadina Expressway Controversy in Toronto, Ontario ca. 1960–71.' *Canadian Historical Review*, 92, no. 2 (2011): 295–322.

Robinson, H. Basil. *Diefenbaker's World: A Populist in World Affairs.* Toronto: University of Toronto Press 1989.

Roy, James. 'Support Pending: The Canadian Autoworkers' Struggle for Adjustment Assistance at a Time of Industrial Change, 1960–1965.' MA thesis, Carleton University Press 2000.

Rubenstein, James. 'The Changing Distribution of US Automobile Assembly Plants.' *Focus*, 38, no. 3 (1988): 12–17.

– 'The Impact of Japanese Investment in the United States.' In C. Law, ed., *Restructuring the Global Automotive Industry: National and Regional Impacts.* New York: Routledge 1991. 114–42.

– *Making and Selling Cars: Innovation and Change in the US Automobile Industry.* Baltimore, JHU Press 2001.

Rubenstein, James, and Thomas Klier. *Who Really Made Your Car? Restructuring and Geographic Change in the Auto Industry.* Kalamzoo, Mich.: W.E. Upjohn Institute 2008.

Ruffilli, Dean. 'The Car in Canadian Culture.' PhD thesis, University of Western Ontario, 2006.

Rutherford, Tod. 'Re-Embedding, Japanese Investment and the Restructuring Buyer-Supplier in the Canadian Automotive Components Industry During the 1990's.' *Regional Studies*, 34, no. 8 (2000): 739–51.

Rutherford, Tod, and John Holmes. '"We Simply Have to Do That Stuff for Our Survival": Labour, Firm Innovation, and Cluster Governance in the Canadian Automotive Parts Industry.' *Antipode*, 39, no.1 (2007): 194–221.

Safarian, A.E. *Foreign Ownership of Canadian Industry.* Toronto: McGraw-Hill 1966.

Sandberg, L. Anders. 'Missing the Road: Working Life at Volvo Nova Scotia.' In Äke Sandberg, ed., *Enriching Production: Perspectives on Volvo's Uddvalla Plant as an Alternative to Lean Production.* Brookfield, Vt.: Avebury 1995. 269–82.

Savoie, Donald. *Regional Economic Development: Canada's Search for Solutions*. Toronto: University of Toronto Press 1992.

Saywell, J.T., ed. *The Canadian Annual Review*. Toronto: University of Toronto Press, various years.

Schmandt, Jurgen, Judith Clarkson, and Hilliard Roderick, eds. *Acid Rain and Friendly Neighbour: The Policy Dispute between Canada and the United States*. Durham, N.C.: Duke University Press 1988.

Sekaly, Raymond R. *Transnationalization of the Automotive Industry*. Ottawa: University of Ottawa Press 1981.

Shapiro, Helen. *Engines of Growth: The State and Transnational Auto Companies in Brazil*. Cambridge, Mass.: Cambridge University Press 1994.

Sharp, Mitchell. 'Canada's Independence and U.S. Domination.' In Edward R. Fried and Philip H. Trezise, eds., *U.S.-Canadian Economic Relations: Next Steps?* Washington, D.C.: Brookings Institution 1984. 11–20.

– *"Which Reminds Me ... A Memoir*. Toronto: University of Toronto Press 1994.

Shepherd, J.J. *The Canada-U.S. Auto Pact: A Technological Perspective*. Ottawa: Science Council of Canada 1978.

Shimokawa, Kōichi. *The Japanese Automobile Industry: A Business History*. New York: Continuum International Publishing Group 1994.

Shook, Robert. *Honda: An American Success Story*. New York: Prentice Hall 1988.

Smith, Denis. *Gentle Patriot: A Political Biography of Walter Gordon*. Edmonton: Hurtig Publishers 1973.

Smitka, Michael. 'Foreign Policy and the US Automotive Industry: By Virtue of Neccessity?' *Business and Economic History*, 28, no. 2 (1999): 277–85.

Sobel, David, and Susan Meurer. *Working at Inglis: The Life and Death of a Canadian Factory*. Toronto: James Lorimer 1994.

Steed, Judy. *Ed Broadbent: The Pursuit of Power*. Toronto: Viking Publishing 1988.

Stevens, Peter. 'Cars and Cottages: The Automotive Transformation of Ontario's Summer Home Tradition.' *Ontario History*, 100, no. 1 (2008): 26–56.

Stone, Frank. *Canada, the GATT and the International Trade System*. Montreal: Institute for Research on Public Policy 1992.

Stuart, Reginald. *Bailout: The Story Behind America's Billion Dollar Gamble on the 'New' Chrysler Corporation*. South Bend, Ind.: And Books 1980.

Studebaker Corporation. *Annual Report for 1962*. Historical Collections, Baker Library, Harvard Business School. 16 October 1962.

Studer-Noguez, Isabel. *Ford and the Global Strategies of Multinationals: The North American Auto Industry*. New York: Routledge 2002.

Stursberg, Peter. *Diefenbaker: Leadership Lost, 1962–1967*. Toronto: University of Toronto Press 1976.

– *Lester Pearson and the American Dilemma*. Toronto: Doubleday Canada 1980.

– *Lester Pearson and the Dream of Unity.* Toronto: Doubleday Canada 1978.

Sugiman, Pamela H. *Labour's Dilemma: The Gender Politics of Auto Workers in Canada, 1937–1979.* Toronto: University of Toronto Press 1994.

Swacker, Frank, Kennth Redden, and Larry Wenger. *World Trade without Barriers: The World Trade Organization and Dispute Resolution.* Charlottesville, Va.: Michie Butterworth 1995.

Swanson, Roger Frank, ed., *Canadian-American Summit Diplomacy, 1923–1973: Selected Speeches and Documents.* Toronto: McClelland and Stewart 1975.

– 'The United States Canadiana Constellation I: Washington D.C.' *International Journal,* 27, no. 2 (1972): 185–218.

Tabachnick, Mark. 'The Impacts of Lean Production and Continental Economic Integration on the Geography and Organizational Structure of the Canadian Automotive Parts Industry.' MA thesis, Queens University, 1998.

Tate, John. *Driving Production Innovation Home: Guardian State Capitalism and the Competitiveness of the Japanese Automobile Industry.* Berkeley, Calif.: University of California Press 1995.

Tedlow, Richard, and Reed Hundt. 'Cars and Carnage: Safety and Hazard on the American Road.' *Journal of Policy History,* 4, no. 4 (1992): 435–52.

Thomas, Kenneth. P. *Capital beyond Borders: States and Firms in the Auto Industry, 1960–1994.* New York: St Martin's Press 1996.

– 'Capital Mobility and Trade Policy: The Case of the Canada-U.S. Auto Pact.' *Review of International Political Economy,* 4, no. 1 (1997): 127–53.

– *Competing for Capital: Europe and North America in a Global Era.* Washington, D.C.: Georgetown University Press 2000.

Thompson, John Herd, and Stephen J. Randall. *Canada and the United States: Ambivalent Allies.* Montreal and Kingston: McGill-Queen's University Press 1994.

Thordarson, Bruce. *Lester Pearson: Diplomat and Politician.* Toronto: Oxford University Press 1974.

Tomlin, Brian. 'Leaving the Past Behind: The Free Trade Initiative Assessed.' In Nelson Michaud and Kim Richard Nossal, eds., *Diplomatic Departures: The Conservative Era in Foreign Policy.* Vancouver: UBC Press 2002. 45–58.

Toner, Glen, and Bruce Doern. 'The Two Energy Crises and the Canadian Oil and Gas Interest Groups: A Re-Examination of Berry's Propositions.' *Canadian Journal of Political Science,* 19, no. 3 (1986): 467–93.

Toyota Motor Corporation. *A History of the First Fifty Years.* Tokyo: Toyota Motor Corporation 1988.

Traves, Tom. 'The Development of the Ontario Automobile Industry to 1939.' In Ian Drummond, ed., *Progress without Planning: The Economic History of Ontario from Confederation to the Second World War.* Toronto: University of Toronto Press 1987. 208–23.

– *The State and Enterprise: Canadian Manufacturers and the Federal Government, 1917–1931.* Toronto: University of Toronto Press 1979.

Trezise, Philip H. 'The Relevance of the Auto Pact to Other Sectoral Arrangements.' *Canada-United States Law Journal*, 10 (1985): 63–74.

United Automobile Workers, Canadian Region. *The UAW in Canada.* Windsor, Ont.: UAW Publishing 1960.

Upgren, Arthur R., and William J. Waines. *The Mid-Continent and the Peace: The Interests of Western Canada and Central Northwest United States in the Peace Settlements.* Minneapolis: The University of Minnesota Press 1943.

Van Ameringen, M. 'The Restructuring of the Canadian Auto Industry.' In D. Cameron and F. Houle, eds., *Canada and the New International Division of Labour.* Ottawa: University of Ottawa Press 1985. 267–87.

Van Nostrand, John. 'The Queen Elizabeth Way: Public Utility versus Public Space.' *Urban History Review*, 12, no. 2 (1983): 1–23.

Vernon, Raymond. *Sovereignty at Bay: The Spread of Multinational Enterprises.* New York: Basic Books 1971.

– *Storm over the Multinationals: The Real Issues.* Cambridge, Mass.: Harvard University Press 1977.

– 'US Direct Investment in Canada: Consequences for the US Economy.' *Journal of Finance*, 28, no. 2 (1973): 407–17.

Volti, Rudy. 'A Century of Automobility.' *Technology and Culture*, 37, no. 4 (1996): 663–85.

Wagenber, R.H., ed. *Canadian-American Interdependence: How Much? Proceedings of the 10th Annual Seminar on Canadian-American Relations, 1968.* Windsor, Ont.: University of Windsor 1968.

Waverman, Leonard, and Melvyn Fuss. *The Canada-U.S. Auto Pact of 1965: An Experiment in Selective Trade Liberalization.* Toronto: Institute for Policy Analysis 1986.

Wearing, Joseph. *The L-Shaped Party: The Liberal Party of Canada, 1958–1980.* Toronto: MHR 1981.

Weaver, Paul. *The Suicidal Corporation: How Big Business Fails America.* New York: Simon and Schuster 1988.

Weintrub, Sidney, ed. 'Canadian Anxieties and U.S. Responses: Introductory Thoughts.' In Peter Karl Kresl, ed., *Seen from the South.* Provo, Utah: Brigham Young University Press 1989. 1–14.

– *The U.S.-Canadian Automotive Products Agreement of 1965: An Evaluation for Its Twentieth Year.* Austin: University of Texas at Austin 1985.

Weintrub, Sidney, and Christopher Sands, eds. *The North American Auto Industry under NAFTA.* Washington, D.C.: CSIS Press 1998.

Wells, Don. 'The Impact of the Postwar Compromise on Canadian Unionism:

The Formation of an Auto Worker Local in the 1950s.' *Labour/Le Travail*, 36 (fall 1995): 147–73.

– 'Origins of Canada's Wagner Model of Industrial Relations: The United Auto Workers in Canada and the Suppression of "Rank & File" Unionism, 1936–1953.' *Canadian Journal of Sociology*, 20, no. 2 (1995): 193–225.

Whitaker, Reg. *The Government Party: Organizing and Financing the Liberal Party of Canada, 1930–1958*. Toronto: University of Toronto Press 1977.

White, Bob. *Hard Bargains: My Life on the Line*. Toronto: McClelland and Stewart 1988.

White, Richard. *Making Cars in Canada: A Brief History of the Canadian Automobile Industry, 1900–1980*. Ottawa: Canadian Science and Technology Museum 2007.

Whiteside, Thomas. *The Investigation of Ralph Nader: General Motors vs. One Determined Man*. Ann Arbor. Mich.: Arbor House 1972.

Wilkins, Mira. *The Emergence of Multinational Enterprise: American Business abroad from the Colonial Era to 1914*. Cambridge, Mass.: Harvard University Press 1970.

– *The Maturing of Multinational Enterprise: American Business Abroad from 1914 to 1970*. Cambridge, Mass.: Harvard University Press 1970.

Wilkins, Mira, and Frank Ernest Hill. *American Business abroad: Ford on Six Continents*. Detroit: Wayne State University Press 1964.

Wilkinson, Bruce. 'Canada-US Free Trade and Some Options.' *Canadian Public Policy*, 8 (October 1982): 428–39.

Wilson, John. 'Capital Mobility and Environmental Standards: Is There a Theoretical Basis for the Race to the Bottom? In Jagdish Bhagwati and Robert Hudec, eds., *Fair Trade and Harmonization: Prerequisites for Free Trade?* Cambridge, Mass.: MIT Press 1996. 393–428.

Wilton, David A. *An Econometric Analysis of the Canada-United States Automotive Agreement: The First Seven Years*. Ottawa: Minister of Supply and Services 1976.

Winham, Gilbert, and Alizabeth DeBoer-Ashworth. 'Asymmetry in Negotiation: The Canada-US Free Trade Agreement 1985–87.' In William Zartman and Jeffrey Rubin, eds., *Power and Negotiation*. Ann Arbor: University of Michigan Press 2002. 35–52.

Wolfe, David. 'Harnessing the Region: Changing Perspectives on Innovation Policy in Ontario.' In Trevor J. Barnes and Meric S. Gertler, eds.' *The New Industrial Geography: Regions, Regulation, and Institutions*. New York: Routledge 2002. 127–154.

– 'Networking among Regions: Ontario and the Four Motors for Europe.' *European Planning Studies*, 8, no. 3 (2000): 389–407.

– 'The Role of Cooperative Industrial Policy in Canada and Ontario.' In Richard Braudo and Jeffrey MacIntosh, eds., *Competitive Industrial Development in the Age of Information: The Role of Cooperation in the Technology Sector.* London: Routledge 1999. 30–63.

Womack, James, Daniel Jones, and Daniel Roos. *The Machine That Changed the World: The Story of Lean Production.* New York: Harper Perennial 1991.

Wonnacott, Paul. 'Canadian Automotive Protection: Content Provisions, the Bladen Plan, and Recent Tariff Changes.' *Canadian Journal of Economics and Political Science*, 31, no. 1 (1965): 98–116.

– *U.S. and Canadian Auto Policies in a Changing World Environment.* Toronto: C.D. Howe Institute 1987.

Wonnacott, Paul, and Ron Wonnacott. 'The Automotive Agreement of 1965.' *Canadian Journal of Economics and Political Science*, 33, no. 2 (1967): 269–84.

– *Free Trade between the United States and Canada: The Potential Economic Effects.* Cambridge, Mass.: Harvard University Press 1967.

– *US-Canadian Free Trade: The Potential Impact on the Canadian Economy.* Montreal: Canadian-American Committee 1968.

Wonnacott, Ron. 'The Canada-US Free Trade Agreement and the Auto Pact.' *Trade Monitor*, no. 2 (March 1988): 1–12.

– 'The Canadian Content Proposals of the Task Force on the Automobile Industry.' *Canadian Public Policy*, 10, no. 1 (1984): 1–9.

– *The United States and Canada: The Quest for Free Trade: An Examination of the Issues.* Washington, D.C.: Peterson Institute 1987.

Wright, Gerald, and Maureen Appel Molot. 'Capital Movements and Government Control.' *International Organization*, 28 (1976): 671–88.

Wright, Richard. *Japanese Business in Canada: The Elusive Alliance.* Montreal: Institute for Research on Public Policy 1984.

Yanarella, Ernest, and William Green. 'Canadian Recruitment of East Asia Automobile Transplants: Cultural, Economic and Political Perspectives.' *Canadian Journal of Sociology*, 18, no. 4 (1993): 359–81.

– *The Politics of Industrial Recruitment: Japanese Automobile Investment and Economic Development in the American States.* New York: Greenwood Press 1990.

Yates, Charlotte. *From Plant to Politics: The Autoworkers Union in Postwar Canada.* Philadelphia: Temple University Press 1993.

– 'Public Policy and Canadian and American Autoworkers: Divergent Fortunes.' In Maureen Appel Molot, ed., *Driving Continentally: National Policies and the North American Auto Policy.* Ottawa: Carleton University Press 1993. 209–30.

Yergin, Daniels. *The Prize: The Epic Quest for Oil, Money, and Power.* New York: Simon and Schuster 1991.

Young, Stephen, and Neil Hood. *Chrysler UK: A Corporation in Transition.* New York: Praeger 1977.

Zeiler, Thomas. *Free Trade, Free World: The Advent of GATT.* Chapel Hill, N.C., and
   London: University of North Carolina Press 1999.

Trade Journals, Periodicals, and Newspapers

Business Quarterly Magazine
Businessweek
Calgary Herald
Canadian Automotive Trade
Canadian Business
Canadian Classics
Canadian Consumer
Canadian Dimension
Canadian Forum
Canadian Journal of Economics
Canadian Labour
Canadian Press
Daily Labor Report
Detroit Free Press
Detroit Magazine
Detroit News
Financial Post
Foreign Direct Investment
Foreign Trade
Fortune
The Futurist
Globe and Mail
Guelph Mercury
Halifax Chronicle-Herald
Hamilton Spectator
Harper's
Kingston Whig-Standard
Le Devoir
Maclean's
Montreal Gazette
Mother Jones
Motor Age
Motor Magazine
New Maritimes
New Republic

Newsweek
New York Journal of Commerce
New York Times
New York Times Magazine
Oriental Economist
Oshawa Times
Ottawa Citizen
Policy Options
Queen's Quarterly
Report on Business Magazine
Sarnia Observer
Saturday Night Magazine
Solidarity Canada
Tariff Media
This Magazine
Time
Toronto Star
Toronto Sun
Toronto Telegram
US News & World Report
Vancouver Sun
Voice of Local 212
Wall Street Journal
Ward's Automotive Reports
Washington Post
Windsor Star

Interviews

C.D. Arthur, 29 November 1999
William Davis, 7 August 2008
DesRosiers, 20 April 2001 and 1 August 2006
Michael Dube, 14 August 2003
Jean de Grandpré, 14 August 2006
Patrick Lavelle, 29 August 2008
E. Lumley, 28 May 2008
Felix Pilorusso, 14 August 2003
Simon Reisman, 19 and 20 December 1997
Philip Trezise, 24 December 1999
Lyndon 'Red' Wilson, 27 June and 19 September 2006

Internet Sources

ABC Group. 'Corporate Profile.' 2007. http://www.abcgroupinc.com/en/
default.htm (accessed 3 December 2010).

AGS Automotive Systems. 'Our Heritage.' http://www.agsautomotive.com/
heritage.cfm (accessed 3 December 2010).

Anastakis, Dimitry. 'Hubris, Nepotism, and Failure: The Bricklin Car Company
and the Question of Inevitability.' *Business and Economic History*, 8 (2010).
http://www.h-net.org/~business/bhcweb/publications/BEHonline/2010/
anastakis.pdf (accessed 29 August 2011).

ATS. 'Corporate Profile: ATS Founder, Klaus Woerner.' http://www.atsauto-
mation.com/profile/news/founder.asp (accessed 3 December 2010).

Canadian Institute of Public Opinion. http://www.library.carleton.ca/ssdata/
surveys/doc/gllp-74-mar364-doc (accessed 21 February 2008).

CBC Archives. 'Americans Disenchanted with Auto Pact.' 1 April 1987. http://
www.archives.cbc.ca/economy_business/trade_agreements/topics/326/
(accessed 14 December 2010).

– 'Canada Fights for Auto Pact.' 22 June 1987. http://www.archives.cbc.ca/
economy_business/trade_agreements/topics/326/ (accessed 14 December
2010).

CBC Newsmagazine Television Report. 'Before the Auto Pact.' 2 October 1960.
http://www.archives.cbc.ca/economy_business/trade_agreements/
topics/326/ (accessed 17 August 2010).

Cronkwright, Paul, and Mike Emmerich. 'Studebaker Canada 1910–1966.'
March 2010. http://www.thehamiltonchaptersdc.ca (accessed 3 April 2009).

Environment Canada. 'Criteria Air Containments and Related Pollutants.'
http://www.ec.gc.ca/cleanairairpur/Criteria_Air_Contaminants-
WS7C43740B-1_En.htm (accessed 6 March 2008).

Fraser Institute. 'Air Pollution Policy in Canada: Improving on Success.'
www.fraserinstitute.org/Commerce.Web/product_files/AirPollution
PolicyinCan.pdf (accessed 6 February 2008).

Historical Statistics of Canada. 'Motor Vehicle Traffic Accident Victims,
1921–1975.' http://www.statcan.ca/english/freepub/11-516-XIE/sectiont/
T271_284.csv (accessed 4 March 2008).

– Table G227-243, 'Foreign Direct Investment in Canada, 1926–1974.' http://
www.statcan.gc.ca/cgi-bin/affdr.cgi?l=eng&loc=G227_243b-eng.csv
(accessed 27 December 2010).

Holmes, John, Tod Rutherford, and Susan Fitzgibbon. 'Innovation in the Auto
Industry: A Case Study of the Windsor-Essex Region.' Originally presented
at the 6th Annual Conference of the Innovation Systems Research Network,

2004. http://www.utoronto.ca/isrn/publications/WorkingPapers/
Working04/Holmes04_Automotive.pdf (accessed 1 December 2010).

Japanese Automotive Manufacturers Association (JAMA). 'A Short History of
the Japanese Auto Industry in Canada.' Toronto, 2004. http://www.jama
.ca.industry/history (accessed 5 December 2010).

Krikorian, Jacqueline. 'Canada and the WTO: Multilevel Governance, Public
Policy-Making and the WTO Auto Pact Case.' http://www.wto.org/english/
res_e/booksp_e/casestudies_e/case9_e.htm#auto (accessed 13 December
2010).

Local 444, Windsor, Ont. 'Auto Pact- Industrial Policy.' In *Recognizing Pillette:
Its History, Its Pride, Its Determination, Its People* (Windsor, 2003). http://
local444.caw.ca/444/images/stories/publications/pillettememories.pdf
(accessed 9 May 2012).

McKitrick, Ross. 'Air Pollution Policy in Canada: Improving on Success.' Vancouver: Fraser Institute. http://www.fraserinstitute.org/Commerce.Web/
product_files/AirPollutionPolicyinCan.pdf (accessed February 2008).

Natural Resources Canada. 'Canada's Emissions Outlook: An Update.' http://
www.nrcan.gc.ca/es/ceo/outlook.pdf (accessed 22 March 2008).

Organization for Economic Co-operation and Development. 'Text of the OECD
Declaration on International Investment and Multinational Enterprises.'
http://www.oecd.org/document/53/0,3343,en_2649_34887_1933109_
119672_1_1_1,00.html (accessed 12 November 2010).

'Toyota's Managing Director at U of G.' *Guelph Mercury*, 11 March 2009. http://
www.news.guelphmercury.com/News/article/450846 (accessed 14 December 2010).

Transport Canada. 'Motor Vehicle Fuel Consumption Standards Act Proclaimed.' http://www.tc.gc.ca/eng/mediaroom/releases-nat-2007-07-
h215e-2339.htm (accessed 22 December 2010).

Wescast Industries Inc. 'Heritage.' http://www.wescast.com/en/heritage
(accessed 3 December 2010).

World Trade Organization. 'The General Agreement on Tariffs and Trade (GATT
1947).' http://www.wto.org/english/docs_e/legal_e/gatt47_01_e.htm
(accessed 12 November 2010).

– 'Report of the Panel: Canada – Certain Measures Affecting the Automotive
Industry.' http://www.wto.org. (accessed 11 February 2000).

Index